MAPPING
MULTICULTURALISM

MAPPING
MULTICULTURALISM

AVERY F. GORDON AND
CHRISTOPHER NEWFIELD,
EDITORS

UNIVERSITY OF MINNESOTA PRESS
Minneapolis / London

Published by the University of Minnesota Press
111 Third Avenue South, Suite 290, Minneapolis, MN 55401-2520
Printed in the United States of America on acid-free paper

Library of Congress Cataloging-in-Publication Data

Mapping multiculturalism / Avery F. Gordon and
Christopher Newfield, editors.
p.   cm.
Includes bibliographical references (p.   ) and index.
ISBN 0-8166-2546-8 (hc. : alk. paper)
ISBN 0-8166-2547-6 (pbk. : alk. paper)
1. Multiculturalism—United States. 2. Minorities—United States—
Social conditions. 3. Pluralism (Social sciences)—United States.
4. United States—Ethnic relations. 5. United States—Social
conditions—1980– 6. Multiculturalism. I. Gordon, Avery F.
II. Newfield, Christopher.
E184.A1M29   1996
305.8—dc20   95-39877

Contents

v

~

Preface

This book grew out of a large conference, "Translating Cultures: The Future of Multiculturalism?" organized by the two editors and held at the University of California, Santa Barbara from November 11 through November 14, 1992. In addition to those included here and a couple of conference attendees who are not present in the volume, the conference included a wonderfully engaged and provocative panel on Women Rebuilding Los Angeles with Cynthia Hamilton, Shirley Kennedy, Angela Oh, and Esther Valadez. Film screenings and a concurrent exhibition at the University Art Museum, *Mistaken Identities,* were also part of the event. The audiences were memorable from beginning to end. The papers included in this volume have been substantially revised since the conference, although a few contributors have maintained the character of their conference presentations.

A project of this scope requires the generous support and assistance of many people. For help in making the conference possible, we would like to thank our valuable graduate assistant Julia Garrett, as well as the other UCSB students who helped us with everything from publicity to student outreach to ushering to cleaning up: D. A. Dixit, Crystal Griffith, Patty Ingham, Helen Quan, Chivy Sok, Suran Thrift, and the women of AKANKE. Special appreciation for all their energetic efforts on our behalf go to Barbara Harthorn of the UCSB Interdisciplinary Humanities Center, and Zaveeni Khan, Director of the UCSB Multicultural Center. We would also like to acknowledge the kind assistance of Marla Berns, Director of the University Art Museum, Roman Baratiak and Susan Gwynne at Arts & Lectures, Corey Dubin and Kris Peterson of Coyote Radio, Randi Glick and Linda James at the UCSB Interdisciplinary Humanities Center, Elizabeth Robinson and Jamon O'Brien of KCSB, and Michael Young, Vice-Chancellor for Student Affairs. For chairing panels and hosting our guests, thanks to Tomás Almaguer, Kum-Kum Bhavnani, Yolanda Broyles-Gonzalez, Sarah Fenstermaker, Gerald Horne, Shirley Kennedy, Shirley Lim, Charles Long, Constance Penley, Judith Raiskin, Beth Schneider, Denise Segura, and Mayfair Yang. For sending his film when he couldn't be there, we are grateful to the late Marlon Riggs. For our beautiful poster, we thank Karen Shapiro, its designer, and Jimmie Durham for allowing us to reproduce his work *New Clear Family.* For their conversations during the planning stage, we would like to thank Elliott Butler-Evans, Antonia Castañeda, Ward Churchill, Rosa Linda Fregoso, Herman Gray, Carl Gutiérrez-Jones, Barbara Harthorn, Wahneema Lubiano, and Gerard Pigeon. Financial support came from the UCSB Interdisciplinary Humanities Center, the University of California Humanities Research Institute's Minority Discourse Initiative, the Chancellor, the Vice-Chancellor for Academic Affairs, the Provost of the College of Letters and Sciences, the Affirmative Action Office, the Academic Senate, the Office of Research, the departments of Sociology, English, Asian-American Studies, Chicano Studies, Film Studies, and Women's Studies, the Center for Black Studies, the Multicultural Center, and the Women's Center, all at UCSB. For financial support in preparing the book, we thank the UCSB Academic Senate, the UCSB Office of Research, and the UCSB Interdisciplinary Humanities Center. Darryl B. Dickson-Carr has been an invaluable and professional assistant to us and we thank him for all his efforts in making this book possible. Rachel Luft stepped in during the final stages of manuscript preparation, and for her talented perseverance we are very grateful. Finally, we would like to extend our appreciation to all the contributors to the volume for their hard work and patience in creating this book.

CHAPTER ONE

Introduction

AVERY F. GORDON AND CHRISTOPHER NEWFIELD

Multiculturalism has established itself as a major framework for analyzing intergroup relations in the United States at a time when it seems more obvious than ever that we cannot advance one inch as a society, or even remain where we are, without major changes in race relations in all their dimensions and new confrontations with racism. Yet as the term "multiculturalism" has appeared more and more frequently in current social and cultural debates, its meanings have become less and less clear. It acknowledges cultural diversity, but what else does it do? For some, it means renewed demands for assimilation in disguise. For others, it means a rejection of all the good things about "Western culture" that made America great. For still others, it is a simple descriptive fact about U.S. society that could serve as an everyday term for the interaction among the country's five major "racial" or "panethnic" groupings: African Americans, American Indians, Asian Americans, European Americans, and Latino Americans.

The term "multiculturalism" has become current in the last five years, but little has been resolved about its meanings and effects. Why does multiculturalism still produce so much simultaneous rejection, ambivalence, and interest? How do its meanings vary? What cultural and political traditions is multiculturalism replacing or displaying? What are the promises and limitations of multiculturalism as a rubric for new knowledges? What prospects does it hold for racial reconstruction as the United States enters a period of general economic and geopolitical restructuring?

Mapping Multiculturalism is occasioned by these kinds of pressing questions as they surround the increasing ubiquity of the term. The essays collected here map the terrain of multiculturalism in its varied dimensions and effects and discuss its future. They question and challenge the coherence, value, and current uses of multiculturalism as a concept and practice. They engage in the debates over the term. They analyze and criticize. In many cases, they propose alternatives to the priorities that multiculturalism encourages.

Mapping Multiculturalism convenes a range of scholars and artists working, regardless of their formal affiliations, in sociology, history, film, literary criticism, inter-American relations, popular culture studies, political economy, critical legal studies, industrial and labor relations, Women's Studies, Chicano Studies, African-American Studies, Asian-American Studies, and American Indian Studies. One hallmark of the volume's contributors is that they link race's complex cultural questions to questions of power and institutional authority. They see race and racism not only as intricate cultural issues that involve all aspects of individual and group life, but as immersed in economic, international, political, and policy dynamics. These scholars and artists not only connect dimensions too long separated by the artificial boundaries and restricted missions of academic departments. They also put culture at the center of politics and society and thus change what culture itself means for the humanities and social sciences. Their endeavors suggest the prospect of the wholesale restructuring of social and cultural knowledge—including the establishment of alternative methods, histories, and future projects—to better fit the often suppressed actualities that are the United States.

Multicultural Dilemmas

Since multiculturalism resurfaced in the late 1980s, commentators have offered a series of conflicting accounts of the term's basic meaning. The authors of the present essays came together for a conference called "Translating Cultures: The Future of Multiculturalism?" at the University of California, Santa Barbara in November 1992, and since that time the debate has only become more involved. As background for the following essays, we offer here a short outline of some of these accounts. We proceed two by two for the sake of a little exaggerated clarity, and we do not hereby imply a consensus among the contributors about the meaning or the value of the term multiculturalism or their agreement with our description of its most commonly expressed internal conflicts.

1. *Is multiculturalism antiracist or oblivious to racism?* Multiculturalism in the 1980s sponsored renewed protests against white racism, and yet it appeared to replace the emphasis on race and racism with an emphasis on cultural diversity. Multiculturalism rejected racial subordination but seemed sometimes to support it.

On the one hand, multiculturalism was a delayed antibiotic to the race trends of the 1970s and 1980s, but better late than never. This period's attacks on various uses of civil rights gave certain kinds of white racism a new lease on life. The official doctrine of these attacks was not white supremacy, however, but color blindness. The backlash against civil rights achieved its greatest gains not by celebrating white racial consciousness but by officially restricting the relevance of race. It did not defend white racism but claimed that racism had passed from the scene.[1] Conservatives had contended that all Americans were living in a postracist era, and their strong attacks on multiculturalism suggested that the latter had indeed contested this claim. Multiculturalism, to the contrary, implied that race is everywhere. If you thought there were mainly two races, multiculturalism insisted there are at least five. If you thought race was a function of economics, multiculturalism told you race is also central to your personal identity. If you let policy talk convince you that race had been taken care of with antidiscrimination statutes, multiculturalism reminded you that it constitutes all social relations. If you were led to assume that American culture would be better if color-blind, then multiculturalism shocked you by showing that color consciousness *is* American culture. And if you came to believe that avoiding race meant peace, multiculturalism implied that avoiding it meant war. The dispersed and complicated presence of what Michael Omi and Howard Winant call "racial projects" suggested that racial thinking, including the white racist variety, had to be examined with a renewed intensity. Multiculturalism underwrote this broadened investigation.

Well, maybe. For, on the other hand, multiculturalism often avoided race. It designated cultures. It didn't talk up racism. It didn't seem very antiracist, and often left the impression that any discussion of cultural diversity would render racism insignificant. It was ambiguous about the inheritance and the ongoing presence of histories of oppression. It had the air of pleading for a clean start. It allowed "culture"'s aura of free play to attribute a creative power to racial groups that lacked political and economic power. It was propelled by culture's traditional belief in its ability to transcend social forces such as racial discrimination or class antagonism. It often played into the view that became backlash orthodoxy in the 1980s—that whites, in Charles Murray's terms, should "abandon the tenet at the core of liberal racial orthodoxy, that white racism explains black problems."[2] In an era in which the evasion of civil rights proceeded by asserting the already existing equality of all individuals and groups under law, multiculturalism chimed in with a similarly idealized equality, an equality among multiple cultures.

2. *Is multiculturalism cultural autonomy or common culture revisited?* Multiculturalism was an *attack* on America's putative common culture, descended from Europe, and yet it was also regarded as this common culture in drag. It was anti-Eurocentric *and* neo-Eurocentric. It promised independence to various cultures to negotiate their own relations to the national whole, *and* it looked like a cornerstone of national union in a more flexible guise. It underwrote alliances among racial minorities grounded in resistance to Euro-American norming, and yet also it gave white people a new way of horning in on the action.

The Canadian philosopher Charles Taylor, on behalf of the first possibility, wrote that "the demands of multiculturalism build on the already established principles of the politics of equal respect. If withholding the presumption is tantamount to a denial of equality, and if important consequences flow for people's identity from the absence of recognition, then a case can be made for insisting on the universalization of [equal respect] as a logical extension of the politics of dignity."[3] Equal respect would replace common culture as a nation's social cement. It would cope with the divisiveness so greatly feared by the common culture crowd, yet would do so by ensuring communities of color a position of independence and strength. Governance would flow from free cooperation and negotiation rather than from coercion or from traditions of white preeminence.

On the other hand, many noted that multiculturalism had a secret longing for the kind of commonality it pretended to replace. Liberal multiculturalism, in particular, had a very difficult time keeping its abstract principle of egalitarian plurality from becoming a set of shared values whose core components were to remain unspoken rules. Proponents sometimes blurted out things like, "If multiculturalism is to get beyond a promiscuous pluralism that gives every thing equal weight and adopts complete moral relativism, it must reach some agreement on what is at the core of American culture."[4] But a good deal of what is "core" to American culture, including the beneficence of capitalist democracy, was unchallenged by multiculturalism's emphasis on cultural respect. In general, granting reciprocity and diversity was compatible with insisting on some underlying cultural unity, as the history of cultural pluralism attests. Behind the celebration of diversity, then, lurked an ambivalent attachment to *e pluribus unum*, with *unum* regaining command when white-majority rule was disrespected or challenged.

3. *Is multiculturalism grounded in grassroots alliances or diversity management?* Multiculturalism sponsored contacts among people of color that avoided white mediation and oversight by white opinion. And yet, it became a popular term in managerial circles for controlling a multiracial and gendered workplace.

Sounding relatively upbeat, Kobena Mercer wrote that while the British version of multiculturalism was a Thatcherite tillering through the shoals of minority demands, "in the United States in the 1980s, against the background of neo-conservative hegemony, [multiculturalism's] connotations suggest a breakdown in the management of ethnic pluralism and draw attention to the question of possible alliances and coalitions between various groups."[5] Multiculturalism might not only support coalitions between groups but could also explore how intermixed and hybrid these groups were in the first place. As Trinh T. Minh-ha put it, "Multiculturalism does not lead us very far if it remains a question of difference only between one culture and another. Differences should also be understood within the same culture . . . Intercultural, intersubjective, interdisciplinary. . . . To cut across boundaries and borderlines is to live aloud the malaise of categories and labels; it is to resist simplistic attempts at classifying, to resist the comfort of belonging to a classification, and of *producing classifiable* works."[6] Or in Lisa Jones's terms, "First I arrived, fatter than an A&P chicken, just another black child in New York City born to a Jewish woman and a Negro man. . . . For many years I thought the entire world was a band of Latin, black, and Chinese children dancing around the maypole and singing 'Qué Bonita Bandera' and the few Ukrainians who served us lunch."[7] Moving from fixed to mixed, multiculturalism sponsored an official identity that seemed to reflect social reality, and that enabled alliances to emerge from everyday life. The crisscrossed and in-from-everywhere things you do already were a better frame for coalitions than the formal categories of institutional processes, multiculturalism suggested. Hence so many explosive developments in concepts like the boundary-shattering borderlands, biraciality, and intersectionality. Multiculturalism reflected how coalition politics and even personal identity itself could evade the regulating effects of official procedure.

But at the same time multiculturalism was another name for that regulation. Driven by the imperatives of "global competition" and "changing de-mographics," diversity management arrived on the corporate scene to help business get, in R. Roosevelt Thomas's words, "beyond race and gender." Putting a spin on a Taylor-type liberalism of recognition, he argued that the "recognition of the uniqueness" of all individuals and groups could be a boon and not a hindrance to the corporate mission. Diversity management explicitly dehistoricized culture, race, and gender in order to offer *management* itself as the instrument for organizing differences. Employee differences would be encouraged but employee sovereignty over the use of difference would not. Multiculturalism alternately encouraged and suppressed the use of cultural difference to expand political democracy.

4. *Does multiculturalism link politics and culture or separate them?* Multiculturalism reinjected culture into politics and politics into culture, and yet it seemed just another page in the book of cultural substitutes.

Although acknowledging that cultural and political activity are by no means interchangeable, many thought multiculturalism might be a way of clarifying the broad sociopolitical relations that are woven into the ties among different cultures. This did not necessarily mean less attention to cultural artifacts themselves but more attention to their stakes. Cary Nelson noted that while "inclusion in an anthology is not equivalent to wielding effective political power," a multicultural anthology's "role in promoting core values that are ... inclusive, in valuing ... minority cultures, in familiarizing readers with different traditions, and in imaging a multicultural body politic can be significant."[8] Multiculturalist educators often saw cultural change leading to political change. "One of the central ways power is exercised in democratic societies," wrote Theresa Perry and James W. Fraser, "is in structuring discourse." By "defining a new conversational terrain," multiculturalism can "fundamentally reorder the ruling definitions of culture" and the distribution of power and resources.[9] Perry and Fraser's book on multicultural education has a number of chapters devoted to teaching, to the curriculum, and to "Shifting the Power, Shifting the Players" in school structures. Even Diane Ravitch, best known for her attacks on what she viewed as politicized, race-conscious education—especially the Afrocentric kind—argued that multiculturalism should pay attention to issues like "intergroup conflict" and "liv[ing] together in peace," although these are as political as they are cultural.[10] Multiculturalism regarded these as systematically interlinked.

But it also separated them. Multiculturalism sometimes celebrated cultural diversity while preserving a political core from being affected by this diversity. Gary Nash argued that *"pluribus* can flourish in these ways only if *unum* is preserved at the heart of the polity—in a common commitment to core political and moral values."[11] Cultural diversity often regarded culture, in Chandra Talpade Mohanty's terms, "as noncontradictory, as isolated from questions of history," as a realm of individual attitudes in which diversity leads to the reduction of prejudice but not to any change in the relative positions of various groups.[12] Cultural diversity noted differences in values and outlooks while ignoring the differences of social position that influence those values. Commentators on multiculturalism have repeatedly warned that it teeters on the brink of lapsing into insipid encouragement of variation with little idea of what difference it makes, like quality-of-life rankings that give more points to the city that has all four kinds of major-league sports teams rather than just two or three. Multiculturalism seemed torn between demanding and avoiding the full conjuncture of political, social, and cultural elements that affect our racialized everyday lives.

Some of these conflicts over the basic meaning of the mere word "multiculturalism" follow from the remarkable range of uses to which it's been put. It has indeed referred to "the life of various ethnic groups, racial diversity, gender differences, international issues, non-Western culture, cross-cultural methodologies, sexual preference, and the physically challenged."[13] But the term also manifests mainstream American irresolution about these four conflicts. Does a democratic United States require orderly racial hierarchy or racial equality? Does American society have one or many centers? Will the bottom or the top control intergroup conflict—will control be relatively popular or relatively elite? Finally, is cultural knowledge intrinsic to or outside of social relations and political life?

Obviously actual choices are not as binary as these heuristic questions suggest. There are combinations, and these vary from place to place. But the elements of these combinations are often at odds with one another, and reflect a profound and gendered ambivalence about these issues. It is simply not possible to invoke an "American Creed" of equality and democracy that rejects racist and exclusionary attitudes, for any such creed is in fact divided within itself. The creed is itself incessantly dubious about the benefits of racial equality, a nonhierarchical society, grassroots control of intergroup relations, and culture's influence on politics. Multiculturalism was hatched into an ambiguous relation to a "post-civil rights" white racial consensus that does not oppose but instead produces the Janus-faced—or Hydra-headed—contradictions around race, racism, and culture. Were there indeed a set of "core American values" ready to assert unambivalent antiracism and democratic equality against their opposites in American life, we would not be in our fourteenth decade of working toward racial Reconstruction of an America without slavery. Multiculturalism, adopting something like the eight stances we've described, has not escaped the conflicts within the consensus it attempts to revise.

The end of the Cold War has not brought the openings for national redevelopment that many hoped for. Part of the reason has been the successful replacement of the communist threat with equally global "ethnic threats" in the minds of many important opinion makers. The columnist Charles Krauthammer fired an early shot against an "intellectually bankrupt 'civil-rights community,'" which he claimed "poses a threat that no outside agent in this post-Soviet world can match"—"the setting of one ethnic group against another, the fracturing not just of American society but of the American idea."[14] Economic and social decline have been attributed not to inefficient and inequitable domestic policy but to allegedly uncontrollable international forces such as world wage competition and ethnic hatred. As we complete this introduction, anti-immigration sentiment in California has managed to link a pervasive sense of economic disintegration to undocumented minimum-wage laborers rather than, say, to avoidance of urban investment or the investment strategies of aerospace firms.

Current trends are tipping ambivalence into retrenchment and restriction. We recur to the four dilemmas listed earlier. First, around the pursuit of antiracist projects, the dominant tendency has recently been to define race not as a social force flowing from center to margins, from the powerful to the less so, but as the threat of chaos wielded by the margins and the powerless against the center. Mainstream common sense in post-Cold War America increasingly ties race consciousness not to First World sovereignty over other peoples (including others within) but to the others' power to transform the globe into a smoldering ruin.[15] "Race" and ethnicity are being radically remodeled into synonyms for the weak's senseless and self-destructive threats to the strong.

Second, recent years have enhanced the prestige of common culture as the primary defensive barrier to the dangers posed by the existence of ethnicity and race. Plurality is increasingly seen as a dangerous thing. Although Lynne Cheney, once christened by George F. Will as the "secretary of domestic defense," has temporarily shed her armor, excessive domestic differentiation remains a threat.[16] Cheney's liberal replacement at the National Endowment for the Humanities, Sheldon Hackney, was unable to devote his confirmation hearings to a theme like increased independence of and representation for "minority" cultures. He was instead compelled to denounce that form of "political correctness" that is "overly solicitous of minority groups and fashionable and trendy concerns."[17] Common values, shared principles, core beliefs, national purpose, bringing people together—all these, in this prescription to transcend actual economic and political processes, are invoked repeatedly against a nameless but standing threat of civil war.

Third, the post-Cold War policy mainstream traces domestic and international poverty and war to excessive local control. It rarely blames histories of excessive management or current top-down alliances of international and local officials. Manufacturing failures are attributed to union demands in a global economy rather than to the international institutions and behaviors that comprise that economy itself. Or trouble in the Los Angeles Unified School District is attributed to disruptive teachers, students, and unions rather than to funding decisions in Sacramento. Diversity management is thought to balance impartial and uniform structure with inclusion and openness; it supposedly offers the best virtues of moderation, in which the clash of vibrant, creative energies can be organized and reconciled by the comprehensive and balanced overview provided by the leadership above. Direct coalitions, on the other hand, attempt to make a supervisory wisdom amongst themselves. In the last few years, they have been repeatedly castigated as at worst divisive and at best antiquated in today's interconnected and transnational flows of resources and information.

Finally, the post-Cold War period has seen a circling of the wagons around increasingly ossified political processes, defending them against direct forms of participation and expression. One famous symptom was the attack on "political correctness," which amounted to an attack on the relevance of cultural identity, experience, and history to the governance of institutional affairs. Culture would be encouraged when controlled by a resurgent emphasis on "Western culture" as a repository of unchanging values, a giant "book of virtues." This meant keeping politics out of culture. Culture would be discouraged when it represented a local, changing, spontaneous, unregulated compilation of historicized individual perspectives. This meant keeping culture out of politics. Strong forms of multiculturalism see culture as expressing and changing how people see their place in the world. The aftermath of the Cold War tends to make the logic of the world invincible. The political process becomes inaccessible to everyday culture and the latter's insights into desire and need.

So we could end up with this conglomeration of the restrictive side of these four dilemmas. American society declares itself postracist and blames all racializing stigma on its targets, declaring exclusions to be the benefits of a common culture while managers supervise a self-perpetuating political and economic process in the name of diversity. That would be terrible. On the other hand, we're used to it. It's what's been going on, and for quite some time. Too many other countervailing things are happening in every kind of community in the United States for these four developments to achieve any simple success.

The essays in this book, though fully aware of problems like these, attempt to circumvent their conditions and outcomes. The essays have been grouped under general rubrics intended to highlight the ways in which they are *not* confined by the dilemmas we've been outlining here.

Overview of Organization

The book is organized into several sections.

Part I, "Mapping Multiculturalism," situates the concept in connection with a range of related discourses about race, culture, and power. It offers essays that link multiculturalism to existing race-based and/or oppositional discourses. How does multiculturalism connect to the history of antiracist struggle in the United States? How does its structure and efficacy compare to the oppositional narratives of postcolonial discourse? Does it build and improve upon Marxist notions of the liberation of oppressed groups, or does it reject (or sidestep) Marxism? Would such a sidestepping be helpful or not? Does multiculturalism continue civil rights protests, or is it a characteristic product of the post-civil rights period? How does it aid or hinder the civil rights effort to establish party-based social movements? Does it successfully expand race-based political activism into the cultural realm?

In "From Farce to Tragedy," Jon Cruz considers multiculturalism's relation to Marxist and post-Marxist forms of social critique. What has multiculturalism given up through its distance from Marxism? What role does multiculturalism play as it negotiates between global capitalism and the fiscal crisis of the state? Angela Y. Davis's "Gender, Class, and Multiculturalism" asks whether multiculturalism hasn't traded in the critical insights of the distinguished histories of antiracist and antisexist struggle for the dubious prerogatives of diversity management. She suggests that multiculturalism cannot accomplish the necessary transformation of social relations, and falls far short of the coalition work performed by women of color. M. Annette Jaimes Guerrero argues in "Academic Apartheid" that multiculturalism develops its notions of multiracial cultural interaction by ignoring the specifically colonial history of American Indian subjugation. She explores the reasons why decolonization remains the necessary theoretical and political model for the liberation of Native peoples. In "Like Being Mugged by a Metaphor," Wahneema Lubiano analyzes the role of state narratives in cultural projects of dominance and resistance. She makes a case for a radically transformative version of multiculturalism that, critically engaging the intersection of race, class, and gender, addresses the state directly. In "Multiculturalism's Unfinished Business," Christopher Newfield and Avery F. Gordon analyze multiculturalism as part of cultural pluralism's erratic attempts to diverge from white-norm assimilationism. They argue that if multiculturalism can build on the overlapping antiassimilationist insights of pluralism and nationalism, it can serve as a useful *starting point* for multiracial, democratic initiatives. Finally, Cedric J. Robinson's "Manichaeism and Multiculturalism" situates the current multiculturalism debate in the history of Western "specular imaginings" of racial difference. Focusing on the politics of knowledge, he argues that Manichaeism has produced atrocities *and* underwritten countervailing understandings of oppression; multiculturalism, Robinson suggests, has the potential to go beyond it.

Part II, "Rethinking the Political Subject," inquires into the ways that politics forms subjectivity and subjectivity informs politics. It brings both empirical and theoretical vantages on gender, class, and sexuality to the analysis of racialized and oppositional subjects. These papers ask a number of questions: How are contemporary events forming new types of collective political subjects? What are the effects of multiculturalism on established and newer modes of identity? What is a "minority" in a multicultural society? How does multiculturalism affect the ongoing projects of recovering historical and cultural identity in nondominant cultures? Are women of color a political class? Does multiculturalism reinforce traditional identity politics and individualistic political modes, like resentment? What are the current relations between theories of the subject and ethnic and gender studies?

Naming the impulse for a different world, Norma Alarcón calls it women of color. In "Conjugating Subjects," she describes how the concept "women of color" establishes a paradigm of multiple determinations and incommensurability for the project of coalition politics. By offering a form of affiliation that has shifted from sameness and commonality to the recognition of distinct social histories, such a concept goes beyond multiculturalism's merely pluralistic "politics of difference." Wendy Brown's "Injury, Identity,

Politics" elaborates, through reconsideration of Nietzsche's genealogy of the logics of *ressentiment*, the ways in which some of the emancipatory aims of politicized identity are subverted not only by the constraints of the political discourses in which its operations transpire, but by its own wounded attachments. Less a critique of identity politics than an analysis of its investments, Brown's essay calls for a reevaluation of the relationship between pain, political recognition, and the agonistic theater of forging alternative futures. In "Multiculturalism as Political Strategy," Cynthia Hamilton discusses the history of the manipulation of racial and ethnic identity as a management tool in the workplace. She argues that multiculturalism fails to see how multiracial workers are made political citizens of U.S. capitalism's "work culture," and thus can't imagine how racial or cultural differences might offer a real alternative. In "Racialization in the Post-Civil Rights Era," Michael Omi notes that in recent years the racial dimensions of political and social life have expanded rather than declined in significance. Omi identifies three key examples of this trend—the development of new racial subjects as a result of panethnic consciousness, the emerging crisis of white identity, and the increasing racialization of electoral politics—and discusses their implications for mainstream politics. "Screening Resistance," a conversation between filmmaker Lourdes Portillo and scholar Rosa Linda Fregoso, situates the formation of Latina/o identity in an international Latin American context.

Part III, "Reading Multicultural Narratives," examines already existing descriptions of U.S. culture as multicultural. These narratives have been around for a long time—they have played a central role in the survival of nondominant U.S. cultures. What do their readings of the country's multicultural past say about the uses of multiculturalism as a guide to the future? Do accounts of the U.S.-Mexico border imagine a multicultural entity? Does multiculturalism add to or detract from the realities of cultural conflict? How do these narratives locate individuals in racial groups? Does a "border" sensibility improve interaction across cultures and teach cures to fear and loathing? How has linguistic and cultural translation served as a paradigm of multiculturalism? What do existing narratives say about improving cross-cultural relations within and across national boundaries?

In "Language and Other Lethal Weapons," Antonia I. Castañeda examines the experience of children, principally Tejana farmworker children, as translators of culture. Basing her analysis on interviews with women whose families lived in various labor camps in the state of Washington during their childhood in the 1950s, Castañeda examines the cultural and political effects of that experience, suggesting that such translation is a process so fraught with conflict, subordination, and pain that it may not be understood by multiculturalism's notions of enlightening cultural exchange. Angie Chabram-Dernersesian's "The Spanish Colón-ialista Narrative" discusses an international form of multiculturalism, Spain's "Colón-ialista narrative" of 1992. Chabram-Dernersesian offers a multinational analysis that demonstrates how the Colón narrative enlists subjugated U.S. identities to develop a fully Eurocentric paradigm of Hispanic multiculturalism. In "Multiculturalism and Racial Stratification," Neil Gotanda reads Judge Joyce Karlin's sentencing colloquy in the widely publicized case of *People v. Soon Ja Du.* Gotanda shows how Karlin, justifying probation in the shooting of African-American teenager Latasha Harlins by Korean grocer Du Soon Ja, used multi*cultural* techniques to establish a racial hierarchy of model and monitored minorities. Ramón Gutiérrez's "The Erotic Zone: Sexual Transgression on the U.S.-Mexican Border" argues that many borderland Americans use negative sexual stereotypes to suppress the dependence of white middle-class prosperity on the intimate presence of Mexicans. Gutiérrez suggests that "multicultural" contact easily coexists with polarizing domination and paranoia, leaving the conjunction of sexuality and economics untouched. In "Site-seeing through Asian America," Renee Tajima explores the complexities of Asian-American identity across the major changes in Asian-American social positions over the last four decades. The themes of her partly autobiographical narrative include the decline of Asian-American assimilation and the continual interaction between Asian- and African-American histories of protest.

Part IV, "Multi-Capitalism," connects group and individual identity to recent changes in national and international economics. The section brings diverse expertise to bear on concrete questions of the relation of culture to political economy. Multiculturalism arises in a context in which culture is a commodity to be bought and sold in a multinational marketplace altered by the globalization of production, the rapid development of international finance, the simultaneous advance of high-tech and sweated labor in the United States, U.S. domination of cultural markets, and the hybridization of nearly all cultures around the world. How does multiculturalism translate this rapidly changing political economy? What is the future of local culture in the context of the internationalization of culture and economy? Can local cultures resist transnational capitalism without directly confronting it? Does connecting culture to economics improve the opportunity for cross-cultural alliances, or not, and why?

Richard P. Appelbaum, in "Multiculturalism and Flexibility," reviews Marx's arguments about globalization in order to investigate the emergence of new transnational forms of labor exploitation, the "information-based economy," and the meaning of flexibility. Drawing on his study of apparel production in Los Angeles and Asia, he reflects on multicultural capitalism. In "The Class Question in Global Capitalism," Edna Bonacich argues that class remains a life-threatening aspect of social organization and social dynamics in the profoundly racialized manufacturing sectors that thrive in Los Angeles. She suggests ways multiculturalism might link race and gender to union struggles and other kinds of worker response to the ongoing consequences of the capital-accumulation process. Appelbaum and Gregg Scott's "Travelogue" offers a short visual essay on the factory districts in Los Angeles and various Asian cities. In "Unified Capital and the Subject of Value," Paul Smith explores the meaning of German reunification. Focusing on the rise of racism and xenophobia and the struggle over the stakes of an authentic German culture, Smith argues that these are aggravated by factitious unifications of capital and labor; the need to oppose these while opposing white supremacy may be a major lesson for U.S. multiculturalists. Patricia Zavella's "Living on the Edge" examines the problems of Chicano families living in poverty in the American Southwest. Arguing against "culturalist" arguments that attribute Chicano employment patterns to having better work attitudes than African Americans, Zavella indicates how culturalism, in conjunction with American family ideology, veils institutional discrimination and exclusion, and ignores the differences between the specific situations of different communities of color.

Part V, "Multiculturalism and the Production of Culture," explores artistic production as a type of social movement that can not only represent traditionally marginalized groups and individuals but refashion public policy. Here, the papers address such questions as: How can multiculturalism be reworked to more closely suit the needs of the cultures it claims to defend? What lies beyond multiculturalism? What will the future of cultural self-determination look like? How do nondominant cultures define winning cultural contests? How do we define a cultural community? What are the histories that have created cultural identities and movements? What is an artistic coalition, especially across cultural difference? How is multiculturalism produced by cultural institutions?

Steve Fagin's "Machine Talk" reflects on his experiences with presenting his video on the overthrow of Philippine president Ferdinand Marcos in 1986, *The Machine That Ate Bad People*. Fagin discusses his efforts to enact political expression through televisual fragmentation rather than coherent metanarratives and interacts with a UCSB audience that is sometimes critical of his format. In "'It's All Wrong, but It's All Right,'" George Lipsitz explores the question of what popular culture consumers and artists do not know, and the "mistakes" they make while trying to figure things out. He suggests that "mistaken" ideas often contain crucial insights about the social construction of identity and the unreliability of surface messages. Lisa Lowe's "Imagining Los Angeles in the Production of Multiculturalism" analyses how the Los Angeles Festival of the Arts (1990) obscured the divergence between the aesthetic representation of cultural difference and differences in material resources. She identifies multiculturalism's tendency to produce consensus by homogenizing differences while also identifying oppositional moments in the festival, ones growing out of juxtapositions of different cultures that acknowledge contradiction without asserting generalizable oppressor/oppressed relations. And in "A Style Nobody Can Deal With," Tricia Rose investigates the postindustrial urban context of hip-hop culture and the political implications of hip-hop style. Analyzing the South Bronx as a critical symbol for urban ruin in the United States, Rose shows how hip-hop artists, who were designated as surplus labor, instead transformed obsolete vocational training skills in such fields as printing, drafting, electronics repair, and auto mechanics into the basis for artistic commentary on the crossroads of lack and desire in African-Diasporic communities.

These essays explore the contradictory and powerful meanings of the concept of multiculturalism and reject its terms altogether when that becomes necessary. Above all, the forces they describe, and the force of the work itself, suggest a comprehension, a momentum, a passion that means come what may, there shall be no going back.

Notes

1. Joe R. Feagin and Melvin P. Sikes recall that "in a 1981 book *Wealth and Poverty*, once called the 'Bible of the Reagan-Bush administrations,' economist George Gilder declared there was no need for government action to assist black Americans because it was virtually impossible to find a serious racist in a position of power and because major discrimination had been effectively abolished in the United States" (*Living with Racism: The Black Middle-Class Experience* [Boston: Beacon Press, 1994], 6).

2. Charles Murray, "The Reality of Black America," *Times Literary Supplement*, 22 May 1992: 10. Murray, reviewing Andrew Hacker's *Two Nations*, is claiming that "white upper-middle-class society" is in the process of abandoning this tenet.

3. Charles Taylor, *Multiculturalism and "The Politics of Recognition,"* with commentary by Amy Gutmann, ed., Steven C. Rockefeller, Michael Walzer, and Susan Wolf (Princeton, N.J.: Princeton University Press, 1992), 68.

4. Gary B. Nash, "The Great Multicultural Debate," *Contention* 1:3 (spring 1992): 24.

5. Kobena Mercer, "'1968': Periodizing Postmodern Politics and Identity," in *Cultural Studies*, ed. Lawrence Grossberg, Cary Nelson, and Paula Treichler (New York: Routledge, 1992), 449.

6. Trinh T. Minh-ha, *When the Moon Waxes Red: Representation, Gender and Cultural Politics* (New York: Routledge, 1991), 107–8.

7. Lisa Jones, "How I Invented Multiculturalism," in *Bulletproof Diva: Tales of Race, Sex, and Hair* (New York: Doubleday, 1994), 7.

8. Cary Nelson, "Multiculturalism Without Guarantees: From Anthologies to the Social Text," *Journal of the Midwest Modern Language Association* 26:1 (spring 1993): 48.

9. Theresa Perry and James W. Fraser, "Reconstructing Schools as Multiracial/Multicultural Democracies: Toward a Theoretical Perspective," in *Freedom's Plow: Teaching in the Multicultural Classroom,* ed. Perry and Fraser (New York: Routledge, 1993), 18.

10. Diane Ravitch, "In the Multicultural Trenches," *Contention* 1:3 (spring 1992): 31.

11. Nash, "Multicultural Debate," 25.

12. Chandra Talpade Mohanty, "On Race and Voice," in *Beyond a Dream Deferred: Multicultural Education and the Politics of Excellence,* ed. Becky W. Thompson and Sangeeta Tyagi (Minneapolis: University of Minnesota Press, 1993), 56.

13. Jerry G. Gaff, "Beyond Politics: The Educational Issues Inherent in Multicultural Education," *Change* (January–February 1992): 32.

14. Charles Krauthammer, "An Insidious Rejuvenation of the Old Left," *Los Angeles Times,* 24 December 1990: B5. Conservatives frequently attack women's studies programs in tandem with ethnic studies. Culturally conservative journalists, during 1990–92, seemed more wary of the danger to national unity posed by multicultural programs, but this does not imply reconciliation with women's studies in the least. For an interesting set of responses to the PC-bashing rejection of feminism, see the *Women's Review of Books* for February 1992.

15. For the matching graphics, see the punctured and burning beach-ball globe illustrating Robert D. Kaplan's cover story, "The Coming Anarchy," *Atlantic Monthly* 273:2 (February 1994): 44–76.

16. George F. Will, "Literary Politics," *Newsweek,* 22 April 1991: 72. As a paranoid rapture, the passage stands the test of time: we must attend, Will wrote, "to the many small skirmishes that rarely rise to public attention but cumulatively condition the nation's cultural, and then, political, life. In this low-visibility, high-intensity war, Lynne Cheney is secretary of domestic defense. The foreign adversaries her husband, Dick, must keep at bay are less dangerous, in the long run, than the domestic forces with which she must deal. Those forces are fighting against the conservation of the common culture that is the nation's social cement."

17. Sheldon Hackney, quoted in Adam Clymer, "Clinton Nominee Defends Himself," *New York Times,* 26 June 1993: A6.

PART I

Mapping Multiculturalism

CHAPTER TWO

From Farce to Tragedy

Reflections on the Reification of Race at Century's End

JON CRUZ

This essay is about multiculturalism. But it is not written in the spirit of benevolent engineering, or as a celebration of ethnotourism, or as added applause to cultural pluralism as a goal in itself. These sensibilities have their virtues and champions. What I propose is that we step back and look at multiculturalism as part of a *social logic* of late capitalism and as a cultural feature at the intersection of economic globalization and the fiscal-domestic crisis of the state. This conjuncture is culturally charged, and part of this new charge is conveyed in the promises and the antagonisms surrounding multiculturalism. As a term that hosts competing claims, multiculturalism is more than a cultural site for pluralism; it is also a cultural fact under siege. There are many ways to approach multiculturalism. The one offered here evaluates multiculturalism as *symptomatic* of our particular historical conjuncture within the social formation of late capitalism.

To present this perspective I have chosen to return first to some well-worn—and, many might argue, worn-out—issues that are central to Marx: *fetishization, reification,* and the importance of *critique.* I proceed with some trepidation since so much of contemporary cultural theory frames itself as "post-Marxist." Plagued by its own history, Marxism is in disrepute, and so to draw on Marx is a troubled and troubling enterprise these days. Marxism's problems are numerous, but there are two very general and over-

lapping developments, one worldly, the other quite academic, that compromise any use of Marx. In the first case, the humanist and emancipatory
vision that oriented much of Marx's writings, meant to flourish in proportion to the withering away of the state, instead atrophied into authoritarian
statism. Accompanying the rise and fall of Stalinism is a history of ideas
quick to argue that Marx authorized the politics and practices of Stalin.
Conflation aside, for those who detest any aspect Marxism as an interpretive
tool, the withering away of the Soviet superpower is seen as a glorious testimony to the triumphant virtue of a corporate capitalism that is now even
more free to move beyond its national confinement to an even larger global
reach.

Joining the recoil from Marxism is the much larger intellectual indictment of the entire epistemological and ideological underpinnings of the Enlightenment in which Marx's writings are embedded. In this criticism, the
roots of rationality have been argued to be nothing more than a set of moral
fictions that underwrite power and domination. In the interrogation of the
Enlightenment, the rationalist table has been turned: Descartes's *Discourse
on Method* has been overtaken and inverted by the methods of discourse;
Kant's *Critique of Pure Reason* has been undermined by the dismissal of
Reason. Certainly the theoretical moves have been significant. In its classical
conception, Reason was to have purged metaphysics; at least that was the
dream of rationalism. But Reason turned out to be just another metaphysical facade. We have come to distrust the not-so-hidden hands of essentialism, universalism, patriarchy, sexism, and racism that prop up modernity
(inasmuch as they prop up social formations in general). In the new spirit of
antiuniversalism and antiessentialism, we have moved away from Grand
Reason and Big Truth in exchange for multiple, increasingly proliferating,
and characteristically embattled arenas occupied by lots of little reasons and
little truths. In the process, the notion of a post-Enlightenment antiuniversalism has fostered a new notion of reason (spelled with a small "r"), and endorses a sense of epistemological safety in the turn to local knowledge in the
present. Theoretical downsizing appears to compete in the atmosphere of a
new and peculiar uneasiness, and in a world of flux where few things come
with guarantees. The lesson is registered in the most reflexive theorizing,
which displays a shrewd wariness for the metaphysics residing in all rational
fronts.[1] In this larger scenario of epistemological crisis, Reason has been
strip-searched to reveal the naked profile of patriarchy behind the ideological fig leaf and the justifications used to hold up class, racial, and cultural
domination have been rendered visible. This critical assessment has been

carried over ecologically to Marxian theory and has, in some cases, war-ranted Marx's total dismissal. Today we are awash in the glee of market vin-dication touted in the references to a "new world order" and "globalization," while the best and brightest seek an interpretive haven in cultural identities and cultural fragments. Yet it is precisely because of the new developments tying capitalism and cultural forces together that Marx's insights warrant revisiting.

As capitalism expands, so too do new identity formations. Both work within newly expanded political economies of money and meanings. But as long as there is the perception of open territory for the movement of eco-nomic capital and symbolic capital, and where money and identities can be made and allowed to circulate, there is a sense of progress (understood as economic and psychocultural growth). Both logics thrive on the achieve-ment of something tangible and substantial. But what if we view these as two social constellations yoked to a deeper ideology of the marketplace? For if liberal democracy can be likened to an open market that sells investment stock in the new currencies of political pluralism, then it would appear that multiculturalism is part of a paid dividend to be enjoyed collectively by civil society. Market metaphors aside, there is perhaps much wishful thinking here.

I am sympathetic with and yet troubled by the theoretical predicaments and the societal contexts in which multiculturalism is currently configured. Coming together in both are mixtures of emancipation and paralysis, and a sense of intellectual freedom accompanied by political default. In the con-temporary context, capitalism and social identities tend to appear as sepa-rate and distinct realms with little to tie them together. But perhaps multi-culturalism is this link. This proposition deserves to be examined. I will argue that, in the American context, multiculturalism now mediates capital-ism and modern social identities, and these spheres, in turn, are connected in a conjuncture that was first opened by the political liberalism of the civil rights era but is now being joined by a deepening fiscal crisis of the state associated with large-scale social disinvestment over the last two decades. Understanding this connection may also give us a way to assess (borrowing from Raymond Williams) the structure of not-so-good feelings in which multiculturalism takes on a double life of troubled parentage.

I turn to Marx in order to bring these mixed sensibilities associated with multiculturalism into a particular kind of focus. The premise is that some aspects of Marx's analytical vision are helpful in framing and elucidating problems that come with identity formations and multiculturalism. Given what I've already said about the critique of Enlightenment, I confess in advance to indulging in what some might call the temptation of retrograde humanism and unoriginal sin.

Retrieving Critique: An Excursus

Two concerns need to be raised. First, the kind of *critique* carried out by Marx—specifically the attempt to interpret the modern social formation we call capitalism—seems to have atrophied within contemporary cultural theory.[2] The result appears as an erosion of the interpretive will to think through the fragments of modernity and to forge linkages between cultural forms and sociohistorical formations. In some cases this abandonment of critique is condoned through selective interpretations of poststructuralism.[3] This move is not innocent or naive in associating the theoretical framing of "structures" with a teleologically contaminated *structuralism* (and, by extension, essentialism). In some cases, essentialism is avoided by a retreat from systems and histories to the present and the local. There are analytical virtues to this move. It has restored the problem of meaning, retrieved the value of hermeneutics, and brought social and cultural analysis back to an appreciation for the nuances of flesh-and-blood subjects who must negotiate through sensuous knowledge-making the conditions of everyday life.

My second concern is that there are also costs in the move to jettison Marx as damaged progeny of the Enlightenment. One such cost is that the insights made possible by Marx's notions of *fetishization* and *reification* under capitalism have been eclipsed.[4] I want to retrieve some of these insights because I think they are needed in order to bring some important aspects of multiculturalism into relationship with economic globalization and the new kind of cultural work facilitated by the state. To do this requires a brief excursus into some key aspects of Marx's concepts of *critique, fetishization,* and *reification.*

For Marx, the rise of capitalism was more than an economic system; it was fundamentally a new, socially organized form of life. Understanding capitalism as a social system required an analysis of the commodity, the most discrete but analytically crucial *fragment* within the capitalist social formation. What is pertinent in Marx's starting point is how commodities as the keys to the social could be *thought*—not simply as distinct and discrete items or things in themselves, with self-enclosed identities and essential attributes, but as embodiments of practical human activity. As moments within a larger continuum, commodities refracted human practices enmeshed in historically specific social relations; commodities functioned as *social hieroglyphics*.[5] Individuals, groups, and classes, however, are seldom able to comprehend themselves as embedded in the larger web of social relations, or to grasp critically the modes of domination that hold and shape these relations in their social form. What reigned instead was the triumphant effect of the market conceived as a natural and autonomous reality. Under capitalism and commodity production, the social identities of individuals were increasingly mediated by commodity production and regulated, too, as if they were *things*, reified along with commodities. Marx called this fundamental misrecognition *commodity fetishization*. Understanding and grasping the conditions that generate specific social relations and the forms that they take—commodities, value, production, circulation, identity, and so on—is included in what Marx meant by *critique*.

Weberian and Western Marxist social theory from Lukács and Gramsci to Adorno and Althusser expands upon these insights, though with different accents. By blending Marx's method of critique, Weber's theory of rationalization, and Freud's contributions to the problem of the unconscious, Western Marxism, while not a unified theory, was able to think through the processes of modern capitalist bureaucratization and the further developments of social fragmentation and atomization. With the growing emphasis on the cultural sphere, Western Marxism identified ways in which an expanding and changing capitalism was able to create new requirements of knowledge and specialization, including more distinctive and specific mechanisms of identification. Individuals under modernization (though still conceptualized in the framework of class reductionism) also became increasingly more *reflective* and *contemplative* of their own particular activity.[6] This activity, however, was not based on a consciousness that grasped the wider, underlying, and systemic social relations that generated one's identity. On the contrary, as capitalism penetrated deeper and deeper into the social formation, modern consciousness was increasingly pushed away from the capacity for critique. Driven to the surfaces as a *social effect*, the contours of consciousness through individuality became increasingly fragmented.[7]

This kind of perspective is like salt in an open wound. It is disconcerting to think that we have such little autonomy and self-control. It grates against and casts aspersions on the civil religion of individualism (American or otherwise). But while it has its problems, the concept of critique is a tool we can use to help us think through the fragmented surfaces of cultural forms that we inherit, and in which we live out our lives. It can give us ways to pose and grasp the links between different social sites, and see them as relations. Most important, it helps us come to terms with the historically specific and materially grounded modes of *power* and *inequality* that condition social relations and underwrite ostensibly distinct and discrete cultural forms—like identity formations and multiculturalism.

I do not want to suggest, however, that simply stepping back to Marx is enough. There has been and there continues to be great debate around what should be jettisoned as well as retained and reconstructed in Marx's very sweeping notions of historical materialism. Marx may have criticized religion, but the presupposition that human history has a transcendental telos that unfolds initially with the transgression of innocence through alienation is a variation on the thesis of original sin, and the idea that the human predicament is eventually to be overcome by final redemption shares an eschatological vision as much as any great religion. The inherent teleology and appeal to transcendentalist solutions places *part*—but not the whole—of Marxian theory squarely in the larger tradition of Western Judeo-Christian metaphysics. Marxism is also shaped by the Romantic movements of the late eighteenth and early nineteenth centuries. From these layered teleological legacies it takes on the dual pressures of dread and euphoria that mark the transition from modernity to postmodernity. Furthermore, race and gender, now recognized as major social, cultural, and historical mountains, were barely envisioned due to the peculiar blind spots induced by the privilege of what C. W. Mills called the "labor metaphysic."

The theory of reification is just as much a way of seeing as it is a crude overstatement. Indeed, overcoming reification is precisely what is attempted in the critical self-reflective dimensions within identity formations where individuals reject the inherited categories and social classifications that are structured in domination and marginalization. This is particularly the case in the United States for racialized groups. These problems and limits noted here mark many of the tensions that run through the whole of Western Marxism, and much of poststructuralism, postmodernism, and feminist and race theorizing. Such theoretical developments represent, in part, a series of complicated and overlapping moves that use as well as reject Marxian notions. These problems aside, historical materialism suggests a way to decenter everyday consciousness by rethinking the immediate, practical, experiential, and concrete in relation to social and historical developments. And this angle of analysis is where Marx suggested we should hedge our analytical bets about where things might matter.

Multiculturalism as a Social Hieroglyphic

I go through the motions of this perhaps tedious retrieval because we have moved lately into new modes of theorizing that restore what Marx tried to reverse. For in cultural analysis today there is an end-of-century intellectual nervousness that seeks a presumed epistemological safety in the ahistoricism of the temporal, the turn to the *local,* and the *cultural fragment.* In essence, cultural fragments—abstractions—have been exonerated as the sites of new (misplaced) concreteness. The surfaces of the social have been restored with a new sense of cultural depth. These theoretical sensibilities sometimes overlap the anguished struggle over the meanings *inside* identity formations. To be safe, to avoid metaphysical contamination, there is sometimes comfort in being wary of the global, the historical, and the structural. This, I think, is one of the conditions we must acknowledge and work to contextualize if we are to begin a critical assessment of the tensions associated with identity formations and multiculturalism, especially when the latter involves the evacuation of any critical reflection on the social formation.

Identity formations are not strictly comparable to commodities. Yet they come into being as political, social, moral—and classed, raced, and gendered—currencies; they draw their value not in and from themselves as isolated entities, but from within a socially and historically embedded grid of meanings and multiple powers of investment, brokerage, and exchange. Their values are not fixed and frozen, but subject to shifting configurations of power and multiple modes of appropriation that refract underlying social relations. This is so, not because social identities are distinct and unique, or based on pristine and preformed essences, but because they are constructed in the shifting field of historically constituted social relations. Governed by *socially embedded transactions,* cultural distinctions through difference function as temporal, transient elements. This means that identity formations are not the result of autonomous, self-fashioning subjects engaged in a pluralist field of options. Theoretical reflection might enable us to generate great inventories of existing and possible combinations of identity formations, but situated subjects are not necessarily free to pick and choose among the cornucopia of options to make themselves anew. (The desire to make the world anew, to scrap bad histories and begin over again, with the belief that this involves not much more than self-willed redefinitions of identity, is fundamentally American. This is as much a part of John Winthrop's vision in 1630 of a Puritan-inspired "city upon a hill" where a new liturgy could be practiced, as it is of the most recent notion of dramaturgy where new selves can be self-fashioned through conscious, reflexive performativity.)[8] On the contrary, social identity formations are subject to the conditions of social surroundings and are traversed (unevenly, of course) by various institutional forces and relations. Identity formations are shaped not by fiat but by social limits and determinations. This underscores the importance of assessing *identity formations* as *social hieroglyphics*.

If the commodity as a social hieroglyphic refracts *class* formations, identity politics under late capitalism refracts the field in which antagonistic relations orbit around struggles over social and cultural—hence political— *classifications* as well as class relations. The analytical sensibility inherent in Marx's notion of critique, however, is not what characterizes the debates and analyses surrounding multiculturalism. Instead, what seems to be more common are frameworks of fragmentation, particularization, fetishization, and reification. In the absence of attempts to ground these developments in the context of historically specific social formations, analyses too frequently begin—and end—with invoking yet abandoning the social through identity politics. Here, Lukács's claim that reification is tantamount to forgetting comes back to haunt.

Economic Globalism versus the Cultural State

What kind of social formation is useful for assessing multiculturalism in the contemporary American context? I would like to sketch an analytic framework that begins to frame just how and why reification and fetishization capture much of the contemporary terrain upon which our understanding of multiculturalism and identity formations unfolds. Let me begin with *race* and the American state. It cannot be denied that race in the United States is a state-constructed and state-sanctioned mode of institutional materiality anchored in the fine print of juridical-legal language and shored up by apparatuses of what Weber called *legitimate force.* Let's just quickly recap the longer legacy. The state stood firmly behind slavery until the Civil War fractured the juridical-legal basis for the "peculiar institution." But even after abolition, the state turned its back to the systematic practices of social control exercised (de facto as well as de jure) over African Americans through institutionalized terror and violence. It was in the name of the state that the military conducted the ethnic cleansing of American Indians and the installment of the reservation system; we still have racial *nations* within the state. It was military conquest and then the imposition of the juridical-legal courts that rationalized the expropriation and transference of Mexican-held land out of Mexican hands. With the Chinese, the state denied citizenship to and excluded already emigrated people, by a series of acts culminating in the Chinese Exclusion Act of 1882, a policy that was modified and extended in various ways to Japanese, Filipino, Korean, and Asian-Indian immigrants in the United States. And many states enforced antimiscegenation laws well into the twentieth century. These examples all hinge on highly institutional-ized and formalized juridical-legal racial codifications that operated as state law (which is precisely why "race" and "ethnicity" should not be conflated as interchangeable terms, a tendency common in the social sciences).

But shortly after mid-century a qualitatively and formally new *cultural transformation* of the polity took shape. With the African American-led civil rights movement during the 1960s—a mere thirty years ago—and the ensu-ing "rights" legislation, the state began to alter substantially its long history of much older racializing strategies that predate the modern national for-mation and reach backward some three centuries. What is interesting about this modern conjuncture is that the state began to adopt, rather feebly, what we might call an ideological-culturalist realignment in terms of *race,* by re-coding and reframing the meaning of race with the rise of "rights" rhetoric and legislation.[9] It is in this conjuncture that the rhetoric and symbols of egalitarianism, long a site of deep contention, were given greater ideological weight, were thrust into broader circulation, and were invested with a new sense of cultural and political capital for *raced* groups and new sociopolitical social alliances (e.g., the New Left vis-à-vis "free speech," and what was ini-tially called the "women's movement"). None of these groups looked like the classic proletariat, a fact that also quickened the broader cultural turn in Marxian theory. These new groups and their affiliated social movements in-terrogated not just corporatism and the bourgeois social contract, but the entire institutional infrastructure of civil society.

Emerging in tandem with the impact of the civil rights movement was the politicized reemergence of additional raced groups—Chicanos, Native Americans, and Asian Americans (hitherto "Orientals")—each holding to, and in some cases making for the first time, their historical memories and raced identities in more reflexive ways. This cultural development is also im-portant because it marks the high point of modern democratic liberalism. The state's response to political struggles over the Enlightenment-rooted bourgeois social contract altered the *political surfaces* of the social terrain and made possible—indeed began to sanction—the modern framework within which identity formations took shape in dialogue with state power. This process has since expanded into multiculturalism. Of course American society (not the polity) has always been "multicultural," but only recently has this been recognized and *named* as such in the context of the modern state's attempt to work with a politically pragmatic blend of cultural benevolence and statecraft to configure its own legitimacy. In negotiating radical egalitarian struggles launched by raced and gendered constituents, the "racial state" took a significant cultural turn.[10]

Centrifugal Capitalism and Centripetal Culture

But there is more to the conjuncture. Just as the cultural dimensions of the state opened up new spaces for raced and gendered identity formations to be understood as such—that is, *in themselves* and *for themselves*—the fiscal crisis of the state began to register. At this point two antagonistically spiraling dynamics began to expand. On the one hand, a *centrifugal capitalism* began to push outward, disengaging from domestic commitments in pursuit of transnational strategies. On the other hand, a *centripetal culture* shaped in part by political developments and aided by new tiers of internal mass-media development augmented the process of identity formations. But key in this conjuncture was the beginning of a significant social split between global forces and domestic developments. It is with the deepening antagonisms as well as intimate ties between *global capitalism* and state-sanctioned *domestic culturalism* that the problems of racial reification—first as historically constructed farce, and now as deepening tragedy—begin to unfold along modern fetishized and reified lines. For as the polity began to give racial groups the recognition of political subjects with civil rights, the economy began to move in directions that would quite quickly strip away the political resolve to underwrite this important cultural turn. As capitalism began to spin centrifugally outward, dispersing and dispensing more and more of its material resources to maintain *transnational trenches and alliances*, liberal democracy was challenged by conservative realignments, and in some spheres became increasingly frail, embattled, and brittle, particularly over public expenditures associated with fiscal liberalism. Deindustrialization began to take its toll in the 1970s and throughout the 1980s. With the Reagan-Bush administration, economic deregulation promoted and intensified capital flight. But coupled with this is what we might call *social deregulation*—best understood as the *deregulation of the bourgeois-liberal social contract*. Many analysts have noted the ties between deindustrialization, capital flight, and the erosion of jobs and tax bases, all of which have been increasingly linked to the globalization of late capitalism. But social deregulation entails increasingly the shriveling of the state's commitment to domestic support, including the domestication of social conflict through public spending. The surplus populations of abandoned social zones have expanded with the deteriorization of capital investment. These developments reflect the erosion of the state's capacity to keep capital investment at home.[11] In this dystopian scenario, the logic of law and order surges to the forefront of public discourse as the primary form of legitimate social spending and as the fiscal policies of domesticity under siege. Today, the construction of prisons outpaces that of schools and universities, and the expansion of the carceral society signals the response of power to social change through state intervention and the necessity of "policing the crisis." In this framework, the massive conflagration in South-Central Los Angeles that came on the heels of the Rodney King verdict was not simply about the perception of a miscarriage of justice, but signaled instead the subterranean mass frustration of those social sectors most bypassed by the new globalism's obvious disinterest in them, and the failure to include them in the cornucopia of late capitalism's new worldly post-civil rights, post-Cold War prowess. Rage, the fruit of long, structural disenchantment, seizes opportunities to engage in what is left of a rapidly contracting public sphere. Incidently, the chants in the streets of "No justice, no peace," in the context of the largest urban upheaval in postwar American history, should be read against the erroneous postmodern claims that grand narratives no longer exercise their ideological grip and collective affect has withered.[12] That such social conflagrations stop short of what Hobsbawn called "collective bargaining by riot" aids the hasty and ahistorical analysis of these actions as nothing but mass criminal hooliganism. The poorest of the poor are too quickly conceived of as primarily a symptom of demographic mobility,[13] and come to signify the worst-case scenario of the arrested development or collapse of traditional communitarian morality.[14] In the process, the social deregulation of a society paralyzed by fiscal hemorrhage and the multiplication of "cultural differences" lends itself to the political opportunism of quick fixes.

The crisis in which we are now steeped is shaped by a deepening contradiction. On the one hand, there is the growing refusal to pay for the egalitarian reformism of the culturalist move launched and sanctioned during the civil rights movement with the state's attempt to amend the history of racial exclusion through policies addressing class, racial, and gender inclusion. On the other hand, there is the globalizing pressure of capitalism to *abandon the will to social investment within the national-domestic sphere*. It is in this conjuncture that neoconservatism as a post-civil rights-era discourse emerged to broker this crisis in the form of conservative populism. From the rise of the Moral Majority to Rush Limbaugh's mass-mediated conservative forum, conservative populism has moved forward with an interrogation of what Samuel Huntington some time ago called the "democratic distemper," by which he meant the state's willingness to *tolerate* the civil rights movement and related liberalist-driven cultural aberrations of American politics.[15] In the conjuncture, the academic squabbles over "political correctness" take on their amplified sound and fury, but are seldom understood as skirmishes in the shadow of what has come to matter much more: the apparent triumph of the new and deepening refusal of liberal democracy to embrace and pay for its own social ideals. In essence, any ideals outside of individuals in the marketplace appear in eclipse. A most revealing symptom of this junctural crisis is the rhetoric of "privatization," the lingua franca of social deregulation.

In the conjuncture, numerous clever diatribes in the form of misplaced concreteness chastise the academy for the decline in intellectual property values induced by too many resident aliens in the academy.[16] Here lies the rub: the academy is one of the only places left in modern civil society where reason, power, and tradition are supposed to be interrogated, examined, made transparent, and held accountable to publics in whose name they purport to operate. And not every voice in the academy is willing to sing praise to either statecraft or the now globally shaped forces of technocratic rationality. The flash points appear, not surprisingly, around themes of institutional contamination—and nothing these days grounds debates quicker than racialized topics like multiculturalism. Behind the manifest argument that "diversity" promotes a decline in standards, a falling rate of intelligence, and thus an increasingly dulled faculty, is a more latent realization: the academy's *critical* faculties have expanded in their sharpness as they take on increasingly more democratic representation. New angles of vision, additional and competing interpretations, and expanded debate give a vibrancy to democratic institutions, and democratic vibrancy is, by definition, hard to manage. The harangues against the academy, which too often pivot on multiculturalism, convey a nostalgia for cultural boundaries that were once less pervious. In this regard, the voices against multiculturalism echo with what they purport to detest: *tribalism.* It is through modernity's transformations that an older "insiders" tribalism of the *familiar,* hitherto beyond reproach, is being challenged by the new and problematic tribalism of social and cultural "outsiders."

The Social Logic of Multiculturalism

But multiculturalism is by no means a panacea. Ironically—and tragically—the ideology of privatization permeates the reification of identity formations: social groups are increasingly compelled to define their identity boundaries, which locate them and mark them as distinct. Moreover, these boundaries of distinction have to be increasingly defended. Multiculturalism is, in part, about groups struggling to achieve moral solidarity, a precious good in an era of profound transformation and instability. But there is a deeper social logic to this development that makes the antagonisms of identity formations much more complex than being composed simply of self-willed acts of collective volition or cast in terms of misguided "tribalism." Stripped of more and more of its resources, the cultural state has been left holding the bag, a bag stuffed mainly with symbols and sound bites for managing diversity as a rhetoric of moral consent, but backed (feebly) by state sanctions. What is key here is that the state contains precious little domestic fiscal capital. And under the new centrifugal flows of capital, the state is increasingly threatened with being reduced to a shell within which the politics of culture and the contentious ground of sprawling and multiplying identity formations become the major forms of symbolic and political capital in a context in which the notion of nation is what remains up for grabs—after capital flight. Culturalism becomes one of the few weapons of the weak,[17] but within an economically abandoned and fragmented civil society. In this dystopian scenario, symbols and the busywork of social differentiation and distinction fill in where money and social institutions cannot, and groups hailed by the new multiculturalism chase after their own interests in a domestically receding economy. As capitalism takes on a new worldly "postfordist" flexibility,[18] American civil society takes on an increasingly illiberal and intolerant moral ecology, and with signs of a growing populist inflexibility.

It is in this conjuncture that identities take on their signs as social hieroglyphics and where multiculturalism is formed and caught in crossfire. For in this conjuncture multiculturalism appears as both a surface promise and a deeper symptom. Multiculturalism signals a concession to earlier modes of exclusion and a cashing in on long-held promissory notes—back pay, if you like—as it gives us currencies that are seen internally as precious to those who have struggled to "own" the notes with their own names and pictures on them. For this is certainly part of what takes place in the struggle over the retrieval of "culture" and a usable past for a troubled present. None of this is trivial. The educational system—from kindergarten classes to the univer-sities—has manifestly entered the important promotional work of encour-aging toleration, pluralism, and diversity. But in a latent sense, this work is simultaneously engaged in rearguard damage control, juggling the domestic tensions brought by the post-civil rights legacy that now reaches into the dovetailing developments of centrifugal capital flight and centripetal cul-tural crisis.

If economic capital seeks flight, cultural capital seeks stable moorings. What we call "culture" in identity formations and multiculturalism operates as a kind of psychosocial currency—or, better yet, as multiple currencies. These currencies, however, are *not* meant to be recognized as equivalent. On the contrary, identity currency has value for its possessors precisely because of its distinctiveness and, in some cases, its purported and cherished incom-mensurableness. Identity is about own-ness, owning, possession, and not about dispossession. In some cases, identity struggles are responses to dis-possession. In addition, *difference* signifies an expanded notion of *cultural freedom*. Yet cultural distinctions operate upon a social terrain that is encir-cled by conditions of exchange; as currencies, they are limited in both their purchasing power and their circulation. Distinctions are meant to be partic-ular, not universal (even though they unwittingly invoke universalisms).[19] However, there are now lots of newly minted currencies vying for circula-tion and exchange: like economic capital, such forms of symbolic capital ex-pect to flourish in a restricted public sphere where they struggle in the con-text of a shriveling domestic realm that is crisscrossed by more and more trenches.

Multiculturalism is thus much more than "identity politics." In the dis-junction of economic expansion and cultural compression, multicultural-ism becomes a new and profoundly contentious social mixture that is not captured—indeed it is obscured—in the framework of pluralism. On the one hand, it appears—and rightly so—as a settling of accounts, a return of the repressed, an admission of diversity, a deepening of tolerance, an expan-sion of social membership, and an empirical sign of an enlarged civil society. Within the framework of liberal democracy, the ideology of egalitarianism positions us to applaud the expansion of the social bases of identity as im-portant, overdue, and progressive. For as promise, multiculturalism has the potential to manifest its best political moments by allowing raced groups to move beyond the show-and-tell domestication of late nineteenth-century folklore and the externally imposed caricaturizing of people into cultural texts and artifacts. It does this by bringing into political discourse the promises dangled in the ideology of a larger equality enshrined at the core of bourgeois liberal democracy, by giving groups a sense of place in society and in history, by offering the comfort that comes (tendentiously) in being able to say something about who they are, by attempting to rethink morally and reconstruct institutionally the meanings behind egalitarianism, and by insisting that social power be truly empowering, enhancing, and protecting for all.

On the other hand, it indicates just as much an unsettling of the presumed homogeneity of American society, signals a call for more cultural repression to nip an emerging "tribalism" in the bud, and equates the renewal of civic virtue and a return to *traditionalism* with an antimodernist intolerance articulated in the shadows of a receding American dream. As the conservative populist Rush Limbaugh sums it up, multiculturalism is the label for all those groups who have failed to make it in America.[20] The sensibility behind Limbaugh's diagnosis feeds into and off of a "differential racism" that substitutes "culture"—and by extension ideology—for "biology" by insisting on insurmountable "cultural differences" for those who imagine a social order in which undesired "mixing" can be prevented by the dismantling of the liberal state.[21]

Taken together, all of these aspects enable multiculturalism to register the full gamut of appropriations—from celebration to demonization. No wonder multiculturalism reverberates antagonistically across virtually every major social institution. It is an overloaded term, a symbolic container that is not capable of containing the range of investments that it attempts to carry. If it is a social hieroglyphic, it is one that is in the process of rupturing under the pressure of multiple conflicting meanings. The strains are now acutely visible. In the conjuncture between economic globalism and cultural crisis, we might begin to look at multiculturalism in two ways: in terms of its own *internal identitarian logic* and as a *symptomatic condition of the disjunction between global and domestic realms within the social formation of late capitalism.* Multiculturalism operates simultaneously as *identity politics* and as *sociosystemic politics.* Both are intimately entwined. As identitarian logic, multiculturalism locates the internal, psychic, and culturally collective desires for, and contestations over, a sense of social place—an arena of protection—in an increasingly turbulent social formation. Here—which is where the term "identity politics" takes hold—piecemeal meanings are fought out, lines of identity demarcations are struggled over. For here is where identities mirror to an extent the identifications imposed from above and outside, and juggle the fact that they are not self-made, but "constrained to see themselves as a community."[22] On the terrain of racialization, gender, and sexuality, we call these *social places* Asian American, Chicano, African American, Native American, feminist, lesbian, gay, and so on. Certainly the list expands with decreasing social stigma beyond the raced and gendered frameworks to include ethnicities and political orientations. Moreover, as dimensions within a social spectrum, none of these sites are airtight and hermetically sealed (even though, upon closer internal examination, they can include, but are never totally encompassed by, wrenching schisms along micromanaged lines of hyperidentified demarcations and over criteria of authenticity, taking on a spirit kindred to nationalism but without reference to a state). In a sense, these identity demarcations are more like landmarks that are erected upon and driven into a social chunk of very sprawling terrain; they attempt to capture and mark the vast surroundings and the deep layers of social lives as *categorical imperatives* (just when Kantianism was thought to have been abandoned). Nonetheless, they overlap and move outwardly and unevenly across institutions and in relationship to various social movements.

It would be the height of arrogance to dismiss as socially constructed moral fictions the meanings that are charged in the identities we inherit and inhabit, for it is in these cultural interstices that we live our socially and institutionally marked everyday lives. On the surface is where we do the bulk of our thinking, swim in our emotions, navigate with our institutionally traversed common sense. We dwell in the inner logic of these surface spheres, our modern social cells; they govern experience and enable us to feel so deep. Historical forces much larger than our individual or collective selves compel us to take on our raced, gendered, and classed places, and to adjust to the fields in which these identities are located. We live and act in their names, working with the combination of plus or minus signs that accrue around them. As modernity churns on, new identity formations hitherto nonexistent, or previously denied, denigrated, devalued, undermined, punished, and repressed, continue to emerge. They register, understandably so, as major psychic as well as social victories. The indulgence in identity politics afforded by multiculturalism can make us feel more whole, more like subjects than objects. Yet could it be that our sense of the social whole may be shrinking? For multiculturalism also appears now to be the latest unfolding of a half-gratifying, half-debilitating social logic. It functions in the contemporary context as a political-demographic fix, and as a patching of fissures that have opened on the social surfaces over the last quarter century. Inheritors of this cultural logic speak in a language of subjectivity and place, and are busy maintaining popular memory; overseers of the new multicultural workforce speak of diversity management. These seem to be the preferred views that embrace the notion of social autonomy and domestic(ated) pluralism.

From Farce to Tragedy?

As with all social identities, raced identities—those that are probably most associated with the term "multiculturalism"—are the result of historical constructions. Marx once suggested that history first unfolds as tragedy, and then repeats itself as farce. In rethinking the historical development of *race* as an organizing operation configured in power relations, we might reverse Marx's summary statement: race as a social category emerges first as a fabricated symbolic construction (farce), and then operates through objectified and mediated institutional practices as social "truth effects" (tragedy). Once put into motion, the fabrications of racialization take on the power of truth as they wind along socially tragic paths. Farce has taken on great power. Through it we are forced to squeeze symbolic virtues out of historical, social, and institutional coercion; we are compelled to weld *artificial* identities into *natural* ones. But we work with raced identities on already reified ground. In the context of domination, raced identities are imposed and internalized, then renegotiated and reproduced. From artificial to natural, we court a hard-to-perceive social logic that reproduces the very conditions we strain to overcome. When most effective, ideology *dehistoricizes* historical developments and fixes through *naturalization* what is historically constituted. Multiculturalism refracts both the attempt to overcome historical fixity and naturalization, and the seduction of reification.

There is, it seems, another potentially tragic outcome. The multiplication of identity formations can also purge the desire for something bigger, and *bigger for all.* As localized identities become more numerous and compressed, the capacity to achieve a larger social identity appears to be compromised. In building more and more symbolic arenas filled with more and more symbolic strategies of distinction, the vision of a transformed society that is substantively better for all atrophies against the velocity and force of the superficial and feebly institutionalized identities. What is troubling in the conjuncture is how *surfaces* of culture in general, and multiculturalism in particular, seem now more capable than ever of continued expansion as our "preferable" identity locations begin to compress and contract. This development is likely to be the most pressing challenge to a radical democracy, for the very principles of a shared framework of political universalism that protects the raison d'être of particularisms are in the process of cultural eclipse. Ironically, with the critique of reductionism, the distaste for the structural side of things, the disdain for universalism, and the dismissal of history as a narrative trope, we seem all too tempted to adopt a reduced if not pulverized notion of the social contract. What is more salient is the growing urgency of patrolling the borders of besieged identities. And as our general, worldly political horizons shrink, our internal identities compress more and more along aestheticized—and ascetic—lines of meaning and distinction, where a sense of certainty and place can be had in a world in which uncertainty and dislocation deepen and intensify. In this regard, there is a disturbing parallel, or kindred cultural spirit—notwithstanding the blatant contradictions here—between the deepening *psychic interiorization* that characterizes identity politics and the fear of the *national interior* being threatened by unwanted, border-crossing immigrants.

Conclusion

If the globalization of late capitalism continues to develop in ways that strip liberal democracy of the domestic capacity to maintain a vision of the social, of "society," while eviscerating the will to use social resources to mitigate the social conflict rooted in the seeming intractability of inequality, then the cultural trenches will likely multiply, deepen, and widen. As corporations rush to secure new positions of strategic power in the global economy (a "strategic essentialism" for the transnational capitalist class willing to forsake domestic peace!), and the draining of fiscal resources for the domestic-national sphere continues, the work of bridge building across the social fissures of *socioeconomic classes* as well as *cultural classifications* will grow in urgency precisely because such *social work* is just as likely to shrivel in importance as it becomes overwhelmed by the decomposition of the economic infrastructure and the spiraling inflation of symbolic capital. The hand-wringing over essentialism and metaphysics that surrounds us and from which we have learned much also tends to abdicate the political challenges over the larger social contract to forces inimical to the egalitarianism that drives the most important facets of multiculturalism and its important place within an expanding democracy.

I want to underscore the need for taking our location in the academy seriously—for this is where we work. We are linked intimately to the problems I've sketched. There is no avoiding them. It is the fate of our work—whether we work with or ignore the larger fate of modern American civil society. I suspect that the split will deepen between the culturalist state and economic globalization, and this will make our work as critical intellectuals within the academy increasingly charged. If I understand our historical context and our institutional location correctly, we, as *cultural workers* working in the cultural infrastructure, have to see to it that the road signs that help us map out the emerging struggles surrounding identity politics and multiculturalism do not point toward our own little Sarajevos. We are nowhere near this dismal example. But it would be quite unwise for us to think that we are exempt from such possibilities.

We live in the conjuncture. It is also our context that presents us with a window of opportunity in which to rethink and rework new social possibilities for a greater social contract, one that builds from multiculturalism toward substantive egalitarianism and political protection for cultural, racial, gender, and sexual differences. The challenge is to recognize that the identity formations that have come about are important. But if we are to weather the crisis between globalization and domestic erosion, such identity formations simply will not be enough to ensure the greater collective forms of engagement in the critical transformation of civil society. Put another way, multiculturalism is necessary but not sufficient. Multiculturalism is not enough. It has to be reconceptualized as *means* rather than *ends*. This is where we might begin: as a key element in our social formation, multiculturalism presents new challenges for us to see to it that the fetishization of identities and the reification of differences do not take hold in ways that deny us *in our partial differences* the mutually enhancing chances to reconfigure the crisis-ridden social contract.

Notes

1. See Stuart Hall, "The Problem of Ideology—Marxism without Guarantees," in B. Matthews, ed., *Marx: 100 Years On* (London: Lawrence & Wishart, 1983); Ernesto Laclau and Chantal Mouffe, *Hegemony and Socialist Strategy: Towards a Radical Democratic Politics* (New York: Verso, 1985); Pierre Bourdieu, "Objectification Objectified," in *The Logic of Social Practice* (Stanford, Calif.: Stanford University Press, 1990), 30–41.

2. But see Frederic Jameson, *Postmodernism, or, The Cultural Logic of Late Capitalism* (Durham, N.C.: Duke University Press, 1991), and Anthony Giddens, *Modernity and Self-Identity: Self and Society in the Late Modern Age* (Stanford, Calif.: Stanford University Press, 1991).

3. Bryan D. Palmer, *The Reification of Language and the Writing of Social History* (Philadelphia: Temple University Press, 1990).

4. Karl Marx, *Capital*, vol. 1 (New York: Vintage Books, 1977), 163–78; Gajo Petrovic, "Reification," in *A Dictionary of Marxist Thought*, ed. Tom Bottomore (Cambridge: Harvard University Press, 1983), 41–43.

5. Marx, *Capital*, 167.

6. Georg Lukács, "Reification and the Consciousness of the Proletariat," in *History and Class Consciousness: Studies in Marxist Dialectics* (Cambridge: MIT Press, 1971).

7. For Lukács and Gramsci, this was registered as the fragmentation of the historical subject. Lukács and Gramsci are perhaps the last of the major Western Marxists to hold firmly to the notion of the proletariat as the historical subject. In the context of an expanding mass culture, the emergence of fascism underwritten by working-class populism was enough to install a deep distrust in the belief that exploited classes occupied the most privileged social location for the development of critical subjectivity. This indeterminacy of class undermined the Marxian prop of the labor theory of value and the automatic and unproblematic reliance on economism. From here on, social and cultural theory register this unraveling of economic reductionism through the increasingly focused lenses of "ideology," "discourse," and "culture."

8. Judith Butler, *Gender Trouble: Feminism and the Subversion of Identity* (New York: Routledge, 1990).

9. I am not suggesting that the state took on a cultural dimension in the context of the civil rights movement. As a primarily political institution, the state is by definition a cultural enterprise and is deeply enmeshed in the making and brokering of cultural relations. Politics is thus never an arena removed from questions of culture; rather, it is a key site that registers and hosts cultural as well as other struggles.

10. On the "racial state," see Michael Omi and Howard Winant, *Racial Formation in the United States*, 2d ed. (New York: Routledge, 1994). Here, it needs to be pointed out that the problems associated with what could be called the "cultural turn" in the social sciences and the humanities are not simply the creations of schools of thought (e.g., British Cultural Studies, deconstruction, or feminist theory). More consideration deserves to be given to how we might situate theoretical shifts and new social knowledge formations in the junctures of social change. Theoretical shifts are thus more than cases of intellectual innovation unfolding as paradigm shifts.

11. Robert Reich, President Clinton's secretary of labor, views global capitalism as based in the forms of transnational tiers of management, and these forms operate beyond the notion of traditional state boundaries. According to Reich, in the modern economy there is little government can do to stem the flexible mobility of corporate investments from one country to another. Global multinational corporatism transcends the state. In Reich's view, there "will be no national products or technologies, no national corporations, no national industries. There will no longer be national economies, at least as we have come to understand the concept. All that will remain rooted within national borders are the people who comprise a nation" (*Los Angeles Times*, 12 December 1992: A22). See also Robert Reich, *The Work of Nations* (New York: Alfred A. Knopf, 1991).

12. On the withering away of grand narratives, see Jean-François Lyotard, *The Postmodern Condition: A Report on Knowledge*, trans. Geoff Bennington and Brian Massumi (Minneapolis: University of Minnesota Press, 1984). The thesis on the waning of affect can be found in Jean Baudrillard, *Simulations*, trans. P. Foss, P. Patton, and P. Beitchman (New York: Semiotext[e], 1983), and *In the Shadow of the Silent Majorities . . . or the End of the Social and Other Essays*, trans. P. Foss (New York: Semiotext[e], 1983).

13. William Julius Wilson, *The Declining Significance of Race: Blacks and Changing American Institutions* (Chicago: University of Chicago Press, 1978).

14. Amitai Etzioni, *The Spirit of Community: Rights, Responsibilities and the Communitarian Agenda* (New York: Crown Publishers, 1993); Robert N. Bellah et al., *The Good Society* (New York: Vintage Books, 1992).

15. Samuel Huntington, "Chapter III: The United States," in *The Crisis of Democracy: Report on the Governability of Democracies to the Trilateral Commission*, ed. Michel Crozier, Samuel P. Huntington, and Joji Watanuki (New York: New York University Press, 1975).

16. Cf. Alan Bloom, *The Closing of the American Mind* (New York: Simon and Schuster,

1987); Dinesh D'Souza, *The Politics of Race and Sex on Campus* (New York: Free Press, 1991); Jon Weiner, "Campus Voices Right and Left," *Nation,* 12 December 1988: 644–45.

17. I draw the phrase from James C. Scott, *Weapons of the Weak: Everyday Forms of Peasant Resistance* (New Haven: Yale University Press, 1985).

18. David Harvey, *The Condition of Postmodernity: An Enquiry into the Origins of Social Change* (Cambridge, Mass.: Basil Blackwell, 1989).

19. Ernesto Laclau, "Universalism, Particularism, and the Question of Identity," *October* 61 (summer 1992): 83–90. See also Joan Scott, "Multiculturalism and the Politics of Identity," *October* 61 (summer 1992): 12–19.

20. Rush H. Limbaugh, *The Way Things Ought to Be* (New York: Pocket Books, 1992).

21. Etienne Balibar, "Is There a 'Neo-Racism'?" in Etienne Balibar and Immanuel Wallerstein, *Race, Nation, Class: Ambiguous Identities* (New York: Verso, 1991), 21–23.

22. Ibid., 18. Cf. also Joan W. Scott, "Experience," and Jane Flax, "The End of Innocence," in *Feminists Theorize the Political* (New York: Routledge, 1992).

CHAPTER THREE

Gender, Class, and Multiculturalism

Rethinking "Race" Politics

ANGELA Y. DAVIS

Last week, during the television coverage of election night, I saw a black and white choir singing black gospel music at the Arkansas state capital. Just then, something struck me about the multicultural veneer of the Clinton victory, and the use of the televisual presence of black people to create an illusion of victory over racism. Considering the virtual absence of discussions on racism (outside of Clinton's encounter with Sister Souljah in which she was portrayed as an archetypal racist), this not only camouflaged the persistence of anti-black racism, but it effectively rendered more palatable the absence of Latino, Native, and Asian Americans. In fact, many of the current strategies that propose to make marginal cultures visible and accessible tend to reproduce ideologies of racism, as well as male dominance and middle-class privilege. I therefore want to suggest a number of ways we can look critically at multiculturalism, not in order to adopt a general position against multiculturalism, but in order to predict and identify possible strategies of containment and co-optation. This will hopefully enable us to move toward a vision that incorporates multiculturalism within a context of powerful political resistance to racism, as it is informed by and in turn informs economic exploitation and male dominance.

I will begin by sharing with you an excerpt from an article that recently appeared in the *Kennedy Career Strategist* by Linda Mitchell entitled "Get Ready to Manage a Salad Bowl":

> In the past, managing a labor force really meant managing white males. However, experts tell us we have jumped out of the "melting pot" and into the "salad bowl." The once-homogeneous workforce is becoming decidedly heterogeneous, and the parts of the whole are determined to retain their own cultures and customs. . . . Some African-Americans will "signify" when they are curious, but their etiquette prevents them from asking a direct question. . . . Some Asians may prefer not to speak unless thoroughly knowledgeable about the subject—research first, then talk—and even then, only when invited to speak. . . . How is corporate America dealing with this? A number of megacompanies have complex training programs. . . . These multicultural programs generically are termed "workforce diversity management." . . . Progressive firms want every employee to receive diversity training.[1]

Of course, the most obvious flaw in this notion of corporate multiculturalism is the assumption that until recently the U.S. workforce consisted primarily of white men. But what I want to suggest is that the concept of "diversity management" may not merely reflect the way multiculturalism is being translated into corporate workplace strategies. Additionally, it may reveal the potentially problematic character of the popular presentation of multiculturalism discourse as an overarching strategy for putting racism to rest. "Diversity management" assumes that a racially, ethnically, and culturally heterogeneous workforce needs to be managed or controlled in ways that contain and suppress conflict. This process is precisely a means of preserving and fortifying power relations based on class, gender, and race. Such disciplining of diversity is, in fact, a strategy for more exhaustive control of the working class. Recall the debates during the last century on the abolition of slavery. Northern industrialists foresaw the end of slavery as providing conditions for a more effective exploitation of the entire labor force, black and white alike.

In the debates around workplace multicultural strategies, there is little discussion about persisting economic inequities, dead-end jobs, unemployment, job hazards, environmental disease, and sexual harassment. Although these may be acknowledged as problems, they are rarely presented as integral to "multicultural programs."

Looking at another constellation of institutions, the so-called correctional system, strategies explicitly named multicultural are even more unabashedly subordinated to the discipline process. Because of the pervasiveness of "racial conflict"—between white and black, white and Latino, and Latino and black prisoners—current multicultural programs (which aim to prevent the violent explosions in which guards and administrations are often implicated) strive for ways to reestablish control over inmate populations. Since jail and prison populations are represented as increasingly more racially and culturally heterogeneous, efforts are under way to reorganize them as racially and culturally harmonious institutions. Actually, we are confronted with increasing racial homogeneity in the incarcerated population. It is fairly common knowledge that young black men are more likely to be found in jails and prisons than in colleges and universities. In a way that parallels the corporate compartmentalization of multiculturalism, correctional institutions rarely if ever address the underlying reasons for vast increases in the incarcerated population and for the ideological process of criminalization that leads so many people of color into the jails and prisons of this country.

I have alluded to workforce and prison strategies for the purpose of suggesting ways of looking at multicultural educational practices in terms of the power relationships they may implicitly affirm, conceal, or reconfigure. Ultimately, I want to pose the question of whether, or what kind of, multicultural approaches can potentially take on the political task of challenging the gender, class, and race hierarchies that continue to shape the institutions of this country.

Progressive approaches to nonracist education that attempt to contest white monocultural dominance are generally referred to as multicultural. The debate around multiculturalism has unfolded within the United States around such notions as "diversity," "political correctness," "pluralistic multiculturalism versus particularistic multiculturalism," and so on. As progressive students, staff, and faculty, we generally have positioned ourselves as advocates of diversity and multiculturalism, in opposition to the defenders of a monolithic notion of education that privileges a white Western intellectual tradition. In the process of fighting these battles around elementary, secondary, and higher education, and specifically around the most immediate policies implemented in these institutions, we sometimes ignore the historical and political context within which these debates and campaigns have taken shape.

In thinking about multiculturalism, I found it helpful to revisit some of the more salient moments in the recent history of race discourse and in a relatively unsystematic way I want to evoke some of the terms that have been used over the course of the last half century or so to represent challenges to the persisting problem of racism: "Assimilation," "Cultural Pluralism," "Desegregation," "Integration," "Black Nationalism," "Black Power," "Chicano

Power," "Puerto Rican Independence," "Indian Sovereignty," "Affirmative Action," "Reverse Discrimination," "Difference," "Diversity," "Multiculturalism." With some obvious exceptions that represent the input of militant oppositional movements, what these terms have in common are implications of "overcoming" racism without necessarily shaking up the power structures that are expressed through and that constitute the social context of racism. In the 1960s, Malcolm X made the observation that integration demands, as advocated by the early civil rights movement, did not take into consideration the fact that we might well be fighting for embarkation onto a sinking ship. What they all have in common, however, including the slogans addressing issues of power, independence, and sovereignty, is a failure to address the ways in which gender, race, and class intersect and inform each other in complex, mutating ways. As Kum-Kum Bhavnani and Margaret Coulson have asked, "How do ['race,' class, and gender] combine with and/or cut across one another? How is gender experienced through racism? How is class shaped by gender and 'race'?"[2]

I am not suggesting that we throw out all these concepts. As historical evidence of important contestations around demands raised by social movements, they reveal the extent to which what we count as victories often challenge us to rethink and reorganize the terms and terrain on which battles against racism, sexism, and class exploitation are fought.

"Race" has always been difficult to talk about in terms not tainted by ideologies of racism, with which the notion of "race" shares a common historical evolution. The assumption that a taxonomy of human populations can be constructed based on phenotypical characteristics has been discredited. Yet we continue to use the term "race," even though many of us are very careful to set it off in quotation marks to indicate that while we do not take seriously the notion of "race" as biologically grounded, neither are we able to think about racist power structures and marginalization processes without invoking the socially constructed concept of "race." Obviously, there is a reason we are stuck with the term "race," and that has to do with the persistence of racism and processes of racialization that perpetuate race-based oppression, even as they appear to move beyond it.

I am convinced that the category "race" is so laden with contradictions that it no longer works in the way it used to, at least within the context of radical theories and practices. Until the fifties and sixties, one way of indicating one's opposition to policies of segregation in the black community was to identify oneself as an upholder of the "race." Billie Holiday, for example, referred to herself as a "race woman." That this has become an obsolete way of identifying oneself is also indicative of the fact that many of us find the term "the black community" problematic in ways that could not have occurred to us thirty or forty years ago. That "race" no longer works as a focus of resistance organizing does not mean that racism has become obsolete and that we should discard it as a concept. I certainly do not wish to associate myself with those who claim that a rising importance of class relations has led to "the declining significance of race" or with those who see no other way of moving away from victimization paradigms than by means of individualistic notions like the precedence of character over race.

But many of us who persist in raising charges of racism—whether in relation to the configuration and exploitation of labor, the educational system, housing, health and welfare issues, or the legal, law-enforcement, and penal systems—are regarded as relics from the past. Even within progressive movements around reproductive rights, sexual harassment, gay and lesbian rights, and trade-union campaigns, charges of racism are often viewed as old and tired arguments. The arguments may be old—and certainly those of us who propose them are tired of always having to point to racism— but there is a sense in which the term "racism" still maintains its ability to ruffle people's feathers. There is a persistently piercing character about the term "racism" that is one sign of the perseverance of power relations based on race.

The term racism itself sharply calls for redress of historical and current grievances. It places blame in institutional structures and policies as well as in attitudes and behavior. But what happens when we shift our arguments away from charges of racism and begin to talk about difference, diversity, and multiculturalism? "Difference" and "diversity" are descriptive: people are different; cultures are diverse. In this context, we must be aware of the fact that multiculturalism can easily become a way to guarantee that these differences and diversities are retained superficially while becoming homogenized and harmonized politically, especially along axes of class, gender, and sexuality. Although this is not an inevitability, multiculturalism can become a polite and euphemistic way of affirming persisting, unequal power relationships by representing them as equal differences. Somehow, I get more excited at a Public Enemy concert when I hear young people chanting "Fuck racism" (even though I might find problematic moments in the performance) than in a discussion on "recognizing diversity."

These unequal power relationships are not only those based on white supremacy. Sexism is often glossed over or even justified by invoking multiculturalism. Nira Yuval-Davis argues that in Britain, various kinds of funda-

mentalism have been "the main beneficiaries of the adoption of multiculturalist norms." Multiculturalism, she argues, "has provided [fundamental-
ism's] chief ideological weapon. . . . The multiculturalist consensus . . . sees
racism not as a form of institutionalized inequality, but as a matter of different mutually exclusive ways of life which must be preserved." She continues
to point out that "Women's demands for freedom and equality are seen as
being outside 'cultural traditions' (often themselves only half understood),
and therefore not legitimate. The most conservative versions are often considered to be the most 'authentic.' Appeals to culture and tradition have been
used to attack women's autonomous organizing."[3]

Multiculturalism often emphasizes what Barry Troyna calls "the expres-
sive features of ethnic minority cultures" and is thus associated with what he
calls "voyeuristic imperatives."[4] In Canada, where multiculturalism has a
history that defined it as a strategy for containment of the separatist demands of the Front de Libération Québécois during the late 1960s, it is often
referred to by community activists as "multivulturalism." In Ontario, the
most visible face of the federal multicultural policy is a caravan that is organized each year in which each "culture" has its own float—to use Faith
Nolan's words—"for the Wasps to gaze upon, for the vultures to devour." Interestingly enough, last year a memo from the Ministry of Multicultural Affairs—where the minister, by no coincidence, is white—circulated among
the provincial offices declaring that gay and lesbian projects were not to be
funded, because they do not represent cultures and therefore are not to
be included under multiculturalism. This meant, for example, that if a
Jamaican lesbian project applied for a grant, it would not be considered
fundable as multicultural. In a related move, indigenous peoples' projects
are not funded by the Ministry of Multiculturalism because there is a
Department of Indian Affairs. Needless to say, there is a great deal of progressive grassroots opposition to the multicultural policies of the Canadian
government.

Multiculturalism has acquired a quality akin to spectacle. The metaphor
that has displaced the melting pot is the salad. A salad consisting of many ingredients is colorful and beautiful, and it is to be consumed by someone.
Who consumes multiculturalism is the question begging to be asked. This
leads us back to the corporate multicultural strategies, wherein the purpose
of acknowledging difference is to guarantee that the enterprise functions as
efficiently as it would if there were no cultural differences at all. As R. Roosevelt Thomas put it in an article in the *Harvard Business Review*:

The correct question today is not "How are we doing on race relations?" or "Are we promoting enough minority people and women?" but rather "Given the diverse work force I've got, am I getting the productivity, does it work as smoothly, is morale as high, as if every person in the company was the same sex and race and nationality?"[5]

Thomas is the executive director of the American Institute for Managing Diversity, Inc. at Morehouse College in Atlanta. As this approach discards the melting pot analogy in favor of the "unassimilated diversity" of the metaphorical salad, the assumption is that not only is it not necessary to be a straight white male in order to participate in this process, you need not even pretend to be one. Yet, although you are permitted to be an "other," you must work "as if" you were not a member of a marginalized group. Corporate culture, Thomas argues, should not attempt to "assimilate diversity into the dominant culture," but rather should "build a culture that can digest unassimilated diversity." But the end result should be the same as if racial, gender, and sexual homogeneity prevailed. Workers may look different and talk (even signify), eat, dance, and act differently from one another, but they will be expected to be as productive "as if" they were all the same. This is a process reminiscent of the Hegelian Idea that externalizes itself and unfolds in wondrous historical heterogeneity, but in the final analysis, it returns to itself and remains its unified self.

Diane Ravitch's defense of cultural pluralism in opposition to cultural particularism has a similar ring. Pluralists, she claims, seek a "richer common culture," while the particularists insist that "no common culture is possible or desirable." While she opposes reconfiguration of school curricula, she applauds such celebrations as Black History Month and Women's History Month: "The point of those celebrations is to demonstrate that neither race nor gender is an obstacle to high achievement. They teach all children that everyone, regardless of their race, religion, gender, ethnicity or family origin, can achieve self-fulfillment, honor, and dignity in society if they aim high and work hard."[6]

Both of these conceptions imply that difference doesn't make any difference, if only we acquire knowledge about it. If our difference is understood, consumed, and "digested," we simultaneously can be different and perform "as if" we really were middle-class, straight white males. Difference as object of "distaste," "dislike," or "hate" must be transformed into difference as object of knowledge. In other words, the locus of racism is in the attitudes of individuals. White racists "hate" Latinos, Native people, Asians, and black people because they have internalized negative stereotypes of our respective cultures. And we, as people of color, have internalized negative stereotypes of each other. Although it is certainly the case that racist representations inform attitudes of hostility, the notion that if we simply correct those stereotypes with knowledge of the "true" cultures, we will no longer be hated and will no longer hate each other, is extremely dangerous. I am certainly not opposed to enlightenment, but policies of enlightenment by themselves do not necessarily lead to radical transformations of power structures.

In fact, some of us already have learned how not to hate each other. There are now harmonious multiracial formations that continue to develop and implement antiracist projects in the context of the law. Here I cannot resist the temptation to evoke Clarence Thomas. Not that I claim a relationship with Clarence Thomas, even though we are racially marked in the same way and to a certain extent share a common historical culture. For example, he claims a relationship to Malcolm X. So do I. He claims a relationship to the Black Panther Party. So do I. But there is a political demarcation that defines my relationship to that political culture in a way that is very different from his. Cultures are not politically neutral. A multiculturalism that does not acknowledge the political character of culture will not, I am sure, lead toward the dismantling of racist, sexist, homophobic, economically exploitative institutions.

As a black woman, I am aware of the extent to which the politics of "race" have evolved around black-white constructions: black versus white or white versus black or black and white. These binary constructions tend to ignore everyone who does not fit into them. Since women, gay men, and lesbians have not been historically acknowledged on the black side of this binary, not even all black people get included. But what I want to refer to here is the way in which relationships among communities of color are being crowded into this paradigm as the object of multiculturalism's reconciliation. Relationships between Asian and black communities, for example, are currently represented through the media in simplistic terms that draw upon the antagonistic representation of black-white relationships, with black people occupying the "white" space and Asians occupying the "black" space, or vice versa. The cover of the October 1992 issue of *Atlantic Monthly* depicts two faces in profile confronting each other, one colored black and the other brown, with the bold caption "Blacks vs. Browns." This is the way the cover advertises a disturbing article by Jack Miles entitled "Immigration and the New American Dilemma." To criticize this rigid way of thinking about relationships among people of color across racial boundaries is not to deny the real conflicts and the all too prevalent racist attitudes in many of our communities. Rather it is to say that a multiculturalism that posits itself as the solution to racial conflict, based on the black-white model, will hardly move us forward.

If multiculturalism is to be liberated from historically outmoded ways of conceptualizing race, it may be helpful to consider some of the theories and practices associated with women of color over the last decade. Departing from the publication of *This Bridge Called My Back*, a great deal of work on class, gender, and sexuality has emerged in relation to women of color feminist theory.[7] The political construction of women of color as a new historical subject has served as an important rallying point for new social movements. Among others, Avtar Brah's notion of "differential racialization" and Chela Sandoval's theory of "differential consciousness" may be helpful to those of us who want to build upon what Wahneema Lubiano calls a "strong multiculturalism."[8] This conclusion is, of course, a point of departure. I will simply say that the kind of multiculturalism that makes sense in 1992 is a multiculturalism that, in Manning Marable's words, not only informs but transforms: a multiculturalism in which difference does make a difference.[9]

Notes

1. Linda Mitchell, "Get Ready to Manage a Salad Bowl," *Kennedy Career Strategist* 5 (January 1990): 3.

2. Kum-Kum Bhavnani and Margaret Coulson, "Transforming Socialist Feminism: The Challenge of Racism," *Feminist Review* 23 (May–June 1986): 81–93.

3. Nira Yuval-Davis, "Fundamentalism, Multiculturalism and Women in Britain," in *"Race," Culture and Difference*, ed. James Donald and Ali Rattansi (London: Sage Publications, 1992), 284.

4. Barry Troyna, "Can You See the Join?: An Historical Analysis of Multicultural and Anti-racist Education Policies," in *Racism and Education*, ed. Dawn Gill, Barbara Mayor, and Maud Blair (London: Sage Publications, 1992), 70.

5. R. Roosevelt Thomas Jr., "From Affirmative Action to Affirming Diversity," *Harvard Business Review* (March–April 1990): 109.

6. Diane Ravitch, "Multiculturalism: E Pluribus Plures," *American Scholar* (summer 1990): 340.

7. Cherríe Moraga and Gloria Anzaldúa, eds., *This Bridge Called My Back: Writings by Radical Women of Color* (Watertown, Mass.: Persephone Press, 1981).

8. Avtar Brah, "Difference, Diversity and Differentiation," in *"Race," Culture and Difference*, 126–49; Chela Sandoval, "U.S. Third World Feminism: The Theory and Method of Oppositional Consciousness in the Postmodern World," *Genders* 10 (spring 1991): 1–24; Ted Gordon and Wahneema Lubiano, "The Statement of the Black Faculty Caucus," in *Debating P.C.: The Controversy over Political Correctness on College Campuses*, ed. Paul Berman (New York: Laurel, 1992), 249–57.

9. Manning Marable, "Multicultural Democracy: The Emerging Majority for Justice and Peace," in *The Crisis of Color and Democracy: Essays on Race, Class and Power* (Monroe, Maine: Common Courage Press, 1992): 249–59.

CHAPTER FOUR

Academic Apartheid

American Indian Studies and "Multiculturalism"

M. ANNETTE JAIMES GUERRERO

Sweet America ... To me I see you Naked,
While Others see just what they want to See.

Buffy Sainte-Marie, "Sweet America"

Multiculturalism or Decolonization?

It is an unfortunate state of affairs that ethnic scholars, as well as nonethnic academicians and educators, are advocating a "multicultural" vision for American education without challenging the paradigmatic status quo that creates such problems as educational disparity and social hegemony in the first place. These well-known and respected educators are aware of the racism and sexism rampant in our social institutions, but are still advocating accommodationist resolutions to those with a non-"ethnic" and even anti-"minority" mindset, a mindset that perpetuates these social ills, Euro-American privilege, and the presumed superiority of "Western civilization."

For American Indians, there is a substantial case to be made for the necessity of *decolonization before any genuine multiculturalism* can take place. Decolonization is a necessary first step in countering the relations of subordination imposed on Native peoples and established by U.S. colonizers through federal Indian policy. Putting decolonization before multicultural-

ism would ease the tension produced by the mandated policies of assimilation *and* marginalization to which Native peoples have been subject in the
process of their colonization. It would allow for compensatory reparations
to be made to be used for educational restoration and preservation programs. This would, in turn, counter the hegemony that perpetuates the
myth of the intellectual superiority of "Western civilization" at the expense
of indigenous peoples, our cultures and contributions to modern society,
and our sophisticated *traditional* knowledge bases. Such an educational plan
would have to be community-centered, and concerned with providing survival skills for employment and opportunities for academic and intellectual
endeavors. Such a plan would be conceptualized from an indigenous worldview of balance with and within the natural order, what some active scholars
are calling *Indigenism*.

American Indian Studies solutions to the problems wrought by U.S. colonization will have to address, therefore, the cultural, economic, and environmental spheres with sociopolitical agendas from Native peoples, and will
have to challenge the conventional wisdom of academic dogma and orthodoxy that has institutionalized a kind of *academic apartheid*. These challenges require an indigenous interpretation of knowledge bases that is predicated on indigenous experiences of both animate and inanimate phenomena,
access to funding and accreditation, and consideration of the rights and national responsibilities of indigenous peoples in an international context and
within international forums such as the United Nations. In short, American
Indian Studies helps begin the work of decolonization that must take place
before a genuine multiculturalism is established.

Colonization and Indian Education

In 1792, Benjamin Franklin recorded the reply of Cornplanter, a Seneca
leader, to Thomas Jefferson in response to Jefferson's overture to provide
free education for selected Iroquois youth:

> You who are wise, must know that different Nations have different Concep-
> tions of things; and you will therefore not take it amiss, if our ideas of this
> kind of Education happens not to be the same as yours. We have had some
> experience of it; Several of our young people were formerly brought up at the
> Colleges of the Northern Provinces; they were instructed in all your Sciences;
> but, when they came back to us, they were bad Runners, ignorant of every
> means of living in the Woods, unable to bear either Cold or Hunger, knew
> neither how to build a Cabin, take a Dear, or kill an Enemy, spoke our Lan-

guage imperfectly, were therefore neither fit for Hunters, Warriors, nor Counsellors; they were totally good for nothing. We are however not the less oblig'd by your kind Offer, tho' we decline in accepting it; and to show our grateful Sense of it, if the Gentlemen of Virginia will send us a Dozen of their Sons, we will take great Care of their Education, instruct them in all we know, and make *Men* of them.[1]

Contemporary Native American scholars, the most prominent being Vine Deloria Jr., have built upon Cornplanter's diplomatically expressed critique of why Euro-American educational ways are not appropriate for a traditionally proper "Indian education"—an education that is community-oriented, predicated on cultural traditions, and focused on survival skills. Deloria even went so far as to call the Euro-American indoctrination of Indian youth in the U.S. school system a form of "cultural imperialism" intent on eradicating Native cultures and belief systems.[2] From the infamous mission and boarding schools to the present-day situation of Indian students denigrated in U.S. public schools, the historical record of federal Indian policy has substantiated the charge of cultural imperialism.[3]

The history of colonialism in North America, the expropriation of Indian lands and resources, parallels the history of U.S.-Indian relations in education and in related areas such as health and social services. As Jorge Noriega has pointed out, from the mission schools of the sixteenth century to the block grant system of today, despite the variation in educational policies and levels of federal funding, these policies have pursued assimilationist goals at the expense of indigenous cultures and belief systems.[4]

As shown by Felix Cohen, author of the seminal treatise that laid the legal ground for tribal sovereignty, *The Handbook of Federal Indian Law* (1941), the original relationship between the Treaty Indians and the early American colonialists was meant to be a bilateral arrangement and was understood by Indians to be such. But major court decisions in the 1830s comprising the Marshall Doctrine revised this arrangement into a unilateral one that enabled the United States to subordinate Indian nations (called tribes since the 1903 *Lonewolf* decision) into what John Marshall called "domestic dependent nations."[5] Initially through this doctrine, the U.S. government constructed a unilateral relationship with Native peoples as tribal groups that established a wardship, or what is often called a "trusteeship." First established after the Indian Settler Wars through the Office of War and later implemented by the Department of the Interior via the Bureau of Indian Affairs (BIA), the authority to act "on behalf" of Indian groups' "best interests" created what I call a dominant-subordinate construction in U.S.-Indian relations. Operated at Indian people's expense, the assumption of U.S. "eminent domain" to Indian lands led to the expropriation of land and resources, the diversion of water, and the later devastation of reservation-based communities.

Federal policies toward Indian education have historically taken place in this colonial context and have been a major part of its organization. Included in certain treaty agreements between Indian nations and the U.S. government were educational appropriations to build schools and services for Indian youth. Indeed, as Jorge Noriega points out, "the real contours of what might be described as the U.S. model of colonialist education began to emerge" in the early nineteenth century with the Civilization Fund:

> In 1819, Congress established the "Civilization Fund," an annual appropriation of $10,000—in addition to those monies already allocated for the purpose—for "education of the frontier tribes." This was followed, in 1820, by acceptance of a proposal by Secretary of War John C. Calhoun that future treaties with indigenous nations be required to directly incorporate provision of additional cash annuities for instruction so that Indians might "be initiated in the habits of industry, and a portion taught the mechanical arts." For delivery of the intended program, the government relied primarily on missionaries supplied by the American Board of Commissioners for Foreign Missions, established collectively by the Congregational, Presbyterian, and Dutch Reform churches in 1810.[6]

The nineteenth century saw the further elaboration of these policies and their combination of coercion and assimilation. With the endorsement of President Teddy Roosevelt, leading intellectuals of the nineteenth and early twentieth centuries called themselves "Friends of the Indians." Several of these educational leaders were also members of his cabinet that gathered in upper New York State in 1889 to discuss the future of educational opportunities for American Indians.[7] The members of the Mohonk Proceedings, a public policy forum, believed their intentions to counter the harsher years of the so-called Indian Wars and the containment of Indian peoples on reservations were honorable and good. However, the history of the boarding school system tells a different story. During the years of the boarding school system, Indian children were kidnapped from their communities by the military and taken to faraway places where they were punished for being "Indian," for speaking their native languages, or for practicing their cultural traditions. In these schools, infamous schoolmasters, men and women of missionary zeal, used Indian youth as factory and farm labor to pay for their upkeep. This was the case, for example, in Chico, California, where a school for Native young women turned out to be a textile factory. One of the particularly pathological headmasters was Eleazar Wheelock, founder of Dartmouth College, who attempted to induce Indian youth to become Christians and missionaries, in effect using them as psychological guinea pigs. Overall, these military-regimented institutions implemented punitive corporal punishment when Indians resisted, often leading to early death and a high incidence of suicide among Indian youth. A gruesome sign of these schools' true nature was the adjoining cemeteries where Indian youth were buried.

The late nineteenth and early twentieth centuries witnessed the popularity and implementation of "scientific racism," manifested in, among other things, U.S. laws against miscegenation and for the protection of the "purity" of the "white" citizen-race, incorrect assumptions about the unified racial nature of all Native groups,[8] and perhaps most pointedly, the racist pseudoscience, *Crania Americana.* "Selected" Indian skulls were compared and contrasted with other "racial" groups and the results were used as a rationale to substantiate the biologically grounded "inferiority" of American Indians as a race. What's more, the Indians were sometimes compared with the African "race," so that white scientists could determine which was considered the more inferior.[9] These race scientists were extremely influential in establishing the scientific grounds for the eradication of "Indianness" that so characterized the concerted federal policy campaign to assimilate Indian students. This assimilationism was the preparation for their return to the reservations as second-class citizens or for their role as a labor force for a first-class citizenry in the predominantly Euro-American society.

Continuing distortions and bias in academic scholarship on American Indians is a direct result of this early colonizing history and the attempts to justify it. The manipulation of demographic data to establish the minimum presence of indigenous peoples prior to Columbus and European conquest, the perpetuation of stereotypes of Indian primitiveness, especially with regard to European standards of civilized agriculture, engineering, metallurgy, and religion,[10] and the marginalization or outright rejection of the Native nations' contribution to democratic governance, particularly the role of the Iroquois Confederacy,[11] all contribute to the legitimacy of the "rights of conquest" by Euro-Americans.

Only in recent years has Native scholarship made inroads into correcting this version of American history. These scholars have sought to counter what Ward Churchill calls these "sins of omission and commission." Alternative facts about the extent of indigenous occupancy in America and about the role of disease in decimating Native populations, the critique and inversion of the judicial theory that underwrites the Discovery Doctrine, and the debunking of Indian stereotypes in history and in contemporary popular culture[12] have sought to challenge the outright denial of inconvenient patterns of events, to reject the "both sides were guilty" rationalization, and in general to reject the standard methodologies in assessing the motives, policies, and impact of Euro-American conquest and colonization on Native America.

The Modern State of Affairs and the Politics of "Indian Identity"

The modern years began with the systematic campaign to mandate American education in public school systems for all Indian students. The 1928 Snyder and Johnson-O'Malley Acts established Indian education programs and provided for federal funds to go directly to school districts for the express purpose of servicing this new student population. At first, Indian youth and their parents resented and resisted this new education mandate and there was a high truancy rate among Indian students living on reservations. In addition, before more watchful oversight by the school and district administration was implemented under pressure from Indian parent committees, there was considerable mismanagement of funds designed for library acquisition and gym equipment. Overall, by the 1970s, federal Indian education policy had become more liberal, reflected in, among other things, the recognition of the growing population of Indians in urban metropole areas. The liberalization of federal Indian education policy was a direct result of the activities and leadership of the American Indian Movement (AIM) across the country in the 1970s. Particularly in the aftermath of the Wounded Knee occupation by AIM in 1973 on the Pine Ridge Reservation in South Dakota, considerably more attention was paid to quelling unrest among Indian peoples in the United States.

The legacy of coercive benevolence is nowhere more apparent than in the debates over federal Indian identification, a highly political issue for American Indians today. All those who claim Indian identity have to have a tribal enrollment number or BIA certification in order to be considered a federally recognized Indian or tribe. In order to receive federal monies and services, the state requires such certification. Prior to the 1970s, the tribes themselves determined who were members and thus would receive educational services as federal benefits. But during the 1970s, legislation was introduced that resulted in the infamous 506 forms, which were used to certify proof of tribal membership. This process was regulated by the BIA and required considerable paperwork for Indian parents and the tribes.[13] Certification demands have created serious problems for younger generations of Indians who have what are called "pending enrollments" for closed tribal rolls. These pending enrollments were exacerbated by a series of termination cases in the 1950s when the federal government declared whole tribes, as well as individuals, "extinct" and removed others from its list of those federally recognized. More recently, the Bush administration announced that the federal government has the power to "declare any Indian tribe in the nation extinct, even if the tribe has been recognized by a congressionally ratified treaty."[14] To make matters worse, the BIA is again being threatened by closure, this time, by Senator Daniel Inouye from Hawaii, who chairs the Senate Select Committee for Indian Affairs. Despite numerous complaints by Indians about the BIA and despite the fact that state certification of identity does not promote tribal self-sufficiency, Indians have generally held that a federal bureau to represent Indian peoples is better than none at all.

The political struggles and dealings around federal Indian identification policy have an important impact on educational policies since they affect the hiring of Indian faculty, administration, and staff to meet ethnic/minority quotas and affirmative action guidelines, as well as who will qualify for educational services and fellowships. Federal Indian identification policies have also contributed to the production of what I call the cloning of "Indian Identity Police," those who circulate in institutional settings, usually behind closed doors rather than in face-to-face interactions, to denounce the hiring of others who are not "real" Indians because they can't produce their certification cards or tribal enrollment numbers. Today, one finds professional Indian organizations and professors claiming "ethnic fraud" among those suspected of not having the proper pedigree or papers to call themselves American Indian or Native American.[15] This has encouraged the "Indian Identity Police" to instigate "hit" lists and "witch-hunts" on university campuses, accusing selected individuals of impersonating or masquerading as Indians. In my view, this "ethnic fraud" is at best a premature assessment and is at worst motivated by self-interest and other personal agendas, including tribal partisan policies in the Indian communities that have little to do with "genuine" Indians or cultural integrity. There are, in reality, many historically grounded reasons why Native peoples do not have BIA certification, reasons that do not generally involve their choice in the matter. Indeed, there are exceptions where individuals have made the choice not to register, but in many cases, this choice is based on the view that the U.S. government should not interfere with the internal affairs and sovereignty of tribal membership. Rather than pursue divisive strategies that ultimately presume that the fewer Indians there are, the more federal support there will be for the remainder, I would propose that the various tribal groups reestablish their traditional kinship systems to determine their tribal membership based on traditional cultural criteria and in this way counter the prevailing federal control of and regulation in this area. This is especially needed in light of the fact that the terms "American Indian" and "Native American" are state constructions that began with the Columbian invasion. The reappropriation of these terms, particularly in the context of an increasingly acknowledged pan-Indian experience, is an ongoing process that must be led by considerations of tribal sovereignty and cultural integrity.[16]

The political difficulties surrounding the role of the state in Indian identification are a sign of the ongoing coerciveness in what are now liberal education policies that encourage assimilation. This assimilation is often promoted as multicultural education. But the history of federal Indian education policies demonstrates the need for a decolonization of prevailing Euro-American rules and norms through a more genuine self-determination of ethnic/minority experiences, or, what I prefer to describe as the experiences of peoples of culture among indigenous groups.

American Indian Studies: Indigenism and Multiculturalism

Multiculturalism favors treating American Indians as ethnic minorities, rather than as descendants of indigenous peoples and members of tribal nations, whether the latter have federal recognition or not. But the history of indigenous peoples in the United States is, as I have shown, one of colonization. Although multiculturalism offers access to new knowledge bases, only a decolonization approach can link the critique of Eurocentrism to the particular experiences of Native peoples. And it is the displacement of Eurocentrism and its replacement by an indigenous worldview that must guide the radical work that some multiculturalism claims to want. To the extent that multiculturalism fosters the assimilation of American Indian Studies into the academic mainstream as a polite pseudo-intellectual vehicle maintained for purposes of providing the appearance of "ethnic diversity" on campus and for providing "Indian validation" to the supposed insights and conclusions of Euro-American academia, it hinders the crucial task of American Indian Studies. That task is to build an autonomous Indian tradition of scholarship and intellectualism that carries a viable conceptual alternative to Eurocentrism and its institutions.

The central dilemma of American Indian Studies was summed up neatly by Marlys Duchene when she observed that the designers of standard academic curriculum were/are Euro-Americans. "This resulted in academic curricula that embodied beliefs and routines that were strictly Euroamerican, the basis of which provided the 'object' for self-reflection."[17] For Native peoples who want to preserve and restore cultural traditions and belief systems that are different from the prevailing Eurocentric ones, any educational reform must challenge, at root, this dominant-subordinate construction. This construction is a social hegemony and moral philosophy that perpetuates the myths of Euro-American superiority at the expense of Native cultures/ cosmologies and at the expense of the indigenous worldview, which holds that all living entities are interrelated and integrated for the whole of the universe.

The problem at hand was perhaps most profoundly described by Ward Churchill when he articulated the nature of the "educational imperialism" inherent in the contemporary functioning of the academy, a condition he terms "white studies." Within Churchill's schema, the "linear conceptual model" marking European culture dominates modern U.S. academic life, extracting conformity to its structures and conclusions as the price of intellectual legitimacy. American Indian intellectualism, which he defines as being structured in a "circulinear" fashion and belonging to the tradition of "the relational indigenous worldview," is thus excluded by institutional mandate.[18] Churchill observes that,

> as currently established, the university system in the United States offers little more than "white studies" to students, minority and mainstream alike. This is to say that curriculum is very nearly monolithic in its focus upon European conceptual modes as being the "natural" formation of knowledge/ means of perceiving reality. In the vast bulk of curriculum content, Europe is not only the subject (conceptual mode; process of learning to think), but the object (subject matter) of investigation as well.[19]

Nowhere is this more evident than in the epistemologies of Western philosophy that permeate most academic disciplines and define our conventional notions of truth. Significant in this regard are the time/space/place constructions as human-derived.[20] By contrast, indigenous knowledge and traditional practice emphasize natural and seasonal rhythm. Native scholars like Churchill highlight the Eurocentric bias that is upheld by linear modes of thinking that rationalize an ideology of Indo-European and Euro-American superiority over indigenous reality and approaches or lifeways. The presumed universality and universal beneficence of the Western scientific and philosophical paradigm is Eurocentrism and it remains, for Native peoples, the dominant example of the power of knowledge to determine reality and to secure the subordination of Indian peoples. *Not all people "know" the same way.* As many have suggested, "superior" reasoning does not determine whether one group's way of thinking dominates another's. Rather, control over institutions and socioeconomic resources usually determines the ability to rule. But Eurocentrism, the ethnocentrism of European-descended populations, plays a part in creating hierarchies of social knowledge and in creating inequalities in resources and in institutional power. Historically, the ideological rule of Anglo-Saxon ethnocentrism was a major force in the European colonization of nonwhite populations and in the resulting inequalities in the distribution of resources and privileges. Increasingly sophisticated versions of Eurocentrism assist in smoothing the transition from traditional colonialism to Third World neocolonialism.[21]

It is difficult to imagine a way of looking at and relating to the world more antithetical to the holistic totalism marking indigenous worldviews than Eurocentrism, which forces American Indian Studies to be evaluated by conformity to conceptual standards and methods that are patently in opposition to Native American realities. What ethnocentrism has wrought in academic institutional settings is a form of *academic apartheid* that marginalizes Ethnic Studies or American Indian Studies or Gender Studies as fringe programs of less merit and credibility. This determines its overall status in hiring, course development, departmental determination, and budgetary allocations. Indigenous knowledge is contrasted with Eurocentric knowledge, and the subordination of the former is justified when it doesn't meet the tests of "rigorous" science and "objective" standards.

Efforts to correct this situational and institutionalized academic apartheid are being undertaken by Native scholars and some non-Native academic allies in all disciplines, from both a historical and a contemporary perspective, and with alternative ethnic as well as interdisciplinary approaches. Hence inroads are being made in demographics and education, in sociology and indigenous ("ethnic") studies, in anthropology, in religious studies, in history and politics, in American studies, in law, in environmental studies and ethics, in cultural philosophy, in art, poetry, and literature.[22] These efforts are driven by a basic fact of American Indian life:

> If, as they say, knowledge is power, then American Indians in the U.S. have been very thoroughly disempowered. Outside a relatively narrow range of traditionalists, mostly on a handful of reservations, our knowledge of ourselves, our histories, our cultures, and the nature of the process by which we

have been subordinated, has been appropriated by the dominant society for its own purposes. Knowledge not just of who we are, but of the nature of the system which dominates us, is consistently denied us, leaving us in near total ignorance of our true situation, more-or-less permanently at the mercy of our domination. In order to change this condition for the better, we must first and foremost recover the knowledge which has been taken from us and our ability to put this knowledge to use. In effect, we must regain our ability to think clearly, and to share this power with others. This, more than anything, is the "mission" of American Indian Studies.[23]

A good deal remains to be accomplished before a viable canon of American Indian Studies can emerge as a coherent whole. American Indian Studies will need to be able to stand on its own as a fully accredited discipline with departmental status and even with a broader institutional standing. Before this can happen, however, institutional standards that support structural barriers and preserve academic apartheid must be challenged. Questions about what kinds of models will prevail (multiethno program centers, autonomous departments, subordination to conventional disciplines, or some combination) will need to be answered. So too issues of hiring, promotion, and tenure, and the composition of degree-granting programs, require careful consideration. American Indian Studies usually gets the short stick in any multiethnic program or center, and often attention is focused on the hiring of "big guns" at the expense of programmatic development; issues of equity will require hard discussion. In addition, gender parity will need to be dealt with. Ethnic women in the academy are the last to be hired in Ethnic Studies and Women's Studies programs; Native women find themselves at the very bottom of a hierarchy that displays little interest in our experiences or perspectives, much less in the wherewithal to initiate permanent faculty positions for us. In addition, any viable American Indian Studies will need to reassess the publish-or-perish structure that consumes academics. In general, we will need to make decisions about how best to disseminate indigenous research and scholarship to the academy and the larger public— whether to operate within mainstream presses and media or whether to seek out alternative enterprises or establish independent Native-determined journals and book publications.

American Indian Studies will also have to take a global perspective so that it can incorporate the experiences of all indigenous peoples. Inter-American Indigenous Studies or Indigenous Global Studies would provide a broader international and interdisciplinary foundation for a more enlightened comprehension of the affairs of humankind. The global reconceptualization of the discipline can help counter the parochialism and ethnocentrism that abound and that perpetrate political factionalism and divisiveness within ethnic communities, reservation-based communities, and American society as a whole.

Most important, the indigenous worldview of American Indian Studies is grounded in the principles of intellectual decolonization long espoused by such theorists as Frantz Fanon and in the more recently emerging perspective of Indigenism elaborated by writer/activists such as Guillermo Bonfil Batalla.[24] As Vine Deloria puts it, "Indian Studies programs should . . . define their goals as encompassing all the relevant knowledge and information concerning the relationship between American Indians and the rest of the world, be it the federal government, other religions, the world of art and music, or international and domestic economics."[25] To decolonize Eurocentric knowledge, American Indian Studies approaches these tasks through the deployment of the "Native American Conceptual Mode" itself:

> With such a conceptual structure . . . there is really no compartmentalization of "spheres of knowledge." All components or categories (by European definition) tend to be mutually and perpetually informing. All tend to concretize human existence within reality (nature) while all are simultaneously informed by that reality. This is the "Hoop" or the "Wheel" or "Circle" of life referred to within the (continuing) oral traditions of so many indigenous peoples. Reality is not something "above," but an integral part of the living/knowing process itself.[26]

What both Deloria and Churchill are insisting on is not merely the inclusion of Indians and Indian programs in academia (although both certainly demand these), but a fully interdisciplinary approach to American Indian Studies as a discipline. This involves reaching a coherent *Indian* understanding of law or political science with a firm grasp of the spiritual principles governing Indian life. These spiritual principles can only be apprehended via a grounding in the Indian relationship to the environment. Indian philosophy cannot be approached without a solid appreciation of all these elements.

In its global context, this approach has led some Native scholars to call for Indigenism, a liberation movement and a worldview that provide an integrated orientation to life with nature.[27] This worldview sees an indigenous "Fourth" or "Host" world on the planet, composed of a multitude of distinct peoples ranging from the Indians of North and South America to the Inuits and Samis of the Arctic Circle, the Maori of New Zealand and the Koori of Australia, the Karins and Kachins of Burma, the Kurds of Persia, the

Bedouins of the Sahara and onward, the Zulus and Bantus of southern Africa, and many others. Even in contemporary Europe, peoples such as the Basques of Spain and the Gaels of the Scottish Highland region may be viewed as indigenous nations. The modern, industrialized and industrializing states of the First, Second, and Third Worlds are seen as sitting squarely atop the Host World.[28] The perspective of Indigenism presumes that indigenous peoples share a common experience of colonization and incorporation into a modern nation-state, a shared interest in the rights of all indigenous people to the right of sovereign nationhood, and a nondisruptive way of relating to the habitat.

This vision of American Indian Studies presumes the necessity of decolonization and seeks universal truths from the contributions of indigenous knowledge and the ancient wisdom that has been passed down through the ages. It is a positive alternative to a multicultural movement that has not yet done what it needs to do to challenge the denigration of ethnic/minority populations who still are forced to meet Euro-American standards and be ruled by Euro-American values for educational and life success. The indigenous worldview of American Indian Studies recognizes collective commonalties with each other at the same time that it acknowledges and respects our differences so that a rich cultural diversity and creative expression of individuality can flourish without sacrificing our universal holism. This is what is meant by the Lakota blessing *metakuyeayasi*, "All My Relations."

Notes

1. Excerpted in Leonard W. Larabee et al., eds., *The Papers of Benjamin Franklin* (New Haven: Yale University Press, 1961), 481–83.

2. Vine Deloria Jr., "Education and Imperialism," *Integrateducation* 19 (January–April 1981): 58–63.

3. See M. Annette Jaimes, "American Indian Identification/Eligibility Policy in Federal Indian Education" (Ph.D. diss., Arizona State University, August 1990).

4. Jorge Noriega, "American Indian Education in the United States: Indoctrination for Subordination to Colonialism," in *The State of Native America: Genocide, Colonization and Resistance*, ed. M. Annette Jaimes (Boston: South End Press, 1992), 371–402.

5. For the Marshall cases, see Vine Deloria Jr., "Trouble in High Places: Erosion of American Indian Rights to Religious Freedom in the United States," in *The State of Native America*. For the *Lonewolf v. Hitchcock* case, see Ward Churchill, "Perversions of Justice: Examining the Doctrine of U.S. Rights to Occupancy in North America," in *Struggle for the Land: Indigenous Resistance to Genocide, Ecocide and Expropriation in Contemporary North America* (Monroe, Maine: Common Courage Press, 1993). For a deconstruction of the original meanings and contemporary terminology of "tribe" and "nation," see Ward Churchill, "Naming Our Destiny: Towards a Language of Indian Liberation," *Global Justice* 3 (summer–fall 1992): 22–33.

6. Noriega, "American Indian Education in the United States," 377.

7. See Alexandra Harmon, "When Is an Indian Not an Indian? 'Friends of the Indian' and the Problem of Indian Identity," *Journal of Ethnic Studies* 18 (summer 1990): 95–123.

8. The myth of Native peoples being a single "race" of people actually began with the Bering Strait theory, which purports that all indigenous peoples are relative newcomers to the American hemisphere since we are presumably all Asian immigrants. Such Eurocentric hype, which tries to make indigenous peoples into immigrants, is now being supported by geneticists who claim to be deconstructing DNA in various racial groups. See Tim Friend, "Genetic Detectives Trace the Origin of the First Americans," *USA Today*, 21 September 1993: 5D, and Russell Means and Ward Churchill, "About That Bering Strait Land Bridge (Turn the Footprints Around)," statement by American Indian Movement leaders (1993).

9. See Stephen J. Gould, *The Mismeasure of Man* (New York: W. W. Norton, 1981), 20–60.

10. See M. Annette Jaimes, "Re-Visioning Native America: An Indigenist View of Primitivism and Industrialism," *Social Justice* 19 (summer 1992): 5–34.

11. See Bruce E. Johansen, *Forgotten Founders: Benjamin Franklin, the Iroquois and the Rationale for the American Revolution* (Ipswich, Mass.: Gambit, 1982); Donald Grinde Jr., *The Iroquois and the Founding of the American Nation* (San Francisco: California Indian Historian Press, 1977); Donald Grinde Jr. and Bruce E. Johansen, *Exemplar of Liberty: Native America and the Evolution of Democracy* (Los Angeles: American Indian Studies Center, 1991); and Donald Grinde Jr., "Iroquois Political Theory and the Roots of American Democracy," in *Exiled in the Land of the Free: Democracy, Indian Nations and the U.S. Constitution*, ed. Oren R. Lyons and John C. Mohawk (Santa Fe, N.M.: Clear Light Publishers, 1992), 227–80.

12. See M. Annette Jaimes, "False Images: Native Women in Hollywood Cinema," *Turtle Quarterly* (fall 1993).

13. See Jaimes, "American Indian Identification/Eligibility Policy in Federal Indian Education," chapter 1. This situation has escalated dramatically. The Indian Arts and Crafts Act of 1990, signed into law during the Bush administration, requires certification of Indian artists. It states that it is now a criminal act to proclaim oneself an "Indian" artist if one is not able to show BIA certification. Uncertified individuals can now be fined and jailed for impersonating an "Indian," and galleries that sell their art as "Indian" can be fined into bankruptcy. This certification is based on a race formula in contrast to the cultural criteria that has traditionally determined one's membership in a tribal group.

14. "BIA Can Declare Tribes Extinct," *American Indian Anti-Defamation Council* (AIADC) *Newsletter*, Denver, Colo. (July 1992): 13. "The new policy is stated deep in the text of a (BIA) decision last month denying recognition to the Miami tribe of Indiana. The BIA . . . says it has no plans to use the power to disqualify already-recognized tribes, though it claims the right to do so if they fall short of agency requirements on continuing existence" (ibid.). It should be noted that an Indian community can petition the Congress for federal recognition or for reinstatement of past recognition, but it is a long and expensive process, with no guarantees that the goal will be attained.

15. Elisabeth Lynn-Cook, "Meeting of Indian Professors Takes up Issues of 'Ethnic Fraud,' Sovereignty and Research Needs," *Wicazo Sa Review* 9 (spring 1993): 57–59.

16. See Robert K. Thomas, "On Pan-Indianism," in *The Emergent Native Americas: A Reader in Culture Contact*, ed. Deward E. Walker (Boston: Little, Brown, 1972), 741–76.

17. Marlys Duchene, "Problems in Curriculum Development in Indian Community Schools," paper presented at the Western Social Science Association Annual Conference, Albuquerque, New Mexico, 1980: 3.

18. Ward Churchill, "White Studies: The Intellectual Imperialism of Contemporary U.S. Education," *Integrateducation* 19 (January–April 1981): 51–57.

19. Ibid., 51.

20. See Vine Deloria Jr., *God Is Red: A Native View of Religion*, 2d ed. (Golden, Colo.: North American Press, 1992), 62–77; M. Annette Jaimes, "Native American Identity and Survival as 'Indigenism': Environmental Ethics for Economic Development" (forthcoming). See also the non-

Indian authors Anthony F. Aveni, *Empires of Time: Calendars, Clocks, and Cultures* (New York: Basic Books, 1989), and Michael O'Malley, *Keeping Watch: A History of American Time* (New York: Viking Press, 1990).

21. See Edward Said, "The Politics of Knowledge," in *Debating PC: The Controversy over Political Correctness on College Campuses*, ed. Paul Berman (New York: Dell Publishing, 1992), 172–89.

22. See, for example, work by George Moriega, Antonio Barriero, Vine Deloria Jr., Jimmie Durham, Ward Churchill, Louise Erdrich, Jack Forbes, Donald Grinde Jr., Joy Harjo, Linda Hogan, M. Annette Jaimes, Clara Sue Kidwell, Hans Koning, Winona LaDuke, John Mohawk, Glenn Morris, Jorge Noriega, Simon Ortiz, Rebecca Robbins, Wendy Rose, Kirkpatrick Sale, Leslie Marmon Silko, David Stannard, Lenore Stiffarm, Ines Talamantez, Russell Thornton, Dagmar Thrope, George Tinker, Haunani Trask, Laurie Whitt, and Winona Stevenson.

23. Ward Churchill, quoted in M. Annette Jaimes, "American Indian Studies: Towards an Indigenous Model," *American Indian Culture and Research Journal* no. 3 (fall 1987): 1.

24. Frantz Fanon, *The Wretched of the Earth* (New York: Grove Press, 1965); Guillermo Bonfil Batalla, *Utopia y revolución: El pensamiento político contemporáneo de los Indios en América Latina* (México: Editorial Nueva Imagen, 1981).

25. Vine Deloria Jr., "Indian Studies—The Orphan of Academia," *Wicazo Sa Review* 2 (fall 1986): 6.

26. Ward Churchill, "White Studies," 54.

27. See M. Annette Jaimes, "Native American Identity and Survival as 'Indigenism,'" and Ward Churchill, "I Am Indigenist," in *Struggle for the Land*. Churchill was perhaps the first to begin to employ this term with consistency in the United States. For example, see his "The New Genocide: An Indigenist Perspective on Native American Environments," *Akwesasne Notes* 18 (1986).

28. The World Council of Indigenous Peoples was one of the first entities in North America to start using this terminology with regularity. See, for example, J. R. Diabo, "The Emergence of Fourth World Politics in the International Arena," paper presented at the Western Social Science Annual Conference, San Diego, 1984.

CHAPTER FIVE

Like Being Mugged by a Metaphor

Multiculturalism and State Narratives

WAHNEEMA LUBIANO

Recently, I have been thinking about political subjects as subjects who imagine their position in the world and act, but who are also subject to state power. I have been thinking about the way the state manifests its power, especially when it does not call attention to its presence.[1] My title, then, was inspired by my interest in the presence of the state in the cultural narratives with which we imagine the world and the social constructions that act as mystifications. Some mystifications can kill or maim us. "Like being mugged by a metaphor" is a way to describe what it means to be at the mercy of racist, sexist, heterosexist, and global capitalist constructions of the meaning of skin color on a daily basis. Whether or not I am a card-carrying believer in distinctions of racial biology, I am nonetheless attacked by the hegemonic social formation's notions of racial being and the way those notions position me in the world. Like a mugging, this attack involves an exchange of assets: some aspect of the social order is enriched domestically and internationally by virtue of material inequities stabilized and narrativized by race oppression and I lose symbolically and monetarily. Further, I am physically traumatized and psychologically assaulted by an operation that is mystified. It goes on in the dark, so to speak—in the dark of a power that never admits to its own existence.

Michael Hanchard has argued that the analytic space between names and appearances and "real problems" is socially traversed by collective and individual narratives.[2] He builds on Raymond Williams's assertion that "the conventional distinction between the material and the symbolic does not correspond to the social reality of language and signification as indissoluble elements of material process."[3] Hanchard makes this argument to remind us that changes in name, in construction, are contextual and not necessarily— but they can be—the mystification of other operations. For example, take the nineteenth-century use among Black people of the sign "American." The construction of Black people as Americans signified a specific refusal to go back to Africa at the urging of white people. It is true that some Blacks were also interested in emigration, but here Hanchard is referring to a set of polemics directed against white supremacists who insisted that Blacks go back to Africa. He is arguing that U.S. race relations have been a dance of meanings not necessarily about, but not excluding, pigmentation. In a similar vein, Michael Omi and Howard Winant argue, along with Stuart Hall, that race is "an unstable and 'decentered' complex of social meanings constantly being transformed by political struggle."[4] Furthermore, they argue that the U.S. state is a racial formation, part of an entire social order equilibrated unstably to preserve the prevailing racial order, and that race is neither an illusion nor an essence that an ideal social order would eliminate. Thus, while there is no universally accepted definition of race, nor a universally accepted position against racism, race can simply be thought of as any group of people generally believed to be, and generally accepted as, a race in any given arena of ethnic competition. As the sociologist Oliver Cox put it, if a person looks white but is in America called a Negro, that person is a Negro American.[5]

This understanding of race has all kinds of ramifications for state deployments of narratives that ensure a particular global economy. Within the terms of race relations in the United States, the tendency, then, of a white bourgeoisie is to proletarianize the whole racial group "Black" or "African American" so that it functions socially and politically as a *class*. In other words, there appear no easily discernible class differences among a racialized group's members in the eyes of the dominant group. Of course, this does not mean that there is no class stratification within the group, but rather that the state's narratives of power empty the meaning of the effects of class stratification on racially marked groups. I mention this as background because I am interested in under what circumstances, for whom, and to do what in the world the political subject is constructed. In other words, the state thinks the subject too. Thus, to some extent, what we think of ourselves in relation to the world, what we imagine ourselves to be in relation to the world, is also, under most circumstances, at least partially a state project. In my discussion of multiculturalism here, I am going to suggest what it means to be an intellectual affiliated with the university system; in doing so I want to remind us of the relationship of that work to the larger operations of state power.

What political work does insistence on a difference, on an identity, do? What political work does staging, performing, foregrounding, articulating, or criticizing recognition of an identity do? In a recent article entitled "Critical Multiculturalism," the Chicago Cultural Studies Group wrote: "What do subalterns have in common except that somehow they are dominated?—a statement so general as to be nearly useless."[6] The statement they sneer at is so important that I am amazed that they could not see it. *What do subalterns have in common except that somehow they are dominated?* "Somehow they are dominated" is the simplicity that is supposed to render the statement itself useless, when in fact it is that statement that signifies what subalterns have in common as individuals in groups attempting to project some form of political agency for themselves. Domination may not determine the specificity of a particular cultural, racial, gendered, sexualized, or classed group, but domination has everything to do with how we think about the internal complexities of those groups and their relationships to larger dominating groups. Somehow the statement "all they have in common is domination" empties out the very thing I want to focus on: what it means to be dominated. Domination is complicated and varied. But domination is so successful precisely because it sets the terrain upon which struggle occurs at the same time that it preempts opposition not only by already inhabiting the vectors where we would resist (i.e., by being powerfully in place and ready to appropriate oppositional gestures), but also by having already written the script that we have to argue within and against.

Part of that script includes what counts as "authentic" opposition, a partial result of that tendency to proletarianize the whole group I mentioned earlier. Our political imaginary always focuses on the non-middle-class person of color, and this focus is part of the reason why I want to highlight the university and the role of the activist intellectual there: one place the state makes its presence felt, but is not necessarily named, is the university. We need to articulate a political imaginary for the middle-class person of color in the university, where we still have a form of political agency, despite the onus that is demonized under the name of "elite intellectual activity." When I am accused of that, on my home ground, I say, "Yes, indeed. There's no getting around it. I not only occupy this hybrid, historically produced position of being an intellectual of color at an Ivy League university, but I'm not leaving it either. And I am not leaving it precisely because it seems to me that if we are willing to have the stain on our honor as people of color who are not 'authentic' political subjects, then there is a certain kind of work we can do there." I also admit to enjoying being in these places because part of what I have learned is that as incredibly corrupting as power is, there is something about it that we can use to help us stave off those corruptions if we are willing to be tainted by them. In a way, this work is another form of rugged bourgeois individualism, instilled in me by virtue of my great training in the U.S. educational system. But part of the impulse for this position comes from growing up in a particular set of circumstances. When I was six years old and I saw someone stomped to death in front of me as a result of a gang war, then I thought I knew what goodness was and what badness was. In the community's response I thought I saw that power was something you used in order to make sure that everybody was good in your imagining of what the good could be. Over the years, I've been traumatized in other more subtle ways and always my response to it has been that you must get in and grapple with the trauma, as opposed to allowing yourself simply to feel the injustice of it, or feel your own implication in the exercise of it. In other words, my complicity in the production of an elite research university system is not all I can be or do.

My understanding of multiculturalism against this context is guided by my troubled response to two questions: Can we affect any change in institutions aimed at the state through education? and Haven't some of us, to some extent and in some places, already begun to try to, if not transform the academy, then at least stage an opposition from within it? Haven't some of us also tried to stage opposition from within our entire educational system, including the K-12 schools? Haven't we tried to extend the knowledge that is produced and disseminated from the agreed-upon but inadequate re-creations of the status quo and its world dominance to something better? My response to these questions is always "yes and no." This double-edged response is true for multiculturalism as well. Can multiculturalism be reduced to cultural relativism, to an empty noncritical pluralism, or to an intellectual and social smorgasbord offered to particular clients by elite institutions or corporations for the purposes of elites, elite institutions, or corporations? Of course it can. But part of the work of those who have been and are engaged in radical multiculturalism is to keep it from being reduced to slogans, to meaning things like "Different strokes for different folks," or "To understand all is to forgive all," or "All we need is peace, love, and understanding."[7]

Within the parameters of the present hierarchical structure of the university, multiculturalism can be and has been in some places and in many ways thoroughly appropriated, diluted, and neutralized so that the domination of Eurocentric knowledge remains completely unchallenged. More to the point for my purpose is the connection between Eurocentric knowledge and the operation of international economies in the name of multiculturalism. For example, any university can simply continue business as usual by making available a selection of ethnic or racially specific courses without ever addressing the ways in which the focus of what we understand as Western culture is itself incomplete and distorted and has a political relationship to the ways in which our world is constructed. Nonetheless, to some limited extent, many universities and colleges are already multicultural. The constituencies that represent the marginalized multiplicity of U.S. culture are present there in some numbers, but—and this is a huge "but"—neither their presence nor the specific knowledge that inheres within the terms of those constituencies has any real curricular or institutional presence or force. Therefore, in order for multiculturalism to be something other than an empty abstraction used by administrators to take the political heat off their institutions, those of us interested in transformative multiculturalism must insist that it cannot be held to exist within dominance at the same time that we use multiculturalism as a way to intervene in that dominance. Multiculturalism is, then, an organizing principle, a tendency to use the space opened up by discussions under rubrics previously marginalized, or not known at all, to do particular work for particular people, including the middle-class intellectuals of color, who have not known previously to think of themselves as operating within a political imaginary.

Multiculturalism is a deliberate attempt on the part of the historically marginalized to reconstitute not simply particular curricula, but the academy itself as part of what George Lipsitz has called "the enormous industry of meaning making."[8] The pressure that is organized under the sign of multiculturalism and placed on universities, colleges, and the public school system to change curricula, admissions, and faculty and staff composition, has forced such institutions to respond, in however inadequate and attenuated a fashion, to the demands of traditionally marginalized cultures for the inclusion of individuals, for group power, and for some reorganization of these institutions. It can be made to do more. But why would we want to make a sinking ship do more? Apart from the fact that the ship is something that is going to pull us down if it doesn't transform, if it isn't made to transform, we will have abandoned it to others. To abandon the university as a site for this kind of work is to abandon the incredibly powerful if co-effected relationship between the university system, the primary and secondary educational system in the United States, and a military and international global economy.

I am not only referring to public relations assistance to the movement of global capital that depresses the wages of labor everywhere to bring you baskets and blouses from Thailand and Buicks from Mexico, and which sends fuel air explosives from the United States to the rest of the world. Nor am I referring only to liberal tolerance of difference, necessary for discussion, but insufficient to effect change. Instead, I am trying to describe a field of inevitable ongoing contestation, argument, and reformation. In regard to the particular criticism that multiculturalism can assist the perpetuation of Western dominance through the creation of a new pluralism to be consumed by elites, I suggest that we remember that even without multiculturalism, other forms of state and elite management continue business as usual. If elites manage business as usual and can't call it multiculturalism, they will simply call it something else. We cannot give up the ground because of what they can do in the name of the ground on which we have chosen to fight. The process of normalization or the work of oppositional gestures is an ongoing dynamic of our system and, of course, multiculturalism can be used to continue such management. Radical multiculturalism, however, turns its attention to demystifying just such management and to fighting it. Contestation is the driving force of such a dynamic. As David Lloyd has argued, "Culture is the ground for both accommodation to and contestation of state desires."[9] As such, it's an important ground for the work of those of us who think of ourselves as progressives engaged in both domestic social justice and international economic justice.

I want to be specific about the complexities of multiculturalism and its negotiation of politics and epistemology. For instance, radical multiculturalism is not just an attempt to make sure that the estimates of genocidal oppression are correct. The work of revising our notions of New World discovery in order to include the knowledge that the North American Indian population was decimated by 1900, and that the twelve million slaves shipped to the New World by 1870 represented less than a third of those captured, is important work, not only for reasons of intellectual accuracy, but also because the work of de-aestheticizing the myth of a glorious New World (or a New World Order) has something to do with establishing the cost of imperialism, including the cost to the peasants back in the Old World of the skewed fifteenth-, sixteenth-, and seventeenth-century conquest economies.

This work has something to do with influencing how priorities are set by the state and with articulating how the U.S. national subject understands the nation's place in the world and its history. De-aestheticizing the myth of America is one of the means by which we do cultural work to oppose the incredibly powerful state myth of a romantic and conquering American past.

But multiculturalism's work is not just epistemological. Universities are corporate in their very structures. They are workplaces for hundreds of thousands of workers and they are legitimation factories at the same time. What kind of work can and ought those of us engaged in radical multiculturalism do in these places? Universities are in the business of investments, of initiating and cooperating in corporate business projects, and are producing research that contributes to the way in which the United States shapes and controls the world economy. It is important, therefore, that we target for pressure the makeup of decision-making bodies in that corporate university, and that the new knowledge produced by multicultural intellectualism be used as part of that pressure. Radical multiculturalism, for example, can include attempting to influence decisions such as whether to focus on high-tech military research, Department of Defense contracts, or fuel air explosives instead of contributing to research based on meeting housing needs. It can influence decisions on whether to reconsider not only lopsided hiring practices at all employment levels in the university, but also the means by which the marginalized are represented in the policy-making entities of the university.

Multiculturalism can of course be appropriated. It can be normalized in ways that lend themselves to static and conservative politics. So can democracy, or the discourse of democracy, or specifically deployed uses of democracy. At the sound of the word "democracy," for example, some people in different parts of the world, including parts of the United States and its sphere of influence, either reach for their wallets or their guns or duck and cover while they grab their loved ones. Yet, both of the academic organizations established over the past three years to oppose "political correctness" bashing and assaults by conservatives on the generation of new knowledges in the academy have made the word "democratic" part of their names: the Teachers for Democratic Culture and the Union of Democratic Intellectuals. Those of us who are part of either or both of those organizations, or those of us who are determined not to let democracy stand for the operation of laissez-faire capitalism, have a stake in claiming the word, its meaning, and its vision. Within the terms of this vision of democracy, multiculturalism is a term worth fighting over also. The analogy to democracy is meant to demonstrate that multiculturalism does not have to displace other ways of describing the projects outlined within the terms of this essay, but neither is it dismissable on the basis of its appropriability by corporations or even by sites within the academy that are hostile to its political force.

By the time I came to undergraduate study at Howard University, being a Black Studies major meant, among other things, studying slavery in a two-semester comparative course so that we could see American slavery in a world context. When we studied imperial American cultures, it meant thinking about movements through history and within race differences. We studied Black history not simply to understand what was left out of many American history books—Black relations to whites, for example—but to understand Black relations to other nonwhite groups. Doing so meant facing up to what was painful for a lot of the students, facing up to what the Western frontier meant to Blacks, for instance. The Western frontier meant, on one hand, escape from the South after Reconstruction failed. On the other hand, it also meant participation for some Blacks in the wars against the Native peoples and the massacres of those peoples. Conquest, then, was not just something that Euro-Americans did to other people. Blacks, too, had a complicated and sometimes complicitous relation to that conquest. I use that as one small example of what radical multiculturalism can make its object of business.

Although multiculturalism cannot fix all that ails the U.S. polity in general, or the education system specifically, it is a way to intervene at the site of education and in the tensions that tie larger structural global concerns and policies to intellectual and cultural work. We should remember that the military and prisons, for example, places where the state is present, both create and rely on knowledge produced by universities about marginalized groups. Radical multiculturalism offers the possibility of countering the state's use of the intellectual and cultural productions of and about marginalized groups and thus offers institutionally transformative possibilities for middle-class people of color affiliated with universities who, as I've suggested, are also themselves bound up with this state-sponsored knowledge.

What is involved in imagining the university's relationship to an international military capitalist economy and a domestic prison economy? What role do culture and cultural opposition play in this imagination? Remember that I have been arguing that the state is involved in these imaginings. One job of the state is to make its manifestations of power in the operation of the economy culturally acceptable. Part of the way the state accomplishes this acceptance is to make culture the terrain, the place, where we imagine our relationship to the world. When we think of state power we do not tend to consider gender socialization and homophobia as constitutive to the way in which the state authorizes itself, partially because the effects of class are obscured, and partially because our gendered and sexualized identities are often the means through which we imagine ourselves outside of the purview of the explicitly political. But, imagining ourselves to be outside of the purview of the explicitly political allows us to participate in concrete ways in an international military economy and a domestic prison economy.

Consider Black males in prison, who are visible and overwhelmingly identified as Black men, as racial subjects. Ninety-three percent of the Black male prison population is comprised of people who were poor, unemployed, or underemployed. Of those who were employed, their average incomes were less than ten thousand dollars a year. Among all people in prison, roughly 85 percent are poor.[10] Black male prisoners or those who will be in prison (or could be as a result of their participation in illegal alternate economic activities) are not identified as poor: they are identified as a Black transgressive outlaw group. The state's identification of them as such and the generalization of that identity are an imposition, a means by which the state dominates culturally, you might say. But it is also the case that Black male prisoners or those who will be in prison or could be in prison internalize a warrior ethos, with its attendant homophobia and patriarchalism, that is relayed elsewhere. This is in large part a result of the invisible cultural hand of the state, which imposes upon the most imposed group its own ethos, an ethos that seems to exist as if it did not have state sponsorship.

This dynamic has implications for Black women who are, as a group, dominated economically and politically regardless of whether each woman or all women are always at the mercy of the same types and degrees of oppression. Black women must function within the Black community where the warrior ethos finds its cultural expression. The warrior ethos remains unchallenged partially because the state seems so absent at its most local articulations. The inability to challenge the state sponsorship of the warrior ethos leads the community as a whole, including those not explicitly engaging in a warrior ethos, to reproduce patriarchal relations that cannot be recognized as state-sponsored. An example: gangs are not only the means by which the drug economy organizes itself ostensibly outside the realm of the state, they are also concentrations of gender socialization and one means by which the drug economy romanticizes itself in the community at large. Women become, willy-nilly, part of this cultural economy that perpetuates a warrior ethos through their roles as socializing agents. This socializing takes place not only in the context of the attenuated history of patriarchy within the community, but within the constraints imposed on Black women to prove to the state that they are not "culturally poor" mothers and can produce "strong" men.

In other words, the constructions of our various beings as a group are both material and cultural. The material and the cultural are neither completely separate nor do they operate autonomously. The idea "Black people" is a social reality. Black people are a dominated group politically and economically, even if every member is not always dominated under all circumstances. Individuals who think themselves part of the social and historical consciousness of the group are claimed by that group and/or accused by others of being part of the group. These claims to group membership, or accusations of group membership, whether imposed or voluntary, function as cultural narratives that make the operation of a political economy possible. Insofar as these narratives are tied to a prison economy, a warrior ethos, and a patriarchal structure within the community *that makes itself known to the community as part of an empowering device for the group as a whole, the cultural apparatus of the state is doing its work.* To put it bluntly, Black people who consciously think of themselves as part of a Black group often think of themselves as oppositional at the very same time as they are internalizing precisely the state's most effective narratives, narratives that are the medium by which the state dominates the group in ways the group does recognize.

Black men and women as an outlaw group: this metaphor is part of a cultural narrative that builds a domestic economy. Think of the prison economy as a capital investment project that rests on the particular manipulation of a group of people. Think of the drug trade as posing such a necessity for disciplinary measures that the whole group's identity is wrapped in this disciplinary necessity. Think of the "culture of poverty" and its ethnographic knowledge as the grease that makes the engine of the United States' racial imagination run more smoothly. Think about how the international circulation of all these narratives forces those of us who are temporarily not in prison, or temporarily not being targeted, but who are concerned about the drug trade's ravaging of our neighborhoods, to participate in the state's disciplinary apparatus, sometimes without our even knowing it.

What does a prison economy have to do with an international military economy, and what does that have to do with selecting the university as a site for radical multiculturalism? In the dominant imaginary, the United States is threatened from within by Black men and the drug trade and by Black women and their culture of poverty. The threat from within prepares the ground by which the American public recognizes the threat from without. And how do people learn something new? By analogy, by reference to what is already understood. The bogey man in the closet is prepared for by the various fears already available to us. Black men and Black women are highly visible in the media, but they are also highly visible *to themselves as metaphors for deviance* and for transgressiveness. These metaphors are so visible within the group that they function as the grid through which we check our concrete reality. Consider how many times certain Black intellectual work has been dismissed because (*a*) it won't save crack babies in the ghetto, or (*b*) it won't reach the brother on the street corner selling crack. This dismissal depends on the renarrativization of all possible effects of epistemological change by virtue of a larger narrative that is so highly visible before us that we think everything through that narrative. The socially, economically, and politically constructed issue of Black pathology becomes, then, the extended metaphor that explains the world and delimits what we could do to change it. That metaphor prevents us from seeing how Black pathology as an explanation is state-derived. But it also prevents us from understanding *the general power of the state to provide, to the public imagination, metaphors for explaining how the world works.*

What does this have to do with multiculturalism and the university? Over the past 250 years, university scholars have created and legitimated the knowledge that has justified the particular oppression I have been discussing. University scholars have provided the necessary cultural justifications for the movement of capital and for state imperatives and policies. University scholars have provided fodder for the cultural narratives that tell the stories of Black people. The university generates and disseminates the metaphors and narratives that thoroughly imagine our world. Those metaphors and those narratives are the very stuff of our educational system, our media representations, our state policy, our individual lives. Black pathology is a thoroughgoing and useful academic production for the state.

I have five brothers. All five have been in the military, four of them in the Korean War, one in the Vietnam War. Their military participation is not at all unusual for working-class Black families. The military is one of the ways that one ensures oneself a job for the time being and possibly the chance at a better job afterward. But the military is also the romantic manifestation of a warrior ethos for individuals concerned that their position within a socially and politically dominated group means that somehow they're female and not male. I have a seventeen-year-old niece who is a community college student. She tells me, "I want to become a prison guard." She tells me, "The prison system is the fastest growing sector in the U.S. economy." She tells me, "I want a job with some chance for career advancement." She tells me, "I do not want to just work in McDonald's. I do not want to just have babies like my friends. I do not want to clean anybody's house like Grandma did." She tells me, "I don't understand why you're so upset." Part of what I have said to her in response I have been trying to convey here. The water is being poisoned right here at the epistemological well. It is important to make a stand right here at that well. These life-directing narratives are produced by a political economy and by an educational system where the state's presence is most dangerous because it is where it is most unnamed.

Notes

This essay includes some material previously published in *Concerns: Women's Caucus for the Modern Languages* 22, no. 3 (1992): 11–21, and in *Debating P.C.: The Controversy over Political Correctness on College Campuses*, ed. Paul Berman (New York: Dell, 1992).

1. See, for example, Wahneema Lubiano, "Standing in for the State: Black Nationalism and 'Writing' the Black Subject," *Alphabet City* 3 (1993): 20–23.

2. Michael Hanchard, "Identity, Meaning, and the African-American," *Social Text* 24 (1990).

3. Raymond Williams, *Marxism and Literature* (New York: Oxford University Press, 1977), 99.

4. Michael Omi and Howard Winant, *Racial Formation in the United States: From the 1960s to the 1990s*, 2d ed. (New York: Routledge, 1994): 55.

5. See Oliver Cox, *Caste, Class, and Race* (New York: Monthly Review Press, 1970 [1948]).

6. Chicago Cultural Studies Group, "Critical Multiculturalism," *Critical Inquiry* 18 (1992): 543.

7. For a program of radical multiculturalism, see Ted Gordon and Wahneema Lubiano, "The Statement of the Black Faculty Caucus," in *Debating P.C.: The Controversy over Political Correctness on College Campuses,* ed. Paul Berman (New York: Dell, 1992), 249–57.

8. George Lipsitz, discussion at the "What Is an Oppositional Left?" conference at the University of Vermont, March 8, 1991.

9. David Lloyd, discussion at the "Americanist Vision of Cultural Studies" conference at Columbia University, March 7, 1992.

10. See *The Fortress Economy: The Economic Role of the U.S. Prison System*, Alexander C. Lichtenstein and Michael A. Kroll (Philadelphia: American Friends Service Committee, 1990), 6–12.

CHAPTER SIX

Multiculturalism's Unfinished Business

CHRISTOPHER NEWFIELD AND AVERY F. GORDON

Contrary to its media image, multiculturalism wasn't born yesterday. Its most important but largely forgotten development took place in the early and middle 1970s in work on primary and secondary education. This earlier work was developed far from the newly multicultural humanities programs at highly selective private universities like Stanford that received most of the coverage in the late 1980s. As expressed in statements by the American Association of Colleges of Teacher Education or in articles in the *Journal of Teacher Education,* 1970s multiculturalism was a grassroots attempt at community-based racial *reconstruction* through that vital local institution, the neighborhood public school. It attempted a multidimensional approach relatively foreign to the compartmentalized knowledges of universities, addressing institutional factors along with questions of personal identity, bi- and tricultural relations, community culture, teacher attitudes and behavior, school administrative structures, and local politics and economics, among others.

In its strongest 1990s versions, multiculturalism continues to have a similar potential to reform racial inequalities within existing institutions. As we mentioned in the Introduction, the meaning of multiculturalism remains varied and often vague despite its growing presence as a policy rubric in schools, businesses, arts and other cultural institutions, the military, and various local and national political organizations. In this essay, we don't survey all the possible meanings of multiculturalism or its institutional practices. Instead, we focus on a general conceptual source for multiculturalism's limited but positive potential to describe one of the baseline conditions necessary for the establishment of multiracial democracy in the United States.

The prominence of multiculturalism in the late 1980s and 1990s can be traced to many complex economic, political, and cultural factors, some of which are discussed by the other contributors to this volume. From the point of view of the popular imagination, multiculturalism's most insistent reason for being is a recognition, however belated, of the fundamentally multiracial and multiethnic nature of the United States. This recognition, though often divorced from the long-standing and broader struggles that produced it, is occurring in what is now called a post-civil rights context, a context in which most Americans believe themselves and the nation to be opposed to racism and in favor of a multiracial, multiethnic pluralism. Whatever delusions and contradictions attach to this belief, and there are many, it nonetheless remains a deeply held structure of feeling. It is in this environment that this essay offers a conceptual source for multiculturalism's potential to describe how to achieve even the limited result of a true cultural pluralism. True pluralism is the surprisingly rare precondition for the democratic debate of a range of economic, political, and cultural problems. It involves taking the widely accepted notion of cultural pluralism and divorcing it from its longtime companion, *assimilationism*. It involves rejecting assimilationist forms of pluralism, particularly what we'll call the supremacist and unionist variants that use pluralism to conceal repressive effects.

Problems and Limits

Multiculturalism's most general goal in the 1970s was to reorganize education for the benefit of minority students. Its proponents saw it as an idea that supported other everyday work toward antiracist social and cultural life. Multicultural education served as an umbrella term for a variety of racial equity projects. It did not envision revolutionary change, but did seek to dismantle white-majority control of schools and the use of white backgrounds and values as the sole yardstick of excellence. It sought to recover lost knowledge and thereby produce new understandings of U.S. history and social life. At its broadest reach, multiculturalism imagined the building of racial democracy through popular pluralism. Its cultural pluralism was popular in that it imagined ways in which intercultural rules would be drawn and re-drawn by those affected by them, particularly by people of color, rather than by experts, bureaucrats, and managers, particularly white ones.

Multiculturalism sought the means through which, in Manning Mar-able's phrase, "people of color [could] radically redefine the nature of democracy."[1] But there are good reasons to be suspicious of multicultural-ism's ability to perform such a redefinition of the national framework. Many of this volume's contributors see multiculturalism as obstructive or irrele-vant to the progressive work they deem most essential. We heartily share their concerns. Marable himself, who defends multiculturalism as an ally of genuine and multiracial democracy, calls for an interconnected set of pro-jects that does not obviously need the concept of multiculturalism, even though expanded multiculturalism needs them: the completion of civil and human rights movements, the enactment of feminist visions, opposition to homophobia, international resistance to tyranny and exploitation, ex-panded critiques of capitalism, and situation-specific cross-racial alliances among people of color.[2] Each of these crucial projects has a life of its own as well as numerous practitioners, and each seems like exactly the kind of po-litical and social movement that is doing just fine without multiculturalism's *cultural* focus.

Multiculturalism's cultural turn has been highly significant in advancing our understandings of race, power, identity, and social institutions. It has helped to displace biological notions of race and is compatible with anti-essentialist notions of racial, ethnic, gender, class, and sexual identity, in which one's identity is real and determinate without being fixed or defined by inherent properties supposedly shared by every member of the group. It has allowed us to focus on how internal differences comprise a group with-out undermining that group's reality. It has helped us to see how porous and flexible group boundaries are, allowing for explorations of hybridity, bor-derlands, and imaginative coalitions, while at the same time helping us to understand how intersectional identities are both constrained and creative. The turn to culture has fostered the exploration of identity as a process of identification, a partly voluntary, partly contradictory, always constructed set of multiple ties to a group or groups. Culture has also shown how per-sonal identity and group formation are themselves political, being directly involved in the application of resources and power. In short, the turn to cul-ture has given us a whole new vocabulary for describing the experiences, ar-tifacts, values, struggles, and history of various groups who are marked and subordinated by race, gender, and sexuality. And, it has, of course, been an important component in the extraordinary efforts to redefine the nature and content of knowledge itself.

But culture has its own history of dubious battles. Although the concept of culture can insist on the sociocultural reality of race and racism, it doesn't always do so. The culturalism of multiculturalism threatens to shift attention from racialization to culture and in so doing to treat racialized groups as one of many diverse and interesting cultures. This makes racism more difficult to acknowledge and control: phenomena that might be at least partially attributed to racism, such as crime in racially segregated, low-income neighborhoods, can be attributed in a culturalist approach to the deficient, or just different, values of the sufferers. Seeing whiteness as cultural produces a complementary blindness. While the attention to whiteness as a cultural system has been a very important move in the reconceptualization of race problems, it downplays the ongoing existence of white supremacy as a system of privilege, favoritism, discrimination, and exclusion. Indeed, given existing racial inequalities and the continuing segregation of most social institutions, the reduction of all racial groups to a nonexistent level playing field poses serious problems. Multiculturalism has also been very uncertain about where gender and sexuality fit into its notion of cultures. When the culturalization of race meets up with a de-gendered and de-sexualized notion of race, the cultural move takes us two steps backward in our efforts to develop complex understandings of intersecting identities and social power.

The most severe problem with multiculturalism's culturalism is that it can be satisfied with bracketing or avoiding institutional and structural determinants of inequality. Social scientists, in particular, are very familiar with the ways in which cultural emphases have mistaken symptoms for causes and promoted an individualized understanding of advantage and disadvantage. For example, explanations of urban poverty that invoke a culture of poverty have allowed researchers to ignore poverty's institutional causes. Ignoring factors such as the loss of urban industry to cheap labor zones abroad, culturalists have blamed poverty on the unemployed and underemployed's bad attitudes toward work (see Zavella in this volume). At the most general level, multiculturalism's culturalism can allow for the segregation of culture from systematic social relations of power like capitalism, patriarchy, and neocolonialism. This segregation both subjectivizes the concept of culture, treating culture not as a structure but as an "ephemeral set of behavioral attitudes and values,"[3] *and* de-culturalizes economic and political structures, treating the latter as transparent objective forces.

Multiculturalism is plagued with doubts arising from these weaknesses and others superbly analyzed elsewhere in this volume. Whether it will be able to provide the conceptual and practical tools necessary for a multiracial democracy is uncertain at this time. What multiculturalism does do is address the need to avoid even benevolent white oversight over the process by which various groups reconstruct democracy and social justice. Multiculturalism's tradition does specifically challenge the most lethal *cultural* aspect of white rule—assimilationism—which allows the mere presence of white people to be a form of control. As we'll try to suggest, a strong multiculturalism can at least extract cultural equity out of the pluralism such a multitude of Americans claim to favor.

Assimilationism

Multiculturalism arises largely from the tradition of cultural pluralism. Although it might seem surprising, cultural pluralism has frequently been a determined opponent of white-norm assimilationism. By assimilationism we do not mean *assimilation*, the means and ends pursued by immigrants or marginalized citizens who wish to join the existing economic and political mainstream. Wanting assimilation often indicates a desire for the kinds of interesting jobs, pleasant neighborhoods, home ownership, financial security, personal leisure time, good health care, vacations, community influence, and other benefits that in the United States are reserved for the proverbial middle class. We are not here passing any kind of judgment on the wish to assimilate in this sense. We are instead criticizing the *terms* that *assimilationism* extracts from those who need and want its rewards. Assimilationism likes to portray itself as nothing more than the innocent desire for a good life, and indeed this is the foundation of its social influence. But as we use the term here, assimilationism refers to a specific ideology that sets the fundamental conditions for full economic and social citizenship in the United States. It is this ideology that we criticize here, and that multiculturalism and cultural pluralism have often pointedly opposed.

Assimilationism has three main features, all of which are contested by the genuinely pluralist traditions we will discuss. Assimilationism requires adherence to core principles and behaviors. It rejects racialized group consciousness. And it repudiates cultural equity among groups. These three features are profoundly interconnected. The demand for a common core displaces both demands for equality and the effects of racial difference. Lacking any notion of cultural equality, assimilationism encourages functional ranking of various cultures. Downplaying the effects of racial marking, assimilationism ignores the way supposedly neutral institutions are pro-white.

Through the interaction of these features, assimilationism continually militates against demands for enhanced equality. It declares these a threat to social harmony and peace, and requires instead the kind of individual upward mobility that, though individually beneficial, does not challenge unjust ground rules since it is contingent on obeying them. Assimilationism requires different groups to follow standards they had no share in making and that they may dislike, even as it presents these requirements as the bedrock of orderly freedom. These standards are very difficult to criticize because they seem inclusive, neutral, and unifying rather than racial and divisive. Assimilationism is the general operating system for everybody's different software of cultural interaction. And it is an immensely powerful opponent of all kinds of equity movements in American life.

Assimilationism is compatible with pluralism, but it is *antipluralist* in a fundamental sense. Pluralism, in the words of one college dictionary, holds that "no single explanatory system or view of reality can account for all the phenomena of life."[4] In the United States, pluralism has been translated as *e pluribus unum*, meaning that multiple groups are subsumed into a single whole. But the strong version of pluralism *rejects* what goes by its name in the United States, since it denies that the many are finally united by the one. What we usually call pluralism in this country is a pluralism of form leading to a monism of rules. It should be called *assimilationist pluralism*, where the outcome is not actually irreducibly plural, but a union or core. Assimilationist pluralists continually insist on conformity to this core even as they profess their belief in plurality. This assimilationist-pluralist position is contradictory, and yet it forms a pillar of the American Creed, standing next to its fellow pillars "democracy" and "free enterprise" and transforming these into elements of a core political culture. Strong versions of cultural pluralism, like the 1970s multiculturalism developed largely by people of color, tried to rehabilitate pluralism as an *alternative* to assimilationism.

The contrast between the two is not so easily sustained. Assimilationism generally tries to endorse pluralism and accuses its adversaries of failing to do so. It charges those who attack the inequalities of assimilationism with attacking pluralism itself.

The recent multiculturalism debates provide an excellent example of this dynamic, which has typified post-World War II racial discourse. One side— call them race progressives—challenged multiculturalism as Eurocentric assimilationism in disguise. It believed that multiculturalism tolerated harmless kinds of diversity while continuing to enforce Euro-American norms. This side called for rejecting weak multiculturalism in favor of cultural equal time and a redistribution of institutional space and power. A second group treated these criticisms of assimilationism as an (ironically, "multicultural") attack on pluralism itself. Group two denounced multiculturalism as a stalking horse for cultural separatism, which it believed to be perennially responsible for civil unrest and national decline. Thus "multiculturalism" in the 1990s came to denote not so much any particular position in an argument about race relations but the argument itself.

This argument has a general postwar form: An opposition group suggests that beneath the borrowed mantle of pluralism is the old emperor of assimilationism militating against cultural and social equality. The emperor says that his critics are not really complaining about the alleged assimilationism beneath his pluralist mantle, but about his pluralist skin itself. His skin, he says, is not merely white, but a neutral tone that harmonizes many colors. Asserting his nakedness, he continues, is a cheap way of denying his ingrained pluralism. As soon as his opponents are successfully branded separatist or nationalist or otherwise blind to pluralism, they lose. This outcome remains a major media hit. Much of the media seems convinced that multicultural research, teaching, and art that put racial power and inequity on the table undermine not so much the wrongs of assimilationism but the rainbow harmonies of a post-civil rights pluralism. Social unrest is traced to calls for racial equity rather than to the emperor's efforts to contain them.

We side with those who are wary of anything that seems like assimilationism in disguise. Many versions of multiculturalism have indeed been this. Even at its closest approach to the popular pluralism we will elaborate, multiculturalism is not likely to be a radical force that undermines the existing ensemble of social relations. It is reformist, and its reforms, though they go beyond a narrow definition of culture, cannot substitute for other kinds of political and social activity. Nonetheless, multiculturalism has the crucial job of constructing a new nonwhite majority without the assimilationist premises being so warmly defended today. Multiculturalism has at times been very good at making white people mean the good things they say about pluralism. Fortifying itself with various race-based nationalisms, and retaining its interest in antiessentialist and hybridized forms, strong multiculturalism can continue to develop its long-standing *rejection of assimilationism from within cultural pluralism itself.* Pluralism remains something like a majority ideology in the United States. Reconditioning it could link large numbers of people to pluralism's most important idea—the never-ending designing and redesigning of "America" out of the *equitable* interaction of its multiple and racialized centers.

Our essay, then, investigates this imperfect tradition within cultural pluralism, from its 1920s roots to its development in the 1970s as "multiculturalism" on through its most hopeful elements today.

Kallen's Pluralist Attack on Assimilationism

Multiculturalism is saddled with the weight of its major precursor, *cultural pluralism*. Cultural pluralism has come to signify cultural "multiplicity in a unity," in the phrase of the term's official source, Horace Kallen, writing in the *Nation* in 1915.[5] Defined in this way, cultural pluralism redivides the public along familiar lines. Some stress multiplicity and some stress unity. The former are wary that pluralist *unity* is a nice word for the assimilation of all U.S. groups to Euro-American or even Anglo-Saxon norms. The latter insist that *pluralist* unity can dissolve our national institutions into partisan tools of interest-group bickering and even civil war. The former group worries about cultural *autonomy;* the latter is preoccupied with cultural *commonality*. The former denounces the cultural *dominance* of the majority, while the latter rejects the cultural *separatism* of the minority.

This argument has gone back and forth for most of this century, with each side laying claim to the mantle of pluralism, though always a pluralism fortified with some other principle (like a core American "creed"). This kind of bipolar arrangement tempts people to split the difference and say the truth lies in the middle, in a combination of autonomy and commonality, of multiplicity and unity. Recently, for example, the respected sociologist Troy Duster, drawing conclusions from the University of California, Berkeley's "Diversity Project," invoked Horace Kallen as a forebear of a kind of third way (a "third experience") of diversity between the untenable poles of separatism and assimilation: "In a pluralist society, ethnic and racial groups can maintain distinctive cultures, organizations, and identities while they participate in the larger community. Individual members of ethnic and racial groups may choose to live in delimited communities, marry within their own group, ... [but] they also relate to others."[6] Multiculturalism needs to update Kallen's "differences in a symphonic blend or harmony" to acknowledge more conflict and ongoing difference. But it remains tied to the project of balancing independence and interaction.

But cultural pluralism, in Kallen's usage, was something more precise than multiplicity in unity. It was formed in opposition to some subtle updates of the stress on "unity." We can clarify the current dispute somewhat by noting that Kallen defined cultural pluralism in *opposition* to one kind of thought that currently claims the name. His most lasting contribution to pluralism is not his encouragement of a third way that balances difference and unity, but his strong tilt away from unity, which writers like Arthur Schlesinger Jr. ignore.

In his later elaboration of cultural pluralism, Kallen makes clear that the idea came into being as the enemy of assimilationism. At one time, he claims, "Americanization" sought "cultural monism" as its outcome: "Any immigrant on whom difference from the natives lays a burden of inferiority will take Americanization for identification, for digesting differences from them into sameness with them. From this point of view equality *is* identity"—no actual equality between different groups exists, for difference is replaced by emulation and replication.[7] Kallen periodically casts doubt on phrases like "the union of the diverse" and the "American Idea" in distinguishing pluralism from monism, which of course raises the prospect of a subtler kind of assimilationism happening all over again.[8] How does Kallen draw a line between his version of pluralism, always flirting with unity, and the kind of unity denoted by traditional assimilationism?

Three features are particularly important. First, cultural pluralism opposes the idea of a *core culture*, one that defines a true national identity. Kallen traces this notion to what he calls "cultural racism":

> A new sort of racism emerged [in the late nineteenth century] to segregate and account for the American past and to rationalize present claims. This has its analogies with the racism of Kipling's "white man's burden." But it was not a racism of color as in imperial Britain and America's Southern states. It was a racism of culture. It claimed that the American Idea and the American Way were hereditary to the Anglo-Saxon stock and to that stock only; that other stocks were incapable of producing them, learning them and living them. If, then, America is to survive as a culture of creed and code, it can do so only so long as the chosen Anglo-Saxon race retains its integrity of flesh and spirit and freely sustains and defends their American expression against alien contamination. Universal suffrage, for example, *is* such a contamination [in this view].[9]

Kallen rejects what he takes to be a biological claim that "Anglo-Saxon" honesty and so on arise from its "stock." But his major complaint is with the identification of the American Way with one particular group. Such a view acknowledges U.S. diversity while identifying the real national culture with the culture of only one group. No less dangerous than biological racism is a cultural racism that assumes that institutions pervaded by Anglo-Saxon persons or ideas can stand for the American Idea. For Kallen, an institution can be "American" only when it is *not* Anglo-Saxon. The American always includes the plurality of America's actual groups. Whatever Kallen means by the unity of diversity, this unity cannot have any one cultural center. The grounding of the American in an Anglo-Saxon or other core is not only monoculturalism; it is cultural racism or what we might call *cultural supremacism.*

Second, Kallen's cultural pluralism insists on the irreducible social reality of *group life.* He rejects the idea that one's group identity must finally dissolve into a larger whole or that one's "individuality" is separate from one's membership in a group. A "group-life prolongs and redirects the lives of the individuals whose association generates, sustains and impels the formations of the group. Individuals not only live and move and nourish their being amid traditions, they are themselves traditions."[10] Kallen is not what we would now call an essentialist on groups: they overlap, move, and mix. Even the word tradition itself, he says, means "a carrying on, a continuous ongoing—but a carrying on, or ongoing, as any person's life goes on, not changelessly, but as a process of changing."[11] Nor is he a determinist: "In freedom, commitment and withdrawal are collaborative decisions of the individual, not compulsions of his group or of any of its institutions."[12] Groups are a fundamental feature of American life, and indeed of culture itself. Cultural groups cannot be dismissed as artificial political factions or as corruptions of the American Idea, because they are the American Idea itself.

Third, many of Kallen's "unifying" moments demand equality among diverse cultures. Cultural pluralism marks "an orchestration of diverse utterances of diversities . . . each developing freely and characteristically in its own enclave, and somehow so intertwined with the others, as to suggest, even to symbolize, the dynamic of the whole. Each is a cultural reservoir whence flows its own singularity of expression to unite in the concrete intercultural total which is the culture of America."[13] Kallen retains concepts like the "whole," although these concepts will betray his better purpose. But orchestration does not necessarily mean the subordination of lesser cultures to one with a broader perspective or higher wisdom. "Note the word 'intercultural.' . . . The intent is in the . . . prefix: *inter,* which here postulates the parity of the different and their free and friendly communication with one another as both co-operators and competitors."[14] *Equality precedes "unity,"* and the unity is the "total" outcome of these interactions, a result that follows from independent *cultural* activities encountering each other. Unity thus does not guide these encounters.

Writers who summon Kallen's cultural pluralism as a mainstream of racial thought are not, whether they know it or not, authorizing diversity subsumed by cultural union. They are also, whether they mean to or not, conjuring some pretty specific criteria for genuine pluralism: a *multicentered* national culture, which cannot be identified with the values of a dominant group or groups; the inevitability of *cultural groups*; and *cultural parity* among these different cultures, rather than implicit hierarchy. Kallen's cultural pluralism has some serious deficiencies, which we will discuss. But it comprises a much more rigorously democratic model of multigroup negotiations than do most that go by its label today.

In fact, it was precisely this kind of cultural pluralism that came under fire in the 1980s in the name of pluralism. With Kallen's efforts in mind, we can find choicer names for these recent detractors.

The Struggle for Pluralism (1): The New Supremacists

Kallen's work on cultural multiplicity perpetuated some serious flaws. One appeared in his silence on the difference between white ethnic and racialized groups.[15] Taking white ethnics as his standard, he overlooked the importance of racial exclusion and subordination in American life. Complacent about the increasing political equality among whites, he did not explore the dependence of genuine cultural pluralism on political and economic parity. He assumed that American capitalism was not subject to the diversity principle and would foster the economic mobility required to integrate ethnic groups into a culturally variegated society. He was also so drawn to concepts of union, harmony, and the One that there was plenty of room for later writers to read him, as Schlesinger does, as grounding plurality in a higher unity. Nonetheless, subsequent theorists of pluralism could have attempted to refine Kallen by eliminating his residual Eurocentrism. Instead, although he launched cultural pluralism as an attack on assimilationism, the bulk of the white pluralist thought that has followed Kallen has attempted to *reconcile* pluralism and assimilationism.

When multiculturalism began to hit the news in the late 1980s, it seemed a relatively mild reform movement. It was pro-diversity *and* it defined diversity not in racial or political but in cultural terms. Although it was enacted, often with the encouragement of radical student protest, it took such forms as Stanford's "Western Civilization" courses, now revised to include

"non-Western" or "minority" materials, or the University of California,
Santa Barbara's "ethnicity requirement," or New York State's report on the
schools, "A Curriculum of Inclusion," or the University of California, Berkeley's "American Cultures" sequence, whose innovation stemmed from the
pluralization of American "culture." Such changes were a real improvement
at schools where student bodies, curricula, and faculty were disproportionately white and casually segregated. But this multiculturalism looked like
curricula reforms and not at all like a social movement. One assessment, by
Arthur Levine and Ette Cureton in early 1992, expresses the calmness of
multicultural reality: "The sheer quantity of multicultural activity . . . belies
the belief that the traditional curriculum has been largely impermeable to,
or has simply marginalized, diversity. And the character of the change—
principally add-ons to, rather than substitutes for, existing practice—makes
untenable the notion that multiculturalism is replacing the historic
canon."[16] Much criticism centered on multiculturalism's ideological timid-
ity: since nonwhite materials were "add-ons" to white structures, they did
not address the centrality and dominance of the latter. As we've noted, multiculturalism seemed to many a kinder, gentler form of assimilationism,
with some expansion of a commitment to a mostly cosmetic pluralism.
Levine and Cureton called this the "quiet revolution," quiet like the tenth
draft of a committee memo coming out of a laser printer.

   Real noise came instead from those proclaiming that this multiculturalism had already gone too far. Some amazing statements were made.

> Counterposed to the traditional idea of American culture—"the melting-
> pot"—is multiculturalism, the United States as a cartel of tribes, of separate
> cultures existing side by side. Accordingly, individual rights in civil society
> must yield to group or corporate rights—the citizen related to the state and
> society through his ethnic or interest group. Though it would come as a sur-
> prise to the trend-setting multiculturalists, their true ideological forefather is
> not Gramsci but Mussolini.[17]

Here, multiculturalism is fascist because it opposes American pluralism. In
Roger Kimball's words, "'Multiculturalism' as used in the academy today is
not about recognizing genuine cultural diversity or encouraging pluralism.
It is about undermining the priority of Western liberal values" on which real
pluralism rests.[18]

   Attacks like this were so common that Burger King could have used them
as hamburger wrappers. But though they tended to substitute hyperbole for
evidence of their clear and present dangers, their targets were precise. Both
of the passages just cited are attempting to recover the meaning of a true

pluralism. The first claims that the "traditional idea of American culture" is assimilationism (the "melting pot") rather than separate cultures. It goes on to subordinate group to individual rights. The second bases pluralism on "the priority of Western liberal values" to others. Taken together, these passages reject all three of the features we extracted from Kallen's strong version of cultural pluralism. They deny the multicentered structure of American culture, the irreducible reality of group identity and social life, and the presumptive equality of different U.S. cultures. Crucially, these statements also claim the title of pluralism. They reassert the unity of pluralism and assimilationism that they find besieged by multicultural tendencies.

The attractions of this pluralism-assimilationism alliance are not limited to the political right, but cut across the political spectrum. The most famous example is probably the longtime liberal Arthur Schlesinger Jr., whose 1991 book *The Disuniting of America* rendered him the theoretical mastermind of those that feared that renewed civil unrest could spring from excessive race consciousness. Schlesinger admits the reality of America's diverse "ethnic" cultures but insists on the need for these to subordinate themselves to an overarching American Creed. The three key ingredients of assimilationist pluralism are there well expressed. First, he calls for a return to George Washington's ideal of a "new race" forming "one people" in the New World.[19] This depends on ending "the attack on the common American identity" and on respecting "the assimilation process" that produces "an acceptance of the language, the institutions, and the political ideals that hold the nation together."[20] Second, American values place the individual above and apart from group life: we must remain aware that "individualism itself is looked on with abhorrence and dread by collectivist cultures in which loyalty to the group overrides personal goals."[21] Finally, cultural equality is bogus; the West is Best. "Whatever the particular crimes of Europe, that continent is also the source—the *unique* source—of those liberating ideas of individual liberty, political democracy, the rule of law. . . . There is surely no reason for Western civilization to have guilt trips laid on it by champions of cultures based on despotism, superstition, tribalism, and fanaticism."[22] Schlesinger's pluralist sense that there are indeed other systems of values that might be (or might seem to be) better for other people easily coexists with his belief that ours *are* "absolutely better."[23] The highest payoff of this strain of cultural pluralism is that it combines tolerance and hierarchy, difference and inferiority, into a pluralist, democratic supremacism.[24]

The assimilationist pluralists veer quite close to what Kallen called the "racism of culture." Other groups are not biologically but culturally inferior.

These pluralist supremacists do not favor racial segregation and skin-color exclusion, and on this point their sincerity need not be doubted. But their sense of the superiority of a consensual creed that they insistently associate with Euro-American ways underwrites a sense of the historical fitness of white or European rule.[25] A "racism of culture" justifies the de facto priority of white concerns and values in U.S. society, including ostensibly neutral institutions. Indeed, it defines this de facto priority of white concerns *as* neutrality itself, where whiteness is nothing other than American standards of democracy and procedural fairness. Cultural racism allows political and economic factors to seem irrelevant, since they merely reflect the relative strength of different cultures. It depicts criticisms of the impartiality or equity of these preponderantly white institutions as the product of inferior cultural values. The absence of de jure white control is touted as evidence of genuine neutrality. So is white indifference to the racialized dimension of this neutrality, an indifference sometimes called "color blindness."[26] Such supremacism, calling itself pluralism, has tremendous influence. Its trinity— one-culture national unity, individualism, and a supremacism cleansed of biology and Jim Crow—forms the intellectual baseline for race talk today.

The Struggle for Pluralism (2): Cultural Unionists

But what about the moderates who seek a balance between assimilation and pluralism, interaction and autonomy? The recent multicultural debates featured a number of writers who reject the visible chauvinism of the emperor mentioned earlier. They are closer to Kallen's original position, as we noted regarding the remarks of Troy Duster. Do they avoid assimilation and find a genuine third way between it and separatist nationalism?

One test case is "The Great Multicultural Debate," whose author, Gary B. Nash, is a nationally renowned historian of American colonial and antebellum history who has placed race at the center of his research for at least twenty-five years.[27] He has more recently served as general editor of a series of systematically multicultural history textbooks for California schoolchildren that has taken a critical and revisionist stance toward earlier, Anglocentric versions of history. He is also director of a congressionally mandated National Standards for the Teaching of United States History, which as we write is pending certification. Nash speaks as a proponent when he says, "Multicultural curricula, 'stressing a diversity of cultures, races, languages, and religions,' and eliminating 'ethnocentric and biased concepts and materials from textbook and classroom,' have been adopted by school systems throughout the United States" (11). He argues that the history profession has often disseminated misinformation about the racial past, and sees multiculturalism's ongoing task as criticizing this ethnocentrism in order to tell a larger truth about such issues as Anglo-Mexican and European-American Indian relations and the centrality of cultural and racial diversity to the creation of the past.

Nash rejects one of the assumptions of assimilationist-pluralism: its individualism. Groups are also important actors in history, which cannot be reduced to the tale of various individuals succeeding or failing on their own personal terms. Unlike Schlesinger, he makes allowances for the fact that many of these groups are racialized instead of "ethnic," which alters their relations to the white cultures they encounter. In order to understand these groups, one can legitimately be "race-conscious"; that is, one must *not* be color-blind in order to understand the place of Mexican Americans or Korean Americans in the past and present United States, for so much of that past and present has been affected by racial difference. Individuals have a group life that, for Nash, must be considered through race consciousness.

Nash also avoids white cultural supremacism even as he avoids endorsing Kallen's cultural parity or equality. He does *not* associate preferred American values with the "West" or the "European origins of American civilization" that Schlesinger claims.[28] But he does denounce "a promiscuous pluralism that gives every thing equal weight."[29] Henry Louis Gates Jr., writing in a later issue of *Contention,* also opposes the thesis of "cultural equity," which holds that "as people enjoy equal standing under the law, so too must the cultural products of different groups be considered both as representative of those groups and as of at least equal value to those other groups."[30] But Gates regards the likely hierarchy of cultural products as something to be mutually established through "the contraposition of different interests, different perspectives," rather than as a rank already known via an artifact's culture of origin. Sharing Kallen's rejection of cultural supremacism, these writers nonetheless do not insist that the best alternative is cultural parity. They endorse multisided cultural *interaction* as a kind of middle way between hierarchy and equality.[31] Interaction suggests two-way contact without making any assurances about the relative positions of the parties involved.

But these writers reject the principle of a multiple core culture in favor of a single, unifying center. Nash's vexed encounter with his version of Afrocentrism leads him to conclude that we need to teach students "the common humanity of all individuals while discovering the historical relevance of gender, race, religion, and other categories that help shape their identity."[32] He explicitly replaces cultural equality with a cultural core: "If multiculturalism is to get beyond a promiscuous pluralism that gives every thing equal weight and adopts complete moral relativism, it must reach some agreement on what is at the core of American culture."[33] "Pluribus can flourish in these ways only if unum is preserved at the heart of the polity—in a common commitment to core political and moral values."[34] In Nash's view, diversity and egalitarian negotiation among various groups do not make common culture unnecessary, but require a common culture to furnish appropriate ground rules. Common or core culture *transcends* cultural difference. It manages diversity via a set of principles that is neutral to the distinctive qualities of the various cultures it manages. The core culture is not, in this view, undergoing continual modification at the hands of everyday group life, but is the unchanging heart that regulates diversity's flow.

The tricky thing about this position is that it does not crudely establish the superiority of white culture to which it then demands conformity. It insists on irreducible cultural diversity. Nash defines his core as "political and moral values"—government by the people, a government of laws, and "common entitlement as individuals to liberty, equal opportunity, and impartial treatment under the law."[35] This requires *political* unity, which means not just holding particular common values, but the fact of holding common values in itself. These common values rule any conceivable negotiations a person or group would conduct with other persons and groups. New values would not emerge from the negotiations to mediate them, for the mediation would already be in place. Diane Ravitch, to cite another example, endorses criticism of racial regimes and practices as long as they do not threaten the core with one view's excessive autonomy. "Segregation of, or separatism by, any group is not multicultural; Afrocentrism is a sort of intellectual apartheid, and as such is the antithesis of multiculturalism."[36] Multiculturalism properly focuses on "the interaction of diverse peoples," the social condition of cultural mixing. This mixing implicitly takes place on some kind of common ground. Todd Gitlin traces the decline of a progressive national agenda to "the fragmentation of commonality politics."[37] Gates cites Cardinal Newman to envision the desired intensity of union: although society cannot achieve such a state, "the university should promote 'the power of viewing many things at once as one whole, of referring them severally to their true place in the universal system, of understanding their respective value, and determining their mutual dependence.'"[38]

While these writers are reluctant to state the system of positive norms to which different cultures must adhere (even Nash's are largely procedural), they claim that a proper sense of common features will create an orderly foundation. Cultural difference rests on political unity, and does so not through coercion or exclusion so much as through consensus about what the "mutual dependence" will look like. These writers support multi-culturalism while rejecting multi-politics. They are concerned lest diverse cultures express not underlying oneness but separate polities, distinctive political principles, and political autonomy. Some principle of commonal-ity must govern the relation between culture and politics.

No formula can predict the assimilative intensity of any particular vision of such underlying unity, which varies. The assimilative power depends on a structure of feeling about what comes first, about what is most urgent. A re-mark by Stephen Steinberg suggests the stakes: "If there is an iron law of ethnicity, it is that when ethnic groups are found in a hierarchy of power, wealth, and status, then conflict is inescapable. However, where there is so-cial, economic, and political parity among the constituent groups, ethnic conflict, when it occurs, tends to be at a low level and rarely spills over into violence."[39] Steinberg thinks *parity* is the most important prerequisite to so-cial peace; it is more important than shared values. Nash et al. put shared values ahead of parity, which they leave virtually unmentioned. Assimilation sufficient to produce a cultural or moral core is, for them, the precondition of equitable rules. But for Steinberg and the multiculturalists we will dis-cuss, equity is the precondition of any kind of valuable common ground.

Although the second kind of contemporary pluralism (that of Nash et al.) is an improvement over the first, it retains the three-part assimilationist-pluralist alliance in a more generous form. First, it encourages cultural diversity as long as that does not affect political unity. Second, it grants the legitimacy of group consciousness around racial as well as ethnic difference, but casts a perpetual shadow of a higher unity over such differences. Group life carries the stigma of something rich but incomplete and partial com-pared to life in common.

Finally, these pluralists generally reject cultural parity. They try not to make a big deal out of this, and offer a substitute for parity—cultural *inter-action*. This is fine in itself, but it says nothing about the conditions, equal or unequal or some combination, under which interaction takes place. Do, say, Hopi culture and Anglo-American culture meet and intermingle as though meaningfully equal? Does the long history of political inequality and subor-dination play *no* role in controlling the cultural outcome? How might the distortions of such inequality be overcome? These pluralists avoid the question. Sometimes they act as though "interaction" takes care of it, sometimes they claim that the issue is epistemologically misguided, sometimes they suggest that the real issue is aesthetic value that is unrelated to "politics," sometimes they critique equality without proposing an alternative. In any case, the issue of parity hangs in midair.

Or so it hangs until the question of parity becomes more obviously political. A crucial example is the moderate pluralists' response to the old issue of nationalist separatism. For Ravitch, Afrocentrics are not entitled even to sit at the negotiation table, and her reason is their alleged separatist agenda. The problem with nationalism for white people has generally been the reverse of separatism: Chicano, Indian, and Black militancy has threatened not to separate and go away but to stay and change society's basic ground rules. The moderate pluralists' hostility to separatism suggests the importance they vest in unity. It also suggests what unity supposedly guarantees: that these ground rules will remain the same. The idea of a core culture rejects separatism by reasserting that these fundamental rules are not open to change. (One of the rules, to offer only one instance, has been that the prevailing forms of due process in university admissions, police procedure, criminal trials, job promotion, and so on, are color-blind, even though critics have charged that these processes are unconsciously pro-white.) The priority of a core to multicentric negotiations stigmatizes those who want to change the core as attacking the structure of civil society. Hence Ravitch's categorical rejection of Afrocentricity. By challenging core Western or white American values, whether well or badly, Afrocentricity seems to challenge white political governance of at least school curricula. She calls Afrocentricity apartheid, apparently imagining the same total loss of political sovereignty that term meant for Black South Africans, this time applied to whites.[40]

We could continue to call the Schlesinger group and the Nash/Ravitch group "pluralists," since they all are. The latter group in particular is responsible for significant cultural and intellectual improvements.[41] But to call all of them pluralists would be to endorse the illusion that "pluralism" has a single, definable meaning. It would also encourage the incorrect view that pluralism consists of a benign balance between unity and multiplicity that can be fair and good to all groups in America. In the face of dissent from some groups, these two kinds of pluralists use unity to control whatever serious autonomy and shifts in power multiplicity might generate. To object to such uses of unity is not to say that all Euro-American norms are bad. It is to say that these forms of pluralism diminish our ability to discuss the harm they may do to others.

These major variants of pluralism are fundamentally assimilationist. Clearer names for the teams will help: let's call Schlesinger's the *cultural supremacists*, and Ravitch's the *cultural unionists*. Their modes are different, but they both mix assimilationism with pluralism and naturalize (a more or less benevolent) white-majority rule. Sure, they're all pluralists, but it would help discussion to get their fundamental companion assumptions up front.

We'd like to turn now to *multiculturalism*, and reserve the word for those who oppose crucial elements of these two variants of pluralism. Multiculturalists, in the strict sense, do this not by rejecting pluralism, as some like to suggest, but by building the alliance missing from the mainstream consensus, the alliance between pluralism and nationalism.

Multiculturalism in Education: The 1970s

A number of trends converge in multicultural educational thought in the early 1970s, and our brief account here can only focus on some common elements without doing justice to the concept's variety.[42]

The word "multicultural" had a fitful beginning in the World War II era, appearing in non-trendsetting situations such as a *New York Herald-Tribune Books* attack on prejudice on 27 July 1941, or, in 1959, a description of Montreal as multicultural (*Oxford English Dictionary*). The word had a far more developed existence in British Commonwealth countries such as Canada and Australia. The Canadian case is particularly interesting, as multiculturalism is one of the ways in which that nation has sought to see itself as comprised of many nations, including the First Nations (indigenous peoples) and a largely separate society, Quebec. A proper survey of these countries unfortunately lies beyond our scope. Nonetheless, the United States' understanding of multiculturalism will remain incomplete until it develops a picture of other international varieties.

In the United States, multiculturalism had arisen most directly from a concern with the experience of schoolchildren. For children of American Indian, Mexican-American, African-American, or Asian-American backgrounds, there is never a single America, in the view of multicultural educators, but always at least two. Such children live in the culture of their home or community, and they go to school in a culture that is sharply distinct. Multicultural theory focuses on children who were not considered white by their schools or society. Their two worlds are more sharply polarized than those of white ethnics like Polish Americans, whose home culture and language are also distinct from the English-speaking Anglo sphere of school. Mexican-American children, for example, are divided from white or Anglo society not so much by "ethnicity" in the traditional sense as by race and color. This means that their community is designated inferior in a way that the Polish or Italian community is not. A number of writers pointed out that African-American and Mexican-American children have almost always been considered "culturally deficient," and this divides their lives.

In this situation, assimilation was generally impossible, since white society regarded children of color as culturally defective as a group (although, of course, unusual individuals would always rise out of difficult circumstances). Or if not impossible, assimilation would be undesirable from the other side, since it would require the wholesale rejection of the home culture that the majority culture regarded as little more than a handicap. Starting from the "bicultural" lives of racialized children, multicultural education theorists distinguished "cultural pluralism" from assimilationism:

> The form of cultural pluralism we wish to describe more fully concentrates on the *bicultural* reality of many Mexican American children living in the United States today. . . . The basic educational issue in our interpretation of cultural democracy concerns the need for providing Mexican American children with the educational experiences necessary to enhance their right to be able to function in *both* cultural worlds, the cultural world of the Mexican American as well as the cultural world of the Anglo-American.[43]

Assimilation to a single national culture is to be replaced by mobility between related but discrete spheres of everyday life. Many Americans lead lives in which their world is at least dual, and multicultural theorists rejected ideals of assimilationism that ignored this ordinary reality. Schooling should not, in their view, take bicultural children and turn them into monocultural Anglicized adults, but should endorse biculturality as a way of life. Multiculturalism in the 1970s endorsed it as an *American* way of life, and called for cultural assimilation to be replaced by cultural democracy. This meant that "an individual can be bicultural and still be loyal to American ideals."[44]

As cultural democracy, 1970s multiculturalism built on a strong version of cultural pluralism. While noting the continual *interdependence* of various cultures, it insisted on each culture's *independence*.[45] "Cultural pluralism is neither the traditionalist's separatism nor the assimilationist's melting pot. It is a composite that recognizes the uniqueness and value of every culture. Cultural pluralism acknowledges that no group lives in isolation, but that, instead, each group influences and is influenced by others."[46] Unlike the su-

premacist and unionist pluralism discussed earlier, this *multicultural pluralism* did not attempt a balance between diversity and unity, but eliminated
the pole of unity altogether. The single core (interacting with multiple cultures) is replaced by a multiplicity of distinct cultures at the level of everyday
life. The Mexican-American child would then no longer be conceived of as
moving from her "subculture" into a "common culture" but as moving between partially overlapping and yet distinct cultures. She would be well aware
that the latter, "Anglo" culture is dominant, supplying the national language,
the law of the land, the structure of economic opportunity, the mainstream
office behaviors, and so on. But this Anglo culture would not be seen as the
unifying, official culture so much as another and socially more powerful
one. The important point was that the Mexican-American child would be
conceived as moving between two sides of her bicultural life rather than
balancing a particularistic identity with a common culture. Multicultural
pluralism replaced a single cultural core with multiple cultural domains.

A second feature distinguishes 1970s multiculturalism. While weaker
forms of pluralism regard group identity as a threat to individuality, 1970s
multiculturalism saw the two as compatible and complementary. Arturo
Pacheco describes "democratic pluralism" as distinguished by "a balance of
power between competing and overlapping religious, ethnic, economic, and
geographical groupings." It is "a more accurate description of actual democracy in America than is classical liberalism, which bases itself on a notion of
individual, rather than group, participatory democracy."[47] Pacheco does not
see this as a threat to individualism but as a description of the multicentered
political bargaining process. Manuel Ramírez and Alfredo Casañeda clari-
fied Milton Gordon's position on the link between group and individual
rights in *Assimilation in American Life* (1964). Gordon writes that "the system of cultural pluralism . . . has frequently been described as 'cultural
democracy,' since it posits the right of ethnic groups in a democratic society
to maintain their communal identity and their own subcultural values. . . .
However, we must also point out that democratic values prescribe free
choice not only for groups but also for individuals."[48] Ramírez and Casañeda
emphasized the falseness of any choice between remaining ethnic (part of a
group) and assimilating (becoming an individual without alliances in a
mixed group). When one is not compelled to assimilate one's individuality
to a particular "core" culture, one can retain one's own racial or ethnic identity while circulating among other races and ethnicities.

We could say, then, that *the unnecessary choice between individual and
group identity is imposed by assimilationism itself.* The wedge between oneself

and one's group is driven *only* by the demand that you be more like the dominant culture than you are. If a Mexican-American can interact with Anglo culture without having to resemble that culture wholesale, then she can retain her ethnic/racial identity as Mexican-American while being treated as an individual by both her own and Anglo culture. The bifurcation here is of course awkward and artificial, but that's the problem such talk addresses. Anglo-American and Mexican-American cultures intersect, differ, overlap, and diverge. Multiculturalism in the 1970s often claimed that in such cases, the dual-culture person should not be divided by a false choice between individuality and group life.

Imagining that one can be one's peculiar self and circulate generally, free of assimilationism, multicultural education theorists thus found no educational loss in retaining racial and ethnic identities in all their local particularity. Indeed, they saw this as a gain. Many educators had assumed that particularity breeds intellectual mediocrity. By contrast, the multiculturalists argued that the presence of local culture enhanced "general" knowledge. For example, if a community's adults have remarkable math skills in ordinary instances of calculating the costs of buying different amounts of different foods for their families, but lack formal training in abstract math, then teaching math through these concrete problems could enhance not only learning but the meaning and uses of math. Race consciousness and local life made one smart and mobile, not stuck and limited.

A third feature of 1970s multiculturalism is that multiculturalists were militant in their opposition to cultural supremacism and insisted on some form of cultural equality. They vigorously opposed all forms of the cultural deficiency thesis when applied to non-Anglo cultures. James A. Banks defines the "cultural-difference (or multicultural) hypothesis" as rejecting both cultural deficiency and assimilationism on the grounds that "ethnic minorities have rich and diverse, not deprived, cultures."[49] Other authors invoked Kallen's cultural pluralism in defense of the general equality of different cultures. "Kallen interpreted the term 'equal' as it appears in the Declaration of Independence, and the Preamble and the Amendments to the Constitution, as affirmation of the right to be different."[50] Pacheco defined strong multiculturalism as producing "students who can function in a culturally plural society, one in which there is parity between various cultural groups."[51]

It is at this point that these writers made their most fundamental move. Rather than calling for mutual cultural respect or cultural parity in the abstract, they tied cultural parity to empowerment and the equalization of power relations. Pacheco, for example, founds pluralism on parity in this way:

> More sensitive to the lack of parity in real life, [multiculturalism] attempts, through a variety of structural arrangements in the school, to aggressively support the right of a cultural group to maintain itself, it perceives that parity of power and decision making among groups is crucially important, and it assumes that the school has a critical role to play in bringing cultural pluralism about in the greater society.[52]

Again and again, multicultural educators insisted on a *multidimensional* approach to cultural parity. This approach entailed not only the affirmation of a student's cultural identity and heritage, but required consideration of curriculum, teacher attitudes, racial views, gender relations, school administration, the features of the community, and economics. In their literature review of the fifty-four articles and twenty-two books they consider fully multicultural, Sleeter and Grant summarize the main issues as "institutional racism in society and schools, unequal power relationships among racial groups, and economic stratification and social class."[53] The authors of these articles and books generally regard these issues as indissociable from the more conventional educational domain of curriculum or heritage. Although Sleeter and Grant think the issue of social stratification is often underplayed, they noted that "social stratification, as well as racial oppression, has provided much of the impetus for recognizing the need for multicultural education" in the first place.[54] At every point in this work, the "desire not to have to assimilate culturally" went hand in hand with "the desire to have power and economic resources equal to Whites."[55] Multicultural education, always focusing on benefiting people of color, saw such benefits depending on the combination of equitable cultural interaction with changed social and economic relations. "Cultural equality" or equity entailed genuine political parity and power sharing.

Pluralist Nationalism in the 1960s

We've emphasized the existence of a strong pluralist tradition that sees cultural differences finding their "resolution" in equity rather than assimilationist unity. But this *multicultural* pluralism owes most of its public life and development to the history of nationalist thought among people of color in the United States. Here we are unable to do justice either to criticisms or to the richness and complexity of nationalist thought. As is the case with Afrocentricity, important critiques and even major overhauls of nationalism from within Native American, African-American, or Chicano communities have been drowned out by wholesale white rejection. The latter skips over nationalism's focus on white racist political and cultural views in favor of charging it with all kinds of race-based divisiveness, the suspiciously simple mirror-image of features nationalism attributes to whites. Although some nationalist thought is separatist *and* militantly antipluralist, this usually follows from its regarding pluralism as an instrument of white supremacism.[56] Given our argument thus far, it will be clear that we think this view is often correct, since whites have so often failed—and downright refused—to separate pluralism from Anglo-norm assimilationism. Strong multiculturalism picked up some good portion of its hostility to supremacist and unionist pluralism from the nationalist attack. It was nationalist thought, Black nationalist thought in particular, that by the early 1970s demanded autonomy from white America on the basis sometimes of separatism but also of *equalized* interaction.[57]

We can invoke only a couple of examples, and we pick two icons precisely because they are emblems of nationalism at its supposed climax of militant separatism.[58] Black Panther leader Huey Newton rejected "cultural nationalism, or pork chop nationalism," which he attributed to those "concerned with returning to the old African culture and thereby regaining their identity and freedom."[59] Cultural nationalists turned out for Newton to have two major blindnesses. They overlooked the socialist project of "revolutionary Nationalism," which knows that "we must destroy both racism and capitalism."[60] And they didn't "understand the white revolutionaries because [they] can't see why anyone white would turn on the system. So they think that maybe this is some more hypocrisy being planted by white people."[61] Newton desired separatism as the basis of revolutionary Black solidarity even as he sought cross-racial support from white radicals. As he put it, "we feel as Malcolm X felt that there can be no black-white unity until there first is black unity."[62] Newton's rejection of the cultural nationalist is a rejection of separatism as a final goal. At least in his official statements, separatism was a means to equality among racial groups. Once Black America had power enough to be treated equitably by whites, Black autonomy could survive and vitalize interaction with whites. Once in this condition of egalitarian pluralism, to use a phrase foreign to Newton's vocabulary, Black America not only would better endure white America but would change it. It is pluralism rather than separatism per se that leads to the hoped-for Black influence over white. Newton envisioned not reverse racism but reverse power, not the drawing of essentialist racial lines but the crossing of history's color line with new political equality.

Much 1960s Black nationalist thought—to stick with one of the United States' several nationalist traditions—anticipates the major features of the strong version of pluralism we've noted in 1970s multiculturalism. First, it rejected white-norm assimilationism as racist and oppressive to Black people. Black Power meant insisting on the "ethnic basis of American politics," which had extended beyond white ethnicity to describe U.S. institutions as color-blind and race-neutral. Vivid condemnations of white racism, reintensified in the Black Power period, are exactly that: condemnations of white racism. Quite often, whites had felt that these spilled over into condemnations of white presence or white existence. They did, particularly where assimilationism had enabled whites to suggest that their own perspectives and interests could stand for those of the nation. In these quite common cases, a white presence made the discussion of racial differences and inequities impossible. Black and other nationalisms were calling for a genuine political pluralism to replace white supremacy.

Second, nationalism regarded individualism's rejection of group consciousness as an obstruction of the racial facts of life. Kwame Toure (formerly Stokely Carmichael) and Charles V. Hamilton cite a statement of the National Council of Churches on this point. "America," the council suggests, "has asked its Negro citizens to fight for opportunity as *individuals*, whereas at certain points in our history what we have needed most has been opportunity for the *whole group*, not just selected and approved Negroes. . . . We must not apologize for the existence of this form of group power, for we have been oppressed as a group and not as individuals."[63] Since racialization operates through a Black American's group affiliation, civil rights premised on a color-blind ignorance of that affiliation will always be inadequate. "It is a commentary on the fundamentally racist nature of this society that the concept of group strength for black people must be articulated."[64] Nationalism spreads awareness of the direct transmission between one's group affiliation and one's individual identity. As Wahneema Lubiano more pointedly puts it, "black nationalism has been the articulated consciousness of black Americans' awareness of their place in the state's intentions."[65]

Third, Black Power continually sought cultural and political equality. Toure and Hamilton sharply distinguished between the presence of Black people under white control and equal Black community control. "Black visibility is not Black Power. . . . The power must be that of a community, and emanate from there. . . . The goal of black self-determination and black self-identity—Black Power—is full participation in the decision-making processes affecting the lives of black people."[66] Toure and Hamilton write that the "concept of Black Power rests on a fundamental premise: *Before a group can enter the open society, it must first close ranks.* By this we mean that group solidarity is necessary before a group can operate effectively from a bargaining position of strength in a pluralistic society."[67] Self-rule requires political equality between the races, and on this count Black nationalism is pluralist, and yet pluralist in a way that would indeed revolutionize American society. The revolution would consist of basing peace on justice by putting group autonomy and equity ahead of traditional demands for assimilation to the core that seems to many to be so biased toward white people and their preferences.

In short, Black Power and related movements had developed a historically pivotal conjunction of *pluralism and nationalism* when their public influence began to wane.[68] These movements combined group autonomy and interaction with other groups, but further insisted that the combination rested on a continual striving for intergroup political equality. Rather than moderate pluralism's balance between unity and multiplicity, they envisioned a federation based on equitable negotiation among multiple groups. Such a federation would protect group autonomy and the still-dreaded "group rights." Nationalism in the 1960s amplified the second and third traits we've been considering beyond moderate recuperation. Race consciousness and political equality, given U.S. racial history, went well beyond the loosening of the core that moderate pluralists had imagined. The pluralist-nationalist sense of the minimum requirements of true pluralism incorporates social and cultural *equity* into the obvious *diversity* of racial groups. Nationalist elements have been subject to unceasing attempts at expulsion on the trumped-up charge that they entirely reject the pluralism that, to repeat, they have in fact attempted to make real.

We've been suggesting that a continuity exists between the strong version of cultural pluralism that was born to oppose assimilationism, 1970s multiculturalism, and nationalism. This nationalism includes some completely reconstructive attacks (feminist especially), which we will touch on later. Were this tradition to have prevailed, our point here would be obvious to white racial common sense: the multiculturalism that built on both pluralism and nationalism is the *only* meaningful form of cultural pluralism in existence, for it is the only form that is not a variant of assimilationism.[69]

Multiculturalism in the 1990s

> The primary criterion for a strong version of multiculturalism is that it
> not be reducible to a pluralism structured in dominance.
> Peter Erickson[70]

These days, anything slightly less white than *Dr. Zhivago* can bill itself as multicultural. This sprawling, meaningless usage makes even the narrowest material seem more inclusive and equitable than it actually is. But the history we have outlined should make it relatively easy to pick the real antiassimilationist out of the crowd of pretenders. It may also make it easier to see the kind of reconstructive research the concept could sponsor.

In colleges and universities, multiculturalism would have gotten nowhere without the decades-long work of ethnic studies and women's studies departments. In the 1970s, multicultural educators and ethnic studies college faculty tended to work at a distance, and ethnic studies programs, in our unsystematic opinion, continue to keep multiculturalism at arm's length, judging it a treacherous ally, and with many good reasons, some of which are spelled out in the essays collected here. This does not change the fundamental historical fact that mild reforms, such as "diversity" in general education requirements, came only after long years of effort on the part of faculty and students in these small race and gender programs. From the mid-1960s onward, ethnic studies programs demanded the integration of all levels of the university and the curricular inclusion of the histories of people of color in the United States. They also went beyond inclusion per se, calling for structural changes in the university as well as in the methodological foundations of their neighboring, more traditional disciplines. Ethnic studies scholars uncovered the signs of American race relations in social science and humanities research that generated major empirical and interpretive errors about communities of color. Most generally, they produced a powerful version of the three-part alternative to assimilationism-based social research. They established the autonomy of culturally specific knowledges from traditional "core" disciplines. They suggested that community ties and local knowledge improved rather than spoiled research. And they claimed that Anglo-European cultural supremacism or just plain old racism obscured these truths with their traditionalist epistemologies.[71] Ethnic and women's studies are slightly to one side of our subject here, but their contributions have been indispensable to the content and conditions of multiculturalism's appearance in the university.

The recent attacks on multiculturalism sensed that one wing of the multicultural house was not only promoting cultural diversity and tolerance but reviving alternatives to assimilationism as a basis of social peace and justice. The three general aspects of strong pluralism or multiculturalism we've been describing acquired new life and emphasis in the late 1980s.

First, multiculturalism was more hospitable than some variants of nationalism and pluralism to a whole range of perspectives for which assimilation was poison. A concept whose major adversaries had at one time been identified mostly through race and ethnicity now had to take on challenges of gender, sexuality, new panethnicities, and new "nations" like Queer Nation in unpredictable combinations. By 1990, over twenty-five years of work had made visible a whole raft of exceptions to the veiled universalism and group unity on which assimilationist pluralism had relied. The women's movement put gender difference on the table. Gay and lesbian activism and research made heterosexuality seem as much a limitation as an artificial norm. Research on class and economic segmentation continued to produce startling results. Socialist feminism tried to think through the complex interrelations of gender and class. African-American women had been crucial to the formulation of the civil rights and Black Power moments from the beginning, and, like Chicana feminists, became increasingly visible critics of the masculinist politics of nationalism and the usual understanding of racialized communities.[72] Feminists of color placed race at the center of the study of gender; one turning point came in the early 1980s with the publication of two widely noted anthologies, *This Bridge Called My Back: Writings by Radical Women of Color* and *All the Women Are White, All the Blacks Are Men, but Some of Us Are Brave: Black Women's Studies.*[73] And lesbian and gay thinkers injected sexual difference into revised understandings of raced, gendered, or classed communities. The current hue and cry about social fragmentation and special interests testifies to a growing sense of sociocultural complexity even in the more obtuse reaches of the high-velocity media world.

The apparent chaos of multicultural knowledge has been a huge conceptual step forward and even signals a modest success. It promotes new degrees of subtlety in the understanding of social and cultural life. Crossover developments like those listed earlier each transformed an apparently neutral, generalizable feature of the American norm—such as heterosexual marriage—into a particularity, a partiality, a perspective, a potential discriminatory bias. The 1980s backlash against "difference" was a tacit response to the loss of the assimilative power of a presumptive common culture. One could detect a dread of *cultural* coexistence with the different, even when the different ones could still be *economically and politically* subordi-nated. Something like Rush Limbaugh's panicky ridicule of ever less politi-cized differences, like vegetarianism, suggests a continual concern that the old normalcies face challenges on a hundred fronts. How else to explain this kind of mournful lament: "Most often, what we believe in is made fun of, lampooned, impugned, and put down. Then, we don't want to feel that way. We want to feel as much a part of the mainstream as anybody else"?[74] Al-though he is winning nearly all his political battles, Rush rightly feels mar-ginal to a diversity that is becoming an accomplished fact in the realm of culture. There, through "identity" and the rest, he is being made to share.

Second, multiculturalism has strongly endorsed racially based group identities and *antiessentialism* at the same time. Antiessentialism describes the way an identity can have a complex social reality without possessing a fixed essence or substance to distinguish it from others. Various nation-alisms, feminisms, and other movements have, to the contrary, been accused of essentialism, of presuming a "core" of Chicanoness or femininity that unites a community around some common, fixed characteristics. Many commentators on identity politics have lived through the abundant political failures of essentialism, but retain the use of *social* identities even as they have long repudiated the dream of sharing essential identities with a passion born of painful experience. Multiculturalism in the 1990s builds on the work of a number of writers and activists who have been devising ways of talking about how identity has social actuality and meaning while being multiple, shifting, indeterminate, and antiessentialist at the same time.[75] So, for exam-ple, in their recently published volume on multicultural education, Cameron McCarthy and Warren Crichlow start things off by saying race is both real and changeable:

> Racial difference is the product of human interests, needs, desires, strategies, capacities, forms of organization, and forms of mobilization. And that these dynamic variables which articulate themselves in the form of grounded so-cial constructs such as identity, inequality, and so forth, are subject to change, contradiction, variability, and revision within historically specific and deter-minate contexts. We maintain that "race" is a social, historical, and variable category.[76]

The lack of a fixed meaning for "race" or for specific uses such as "Chicana" does nothing to diminish the category's social importance and analytic ne-cessity. Quite the contrary: antiessentialism increases and refines it.

A crucial test of antiessentialist race consciousness will continue to re-volve around affirmative action. Some have argued that once we understand the multiple and sometimes contradictory and indeterminate sources of racial identity, we can no longer use race as an index of disadvantage. Antiessentialism has been used in this way by conservatives, who have contested any group-based challenge to a meritocratic identity based on pure individual performance. This argument goes hand in hand with the premature claim of the declining significance of race. The backlash against affirmative action programs has spearheaded the charge against race consciousness of any kind, and the success of renewed explanations for the ongoing need for these programs will largely determine the practical utility of the concept of multiculturalism itself.

In fact, antiessentialist understandings of racial identity as multiply determined make it *easier* to show that white-majority institutions are white rather than neutral. They make it easier to show that white attitudes need not necessarily be racist or supremacist to have a racially differentiating effect, to have a racially marked presence. They help demonstrate how cultural identities are woven into legal and economic procedure so that even supposedly neutral process reflects the culture that produced it. They show that "merit" too consists of a set of choices established within a particular social context: particular test skills may be favored over experience with economic adversity, and so on. More nuanced descriptions of racial influence help show the ways that culture racializes the choices that lie behind all its procedures. These choices can be unconscious, as in the case where blanket "neutrality" is declared. They can be conscious, as in affirmative action programs. In a culture habituated to believing in the neutrality of even the 80, 90, or 95 percent white institution, these more nuanced descriptions of actual racial influence can promote more open decisions about racial policy.[77]

Third, the strong version of 1990s multiculturalism has cemented the conjunction of antiassimilationist cultural pluralism with political parity. In 1990, Ted Gordon and Wahneema Lubiano of the University of Texas at Austin rejected those forms of multiculturalism that overlook political equity: "Multiculturalism . . . is understood at its most simplistic to mean exposure to different cultures. Simple exposure, however, is absolutely meaningless without a reconsideration and restructuring of the ways in which knowledge is organized, disseminated, and used to support unequal power relations."[78] A "transformative multiculturalism" rejects the divide between culture and politics, and links genuine cultural inclusion to political power sharing. This involves more than broadening cultural discourse. It means changing the racial composition of the institution in question: "crosscultural work . . . depends upon the presence of a critical mass of people of color (all levels of the University). . . . multiculturalism demands empowered *people* of color as well as empowered *areas* of knowledge."[79] A real multiculturalism requires political as well as cultural inclusion, requires the sharing of power among relevant groups.[80] Although culture cannot be simply reduced to politics, this multiculturalism argues, cultural diversity within institutions that are still white-dominated lacks redeeming social value.

A lot of valuable research affirmed the indissociability of cultural and social dynamics. Becky W. Thompson and Sangeeta Tyagi begin their edited volume on multicultural education by noting that the "acceptance of new voices and new perspectives goes hand in hand with vigorous and committed efforts at affirmative-action hiring at all levels within educational institutions."[81] In other words, changes in culture are cosmetic without changes in the polity. In the same volume, Chandra Talpade Mohanty writes that a merely "attitudinal engagement with diversity" must be supplemented by the history of inequities that work at the level of racialized groups.[82] Also criticizing a weak multiculturalism that "celebrate[s] diversity without adequately analyzing power differentials among groups positioned by racial categorizations and inequalities," Leslie G. Roman suggests the need for white students and educators to "take effective responsibility and action for 'disinvesting' in racial privilege."[83] Christine E. Sleeter argues that education cannot become truly multicultural "without specifically interrogating the racial identities of a predominantly white teaching force." Further, multiculturalism must regard racism not as an individual "misperception but as a structural arrangement among racial groups."[84]

Strong multicultural notions of education invoke the need to pursue a whole range of goals at the same time. In her comprehensive volume *Affirming Diversity*, Sonia Nieto argues that multiculturalism requires attention to "racism, discrimination, and expectations of students' achievement," to "[s]tructural factors such as school organization and educational policies and practices," *and* to "[c]ultural and other differences such as ethnicity, race, gender, language, and class."[85] Again, multiculturalism is never reducible to a stress on cultural heritage, or to personal identity, or to a more racially balanced school administration, but refers to the dynamic interaction of these features and more. These multiculturalists do not collapse all these terms into one another, but also regard the conceptual isolation of the "cultural," "educational," "scholarly," "political," and so on as falsifying their inevitable interaction.

More general institutional commentary of the multicultural kind has also increasingly insisted on a similar dependence of cultural on economic parity. David A. Hollinger argues that those who criticize multiculturalism as leading to the "Balkanization of America" should focus their complaints not "on the educational and political programs of ethno-racial 'separatists' [but] . . . instead, on the rigidification of the class structure."[86] Mable Haddock and Chiquita Mullins Lee note that "for multiculturalism to become a reality in cultural programming, rather than an empty slogan, there must be a shift in power. Neither arts councils, nor the heads for the Corporation for Public Broadcasting (CPB), PBS, and other corporations are committed to sharing the power to make funding decisions with those outside their immediate purview. Were they to share power equitably with people of color, there would be substantial changes."[87] Politics cannot be seen as something added on to culture here and there as a luxury, a vendetta, a bias. The survival of cultural diversity depends on greatly enhanced political and economic equality.[88]

This multiculturalism draws at the same time on cultural pluralism and the specific kind of nationalism described earlier. In doing so, it has continued to develop a tradition of racial thought that is quite distinct from the assimilationist pluralisms that have sometimes used the same tag of multiculturalism. It takes a *multicentered* national culture as encompassing the intersectionality of race with a range of the identities and forces *in addition to race* that comprise social life. It supports *race consciousness* along with *antiessentialist* notions of identity and social structure, and refines our understanding of the way racial and other dimensions of culture influence even apparently neutral institutions. And it puts *political equity* at the center of any discussion of cultural interaction. The result is not merely criticism of assimilationist wishes on a variety of fronts, though that remains indispensable, but visions of a postassimilationist America. This multiculturalism imagines the necessary transformation of subjectivity itself. It does not seek a hardening of categories. To the contrary, it concentrates on those cultures that are already renegotiating areas of broad overlap from the standpoint of their own independent practices.

A New Starting Point

Racial assimilationism is a pillar of conservative cultural rule in America, and always has been. It preempts full debate on cultural questions and on a range of public policy issues by supporting a majority group making ground rules for everyone before discussion takes place.

By contrast, a basic requirement of power sharing is shared control over definitions of social injury and remedy. This kind of sharing has been mostly impossible.[89] White liberalism has generally consented to the prevailing racial common sense that, after the middle 1960s, race has ceased to be a serious obstacle to the advancement of people of color. This consent has become one of the ground rules. Thus, assimilationism continues to be the preferred solution to the problems of minorities and women. Economic and social control takes a back seat to integration, which has meant ongoing retention of control by the white majority. Liberal consent to assimilationist pluralism has damaged discussions of race, to say nothing of racial progress.

Multiculturalism, in the stronger sense we've described here, has, since the 1970s, not assumed that its primary goal of improving the lives of people of color can be achieved through assimilation. It thus links its promotion of a multiracial terrain to finding alternatives to common culture. It offers a different basis of social interaction and peace than does white norming, which has been hard for its nonwhite subjects to distinguish from the coercions of poverty, exclusion, and second-class citizenship.

Where multiculturalism can combine the best of the pluralist and the nationalist traditions, it offers an alternative to cultural assimilationism. It offers an alternative racial common sense that is complexly figured yet unrelenting about a few starting points. It addresses racism prominently. It respects group autonomy *and* the complicated divisions and differences within and among racially marked groups. It focuses on equity as a primary principle. It is committed to the patience and effort required to let solutions emerge from the process of confrontation and debate. In short, multiculturalism suggests that a new basic structure of intergroup negotiation could replace *e pluribus unum* to good effect.

Multiculturalism is and will remain a type of cultural pluralism. But it promotes norms of its own, alternative ground rules, a different starting point. It offers itself as an alternative jumping-off place. It offers a specific kind of *recognition* as a form of citizenship, in which various parties get to the table in an autonomous and equal state. It does not predict the kind of substantive policy, political and economic alterations, the social *reconstruction*, that could follow. Will multiculturalism promote racial justice? Will it link racial justice to the redistributive project necessary for economic equality? Will it redefine racial justice and economic equality as constitutively feminist and antihomophobic? Will it take its "multi" prefix seriously in grappling with the reality of transracial coalition and conflict? Will it reach for the kind of international perspective no longer readily available in the United States? Will it even lead to the reformation of cultural knowledge that it sometimes promises? No. Not really. Not in itself. But multiculturalism may be viewed as a *precondition* for these different kinds of work. As a form of cultural pluralism, it would be a precondition with a long though obscured tradition in the United States, one with some built-in mass appeal. And it would weaken the assimilationist grip on a multiculturalist ideal that is rapidly being adopted by the state, the corporation, the military, the arts council, the university. Multiculturalism would simply make real cultural pluralism do what it says it means. That in itself would make quite a difference.

Notes

1. Manning Marable, *The Crisis of Color and Democracy: Essays on Race, Class and Power* (Monroe, Maine: Common Courage Press, 1992), 252.

2. Ibid., 252–56.

3. Cornel West, *Race Matters* (New York: Vintage Books, 1994), 19.

4. *The American Heritage Dictionary of the English Language*, ed. William Morris (Boston: Houghton Mifflin, 1980), 1009.

5. Cited in Arthur Schlesinger Jr., *The Disuniting of America* (Knoxville, Tenn.: Whittle Direct Books, 1991), 13. Schlesinger is best known for stressing unity over multiplicity. W. E. B. Du Bois's famous notion of African-American double consciousness in *The Souls of Black Folk* (1903) bears a strong relation to cultural pluralism. Du Bois never uses the term; the term in its white development was often (mis)used against ideas like his, and his own thought moved in a different direction. But note the book's early reference to "the ideal of fostering and developing the traits and talents of the Negro, not in opposition to or contempt for other races, but rather in large conformity to the greater ideals of the American Republic, in order that some day on American soil two world-races may give each to each those characteristics both so sadly lack" (*The Souls of Black Folk*, intro. Henry Louis Gates Jr. [New York: Bantam, 1989], 8). Du Bois simultaneously imagines an interaction between two races that remain separate, and yet veers toward pluralism's perennial assimilationist fascination with American ideals that encompass both.

6. Troy Duster, "The Diversity of California at Berkeley: An Emerging Reformulation of 'Competence' in an Increasingly Multicultural World," in *Beyond a Dream Deferred: Multicultural Education and the Politics of Excellence*, ed. Becky W. Thompson and Sangeeta Tyagi (Minneapolis and London: University of Minnesota Press, 1993), 248.

7. Horace M. Kallen, *Cultural Pluralism and the American Idea: An Essay in Social Philosophy*, with comments by Stanley H. Chapman, Steward G. Cole, Elizabeth F. Flower, Frank P. Graham, R. J. Henle, S. J., Herold C. Hunt, Milton R. Konvitz, Leo Pfeffer, and Goodwin Watson (Philadelphia: University of Pennsylvania Press, 1956), 85.

8. Ibid., 97.

9. Ibid., 82.

10. Ibid., 23. We have omitted Kallen's biologistic continuation, which mixes complicatedly with his culturalism.

11. Ibid.

12. Ibid.

13. Ibid., 98.

14. Ibid.

15. For a brief summary, see Michael Omi and Howard Winant, *Racial Formation in the United States: From the 1960s to the 1990s*, 2d ed. (New York: Routledge, 1994), 15–16. For an account that ties "ethnic pluralism" to the simultaneous assimilation of white ethnics and subor-

dination of African Americans, see Stephen Steinberg, *The Ethnic Myth: Race, Ethnicity, and Class in America*, 2d ed. (Boston: Beacon Press, 1989), 42. Steinberg concludes that "at the same time that the nation pursued a policy aimed at the rapid assimilation of recent arrivals from Europe, it segregated the racial minorities who, by virtue of their much longer history in American society, had already come to share much of the dominant culture."

16. Arthur Levine and Ette Cureton, "The Quiet Revolution: Eleven Facts about Multiculturalism and the Curriculum," *Change* (January–February 1992): 29.

17. Robert Leiken, "O Their America," *Times Literary Supplement* (22 May 1992): 6.

18. Roger Kimball, *Tenured Radicals: How Politics Has Corrupted Our Higher Education* (New York: Harper Perennial, 1990), 193.

19. Schlesinger, *The Disuniting of America*, 6.

20. Ibid., 70, 71. Schlesinger is thinking of immigrants here, but the process is much the same for U.S. citizens who are newcomers to the cultural mainstream.

21. Ibid., 76.

22. Ibid.

23. Ibid., 82.

24. This paragraph is based on a discussion in Avery Gordon and Christopher Newfield, "White Philosophy," *Critical Inquiry* (summer 1994): 753. That essay offers a fuller criticism of pluralist supremacism or liberal racism.

25. For an interesting comparison, see Etienne Balibar's valuable analysis of nonbiological racialist thought in postcolonial France (Etienne Balibar, "Is There a 'Neo-Racism'?" in Balibar and Immanuel Wallerstein, *Race, Nation, Class* [1988; London and New York: Verso, 1991], 17–28). The "neo" should not mislead us into thinking this is a new development, at least in the United States. Kallen, as noted earlier, was already tracing it to antebellum New England culture.

26. Critiques of neutrality in the law were developed by a number of writers in the Critical Legal Studies and Critical Race Studies movements. On color blindness specifically, see Neil Gotanda, "A Critique of 'Our Constitution Is Colorblind': Racial Categories and White Supremacy," *Stanford Law Review* 44 (1991): 1–68. See also Patricia J. Williams, *The Alchemy of Race and Rights* (Cambridge: Harvard University Press, 1991), especially "The Death of the Profane" and "The Obliging Shell"; and Gary Peller, "Race Consciousness," *Duke Law Journal* (1990): 758–847. Peller analyzes the "social compromise" by which "the price of the national commitment to suppress white supremacists would be the rejection of race consciousness among African Americans" (760).

27. Gary B. Nash, "The Great Multicultural Debate," *Contention* 1:3 (spring 1992): 1–28.

28. Schlesinger, *The Disuniting of America*, 71.

29. Nash, "The Great Multicultural Debate," 24.

30. Henry Louis Gates Jr., "Pluralism and Its Discontents," *Contention* 2:1 (fall 1992): 71.

31. For a discussion that seeks to avoid attributing equal value to other cultures while insisting on interaction based on a mutual presumption of (some) value, see Charles Taylor, *Multiculturalism and "The Politics of Recognition,"* ed. Amy Gutmann (Princeton, N.J.: Princeton University Press, 1992), 68. Taylor sees no right to equality but does believe in a right to recognition (as we are formed by being recognized by the other) (36, 64).

32. Nash, "The Great Multicultural Debate," 23.

33. Ibid., 24.

34. Ibid., 25.

35. Ibid.

36. Diane Ravitch, "In the Multicultural Trenches," *Contention* 1:3 (spring 1992): 34.

37. Todd Gitlin, "From University to Difference: Notes on the Fragmentation of the Idea of the Left," *Contention* 2:2 (winter 1993): 22. Gitlin mourns the passing of "the early New Left pol-

itics of universalist aspiration," which were replaced by the "late New Left politics of dispersion and separateness" (32). One could more plausibly argue that universalist aspiration necessarily and justly foundered on the rock of race after 1965, and that "late" New Left politics had to attempt cross-racial connections in the awareness that even the Vietnam War did not provide a universalizing, unifying issue for the Left, much less the Port Huron Statement's 1962 invocation of "human brotherhood" (cited by Gitlin, 30).

38. Gates, "Pluralism and Its Discontents," 74.

39. Steinberg, *The Ethnic Myth,* 170.

40. This says nothing about the virtues of Afrocentric interpretations of historical epochs and peoples. Although white commentary has been little more than one long hatchet job, Black critiques have been more telling. For an excellent analysis of white attacks on nationalism from the position of integration that has influenced our own thinking, see Peller, "Race Consciousness."

41. The value of Nash's position appears clearest when under attack from the Right. The *MacNeil/Lehrer News Hour* devoted a segment to criticisms of his National Standards, voiced in this case by the director of the National Endowment for the Humanities under Ronald Reagan and George Bush, Lynne Cheney. Nash was asked, "When you all were creating this document, you did come under pressure from various groups—women's groups, minority groups—to include politically correct, in their view, views of American history. Is that true? Were you under pressure to change or amend what you were creating?" Nash replied: "I don't know of any politically correct groups. I know of American women. I know of Black Americans and American Indians. I do know that these groups have been absent from most of the textbooks and it is because of the historical amnesia concerning these groups that it is due time to have them restored to their proper place in the making of American history. Ms. Cheney thinks we will disunite America by paying attention to these groups. But we have been disunited, and we're more likely to be united if we take proper and due account of the contributions and the struggles of these forgotten groups." Although we are wary of his ongoing goal of unification (and of national standards), we admire Nash's long-term labor—along with that of his multitude of collaborators on this project—on behalf of greater inclusion in all primary and secondary school curricula.

42. For a valuable survey and taxonomy of multicultural education literature, see Christine E. Sleeter and Carl A. Grant, "An Analysis of Multicultural Education in the United States," in *Facing Racism in Education* (1987), ed. Nitza M. Hidalgo, Caesar L. McDowell, and Emilie V. Siddle (Cambridge: Harvard Educational Review Reprint Series no. 21, 1990), 138–61. The authors use fourteen categories to sort their long bibliography into five types: "Teaching the Culturally Different"; "Human Relations" approaches; "Single Group Studies"; "Multicultural Education"; "Education That Is Multicultural and Social Reconstructionist" (139). We are using the term multiculturalism to cover principally the last three of these categories. In any case, internal differences are smaller than those between the multicultural and other pluralist types we have discussed.

43. Manuel Ramírez III and Alfredo Casañeda, *Cultural Democracy, Bicognitive Development, and Education* (New York: Academic Press, 1974), 28.

44. Ibid., 11.

45. "For example, the statement of the Steering Committee of the National Coalition for Cultural Pluralism defines the concept of cultural pluralism as 'the perspective used by different social groups in their attempt to survive as *independent,* yet *interdependent,* segments of society'" (Arturo Pacheco, "Cultural Pluralism: A Philosophical Analysis," *Journal of Teacher Education* 28:3 [May–June 1977]: 16).

46. The ASCD Multicultural Education Commission, "Encouraging Multicultural Educa-

tion," in *Multicultural Education: Commitments, Issues, and Applications,* ed. Carl A. Grant (Washington, D.C.: Association for Supervision and Curriculum Development, 1977), 3.

47. Pacheco, "Cultural Pluralism," 18.

48. Cited by Ramírez and Casañeda, *Cultural Democracy,* 26. In general, Gordon may stress the priority of group life more than Ramírez and Casañeda concede.

49. James A. Banks, "Multiethnic Education and the Quest for Equality," *Phi Delta Kappan* (April 1983): 584.

50. Ramírez and Casañeda, *Cultural Democracy,* 25.

51. Pacheco, "Cultural Pluralism," 20.

52. Ibid. We have replaced Pacheco's term "cultural diversity" with "multiculturalism" to avoid terminological confusion.

53. Sleeter and Grant, "An Analysis of Multicultural Education," 146.

54. Ibid., 149.

55. Ibid.

56. Even a nationalist anger that trashes cross-racial coalitions criticizes not coalitions per se but the posture of the prospective partner. In a well-known passage, the Chicago office of the Student Nonviolent Coordinating Committee (SNCC) writes, "We have to learn that black is so much better than belonging to the white race with the blood of millions dripping from their hands that it goes far beyond any prejudice or resentment. We must fill ourselves with hate for all white things. This is not vengeance or trying to take the white oppressors' place to become new black oppressors but is a oneness with a worldwide black brotherhood" (Chicago Office of SNCC, "We Want Black Power," leaflet [Chicago: Chicago Office of SNCC, 1967]; reprinted in August Meier et al., eds., *Black Protest Thought in the Twentieth Century,* 2d ed. [Indianapolis and New York: Bobbs-Merrill, 1971], 487). The call for a separate oneness expresses a sense of the impossibility of alliances with a white majority that has such a long history of extreme anti-Black activity.

57. In reverse order, Wahneema Lubiano notes that the message of Black nationalism "has been described variously as either an example of a 'better' world directed at the rest of the actually existing world and/or as a meaning available only within the group" ("Standing in for the State: Black Nationalism and 'Writing' the Black Subject," *Alphabet City* 3 [October 1993]: 20).

58. The case would be somewhat different were we to focus on the American Indian movement, for example, or the Chicano movement, or recent alternations of these traditions. Chela Sandoval, for example, does not contrast assimilationism and separatism with pluralism but with oppositional and then differential consciousness ("U.S. Third World Feminism: The Theory and Method of Oppositional Consciousness in the Postmodern World," *Genders* 10 [spring 1991]: 1–24).

59. *Huey Newton Talks to the Movement* (Chicago: Students for a Democratic Society, 1968; reprinted in Meier et al., eds. *Black Protest Thought*), 495.

60. Ibid., 496.

61. Ibid., 498–99.

62. Ibid., 500–501.

63. National Council of Churches, paid advertisement, *New York Times,* 31 July 1966, cited in Stokely Carmichael and Charles V. Hamilton, *Black Power: The Politics of Liberation in America* (New York: Random House, 1967), 49.

64. Ibid.

65. Lubiano, "Standing in for the State," 20.

66. Carmichael and Hamilton, *Black Power,* 46–47.

67. Ibid., 44.

68. In his afterword to the 1992 reissue of *Black Power,* Hamilton writes, "The call for Black Power in the 1960s was not a call for racial isolation. Yes, it was an honest recognition that for

any group—racial, ethnic, economic—to become a respected, effective player in the American political system, cohesive organization was crucial. . . . When blacks began applying this [common] lesson to themselves they immediately were branded 'separatists' and ill-advised activists who sought to 'go it alone'" (*Black Power* [1967; New York: Vintage-Random House, 1992], 203). This hasty branding continues to control our understanding of nationalist movements that focused on overall political change. (Kwame Toure notes simply that "the book does not advocate Revolution. It preaches reform" [187].)

69. We continue to use "cultural pluralism" in its specific sense. It does not encompass other forms of multiple identities or coalition politics (racial hybridity, women of color, and others). Lubiano uses the concept of Black common sense in for the State" (20).

70. Peter Erickson, "What Multiculturalism Means," *Transition* 55 (1992): 113.

71. For a recent survey of some of these long-standing issues, see Johnella E. Butler and John C. Walter, eds., *Transforming the Curriculum: Ethnic Studies and Women's Studies* (Albany: State University of New York Press, 1991); see especially the essays by Butler, Johnetta B. Cole, and R. A. Olguin.

72. A very interesting early account is Angela Davis, *Angela Davis: An Autobiography* (1974; New York: International Publishers, 1988). See also Toni Cade, ed., *The Black Woman: An Anthology* (New York: New American Library, 1970).

73. Cherríe Moraga and Gloria Anzaldúa, eds., *This Bridge Called My Back: Writings by Radical Women of Color* (Watertown, Mass.: Persephone Press, 1981); Gloria T. Hull, Patricia Bell Scott, and Barbara Smith, *All the Women Are White, All the Blacks Are Men, but Some of Us Are Brave: Black Women's Studies* (New York: Feminist Press, 1982). See also Sara Evans, "Black Power—Catalyst for Feminism," in *Personal Politics: The Roots of Women's Liberation in the Civil Rights Movement and the New Left* (New York: Vintage Books, 1979); and Paula Giddings, "The Women's Movement and Black Discontent," in *When and Where I Enter: The Impact of Black Women on Race and Sex in America* (New York: Bantam Books, 1984).

74. Rush Limbaugh, radio broadcast (1992) cited in Thomas Byrne Edsall, "America's Sweetheart," *New York Review of Books*, 6 October 1994: 9.

75. Nearly all of the contributors to this volume have explored in various places the ways a category like "African American" or "lesbian" or "male" can lack an essence while retaining a systematic, determinate set of social effects. For an interesting exception, see Lourdes Portillo's remarks in chapter 12. Other writers trying to think about social determinacy in antiessentialist ways include Gloria Anzaldúa, Homi Bhabha, Ed Cohen, Diana Fuss, Stuart Hall, Donna Haraway, June Jordan, Duncan Kennedy, Ernesto Laclau, Kobena Mercer, Chantal Mouffe, Gayatri C. Spivak, and Patricia J. Williams.

76. Cameron McCarthy and Warren Crichlow, "Introduction: Theories of Identity, Theories of Representation, Theories of Race," in *Race, Identity, and Representation in Education* (New York and London: Routledge, 1993), xv. See also the discussion of the reality of race in quotation marks in Angela Y. Davis's contribution to this volume.

77. For a persuasive description of the white bias in ordinary medical school procedures, see Joel Dreyfuss and Charles Lawrence III, *The Bakke Case: The Politics of Inequality* (New York: Harcourt Brace Jovanovich, 1979), especially "The Best Doctors."

Medical school admissions are a particularly interesting case because their procedures have frequently landed in court. Scientific competence is obviously of critical importance in the successful practice of medicine, and like other such knowledges has been subject to long and elaborate sequences of objective testing. It seems relatively easy to determine whether a person scored an 80 or an 89 on an exam, and to eliminate most racial bias from such a test. The life-and-death aspects of medical practice make the idea of passing on incompetent physicians for ostensibly political reasons particularly abhorrent, even for those who agree that the medical profession should represent the national population as much as it can. It seems preposterous to claim that testing for the maximum possible medical skill is a white idea, for it appears so obviously to be a desire for objective merit that any culture can share.

But the issue in such famous cases as *Bakke v. Regents of the University of California* has generally been *what* exactly constitutes merit and how to adjudicate the different perception of candidates for admission. One could favor mathematical achievement, or commitment to future service in poor or rural areas, or one's goals as a specialist, or "personal qualities" that would positively affect a medical practice. The Association of American Medical Colleges had singled out one of these, formally recommending that "medical schools must admit increased numbers of students from geographical areas, economic backgrounds and ethnic groups that are now inadequately represented" (19). Competence in all relevant areas was required—applicants committed to rural service but incompetent in math would rarely if ever be admitted. But one candidate with a slightly lower math score than another could be preferentially admitted on the basis of some other quality, such as an interest in bioengineering research, or in public health, and so on.

Given the same pool in which qualified applicants outnumber positions, different kinds of admissions committees working with different assumptions will produce very different classes of medical students. A group dominated by faculty seeking the "smartest" class and who equate smartness with test scores will produce a class of MCAT wizards (although these scores only weakly correlate with future performance as medical students or physicians). A committee with some members also concerned with the inferior collective health of African Americans will produce students with good grades and test scores *and* demonstrated interest in and knowledge about these kinds of medical issues. Members who believe that the United States must keep its technological edge in high-cost treatment of the most serious illnesses will favor students with good grades and test scores *and* strong technical interests. These are complex situations, and clearly the racial and ethnic composition of the committee will not be the sole influence, nor will it have a simple, determinate effect. Nonetheless, the institution is not *neutral* on any of these issues. It defines good doctors as having one set of qualities, or another set, depending on what people and interests operate the institution. Speaking with historical patterns in mind, a 95 percent white committee *may* produce a racially diverse class with more interest in general practice in underserved areas than in highly paid specialization. But it is less likely to than a committee comprised itself of people of diverse backgrounds. Although we are all reluctant to resort to stereotyping, it can nonetheless be said that medical schools are not neutral but either more or less "white," that a white medical school will usually produce different kinds of doctors than one less white, and that such differences can be measured.

78. Ted Gordon and Wahneema Lubiano, "The Statement of the Black Faculty Caucus," in *Debating P.C.: The Controversy over Political Correctness on College Campuses*, ed. Paul Berman (New York: Dell-Laurel, 1992), 249–50.

79. Ibid., 252–53.

80. Similarly, Ray Davis, executive director of the Student Coalition against Apartheid and Racism (SCAR), says, "By the mid- to late '80s, students and faculty recognized that universities as a whole were still Eurocentered. We saw that what we needed to do was to change the university, not just add a department. . . . Multiculturalism will be one of *the* issues in the '90s. . . . [It intersects] the same issues of what is equality and who has advantages over whom" (quoted in Sarah Ferguson, "The Campus and Beyond: Postwar Activists State Their Case," *Voice Class Action, Village Voice* [20 August 1991]: 8).

81. Becky W. Thompson and Sangeeta Tyagi, "Introduction," in *Beyond a Dream Deferred*, xiv.

82. Chandra Talpade Mohanty, "On Race and Voice: Challenges for Liberal Education," in *Beyond a Dream Deferred*, 41–65.

83. Leslie G. Roman, "White Is a Color! White Defensiveness, Postmodernism, and Anti-racist Pedagogy," in *Race, Identity, and Representation in Education*, 71, 84.

84. Christine E. Sleeter, "How White Teachers Construct Race," in *Race, Identity, and Representation in Education*, 157.

85. Sonia Nieto, *Affirming Diversity: The Sociopolitical Context of Multicultural Education* (New York: Longman, 1992), xxvi–xxvii.

86. David A. Hollinger, "Postethnic America," *Contention* 2:1 (fall 1992): 90. David Reiff, on the other hand, doubts that multiculturalism is capable of a conjunction of politics, economics, and culture: "For all their writings on power, hegemony, and oppression, the campus multicul-turalists seem indifferent to the question of where they fit into the material scheme of things. . . . Are the multiculturalists truly unaware of how closely their treasured catchphrases—'cultural diversity,' 'difference,' the need to 'do away with boundaries'—resemble the stock phrases of the modern corporation: 'product diversification,' 'the global marketplace,' and 'the boundary-less company'?" (David Reiff, "Multiculturalism's Silent Partner: It's the Newly Globalized Con-sumer Economy, Stupid," *Harper's* [August 1993]: 64).

87. Mable Haddock and Chiquita Mullins Lee, "Whose Multiculturalism?: PBS, the Public and Privilege," *Afterimage* (September 1993): 17.

88. Los Angeles launched a great deal of discussion of the links between meaningful multi-culturalism and economic reconstruction. About one year after the Los Angeles revolt was cat-alyzed by the acquittal of the white LAPD officers who beat Black motorist Rodney King, the city's citizens replaced Black Democratic mayor Tom Bradley with white Republican Richard Riordan. The *LA Weekly*'s Harold Meyerson comments: "The *Times* exit poll showed that the two issues that mattered most to voters were 'Jobs/the economy,' mentioned by 52 percent, and 'Crime/gangs,' mentioned by 37 percent. From the beginning, [liberal candidate Michael] Woo was playing catch-up on crime; the issue on which he could have gone on the offensive was the economy. It wasn't enough simply to attack [conservative businessman Richard] Riordan as the personification of Reaganomics; Woo had to stand for a distinct economics of his own. He might have borrowed government-as-incubator-of-small-business from primary rival Linda Griego, or government-as-catalyst-for-manufacturing from Nick Patsaouras. . . . [Such] pro-posals would not have assured victory, but Woo could have used any one of them to contrast himself with Riordan. . . . Without them, though, Woo couldn't even provide his union sup-porters with an argument on his behalf. On election day, white voters from households with union members voted for Riordan, 61 percent to 39 percent. . . . The lesson for liberal L.A., for South-Central and the Eastside, couldn't be clearer: multiculturalism, divorced from econom-ics, can get you a government grant or win you a primary. It is not the path to power, or to change" (Harold Meyerson, "The Word on Woo," *LA Weekly*, 18–24 June 1993: 12).

89. For the earlier numbers, see William Brink and Louis Harris, *Black and White: A Study of U.S. Racial Attitudes Today* (New York: Simon and Schuster, 1967), and Dreyfuss and Lawrence, *The Bakke Case*, 108, 144.

CHAPTER SEVEN

Manichaeism and Multiculturalism

CEDRIC J. ROBINSON

History as a value in itself is a very European phenomenon. Europeans are
the ones who go about investigating the history of other peoples.
Michael Landmann[1]

Since even Dinesh D'Souza, one of the most resolute critics of multiculturalism, acknowledges that one of its appropriate uses would be "as a complement to rather than as a substitute for study of the West,"[2] I believe it is per-
missible to initiate our interrogation of the multiculturalist polemic with an
exemplary instance of the specular imagining from a Western interior.[3] Put
in another way, we will begin with an event that was indisputably domiciled
in the West, but we will rely on reports from spectators who, though irre-
trievably and materially positioned in Western society, imagine and realize a
joint and mutually ratified peripheralization with the West. (Momentarily, I
shall provide evidence of the existence of such creatures.) But in the stead of
D'Souza's favorite elite antagonists in the academy ("student protestors, faculty advocates, and ideologically sympathetic administrators"),[4] I intend to
summon less privileged informants.

Leonard Smith, now a retired transit policeman, was a barely twenty-
year-old enlisted man when, in April 1945, he stood before the broken gates
of the concentration camp at Dachau. Smitty's presence at Dachau was ac-

116

counted for by his membership in the all-Black 761st tank battalion of the Third Army, a frontline combat unit in the segregated U.S. Army. That same April, the grotesque scene Smith observed at Dachau was being repeated at Buchenwald, another concentration camp, for the 183rd Combat Engineer Corps, also an all-Black unit. As history has not always recorded, Smitty and his shocked Black comrades were the first American troops to encounter the horrors of the concentration camps. Their reactions are worth noting.

Smitty recalled: "I got angry . . . all of these human skeletons, falling out of the doors, came out. We said, 'Oh my God, what is this?' It made us so angry. I couldn't understand how another human could treat other humans like that."[5] And at Buchenwald, Leon Bass, a twenty-year-old Black corporal, had almost the identical thought: "I just said to myself, my God, what is this? What's happening here? How could people do this to other people?"[6] From another perspective, one of the fifty-three thousand survivors remembered the "black soldiers of the Third Army, tall and strong, crying like babies, carrying the emaciated bodies of the liberated prisoners."[7] At Buchenwald, Elie Wiesel, then a sixteen-year-old prisoner, recalled: "I'll never forget their eyes, the rage, the anger. Their reaction was so profound."[8]

Although it was clear to Smitty and Bass that they were at that moment confronting some sort of moral deficiency that also implicated their own racial experience of American oppression, their anguish was for another. Their anger, and the tears shed by their brothers, resulted from the specular pain of recognition and amazement: this wasteland of broken humanity issuing from the camps was themselves and beyond themselves. It was history, both familiar and exteriorized, which they bore in their arms. Forty years later, a journalist insisted that "none of the young soldiers . . . were prepared for the sights." But Buchenwald, Bass remembered, "made me aware that I was not alone in my suffering" and that "there were a host of other folk out there who for a host of different reasons were being mistreated." The Buchenwald inmates, he said, "reached the ultimate. I saw this and said, 'My God, that could happen to me.'"[9]

Fifty years later, E. G. McConnell, a third witness among the young Black soldiers, peered into the Dachau cremation ovens and pronounced: "This is the ultimate end of slavery. They worked the poor devils to death. Worked them down to the bone. They burned them; they sold the ashes."[10] Bass's and McConnell's reactions to the death camp provide evidence, I submit, for the specular imagining.

What Smitty, McConnell, and Bass and their comrades did not know was that what they had come upon was a reenactment, on a larger, grander scale, of a particular ritual of racial degradation that extended back nearly two hundred years. Londa Schiebinger has recovered the beginnings of this most characteristic manifestation of evil:

> In the 1780s Duke Frederick II of Hessen-Kassel settled a colony of Africans at Wilhelmshohe (near Kassel), high above the Eder river, in order to study their customs and anatomy. Originally intended to house Chinese, the colony was built with pagodas and oriental gardens. Since Chinese were either too expensive or simply not available, the colony was settled with Africans. The medical doctor in charge of the colony, Ernst Baldinger, noted that the Africans settled there did not flourish; most died of tuberculosis or committed suicide. Their bodies were turned over to Germany's leading anatomist: Samuel Thomas von Soemmerring. From his dissections of "several Negro bodies of both sexes" (one woman, one child, and at least two men), along with his earlier observations of them in public baths, Soemmerring prepared his 1784 *Über die körperliche Verschiedenheit des Mohren von Europäer* (Concerning the physical difference between the Moor and the European)—a book that served as a basic text on the African physique until well into the nineteenth century.[11]

In 1945, those young Black troops could not have known, factually, of the existence of this earlier human exhibit and anatomical laboratory. Alternatively, however, I suspect they already comprehended, intuitively and consciously, the profound moral deficit from which it issued: the subordination and perversion of knowledge by its suturing to the interests of power and privilege. Such exercises of prerogative provided the conditions for the emergence of Western racial science. Let me remind you, in Professor Landmann's more genteel imagination, that "Europeans are the ones who go about investigating the history of other peoples."

In the eighteenth century, Europe's most eminent scholars had less need for Landmann's euphemisms for domination: Hegel candidly found nothing worthy of the name of history outside Europe; and Linnaeus and Kant concurred in their own fashion with this appropriation of history by fastening on anatomy as the code for the non-West. With the notable exception of Blumenbach, Europe's scientists found sufficient taxonomic proof of the inferior difference of women, African, and pre-American native males in the simple fact that these assorted creatures lacked beards: "the want," as Richard McCausland reported in 1786 in the *Philosophical Transactions of the Royal Society of London*, "of one very characteristic mark of the [male] sex."[12] As such, Duke Frederick and the doctors Soemmerring and Baldinger joined the illustrious company of Kant, Winckelmann, von Schlegel, Schiller, and a host of others in Germany, of de Buffon, Lamarck,

Fontenelle, and Gobineau in France, and of Tyson, Camper, Knox, Hunt, and Galton in Britain.[13]

And finally, in the mid-eighteenth century (as Donna Haraway has reminded us), Linnaeus, the Swede, had invented the primate order, "the first Order of Nature," by renaming Homo sapiens, monkeys, apes, lemurs, and bats.[14] "Literally and figuratively," Haraway writes, "primate studies were a colonial affair, in which knowledge of the living and dead bodies of monkeys and apes [and now, we must add, African men, women, and children] was part of the system of unequal exchange of extractive colonialism."[15] The imaginary factualities of racism, sexism, and science conspired with colonialism, demonstrating anew that "deeds, as opposed to words, are the parents of facts. That is, human action is at the root of what we can see as a fact, linguistically and historically."[16]

The recovery and exposure of just such deliberate, mean-spirited, and oftentimes consciously self-interested exercises within the history of modernist Western inquiry is one function and one result of multicultural research. The superior instances of multicultural scholarship extend and deepen the emphatic moral revulsion experienced by Smitty, McConnell, Bass, and their brethren at the gates of hell. And in the mirroring images affiliating the casualties of race, ethnicity, class, and gender, multiculturalist inquiry provokes an alternative dialectic of ethics between the desperate particularity of the Same and the anguished universality of the Other. However, it is precisely this desperate particularity that most frequently animates the opposition to multiculturalism.

On this score, consider for a moment William F. Buckley's *God and Man at Yale* (1951), which sought to defend "the Christian and individualist West" from the onslaught of liberalism. Buckley was by no means the first American patrician to lament the appearances of democratic parties in the academy and the falling away of certain privileges of the ruling classes. What distinguished Buckley was his ability to recruit, train, and nurture the polemical skills of his coreligionists in a para-academic domain through such organs as satellite think tanks, the *National Review*, his varied publishing operations, and his nationally televised program, *Firing Line*. Buckley's activities, clearly distinguishable from the more crude fascistic impulses of Robert Welch, Robert Scaife, the Coors family, and others of the John Birch ilk, prepared the ground for Reagan-era right-wing publicists like Edward Shils, Allan Bloom, Dinesh D'Souza, Diane Ravitch, Lynne Cheney, Gertrude Himmelfarb, and the neoconservatives grouped around *Commentary* (Norman Podhoretz, Midge Dichter, Ben Wattenberg, etc.), *Policy Review*, the *New Republic, Academic Questions* (published by the National Association of Scholars), and the American Enterprise Institute.

Thus when Shils's *The Academic Ethic* appeared in 1984, indicting the burdens of "social justice" and "meeting societal needs" and other recent diversions from "the methodological discovery and teaching of truths about important things" within the academy, the terrain was already well tilled.[17] Buckley, Shils, and the more fugitive works of Sidney Hook became the most immediate progenitors to what eventually would become the better-known neoconservative tracts: Allan Bloom's nostalgic *The Closing of the American Mind* and D'Souza's sophomoric *Illiberal Education.*

The thread that sutures these works is the assertion of an imaginary transcendent universal culture—the West—and the near destruction of its cathedral, the academy. As Thomas Short put it in the first issue of *Academic Questions,* what must be emphasized in the academy is "how Western civilization, rather than being racist, sexist, classist, and ethnocentric, is actually the [sole] source of those principles and ideals by which diversity of opinion is sought, diversity of cultures honored, and individuals of all types respected."[18] On the other hand, the proponents of multiculturalism are represented as the barbarians at the wall, laying siege to the cultural canons exhibited and taught in the university of the thirties, forties, fifties, and early sixties, the undergraduate years of neoconservatives' nostalgia.[19] Tactically, what the neoconservatives truly seek to preserve is that conceit which Hayden White has described as "modern Western culture's notions about its own identity, its status as a (or rather *the*) civilization."[20]

The recurring strategy of neoconservatism, according to Joan Wallach Scott, is "to neutralize the space of ideological and cultural nonconformity by discrediting it."[21] In essence, neoconservatives pursue a political agenda that accords with the central premise of the multiculturalist critique "that the production of knowledge is a political enterprise."[22] What concerns neoconservatives, then, is neither culture nor (as Scott and others have put it) "white male privilege." They wish to erase the exposed seam, the nexus between power and regimes of knowledge so forcefully articulated by Michel Foucault.[23] How else can one defend their specious histories of knowledge, which invoke some pristine mythical moment in the life of the American academy? What else might explain the compulsion of Buckley, Shils, Ozick, Bloom, or D'Souza to tortured fantasies of an imaginary edifice they might restore from the predations of "politicization, bureaucratization and government interference"?[24]

To read Dinesh D'Souza, one would never know that Jews were deliberately
excluded from university faculties until after WWII, that women were until
recently systematically denied appointment at most research universities because of their sex, and that blacks were not admitted as students or hired as
faculty at many public and private universities until the 1960s.[25]

And what would Shils make of Yale's involvement in the Office of Strategic
Services (OSS) and the Central Intelligence Agency; Harvard's sympathies
for eugenics; the University of California's involvement in agribusiness; or,
in the nineteenth century, the curricular revolution at Dartmouth in the
early 1880s; the rejection of history, sociology, economics, and political science by the faculty at the University of Pennsylvania; or Thomas Jefferson's
Aristotelian objectives in the founding of the University of Virginia? And
these instances were comparatively small potatoes when we recall the Angli-
can determination of education at Oxford and Cambridge, and Harvard's
and Yale's and Oxbridge's intellectual subsidization of race science in the
nineteenth century.[26]

Perhaps because the majority of the opponents of multiculturalism have
only a tenuous grasp of their own history, they have often resorted to the
most blatant restagings of suppression (e.g., enlisting George Bush in the
attack on "political correctness"; Education Secretary William Bennett's Pla-
tonic pronouncements on American virtue and the Western classics; and
National Endowment for the Humanities chair Lynne Cheney's attacks
on critical scholarship). And though one might be tempted to invoke
McCarthyism, a truer parallel comes from Europe's Middle Ages: the extin-
guishment of heresy. Unlike McCarthyism, during which the "responsible"
classes and their intelligentsia remained in the shadows, feigning embarrassment with the excesses to which popular hysteria drove them, the present
crop of suppressionists makes the boldest and most public claims to the
pursuit of the true faith: intellectual freedom.[27]

The most telling resemblance between the present neoconservatives and
their medieval predecessors, however, is paradox. From Augustine, in the
fifth century, to the first Inquisition in the thirteenth century, Christian intellectuals had rigorously attempted the erasure of such heresies as Manichaeism, the dualistic sect that asserted that "Good was everywhere locked
in conflict with evil . . . with no morally gray areas in between."[28] Eventually,
of course, in the very process of eradicating the dualist heresy, Christianity
appropriated Manichaeism and its stark dichotomous worldview. Indeed,
Manichaean fantasies of existential opposition became a frequent rhetorical
strategy for instantiating social and international interests. As Frantz Fanon

discovered within the colonial apparatuses of the Caribbean and Africa, the irrationalist discursive practices of Western racism assumed a Manichaean presence resistant to class politics.[29]

We must recognize, however, that the Manichaeism of the Right opponents of multiculturalism is mirrored in some of the truth claims of liberal multiculturalist discursive practices (for example, "white male privilege") and particularist cultural studies (the essentialist assertions made on behalf of gender, race, and ethnicity). As Lisa Lowe has indicated elsewhere, Minority Discourse is one mode of connection that rehabilitates multiculturalism.[30] S. P. Mohanty has most effectively captured the thrust of Minority Discourse. Mohanty queries:

> How do we negotiate between my history and yours? . . . our various pasts and presents . . . ? It is necessary to assert our dense particularities, our lived and imagined differences; but could we afford to leave untheorized the question of how our differences are intertwined and, indeed, hierarchically organized? Could we, in other words, afford to have *entirely* different histories . . . in entirely heterogeneous and discrete spaces?[31]

Mohanty argues that we cannot afford such forfeiture. And Jon Cruz has nominated Marxism as that theoretical enterprise that best encompasses the significations of our "various pasts and presents." I am less certain that Marxist theory, with all its Victorian positivistic, scientistic, messianic, and Eurocentric baggage, is up to the task. And Marx himself would have few regrets or legitimate complaints if we moved on. Like the civilization in which it was conceived, and the architectonic world-system it sought to comprehend, Marxism was in actuality composed of antagonistic differences that fracture the economy and the elegance of a unitary or totalizing theory of history. A very different unifying narrative is required, and most certainly not one that presupposes that difference will and ought to be oxidized by the economies of commodity production.

I suggest that a radical impulse in multiculturalism constitutes both a critique of the absences and an appropriation of the positive contributions of Marxism. We are not the subjects or the subject formations of the capitalist world-system. It is merely one condition of our being. Amilcar Cabral recognized that fact when he insisted that " it is generally within the culture that we find the seed of opposition."[32] Multiculturalism, then, is a site of discursive resistance, an emblem and articulation of the several trajectories of "objective" opposition (religious, nationalist, feminist, etc.) mounted by our peoples in the everyday world.

Notes

1. Michael Landmann, "The Means as an End in Itself: Europe as the Perfection of Mankind," *History of European Ideas* 2:3 (1981): 188.

2. Dinesh D'Souza, "Multiculturalism 101: Great Books of the Non-Western World," *Policy Review* (spring 1991): 22.

3. I owe the notion of the specular subject identity to Abdul JanMohamed. See his "Worldliness-without-World, Homelessness-as-Home: Toward a Definition of the Border Intellectual," unpublished manuscript.

4. D'Souza, "Multiculturalism 101," 24.

5. Quoted in Susan King, "A Liberating 'Experience,'" *Los Angeles Times: TV Times*, 8–14 November 1992: 5. In 1985, the *New York Times* substituted Russian troops for the Black American troops who liberated the camps.

6. Quoted in William Stevens, "For Survivors and Liberators, a Commemoration," *New York Times*, 14 April 1985: 28.

7. *New York Times*, 8 November 1992, section 2: 30.

8. Quoted in Stevens, "For Survivors and Liberators," 28.

9. Ibid. At Bergen-Belsen, one survivor, Sigmund Strochlitz, remembered the British liberators as "young soldiers with boyish faces. They seemed confused at the sight of us, their eyes wandering in disbelief. They didn't know what to do."

10. *Fighting on Two Fronts in World War Two*, a documentary film by William Miles and Nina Rosenblum, aired on PBS-TV, 11 November 1992.

11. Londa Schiebinger, "The Anatomy of Difference: Race and Sex in Eighteenth-Century Science," *Eighteenth-Century Studies* 23:4 (summer 1990): 387.

12. Ibid., 391ff.

13. George Mosse, *Toward the Final Solution: A History of European Racism* (London: J. M. Dent and Sons, 1978).

14. Donna Haraway, *Primate Visions* (New York: Routledge, 1989), 9.

15. Ibid., 19.

16. Ibid., 3.

17. Quoted in John Thelin, "The Curriculum Crusades and the Conservative Backlash," *Change* (January–February 1992): 18.

18. Quoted in Edward Jayne, "Academic Jeremiad: The Neoconservative View of American Higher Education," *Change* (May–June 1991): 39.

19. For two instances of neoconservative undergraduate nostalgia, see the quote from Edward Shils in Thelin, "The Curriculum Crusades," 20; and Cynthia Ozick's memories in "A Critic at Large: T. S. Eliot at 101," *New Yorker*, 20 November 1989 (treated in Bruce Robbins, "Othering the Academy: Professionalism and Multiculturalism," *Social Research* 58:2 [summer 1991]: 360).

20. Hayden White, "Between Science and Symbol," *Times Literary Supplement*, 31 January 1986: 109.

21. Joan Wallach Scott, "The Campaign against Political Correctness: What's Really at Stake?" *Change* (November–December 1991): 30.

22. Ibid.

23. Michel Foucault, *Power/Knowledge* (New York: Pantheon Books, 1980).

24. Thelin writes: "For example, Shils' criticism of the external connections of the modern university overlooks the 'Wisconsin Plan' of the early 1900s, whereby campus and capitol in Madison meant that state university faculty often were intended to contribute to policy discussions; at the federal level, New Deal involvement of professors as experts in the 1930s set a precedent that has been followed for well over half a century. The presence of sponsored research in the evolution of such institutions as The California Institute of Technology in the 1920s indi-

cated that the role of professor did not preclude involvement in research and analysis of contemporary public affairs and national projects" ("The Curriculum Crusades," 18).

25. Scott, "The Campaign against Political Correctness," 32.

26. For the histories of the American academy's complicity in race science, secret government, and the suppression of intellectuals, see, respectively, John Trumpbour, ed., *How Harvard Rules* (Boston: South End Press, 1989); Robin Winks, *Cloak and Gown* (New York: William Morrow, 1987); and Ellen Schrecker, *No Ivory Tower* (New York: Oxford University Press, 1988).

27. For McCarthyism's anti-intellectualism, see Richard Hofstadter's *Anti-Intellectualism in American Life* (New York: Alfred A. Knopf, 1965).

28. Frederick H. Russell, "'Only Something Good Can Be Evil': The Genesis of Augustine's Secular Ambivalence," *Theological Studies* 51:4 (December 1990): 699.

29. See Cedric J. Robinson, "Fanon and the West: Imperialism in the Native Imagination," *Africa and the World* 1:1 (October 1987): 33.

30. Cf. Abdul JanMohamed and David Lloyd, "Toward a Theory of Minority Discourse," *Cultural Critique* 6 (spring 1987): 5–12.

31. Quoted in Scott, "The Campaign against Political Correctness," 39.

32. Amilcar Cabral, "National Liberation and Culture" in *Return to the Source* (New York: Monthly Review Press, 1973), 43.

PART II

Rethinking the Political Subject

CHAPTER EIGHT

Conjugating Subjects
in the Age of Multiculturalism

NORMA ALARCÓN

This essay is necessarily layered as I attempt to write and connect circuits of signification arising in specific historical locations, while also attempting to bring into view their relationality through processes of appropriation, translation, and recodification. Terms such as subject(ivity), *différance*/difference, identity, experience, history, resistance, negritude, and *mestizaje* are implicated in such processes. These, however, will be threaded through the term *essential(ism)* to bring into relief the politics of "identity" on the one hand, and the cultural politics of "difference" on the other, as well as the consideration of the complex possibilities of "identity-in-difference" as a privileged nexus of analysis. Moreover, following, implicitly or explicitly, the diverse uses or charge of the vexed term *essentialism* may aid the reader to weave the layered text. (May my "instructions" be simpler to follow than those for assembling a bicycle.)

In the preface to her book *Between Past and Future: Eight Exercises in Political Thought,* Hannah Arendt meditates on the "lost treasure" of the generation that came of age during and after World War II. That "lost treasure," I suggest to you, is the loss of a *grand récit,* or a coherent metanarrative, or exhausted versions of some metaphysics. (As an aside, conquest, displacement, migration, and colonization have had similar effects for non-Europeans. Thus, it may be argued that that global war had the effect of putting in question both in the "center" and the "periphery" the value of modernity, reason, and enlightenment; that is, highlighting their dark sides. Moreover, the unique historical role of the United States in this potential binarization gives its entry into the debates of modernity and postmodernity peculiar twists.)

Arendt points out that the loss is beset by a "namelessness." It is an un-willed situation. It was without testament. It had no story. She resolves the metaphors by suggesting that the "lost treasure" be named "tradition—which selects and names, which hands down and preserves, which indicates where the treasures are and what their worth is." However, because there no longer seems to be a "willed continuity in time and hence, humanly speaking neither past nor future," she asserts that we face a situation totally unforeseen by any tradition, because no "testament had willed it for the future."[1]

Through that moment of virtually total social and political breakdown, Arendt suggests, there set in a recognition of the existential experience of the rupture between "thought and reality"; that is, "thought and reality [had] parted company."[2] Arendt locates the moment of recognition in the after-math of World War II, "when it began to dawn upon modern man that he had come to live in a world in which his mind and his tradition of thought were not even capable of asking adequate, meaningful questions, let alone of giving answers to its own perplexities."[3] In a sense, that West European experience, which promotes the growth of existentialism with its inversion of the "essence-existence" binary (Jean-Paul Sartre, *Search for a Method* [1968]), and which is followed by poststructuralism, attempts to interrogate and contest through these theoretical trends the assertion that "Modern[ist] philosophy began with a loss of the world . . . [indeed] the autonomous bourgeois subject . . . began with the withdrawal from the world."[4]

The most recent challenges to that subject have emerged with a larger de-gree of convergences than we have recognized. Although Arendt was writing in the 1950s, that same decade promotes the proliferation of the "new" social movements on a global scale and their concomitant "politics of identity-in-difference." Thus, for example, even as Arendt is rewriting the epistemologi-cal politics of Western philosophy, Simone de Beauvoir is rewriting the on-tological and epistemological sexual politics in *The Second Sex*.[5] Moreover, in the United States, even as Jacques Derrida was addressing the French Philosophical Society in January 1968 with his groundbreaking theorization of *différance*, people of Mexican descent, under the recodified name Chi-cano, signaling *différance*, were mobilizing in Los Angeles for the school walkouts of March 1968.[6] In brief, with broad strokes I am attempting to convey the convergence of discourses of identity-in-difference as linked to the "essence-experience" binary that it has taken so long to recognize as the patriarchal "West" engages in resistances of its own.

The potential of the discourse of identity-in-difference and its nuances was derailed by the oversimplified hegemonization of a universalized concept of woman aided and abetted by the media, for example.[7] The hegemonization of feminism as woman brought on an attack by a patriarchal media commodification of feminism on the assumption that feminism entailed a strictly recodified appropriation of the autonomous, self-determining, bourgeois, unified subject presumed to be male-owned, as if that kind of subject was essential to maleness—that is, if women claimed that facet of the subject as well, what was man to do? In other words, feminism was read by the Reaganomic media as a mimetic inversion of an essential aspect of maleness, which produced anxiety. These processes of identification and counteridentification between unified man and unified woman barely permitted the articulations (in both senses of the word—enunciation and linkage) of a politics of identity-in-difference by "women of color" to be heard in the United States. Historically, racialized women were not heard until postmodernism in the 1980s invaded the hegemonic 1970s liberal agenda of feminism. Poststructuralist theory made it possible to mis(man-age) a variety of other feminist discourses (i.e., socialist, radical, Marxist, "of color," and so on).[8]

By working through the "identity-in-difference" paradox, many racialized women theorists have implicitly worked in the interstice/interface of (existentialist) "identity politics" and "postmodernism" without a clear-cut postmodern agenda. Neither Audre Lorde's nor Chela Sandoval's notion of difference/differential consciously subsumes a Derridean theorization— though resonance cannot be denied and must be explored—so much as represents a process of "determinate negation," a nay-saying of the variety of the "not yet," that's not it. The drive behind the "not yet/that's not it" position in Sandoval's work is termed "differential consciousness," in Lorde's work, "difference," and in Derrida's work, *différance*. Yet each invokes dissimilarly located circuits of signification codified by the context of the site of emergence, which nevertheless does not obviate their agreement on the "not yet," which points toward a future. The difficulties of articulating these sites across languages, cultures, races, genders, and social positions are painfully hard but yield a space for debate beyond "ethnocentrisms" without denying them.

Arendt herself, in an effort to theorize the critical interstitial intervention

of the existential and historical subject who has lost the testamental "treasure," turns to Kafka to provide her with the poetics for a theorization of the
gap. It is there, in the interstice, that Arendt thinks the simultaneity of time-
and-space, thought-and-event will henceforth take place. Kafka's valuable
parable is as follows:

> She has two antagonists: the first presses her from behind, from the origin.
> The second blocks the road ahead. She gives battle to both. To be sure, the
> first supports her in her fight with the second, for it wants to push her for-
> ward, and in the same way the second supports her in her fight with the first,
> since it drives her back. But it is only theoretically so. For it is not only the
> two antagonists who are there, but she herself as well, and who really knows
> her intentions? Her dream, though, is that some time in an unguarded
> moment—and this would require a night darker than any night has ever
> been yet—she will jump out of the fighting line and be promoted, on
> account of her experience in fighting, to the position of umpire over her
> antagonists in their fight with each other.[9]

Arendt translates Kafka's forces into past and future. The fact that there is
a fight at all is due to the presence of the (wo)man. Her insertion, her inscription, breaks up the motion of the forces, their linearity. This causes the
forces to deflect, however lightly, from their original direction. The gap
where she stands is an interstice or interval.[10] It is a time-space from which
she can simultaneously survey what is most her own and that "which has
come into being" through her "self-inserting appearance." Arendt falters, as
does every theorist including Derrida, as to what precisely drives one to that
differential self-insertion through which "a double gesture, a double science,
a double writing, practice an *overturning* of the classical opposition *and* a
general displacement of the system."[11] (Psychoanalysis and its theory of the
unconscious provide for some a venue for understanding such impulses
within the subject; for others it is the experience of "otherization" *between*
subjects.) However, anyone outside of contexts that entail "classical oppositions" proper to the West's systematizing reasoning processes is likely to
practice more than "double" gestures and writings. Thus Gloria Anzaldúa,
through the textual production, self-insertion, and speaking position of a
"mestiza consciousness," disrupts the possibility of such tidiness.[12] A different tactic with similar effects is that of Luce Irigaray, who disrupts the tidiness of deconstruction's use of the feminine by introducing the contingent
woman outside of metaphysical circuits of representation and meaning.[13]
She is the one who engages the essentialization of Woman and renegotiates
symbolization.

Both Anzaldúa and Irigaray have been suspected of essentializing: the first on the basis of race, that is, *mestizaje*, and the second on the basis of the female body. The charges against Anzaldúa are made at conferences, or muttered in classrooms and academic hallways, while those against Irigaray are subject to extensive debates with a healthy bibliography.[14] (In the United States, the debate on race and [anti]essentialism has been largely left to African-American theorists and Diana Fuss, while the debate with respect to Chicanas and Latin Americans and other groups is largely obscured as the discourses of race continue to binarize into black and white.)

Taking up the question of essentialism and race from another angle, Jean-Luc Nancy resists the possibility of turning *mestizaje* into "a substance, an object, an identity . . . that could be grasped and 'processed.'" He deplores the notion that one could be a mestiza or a mestizo. "Everything," he continues, "everyone—male, female—who alters me, subjects me to *mestizaje*. This has nothing to do with mixed blood or mixed cultures. Even the process of 'mixing' in general, long celebrated by a certain theoretical literary and artistic tradition—even this kind of 'mixing' must remain suspect: it should not be turned into a new substance, a new identity."[15]

Even as he wants to valorize the notion of *mestizaje*, indeed claim the term mestizo for himself, he cautions against "biologisms," or even cultural mixing, and cautions against ultimate *meaning* by having us place ourselves "on the border, on the very border of *meaning*."[16] To be pinned down by meaning and intentionality, to mean, is to essentialize. The pursuit of identity as a quest for meaning closes off possibility. This quest for meaning can also appear, in postmodernist terms, as the drive to privilege our constructedness through the deconstruction of our essential(izing) quest for identity meaning. Nancy speaks of the constructed subject who is traversed by the world and by others in such ways that he is never pure. The subject is unbounded and open to the other through *mestizaje*, "[s/he who] alters me, subjects me to *mestizaje*."[17] Significance cannot come to rest, cannot stop; intersubjectivity as well as interaction with the world is always at play. However, we are indeed in the face of a paradox/contradiction. For Nancy does not want us to mistake his meaning of the term. In wanting to set it free and make it open to the future in specific ways, we are cautioned that this does not mean "mixed blood," or "mixed cultures," one of the modes in which Anzaldúa, for example, employs the term. With that prohibition he closes up the time and space of *mestizaje*; it is now under control, yet of course open to the future "toward infinity." Thus is Nancy subjected to the politics of his own location, "a twentieth-century Frenchman, . . . of Spanish and Viking, of

Celt and Roman." What I mean to say is that the politics of his own location, his own time and space, leads him to appropriate and recodify the notion such that now it refers to the specificity of his own history, the "melting pot" that is France. Although he too is a mestizo, it is a kind open to the drift of the future, "on the border, on the very border of *meaning*." Indeed, one may view Anzaldúa's work as doubly located on the "border of meaning"—that is, the U.S.-Mexican geopolitical border as juridical sociopolitical division, which simultaneously opens up the past and the future as unfolding "borders of meaning" wherein Kafka's (wo)man struggles; insofar as there is meaning, it emanates from the prohibition itself. The historical discussion of "mixed blood" in the Americas, including its juridical normalizations, further problematizes Nancy's prohibition since it might silence the legal history of the racialization of the pre- and post-Columbian subject, of (post)slavery African Americans, and of the migratory/diasporic travails of others such as Chicanos.

Another example of a different kind of prohibition, yet with similar silencing effects, appears in Frantz Fanon's rejection of Jean-Paul Sartre's translation of negritude into class on the grounds that the former is too particularistic/concrete and the latter abstract and universal, whereas Fanon suggests that the former is a "psychobiological syncretism," a methodical construction based on experience.[18] Fanon cites Sartre saying that negritude

> "appears as the minor term of a dialectical progression: The theoretical and practical assertion of the supremacy of the white man is its thesis; the position of negritude as an antithetical value is the moment of negativity." ...
> Proof was presented that my effort was only a term in the dialectic. ... I defined myself as an absolute intensity of beginning. So I took up my negritude, and with tears in my eyes I put its machinery together again. What had been broken to pieces was rebuilt, reconstructed by the intuitive lianas of my hands.[19]

The very inflected force of the selected theoretical frameworks from a universalizing center expels the narratives and the textualization of difference and resistance.

It may be true that the expulsion itself produces a resistance; that is, resistance becomes the site of the emergence of meaning itself and its concomitant practices should there be no other resistance to deflect the projected course of meaning. But in Sartre, as Fanon reads him, the coexistence of prohibitions and resistances forecloses conditions of possibility for the renegotiation of relations and structures. The very emergences of syncretic new subjects, recodified on their own terms and rehistoricized anew, are dismissed without taking up the task of piercing beneath, uncovering the structure, relations and possibilities that present themselves as the conditions of the possibility of the [new subject's] appearing as it does. The maneuver to avoid the probing is done through a reobjectification of the "new subject," a reification or a denial of the historical meaning posited by the differential signifier. As a result the difference is not fully engaged as a resistance to the monologizing demands of the West. The desire to translate as totalizing metaphorical substitution without acknowledging the "identity-in-difference," so that one's own system of signification is not disrupted through a historical concept whose site of emergence is implicated in our own history, may be viewed as a desire to dominate, constrain, and contain. Sartre's desire reflects the "center"'s own resistance to negotiating meaning and structure.

Sartre allows the possibility that racial difference may be ontologized in the process of exploring *mestizaje* or negritude as "psychobiological syncretism" to lead to a prohibition rather than a careful evaluation of how the drive to decolonize, to free up the subject from subjection, has embattled her inscription as represented by Kafka's allegorical parable. If to "ontologize difference" in the pursuit of identity and meaning as modes of resistance to domination entails essentializing by relying on the concept of an authentic core that remains hidden to one's consciousness and that requires the elimination of all that is considered foreign or not true to the self, then neither Anzaldúa nor Fanon are essentialists at all. Both are quite clear that the pursuit of identity through "psychobiological syncretism" is one engaged through the racial difference imputed to them as a stigma that is now revalorized through reconstruction in historical terms.

Where does the terror of the "ontologization of difference" come from if not from the possibility that the result will continue to be inequality in the face of a liberal legal subject that has been naturalized on masculine terms? This particular fear is more pronounced in feminist theory than in anti-essentialist theories of race because, as I stated earlier, the latter is dominated by men who do not bother to remark gender. The possibilities that the combination of gender with race may transform our mode of speaking about the constructedness of the subject from both the outside *and* the inside are virtually unexplored by men.

One sign of this is that Derrida's considerations on the two interpretations of interpretation have not been explored as simultaneous *and* irreconcilable in conjunction with the "obscure economies" that emerge in instances such as Kafka's parable.[20] Derrida describes these "two interpretations of interpretation": "The one seeks to decipher, dreams of deciphering a truth or an origin which escapes play and the order of the sign, and which lives the necessity of interpretation as an exile. The other, which is no longer turned toward the origin, affirms play and tries to pass beyond man and humanism."[21] Further, it is not a question of choosing one or the other since both are irreducible and to choose is to trivialize. Thus, Derrida continues, "we must conceive of the common ground, and the *différance* of this irreducible difference."[22] The fact that the resistant texts of minoritized populations in the United States are often read as interpretation number one and charged with essentializing, as is the case in Fuss's treatment of African-American women critics and the debate on Irigaray, is a misreading in light of the theorists' own resistance to conjugating both interpretations of interpretation and its significance for the present. It is often the case as well that no one claims an "immutable origin"; however, the anxiety of pursuing the "différance of this irreducible difference" continues to surface as a charge of essentialism on the one hand, and a fear of losing ground on the equality battlefront, given patriarchal resistance to equality via a naturalized liberal subject whose criteria we all must be, on the other; that is, while identity now labors under a charge of essentialism, difference is now checked by the charge of inequality. The double bind of *différance* emerges in the struggle between the old-age metaphysics of *being* and the liberally inspired politics of *becoming*—dare I say the past and the future?

Fuss struggles with this double bind, justifying "the stronger lesbian endorsement of identity and identity politics" on the basis that it may indicate that "lesbians inhabit a more precarious and less secure subject position than gay men."[23] Interestingly, she argues for the progressiveness (i.e., antiessentialism) of lesbian scholarship by arguing via Heidegger for the metaphysical unity of identity as a fictional coherence that "theories of 'multiple identities' fail to challenge effectively." The unity of identity even as fictional coherence can be maintained and thereby make "identity politics" theoretically acceptable if one does away with the claim of "multiple identities"; that is, *différance* must be relocated to the "space *within* identity" and withdrawn from the "spaces *between* identities."[24] A theory of the fictional unity of identity via the Freudian-Lacanian unconscious is selected by Fuss, in my view, in order to salvage, through complementariness, the autonomous, self-determining, liberal bourgeois subject that is important to the kind of struggle made necessary by currently hegemonic views of juridical equality.[25] In the process, however, she discards "the spaces *between* identities," which are paramount to cross-cultural exploration and analysis of "women of color." Thus, one of the major questions that arises in these theoretical debates is, What is behind the antiessentialist position? Certainly it is one that too readily assumes that the other is, of course, being essentialist. What are the stakes in such oppositional arguments wherein one is either implicated in Derrida's interpretation number one or interpretation number two, but not, shall we say, engaged in a struggle such as that of Kafka's (wo)man?

In Anzaldúa's terms, "mestiza consciousness" reveals a "tolerance for contradictions," paradox, and ambiguity because the term "mestiza" projects a confluence of conflicting subject positions that keep "breaking down the unitary aspect of each new paradigm."[26] M. Y. Mudimbe designates an "intermediate space between the so-called . . . tradition and the projected modernity of colonialism." It is apparently an urbanized space in which "vestiges of the past, especially the survival of structures that are still living realities (tribal ties, for example), often continue to hide the new structures (ties based on class or on groups defined by their position in the capitalist system)"; at any rate, this intermediary space "could be viewed as the major signifier of underdevelopment. It reveals the strong tension between a modernity that often is an illusion of development, and a tradition that sometimes reflects a poor image of a mythical past."[27] These in-between/interstitial zones of instability present us with paradigms of "obscure economies." In these zones theoretical frameworks are both affirmed and resisted, especially when experiential and historical meanings are erased and differences go unengaged, their irreducibility unnamed despite the risk of misnaming.

In resonance with Anzaldúa, Chela Sandoval claims that

> U.S. Third World feminism represents a central locus of possibility, an insurgent movement which shatters the construction of any one of the collective ideologies as the single most correct site where truth can be represented. . . . What U.S. Third World feminism demands is a new subjectivity, a political revision that denies any one ideology as the final answer, while instead positing a *tactical subjectivity* with the capacity to recenter depending upon the kinds of oppression to be confronted. This is what the shift from hegemonic oppositional theory and practice to a U.S. third world theory and method of oppositional consciousness requires.[28]

Sandoval calls attention to the many "women of color" who have pointed the way toward the development of a "new subject of history" and as such a "new political subject." Aída Hurtado has claimed that "women of color" develop political skills "like urban guerrillas trained through everyday battle with the state apparatus."[29] For Cherríe Moraga, feminist "guerrilla warfare" is a way of life. "Our strategy is how we cope" on an everyday basis, "how we measure and weigh what is to be said and when, what is to be done and how, and to whom . . . daily deciding/risking who it is we can call an ally, call a friend."[30]

Citing Audre Lorde's remarks at a 1979 conference commemorating the thirtieth anniversary of the publication of *The Second Sex*, Sandoval points to the fact that "ideological differences" must be seen as "a fund of necessary polarities between which our creativities spark like a dialectic. Only within that interdependency" of historical and ideologically positioned differences "can the power to seek new ways of being in the world generate . . . the courage and sustenance to act where there are no charters."[31] In a sense, if, as Moraga also claimed, feminists of color are "women without a line," coalescing with Sandoval, then the "new subject of history" is the one who struggles "to insure our survival," who is always "challenging women to go further," who in my view engages a politics of the "not yet," in the interstice between past and future.[32] As Sandoval herself states, the "politics of the not yet" waged by U.S. Third World feminists is that of "differential consciousness" that posits no "ultimate answers, no terminal utopia . . . no predictable final outcomes. . . . Entrance into this new order requires an emotional commitment within which one experiences the violent shattering of the unitary sense of self, as the skill which allows a mobile identity to form. . . . Citizenship in this political realm is comprised of strategy and risk."[33]

Who is this "new subject of history" whose "identity-in-difference" politics was so dramatically documented in *This Bridge Called My Back* and given form in the context of second-wave, that is, contemporary, feminism, whose existential writings foreshadowed, *avant la lettre*, the poststructuralist subject, yet emerged as a paradoxical, contradictory subject whose own pursuit of "identity politics" was fissured by every other sentence through an affirmation of difference that questioned every category of import to the formation of a new society? Categories such as nation, class, race, gender, sexuality, and ethnicity were intermittently questioned and disrupted. In brief, her very constitution as a "speaking subject" called attention to contradiction and difference as her constitutive ground through discursive political and intersubjective practices. When Sandoval publishes her essay ten years later, she calls it "differential consciousness." She gives it a name that at its core signals a situated (located in the interval/gap/interstice/time-space) subject whose practice "cannot be thought *together*."[34] It cannot be thought simultaneously because the reinscription is thought out from the site of displacement, which is subject to misnaming, misrecognition, misalliance, as

well as hitting the mark. It cannot be thought together because it aims to situate that which has no place and through naming may fall short of the
mark. The name may never be quite "it" because names are "relatively unitary . . . structures" whose oppositional status one may not intend, yet may
take over. When Sandoval claims that the differential consciousness that
calls for entering the "between and amongst" demands a mode of consciousness once relegated to the province of intuition and psychic phenomena, but
which now must be recognized as a specific practice, she is in effect moving
us toward and/or finding the relationality between the inside, as affirmed by
Fuss (per the discussion earlier), and the outside as the cross-cultural, intersubjective site; that is, she poses the challenge of resistance to oppositional
hegemonies through a *différance* that works inside and outside on multiple
planes—a factor that works itself out through a "speaking subject" conscious that she can be "constituted by discourse and yet not be completely
determined by it." Benhabib asks, "What psychic, intellectual or other
sources of creativity and resistance must we attribute to subjects for such
[agential variation to discursive subject determination] to be possible?"[35]
Hannah Arendt called it "spirit," others call it "aesthetics," yet others have
called it a "project," a "sparking dialectic." Anzaldúa calls it the "Shadow
Beast." All grope for the impulse; as stated earlier, some have settled for the
"unconscious"—a metaphor for the drives and impulses toward structural
and symbolic change in the name of feminism.

The critical desire to undercut subject determination through structures
and discourses, in my view, presupposes a subject-in-process who constructs *provisional* identities, or Sandoval's *tactical subjectivity,* which sub-
sume a network of signifying practices and structural experiences imbri-
cated in the historical *and* imaginary shifting national borders of Mexico
and the United States for Chicanas, for example. (Other "borders" that mediate [im]migration might be invoked.) A subject-insertion into such a geographical economy and politics may presuppose not only specific historical
sociosymbolic texts but a situated contemporaneous horizon of meanings
and intentions that swerve away from those produced and enunciated by
Euro-Americans and Europeans, especially when the latter produce structures and discourses of containment that resist change. Identity formations
through differentially theorized experience and history—in this instance,
through the term Chicana, thus signaling a historically raced/gendered/
classed position forged through the interstices of two nation-states—propose
a subject-in-process, desirous of self-determination yet "traversed through
and through by the world and by others. . . . It is the active and lucid agency

that constantly reorganizes its contents, through the help of these same contents, that produces by means of a material and in relation to needs and
ideas, all of which are themselves mixtures of what it has already found there
before it and what it has produced itself."[36] Through the speaking critical
subject-in-process, cultural production reintroduces what was there before
in new and dynamic combinatory transculturations. A bi- or multiethnicized, raced, and gendered subject-in-process may be called upon to take up
diverse subject positions that cannot be unified without double binds and
contradictions. Indeed, what binds the subject positions together may be
precisely the difference from the perceived hegemony and the identity with a
specific autohistory. The paradoxes and contradictions between subject positions move the subject to recognize, reorganize, reconstruct, and exploit
difference through political resistance and cultural productions in order to
reflect the subject-in-process. It is not a matter of doing away with the discourse of the other "because the other is in each case present in the activity
that eliminates [it]."[37] The traces of a process of elimination may construct
the subject as much as the efforts to incorporate. A critical subject-inprocess who reorganizes "contents" upon the demands of the contingent
moment and context may discover that it is in the inaugural transitional
moment from being traversed to reconfiguration that the political intention
as well as the combinatory transculturating takes place. Through such time-
spaces one can discover diverse cultural narrative formations, translations,
appropriations, and recodifications, which generate texts that are "hybrid"
or "syncretic" and, far from wanting to remain at rest in that taxonomy,
make a bid for new discourse formations bringing into view new subjects-
in-process. In Gloria Anzaldúa's terms, these are the "borderlands" through
which the "theory circuits" of geopolitics and critical allegories find resonance but the zones of figurations and conceptualizations remain nonequivalent; that is, the very contingent currents through which the geopolitical subject-in-process is dislocated and forced into (im)migration will
retain an irreducible difference that refuses to correspond neatly to the
subject's account of herself and the theory we produce to account for her
appearance.

As transnational geopolitics with a concomitant production of "new" subjects of history come into contact with theoretical and critical allegories of
the liberal political subject, the "new citizen subject," in Chela Sandoval's
terms (see earlier discussion), and the "cultural politics of difference, or
identity-in-difference," are subsumed under "multiculturalism." However, as

I will argue, "multiculturalism" and the "cultural politics of difference" are neither equivalent nor homologous. The term "multiculturalism" appears to be a quick metaphoric fix signaling inclusion that both comprehends the commodifications of difference and refuses to hear the implications for the production of knowledge and the material grounds that give rise to revised social and political histories as well as the "cultural politics of difference"; that is, "multiculturalism" serves a functional end in the political economy of culture that fails to grasp the substantive claims generated through what Cornel West has named "the new cultural politics of difference." Yet, "multiculturalism" has, in our time, become the discourse of choice for a multiplicity of national and transnational agendas to name the traffic in goods and peoples, the referential subjects of this complex discursive economy. Like most ideological formations, "multiculturalism" harnesses and distorts the production of the interpellated.[38]

Etienne Balibar suggests that the current multiculturalism has become a lightning rod that produces a neoracism. It is, after all, the "unmeltables" who are the metaphoric subjects, daily in the media, of multiculturalism's discourse. The currently renewed, "genetic"-based attack on African Americans' "measured" IQ levels suggests that, at the end of the twentieth century, the so-called nineteenth-century racist biologism converges with the end-of-the-twentieth-century culturalism to bespeak the racialized panic of our "liberal" society and the age-old questions of administering heterogeneity. As the media "educates" the public, both IQs and multiculturalism are raced, permitting "liberal" discourse to assume a mediating position in the face of right-wing attacks on "unmeltables." How, one might ask, is that position articulated, and is it possible to make productive critical interventions in the contemporary discourse of multiculturalism as mediated by politically liberal critiques, or is it the kind of octopus that ensnares one in its multiple tentacles? Jürgen Habermas, I think, does a creditable job of outlining the potential multicultural tentacles—feminism, ethnic minorities, nationalism, Eurocentrism as Western cultural hegemony, philosophical discourses, the question of rights and political correctness—especially as these are embroiled in producing discourses that also narrate the "cultural politics of difference."[39] However, the point of my analysis at this juncture is to do a preliminary mapping of how liberal academic thinkers mediate the "cultural politics of difference" and have it end up recodified as "multiculturalism." In brief, the question might well be, What is the ground for the formation of a critical and political culture that is not equivalent to a recodification as "multiculturalism?"[40]

Even an eminent intellectual such as Arthur Schlesinger Jr., for example, is reduced to incoherent, murky thinking when faced with multiculturalism and its implications for the location from which he reads it. He fears a dismantling of "his" institutions. Insofar as he reads Afrocentrism as the total negation of what he thinks he stands for, clear thinking collapses and his text, *The Disuniting of America*, becomes the occasion for hysteria and paranoia. The hysteria enters in when he deploys unremarked contradictory arguments in a surreal stream-of-consciousness fashion, and the paranoia when he sees the nation-state crumbling before him as a result of the "cultural politics of difference" or of "multiculturalism," as school boards have recoded it.[41] The recoding in itself is a disservice to a complex cultural and political questioning that at a minimum goes back to the constitution of the nation-state, leading up to and unfolding from the Constitution itself. In this context, "multiculturalism" becomes a wimpy kind of name that returns one to the notion of cultural contribution to the making of the nation, which permits a kind of blindness in which "American" culture becomes fused with the "political contract" and the rest is pasted on such that most nonwhites will remain not-American, but "raced ethnics" in perpetuity. There is, however, the possibility of seeing "American" culture as the consistent failure to make good on its ideal horizon of meanings and on the institutional interpretation of the political contract. "We the people" can be analyzed along its historical trajectory as in effect meaning some and not others, hence the desire for a strong revisionist historical and social map that is tied to a reconstructionist project. On the other hand, when "the cultural politics of difference" are practiced as a strictly oppositional formation of a minoritized "we the people" held up to a capitalized "We the People," another kind of boundary is constructed, which in effect converges as well with some liberal understandings of multiculturalism as celebratory heterogeneous representations. These responses, in my view, are symptomatic of deep dialogic complicity in the formation of all "American" subjects, though some are constantly on trial as to their "Americanness." To see one's self-representation textualized is not to come to terms with its dialogic construction and contestation. Grasping the dialogic constructions, however, creates passages that undermine, for example, Stuart Hall's observation that "far from collapsing the complex questions of cultural identity and issues of social and political rights, what we need is *greater distance between them* [sic]. We need to be able to insist that rights of citizenship and the incommensurability of cultural difference are respected and the *one is not made a condition of the other* [sic]."[42] How can we simultaneously deal with the contemporary desire

to renegotiate the "political contract," maintaining distant equilibrium between equal citizenship rights and cultural difference, when faced with a
history where "rights of citizenship" have been conditioned by identitarian
sameness with the contingently historical bourgeois liberal subject and not
in conjunction with difference—that is, race, gender, sexuality, and social
position—but its expulsion? At this juncture the traffic between cultural and
political practices is heightened and highly dependent on whether one is or
is not viewed as a social equal and on asking what is producing social and
political inequality. Moreover, if indeed the construction of differences has
been historically produced in a dialogical manner between discrete sets of
social relations, one must question, as I have earlier, the boundaries that
such an analytic and interpretative nexus produces and that make it impossible to grasp articulations across the "cultural politics of difference or identity-in-difference." The fact that the latter often appears virtually impossible,
indeed, does tend to make it homologous to "multiculturalism."[43]

Consequently, and in fairness to Stuart Hall, I would argue that although
there may be a distinction to be made with respect to the "incommensurability of cultural difference" and "rights of citizenship," the struggle of the
"cultural politics of difference" is precisely about the "distance between
them" and how the distanced is functioned. What is involved in the "distance
between them" that we take, or what is at stake in making or not making one
"a condition of the other"? Such "distance" should be functioned in more as
an analytical pause for critique and productive resolutions than as unquestioned separation of spheres of interest. It would be more productive, then,
to ask with Cornel West, what the political consequences are of (strategic)
cultural identity-in-difference formations as an effect of previous overdeterminations of culturally raced identities. As distinct from liberalized "multiculturalist" discourses, the "cultural politics of difference" "acknowledge[s]
the uphill struggle of fundamentally transforming highly objectified, rationalized and commodified societies and cultures in the name of individuality
and democracy."[44] In effect the raced-ethnic overdeterminations have taken
place a priori in the Americas, certainly in the United States, "in the name of
individuality and democracy," as tied to economistic opportunity and
desire.

Multiculturalism is only the latest discourse on the "table" to rehearse
once again the discursive positional traps that emerge from deep-seated
structural inequalities, which, moreover, have been sedimented over hundreds of years. Because "multiculturalism" in the United States is often perceived through the ongoing ethnic genocide and fighting in Eastern Europe,

it gives rise in the United States to paranoia, on the one hand, which only seems to have the effect of triggering more racism, on the other, especially in light of a much-publicized economic decline and restructuration.[45] Thus, "multiculturalism," a name never advanced in the first place by U.S. activists and intellectuals of the "cultural politics of difference," has moved from revising the K-12 curriculum to focusing on the academy, and is served up as rethinking the foundational epistemology, but not practice, of liberalism. As demonstrated in the recently reissued meditation on "the politics of recognition" by Charles Taylor in a collection sold as *Multiculturalism and the Politics of Recognition,* liberalism is not the same for the Canadian thinker as it is for Jürgen Habermas, a German one. (The question, What are the historical and political conditions that make the difference possible? is beyond the scope of this essay; certainly, however, the geographic position of each exerts pressure on his thinking. In short, the Americas are not Europe.) While, on the one hand, Taylor appears as a benign patriarch for whom boundaries may be blurred, questioned, or reasserted periodically, and who even invokes, though he doesn't account for, a dialogic subject/group formation, Habermas, on the other, wants to draw boundaries everywhere and exercise a strong control over their porosity and permeability. "Constitutional patriotism" and "procedural consensus" are the twin pillars for the hard-and-fast universalism Habermas proposes.[46]

Charles Taylor provides philosophical merit to the discourse of multiculturalism with his meditative and critical essay "The Politics of Recognition," which has been translated into Italian, French, and German. In a sense this signals the modes through which some European and Euro-American thinkers understand what I've been calling with Cornel West "the cultural politics of difference." To codify the latter as "multiculturalism" is tantamount to an effort to displace "the cultural politics of difference" embraced by many intellectuals in the United States and to rethink them through an invocation of liberal epistemological foundations. At the core of this rethinking is the question of individual rights and citizenship as a unit.

Taylor's invocation of liberal epistemological foundations has the virtue of sincerely trying to explore the contradictions that "the cultural politics of difference" (or, as he entitles them, "the politics of recognition") has uncovered in the liberal political agenda. Taylor perceives two modes of politics: (1) the politics of difference "as an individual and also as a culture"; and (2) the claim to cultural equal worth.[47] He admits that the liberal principle of blindness to difference has not been successful in its application and that perhaps "the very idea of such a liberalism may be a kind of pragmatic con-

tradiction, a particularism [of liberal thought] masquerading as the universal."[48] Moreover, he cannot imagine a "common project" that is compatible
with differentiation, but he would like to. As a result, he wonders if there is
not middle ground wherein there is a "willingness to be open to comparative
cultural study of the kind that must displace our horizons in the resulting
fusions."[49] Borrowing from H. G. Gadamer, he hits upon the possibility of a
coming "fusion of horizons" that "operates through our developing new vo-
cabularies of comparison, by means of which we can articulate these contrasts."[50] The gesture to dialogism and conversation is not given up by Taylor
even though "equal worth" cannot be demanded as a right. Such "equal
worth" can only be accomplished or established through conjunctural conversations, otherwise they polarize into demands of cultural "equal worth"
and "self-immurement within ethnocentric standards."[51] Stated from this
angle, there is a strong desire on Taylor's part to understand the "cultural
politics of difference" and the flaws it uncovers in the liberal political and
aesthetic project. He questions procedural liberalism and finds it inhos-
pitable because it continues to pretend a blindness to differences and "pre-
tends to offer a neutral ground in which people of all cultures can meet or
coexist."[52]

In appropriating G. H. Gadamer's notion of "fusion of horizons," Taylor
is actually proposing, though not specifying, different "reading" practices.
Gadamer's project is to outline the reading practices appropriate to the
"hermeneutic experience" wherein the "conversation" takes place between
the critical reader and the literary object. It is a practice that, in his view, may
account for but surpasses historicism, such that the aesthetic is the teleological site for the "fusion of horizons" between reader and text.[53] Taylor
swerves from this ethnocentric project to insist on conversation between diverse ethnocultural critical readers and claimed texts. From this point of
view, "equal [cultural] worth" is deferred through the conversation and the
criterion of worth is as yet undetermined. Gadamer's ethnocentric project is
undergirded by an insulated diachronism that insists, as Habermas notes in
another context, on "the ontological priority of linguistic tradition before all
possible critique."[54] Taylor's repositioning of "fusion of horizons" as the outcome to be achieved through conjunctural conversations between critical
readers of different cultural formations disrupts and displaces Gadamer's
map of the "hermeneutic experience." In fact, it opens it up to the possibility
of a nonethnocentric critical discourse.

Given the desire for dialogism, Taylor's good intentions are too slippery
for his interlocutors. His implicit understanding that there's more here than

a "politics of recognition," which is only a first step for the conversation to take place, leads to a concomitant reciprocity of I's and We's that become polylogical given their formations in the context of nation making, which, no matter how veiled, is understood in the context of Canada, as I then understand it in the context of the United States; that is, a history hovers throughout the discussion. His interlocutors, however, panic over the emphasis given to collective groups' goals, which perhaps undermines the attachment to individual rights and individual freedom and the construction of citizenship on these grounds rather than collective goals. (See, for example, the comments by Steven Rockefeller and Michael Walzer in the volume.) The possibility of conversations that may give rise to uncontrolled "fused horizons" is a source of panic to them. And perhaps no one in the volume speaks to it more forcefully than Jürgen Habermas, while Rockefeller and Walzer retreat to notions of "universal identity as human beings," completely divorced of the nation-form that confers identities, whether they be a "matter of citizenship, gender, race, or ethnic origin."[55] The more sophisticated Habermas understands that the question of the nation-form cannot be obliterated. The nation-form cannot eschew its relationality to its subjects. Given this, then, one has to return to that which is fundamental for the nation, its legal system and its conferring of basic rights, which are individual and in contradiction to collective rights. The latter may be protected as cultural lifeworlds, but subject to the political culture of the nation-form, "the ethical integration of groups and subcultures with their collective identities must be uncoupled from the abstract political integration that includes all citizens equally."[56] What is that "abstract political integration"? Isn't that often made substantive and hence not abstract through the narrative of the nation-form, which continually strategizes to include or exclude citizenship and aestheticized "hermeneutic experience"? What does it mean to have "constitutional principles" interpreted or thoroughly distanced "from the perspective of the nation's historical experience" when the narrative of that very national experience is in question, as is the case in Canada, the United States, and the Americas?

Taylor sees the "common political culture" as something to be achieved, while Habermas takes it to be in place, resting on the constitutional rights and principles "form the fixed point of reference of any constitutional patriotism that situates the system of rights within the historical context of a legal community."[57] We get closer to Habermas's desire here, since it would appear that it is not so much the "nation's historical experience" in general and the formation of its subjects, as it is the "historical context of a legal community" that should prevail. I take this to suggest that it is the "historical legal community" that will have priority over any other notion or version of history. This is confirmed by the assertion that "in complex societies the citizenry as a whole can no longer be held together by a substantive consensus on values but only a consensus on the procedures for the legitimate enactment of laws and the legitimate exercise of power."[58] A strong proceduralism is the glue that will hold society together, not conversations over time that seek "fusion of horizons" as utopic possibility. In the age of poststructuralist thought, the question of universality will now reside in the rationality of the legal community.

In a sense, Habermas faults Taylor for too much philosophical thinking and not enough legalistic politics. At stake in the latter is the strong preservation of individual rights and freedom as the hallmark of citizenship. The swipes at poststructuralist thought that are taken by most in the book are conditioned by its deconstruction of the transcendental and sovereign subject on which "enlightened" modernity has depended for the maintenance of its self-contradictory empowered legitimacy and which subsequently makes it necessary to speak of two levels of integration, those that aspire to "our" political culture and those that remain in a "subpolitical level," that is, "ethnics" or, as Habermas refers to these, "lifeworlds" as a reconfiguration of pluralism now coded as multiculturalism. Consequently, the latter are misrecognized as culturally bounded in discrete forms and may claim the right to participate in the "political culture" by discarding "difference." What difference is at this level of discourse, I presume, is adjudicated by the modern liberal subject of the contingently prevailing political culture-in-law. What is citizenship continues to be on trial and, I suppose, will be juridically administered by the self-legitimated "political culture." While Taylor emphasizes the cultural discussion and postpones the political outcome, Habermas emphasizes the political legal culture and contains rather than postpones the cultural outcome. The former is portrayed as too philosophical and involved in questions of intersubjectivity; the latter ultimately and implicitly discards the intersubjective dimension except in a discussion of feminism, a version that appears to be already and conveniently homogenized by Habermas into his liberalism—a curious exception, to say the least, yet a minimalist gesture to the epistemological problems that feminism has raised so successfully.[59] That gesture remains too isolated from the a priori of legal history and its production of the "political culture" already in place. On the other hand, the "cultural politics of difference" is already embroiled in claims of the historical experience of the nation-making form, which is also a political culture whose adjudications have indeed been intersubjective throughout.[60] The clarity of thought in Habermas should not be underestimated, especially its apparent administrative resolutions in "the historical context of a legal community." It interpellates a historically constructed Anglo-America and those who have been able to seek protection and entitlement through that proceduralism. Insofar as the theorists and practitioners of the "cultural politics of difference," each in turn and formed around their historical constitutedness, have engaged in a dialogism with the proceduralist "center," we have not been able to produce a notion of the coalitional subject. White paranoia and panic have reached extreme proportions in California, as reflected in the negative adjudication of Rodney King's rights[61] and those of (im)migrants via the passage of Proposition 187 and of the upcoming (irony not intended) California *Civil Rights* Initiative.

Notes

1. Hannah Arendt, *Between Past and Future: Eight Exercises in Political Thought* (New York: Penguin Books, 1978), 6.

2. Ibid.

3. Ibid., 9.

4. Seyla Benhabib, *Situating the Self: Gender, Community and Postmodernism in Contemporary Ethics* (New York: Routledge, 1992), 205–7.

5. Simone de Beauvoir, *The Second Sex*, trans. H. M. Parshley (New York: Vintage Books, 1974).

6. Carlos Múñoz, *Youth, Identity, Power: The Chicano Movement* (London: Verso, 1989).

7. See Susan Faludi, *Backlash: The Undeclared War against American Women* (New York: Crown Publishers, 1991).

8. See Alison M. Jaggar, *Feminist Politics and Human Nature* (Totowa, N.J.: Rowan and Allanheld, 1983).

9. Cited in Arendt, *Between Past and Future*, 7.

10. Jacques Derrida, *Margins of Philosophy*, trans. Alan Bass (Chicago: University of Chicago Press, 1982).

11. Ibid., 329.

12. Gloria Anzaldúa, *Borderlands/La Frontera: The New Mestiza* (San Francisco: Spinsters/Aunt Lute, 1987).

13. Luce Irigaray, *Speculum of the Other Woman*, trans. Gillian C. Gill (Ithaca, N.Y.: Cornell University Press, 1985). For commentary on deconstruction's use of the feminine, see Rosi Braidotti, *Patterns of Dissonance: A Study of Women in Contemporary Philosophy*, trans. Elizabeth Guil (New York: Routledge, 1991); and Gayatri C. Spivak, "Displacement and the Discourse of Woman," *Displacement: Derrida and After*, ed. Mark Krupnick (Bloomington: Indiana University Press, 1983), 169–96.

14. See, for example, Judith Butler, *Gender Trouble: Feminism and the Subversion of Identity* (New York: Routledge, 1990); Nancy Fraser and Sandra Lee Bartky, *Revaluing French Feminism: Critical Essays on Difference, Agency & Culture* (Bloomington: Indiana University Press, 1992); and Toril Moi, *Sexual/Textual Politics* (London: Methuen, 1985).

15. Jean-Luc Nancy, "Cut Throat Son," *An Other Tongue*, ed. Alfred Ortega (Durham, N.C.: Duke University Press, 1994).

16. Ibid., 123.

17. Ibid.

18. Frantz Fanon, "The Fact of Blackness," in *Anatomy of Racism*, ed. David Theo Goldberg (Minneapolis: University of Minnesota Press, 1990), 120.

19. Ibid., 120, 124.

20. Jacques Derrida, *Writing and Difference*, trans. Alan Bass (Chicago: University of Chicago Press, 1978), 293.

21. Ibid., 292.

22. Ibid., 293.

23. Diana Fuss, *Essentially Speaking: Feminism, Nature and Difference* (New York: Routledge, 1989), 98.

24. Ibid., 103.

25. See Kimberlé Crenshaw, "Demarginalizing the Intersection of Race and Gender in Anti-discrimination Law, Feminist Theory, and Antiracist Politics," *Chicago Legal Forum* (1989).

26. Anzaldúa, *Borderlands/La Frontera*, 79–80.

27. M. Y. Mudimbe, *The Invention of Africa* (Bloomington: Indiana University Press, 1988), 5.

28. Chela Sandoval, "U.S. Third World Feminism: The Theory and Method of Oppositional Consciousness in the Postmodern World," *Genders* 10 (spring 1991): 14.

29. Aída Hurtado, cited in ibid., 14–15.

30. Cherríe Moraga and Gloria Anzaldúa, *This Bridge Called My Back: Writings by Radical Women of Color* (Watertown, Mass.: Persephone Press, 1981), xix.

31. Sandoval, "U.S. Third World Feminism," 15.

32. Moraga and Anzaldúa, *This Bridge Called My Back*, 127.

33. Sandoval, "U.S. Third World Feminism," 23.

34. Derrida, *Margins of Philosophy*, 19.

35. Benhabib, *Situating the Self*, 218.

36. Cornelius Castoriadis, *The Imaginary Institution of Society*, trans. Kathleen Blamey (Cambridge: MIT Press, 1987), 102–3.

37. Ibid., 106.

38. I use the term "transnational" as a mediating analytical category that enables a nexus for critical intervention across and between nation-states and opens up a ground for the critique of the representations, practices, and discourses that emerge in the conjunctural constitutiveness of historical subjects. This approach would beg the question of how one can generate a post-nationalist critical discourse. For further discussions of transnational critique see Frederick Buell, *National Culture and the New Global System* (Baltimore: Johns Hopkins University Press, 1994). For further discussion of "The New Cultural Politics of Difference," see Cornel West, *Keeping Faith: Philosophy and Race in America* (New York: Routledge, 1993), 3–32.

39. Etienne Balibar, "Is There a 'Neo-racism'?" in Etienne Balibar and Immanuel Wallerstein, *Race, Nation, Class: Ambiguous Identities* (London: Verso, 1991), 17–28; and Richard J. Herrnstein and Charles Murray, *The Bell Curve: Intelligence and Class Structure in American Life* (New York: Free Press, 1994).

40. Charles Taylor et al., *Multiculturalism and the Politics of Recognition* (Princeton, N.J.: Princeton University Press, 1994), 116–22. David Palumbo-Liu is congnizant of the fact that once a discourse such as multiculturalism makes a bid for hegemonic mediation of identity-in-difference, perhaps the best that minoritized intellectuals can do is to turn our critical mapping lens through it as well. Consequently, he calls for a critical multiculturalism. As he notes, ideologically, multiculturalism becomes a recodification of pluralism for the era of trans-

148   NORMA ALARCÓN

nationalisms and globalisms. See his edited anthology, *The Ethnic Canon: Histories, Institutions, and Interventions* (Minneapolis: University of Minnesota Press, 1995), 1–27.

41. See Michael Bérubé, "Disuniting America Again," in *Public Access: Literary Theory and American Cultural Politics* (London: Verso, 1994), 225–42.

42. Stuart Hall and Martin Jacques, eds., *New Times: The Changing Face of Politics in the 1990s* (London: Verso, 1990), 35.

43. Carl Gutiérrez-Jones makes a solid argument for the interfacing juncture of aesthetics and legal culture in *Rethinking the Borderlands: Between Chicano Culture and Legal Discourse* (Berkeley: University of California Press, 1995).

44. West, *Keeping Faith*, 30.

45. See Michael A. Bernstein and David E. Adler, eds., *Understanding American Economic Decline* (Cambridge: Cambridge University Press, 1994).

46. Taylor et al., *Multiculturalism and the Politics of Recognition*, 135.

47. Ibid., 42–43.

48. Ibid., 44.

49. Ibid., 68.

50. Ibid., 67.

51. Ibid., 68, 72.

52. Ibid., 62.

53. H. G. Gadamer, "The Hermeneutical Experience," in Joseph Margolis, ed., *Philosophy Looks at the Arts: Contemporary Readings in Aesthetics*, 3d. ed. (Philadelphia: Temple University Press, 1987), 501.

54. Cited in Christopher Norris, *Contest of Faculties: Philosophy and Theory after Deconstruction* (London: Methuen, 1985), 26.

55. Taylor et al., *Multiculturalism and the Politics of Recognition*, 88.

56. Ibid., 133–34.

57. Ibid., 134.

58. Ibid., 135.

59. Ibid., 115–17.

60. See Priscilla Wald, "Terms of Assimilation: Legislating Subjectivity in the Emerging Nation," in Amy Kaplan and Donald E. Pease, eds., *Cultures of United States Imperialism* (Durham, N.C.: Duke University Press, 1993), 59–84.

61. See Robert Gooding-Williams, ed., *Reading Rodney King, Reading Urban Uprising* (New York: Routledge, 1993).

CHAPTER NINE

Injury, Identity, Politics

WENDY BROWN

Taking enormous pleasure in the paradox, Stuart Hall tells this story of the postwar, postcolonial "breakup" of English identity:

> In the very moment when finally Britain convinced itself it had to decolonize, it had to get rid of them, we all came back home. As they hauled down the flag [in the colonies], we got on the banana boat and sailed right into London. . . . [T]hey had ruled the world for 300 years and, at last, when they had made up their minds to climb out of the role, at least the others ought to have stayed out there in the rim, behaved themselves, gone somewhere else, or found some other client state. But no, they had always said that this [London] was really home, the streets were paved with gold, and bloody hell, we just came to check out whether that was so or not.[1]

In Hall's mischievous account, the restructuring of collective identity and political practices required by postcoloniality did not remain in the hinterlands but literally, restively, came home to roost. The historical "others" of colonial identity cast free in their own waters sailed in to implode the center of the postcolonial metropoles, came to trouble the last vestiges of centered European identity with its economic and political predicates. They came to make havoc in the master's house after the master relinquished his military-political but not his cultural and metaphysical holdings as *the* metonymy of man.

Hall's narrative of the palace invasion by the newly released subjects might also be pressed into service as metaphor for another historical paradox of late twentieth-century collective and individual identity formation: in the very moment when modern liberal states fully realize their secularism (as Marx put it in "On the Jewish Question"), just as the mantle of abstract personhood is formally tendered to a whole panoply of those historically excluded from it by humanism's privileging of a single race, gender, and organization of sexuality, the marginalized reject the rubric of humanist inclusion and turn, at least in part, against its very premises. Refusing to be neutralized, to render the differences inconsequential, to be depoliticized as "lifestyles," "diversity," or "persons like any other," we have lately reformulated our historical exclusion as a matter of historically produced and politically rich *alterity*. Insisting that we are not merely positioned but fabricated by this history, we have at the same time insisted that our very production as marginal, deviant, or subhuman is itself constitutive of the centrality and legitimacy of the center, is itself what paves the center's streets with semiotic, political, and psychic gold. Just when polite liberal (not to mention, correct leftist) discourse ceased speaking of us as queers, colored girls, or natives, we began speaking of ourselves this way. Refusing the invitation to absorption, we insisted instead upon politicizing and working into cultural critique the very constructions that a liberalism increasingly exposed in its tacit operations of racial, sexual, and gender privilege was seeking to bring to a formal close.

These paradoxes of late-modern liberalism and colonialism, of course, are not a matter of simple historical accident—indeed, they are both incomplete and mutually constitutive to a degree that belies the orderly chronological scheme Hall and I have imposed on them in order to render them pleasurable ironies. Moreover, the ironies do not come to an end with the Jamaican postcolonials sailing into London, nor with the historically subordinated constructing an oppositional political culture and critique out of their exclusion from the family of Man. Even as the margins assert themselves as margins, the denaturalizing assault they perform on coherent collective identity in the center turns back on them to trouble their own. Even as it is being articulated, circulated, and lately institutionalized in a host of legal, political, and cultural practices, identity is unraveling—metaphysically, culturally, geopolitically, and historically—as rapidly as it is being produced. The same vacillation can be seen in the naturalistic legitimating narratives of collective identity as nationalism. Imploded within by the insurrectionary knowledges and political claims of historically subordinated cultures, and assaulted from without by the spectacular hybridities and supranational articulations of late twentieth-century global capitalism as well as crises of global ecology, nation formation, loosened from what retrospectively appears as a historically fleeting attachment to states, is today fervently being asserted in politico-cultural claims ranging from Islamic to deaf, indigenous to Gypsy, Serbian to queer.

Despite certain convergences, articulations, and parallels between such culturally disparate political formations in the late twentieth century, this essay does not consider the problematic of politicized identity on a global scale. Rather, as an argument for substantial historical and geopolitical specificity in an exploration of the problematic of political identity, this essay examines selected contradictory operations of politicized identity *within* late-modern democracy, considering politicized identity as both a production *and* a contestation of the political terms of liberalism, disciplinary-bureaucratic regimes, certain forces of global capitalism, and the demographic flows of postcoloniality, which together might be taken as constitutive of the contemporary North American political condition. In recent years, enough stalemated argument has transpired about the virtues and vices of something named identity politics to suggest the limited usefulness of a discussion of identity either in terms of the timeless metaphysical or linguistic elements of its constitution or in terms of the ethical-political rubric of good and evil. Beginning instead with the premise that the proliferation and politicization of identities in the United States is not a moral or even a political choice but a complex historical production, a more useful contribution from scholars might consist of elucidating something of the nature of this production, in order to locate within it both the openings and the perils for a radically democratic or counterhegemonic political project.

Many have lately asked how, given the totalizing, regulatory, and "othering" operations of identity in/as language, identity can avoid reiterating such investments in its ostensibly emancipatory mode.[2] I want to ask a similar question but in a historically specific cultural-political register, not because the linguistic frame is unimportant but because it is insufficient for discerning the character of politicized identity's problematic investments. Thus, my focus here will be on selected contradictory operations of politicized identity *within* late-modern democracy, considering politicized identity as both a production *and* a contestation of the political terms of liberalism, disciplinary-bureaucratic regimes, certain forces of global capitalism, and the demographic flows of postcoloniality, which together might be taken as constitutive of the contemporary North American political condition. The specific questions framing the work of this paper are these: First, given the subjectivizing conditions of identity production in a late-modern capitalist, liberal, and disciplinary-bureaucratic social order, how can reiteration of these production conditions be averted in identity's purportedly emancipatory project? In the specific context of contemporary liberal and disciplinary-bureaucratic discourse, what kind of political recognition can identity-based claims seek—and what kind can they be counted on to want—that will not resubordinate the subject that is itself historically subjugated through identity, through categories such as race or gender that emerged and circulated as terms of power to enact subordination? The question here is not *whether* denaturalizing political strategies subvert the subjugating force of naturalized identity formation, but *what kind* of politicization, produced out of and inserted into *what kind* of political context, might perform such subversion. Second, given the averred interest of politicized identity in achieving emancipatory political recognition in a post-humanist discourse, what are the logics of pain in the subject formation processes of late-modern society that might contain or subvert this aim? What are the particular constituents—specific to our time yet roughly generic for a diverse spectrum of identities—of identity's desire for recognition that seem as often to breed a politics of recrimination and rancor, of culturally dispersed paralysis and suffering, a tendency to reproach power rather than aspire to it, to disdain freedom rather than practice it? In short, where do the historically and culturally specific elements of politicized identity's investments in itself, and especially in its own history of suffering, come into conflict with the need to give up these investments in the pursuit of an emancipatory democratic project?

I approach these questions by offering first a highly selective account of the discursive historical context of identity politics' emergence in the United States and then elaborating, through reconsideration of Nietzsche's genealogy of the logics of *ressentiment*, the wounded character of politicized identity's desire within this context. This is not an essay about the general worth or accomplishments of the oppositional political formation called "identity politics." It is, rather, an exploration of the ways in which certain aspects of the specific genealogy of politicized identity are carried in the structure and temperament of its political demands, ways in which some of the emancipatory aims of politicized identity are subverted not only by the constraints of the political discourses in which its operations transpire, but by its own wounded attachments.

The tension between particularistic "I's" and a universal "we" in liberalism is sustainable as long as the constituent terms of the "I" remain unpoliticized— as long as the "I" itself remains unpoliticized on one hand, and the state (as the expression of the ideal of political universality) remains unpoliticized on the other. In other words, the latent conflict in liberalism between universal representation and individualism remains latent, remains unpoliticized, as long as stratifying powers in civil society remain naturalized, as long as the "I" remains politically unarticulated, as long as it is willing to have its freedom represented abstractly, in effect, to subordinate its "I-ness" to the abstract "we" represented by the universal community of the state. This subordination is achieved either by the "I" abstracting from itself in its political representation, thus trivializing its "difference" so as to remain part of the "we" (as in homosexuals who are "just like everyone else except for who we sleep with"), or by the "I" accepting its construction as a supplement, complement, or partial outsider to the "we" (as in the history of women being "concluded by their husbands," to use Blackstone's phrase, or homosexuals who are just "different," or Jews whose communal affiliations lie partly or wholly outside their national identity). The history of liberalism's management of its inherited and constructed "others" could be read as a history of variations on and vacillations between these two strategies.

The abstract character of liberal political membership and the ideologically naturalized character of liberal individualism together work against politicized identity formation.[3] A formulation of the political state and of citizenship that, as Marx put it in "On the Jewish Question," abstracts from the substantive conditions of our lives, works to prevent recognition or articulation of differences *as* political—as effects of power—in their very construction and organization; they are at most the stuff of divergent political or economic *interests*.[4] Equally important, to the extent that political membership in the liberal state involves abstracting from one's social being, it involves abstracting not only from the contingent productions of one's life circumstances but from the *identificatory* processes constitutive of one's social construction and position. We are invited to seek equal deference— equal blindness—but not equalizing *recognition* from the state, liberalism's universal moment.[5] Indeed, as Marx discerned in his critique of Hegel, the universality of the state is ideologically achieved by turning away from and thus depoliticizing, yet at the same time *presupposing*, our collective particulars, not by embracing them, let alone emancipating us from them.[6] In short, "the political" in liberalism is precisely not a domain for social identification: expected to recognize our political selves in the state, we are not led to expect deep recognition there.

While this détente between universal and particular within liberalism is potted with volatile conceits from the outset, it is rather thoroughly unraveled by two features of late-modernity, spurred by developments in liberalism's companion powers: capitalism and disciplinarity. On one side, the state loses even its guise of universality as it becomes ever more transparently invested in particular economic interests, political ends, and social formations—as it transmogrifies from a relatively minimalist, "night watchman" state to a heavily bureaucratized, managerial, fiscally enormous and highly interventionist welfare-warfare state, a transmogrification occasioned by the combined imperatives of capital and the autoproliferating characteristics of bureaucracy.[7] On the other side, the liberal subject is increasingly disinterred from substantive nation-state identification, not only by the individuating effects of liberal discourse itself but through the social effects of late twentieth-century economic and political life: deterritorializing demographic flows; the disintegration from within and invasion from without of family and community as (relatively) autonomous sites of social production and identification; consumer capitalism's marketing discourse in which individual (and subindividual) desires are produced, commodified, and mobilized as identities; and disciplinary productions of a fantastic array of behavior-based identities ranging from recovering alcoholic professionals to unrepentant crack mothers. These disciplinary productions work to conjure and regulate subjects through classificatory schemes, naming and normalizing social behaviors as social positions. Operating through what Foucault calls "an anatomy of detail," "disciplinary power" produces social identities (available for politicization because they are deployed for purposes of political regulation) that crosscut juridical identities based on abstract right. Thus, for example, the welfare state's production of welfare subjects—themselves subdivided through the socially regulated categories of motherhood, disability, race, age, and so forth—potentially produces political identity through these categories, produces identities *as* these categories.

In this story, the always imminent but increasingly politically manifest failure of liberal universalism to be universal—the transparent fiction of state universality—combines with the increasing individuation of social subjects through capitalist disinternments and disciplinary productions. Together, they breed the emergence of politicized identity rooted in disciplinary productions but oriented by liberal discourse toward protest against exclusion from a discursive formation of universal justice. This production, however, is not linear or even, but highly contradictory: while the terms of liberalism are part of the ground of production of a politicized identity that reiterates yet exceeds these terms, liberal discourse itself also continuously recolonizes political identity *as* political interest—a conversion that recasts politicized identity's substantive and often deconstructive cultural claims and critiques as generic claims of particularism endemic to universalist political culture. Similarly, disciplinary power manages liberalism's production of politicized subjectivity by neutralizing (re-depoliticizing) identity through normalizing practices. As liberal discourse converts political identity into essentialized private interest, disciplinary power converts interest into normativized social identity manageable by regulatory regimes. Thus, disciplinary power politically neutralizes entitlement claims generated by liberal individuation, while liberalism politically neutralizes rights claims generated by disciplinary identities.

Contemporary politicized identity contests the terms of liberal discourse insofar as it challenges liberalism's universal "we" as a strategic fiction of historically hegemonic groups and asserts liberalism's "I" as social—both relational and constructed by power—rather than contingent, private, or autarkic. Yet it reiterates the terms of liberal discourse insofar as it posits a sovereign and unified "I" that is disenfranchised by an exclusive "we." Indeed, politicized identity emerges and obtains its unifying coherence through the politicization of *exclusion* from an ostensible universal, as a protest against exclusion, a protest premised on the fiction of an inclusive/ universal community, a protest that reinstalls the humanist ideal insofar as it premises itself upon exclusion from it. Put the other way around, insofar as they are premised on exclusion from a universal ideal, politicized identities require that ideal, as well as their exclusion from it, for their own perpetuity as identities.[8]

   Politicized identity is also potentially reiterative of regulatory, disciplinary society in its configuration of a disciplinary subject. It is both produced by and potentially accelerates the production of that aspect of disciplinary society that "ceaselessly characterizes, classifies, and specializes," which works through "surveillance, continuous registration, perpetual assessment, and classification," through a social machinery "that is both immense and minute."[9] A recent example from the world of local politics makes clear politicized identity's imbrication in disciplinary power, as well as the way in which, as Foucault reminds us, disciplinary power "infiltrates" rather than replaces liberal juridical modalities.[10] Recently the city council of my town reviewed an ordinance, devised and promulgated by a broad coalition of identity-based political groups, which aimed to ban discrimination in employment, housing, and public accommodations on the basis of "sexual orientation, transsexuality, age, height, weight, personal appearance, physical characteristics, race, color, creed, religion, national origin, ancestry, disability, marital status, sex or gender."[11] Here is a perfect instance of the universal juridical ideal of liberalism and the normalizing principle of disciplinary regimes conjoined and taken up within the discourse of politicized identity. This ordinance—variously called the "purple hair ordinance" or the "ugly ordinance" by state and national news media—aims to count every difference as no difference, as part of the seamless whole, but also to count every potentially subversive rejection of culturally enforced norms as themselves normal, as normalizable, and as normativizable through law. Indeed, through the definitional, procedural, and remedies sections of this ordinance (e.g., "sexual orientation shall mean known or assumed homosexuality, heterosexuality, or bisexuality") persons are reduced to observable social attributes and practices; these are defined empirically, positivistically, as if their existence were intrinsic and factual, rather than the effect of discursive and institutional power; and these positivist definitions of persons as their attributes and practices are written into law, ensuring that persons describable according to them will now become regulated through them. Bentham couldn't have done it better. Indeed, here is a perfect instance of how the language of recognition becomes the language of unfreedom, how articulation in language, in the context of liberal and disciplinary discourse, becomes a vehicle of subordination through individualization, normalization, and regulation, even as it strives to produce visibility and acceptance. Here, also, is a perfect instance of the way in which differences that are the effects of social power are neutralized through their articulation as attributes and their circulation through liberal administrative discourse. What do we make of a document that renders as juridical equivalents the denial of employment or housing to an African American, an obese man, and a white middle-class youth festooned with tatoos and fuschia hair?

What I want to consider, though, is why this strikingly unemancipatory political project emerges from a potentially more radical critique of liberal juridical and disciplinary modalities of power. This ordinance, I want to suggest, is not simply misguided in its complicity with the rationalizing and disciplinary elements of late-modern culture; it is not simply naive with regard to the regulatory apparatus within which it operates. Rather, it is symp-

tomatic of a feature of politicized identity's *desire* within liberal-bureau-
cratic regimes, its foreclosure of its own freedom, its impulse to inscribe in
the law and in other political registers its historical and present pain rather
than conjure an imagined future of power to make itself. To see what this
symptom is a symptom of, we need to return once more to a schematic consideration of liberalism, this time in order to read it through Nietzsche's account of the complex logics of *ressentiment*.

Liberalism contains from its inception a generalized incitement to what
Nietzsche terms *ressentiment*, the moralizing revenge of the powerless, "the
triumph of the weak as weak."[12] This incitement to *ressentiment* inheres in a
constitutive paradox of liberalism between individual liberty and social
egalitarianism, a paradox that produces failure-turned-to-recrimination by
the subordinated, and guilt-turned-to-resentment by the "successful." However, it is not only the tension between freedom and equality, but also the
prior presumption of the self-reliant and self-made capacities of liberal subjects, conjoined with their unavowed dependence on and construction by a
variety of social relations and forces, that makes *all* liberal subjects, and not
only markedly disenfranchised ones, vulnerable to *ressentiment*. It is their
situatedness within power, their production by power, and liberal discourse's
denial of this situatedness and production that cast the liberal subject into
failure, the failure to make itself in the context of a discourse in which its
self-making is assumed, indeed, is its assumed nature. This failure, which
Nietzsche calls suffering, must either find a reason within itself (which re-
doubles the failure) or a site of external blame upon which to avenge its hurt
and redistribute its pain. Here is Nietzsche's account of this moment in the
production of *ressentiment*:

> For every sufferer instinctively seeks a cause for his suffering, more exactly,
> an agent; still more specifically a *guilty* agent who is susceptible to suffer-
> ing—in short, some living thing upon which he can on some pretext or
> other, vent his affects, actually or in effigy. . . . This . . . constitutes the actual
> physiological cause of *ressentiment*, vengefulness, and the like: a desire to
> deaden pain by means of affects . . . to deaden, by means of a more violent
> emotion of any kind, a tormenting, secret pain that is becoming unen-
> durable, and to drive it out of consciousness at least for the moment: for that
> one requires an affect, as savage an affect as possible, and, in order to excite
> that, any pretext at all.[13]

Ressentiment in this context is a triple achievement: it produces an affect
(rage, righteousness) that overwhelms the hurt; it produces a culprit re-

sponsible for the hurt; and it produces a site of revenge to displace the hurt (a place to inflict hurt as the sufferer has been hurt). Together these operations both ameliorate (in Nietzsche's terms, "anaesthetize") and externalize what is otherwise "unendurable."

Now, what I want to suggest is that in a culture already streaked with the pathos of *ressentiment* for these reasons, there are several characteristics of late-modern postindustrial societies that accelerate and expand the conditions of its production. My listing will necessarily be highly schematic: First, the phenomenon William Connolly names "increased global contingency" combines with the expanding pervasiveness and complexity of domination by capital and bureaucratic state and social networks to create an unparalleled individual powerlessness over the fate and direction of one's own life, intensifying the experiences of impotence, dependence, and gratitude inherent in liberal capitalist orders and constitutive of *ressentiment*.[14] Second, the steady desacralization of all regions of life—what Weber called disenchantment, what Nietzsche called the death of god—would seem to add yet another reversal to Nietzsche's genealogy of *ressentiment* as perpetually available to "alternation of direction." In Nietzsche's account, the ascetic priest deployed notions of "guilt, sin, sinfulness, depravity and damnation" to "direct the ressentiment of the less severely afflicted sternly back upon themselves ... and in this way [exploited] the bad instincts of all sufferers for the purpose of self-discipline, self-surveillance, and self-overcoming."[15] However, the desacralizing tendencies of late modernity undermine the efficacy of this deployment and turn suffering's need for exculpation back toward a site of external agency.[16] Third, the increased fragmentation, if not disintegration, of all forms of association until recently not organized by the commodities market—communities, churches, families—and the ubiquitousness of the classificatory, individuating schemes of disciplinary society combine to produce an utterly *unrelieved* individual, one without insulation from the inevitable failure entailed in liberalism's individualistic construction. In short, the characteristics of late-modern secular society, in which individuals are buffeted and controlled by global configurations of disciplinary and capitalist power of extraordinary proportions and are at the same time nakedly individuated, stripped of reprieve from relentless exposure and accountability for themselves, together add up to an incitement to *ressentiment* that might have stunned even the finest philosopher of its occasions and logics. Starkly accountable yet dramatically impotent, the late-modern liberal subject quite literally seethes with *ressentiment*.

Enter politicized identity, now conceivable in part as both product of and

"reaction" to this condition, where "reaction" acquires the meaning Nietzsche ascribed to it, namely, an effect of domination that reiterates impotence, or, a substitute for action, for power, for self-affirmation that reinscribes incapacity, powerlessness, and rejection. For Nietzsche, *ressentiment*
itself is rooted in "reaction"—the substitution of reasons, norms, and ethics
for deeds—and suggests that not only moral systems but identities themselves take their bearings in this reaction. As Tracy Strong reads this element
of Nietzsche's thought:

> Identity . . . does not consist of an active component, but is reaction to some-
> thing outside; action in itself, with its inevitable self-assertive qualities, must
> then become something evil, since it is identified with that against which one
> is reacting. The will to power of slave morality must constantly reassert that
> which gives definition to the slave: the pain he suffers by being in the world.
> Hence any attempt to escape that pain will merely result in the reaffirmation
> of painful structures.[17]

If *ressentiment*'s "cause" is suffering, its "creative deed" is the reworking of
this pain into a negative form of action, the "imaginary revenge" of what
Nietzsche terms "natures denied the true reaction, that of deeds."[18] This revenge is achieved through the imposition of suffering "on whatever does not
feel wrath and displeasure as he does"[19] (accomplished especially through the
production of guilt), through the establishment of suffering as the measure
of social virtue, and through casting strength and good fortune ("privilege,"
as we say today) as self-recriminating, as its own indictment in a culture of
suffering: "it is disgraceful to be fortunate, there is too much misery."[20]

But in its attempt to displace its suffering, identity structured by *ressentiment* at the same time becomes invested in its own subjection. This investment lies not only in its discovery of a site of blame for its hurt will, not only
in its acquisition of recognition through its history of subjection (a recognition predicated on injury, now righteously revalued), but also in the satisfac-
tions of revenge that ceaselessly reenact even as they redistribute the injuries
of marginalization and subordination in a liberal discursive order that alternately denies the very possibility of these things or blames those who experience them for their own condition. Identity politics structured by *ressentiment* reverses without subverting this blaming structure: it does not subject
to critique the sovereign subject of accountability that liberal individualism
presupposes, nor the economy of inclusion and exclusion that liberal universalism establishes. Thus, politicized identity that presents itself as a self-
affirmation now appears as the opposite, as predicated on and requiring its
sustained rejection by a "hostile external world."[21]

Insofar as what Nietzsche calls slave morality produces identity in reaction to power, insofar as identity rooted in this reaction achieves its moral superiority by reproaching power and action themselves as evil, identity structured by this ethos becomes deeply invested in its own impotence, even while it seeks to assuage the pain of its powerlessness through its vengeful moralizing, through its wide distribution of suffering, through its reproach of power as such. Politicized identity, premised on exclusion and fueled by the humiliation and suffering imposed by its historically structured impotence in the context of a discourse of sovereign individuals, is as likely to seek generalized political paralysis, to feast on generalized political impotence, as it is to seek its own or collective liberation through empowerment. Indeed, it is more likely to punish and reproach—"punishment is what revenge calls itself; with a hypocritical lie it creates a good conscience for itself"—than to find venues of self-affirming action.[22]

But contemporary politicized identity's desire is not only shaped by the extent to which the sovereign will of the liberal subject, articulated ever more nakedly by disciplinary individuation and capitalist disinternments, is dominated by late twentieth-century configurations of political and economic powers. It is shaped as well by the contemporary problematic of history itself, by the late-modern rupture of history as a narrative, history as ended because it has lost its end, a rupture that paradoxically produces an immeasurable heaviness to history. As the grim experience of reading *Discipline and Punish* makes clear, there is a sense in which the gravitational force of history is multiplied at precisely the moment that history's narrative coherence and objectivist foundation are refuted. As the problematic of power in history is resituated from subject positioning to subject construction, as power is seen to operate spatially, infiltrationally, "microphysically" rather than only temporally—permeating every heretofore designated "interior" *space* in social lives and individuals—as the erosion of historical metanarratives takes with them both laws of history and the futurity such laws purported to assure, as the presumed continuity of history is replaced with a sense of its violent, contingent, and ubiquitous *force*, history becomes that which has weight but no trajectory, mass but no coherence, force but no direction; it is war without ends or end. Thus, the extent to which "dead generations weigh like a nightmare on the brains of the living" is today unparalleled even as history itself disintegrates as a coherent category or practice. We know ourselves to be saturated by history, we feel the extraordinary force of its determinations; we are also steeped in a discourse of its insignificance,

INJURY, IDENTITY, POLITICS   161

and above all, we know that history will no longer (always already did not) act as our redeemer.

I raise the question of history because, in thinking about late-modern politicized identity's structuring by *ressentiment*, I have thus far focused on its foundation in the sufferings of a subordinated sovereign subject. But Nietzsche's account of the logic of *ressentiment* is also tethered to that feature of the will which is stricken by history, which rails against time itself, which cannot "will backwards," which cannot exert its power over the past— either as a specific set of events or as time itself:

> Willing liberates but what is it that puts even the liberator himself in fetters? "It was"—that is the name of the will's gnashing of teeth and most secret melancholy. Powerless against what has been done, he is an angry spectator of all that is past. . . . He cannot break time and time's covetousness, that is the will's loneliest melancholy.[23]

Although Nietzsche appears here to be speaking of the will as such, Zarathustra's own relationship to the will as a "redeemer of history" makes clear that this "angry spectatorship" can with great difficulty be reworked as a perverse kind of mastery, a mastery that triumphs over the past by reducing its power, by remaking the present against the terms of the past—in short, by a project of self-transformation that arrays itself against its own genealogical consciousness. In contrast with the human ruin he sees everywhere around him—"fragments and limbs and dreadful accidents"—it is Zarathustra's own capacity to discern and to make a future that spares him from a rancorous sensibility, from crushing disappointment in the liberatory promise of his will:

> The now and the past on earth—alas, my friends, that is what *I* find most unendurable; and I should not know how to live if I were not also a seer of that which must come. A seer, a willer, a creator, a future himself and a bridge to the future—and alas, also as it were, a cripple at this bridge: all this is Zarathustra.[24]

Nietzsche here discerns both the necessity and the near impossibility—the extraordinary and fragile achievement—of formulating oneself as a creator of the future and a bridge to the future in order to appease the otherwise inevitable rancor of the will against time, in order to redeem the past by lifting the weight of it, by reducing the scope of its determinations. "And how could I bear to be a man if man were not also a creator and guesser of riddles and redeemer of accidents?"[25]

Of course, Zarathustra's exceptionality in what he is willing to confront and bear, in his capacities to overcome in order to create, is Nietzsche's device for revealing us to ourselves. The ordinary will, steeped in the economy of slave morality, devises means "to get rid of his melancholy and to mock his dungeon," means that reiterate the cause of the melancholy, that continually reinfect the narcissistic wound to its capaciousness inflicted by the past. "Alas," says Nietzsche, "every prisoner becomes a fool; and the imprisoned will redeems himself foolishly."[26] From this foolish redemption—foolish because it does not resolve the will's rancor but only makes a world in its image—is born the wrath of revenge:

> "that which was" is the name of the stone [the will] cannot move. And so he moves stones out of wrath and displeasure, and he wreaks revenge on whatever does not feel wrath and displeasure as he does. Thus the will, the liberator, took to hurting; and on all who can suffer he wreaks revenge for his inability to go backwards. This . . . is what *revenge* is: the will's ill will against time and its "it was."[27]

Revenge as a "reaction," a substitute for the capacity to act, produces identity as both bound to the history that produced it and as a reproach to the present that embodies that history. The will that "took to hurting" in its own impotence against its past becomes (in the form of an identity whose very existence is due to heightened consciousness of the immovability of its "it was," its history of subordination) a will that makes not only a psychological but a political practice of revenge, a practice that reiterates the existence of an identity whose present past is one of insistently unredeemable injury. This past cannot be redeemed *unless* the identity ceases to be invested in it, and it cannot cease to be invested in it without giving up its identity as such, thus giving up its economy of avenging and at the same time perpetuating its hurt—"when he then stills the pain of the wound, he at the same time reinfects the wound."[28]

In its emergence as a protest against marginalization or subordination, politicized identity thus becomes attached to its own exclusion both because it is premised on this exclusion for its very existence as identity, and because the formation of identity at the site of exclusion, as exclusion, augments or "alters the direction of the suffering" entailed in subordination or marginalization by finding a site of blame for it. But in so doing, it installs its pain over its unredeemed history in the very foundation of its political claim, in its demand for recognition as identity. In locating a site of blame for its powerlessness over its past—a past of injury, a past as a hurt will—and locating a "reason" for the "unendurable pain" of social powerlessness in the present, it converts this reasoning into an ethicizing politics, a politics of recrimination that seeks to avenge the hurt even while it reaffirms it, discursively codifies it.

Politicized identity thus enunciates itself, makes claims for itself, only by en-
trenching, restating, dramatizing, and inscribing its pain in politics and can
hold out no future—for itself or others—that triumphs over this pain. The
loss of historical direction, and with it the loss of futurity characteristic of
the late-modern age, is thus homologically refigured in the structure of desire of the dominant political expression of the age—identity politics. In the
same way, the generalized political impotence produced by the ubiquitous
yet discontinuous networks of late-modern political and economic power is
reiterated in the investments of late-modern democracy's primary oppositional political formations.

   What might be entailed in transforming these investments in an effort to
fashion a more radically democratic and emancipatory political culture?
One avenue of exploration may lie in Nietzsche's counsel on the virtues of
"forgetting," for if identity structured in part by *ressentiment* resubjugates itself through its investment in its own pain, through its refusal to make itself
in the present, memory is the house of this activity and this refusal. Yet
erased histories and historical invisibility are themselves such integral elements of the pain inscribed in most subjugated identities that the counsel of
forgetting, at least in its unreconstructed Nietzschean form, seems inappropriate if not cruel.[29] Indeed, it is more likely that we have reached a pass
where we ought to part with Nietzsche, whose skills as diagnostician usually
reach the limits of their political efficacy in his privileging of individual
character and capacity over the transformative possibilities of collective political invention, in his remove from the refigurative possibilities of political
conversation or transformative cultural practices. For if I am right about the
problematic of pain installed at the heart of many contemporary contradictory demands for political recognition, all that such pain may long for more
than revenge is the chance to be heard into a certain reprieve, recognized
into self-overcoming, incited into possibilities for triumphing over, and
hence losing, itself.

   Our challenge, then, would be to configure a radically democratic political culture that can sustain such a project in its midst without being overtaken by it, and without abetting the steady slide of political into therapeutic
discourse, even as we acknowledge the elements of suffering and healing we
might be negotiating. What if it were possible to incite a slight shift in the
character of political expression and political claims common to much
politicized identity? What if we sought to supplant the language of
"being"—with its defensive closure on identity, its insistence on the fixity of
position, its equation of social with moral positioning—with the language

of "wanting"? What if we were to rehabilitate the memory of desire within identificatory processes, the moment in desire—either "to have" or "to be"—prior to its wounding?[30] What if "wanting to be" or "wanting to have" were taken up as modes of political speech that could destabilize the formulation of identity as fixed position, as entrenchment by history, and as having necessary moral entailments, even as they affirm "position" and "history" as that which makes the speaking subject intelligible and locatable, as that which contributes to a hermeneutics for adjudicating desires? If every "I am" is something of a resolution of desire into fixed and sovereign identity, then this project might involve not only learning to speak but to *read* "I am" this way, as in motion, as temporal, as not-I, as deconstructible according to a genealogy of want rather than as fixed interests or experiences.[31] The subject understood as an effect of an (ongoing) genealogy of desire, including the social processes constitutive of, fulfilling, or frustrating desire, is in this way revealed as neither sovereign nor conclusive even as it is affirmed as an "I." Might such a deconstruction, paradoxically, be that which reopens a desire for futurity where Nietzsche saw it inevitably foreclosed by the logics of rancor and *ressentiment*?

Such a slight shift in the character of the political discourse of identity eschews the kinds of ahistorical or utopian turns against identity politics made by a nostalgic and broken humanist left as well as the reactionary and disingenuous assaults on politicized identity tendered by the right. Rather than opposing or seeking to transcend identity investments, the replacement—even the admixture—of the language of "being" with "wanting" would seek to exploit politically a recovery of the more expansive moments in the genealogy of identity formation, a recovery of the moment prior to its own foreclosure against its want, prior to the point at which its sovereign subjectivity is established through such foreclosure and through eternal repetition of its pain. How might democratic discourse itself be invigorated by such a shift from ontological claims to these kinds of more expressly political ones, claims that, rather than dispensing blame for an unlivable present, inhabit the necessarily agonistic theater of discursively forging an alternative future?

Notes

1. Stuart Hall, "The Local and the Global," in *Culture, Globalization, and the World System: Contemporary Conditions for the Representation of Identity*, ed. Anthony King (Albany: State University of New York Press, 1989), 24.

2. "An identity is established in relation to a series of differences that have become socially recognized. These differences are essential to its being. If they did not coexist as differences, it

would not exist in its distinctness and solidity.... Identity requires difference in order to be, and it converts difference into otherness in order to secure its own self-certainty" (William Connolly, *Identity/Difference: Democratic Negotiations of Political Paradox* [Ithaca, N.Y.: Cornell University Press, 1991], 64). I cite from Connolly rather than the more obvious Derrida because Connolly is exemplary of the effort *within* political theory to think about the political problem of identity working heuristically with its linguistic operation. I cite from Connolly as well because the present essay is in some ways an extension of a conversation begun at a 1991 American Political Science Association roundtable discussion of his book. In that discussion, noting that Connolly identified late modernity as producing certain problems for identity but did not historicize politicized identity itself, I called for such a historicization. To the degree that the present essay is my own partial response to that call, it—as the footnotes make clear—is indebted to Connolly's book and that public occasion of its discussion. A short list of others who have struggled to take politicized identity through and past the problem of political exclusion and political closure might include Stuart Hall, Trinh T. Minh-ha, Homi Bhabha, Paul Gilroy, Aiwah Ong, Judith Butler, Gayatri Spivak, and Anne Norton.

3. John Locke's *Letter on Toleration* (1689) signals this development in intellectual history. The three-hundred-year process of eliminating first the property qualification and then race and gender qualifications in European and North American constitutional states heralds its formal political achievement.

4. Karl Marx, "On the Jewish Question," in *The Marx-Engels Reader,* 2d ed., ed. R. Tucker (New York: W. W. Norton, 1974), 34.

5. John Locke, *Letter on Toleration*; John Stuart Mill, *On Liberty;* George Kateb, "Democratic Individuality and the Claims of Politics," *Political Theory* 12:3 (August 1984).

6. In "On the Jewish Question," Marx argues: "Far from abolishing these *effective* differences [in civil society, the state] exists only so far as they are presupposed; it is conscious of being a political state and it manifests its universality only in *opposition* to these elements" (*The Marx-Engels Reader,* 33). See also Marx's *Critique of Hegel's Philosophy of Right,* ed. J. O'Malley (Cambridge: Cambridge University Press, 1970), 91, 116.

7. Jürgen Habermas's *Legitimation Crisis,* trans. T. McCarthy (Boston: Beacon Press, 1975), and James O'Connor's *Fiscal Crisis of the State* (New York: St. Martin's Press, 1973) remain two of the most compelling narratives of this development. Also informing this claim are Max Weber's discussion of bureaucracy and rationalization in *Economy and Society,* and Sheldon Wolin's discussion of the "megastate" in *The Presence of the Past,* as well as the researches of Claus Offe, Bob Jessop, and Fred Block.

8. As Connolly argues, politicized identity also reiterates the structure of liberalism in its configuration of a sovereign, unified, accountable individual. Connolly urges, although it is not clear what would motivate identity's transformed orientation, a different configuration of identity—one that understands itself as contingent, relational, contestatory, and social. See Connolly, *Identity/Difference,* especially pp. 171–84.

9. Michel Foucault, *Discipline and Punish,* trans. A. Sheridan (New York: Vintage Books, 1979), 209, 212.

10. Ibid., 206.

11. From a draft of "An Ordinance of the City of Santa Cruz Adding Chapter 9.83 to the Santa Cruz Municipal Code Pertaining to the Prohibition of Discrimination" (1991).

12. A number of political theorists have advanced this argument. For a cogent account, see Connolly, *Identity/Difference,* 21–27.

13. Friedrich Nietzsche, *On the Genealogy of Morals,* trans. W. Kaufmann and P. J. Hollingdale (New York: Random House, 1967), 127.

14. Connolly, *Identity/Difference,* 24–26.

15. Ibid., 128.

16. A striking example of this is the way that contemporary natural disasters, such as the 1989 earthquake in California or the 1992 hurricanes in Florida and Hawaii, produce popular and media discourse about relevant state and federal agencies (e.g., the Federal Emergency Management Agency [FEMA]) that come close to displacing onto the agencies themselves responsibility for the suffering of the victims.

17. Tracy Strong, *Friedrich Nietzsche and the Politics of Transfiguration*, expanded edition (Berkeley: University of California, 1988), 242.

18. Nietzsche, *Genealogy of Morals*, 36.

19. Friedrich Nietzsche, *Thus Spoke Zarathustra*, in *The Portable Nietzsche*, ed. W. Kaufmann (New York: Penguin Books, 1954), 252.

20. Nietzsche, *Genealogy of Morals*, 124.

21. Ibid., 34.

22. Nietzsche, *Thus Spoke Zarathustra*, 252.

23. Ibid., 251.

24. Ibid., 250–51.

25. Ibid., 251.

26. Ibid.

27. Ibid., 252.

28. Nietzsche, *Genealogy of Morals*, 126. In words that could easily characterize the rancorous quality of many contemporary institutions and gatherings—academic, political, cultural—in which politicized identity is strongly and permissibly at play, Nietzsche offers an elaborate account of this replacement of pain with a "more violent emotion," which is the stock-in-trade of "the suffering": "The suffering are one and all dreadfully eager and inventive in discovering occasions for painful affects; they enjoy being mistrustful and dwelling on nasty deeds and imaginary slights; they scour the entrails of their past and present for obscure and questionable occurrences that offer them the opportunity to revel in tormenting suspicions and to intoxicate themselves with the poison of their own malice: they tear open their oldest wounds, they bleed from long-healed scars, they make evildoers out of their friends, wives, children, and whoever else stands closest to them. 'I suffer: someone must be to blame for it'—thus thinks every sickly sheep" (127).

29. This point has been made by many, but for a recent, quite powerful phenomenological exploration of the relationship between historical erasure and lived identity, see Patricia Williams, *The Alchemy of Race and Rights* (Cambridge: Harvard University Press, 1991).

30. Jesse Jackson's 1988 "Keep hope alive" presidential campaign strikes me as having sought to configure the relationship between injury, identity, and desire in just this way and to have succeeded in forging a "rainbow coalition" *because* of the idiom of futurity it employed—want, hope, desires, dreams—among those whose modality during the 1980s had often been rancorous.

31. In Trinh T. Minh-ha's formulation, "to seek is to lose, for seeking presupposes a separation between the seeker and the sought, the continuing me and the changes it undergoes" ("Not You/Like You: Post-Colonial Women and the Interlocking Questions of Identity and Difference," *Inscriptions* 3–4 [1988]: 72).

CHAPTER TEN

Multiculturalism as Political Strategy

CYNTHIA HAMILTON

The intellectual discourse on multiculturalism has focused on the nature of representations of history, culture, and society. Although the objective is one of a general rejection of approaches that present homogeneous and monolithic interpretations, what has been undertaken is no less a task than resisting the commodification of culture projected by the image-making industries of film, TV, and advertising. However, what multicultural writers offer as alternative vision often comes in a particularized form, one that relies on individualized rather than group representations.

Focusing on the conceptual character and challenge of "multiculturalism" has obscured its important political (and policy) function. Universities, governments, corporations all have policies governing multiculturalism in hiring, curriculum, and so on. Can we assume that the objectives of scholars and those of institutions diverge? It might be useful for us to begin to consider the ways in which multiculturalism has been used as an institutional practice to obscure and thereby help preserve existing relations of domination and power. Used this way, multiculturalism redirects—even refashions—social conflict regarding racial inequality. Without discounting the political work and objectives of civil rights reformers, Kristin Bumiller, in her book *The Civil Rights Society,* explores the role of law in shaping/reshaping social conflict. In her discussion of the results of the constitutional revolution that laid the basis for antidiscriminatory law in the post-Civil War period, she acknowledges that "The 'Negro question' became part of a strategy for enlarging the base of federal control."[1] She concludes that antidiscrimination ideology and protective legislation may perpetuate patterns of behavior that maintain discriminatory practice. "Instead of providing a tool to lessen inequality, legal mechanisms, which create the legal identity of the discrimination victim, maintain divisions between the powerful and powerless by means that are obscured by the ideology of equal protection."[2] Similarly, the current use of multiculturalism obscures the historical and ideological role of race. By treating race and ethnicity interchangeably, we lose sight of the historic use of race and ethnicity as a cover for relations of economic domination. In fact, some might argue, little has changed since the turn of the century when industrialists like Henry Ford used race as a mechanism of control and domination by employing Blacks on the assembly line as a way of reminding white workers that he alone would control relations on the job. A similar objective is expressed by Thornton Bradshaw, the late chairman of the board of Atlantic Richfield Company, in explaining his reasons for relocation of the company headquarters from New York to Los Angeles:

> The United States for a long time consisted of fairly rigid groups characterized by the farmer, the small businessman, the New York intellectual, the Jews, the Hamtramack Polish. They were expected to act as groups. That has changed. The West is now the place where history is being made. It's due largely to radio and television. We're developing a common culture. We are no longer these groups bound together. We are individuals. . . . This kind of breaking out, that's what California and the West represent.[3]

The objective, for both Ford and Bradshaw, was to move away from any basis for group identification and toward individualized notions to prevent the formation of distinct cultural group formations by maintaining flux and instability. The workplace of the early twentieth century became the arena in which culture in America was shaped and reshaped. It was and remains the stage on which "differences" are erased or elaborated. When is "multiculturalism" a tool for change? How has it been used to manipulate change in the interest of existing relations of domination? A review of the history of culture in the workplace may help to provide answers.

Culture has always been a process. For immigrants newly arrived in the United States, the culture of their past had to prove useful in their struggle to adjust to urban life and factory work or be discarded. Therefore, ethnic cultures would succumb to the homogenization process that substituted

"Americanization." Only in times of distress do we see elements of ethnic culture being called up as a defense or a tool to fight back. For Black Americans, culture was linked to a material base, to community formations; culture was an essential tool of resistance because it defined the terms of solidarity. In the twentieth century, in urban communities, culture provided a balance for Blacks living with the self-effacement of Jim Crow; culture was an essential counterpoint to the dominant society's debasement and insults, which denied Blacks any social or human worth.

Work and the New "Culture"

In his essay "Racism & Culture," Frantz Fanon describes what he calls the doctrine of "cultural hierarchy."[4] Racism that is phenotypically determined, he says, is transformed into cultural racism in which certain forms of existing, not individual men, become the object of racism. He also says that racism "vitiates American culture."[5] Therefore we get a complete distortion of the many cultures present in the society. By looking at the role of culture in the workplace, we are able to see how this cultural hierarchy is established and how the ruling class achieves a harmony of economic relations and ideology.

Resistance was a natural by-product of culture for those lowest on the economic scale. For many new immigrants to the cities, which included many Black American migrants from the South, their cultures were a result of nonindustrial settings and thereby gave legitimacy to alternative work styles and values. Therefore a "work ethic" had to be imposed. To accomplish this, employers fashioned an environment that gave the appearance of recognizing ethnic cultures. The workplace forged its own culture from a synthesis of stereotypes about ethnic cultures.

The "middle-class, white" ideal is therefore a fiction created in opposition to the multitude of ethnic fictions that dominated the late nineteenth century. For example, a review of the characteristics attributed to immigrant groups reflects a "pecking order" that could be identified in industry and was reproduced in housing and social relations and later marked occupational mobility. Of Germans it was said that "they are a stable group, property/home owners who send their children to school; thrifty, frugal, industrious, and productive."[6] Germans easily assimilated into local culture and politics and were for the most part committed to Bourbon Democracy or stalwart Republicanism. Most belonged to the Lutheran church, but the few Catholics among them dominated the Roman church hierarchy. Poles, on the other hand, were described as "ignorant newcomers; generally considered thrifty and industrious, somewhat less stable than the Germans in times of unemployment, given to quarreling and pilfering."[7] Italians, almost from the beginning, were categorized as itinerant laborers, moving with the seasons in search of work with railroad construction gangs or on the levees of New Orleans. They were described as "untidy in their habits but not destructive; ignorant of English and American methods and technology; suited only for common labor; they were prone to quarreling among themselves and resorted to violence; there was a natural disposition to laziness and they drank too much."[8] Hungarians did not fare much better. Although they were considered industrious and honest, it was said that "Hungarians chose to live in wretched housing. Their habits of cleanliness, regardless of the environment or their personal means, left much to be desired. According to one investigator, they were just too interested in saving as much of their earnings as possible so that they could take their savings back to Hungary."[9] Lastly, the Greeks were said to be even more unstable than Italians and too volatile to accept industrial discipline.[10]

Thus we find that particular ethnic groups were the "favorites" in certain industries. The knitting industry relied heavily on German and Polish girls because "They appeared to have a particular aptitude to the work."[11] Employers in the ice business preferred Poles and Swedes. Railroad bosses preferred "hoboes . . . they can do four or five times the work a gang of Greeks or Bulgarians can do." Korman found that Pabst Brewing Company staffed most of its departments with Germans and hired non-Germans, usually Polish girls, only for the most unskilled tasks in the bottling department. An Italian straw boss in the chipping room of the foundry at International Harvester made sure his department was completely Italian, while a Scottish-born foreman who had worked for about fifty years in International Harvester's foundry believed Poles made the best workers in the department, even better than his own countrymen. All of these examples are from Milwaukee and reflect the composition of the city and the amount of time each group had spent in the area. The patterns, however, were repeated in city after city throughout the United States. Responses to work obviously varied with the circumstances of each group; however, industrialists used these responses to work as a way of generalizing cultures; they explained discontent and conflict in terms of pathological tendencies or innate inadequacies of the groups themselves.

The intentions of immigrants on arrival in the United States certainly would affect their approach to work. Those who saw their stay as temporary would respond quite differently than those who intended to make their homes permanently in new lands. On a mass scale this is quite apparent. As immigrants began to see themselves in a new light and view their status differently in America, the behavior they exhibited changed. They became more concerned with the permanent benefits of work and thus forced employers to change both their attitudes and the work conditions.

The need to inculcate the new work ethic was essential in the United States for the development of capitalist productive relations. Therefore, cultural habits and attitudes (good and bad) were incorporated or transformed by industrialists in an effort to maintain control.

Culture is not a static set or pattern of social relations, beliefs, and attitudes. This becomes clear in looking at the experience of millions of immigrants newly arrived in the United States. In their struggle to adjust to urban life and factory work, the baggage of the past had to prove useful or be discarded. Some immigrants came to the United States with factory experience; others were in fact transplanted urbanites. When these two conditions existed, the newcomer found him/herself at an advantage. But for all immigrants the very process of being transplanted into a new environment without the security of tradition and of that which is familiar and necessary for self-development meant that culture would take on new dimensions and meaning.

The struggle for survival among immigrants was plagued by prejudice. Each successive wave of immigrants was confronted by a form of institutional racism. The Irish, Catholics, Chinese, Italians each faced the contradiction of, on the one hand, needing to preserve their communities—rooted in common language, descent, and custom—and, on the other, feeling the pressure to deny these ties and be accepted as "Americans." Work became the central focus of all political, social, cultural, and economic concerns. It was no longer just a means to other ends. Work had meaning in the new industrial society, in and for itself. It determined what men were, could be, or hoped to be. Therefore, cultural habits and social relations could no longer simply be taken for granted. All traditions had to pass the test of function in a new environment. Social norms had to prove their usefulness in the work arena. For example, company housing and even home ownership did not meet with immediate success with all immigrants. Many preferred the boarding system, not only because of the lack of expense, but also because it provided social relief. For men, many of whom were in the United States without family, it was a surrogate structure. Still others, of course, were simply trapped by the nexus of poverty, which landlords made worse by allowing overcrowded housing to disintegrate on top of its inhabitants.

Culture posed the most serious threat to management dominance. In response, industry had to find ways of involving itself in the personal lives of workers and did so by implementing everything from punitive measures to prevent worker cooperation to wage incentives, welfare programs (like housing and social engineering), and language training.

In many instances, industries were able to reinforce negative work patterns for their own ends as well. For example, steel and railroad industries found themselves, in the period before industrial organization, paradoxically encouraging irregular and undisciplined behavior *off* the job; their workers—men—lived in company boarding arrangements where they had to look outside for food, amusement, and the small comforts of home. These men were completely rootless, with the factory as their only common frame of reference. Without community, wife, or family, they were easy sources of scab and low-wage labor.

On the job, however, industries found undisciplined behavior disruptive. Iron manufacturers resorted to fines for drinking, but could never resolve the problem of absenteeism. They also found it necessary to institutionalize many traditional customs to encourage and ensure good work. Festivals and parades could not be prevented, so they were incorporated by industry and used to celebrate the completion of a product or the construction of a new facility, or to commemorate management. Industries simply made themselves the center of traditional rituals.

The rituals of the "Goose Egg" (heavy drinking) and "Blue Monday" (traditionally practiced by skilled workers and artisans as a day off for sharpening tools) plagued industry most. And in some cases the only solution was new technology and improved machinery, which would make these men expendable. We see here a clear connection between technological advance and the owners' desire for control in industry.

The destruction of the cultural autonomy of ethnic groups was thus achieved indirectly and directly through the work process. Ethnic communities facilitated cultural contact outside the workplace, but inside a new culture of work was being constructed. Over time this has become the standard for behavior and values. As ethnic communities disappear, there is no alternative.

Classless Culture

Contemporary race relations and the most recent expression of racial backlash can only be understood as a reaction, not simply of prejudice and institutional racism but also as a consequence of the increasing state of anomie within society (particularly among whites). As European Americans have lost their ethnic identification and culture, little of substance has been substituted. Racism and white supremacist expressions therefore have come to play a dual function in American society: racism obscures class distinctions and similarities and at the same time provides a source of cultural belonging for Europeans whose culture has been lost.

Analysts have overlooked the work process in discussions of culture and therefore often misapply the ideas of cultural pluralism, which presumably lead to an image of an amalgamation of cultures, the "melting pot" thesis. Far from a mixture of cultures, what has emerged as "American" culture is a set of values and behavior ironically devoid of any references to working-class, ethnic immigrant, or non-Western European influences. What was produced in the United States was a culture of assimilation, which required immigrants to release all of their unique references and transcend their class orientation. To be American, one had to strive to be nonethnic and non-working-class. This process obscured relations of power and the promotion of a new "synthetic" culture that helped to eradicate all references to working-class resistance. This process dramatically transformed culture as a vital adaptive mechanism for all groups.

Social-science views about ethnicity in the United States have been integrated into ideas about mobility to avoid discussion of the organization of power in society. Popular interpretations present the view that immigrants arrived in America with nothing and that they were able to improve their status economically and politically. Two important corollaries to this idea of ethnic immigrant mobility are (1) the idea that groups prospered as whole units rather than as individuals and (2) the idea that one's ethnic identification was and is a function of choice, and one may freely associate rather than be "labeled." The emphasis on mobility and free association has been used repeatedly to deny the existence of institutional racism and class stratification.

Social scientists do concede that these ideas about mobility and free association are a bit optimistic but have not changed their analysis of the ethnic, immigrant experience in America. Therefore, it is important to assess the function of ethnicity and, by extension, race. What we find is that (1) ethnicity was a variable used by employers in an effort to prevent trade unionism; (2) ethnic groups have not been allowed to prosper or survive as whole units but rather as individuals; and (3) ethnic group identity today is a reaction to the social movements of the 1960s and the lack of common sources of identity within the population (for example, job, class, community are no longer sources of identity because they are so impermanent).

Work was the source of a new identity and culture for immigrants early in this century. Black Americans were not part of that homogenization process until after 1965, and then it was to counter the cultural and political movement of the time. But as Blacks were welcomed to the work culture, it was losing its hold on white Americans.

The disappearance of sources of identity was recorded in the reports prepared for the nation's Bicentennial celebration. In the Working Papers of the Rockefeller Foundation, Michael Novak wrote:

> Almost everywhere, people see in their own cultural history . . . a new defense against certain evils of modern life and a reliable resource for some of the humanistic values that have always given life its savor. Too little stands between the solitary individual and the bureaucratic power of the large modern state; intermediate social bonds have been weakening—family, kinship, group loyalties, churches, neighborhoods, regions.[12]

However, even though the report suggests a yearning for a cultural past, it views ethnic group identification as merely a consequence of choice for individuals. The report laments that non-Europeans in the United States (African Americans, Native Americans, and Chicanos) "resorted to militancy" and social movements to express racial identification. Throughout, the report underscores the idea that "ethnicity . . . is a phenomenon to be studied in individuals rather than in groups."[13] The report proposes a method for the standardization of ethnic identification using education as a tool for controlling expressions among "all hyphenated Americans." The Rockefeller report is another testimony to the need to constantly present alternatives to working-class resistance. It treats race and ethnicity as the same. However, there can be little disagreement that those whose appearance physically distinguished them (and who were subject to slavery) have experienced the greatest alienation and exclusion in society. By treating race and ethnicity as synonyms, the report (as well as other such studies) helps justify the vilification of African Americans who have failed the test of assimilation.

Conclusion

Despite the prevalence of the language of diversity and multiculturalism, we find a society still unable to confront race and racism, a society unable and unwilling to recognize structures of domination, and therefore increasingly unable to conceptualize social change. According to Hazel Carby, "Theories of difference and diversity in practice leave us fragmented and divided but equal in an inability to conceive of radical social change."[14]

The philosophy and practice of pragmatism have made it legitimate to transform all discourse into tools for maintaining the status quo (and thereby the interests of the few). This is particularly apparent when we consider legislation resulting from confrontations challenging the status quo. Since 1964 we have seen Republicans and Democrats use such policies (Civil Rights Act, Voting Rights Act, Community Development Act, Affirmative Action, etc.) to build constituencies (and channel public dollars into private hands), often at the expense of serious social needs. Academics provide the perfect cover by continually steering our concerns away from material conditions and emphasizing the individual.

The review of the historical use of ethnicity confirms its political function in the United States. Mobility required a loss or relinquishing of ethnic group identification and its replacement by the philosophy of individualism. This helps to explain the contemporary reaction or racial backlash. When Blacks, for example, call for group access and opportunity for mobility, the reaction in the general population takes the form of renewed group, and thereby racial, identification. The political campaigns of George Wallace, Richard Nixon, Ronald Reagan, and even George Bush, were all symptomatic of this reaction. The tenor of the campaigns was that of a return to "tradition," a cultural reaction to the "outsiders" who represent a threat to the homogeneity of society. But the reaction really results from resentment by those who have been convinced to give up group identification and rights and have gained little in return. When other groups remain cohesive (by choice or default) they (whites) fear the groups' potential power and are confronted with the realization of what they themselves have given up. The new group identification is seen as a threat to individualism, and in some ways this reaction is accurate. Any precedence in the United States for the protection of a class or group of persons would automatically expose the vulnerability of acting alone and thereby discredit individualism.

The dismantling of all of the sources of identity and working-class culture under capitalism left only one arena for collective thought and action, the workplace. Left alone, work could have produced a group consciousness, and for that reason we understand why so much attention was focused on the work environment and work behavior. The revival of ethnicity in the United States, viewed in this light, is no more than an expression of alienation experienced by workers who have no source of identification in the face of the decline of neighborhoods and the transformation of work.

Ethnicity within this context has come to replace occupational identity. Unlike their immigrant ancestors, Americans see no intrinsic value in being identified as workers. Ethnicity is therefore donned as a costume at appropriate times of the year in an effort to create a sense of unity and belonging, a response to alienation.

The height of workers' class consciousness was, of course, 1932–45. The post-World War II era has been important because changes in the domestic political economy have undermined worker consciousness and solidarity. Industry led the way by physically relocating outside of urban industrial cities. The movement of industry to suburbs and the corresponding housing patterns were aided by government subsidy. All new industrial construction financed by government for the war effort, for example, was in plants outside established urban areas. After the war, this relocation escalated. Workers, of course, followed industry, and this was made possible by government legislation that made financing for homes available to the average worker and to returning veterans. As America experienced this new stage of the American Dream—home ownership—the process of developing political consciousness was reversed. Collectivism in the workplace was replaced by individualism in everyday life. Suburban life simply did not lend itself to the shared experiences of urban life. As the workplace was separated physically from the community, workers' lives became even more privatized and group identification became more difficult. Ironically, this loss of group identification now stands as an impediment to the expression of the very individualism Americans value. According to Émile Durkheim, anomie develops when the prerequisites for individuality are absent; these prerequisites are relations between people. In destroying group networks, the United States has placed its own future at risk.

Notes

1. Kristin Bumiller, *The Civil Rights Society* (Baltimore: Johns Hopkins University Press, 1988), 43.
2. Ibid., 2.
3. Joel Kotkin and Paul Grabowicz, *California Inc.* (New York: Rawson, Wade, 1982), 107.
4. Frantz Fanon, "Racism & Culture," in *Toward the African Revolution* (New York: Grove Press, 1967), 31.
5. Ibid., 36.
6. Gerd Korman, *Industrialization, Immigrants, and Americanization: The View from Milwaukee* (Madison: State Historical Society of Wisconsin, 1967), 42.
7. Ibid., 44.
8. Ibid., 45.

9. Ibid.

10. Ibid., 45–46.

11. Ibid., 65.

12. Michael Novak, "On Cultural Ecology: The United States as Nervous System of the Planet's Cultures," in *Working Papers, a Guide to Ethnic Studies Programs in American Colleges, Universities and Schools* (New York: Rockefeller Foundation, 1975), vi.

13. Ibid.

14. Hazel Carby, "The Politics of Difference," *Ms.* (September–October 1990): 85.

CHAPTER ELEVEN

Racialization in the Post-Civil Rights Era

MICHAEL OMI

In May 1991, there were two senior proms at the Brother Rice High School, a Catholic college preparatory academy in Chicago—an official one that was virtually all white, and, for the first time, an alternative all-black one (Wilkerson 1991).

Popular music, in this instance, provided the rallying point for racial consciousness and self-segregation. The trouble began when a white prom committee announced that the playlist for the music to be featured at the prom would be based on the input of each member of the senior class. Each student would list his/her three favorite songs, and the top vote-getters would be played. While this procedure was ostensibly democratic, African-American students (who comprised 12 percent of the school) complained that their preferences would be effectively shut out in a system of majority rule—songs by Marvin Gaye would be overwhelmed by those of Bon Jovi.

But parity was not the only issue. One African-American senior noted that even if they got half the requests, folks would still be unhappy since "we would have sat down during their songs and they would have sat down during ours." So the African-American students organized their own prom against the wishes of school administrators, who disavowed the prom and barred the use of the Brother Rice name. The principal of the school, Brother Michael Segvich, said: "There is only one prom this year at Brother

Rice. [The black prom] is something we don't want. I think it has to do with racism."

Ah yes, but racism on whose part? The controversy over two proms raises a host of questions regarding fairness and representation, the relationship of majority and minority cultures, and, as Aretha Franklin has so eloquently put it, "Who's zoomin' who?" In essence, these are issues that debate the very meaning of racial integration and equality in American life.

Although educational institutions have been formally integrated for decades, we are nonetheless witnessing a growing *balkanization*—a pattern of separation, segregation, and assertion of "difference"—among students of different racial backgrounds, and a parallel increase in racial conflict and tension. Such problems are by no means confined to the schools. Workplaces, neighborhoods, the media, and political parties are equally the sites of conflicts and dilemmas regarding their racial organization and makeup.

Despite legal guarantees of formal equality and access, race continues to be a fundamental organizing principle of individual identity and collective action. I would argue that, far from declining in significance (as William Julius Wilson [1978] would have us believe), the racial dimensions of political and social life have expanded in the post-civil rights era.

Racialization

In my work with Howard Winant (1986), we employ the term *racialization* to signify the extension of racial meaning to a previously racially unclassified relationship, social practice, or group. A historical example is the consolidation of the racial category of *black* in the United States from Africans whose specific identity had been Ibo, Yoruba, or Bakaongo, among other West African tribal identities. Parallel to this was, as Winthrop Jordan ([1968] 1977) observes, the emergence of *white* as a term of self-identity evolving from earlier conceptions of *Christian, English,* and *free.*

In what follows, I extend this notion to account for the complexity of race in the current period. In the post-civil rights era, new forms and expressions of racialization have developed. These include the emergence and consolidation of new racial categories; the phenomenon of groups confronting previously unexamined questions regarding their racial identity and status; and the increasing interpretation of seemingly "nonracial" issues through a framework of racial meanings. To illustrate these developments, I briefly discuss the development of new racial subjects as a result of panethnic consciousness; the emerging crisis of white identity; and the overall racialization of politics.

Panethnicity and the Development of New Racial Subjects

The post-civil rights period has witnessed the rise of *panethnicity* as a phenomenon of racialization. Groups that were previously self-defined in terms of specific ethnic background, and that were marginalized by the seemingly more central dynamic of black/white relations, began to confront their own racial identity and status in a political environment of heightened racial consciousness and mobilization.

Prior to the late 1960s, for example, there were no "Asian Americans." In the wake of the civil rights movement, distinct Asian ethnic groups, primarily Chinese, Japanese, Filipino, and Korean Americans, began to frame and assert their "common identity" as Asian Americans.

The *racialization* of Asian Americans involved the muting of profound cultural and linguistic differences, and of significant historical antagonisms, that existed among the distinct nationalities and ethnic groups of Asian origin. In spite of diversity and difference, Asian-American activists found the political label a crucial rallying point for raising political consciousness about the problems in Asian ethnic communities and in asserting demands on state institutions.

David Lopez and Yen Espiritu (1990) have explored this process and define panethnicity as "the development of bridging organizations and solidarities among subgroups of ethnic collectivities that are often seen as homogeneous by outsiders." While noting that panethnicity is shaped by an ensemble of cultural and structural factors, Lopez and Espiritu conclude that a specific concept of race is fundamental to the construction of panethnicity: "Those . . . groups that, from an outsider's point of view, are most racially homogeneous are also the groups with the greatest panethnic development" (219-20).

I view the rise of panethnicity as a process of racialization that is driven by a dynamic relationship between the specific group being racialized and the state. The elites representing such groups find it advantageous to make political demands by using the numbers and resources panethnic formations can mobilize. The state, in turn, can more easily manage claims by recognizing and responding to large blocs as opposed to dealing with the specific claims of a plethora of ethnically defined interest groups. Within this context, conflicts often occur over the precise definition of various racially defined groups, and their adequate representation in census counts, reapportionment debates, and minority aid.

Panethnic consciousness is unstable and susceptible to strategic manipulation. Recently, in San Francisco, Chinese-American architects and engineers protested the inclusion of Asian Indians under the city's minority business enterprise law (Chung 1991). Citing a Supreme Court ruling that requires cities to narrowly define which groups had suffered discrimination to justify specific affirmative action programs, Chinese Americans contended that Asian Indians should not be considered "Asian." At stake were obvious economic benefits accruing to designated "minority" businesses.

What this demonstrates is that panethnic consciousness and organization are, to a large extent, contextually and strategically determined. At times it is advantageous to be in a panethnic bloc, and at times it is desirable to mobilize along particular ethnic lines. A dynamic of inclusion and exclusion pervades the politics of panethnicity as racial and ethnic definitions and boundaries are drawn and contested.

The Emerging Crisis of White Identity

The 1990 United States Census revealed that the racial composition of the nation changed more dramatically over the past decade than at any time this century (Barringer 1991). Today, nearly one in every four Americans is of African, Asian, Latino, or Native American ancestry. The stunning increase in what used to be thought of as "minority" populations in the United States renders much of the very language of race relations obsolete and incongruous. For example, by 2003, white Americans are expected to make up less than 50 percent of the state of California. And the demographics of the workplace and the campus are changing faster than those of the general population.

The prospect that whites may not constitute a clear majority or exercise unquestioned racial domination in particular institutional settings has led to a *crisis of white identity*. In this respect, whites have been racialized in the post-civil rights era.

By the early 1970s, a backlash could be discerned against the institutionalization of civil rights reforms and the political realignments set in motion in the 1960s. There was a growing popular disenchantment with the civil rights vision—particularly the perceived shift in emphasis from individual opportunity to group preferential treatment. As one respondent noted in Stanley Greenberg's *Report on Democratic Defection* (1985), the "average American white guy" gets a "raw deal" from the government because, "blacks get advantages, Hispanics get advantages, Orientals get advantages. Everybody but the white male race gets advantages now" (70).

The idea that white racial identification could be a handicap seems historically unprecedented. For the most part, prior to the civil rights challenge, white identity, whiteness, was "transparent," its meaning unproblematic. In the wake of the civil rights challenge, however, it became necessary to reevaluate the meaning of whiteness.

In this reconceptualization of whiteness, traditional articulations of ethnicity have proven inadequate. Recent research by Mary Waters (1990) and Richard Alba (1990) suggests that most whites do not experience their ethnicity as a definitive aspect of their social identity. The specifically ethnic components of white identity are fast receding with each generation's distance from the old country. Most are unable to speak the language of their immigrant forebears, uncommitted to ethnic endogamy, and unaware of their ancestors' traditions (if in fact they can still identify who their ancestors are). Waters suggests that whites perceive their ethnicity dimly and irregularly, picking and choosing among its varied strands to exercise an "ethnic option."

The "twilight of white ethnicity" in a racially defined, and increasingly polarized, environment means that white racial identity will grow in salience. The racialization process for whites is very evident on many university campuses as white students encounter a heightened awareness of race that calls their own identity into question. In a recent study on racial diversity (Institute for the Study of Social Change 1991) conducted at the University of California at Berkeley, white students expressed the problematic nature of their racial identity:

> (Student 1): Many whites don't feel like they have an ethnic identity at all and I pretty much feel that way too. It's not something that bothers me tremendously but I think that maybe I could be missing something that other people have, that I am not experiencing.

> (Student 2): Being white means that you're less likely to get financial aid. . . . It means that there are all sorts of tutoring groups and special programs that you can't get into, because you're not a minority.

> (Student 3): If you want to go with the stereotypes, Asians are the smart people, the Blacks are great athletes, what is white? We're just here. We're the oppressors of the nation. (37)

Here we see many of the themes and dilemmas of white identity in the post-civil rights period: the "absence" of a clear culture and identity, the "disadvantages" of being white with respect to the distribution of resources, and the stigma of being perceived as the "oppressors of the nation."

Increasingly, whites are seeing themselves as a new panethnic group—Euro-Americans. Dale Warner, secretary of the European American Study Group in San Jose, states that European Americans who do not start speaking out as European Americans "are not engaged in the public discourse of our times." He goes on: "We've left our chair at the multicultural table empty, and the multicultural table is where the debate is, where the deals are being made—about voting rights, immigrant services, immigration laws, redistricting, health policy. More and more, it's now being built around ethnicity" (quoted in Ness 1992).

I would disagree with the last statement and contend that the issue is race. Nonetheless, the sentiments remain clear. Whites are concerned that their interests as *whites* are not being articulated, advanced, and addressed.

In the post-civil rights era, whites have not been immune to the process of racialization and have had to consider the racial implications of an order that now formally disavows "white skin privilege." The changing demographic scene, global economic competition, and America's overall fall from grace have provoked a profound crisis of white identity. What direction this takes politically—the White Aryan Resistance or opposition to "politically correct" multicultural education—remains to be seen.

The Racialization of Politics

The civil rights movement challenged the racial understandings and practices of the times and ushered in a period of desegregation efforts, "equal opportunity" mandates, and other state reforms. Despite these tremendous accomplishments, the patterns of institutional discrimination have proven to be quite entrenched, and the precise meaning and legal status, if any, race should have in various institutional settings remains undefined. The repressive racial order of legally sanctioned segregation has been overthrown, but no clear and consensual racial order has been consolidated in its place.

One paradoxical result of all this is that, far from decreasing, the significance of race in American life has expanded and the racial dimensions of politics and culture have proliferated. As we have seen, new racial identities and meanings continue to be created as a result of panethnic linkages. And as the "complexion" of American society changes, in a climate of "affirmative" racial policy, whites too are experiencing the contradictions and conflicts of racial identification.

The absence of a clear post-civil rights understanding of race has meant that issues of racial equality and racial identity have been vulnerable to *rearticulation* from political projects on the right. These have ranged from what Ronald Walters (1987) calls "white racial nationalism" to neoconservative critiques of affirmative action and other supposedly "color-conscious" remedies.

Political issues have been increasingly interpreted through a framework of racial meanings. Jesse Helms's come-from-behind Senate campaign in 1990, the late Lee Atwater's "Willie Horton" ad campaign for President Bush, and David Duke's surprising show of support in various Louisiana bids are all eloquent testimony to the fact that the race card can be played effectively and does win elections. Racially "coded" and racially explicit appeals have come to dominate electoral contests and hence there has been an increasing racialization of politics.

Much of this has taken the form of a concerted backlash against the perceived social impact of an increasingly diverse population. David Duke, declaring his candidacy in December 1991, argued that immigration should be a major issue in the presidential election. The time had come, he stated, to severely limit immigration into our society: "What's happening is, we are unraveling. We're losing our way. This country is overwhelmingly European descent. It's overwhelmingly Christian. And if we lose our underpinning, I think we're going to lose the foundations of America" (quoted in Toner 1991).

Other political initiatives are indicative of an overall intolerance toward diversity. In the summer of 1992, U.S. English began a $1.6 million campaign against congressional representatives who oppose a House bill declaring English the official U.S. language. Norman Shumway, the organization's chairman and a former Republican Congressman from California, says, "There are people coming to this country who feel they don't have to learn English, and we think that's a threat" (quoted in Levy 1992).

While the civil disorders in South Central Los Angeles momentarily led to a reconsideration of liberal social policy, a hard line quickly gained ground. Pat Buchanan, in his speech to the 1992 Republican convention, argued that Republicans need to shift their campaign from the Cold War to the cultural war for the soul of America: "As America's imperial troops guard frontiers all over the world, our own frontiers are open, and the barbarian is inside the gates. And you do not deal with the Vandals and Visigoths who are pillaging your cities by expanding the Head Start and food stamp programs" (quoted in Wills 1992).

The overall racialization of politics projects a grim vision of the future in which multiracial and multicultural diversity is openly resisted and legislated against, instead of celebrated.

Toward a New Politics?

Any progressive political project will have to address the racialization of politics and seek to challenge and deconstruct the racial meanings attached to, or embedded in, a range of issues, from immigration to foreign trade imbalances.

In the post-civil rights era, such a progressive racial politics needs to reassess the adequacy of the original civil rights vision to deal with contemporary patterns of inequality. This would include an examination of the impact of class and class relations within and between racially defined groups and of their meaning for race-specific remedies. Such a politics also needs to rethink minority demands in such a way as to avoid a zero-sum game. Group-specific demands need to be articulated in universal terms and an attempt must be made to mobilize and consolidate a majoritarian political bloc.

This does not mean submerging the issue of race, however, nor viewing hints of race consciousness as racism. The prevailing tendency to racialize American politics needs to be challenged directly. As we head into the Clinton years, let us remember that a strategy of economic growth that ignores the specificity and relative independence of racial problems will not solve those problems, nor make them go away.

References

Alba, Richard D. 1990. *Ethnic Identity: The Transformation of White America.* New Haven: Yale University Press.
Barringer, Felicity. 1991. "Census Shows Profound Change in Racial Makeup of the Nation." *New York Times* (11 March).
Chung, L. A. 1991. "S.F. Includes Asian Indians in Minority Law." *San Francisco Chronicle* (25 June).
Greenberg, Stanley B. 1985. *Report on Democratic Defection.* Unpublished report prepared for the Michigan House Democratic Campaign Committee.
Institute for the Study of Social Change. 1991. *The Diversity Project: The Final Report.* University of California, Berkeley (November).
Jordan, Winthrop. [1968] 1977. *White over Black: American Attitudes toward the Negro, 1550–1812.* New York: W. W. Norton.
Levy, Dan. 1992. "U.S. English Goes National with Campaign." *San Francisco Chronicle* (9 July).
Lopez, David and Yen Espiritu. 1990. "Panethnicity in the United States: A Theoretical Framework." *Ethnic and Racial Studies* 13: 198–224.
Ness, Carol. 1992. "Eurocentrism Gains a Voice." *San Francisco Examiner* (2 February).

Omi, Michael, and Howard Winant. 1986. *Racial Formation in the United States: From the 1960s to the 1980s*. New York and London: Routledge.

Toner, Robin. 1991. "Duke Takes His Anger into 1992 Race." *New York Times* (5 December).

Walters, Ronald V. 1987. "White Racial Nationalism in the United States." *Without Prejudice* 1: 7–29.

Waters, Mary C. 1990. *Ethnic Options: Choosing Identities in America*. Berkeley and Los Angeles: University of California Press.

Wilkerson, Isabel. 1991. "Separate Senior Proms Reveal an Unspanned Racial Divide." *New York Times* (5 May).

Wills, Garry. 1992. "The Born-Again Republicans." *New York Review of Books* (24 September).

Wilson, William Julius. 1978. *The Declining Significance of Race: Blacks and Changing American Institutions*. Chicago: University of Chicago Press.

CHAPTER TWELVE

Screening Resistance

LOURDES PORTILLO AND ROSA LINDA FREGOSO

ROSA LINDA FREGOSO: I first met Lourdes Portillo in Santa Barbara in 1987 when I had the honor of introducing her at the premiere of her film *Las Madres de la Plaza de Mayo*. Since then, I have had the occasion to write about her work and to undertake readings of two of her films, *Después del Terremoto* (After the earthquake) (1979) and *La Ofrenda* (The offering) (1990).[1] In my estimation, these two films enact what Chela Sandoval terms "differential consciousness."[2] More properly, they inscribe the tactical subjectivity deployed by U.S. Third World feminists since the 1960s. During the decade of the 1970s, feminist film criticism tended to view cinematic practices in terms of a series of binary oppositions: commercial versus independent, mainstream versus oppositional, documentary versus experimental, or narrative-driven versus avantgarde, nonnarrative cinema. Lourdes Portillo's films resist such rigid binary constructions of cinematic practices. Her films are all narrativedriven; however, they are not straightforwardly didactic; a genuine mix of complexity, self-reflexivity, and a concern for the aesthetics of reception characterize them. Indeed, I have learned from viewing and reviewing Lourdes Portillo's films that each viewing unlocks a different textual door because her films enact the multiple articulations of race, class, and gender. Cultural conflict drives most of Portillo's projects, yet I would argue that she orchestrates an aesthetics of reception and an aesthetics of subtlety that make for polyvocal, multivalent, cultural forms. These cultural forms inscribe Third World feminists as their foremost spectators. Portillo's films are not, however, just about Third World, or, subaltern subjects, but are about subjectivities; her films position spectators on multiple sides and in various locales of conflict and engagement.[3]

RLF: Let's begin with how you got started as a filmmaker in the Bay Area.

LOURDES PORTILLO: Well, it's a very long story. We don't have enough time to hear it and I don't have the patience to retell it after I've lived it. . . . I was always interested in film. I began working in film in Los Angeles as a camera assistant for an educational film company. At that time, I was studying political science and I realized that it was film that I could do best. There are moments in one's life when you find out that there are some things that you can't do—I couldn't type, well, not very fast—and there are other things that feel very natural to do. I realized I could work in a crew with a group of people. And I liked creating an alternate kind of reality. I stopped making films for a while when I got married and had children because I didn't have time to do the work. Instead, I studied film. Later, when I moved to San Francisco, I worked with a collective there called Cine Manifest, which was a group of Marxist filmmakers. I was getting two different kinds of education: a political education and a free associative filmic education. That's how I began working in film.

RLF: You've done commissioned work, but you've stayed pretty much in the independent circuit. Tell us why you made that decision.

LP: Coming from San Francisco and having children made me realize that I couldn't move to Los Angeles and try to make it in Hollywood. It was the 1970s and if I went to the offices of the funders, or to whomever was in charge, I'd probably look like their maid and they wouldn't trust me with a million dollars. So I decided I would make independent film in San Francisco where there was a lot of opportunity for me to grow and to make films. I think that's the real reason. The other reason I realized later as I made more films: I didn't want to compromise as much as one needs to compromise. It was a very big luxury to remain independent.

RLF: Can you elaborate a little bit more about the compromises?

LP: After having worked in television, I realized that your voice is so manipulated to fit into the format they're used to that it is very deadening. I imagined that television was just like a small version of what Hollywood might be.

Después del Terremoto

RLF: Let's talk about your first film, *Después del Terremoto* (1979), which is about a Nicaraguan woman who migrates to San Francisco after the Nicaraguan earthquake of 1976. You've mentioned to me that it is indicative of filmmaking at a particular historical moment. Could you give us some background on why you decided to do a film about a Nicaraguan woman in San Francisco and her desire to purchase a television set?

LP: *Después del Terremoto* was made at the beginning of the Nicaraguan insurrection. I was involved with people living in San Francisco who were involved in the insurrection, one of whom is my friend and collaborator Nina Serrano. We talked to the Sandinistas and told them that we wanted to make a film about what was happening *here*, not in Nicaragua, because it was very dangerous to go to Nicaragua at that time. They said, "Perfect. Do it. We support you." So we proceeded to get funding, including from the American Film Institute, on the basis of a script that Nina and I wrote. It was a script for a narrative film. If you remember, in the late 1970s, most political film, although there were some exceptions, were documentaries and we were proposing a narrative film. We came back to the Sandinistas and said, "Well, we got funded and this is the film we're going to make," and we showed them the script. They said, "Oh, sorry. We can't support you any longer. This is crazy. You have to do something that really expresses what we need expressed." And so that was a parting of the ways.

RLF: You did a docudrama. What made you decide against the documentary format?

LP: It was a practical decision. It was very impractical for us to go to Nicaragua then.

RLF: But, you could have made a documentary about the immigrants' experiences or about the struggle of Sandinistas in exile. Instead, you made more of a fictional docudrama, a scripted narrative film, where you investigate sexual freedom and the freedom to consume within the context of North and Central American politics.

LP: We had a story in mind, so it was harder to find the subjects than just to recreate the story. That's how we came to that decision.

RLF: There's a climactic scene in *Después del Terremoto* I'd like to ask you about. The younger and older women have been preparing for the birthday celebration of the matriarchal elderly Latina. Different genders, generations, and ideological positions are depicted. People are dancing, eating, and celebrating. The scene culminates when Roberto, the protagonist Irene's boyfriend, who has just returned from Nicaragua, is asked to show his slides of the aftermath of the earthquake. In the first series of slides, Roberto provides general information about the earthquake, its effects on people, the casualties, the devastation of homes and schools, and so on. Roberto's tone and demeanor change from a neutral account of the events to a more political analysis of the corruption of the dictator Somoza and the repression of political activists. As we learn, Roberto was imprisoned for stealing food from the government and giving it to the poor. As Roberto voices condemnation of U.S. support for the dictatorship, one of the tamale-making *tías* intervenes. As she stands up before Roberto, the slide show is transposed from the makeshift screen to her white apron, projecting images of Nicaragua onto her body. She says, "Stop this slide show. I don't want to hear anymore." I call this scene the moment of implosion; it's where all the narrative strands come together. But, interestingly, it reveals the kinds of contradictions or divisions that are always part of political communities. Is that what you intended?

LP: Sure. We wanted to give the situation a human depth, to actually contextualize it the way it really was. We wanted to show that there are political concerns, there are contradictions, and there are oppositions. It wasn't just one-way, you know.

RLF: Like Roberto, who's just come from Nicaragua? He has a specific kind of revolutionary discourse, and he's young. You create a situation in which the women are much older. They have had to survive here and are a little more fearful than he: they know the realities. Why did you choose to focus on an older woman to convey these dynamics of the political community?

LP: I think the women in the film represent the women of that time. They were very aware of what happened during the Somoza regime and that's the reason why they were in the United States. Youth is always

Scene from *Después del Terremoto*

much more idealistic and stronger in a certain way, but blinder too. We felt that the older women have traditionally filled that role of consciousness-raising in the community, so we were just representing that.

RLF: Do you believe that is why the Sandinistas didn't want you to do the film the way you proposed?

LP: I think that the Sandinistas had an objective in mind. I don't think that was a bad thing; they might not have won the war without such single-mindedness. In a sense, and I don't mean a negative sense, we were a bit frivolous. At the same time, we were trying to do something that was meaningful beyond the single objective of winning the war and then discarding the film. One of the things that I find so interesting and important about the film is that gender is at the center of cultural conflict.

Las Madres de la Plaza de Mayo

RLF: Lourdes Portillo is best known for her documentary film, *Las Madres de la Plaza de Mayo*, about the mothers of the disappeared in Argentina. The film received twenty international and national awards.

Scene from *Las Madres de la Plaza de Mayo*

Meanwhile, General Rivera had suspended all civil rights. At bus stops, at work and in cafés. People were taken away. Disappeared . . .

LP: The story of the mothers is so poignant and painful that the film sort of made itself in many ways. I mean, there was nothing to do but to record what happened and that was sufficient.

RLF: How was it received in Argentina?

LP: They loved it. They loved the film because we brought it to the Cultural Center in San Martín to screen after the dictatorship had fallen. There was a line nine blocks long to see the film. They wanted to see the truth. They hadn't been told the truth for a long time and this was the first exposure that they had to it. They had never seen on the screen a representation about the disappeared and the struggle of the mothers.

Mirrors of the Heart

RLF: Let's turn now to a commissioned work about identity in Latin America, *Mirrors of the Heart* (1992). Could you share your thoughts with us about this film?

LP: I wanted to make a film about identity from my experience as a Mexican. I was born in Mexico. The Indians in Bolivia had a similar experience and it was their experience I wanted to translate to the screen. The film is about ethnic identity, how the indigenous people of the Americas have defined themselves and how the colonizers define them. It is about the conflict around those two definitions. This film was an Annenberg project, which involved ten, fifteen—I don't remember exactly—academics who were to tell me whether I was correct or not about what I was perceiving, or if it fit within their theories of what identity was. I had a lot of problems with them. This is my vengeance now.

RLF: What did the academics tell you identity was?

LP: They insulted me. They called me an essentialist, which I took as a compliment. In one important scene, we hear Raul Julia reading a stilted narration that I fought over for months and months and never really won. I would win two words and they would win thirty, and it went on like that forever. Does this man choose to have his hair curled because he wants to be up-to-date, or because he wants to seem less indigenous? From my research and from who this man was, he didn't want to be indigenous. He wanted to fit into the urban setting of La Paz. He had come from the country and to be an Indian in La Paz is not a nice thing. Anything one can do to hide that, he will do. He did look better with a perm, though.

RLF: Can you say more about shifting identities?

LP: Yes. One particular scholar from Princeton—I won't name any names, but someday you may find out who she is—had this theory, a

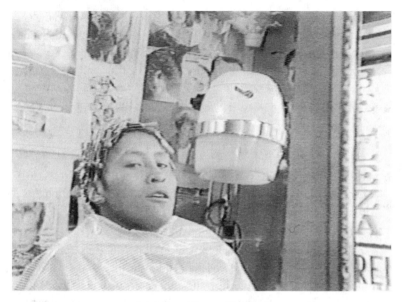

Scene from *Mirrors of the Heart*

theory I think a lot of you also share. This theory says that identity is fluid. From my experience, I don't believe that identity is fluid. Perhaps over a series of generations you can change aspects of yourself or aspects of your children will change; maybe your children will be whiter, or maybe they will look indigenous. But when an indigenous person moves from the country to an urban setting, he is undoubtedly indigenous. The Criollos, or descendants of the Spaniards, will never mistake him for anything other than an indigenous person. The theory implies that if you come to the city, get a perm and a job in which you do somewhat well, and call yourself a Cholo, a mestizo, or a mixed-blood person, then you've changed your identity. In fact, in the eyes of the people around you, your identity has *not* changed. And this was the argument that went back and forth between myself and this particular scholar. She had curly blond hair, in case you ever recognize her, and she said that during the 1970s she had an Afro. I was appalled. I just gave up. I said, "No, I can't do this anymore. I'm going to quit. I don't care." She had an Afro. You know, she's crazy.

RLF: A point to emphasize is that some people, because of their skin color, have the privilege of being able to slip and slide in categories whereas other people do not have that ability.

LP: Exactly.

RLF: A Black man walks into a ritzy store in San Francisco and the electronic cameras go on just because no matter how well-dressed he may be, he still wears his race on his body.

LP: I also think that it's easier for a white person to *feel* like he or she can be indigenous, as in the film *Dances with Wolves*, you know? But an Indian can't be white. That was the argument in very simplistic terms. I am kind of a simple person. No, I mean I like to simplify things. That's why they call me an essentialist.

The Trial of Christopher Columbus

RLF: Lourdes's newest film is called *The Trial of Christopher Columbus* (1992) and stars the Chicano comedy troupe Culture Clash. History has found Columbus innocent, but Portillo has not in this film. Why did you choose comedy for this film?

LP: That is the medium I'm using to try to synthesize my political thinking and my emotional state to bring you some sort of spectacle all at the same time. I thought a mixture of political satire, humor, and experimentation with video would bring something new to the argument. I like to laugh. I really think it makes me feel good. You know, after I laugh I feel better. Maybe I won't get a heart attack after all.

Scene from *The Trial of Christopher Columbus*

List of Completed Works by Lourdes Portillo

The Trial of Christopher Columbus (1992)
An 18-minute video. A political satire with Culture Clash, the comedy trio. Verbal satire, physical comedy, and state-of-the-art video techniques are used to dramatize a faux-trial of Columbus in a present-day courtroom.

Mirrors of the Heart (1992)
A one-hour documentary for WGBH in Boston for *The Americas,* a ten-part series on Latin America broadcast in 1993. *Mirrors of the Heart* explores the notions of ethnic identity, and was filmed on the island of Hispaniola and in the highlands of Bolivia.

"The Aztec Myth of Creation" (1991)
A screenplay for an animated feature for animator Patricia Amlyn. Funded by the National Endowment for the Humanities. It is presently in production.

Vida (1990)
A short narrative film for AIDSFILMS that depicts the struggle of a young Latina woman in New York coming to terms with the dangers of AIDS. Recipient of a Gold Award at the International Film and TV Festival in New York City, a Golden Eagle, and a Silver Apple at the National Educational Film Festival. Vida received an honorable mention at the San Antonio Film Festival.

La Ofrenda (1990)
A lyrical, 16mm documentary film that portrays the attitudes that Chicanos and Mexicans have toward death. The film has received several awards, including a Blue Ribbon from the American Film and Video Association, as well as honors from the Independent Documentary Association and the Latino Film Festival in San Antonio, Texas.

Las Madres de la Plaza de Mayo (1986)
A one-hour documentary depicting the story of the mothers of the disappeared in Argentina. The mothers forced the military regime into an accounting for their disappeared ones. Recipient of twenty national and international awards, including a 1986 Oscar nomination for Best Documentary and an Emmy nomination.

"Chola" (1982)
Original screenplay, commissioned by American Playhouse, about a teenage Salvadoran refugee in San Francisco, an orphaned girl who has come to live with her grandmother in the United States.

Después del Terremoto (1979)
A 16mm, half-hour narrative about a Nicaraguan maid trying to adapt to America and her dilemma over her impending marriage to a Nicaraguan revolutionary. Recipient of awards in Poland and Cuba.

All films distributed by Xochil Films, 918 Esmeralda, San Francisco, CA 94110.

Notes

1. See Rosa Linda Fregoso, "*Nepantla* in Gendered Subjectivity," in *The Bronze Screen* (Minneapolis: University of Minnesota Press, 1993).

2. Chela Sandoval, "U.S. Third World Feminism: The Theory and Method of Oppositional Consciousness in the Postmodern World," *Genders* 10 (spring 1991).

3. I occupy a particularly complicated role as spectator and critic. I have established a friendship with Lourdes Portillo and I was very ambivalent about that friendship because I had to resolve how to separate my critical work from my subjective enthusiasm and admiration for her as a mother (she has been a single mother of three sons; I was a single parent at a very young age). I had to separate this personal human feeling and connection I have with Lourdes from a much more objective assessment of her work. As much as I realize the impossibility of separating the subjective from the objective, it has nevertheless been a problem I have taken very seriously. Those of us who do literary criticism can certainly agree that it is much less conflicting to offer a negative critique of a text written by an author long dead than by one who is living. A nineteenth-century author can be criticized without the danger of retribution. The author won't not talk to you, and she or he won't respond to negative reviews of your book or deny permission for citations. I have always been suspicious of the kind of compromises inherent in befriending one's object of analysis. For example, I had some problems with a scene in Lourdes's film *La Ofrenda* about a cross-dresser. I felt I had to write about its contradictions, but I also felt that I had to talk to Lourdes about it and tell her I was going to do this. My hunch was that she would tell me that I had it all wrong and that I didn't understand what she was trying to do. When I told her how disturbed I was about the scene, she blew me away with her response. She said, "That's fine. Write about its problems and contradictions. I don't have any problem with being contradictory. Rosa Linda, I don't claim to be politically correct."

PART III

Reading Multicultural Narratives

CHAPTER THIRTEEN

Language and Other Lethal Weapons

Cultural Politics and the Rites of Children
as Translators of Culture

ANTONIA I. CASTAÑEDA

Age 7: El doctor[1]

"Dile que no puedo respirar—que se me atora el aire. Dile..." How do I say "atora"?

"Tell your mother that she has to stop and place this hose in her mouth and press this pump or else she will suffocate."

"¿Qué dice? ¿Qué dice?"

He is sitting behind this big desk, and my mother is sitting beside me and holding onto my hand very tightly.

I . . . what does suffocate mean? How do I translate this? I don't have the words.

"¿Qué dice? ¿Qué dice?"

"I . . . uh . . . Dice que... uh . . . Dice que si no haces lo que te dice te mueres."

"Dile que cuando me acuesto por la noche que no puedo resollar."

"Resollar," what does that mean?

Her gasps came out quickly and sounded so awful: a croaking sound that seemed to hurt from deep inside her throat. I sit in front of the big desk remembering, hearing her sounds, and feel again the terror of last night and every time I heard her and could not help. I do not have the words to help her. She will die. And all I could do was sit there and hold her hand and listen to her gasp and gasp for air—for breath that would not reach her, her eyes popping out—and watch her die. She called me her *lengua,* her *voz.* If she dies, it will be my fault.

I tell the doctor she cannot breathe and will die. And he says something I cannot understand about asthmatics and how there is little he can do except give her this pump and that I should be sure to tell her not to panic.

Panic. What does that word mean? How do I say panic?

How does a seven-year-old girl, not yet in the second grade, translate the life and death words "atora," "suffocate," "resollar," "panic"? How does she explain and interpret words she does not know in either language, while knowing at the same time that her mother's life sits on her tongue and on what she does with the words given her? Where in her seven-year-old knowledge does she find the meaning of words that hold the life or death of the mother who calls her "mi lengua"—her tongue—the fleshy, movable organ attached to the floor of the mouth with which words are made? What cultural rites are these in which children become adults long before puberty?

Age 8: La cuenta

"Dile que no le podemos pagar toda la cuenta porque ha llovido mucho y no hemos podido pizcar. Pero que aquí están estos centavitos y luego luego se la pagamos tan pronto que trabajemos... y que queremos llevar una poca comida hoy—que si nos extiende el crédito un poquito. Andale, dile."

He looks at me from behind his counter and says, "What? What'd she say?"

"My mother said we can't pay all the bill today—because of the rain we have not been able to work—and we will pay the rest real soon, as soon as we work . . . and can we have a little more food on credit?"

He looks at me, then he looks at her, and we stand there in front of him. He starts to say something I cannot hear.

"¿Qué dice? ¿Qué dice?" my mother asks. "Andale, dile que sí le pagamos—nomás que ahorita no hay trabajo."

I start to speak to him again. I look up to talk to him, and he stares down at me, and the look I see in his eyes tells me that he does not believe we will pay our bill. I have seen that same look on people's faces in town when we all get out of the back of the truck by the city park, and me and my friends walk down the street—in Toppenish—the people just stare at us and glare at us with eyes that tell us we do not belong there. It is the same look the man at the restaurant gave us—at that place where we stopped on our way from Texas—when he wouldn't sell us milk for the baby's bottle.

"¿Qué dice? ¿Qué dice?" my mother asked.

"Nada mamá. No dice nada. Mejor vámonos. No nos van a dar más crédito."

What cultural issues are at stake for child translators? How do they interpret for themselves the cultures they must translate for others? What are the politics they confront each time they translate cultures? How do they negotiate their culture of origin, which cannot protect them and in which the roles of parent and child are inverted as children become the tongues, the lifeline, the public voice of parents, family, and sometimes communities? How do they negotiate the culture they must translate for their parents—the culture that assaults and violates them, their families, and their communities with its assumptions and attitudes about them as well as with its language and other lethal weapons?

Age 15: El rifle

"Ay tocan a la puerta. Trae rifle. Ha de ser uno de esos gringos que cazan faisanes. Anda ver qué quiere."

I open the door to a man with a hunting rifle.

"Does Raaool Valhenzoola live here? Is he here? I want to talk to him."

"¿Qué dice? ¿Qué dice? ¿A quién busca? ¿Busca a Raúl?"

"Si mamá, busca a Raúl. Quédate adentro. No, my brother's not home. He's working."

"Well, you tell your brother that I came here to order him to stay away from my daughter. You tell him I catch him anywhere near Janice, or even lookin' at her, he'll be sorry. You tell him I have friends, and they know who he is. You tell 'im, girlie, you tell 'im."

I look past him, past the lingering swirls of dust his truck tires had stirred up on the dirt road, and know what the people in the camp meant when they told us stories about the Texas Rangers.

"¿Qué dice? ¿Qué dice? ¿Qué quiere con Raúl?" my mother cries from somewhere behind me.

I tell him to put the rifle down because he is scaring my mother and to please leave. I step back inside the house and close the door. What can I tell her that she doesn't already know?

Who are these children who speak in tongues and live in fire? What happens to them as they move through the educational system—the system of which most of us are products, the system to which we send our children, the system that employs us, the system that does violence to our mental integration, and the system that historically has also done violence to our physical selves precisely because we spoke languages other than English?[2] Although many Chicano/Latino children are pushed out of the public educational system in places like Texas and California, they and all children in the United States are steeped in lessons about rugged individualism, democracy, "American" nationalism, equality, justice, merit, and fair play. What do children of color, children of farmworker families, and other working-class children, whose daily experiences belie the national myths, understand and know about these myths?

If we are to decolonize national myths, we must understand how different people have lived the American myths: the historical myths about inventing America that refer to invasion as discovery (as Angela Davis noted during her keynote address at the Translating Cultures conference held in Santa Barbara in 1992) and the ideological myths that sustain U.S. imperialism, genocide, racialism, and economic exploitation and have done so since the founding of this nation.[3] These myths, and the attitudes and the violence they foster, are intrinsic to the political, economic, social, and cultural values of the United States and are the toxic particles that we ingest with every breath.

These myths include the notion that the United States, symbolized by "The West," is a classless, casteless society where equality and justice for all reign supreme, where merit and hard work are rewarded, and where education—which is free and available to all children—is the key to success. Certainly children are vitally aware of the popular heroes and heroines of the western frontier, including every white-hatted cowboy who ever rode a horse across the vast expanses of the silver screen, dispensing evenhanded justice with his faithful but rather dumb—sometimes ethnic—sidekick and greeted by a blonde beauty at the end of the dusty trail.

Those of us living in California know firsthand how deeply rooted and pervasive are the national myths surrounding the "frontier" and "The American West." Not only is California the most romanticized, mythologized, and distorted of the western states, but the West and how the West was spun, who spun it, how it is now being spun, and who is authorized to spin it, are among the most highly contested issues in the ideological—euphemistically called cultural—wars now being waged on battlefields across the nation: newspapers, popular magazines, academic journals, conferences, public school textbooks, the National Museum of American Art, and the National Museum of American History.[4]

These wars are about national myths, about ideology and who controls it. They are about "The West as America"—to use the title of the bitterly contested exhibit at the National Museum of American Art, site of one of the most acrimonious battles waged during the cultural wars of 1991.[5]

What is the relationship between those myths and the politics of translating cultures? What rites of passage are these that require children to conceive the significance of, construe, and interpret entire cultural universes for adults, universes that include every possible human experience: a nation's mythology and ideology, a sibling's arrest, pregnancy and pre- and postnatal care, an argument with a boss who refuses to pay the wages he agreed to pay? What rites are these in which childhood's boundaries are transgressed each time a child is required to translate—and thus mediate, negotiate, and broker—adult realities across cultures?

These questions are guiding my current research on a social history of Tejana farmworkers. How did Tejana farmworkers and their families who migrated between Texas and the state of Washington live this nation's national myths? Based on interviews with women who lived in five labor camps in different parts of Washington State, this work examines the lives of Tejanas who came of age during the two decades after the Second World War, from about 1945 to 1965.

These were the decades of the Bracero Program, which recruited more than 4.5 million Mexican men to work in agriculture and industry in the western/southwestern United States, and of Operation Wetback, which in 1954 alone deported a million "aliens."[6] These were the decades of aggressive anti-immigrant sentiments, expressed in national efforts such as the McCarran-Walter Act, which aimed to tighten immigration laws and to intensify the screening and deporting of "aliens."

The calls for immigrant labor coincided with the economic booms that began with the First World War and accompanied all major wars in this century. Anti-immigrant laws and waves of deportations were symptoms of the economic downturns that inevitably followed. The first laws restricting immigration were enacted in 1922, after the end of the First World War. In 1930-33, during the Great Depression, three hundred thousand Mexicans and Mexican Americans were forcibly "repatriated" to Mexico; in 1953-54, Operation Wetback deported more than twice the number of Mexicans contracted under the Bracero Program during the same period.[7]

These were the decades in which New Deal spending and subsidies to agriculture—including the building of monumental dams—provided agri-business with cheap water for irrigation and electric power.[8] Irrigation trans-formed arid western wastelands into verdant, fertile agricultural valleys with undulating fields of row crops, fruit orchards, and hop yards endlessly stretching out under liquid blue skies. Twentieth-century agricultural corpo-rations required massive armies of seasonal, mobile manual labor, which they obtained not only through the public recruitment of braceros from Mexico but also through the private recruitment of Mexicano/Chicano fam-ilies, especially from isolated rural communities of South Texas where racism, segregated schools, the hated *rinches*, and "no Mexicans or dogs al-lowed" signs at the front doors of restaurants were the norm.

During these decades, entire Tejano families, both nuclear and extended, began an annual migrant work cycle from Texas, to Arizona, to California, to Washington, to Oregon, to Idaho, and back to Texas. The children of these South Texas communities, where earlier generations of native-born children had often been refused even rudimentary education in English because the town had "no school for Mexicans," were the girls and boys who scrambled onto the beds of tarp-covered flatbed trucks to migrate to *las piscas*, to live in labor camps, and to labor alongside their parents, older siblings, and other relatives in the row, field, and orchard crops of the Yakima, Skagit, and We-natchee valleys. Some of these families settled out early on and, in the late 1940s and early 1950s, began to form the nucleus of Chicano communities in the Pacific Northwest.

Most of the families lived in labor camps—some of which had commu-nal showers, outside toilets, and communal laundries that consisted of large steel tubs with built-in washboards; others had neither showers nor laun-dries. Located at the end of long dusty roads or set far beyond groves of trees that hid the ramshackle structures from view, the labor camps were not vis-ible from the highway. Thus the camps, and their inhabitants, were rendered invisible to the local citizenry. Ostensibly, migrant farmworkers did not exist.

What existed instead were inflammatory newspaper headlines, which decried the threat "illegal Mexican aliens" posed to local resources, and McCarthyism and anticommunist hysteria, which denounced as subversive and/or homosexual anyone even remotely suspected of harboring radical political sympathies and posing an internal threat to national security. His-torically defined as racial, sexual, and political threats, people of color were now at even greater risk. What also existed were Hollywood's countless ren-ditions of the West as America, which Chicano, Amerindian, Black, and

Anglo children could see on Saturday afternoons at the segregated Liberty Theater in Toppenish, Washington—the heart of the Yakima Indian Reservation. Above all, what existed were the myths.

Thus, for people of Mexican descent, whose historical communities had existed under a state of siege since the end of the U.S. war with Mexico in 1848, the repressive politics, policies, and culture of the 1950s were a postwar manifestation of historical patterns of repression, now further justified by nativist as well as racist arguments that Mexicans were foreigners. For the migrant farmworker families of the Tejanas interviewed for this study, the "keep America pure" ideology, the economic and political policy of containment, and the cultural and political repression of the 1950s conveyed the clear message that people of Mexican descent were un-American, subversive, and unwelcome.

During these decades, the women whose stories begin and end this chapter translated for their families and their communities. During the decade of the 1950s, in particular, Cold War politics and the gender, racial, class, and sexual politics of containment further converted these women of color—and, in fact, all people of color—into "the enemy within."

As children, the women I interviewed translated for parents, family, and community, and the question of how they experienced the national myths is a critical political, and thus cultural, question. Their oral histories reveal that the act of translation is informed by unequal power relationships. Translation usually occurs under conditions of conflict and stress. It is frequently traumatic, and the trauma is long-lasting. Children are often at the center of the process of translation, and they experience that trauma more strongly than adults. What, then, do we make of children translating cultures? How do we assess, analyze, theorize, and interpret this experience, which in most cases continues into their own adulthood and generally until their parents' death?

The current body of knowledge and literature on translation privileges the written word. It largely focuses on the translation of written texts, principally all genres of literature, or seeks to teach businesses how to train workers to be translators and thus to digest "unassimilated diversity," to quote Angela Davis again. It yields little of value for examining and understanding the experience of child translators.

Recently, social-science scholars and practitioners—particularly linguists, psychologists, anthropologists, and social workers—have begun to examine and debate issues pertinent to children as translators.[9] Generally, however, these scholars have cast the experience as a recent phenomenon specific to immigrant children and their families. They have centered the debate on the psychological or linguistic "costs and benefits" to the individual child.

One side argues that translating for parents and family is harmful to the child's psychological development and that, because children play an adult role while they are translating, they may grow up too quickly and resent or lose respect for their parents.[10] This perspective is exemplified by Richard Rodriguez's undernourished *Hunger of Memory: The Education of Richard Rodriguez* (1981).[11] Rodriguez accepted and internalized the tenets of a racist, classist society that deemed everything about him—the color of his skin, his language, his physiognomy, and his working-class origins—wrong, unacceptable, and un-American. He internalized these notions and relinquished his Mexican self, choosing education over family, erudite English over Spanish, a "public" Euro-American life over a "private" Mexican one. In rejecting his Mexican self, Rodriguez has, in fact, been accepted by Euro-America and has become the darling of certain segments of the white intelligentsia.

The other side of the debate argues that translating can help children develop language skills and understand American institutions. In 1991, Lowry Hemphill, a specialist in language development at Harvard University, stated that translating is not necessarily something that should be discouraged, since it is "part and parcel of the whole experience of being an immigrant child. People do what they have to do to get by."[12] Ernesto Galarza, whose autobiographical *Barrio Boy: The Story of a Boy's Acculturation* (1971) reveals translating as empowering, learned very early—in a remote, mountainous village in Mexico and in a multiethnic, working-class barrio in Sacramento—to see himself in relation to his family, his community, and his class and to understand and interpret the world in terms of power relationships and class differences.[13] Galarza embraced the experience of translating and transformed it into a powerful tool with which to give public voice to the struggle for the rights of industrial workers, including farmworkers, throughout the world. Within that framework, translating was a powerful, positive, and valuable skill to be used and shared with others.

Most scholars ignore, however, the global history of imperialism in general and the history of U.S. imperialism in particular. In so doing, they reify one of the pivotal national myths that still undergirds U.S. imperialist ideology: the myth that the American continents were largely unpopulated, or only partially inhabited, when Europeans landed on these shores. For California and the West, this reaffirms the myth of the "bloodless conquest" and ignores demographic studies of the last two decades that debunk this myth, provide new data confirming high population density, particularly in Mexico and California, and describe the genocide and demographic holocaust wrought upon native peoples by European conquest and colonization. The myth of unpopulated continents has not only served to rationalize genocide of Amerindians but has also enabled scholars to ignore the fact that Europeans had to communicate with the people living here. Europeans did not initially speak indigenous languages; somebody had to translate, and that somebody was often a child.

Thus, the issue of translating cultures, and specifically the experience of children as translators, is a historical as much as a contemporary issue and experience. It is by no means solely or even principally an immigrant experience, at least not historically. Beginning with Malintzín, or La Malinche, as she is also known—a fourteen-year-old girl who was given, with nineteen other young women, by the Chontal Maya of the Tabasco coast to the Spaniards in 1519 and became translator, lover, and tactical adviser to Hernán Cortés—the experience of translating cultures has been lived by native-born children and adolescents, including Tejana farmworkers.[14]

Throughout the Spanish-Mexican periods, both Amerindian and mestizo children and adolescents captured in war, raids, and slaving expeditions in the northern frontier of Mexico could find themselves translating cultures, as in the case of boys and young men who worked for the military as scouts, horse-breakers, or herders, and in that of young servant girls who worked in the homes of soldiers and settlers. Indian children, in particular, were often captured, traded, or sold into slavery by Spanish-Mexican military forces and, after the Euro-American conquest, by settlers and paramilitary groups.[15]

On another level, but also in terms of culture, children were at the center of the strategies employed by Spanish-Mexicans as well as Euro-Americans to detribalize native peoples. Catholic missionaries and the Euro-American educational system went to great lengths to "denaturalize or deculturalize" native peoples through their children: in missions, in the case of the Jesuits and the Franciscans, and in Indian boarding schools, in the case of Euro-American educators.[16] This is fundamentally what the contemporary English-only movement is all about. Historically, the effort was to subvert the authority of the parents and the community by inverting the parent-child relationship and making the child the authority in certain realms, including the ability to communicate with whoever represented the ruling colonial authority or power.

Although Malintzín's narrative relating her experience is not available, we know that her acts of translation, as well as her sexuality, earned her the opprobrium of a Euro-centered, patriarchal Mexicano/Chicano history and culture, which portrays her—the symbolic mother of the mestizo peoples—as a traitor and a whore. In the past decade and a half, however, Native American and Chicana writers and scholars have reinterpreted the documentary record and inverted the spurious sexualized and racialized image of Malintzín, claiming this Indian woman as our own, even as lesbian.[17]

Reinterpretations of Malintzín by Chicana and Native American scholars Adelaida del Castillo, Norma Alarcón, and Inés Hernández center on issues of subjectivities, translation, and agency. Del Castillo interprets Malintzín as a gifted linguist, a young woman who made well-considered choices based on her realities and those of her people. Alarcón examines La Malinche as a paradigmatic figure of Chicana feminism. Hernández draws upon the syncretic ceremonial dance tradition of the Concheros of "la Gran Tenochtitlán, in which La Malinche is the path-opener—the front(line)—the vanguard," to discuss how in the contemporary period we can choose to be Malinches in a political, social, and intellectual context.[18]

The Malinches of today, she states, are "all of the women who have accepted their role as 'tongues' and demanded that their voices be heard."[19] Including especially Rigoberta Menchú, who learned Spanish—the language of the oppressor—and made it her own, just as she learned and used the Bible as an organizing text and tool in her community; these women join their voices and their skills in the global struggle to end exploitation and oppression in all their forms.

With these very few exceptions, and linguist Frances Karttunen's most recent work, *Between Worlds: Interpreters, Guides, and Survivors* (1994), which discusses the young translators Malintzín and Sacajawea within a global context and experience, scholars have yet to focus on the spoken word and the act of oral translation across unequal relations of power based on age, gender, race, class, and culture. Centering gender and the experience that women have had as child translators and examining the pressures, conflicts, and contradictions that arise when they must translate in a context of unequal power raises critical epistemological and theoretical questions for feminism, and for feminist scholars seeking to theorize history, politics, and culture.

What did a Tejanita of seven summers know and interpret as she broke through multilayered power differentials to translate for a mother facing racist male creditors, doctors, police, or school authorities? What did a teenage Mexican girl of fifteen understand about sexuality, race, and violence when she had to translate her family's needs to a store owner who made sexual overtures to her every time she came into the store in the same town where a white man with a hunting rifle came to threaten her brother away from his daughter. How did these young Tejanas negotiate translating across two patriarchal cultures during the 1950s—their own, which sexualized them, and another, which sexualized and racialized them while disparaging their class origins? How did working-class Mexican girls live and interpret the cultural politics of the Cold War, of which one central ideological tenet, feminist scholars have concluded, was a domestic revival that centered the family, prescribed traditional gender roles, and prized marital stability.[20]

How did these girls and young women assimilate, accept, and/or resist this experience? What did they change, and how were they changed by the act of translating cultures across space, time, and circumstance? Although still in its very early stages, this study of Tejana farmworkers reveals that the act of translating, and the corollary rites that working-class womanchild translators passed through, challenge current feminist theories about consciousness, identity, choice, power, and the politics of culture.

Age 10: La escuela

"Dile que venimos con Doña Chelo para averiguar por qué espulsaron a Mariquita."

"Sí, y dile que..."

The door opens, and the principal comes out, asking, "Who is Mrs. Rodríguez?"

I touch Doña Chelo's arm. She looks at me and steps forward with her hand outstretched.

"We can't have all these Mexican kids disrupting our school."

"¿Qué dice? ¿Qué dice?" Doña Chelo asks.

"If this is Marrría Rodríguez's mother, tell her that her daughter bit the school nurse, and we had to expel her."

"Dile que Mariquita no tiene piojos. Que soy muy limpia—cada noche caliento tinas de agua y baño a todos mis muchachos y los mando muy limpiesitos a la escuela. Y a Mariquita le hago sus trenzas cada mañana. Por qué le echaron todo ese polvo tan apestoso? Dile que la asustaron y la humillaron."

"Doña Chelo says her family is very clean. She heats water every night for baths and sends her children to school clean every day. She braids Mariquita's hair every morning. Why did you pour that ugly powder on her? You scared Mariquita and hurt her."

"Tell her that we do this every year in March when all you kids from the camps start coming in. Tell her that the lice powder is not harmful and that the school nurse tries not to get it in their eyes or mouth. There was no reason for Marrría to cry and scream like she did. And then when the nurse tried to hold her down, she screamed even louder and bit and kicked and hit our poor nurse. Tell her she should send her children to school clean and neat. And she should teach her children to behave, to respect school authorities."

"¿Qué dice? ¿Qué dice? ¿Cuándo puede regresar Mariquita a sus clases? ¿Cómo puede aprender si me la expulsan? Yo no quiero que se queden burros como nosotros, que no nos admitían a las escuelas en Tejas. Dile, Nenita. Dile."

"Les estoy diciendo, Doña Chelo. Les estoy diciendo."

Notes

I thank the Tejanas from El Golding, El Six, Crewport, y los otros campos de labor del valle de Yakima. Their translating stories are the heart of this paper. I thank Arturo Madrid, Alicia Gaspar de Alba, and Deena González for reading and commenting on this essay. I thank Elizabeth Forsyth for editorial assistance.

1. The four translation stories in this paper derive from a larger study of Tejana farmworkers based, in part, on oral histories. These stories are composites of translation stories related by the Tejanas I interviewed and my own childhood experiences of translating.

2. Guadalupe San Miguel, *"Let All of Them Take Heed": Mexican Americans and the Campaign for Educational Equality in Texas, 1910–1981* (Austin: University of Texas Press, 1987); Charles M. Wollenberg, *All Deliberate Speed: Segregation and Exclusion in California Schools, 1855–1975* (Berkeley, Los Angeles, and London: University of California Press, 1978).

3. Angela Y. Davis, keynote address at the conference "Translating Cultures: The Future of Multiculturalism?" University of California, Santa Barbara, 11–14 November 1992.

4. For articles in newspapers and popular journals, see Kay Larson, "How the West Was Done," *New York*, 17 June 1991; Miriam Horn, "How the West Was Really Won," *U.S. News & World Report*, 21 May 1990: 56–65; Kim Masters, "Two Senators Charge Smithsonian with Leaning Left," *Houston Chronicle*, 16 May 1991: 17A; Robert Hughes, "How the West Was Spun," *Time*, 13 May 1991: 79–80; Eric Foner and Jon Wiener, "Fighting for the West," *Nation*, 29 July–5 August 1991: 163–66; Richard Bernstein, "Unsettling the Old West," *New York Times Magazine*, 18 March 1990: 34, 57–59. The scholarly literature on the subject is vast. For recent scholarship, see Susan Lee Johnson, "'A Memory Sweet to Soldiers': The Significance of Gender in the History of the American West," and David Gutiérrez, "Significant to Whom? Mexican Americans and the History of the American West," *Western Historical Quarterly* (November 1993): 495–517 and 519–39,

respectively; Antonia I. Castañeda, "Women of Color and the Rewriting of Western History: The Politics, Discourse, and Decolonization of History," *Pacific Historical Review* (November 1992): 501–33; Brian Dippie, "The Winning of the West Reconsidered," *Wilson Quarterly* (summer 1990).

5. For the publication from this exhibit, see William H. Truettner, ed., *The West as America: Reinterpreting Images of the Frontier, 1820–1920* (Washington and London: Smithsonian Institution Press, 1991).

6. For an overview of twentieth-century Chicano history, upon which this section is based, see Rodolfo Acuña, *Occupied America: A History of Chicanos*, 3d ed. (New York: Harper and Row, 1988). For discussion specific to the Bracero Program, see Erasmo Gamboa, *Mexican Labor and World War II: Braceros in the Pacific Northwest, 1942–1947* (Austin: University of Texas Press, 1990), and Ernesto Galarza, *Merchants of Labor: The Mexican Bracero Story* (Santa Barbara, Calif.: McNally and Loftin, 1964).

7. Abraham Hoffman, *Unwanted Mexican Americans in the Great Depression* (Tucson: University of Arizona Press, 1974).

8. Michael P. Malone and Richard W. Etulain, *The American West: A Twentieth Century History* (Lincoln and London: University of Nebraska Press, 1989).

9. For an important discussion of the politics of linguistic domination, and its centrality to the politics and policies of Spanish colonialism in Mexico, see Jorge Klor de Alva, "Language, Politics, and Translation: Colonial Discourse and Classic Nahuatl in New Spain," in *The Art of Translation: Voices from the Field*, ed. Rosanna Warren (Boston: Northeastern University Press, 1989), 143–62.

10. Zita Arocha, "Like Most Children of Immigrants, I Suffer from a Split Psyche," *Los Angeles Times*, 27 October 1991; Lowry Hemphill, "For Immigrants' Children, an Adult Role," *New York Times*, 15 August 1991.

11. Richard Rodriguez, *Hunger of Memory: The Education of Richard Rodriguez* (Boston: David R. Godine, 1981). Omission of the accent in "Rodriguez" is consistent with the way the author of *Hunger of Memory* spells his family name.

12. Lowry Hemphill, "For Immigrants' Children, an Adult Role," *New York Times*, 15 August 1991.

13. Ernesto Galarza, *Barrio Boy: The Story of a Boy's Acculturation* (Notre Dame and London: University of Notre Dame Press, 1971).

14. Frances Karttunen, *Between Worlds: Interpreters, Guides, and Survivors* (New Brunswick, N.J.: Rutgers University Press, 1994); Inés Hernández, "An Open Letter to Chicanas," in *Without Discovery: A Native Response to Columbus*, ed. Ray González (Seattle: Broken Moon Press, 1992), 153–66; Norma Alarcón, "Tradductora, Traditora: A Paradigmatic Figure of Chicana Feminism," *Cultural Critique* (1990): 57–87; Norma Alarcón, "Chicana Feminism: In the Tracks of 'The' Native Woman," *Cultural Studies* 4 (October 1990): 248–55; Adelaida del Castillo, "Malintzín Tenépal: A Preliminary Look into a New Perspective," in *Essays on La Mujer*, ed. Rosaura Sánchez and Rosa Martínez Cruz (Los Angeles: Chicano Studies Center Publications, 1977), 124–49.

15. L. R. Bailey, *Indian Slave Trade in the Southwest: A Study of Slave-taking and the Traffic in Indian Captives* (Los Angeles: Westernlore Press, 1966). For a collection of captivity narratives, all related from a non-Indian perspective, see the Largland Library of *Narratives of North American Indian Captivities* (New York and London: Garland Publishing, 1976), 311 titles in 111 volumes.

16. For discussion about Jesuit and Franciscan strategies of using children to invert the lines of authority among native peoples, see Karen Anderson, *Chain Her by One Foot: The Subjugation of Native Women in Seventeenth-Century New France* (New York and London: Routledge, 1991), 159–61; Ramón Gutiérrez, *When Jesus Came, the Cornmothers Went Away: Marriage, Sex-*

uality and Power in New Mexico, 1500–1846 (Stanford, Calif.: Stanford University Press, 1991), 74–76.

17. See note 14.

18. Hernández, "An Open Letter to Chicanas," 159.

19. Ibid.

20. Elaine Tyler May, *Homeward Bound: American Families in the Cold War Era* (New York: Basic Books, 1988).

CHAPTER FOURTEEN

The Spanish Colón-ialista Narrative

Their Prospectus for Us in 1992[1]

ANGIE CHABRAM-DERNERSESIAN

As a Chicana Riqueña subject residing in California's semirural Yolo County, I was drawn into the 1492–1992 connection by the particular forms of media knowledge that interpellated Us in culturally specific ways that I could not ignore. After all, I was entrusted to teach Chicana/o culture and its roots. I had labored long and hard with many others on behalf of Chicana/o speakers of Spanish and for a more equitable representation of Chicana/o literature within an overarching "Spanish" curriculum. Like many of my contemporaries, whose situated bodies are crisscrossed by competing transnational interests and histories of colonialism, I reviewed the five-hundred-year celebration with an eye toward understanding the crucial matter of how it framed the cultural and ethnic problematics generally associated with multiculturalism. Following the notion that "identities concern the ways in which we are positioned and in turn position ourselves within the narratives of the past,"[2] I responded to this initial concern with this essay, which proposes a critical examination of a hegemonic construction of national identity: the Colón-ialista narrative and its prospectus for Us in 1992.

This unconventional term, Colón-ialista, was inspired by a Chicana/o art exhibit protesting the celebration of the Quincentenary.[3] As I understand it, this term deliberately breaks with the rhythms of the Spanish word *colonialista* by inscribing a hyphen, which initiates a stop, calling attention to the gender-specific construction of national identity through the naming of a particular masculine subject. Graphing Colón this way enables Us to visualize someone else's body at the center of national identity. At the same time, the hyphen links his particular historical identity to a colonial system and a form of discursive power inscribed in the Spanish language. Thus Colón surfaces as the original colonizer, as visualized in the root of the term, *colón-ialista*, which describes the colonizing *action* by naming within its borders the colonizing *agent*. With this semantic construction it could be said that the Colón-ialista narrative carries forward this function through its recentering of Colón and colonial interests as they are inherited from the colonial system and as they are refurbished, retold, and reenacted under present conditions within the capitalist system and its global representations. Thus the Colón-ialista narrative offers the "authoritative" rendition of a nation's or a continent's "founding" identity narrative; it is the narrative that communicates a "selective tradition" propagated by dominant cultures.[4] Insofar as this narrative counts with the cultural and economic capital of various nation-states and its reenactment is normalized to the point of being a fundamental part of the national patrimony, at times occupying a sacred space, this is by far a supernarrative.

In daily life this Colón-ialista narrative is inextricably linked to officially sanctioned "prepackaged events" and "commemorations" that "contribute to the continuous mythmaking process" of the nation as it is reconstituted with the foregrounding of particular temporal sequences of a hundred years. These sequential commemorations, which reenact the Colon-ialista narrative, are supposed to "adorn the past with certainty," so that the proof of the happening is in the cyclical inevitability of its celebration.[5] Within these commemorative narratives, geographical, political, linguistic, cultural, and ethnic genealogies and boundaries are drawn around Colón, his exploits, and the requisites of shifting Euro-American centers, abroad and at home.

The particular Colón narrative I have selected for analysis is probably not the one generally experienced in the local electronic or print media or on cable's much-watched CNN. I am referring to that revision of 1492 that unfolded in the *Spanish*-language print media in the United States and Spain around 12 October 1992. My focus is deliberate: this is a circuit that is generally overlooked as a productive ground for ideological and political analysis of narrativized identities and the political positions that map out and construct local knowledge about ourselves, the world, and our relationships to one another. This lack of attention has worked to the detriment of critical cultural studies because the analysis of this medium promises to yield a greater understanding of the competing transnational identities that configure Chicanas/os. The critical analysis of this medium also has the potential to problematize the view that cultural productions that speak in partially incorporated, transnational, or alternative "linguistic" realms are somehow outside of the dominant culture's menacing grip. To the contrary, this paper will speak to the existence of multiple effects of various dominant identities that seek to make a home for Us through the narrative rehearsed on Columbus Day. The subhead of this next section ("The Quincentenary Has Put Spain in Her Place") evokes a number of issues surrounding the politics of representation associated with multiculturalism and the translation of cultures across national communities and state-sanctioned borders.

Rather than framing these issues around the counter-Colón-ialista narrative of 1992 and its oppositional identities, I center my discussion around the ways in which the Colón-ialista narrative purposefully enlists subjugated identities "over here" through an international "*Hispanic*" register that intersects predominant multicultural paradigms in the United States. These paradigms frequently revisit cultural pluralism and the melting-pot theories of national culture, and they footnote inequalities (race, class, and gender) as well as the underrepresented social groups that are foregrounded within their critical epistemologies. Not surprisingly, these epistemologies are themselves displaced as the self-proclaimed authors of this multiprolonged and seemingly limitless multicultural framework supplant critical genealogies, racial memories, social hierarchies, and situated knowledges with an ideal essentialist Americana/o subject. This subject is alleged to be amenable to all of Us but is not supposed to be recognized by any of Us in particular.

Thus the demise of the political subject of Chicana/o Studies, African-American Studies, American Studies, Asian-American Studies, Feminist Studies, Native American Studies, and studies of the subaltern is contemplated through its dilution and utter fragmentation into an unrecognizable and equally foreign mixture of traditions and practices. Here transparent social beings are refashioned into an ideal national unity, purported to be universal. In a maneuver typical of those neoconservatives who would oppose the most watered-down forms of multiculturalism as un-American, such a construct is often linked to the preservation of a fabric of U.S. society that is allegedly being threatened by those who might unravel it. How? By openly naming and configuring social privilege and difference and the *distances* that these elements necessarily produce in the lives of human subjects today and in the way they live out and define culture.

The markedly nationalistic movement that has triggered these contradictory processes of fragmentation and reunification within multiculturalism can be seen as offering a reaction to the growth of international and ethnic communities in the United States and the nation's unequivocal and widespread participation in a global economy. In an attempt to ward off the ill effects of these nationalist constructions and, at the same time, incorporate these international dynamics, some cultural practitioners have abandoned multiculturalism because of its insular translation of national culture. Others have sought to reclaim multiculturalism as a viable, although contested, territory by restoring its political ground, communities, intellectual traditions, and potential global dimensions across particular social, cultural, and political linkages. Notwithstanding this response, multiculturalism continues to be constructed primarily as a national phenomenon; thus little attention is paid to the existence of competing forms that originate outside of this now fully transnational context.

The Columbus Day narrative provides an avenue for initiating this kind of inquiry, first because it provoked a host of muticultural readings and/or interpretations in the United States, and second because it furnished a connection with Spanish/European variants of "multiculturalism" that compete with these national readings and offer significant divergences as well. By placing my emphasis here, I seek to call attention to the various fronts on which an effective counter-Colón-ialista narrative can be launched.

"El Quinto Centenario ha puesto a España en su lugar" (The Quincentenary Has Put Spain in Her Place)—Luis Yáñez

In his essay "Good Day Columbus" Michel-Rolph Trouillot describes the naming of "the fact" of 12 October 1492 as a "narrative of power disguised as innocence."[6] A number of newspaper articles appearing in Madrid's *El País* very deliberately offer a "predominant Spanish rendition" of 1492–1992 as a way of fostering a balanced account of the Columbus debate and appear to confirm this assessment. However, in and of itself this assessment runs the risk of contributing to the idea of timeless, universal narratives of power that don't bear the imprint of change or register the traces of their context.[7] If it is true, as John Fiske has proposed, that ideology is "engaged in a constant struggle not to just extend its power, but to hold onto the territory it has already colonized,"[8] then it follows that the narratives that frame them are subject to substantial revision as well. Many of the Spanish-language articles commemorating Columbus Day bear this out. They offer a number of twists in the Colón-ialista narrative that newly interpellate not only Spanish and Latin American but also Chicana/o and indigenous subjects.

To start with, much of the official discourse on 1492 that is intended for popular consumption consciously seeks to distance itself from the old-style colonial discourse normally associated with the Golden Age of Spanish politics: the Empire. In its revised forms, the Colón-ialista narrative tempers its patriotic fervor, mediates its Spanish nationalism with a Euro-Latin American representation, and aggressively seeks to "modernize" itself in the contemporary world order by ridding itself of anachronistic expressions and historic recriminations. This is a Colón narrative that reinvents the legacy of 1492 by minimizing references to the "facts" of the Conquest and its aftermath and seeks to reconcile political opposites by appealing to a new Euro-American unity: *La Hispanidad*/Hispanism or Hispanics.[9] Finally, this Colón has abandoned the Yankee colonizer and his political exploits in Wounded Knee and Aztlán while seeking less accountability for the Spanish colonizer for his exploits elsewhere.

Within this recasting of the Columbus narrative, events of the past are often blurred or confounded with those of the present. That this is the case is not surprising since those who defend the colonial Spanish positionality as the dominant one also consciously seek to distance readers from the historical realities of 1492, and the benefits and/or atrocities they may have engendered for contending groups. At the same time, these realities are translated, often refashioned within cryptic historical reconstructions that are so preposterous—so far from general understandings of the nature of these events—that they often reveal themselves to be outright distortions of history, although this is not the intended effect.[10]

I have pieced together some of the dominant strands of the public discourse around the commemorations of 1492 in order to examine some of its constitutive elements, although it is important to note that not all Colón narratives propose to arrive at his identity in this way. An example can be found in Félix Monteira's interview with Luis Yáñez, the president of the Society for the Celebration of the Quincentenary. At one point in the interview, Yáñez emphatically claims that the "commemoration in Spain isn't a celebration of victory which only seeks to increase her past glory"; at another, he assures his reading public that "the Quincentenary has served to put Spain in her place."[11] Thus, he bolsters the claim made by other newspaper editorials that the Quincentenary has offered the nation "capitalidad cultural europea," roughly, a form of European cultural capital. Following this line of thinking, the editorial, "Octubre del 92," featured by Jesús de

Polanco and company of *El País,* proposes that "five hundred years after the conquest, the day of Hispanism isn't vindicating a model of Conquest or colonization, but rather the importance of *some* exposides that presupposed the *most* important external projection of Spaniards."[12] The editorial proposes that without these transcendental events (which we all recognize despite their erasure), "contemporary history would not be intelligible" and "an important *fact of civilization* would be erased." Thus, the significance of the Conquest and the Quincentenary is magnified to encompass an unprecedented scale and an unwarranted value in singularly forging the political and cultural entity that we recognize as *América.* At the same time, Polanco et al. seek to detach themselves and their readers from the social, political, and cultural process that such a "spectacular external projection" necessarily entailed. Interestingly enough, this logic echoed that of the pope, who kept insisting that his visit to the New World around 12 October 1992 wasn't a commemoration of the Conquest, but a celebration of Christianity, as if the two weren't historically linked.[13]

These reflections not only demonstrate the flawed and contradictory logic that frames the Spanish Eurocentric Colón narratives; they also register the impact of the context of 1992, thus bringing home the reality that even neocolonial discourses require adjustments of the original colonizing mission if they are to close the circuit of consumption with revised Colón identity, or if they are to compete with other Eurocentric interpretations, perceived to be more generous in their constructions. In the case of Spain, this proves to be particularly relevant, since the Spanish public, the target for such a narrative revival, proved to be somewhat divided by a recent poll, with at least 38 percent accepting the Spanish history of colonization *while admitting to errors,* 33 percent claiming pride in the epoch, 9 percent claiming that Columbus Day shouldn't be celebrated, and at least 5 percent claiming, "I'm embarrassed about that part of my history because the Conquest was, after all, a genocide."[14]

Other contextual pressures can also be seen as impinging on the revision of the Colón-ialista narrative, including the undeniable political and cultural significance of the fact of American independence from Spanish colonial rule and the increased transnational visibility of the indigenous resistance movements throughout the Americas and Europe. Significantly, the resistance to Colón incorporated Spanish protests in Barcelona and Toledo and a youth protest in Sevilla that sidestepped official attempts to purge the nation of the guilt of Conquest by openly seeking the *perdón* (forgiveness) of *América* (the continental Americas).[15] From the patrons of local Spanish bars who sported T-shirts reading "No al/to 92" to the young Chicana/o activists in Aztlán who wore *camisetas*[16] with Malaquías Montoya's graphic rendition of a virus-ridden Columbus flanked by the phrase "Chále con Colón" (The heck with Colón), these sectors have not only interrupted the terms of the old-style Spanish colonial discourse, they have also generated a contentious dialogue that carries over into the neocolonial revisions that commemorated 1492 in 1992.

Just as local conservatives have emerged to counteract the progressive agenda associated with Ethnic and Women's Studies in the United States, the proponents of the Colón-ialista narrative in Spanish newspapers actively seek to contest those oppositional framings of *indigenistas*/indigenous peoples that countered "discovery" with "*genocidio*/genocide," "*encuentro*/encounter" with "*colisión*/collision" or "*encontronazo*/crash," and "*España*/Spain" with "*América*." The anti-Colón movement has left a lasting imprint on the popular imagination that even the proponents of Colón cannot ignore: the idea that even in 1992, 1492 is a wound that continues to bleed.[17]

As we shall see, this Spanish revision of the national identity also responds to new social and political objectives, not the least of which is Spain's current efforts to rearticulate her relationship to Europe, Latin America, and the world economy. The Quincentenary and its Colón narrative were, after all, political, state-sanctioned events, and as such they incorporated not only ideological, but also material and institutional, practices. As Javier Solana notes in his editorial "V Centenario, Proyecto Cumplido" (The Quincentenary, the completed project): "In our country, the commemoration of the Quincentenary has been fundamentally a political project, a project of the state. . . . Of the state not only the central administration, but . . . an infinite number of private associations and public ones have participated."[18]

Yáñez's account of the significance of 1492–1992 goes far beyond this particular rendition, for it constructs the Quincentenary and its related programs (the Expo and the Olympic Games) as symbolic re-creations of a Spanish imperial enterprise. When asked whether he took offense at the fact that the Quincentenary was often reduced to the Expo and the Olympics, the president of the committee went a step further and fully embellished the Quincentenary program with the language and characteristics of the Columbus voyage and the Conquest, extending as well the field of its projected influence: "No, because I conceive of the Quincentenary as an arch that includes *many* things. . . . The Olympic Games are secured in 1986 because in 1992 the Quincentenary was being celebrated. And, let's not say anything about the Expo; that is a part of the Quincentenary program. They have been *the flagships,* spectacular projection toward the outside."[19] With this description Yáñez recovers the militaristic interpretation that was played down in Polanco's initial revision of the events commemorating 1492, repeating in this instance the idea that the Conquest was "a spectacular projection." Thus traces of the old-style colonial narrative are reenlisted at the symbolic-imaginary level, this time through a contemporary Spanish register and cultural practice: the Expo. At the same time, the convergence, 1492-1992, seems to offer the possibility for an unprecedented Spanish basking in glory, despite declarations to the contrary, for Yáñez elaborates: "The Quincentenary has put Spain in her place. . . . 1992 can be summarized with a slogan that has been created abroad and used from Japan to the United States: 'The Year of Spain.' The triumph of this strategy . . ."[20]

It is here where the essence of this Colón-ialista narrative is captured: this is a narrative that recenters an imperial Spain while displacing *América,* that speaks itself while pretending to represent a largely unspoken *América.*[21] This is a narrative that envelopes history—that history that hurts Us—within a sanitary colonial mythology that has edited out the realities of the violence of the Conquest and the forms of domination that such an enterprise necessarily entailed. This is a narrative that very deliberately constructs itself as being "measured," as leaving behind the contentious discursive positions of the "sí's/yeses and the noes" and their passion of remembrances, while at the same time taking solace in the brutality of other (especially Anglo-American) conquests.

Finally, this is a narrative that offers a conservative counterdiscourse to resistance, while at the same time carefully privileging its positionality within its founding account to the exclusion of the other narratives protesting against Colón that unfolded on the streets, in the newspapers, and on television. I am referring to counterdiscourses and countercelebrations that were foregrounded in Spanish-language newspapers such as *La Opinión* in articles such as "Marchas, festejos y contrafestejos caracterizan el 'Día de la Raza' en los países latinoamericanos." For example, the following events, documenting resistance in the Americas, were covered in *La Opinión:*[22]

> Mexico City: Amid screams of "Christopher Columbus to the firing line" and throwing eggs, paint, and rocks at the monument of the conqueror . . . hundreds of *indígenas* danced and protested, singing . . . "Thief, we don't want you in the pantheon."

> Guatemala: The natives of this Central American country marched through the center of the capital to commemorate five hundred years of "Indigenous,

Black, and Popular Resistance," and at the end of the march they gave the government a memorial claiming recognition of their identity and rights. . . . The guerrilla leadership of the URNG (Unidad Revolucionaria Nacional Guatemalteca) publishes a declaration . . . commemorating the five hundred years of resistance and struggles of the indigenous peoples of Latin America against "the Conquest, colonization, and oppression."

Panama: Indigenous peoples marched in front of the Spanish embassy, where they danced and demonstrated their anger over the celebration.

El Salvador: A group of Salvadoran aborigines throws red paint on the statues of Colón and Queen Isabella that grace the entrance to the National Palace.

Costa Rica: A peaceful demonstration, including the leaders of twenty-one indigenous groups, took place on the streets of Costa Rica. The protest changed in mood when another angry group burned the flags of the United States and Spain.

Ecuador: Five hundred years of popular and indigenous resistance is celebrated.

Colombia: Groups of Indians from different regions of Colombia gathered today to protest the celebration of the five hundred years of the arrival of Columbus in America. The Indians were in agreement that the cultural rupture between the two worlds was still present. In Popayán, more than ten thousand Indians and farmworkers (mostly Guanbinos) marched silently and blindfolded in protest against the celebration of the "discovery" of America.

Paraguay: Seventeen indigenous tribes refuse to celebrate the Quincentenary while the president, Andrés Rodríguez, declares the occasion a free day . . .

Bolivia: In La Paz, between twenty-five thousand and thirty thousand persons of different ethnicities, most of whom were Indian and who had arrived from the Aymara communities, gathered in a protest against colonization.

Argentina: Representatives of indigenous movements end the four-day hunger strike they were waging in front of the house of the government in the context of a protest against the genocide of the Conquest.

Chile: Indigenous protesters briefly took over various university buildings while leftists exploded a bomb in front of the Spanish embassy.

Santo Domingo: Protests are held throughout the country against a state-funded monument of Columbus that cost twenty-five million dollars.

Aztlán: Students at UCLA offer a countercelebration in honor of the dead in the brutal Conquest.

The narrative of Colón-ialismo is presenced through omissions of such resistance. This narrative does not fashion itself from the force of arrows,

horses, or crosses, but through the power of discourse itself, through the creation of a selective tradition within electronic media and cultural histories,
and through the highly sophisticated mediums of government politics, public relations campaigns, and economic enterprises as they activate the desire
for empire. This particular rendition of the Quincentenary as the "colonial
enterprise" alerts us to the ethnocentric dimensions of this commemoration
that had been shadowed under a diplomatic outreach directed at the Latin
American republics.[23] This dimension also serves to explain the reasons for
the distancing from Old World politics. The positioning of Spain within a
new world order, alongside the United States and Japan, is itself intended to
be a sign of her desired prominence in the contemporary period. This re-
creation of the Quincentenary thus returns a position lost to her through independence and subordination to other Euro-American centers, permitting
her to relive her imperial legacy without the nagging memory of past or present complications.

   An understanding of the re-creation of this brand of Spanish hegemony
is not complete without referring to the cultural, ethnic, and linguistic configurations that play into the equation, for if the United States and Japan are
linked to the economic program of the future where Spain is more than just
a marginal contender, Spain's imperial influence is affirmed in the present at
the sociocultural level through a reconfiguration of her relations with the
Spanish-speaking inhabitants of the Americas. This configuration draws its
inspiration from a colonial past but reaffirms its legacy in the historic present. Spain might be short on hard capital, she may have been displaced as an
imperial power, but, as the proponents of the Colón narrative explicate, she
is rich in culture and language. The extent of her power and influence in
Latin America is confirmed at this level by a series of claims regarding the
extensive domain of the Spanish language; the failure of indigenous dialects
and American republics to marshal up an independent "national" expression; the enduring presence of Spanish colonial institutions in the Americas
and the existence of a Spanish stock through the ethnic identity of *mestizaje*.
For all practical purposes, the Spanish and American republics are characterized through the *same* language, culture, and religion—the ones intentionally associated with an original colonizing culture.

   These perspectives are well illustrated in the "Octubre del 92" *El País*
newspaper article, where the editorial group argues that a "common" language is the legacy Spain has left to Latin Americans and that it is *this*
language that permits Latin Americans to project themselves as political,
cultural, and economic entities and to participate in a joint "unfolding of

civilization" with Spain. Nicolás Sánchez-Albornoz also commemorates the Quincentenary through a politically charged construction of the Spanish language. He charts five hundred years of a continual linguistic expansion that began with the Conquest and continues to the present day and credits this legacy with guaranteeing the "supremacy" of the Spanish language.

Like others, he minimizes the role of the actual Spanish Conquest in unleashing this much-celebrated expansion—he even attributes it to Latin Americans (particularly the dominant classes: the creoles) who seized the colonial impetus. However, to the degree that he appeals to a long-standing, uninterrupted linguistic legacy that coincides with the five hundred-year commemoration, and to the degree that he links this legacy to the acts of those colonizers who purportedly generated its growth from 1500 to 1650 by regrouping into insular nuclei in order to preserve the language intact, his rendition also generates the notion of an original linguistic capital that is unmistakenly Spanish. Only by undervaluing the regional and national variations of Spanish and the force of indigenous languages and by isolating those demographic, political, and communicative necessities associated exclusively with the Spanish language can he chart the "dominion of the Spanish language."[24]

From a quite different perspective, Miguel Oviedo attempts to furnish a more balanced account of the Conquest, exploring its violence toward the indigenous peoples and recording Spanish opposition to its unfolding.[25] However, like many of his contemporaries who support the five hundred-year commemoration, Oviedo adheres to the idea that the Conquest rendered a productive legacy with the by-product of cultural *mestizaje*: the fusion of two cultures into one. As he describes it, this was a "fusion," not an "exclusion," and from this fusion a new culture emerged that was different from the original cultures but shared their roots.[26] It is to Oviedo's credit that he recognizes that *América* is a multicultural and multiethnic construct, that he creates a distance from those who view this fusion as part of an original colonizing design. However, his notion of *mestizaje* is also a flawed and totalizing concept.[27]

Oviedo's assessment of what the Conquest actually left behind after five hundred years confirms the problematic nature of this equitable fusion, for, as he sees it, what's left behind after all is done is a "society that, with its own variations, is a new variation of *Occidental* culture, an inheritor of a vast spiritual and intellectual legacy."[28] Above all, what is left behind, once Occidental culture has become the new centralizing space, is the Spanish language—"the language in which we Spanish Americans can communicate among ourselves and across the Atlantic." Here, from within this Eurocentric lens, *mestizaje does* exclude peoples and cultures,[29] and for Oviedo the Spanish language is capable of becoming a powerful instrument of

> expression, the key to our (their)[30] universal vocation, and the promise that one day, understanding one another, we (they/Hispanics) will never commit the error of the first Spanish *discoverer* who, upon seeing in front of him a naked human being, who was *incapable of reading* and *ignorant of God,* thought he was a monster. That is to say, an aberration of nature, an enemy, a war booty, instead of seeing him for what he was: *his* likeness. [31]

This projected mimesis sins by virtue of its lack of cognizance of the dynamic interplay between similarity and difference that occurs in the relations between fully contested ethnic identities. This description also threatens to reinscribe the civilization/barbarism opposition, so long ago discarded for its racist overtones and stereotyping, by failing to fully interrogate the founding presumptions of the conqueror—not the discoverer—toward the Indian, and by failing to ask: Who was ignorant? Who was incapable of reading or writing another's culture? And: Why should *Spanish* (this code of Spanish) be the key to our/*their* vocation and expression? In addition, in 1992 Oviedo cannot imagine an indigenous viewpoint that is centered in a positionality or a linguistic framework substantially different from the one inherited from the conqueror. He fails to comprehend how this particular rendition of the Spanish language, which is so crucial for those who seek to rescue the Quincentenary from all of its evils in an effort to salvage a productive colonial legacy, promotes not only alliances but also *ruptures* between peoples, how those who do not privilege Spanish in this way are left out of the orbit of transnational communication and a place in the world's representational landscape.

Other problems loom ahead in the literature overtly celebrating the Quincentenary. This linguistic transatlantic network featuring Spanish dominance is often encircled with its own cultural space with the notion of *La Hispanidad,* historically, a euphemism for Spanish-centered. Here the various Spanish, Latin American, and Chicana/o traditions are held to celebrate these inherited "common" cultural and ethnic traditions. At the political level, this global essentialism acts to legitimate Spanish power and to cancel out the growing force of competitive American identities that propose radical deviations from this model, such as the *indigenista* and popular resistance movements, and/or Chicana/o countercelebrations. Rather than functioning as independent ethnic, political, and cultural entities, these ele-

ments become symbolic extensions of Spain's old cultural and political empire as it is recoded and refashioned through the political imaginary and the
Spanish language of "Sí al/Yes to 1992."

Once again the irony is that this is set forth as an entirely *new* multicultural vision. This vision is problematic, not only because it distorts history in the service of revised but nevertheless visible old-style colonial interests, but because its code for doing so has changed. This code has become
more contemporary, more familiar—more "American." In short, it has come
home to newly invade our *casa*/house and to reformulate the terms of political and ethnic relations over here.[32] For Chicanas/os this twist is particularly
challenging since debates on multiculturalism have generally functioned
with reference to contestations of an Anglo-American center and a more recent construction of political domination and whiteness. The framing of
multiculturalism within the confines of the five hundred-year commemoration involves another locus of contestation, another source of ethnic and
political conflict, one that potentially reinscribes hierarchies from centuries
past, renewing them through a centralizing imperial channel: in this case the
Spanish press, as it echoes, reappropriates, and redefines the language of
contemporary social relations.

This "colonial multiculturalism" is jarring, for it is not only a reinvention
of the melting pot that proposed to fuse Chicanas/os into a dominant
Anglo/European Center. This construction also nourishes homogeneous visions of Spanish culture, purist notions of the Spanish language, and a complete denial of cultural, ethnic, and racial differences among the different
mestizo and indigenous populations associated with what we know as
América, before as well as after the Conquest.[33] For Chicanas/os, as well as
for other groups that are constructed under this seemingly pluralistic notion
of His*panidad* (Colón' s), this construction is very problematic. This multicultural border is intersected by another fence/*frontera*/border that also ob-
fuscates the realities of oppression, unequal access to discourse, and the
power of dominant regimes of representation to make us experience ourselves as "other/Colóns."

To put it bluntly, Chicanas/os are simultaneously countering the Colón-
ialista narratives of two empires: one presumed dead (the Spanish empire)
and one known to be alive (the dominant culture here). Although unequal
in strength and influence in the contemporary world, they have nonetheless
configured Us according to their cultural, political, and social designs and
significant capital and ideological investments, but not without resistance.

500 Years of Resistance

Contrary to what is frequently posited in studies of culture—the idea that "transnational" identities are essentially "progressive," "productively" hybrid, and "free" to relocate though mental or physical migrations without border patrols (within the academy, in the streets, or on the border)—I would argue that this particular transnational identity is regressive. It has indeed placed Us within a series of multiethnnic constructions that purposefully stop right where our emergent and oppositional agencies begin. Thus this transnational formation of American identities is unable to offer an alternate avenue of representation, shadowed as it is by the towering frames of the Hispanic or Anglo Columbus.[34] The best it can do is offer bicultural/transcultural options of self-effacement. Cognizant of the double-forked tongue of the neocolonial discourse, many Chicanas/os have resisted these European and North American constructions, identifying the Colón narrative for what it is: a recentering project, an enterprise/*empresa* that places Spain back in its desired place: at the front of the flagship of a new European/American configuration.

Interestingly enough, in the period of its gestation, her promoters have captured a new cultural and linguistic marketplace in the Americas, through which another Spanish hegemony is being mapped out through a renewed European presence. Ironically, this construct is inclusive of Chicanas/os in an essentialist and colonizing way. But this characterization does not suffice if we are to understand the predicament of our double positioning. Although miles apart in terms of their geographic and political configurations, the dominant constructions of the Colón-ialista narrative share a similar characteristic: they commonly polarize their constructions and frequently conceal their partnership and complicity.

I am referring to the way in which the Yankee Columbus and the Spanish Colón work together to produce a type of master narrative of the colonial order: past and present, here and there. In both versions, the Columbus controversy tends to overlook the continued effects of the "imperial" presences in our daily lives and their mediating institutional effects on our own fractured self-representations. For these linkages to be made between the commemorative holiday and every day, for these effects to be visible, it is necessary to go beyond particular celebrations of the Quincentenary and the supernarrative surrounding Colón, to see how these representations are sustained in yearly cultural, educational, and political programs that do not necessarily subscribe to his particular identity directly but that nourish this type of construction of the national identity.

This type of connection was symbolically rendered by a group of students at the University of California, Davis. Four years ago they dramatically encountered these imperial presences as they protested against a Spanish-Castilian-centered curriculum and against cultural disrespect through newspaper campaigns against the Department of Spanish, marches through that academic unit, complaints to the Department of Civil Rights, and finally a hunger strike. Although they did not frame their opposition in terms of a protest against Colón per se, they nonetheless appealed to his afore-mentioned effect: *colonialismo*/colonialism. Ironically, it was the extensive dominion of that language, hailed by Spanish editorials covering the Quincentenary debate as one of Spain's most laudable accomplishments and a unifying force, that was under dispute here. Through their protest the students interrogated the supremacy of Spanish and revealed a transnational institutional complicity, thereby linking educational practices and a Eurocentric view of culture to the kind of cultural logic delivered by Sánchez-Albornoz and Oviedo.[35]

The *Davis Enterprise* described one of the early chapters of this ongoing protest movement in an article by Elisabeth Sherwin: "About 100 Chicano Latino students carried signs and marched at UCD on Jan. 29 to bring attention to their problems. They charged the Spanish department with treating Mexican and Chicano students as second-class citizens, scorned for speaking Street Spanish instead of the more academically acceptable Castilian Spanish."[36] As Sherwin explains, the UCD task force "found that the complaints of many Chicano/Latino students were valid, including the students' perception of an unjustified attitude held by some faculty, teaching assistants, lecturers and students that Castilian Spanish, as opposed to Mexican Spanish, is the preferred regional variety."[37] In reality, the complaints spanned a much broader terrain because "the emphasis of foreign language departments on classic literature and the use of the standard forms of language to the exclusion of contemporary forms of ethnic literature and dialectical varieties used by ethnolinguistic minority groups" were "clearly viewed by . . . students as an attempt to invalidate their language and culture, and to reject their very ethnic identity."[38] Like those who would later counter Colón, these students often complained that access to their national cultural and linguistic traditions, to the images, histories, and tongues of people with an indigenous claim to the language and a local culture, was being subverted by predominant academic constructions of Spanish that reenacted a colo-

nial linkage to Spain and communicated a profound disregard for these native cultures.

Upon breaking with the oppressive silence that marked the Chicano/a experience with Spanish and claiming their right to their cultural and linguistic terrain, these Chicana/o speakers exposed the vestiges of a colonial system in the very heart of a national educational system that long ago rid itself
of England's colonizing grip. Those on the receiving end of exclusion could
have predicted this revelation: the Chicana/o movement had primed Chicanos and Chicanas for this type of contention, with its displacement of the
imperial Spaniard from the center of the *mestizaje* image, its diffusion of
poems that addressed cultural and linguistic displacements with verses such
as "España chingó in Spanish" (Spain screwed us in Spanish),[39] and its recovery of poems that subverted the lingocentrism of standard Spanish and
English by crossing their borders illegally.

Suffice it to say that this protest produced quite a lot of consternation
within the greater reading public, which was amazed to find yet another crisis of Western civilization brewing in Davis, in *Spanish* classes, within a university known for its agricultural programs. Unbeknownst to many, this
protest signaled a rejection of the (peninsular) Spanish-only movement that
had put Spain in her place institutionally across these United States in a wide
array of programs that *claimed* to represent the Spanish-speaking traditions
and diverse cultural identities of the Americas. Long before the unfortunate
birth of the PC narrative in English, long before the lamentable de-Ameri-
canization of Ethnic Studies by nineties-style Rush Limbaugh-type conservatives, the Spanish-only principle had censored Us through its policing of
the Spanish language, its containment of Chicana/o, Mexicana/o, Latina/o
cultures, and its all too effective management of the institutional space we
call Spanish—a space that renarrativizes alternative histories, traditions, and
cultures by inserting our emergent identities into their canonical narratives,
where these Chicana/o identities are either marginalized or made to appear
incompetent against an unfair standard of *their* past, a past commemorated
by the very force of its legitimacy and repetition in U.S. academies.[40] This
space regulated and continues to regulate how Spanish should be spoken and
whose Spanish *lengua*/language merits canonization. This space determines
who is a partner or an outlaw in intellectual discourse. This space fore-
grounds an ethnicity, a body, a subject that is not figured as our own but that
is nonetheless represented as such by most U.S. educational institutions.

However, the student protest, which was covered in newspapers from San
Juan to New Delhi, from San Francisco to New York, countered the domi-

nant Spanish placement in U.S. culture with the responses: "Spanish is *our* language too, and if you don't like it, the hell with you" and "Aquí estamos y no nos vamos/We are here and we're not going anywhere." The Spanish crisis was instructive for others as well, who became attuned to the power-knowledge connection in Spanish through protest chants such as "Equal Rights, Equal Space, Don't Throw Racism in Our Face." They cut through the imperial Spanish register, which promotes not only Colón but also a traditional Spanish canon, coding their transnational resistance and language in terms taken from the civil rights movement over here.

Just as Columbus Day could never be their day from this critical oppositional space, Spanish could never be a neutral zone where tourists prepared for travel to a native land of enchantment, a grammar detached from its producers and their interests, a homogeneous space where stylistics obfuscated the relations of power and dominance and where Castilian dominated *pachuca/o caló* or Chicano/Mexicano Spanish without resistance. Four years before Sánchez-Albornoz would commemorate the Quincentenary by projecting his image of linguistic democracy in America as a type of productive "Hispanic" legacy of the Conquest to be celebrated in 1992, these Chicanas/os had proven him wrong through this protest, which signaled the existence of unequal access to one's own voice and culture in the *Américas*.[41] They would prove him wrong again, along with other indigenous resisters who, on 12 October 1992, wrote "No Colón" in various indigenous languages, disputing the widespread claims of a univocal form of expression defended by the proponents of the Colón-ialista narrative.

What worked against consent to the Colón-ialista narrative at the university in January of 1990 and in the nation's streets in October 1992 was the resisters' exposing of the discrepancy between this dominant Spanish ideology and their social experience and location. This provided the "keywords" with which to unravel the master's narrative, allowing other kinds of readings as well.[42] This kind of critical literacy can be fortified through an examination of how their experiences are implicated in the changing vectors of power that grace transnational relations between global cultures in the nineties. Thus it becomes possible to see the connection between this type of media knowledge and the one we experienced in English, which centered Colón within a Hollywood pantheon of loved movie stars and placed him at the center of national identity through parades, televisual encounters, and the government's blessings.

Television accounts of the controversy often read like a replay of the Conquest, with their images of the voyage to *América*, the pope's journey to

Santo Domingo, Colón's boatlike resting place lighting up the profile of a cross that bordered the shacks of *la gente*/the poor people, the forces of resistance: the modern *indigenista* resisters in San Francisco and Santo Domingo, the combat with the police (the modern conquistadores?). The shifting camera angles take us from here to there (Santo Domingo) and back again.

Thus the spectacle of the Conquest was replayed on 12 October 1992 through a reinscription of fully contested identities within an electronic dramatization of "the original journey." Their political and ideological distances were not blurred with voiced-over news broadcasts, print-media interpretations, and news specials that proposed a multicultural solution that both interpretations were valid and that a "neutral" balance was being furnished by simply telling *both* sides of the story. Instead, televisual images revealed a show of contested might: police on horseback, a display of national legitimacy, what some might call a "mini" *encontronazo*/crash, *conquista*/conquest on the streets of San Francisco that sealed the desired national identity and an Anglo/Hispanic romance with conquest. At the same time, the voices of the protesters seeking recognition of the land, an alternative tradition, and urging the pope to "go home" would not be silenced in this fully engaged struggle over the right to representation within the nation's founding identity narrative.

Whether in English or in Spanish, the state-generated Colón-ialista narrative seeks to redomesticate and silence those who do not call themselves Colón, those who do not call him their *papá*/father, and those who dare call themselves someone else. The Colón narrative locates us in discursive locations that are not ours, that are not home although they are reproduced here, and that seek to evict us from a truly egalitarian multicultural *encuentro*/encounter. It behooves us to define our positionalities with respect to the Colón narrative. Otherwise we might end up dreaming someone else's *sueño americano*/American dream, more appropriately, someone else's American nightmare. José Montoya, a movement poet, referred to this as "the Yankee nightmare"/"la pesadilla yanqui," and the students who protested against hispanization at UC Davis referred to this as "the Spanish nightmare/"la pesadilla española."

This definition also entails recognizing the silencing of the other gender in the gendered constructions of Colón, 1492–1992, and *his América*. The Colón-ialista narrative provides an unprecedented space for this type of examination, for it is *he* who is the essential subject of not one, but five centuries. As the emblematic figure of Old World and New World masculinity, *he* has had the task of embodying and configuring U.S. national identity, something that is unheard of for other underrepresented males who find themselves at the margin/*al margen* of this type of "unequal opportunity." For those of us who call ourselves Chicanas, those who choose to narrate her-story, the *mujer*/woman's story, the Colón-ialista narrative, which inscribes *his* body as the space for national identification, offers even greater levels of violence. Perhaps that is why it is *our* bodies (the young woman assassin who takes charge and kills Colón in the film *The Trial of Christopher Columbus*, for instance)[43] that so often light the match that fuels the flame of resistance to His*panism*—the construction of *his día*/day, *his lengua* (tongue/language), *his* subject, and *his* body/*cuerpo*.

Notes

1. I dedicate this essay to all of those students who valiantly stood up and fought for the rights of Chicana/o Latina/o speakers of Spanish and for equal representation of Chicana/o literature within the Spanish curriculum at the University of California, Davis. I would also like to acknowledge my friend and brother Richard, my compañero Zaré Juan, and my dear colegas Vicki, Mike, and María for their powerful support and wonderful humor during this protracted struggle, which taught me more about the politics of location than I could ever have learned from textual renditions of cultural theories and subjects. Coverage of this struggle spanned several issues of the student newspaper at UC Davis, The *Third World Forum*, from 1990 to 1992.

2. I have taken this idea from Stuart Hall, "Cultural Identity and Cinematic Representation," *Frame Works* 36 (1989): 70.

3. Counter Colón-ialismo is an exhibit that addresses the "Quincentenary of America, the 500 year anniversary of Columbus' (Colón's) discovery of America," according to the brochure announcing the events featured therein. The exhibit was curated by Patricio Chávez, Liz Lerma, and Sylvia Orosco. In the book *Counter Colón-ialismo* (San Diego: Centro Cultural de la Raza, 1991), the curatorial staff elaborates: "The word 'Colón' is also the root of colonialism, colony, colonial, colonist, and colonize. The word colonialism refers to the policy of one nation which seeks to control and dominate the peoples and resources of another nation. Thus the play on words. And the word 'counter' describes our perspective or approach to the concept of colonization or colonialismo" (1).

4. Raymond Williams coined the term "selective tradition" in *Problems in Materialism and Culture* (London: Verso, 1980), 39.

5. For an excellent rendition of this topic, see Michel-Rolph Trouillot, "Good Day Columbus: Silences, Power and Public History (1492–1892)," *Public Culture* 3:1 (fall 1990): 4–20.

6. Ibid., 3.

7. I do not mean to suggest that Trouillot effects this type of strategy in his essay, but rather I caution against the mechanistic application of his arguments in 1992 without the necessary qualifications.

8. John Fiske, "British Cultural Studies and Television," in *Channels of Discourse*, ed. Robert C. Allen (Chapel Hill: University of North Carolina Press, 1987), 260.

9. Although *Hispanidad* is normally associated with the Spanish-speaking American republics and the different groups residing in these countries, this identity is also related to the term "Hispanic." As Jack Forbes explains, the concept of Hispanic means "Spanish" or "Spanish-derived." He later elaborates: "The use of Hispanic or Spanish-origin categories achieves the end of continuing to empower white Spanish-speaking elites at the expense of people of mes-

tizo, Indian, and African origin and of masking the hierarchical, color-ranked class structure and racial ethnic diversity within the Spanish-speaking and Latin American origin populations." See Jack Forbes, "The Hispanic Spin," *Latin American Perspectives* 19:4 (1992): 59–78; 65.

10. As I point out later, the Conquest becomes a contemporary sign for civilization: multiculturalism and a kind of ideal laboratory for the successful diffusion of the Spanish language.

11. These quotes referring to the interview are taken from the Félix Monteira's "Entrevista con Luis Yáñez," *El País*, 12 October 1992: 14. These and all other quotes from Spanish-language newspapers are my translations of the original versions.

12. This line of thinking appears in an editorial piece, "Octubre del 92," following a list of editors, headed by Jesús de Polanco, which reads: "La celebración del V Centenario, del que la Expo ha sido el buque insignia, constituiría un fiasco si no siriviera para reforzar los elementos integradores, a uno y otro lado del Atlántico, de la *aventura* del Descubrimiento, El Día de la Humanidad... A cinco siglos de distancia, no es el modelo de conquista ni de colonización lo que se reinvindica, sino la significación histórica de unos episodios que supusieron el más importante esfuerzo de proyección exterior de los españoles y sin los que sería ininteligible la historia moderna" (*El País*, 12 October 1992: 10). In the typical doublespeak of this narrative, Polanco goes on to state that to celebrate the five hundred years is to celebrate the unfolding of a "project of *civilization* that is shared beween Spain and the Latin American countries." Like many of his contemporaries, he describes the events surrounding 1492-1992 as an adventure story, as a national holiday, reminiscent of our fourth of July.

13. Fernando Orgámbides reported in *El País* that several popular organizations protested the visit of the pope to Santo Domingo, asking him to condem the extermination of Indians that took place during and after the Conquest. As the article reads, the pope avoided the controversy, which mushroomed into a series of street protests, by stating that his mission was "to give thanks to God for these five hundred years of evangelization" and for the "message of salvation to this continent" ("El papa evita la polémica sobre el V Centenario," *El País*, 13 October 1992: 14).

14. "El Rey reclama en Sevilla una mayor integración con Iberoamérica," *El País*, 12 October 1992: 15.

15. For an account of this see "Cuarenta arrestados en Barcelona tras los actos del Doce de Octubre," *El País*, 13 October 1992: 19. According to these reports, those who favored and disputed the five hundred-year celebration clashed in Barcelona. In Sevilla, Spanish youths protested in front of the Expo exhibit, while in Tlavera de la Reina, the committee in solidarity with Latin America dedicated a mural with the words: "500 years of Indigenous and Popular Resistance."

16. The Mexican-Chicana/o word for T-shirt.

17. This description was inspired by José Miguel Oviedo, who characterized the Conquest as "una herida abierta de la cual sigue manando sangre." See "La Conquista, 500 años después," *El País*, 13 October 1992: 18.

18. Javier Solana, "V Centenario, un proyecto cumplido," *El País*, 12 October 1992: 16.

19. Monteira, "Entrevista con Luis Yáñez." The "Octubre del 92" editorial, from the same issue, also incorporates the idea of the Quincentenary as flagship.

20. Ibid.

21. I am influenced here by Stuart Hall's reading of Africa in his essay "Cultural Identity and Cinematic Representation."

22. These translated summaries are taken from "Marchas, festejos y contrafestejos caracterizan el 'Día de la Raza' en los países latinoamericanos," *La Opinión*, 13 October 1992: 7A; "Confusión y controversia por Colón," *La Opinión*, 12 October 1992: 10A; and Robert Lindo, "Contracelebración en la UCLA, entre danzas y cánticos," *La Opinión*, 13 October 1992: 1A.

23. The Colectivo Quijano offered a critique of this type of altruism in its editorial "América

Latina y nosotros" (*El País*, 12 October 1992: 12), where it proposes that the Spanish public abandon and reject a pejorative attitude toward Latin Americans, who are often referred to as "sudacas" and are marginalized and disempowered in Spain today.

24. Nicolás Sánchez-Albornoz summarizes the prevailing sentiment in his editorial "500 años" (*La Opinión*, 12 October 1992: 11), where he emphasizes the perdurability of the Spanish language, noting that it has not lost its prestige in the world with political decline (the independence of the Spanish-speaking Americans, Indians, etc.) but rather fortified itself, leaving behind the indigenous languages. What would Sánchez-Albornoz make of the mushrooming of indigenous dialects through Mexico into the United States that now promises a mixture with Chicana/o Spanish and caló (a youth argot popularized by *pachuchos* and a dialect of Chicana/o Spanish)? This decline of indigenous languages is disputed in another editorial entitled "1492–1992" (*La Opinión*, 12 October 1992), where Ignacio Lozano Jr. and his editorial group suggest that "Cinco siglos de opresión no han logrado, sin embargo, aniquilar a estos pueblos aborígenes. Su reclamo de una identidad propia e inconfundible se hace sentir hoy más que nunca" (11A).

25. Oviedo, "La Conquista, 500 años después."

26. Oviedo appears to be suggesting that multiculturalism did not exist prior to the Conquest, that the Indians were culturally and linguistically the same.

27. Suffice it to say that this notion has been disputed by those *indigenistas* who neither consider themselves to be fused nor to be participants in mestizo cultures or ethnicities.

28. Oviedo, "La Conquista, 500 años después"; italics mine.

29. We can only presume that strands of Native American and indigenous cultures are expressed at the periphery of this construct, although they are not named.

30. I draw these parenthetical comments in order to distinguish between the Colón-ialista narrative that is being reinscribed in this editorial and the plurality of Us's who resist incorporation into such a narrative and its colonial subjectivity in 1992. Italics are mine—they indicate an unfortunate complicity with the old-style colonial discourse.

31. Oviedo, "La Conquista, 500 años después."

32. See, for example, the editorial "500 años," where Sánchez-Albornoz uses Latin American and Caribbean immigration into the United States and its diversifying effect as proof of the widespread dominion and supremacy of the Spanish language as a by-product of the legacy of 1492. Suffice it to say that for Sánchez-Albornoz, this type of construction is not contested by Chicanas/os and other indigenous peoples.

33. This type of national construction has been under attack for years within Spain itself by a number of subordinated groups protesting linguistic, cultural, and political discrimination, with the Basques being the most militant in their opposition to Spanish hegemony. Unfortunately, traditional Spanish language departments, which reinscribe a fictive Spanish center that neutralizes contestation by marginalized cultures in Spain, have worked against the formation of strategic alliances across the Atlantic between subaltern groups on both sides.

34. For an account of the changing image of Columbus, see Trouillot's "Good Day Columbus."

35. It would be important to review this type of linguistic contestation from transnational perspectives, including a comparative analysis of how this resistance is constructed across the national borders of Spain and the American republics and into the United States.

36. Elisabeth Sherwin, "Change Advised in the Spanish Curriculum," *Davis Enterprise*, 15 March 1990: 1.

37. Ibid.

38. Lorena Natt, "U.S. Probes Alleged UCD Hispanic Bias," *Sacramento Bee*, 14 March 1990: 2. The Federal Office of Civil Rights launched its own investigation into allegations of discrimination against Chicana/o Latina/o students. The investigation took into account incidents of

screening by skin color of students who protested against being unfairly singled out in Spanish classes, according to the Trueba Report. Other newspaper reports, including those provided by the student newspaper *Third World Forum,* also included student discontent over being arbitrarily sent to *special* "native speaker classes" because of their Chicano/Mexican/Latin American dialects.

39. Louie the Foot, "Cortés Nos Chingó in a Big Way the Huey," *Festival Flor y Canto,* vols. 4 and 5 (Albuquerque, N.M.: Pajarito Publications, 1980): 95.

40. It is precisely because of the association of the name of the language—Spanish—with the name of the colonizing, ethnic group associated with the Conquest that many Chicanas/os are beginning to rethink the naming of their linguistic expression. In order to avoid these linkages between one's voice and the inscription of a colonial subject, Chicanas/os are exploring ways of engaging the multiplicity of their *lenguas*/languages in order to avoid the narrow nationalistic denominations associated with singular renditions that compartmentalize their hybrid voices.

41. Sánchez-Albornoz argues against those whom he views as proposing that Spanish has degenerated into national languages. He argues: "Los lingüistas conocen, en cambio la existencia de una koiné en la que participan en igualdad de derechos todos los usarios de español." His entire essay is aimed at reinforcing the idea of a linguistic system in which satellite and metropolis enjoy the same linguistic capital regardless of historical circumstances.

42. I have borrowed the term "keywords" from Raymond Williams, *Keywords* (New York: Oxford University Press, 1983).

43. This film was produced by Lourdes Portillo and stars Xochtil Peralta, a Chicana actress, as the successful Colón resister.

References

Chávez, Patricio, Liz Lerma, and Sylvia Orosco. *Counter Colón-ialismo.* San Diego: Centro Cultural de la Raza, 1991.

Colectivo Quijano. "América Latina y nosotros." *El País,* 12 October 1992.

"Confusión y controversia por Colón." *La Opinión,* 12 October 1992.

"Cuarenta arrestados en Barcelona tras los actos del Doce de Octubre." *El País,* 13 October 1992.

"El Rey reclama en Sevilla una mayor integración con Iberoamérica." *El País,* 12 October 1992.

Fiske, John. "British Cultural Studies and Television." In *Channels of Discourse,* ed. Robert C. Allen. Chapel Hill: University of North Carolina Press, 1987. 254–90.

Forbes, Jack. "The Hispanic Spin." *Latin American Perspectives* 19:4 (fall 1992): 59–78.

Hall, Stuart. "Cultural Identity and Cinematic Representation." *Frame Works* 36 (1989): 68–81.

Lindo, Robert. "Contracelebración en UCLA, entre danzas y cánticos." *La Opinión,* 13 October 1992.

Louie the Foot. "Cortés Nos Chingó in a Big Way the Huey." *Festival Flor y Canto,* vols. 4 and 5. Albuquerque, N.M.: Pajarito Publications, 1980.

Lozano, Ignacio, Jr., et al. "1492–1992." *La Opinión,* 11 October 1992.

"Marchas, festejos y contrafestejos caracterizan el 'Día de la Raza' en los países latinoamericanos." *La Opinión,* 13 October 1992.

Monteira, Félix. "Entrevista con Luis Yáñez." *El País,* 12 October 1992.

Natt, Lorena. "U.S. Probes Alleged UCD Hispanic Bias." *Sacramento Bee,* 14 March 1992.

Orgámbides, Fernando. "El papa evita la polémica sobre el V Centenario." *El País,* 13 October 1992.

Oviedo, José Miguel. "La Conquista, 500 años después." *El País,* 13 October 1992.

Polanco, Jesús, et al. "Octubre del 92." *El País,* 12 October 1992.

Sánchez-Albornoz, Nicolás. "500 años." *La Opinión,* 12 October 1992.

Sherwin, Elisabeth. "Change Advised in the Spanish Curriculum." *Davis Enterprise,* 15 March 1990.

Solana, Javier. "V Centenario, un proyecto cumplido." *El País,* 12 October 1992.

Trouillot, Michel-Rolph. "Good Day Columbus: Silences, Power and Public History (1492–1892)." *Public Culture* 3:1 (fall 1990): 1-24.

Williams, Raymond. *Keywords.* New York: Oxford University Press, 1983.

———. *Problems in Materialism and Culture.* London: Verso, 1980.

CHAPTER FIFTEEN

Multiculturalism and Racial
Stratification

NEIL GOTANDA

Overlooked by much of the national media in its coverage of the 1992 Los
Angeles civil disturbances was the case of *People v. Soon Ja Du*.[1] The trial of
Du Soon Ja[2] for the grocery-store shooting of fifteen-year-old Latasha Har-
lins has helped to define subsequent relations between Asian Americans and
African Americans.

Crucial to understanding the role of the courts in this incident is the
statement of the judge that accompanied her pronouncement of sentence.
Instead of their stated goal of reducing tensions, I will argue that the judge's
culturally coded comments show how institutions like the judicial system
may manage "minority-minority" conflict.

Du Soon Ja, a fifty-one-year-old Korean immigrant mother and store
owner, shot and killed a fifteen-year-old African-American girl in a dispute
and fight over a bottle of orange juice. Coming after a national series of incidents involving Korean grocers in African-American neighborhoods, the
case was followed closely in the press.

After a tense jury trial marked by demonstrations and courtroom out-
bursts, Du was convicted of voluntary manslaughter. Attention then focused
on the sentence of newly appointed Los Angeles Superior Court Judge Joyce
A. Karlin. Karlin was widely expected to sentence Du to prison time, with
most speculation centering on the length of the sentence. However, instead

of a prison sentence, Karlin sentenced Du to probation with prison time suspended, a small fine, and a requirement of community service.[3] Judge Karlin immediately became a center of controversy because the sentence was regarded as far too lenient. Many critics accused her of being at best insensitive, and at worst racist.[4] The Los Angeles County district attorney appealed the sentence, but the California Court of Appeal affirmed the decision.[5]

The statement explaining a sentence is referred to as a sentencing colloquy. I will use Karlin's short sentencing colloquy (reproduced at the end of this essay) as a text—interpreting her language to illustrate the hidden assumptions and implications in her statement and sentence.

Recognition and use of the idea of culture are sometimes offered as a positive alternative to the reenshrinement of racial subordination that comes with the repetition of traditional racial usages. The colloquy reveals how multicultural techniques can function to maintain the centerpiece of the old racial order—White privilege. As the racial, ethnic, and cultural complexities of Los Angeles continue to develop, this case illuminates some of the ongoing rearrangements of race, culture, subordination, and power.

Karlin's Multiculturalism

Karlin makes extensive use of particular culturally specific characterizations. The defendant Du is portrayed as a good mother and wife, as a hardworking shopkeeper, as an innocent victim of circumstance acting in self-defense. The real victim, Latasha Harlins, is presented as a criminal shoplifter, as aggressive and violent, as associated with gangs. These portrayals are woven together from fact and speculation and extend existing racial stereotypes.

Judge Karlin structures the sentencing colloquy in a way that illustrates her adherence to the color-blind technique. Karlin specifically recognizes the African-American and Korean communities in the opening and closing paragraphs of the colloquy (¶ 1–2, 41).[6] In her actual sentencing comments, however, Karlin makes no explicit reference to Koreans or African Americans.

Thus, the judge does not make specific reference to Black, African-American, Korean, or Asian in the main body of the colloquy. Instead, it is the use of the cultural characteristics themselves that emphasizes and circumscribes the contrasting groups—Korean and African-American. Links to Koreans and African Americans are made in prefatory and concluding comments. The crucial racial connections lie in the background understanding that these individuals are representatives of communities in conflict.

The use of cultural markers and the avoidance of the Korean and African-

American labels are of particular importance in the legal context. Avoidance of racial or ethnic labels is supportive of the doctrine of constitutional color blindness. Under that ideology, any consideration of race in governmental decision making is either questionable or unconstitutional.[7]

Karlin's use of multicultural markers goes beyond the traditional legal prescription for color blindness. Instead of a judicial fiat that race shall not be taken into consideration in her deliberations, Karlin uses the various cultural attributes and stereotypes as a multicultural alternative to race. Her implicit adoption of these cultural markers as a substitute for race validates the significance of the cultural stereotypes she employs.

The specific content of these stereotypes and cultural attributes is also of significance. Within the boundaries of the cultural markers that substitute for race and ethnicity, Karlin utilizes attributes that differ from traditional Black-White racial subordination. Instead of a model that emphasizes the subordinate position of *all* racial and ethnic minorities, Karlin creates a tiered, hierarchical structure *between* minorities. The cultural attributes of defendant Du are favorable, and portray a sympathetic, Korean "model minority." Placed in opposition is the more familiar cruel stereotype of African American as criminal and gang member.

The difference in this context is that the African-American minority is not judged against the majority society. Rather, the African-American minority is measured against and therefore "monitored" by the Korean minority. The Korean "model minority" is thus the measure of the African-American "monitored minority."

Implicit also is the idea that "monitored" and "model" racial minorities are subordinate to an "invisible majority." That invisible majority is, I believe, the White majority and its position of White racial privilege.

Judge Karlin's Sentencing Colloquy

In this section, my examination of the text of Judge Karlin's colloquy shows how Karlin sympathizes with Du and presents the victim Latasha Harlins in a harsh and unfavorable light. These contrasting portrayals are presented by associating Du and Harlins with various culturally based racial stereotypes.

The individualized racial characterizations of Du coincide with and reproduce the image and structure of Koreans and Asian Americans as a "model minority." Karlin emphasizes Du's "model minority" status by portraying her as an "innocent shopkeeper." Karlin does not articulate, but understands, and expects others to understand, that Du is a Korean shop-

keeper. Du Soon Ja is a representative successful shopkeeper and, by implication, the Korean community is a successful "model minority."

Latasha Harlins is portrayed as a criminal and associated with gangs and
gang violence. Judge Karlin emphasizes the "monitored minority" aspect of
Harlins by improperly balancing Du against Harlins. In the traditional approach to sentencing, valuation of the "worth" of the victim is only one
among many considerations. Judge Karlin, however, makes constant com-
parisons between the two throughout the colloquy. This use of Du as the
"model" against which the victim Harlins is measured emphasizes the mon-
itoring dimension to Karlin's social hierarchy.

Karlin describes Du as a fifty-one-year-old woman who is a victim of circumstances (¶ 29), including gang terror (¶ 29, 33), and a gun altered by unknown thieves (¶ 29). Further, Du was present on the day of the killing only
because of her maternal loyalty to her son (¶ 33–34), to shield her son from
the repeated robberies (¶ 33) and "to save him one day of fear" (¶ 34). And
Karlin is generally sympathetic to the hardships faced by innocent shopkeepers who are under frequent attack (¶ 24–36).

Judge Karlin portrays defendant Du as an innocent victim. In the colloquy, Du is a hard worker and has no criminal record (¶ 19). Gangs terrorize
Du's family while they operate the store (¶ 29–33). The actual killing was the
result of the assault by Harlins upon Du (¶ 38) and the modification of the
revolver by unknown thieves who had rendered the revolver "defective"
(¶ 29, 32).[8]

Harlins is described as having likely committed a criminal assault upon
Du (¶ 26–29) after an act of shoplifting (¶ 25). Harlins is an example of
shoplifters who attack shopkeepers after being caught in the act (¶ 24–26).
Further, Karlin associates Harlins with gang theft and terror (¶ 33); Harlins
is the person who caused Du to commit a criminal act when Du had previously led a crime-free life (¶ 38).

Judge Karlin also stereotypes Harlins through continued references to
gangs and gang terror. These references to gangs are not an allegation that
Harlins was herself a gang member. Judge Karlin connects "gangness" with
African Americans, ignoring the widespread presence of gangs comprised
largely of Asians. Karlin emphasizes her appreciation of "gangness" by using
the word "terror" three times in her colloquy: "victimized and terrorized by
gang members" (¶ 29); "the very real terror experienced by the Du family"
(¶ 33); "repeated robberies and terrorism in the same store" (¶ 33).

Judge Karlin's omission of any humanizing information about Harlins works to demonize her. Karlin might have done well to note a number of facts related by the court of appeal about Latasha Harlins:

> The probation report also reveals that Latasha had suffered many painful experiences during her life, including the violent death of her mother. Latasha lived with her extended family (her grandmother, younger brother and sister, aunt, uncle and niece) in what the probation officer described as "a clean, attractively furnished three-bedroom apartment" in South Central Los Angeles. Latasha had been an honor student at Bret Harte Junior High School, from which she had graduated the previous spring. Although she was making only average grades in high school, she had promised that she would bring her grades up to her former standard. Latasha was involved in activities at a youth center as an assistant cheerleader, member of the drill team and a summer junior camp counselor. She was a good athlete and an active church member.[9]

Another significant dimension of Karlin's "humanizing" of Du and "demonizing" of Harlins occurs in the question of *punishment*. Karlin omits any direct consideration of punishment. Instead, Karlin *balances* Harlins against Du, African American against Asian American.[10]

First, Karlin balances Du against Harlins by noting that in determining whether probation is appropriate, she must determine "the *vulnerability of the victim*" (¶ 23). Although the issue of vulnerability is in theory applicable only to the *victim*, Karlin proceeds to apply it to both Harlins *and* Du. Because Harlins "used her fists as weapons," Karlin declares that she was not vulnerable. Karlin does not mention the fact that Du shot Harlins in the *back* of the head, which demonstrates that Harlins was "vulnerable" to an attack by Du. Karlin follows this with a non sequitur implying that Harlins was not vulnerable because she was an accused shoplifter and therefore had not been justified in her assault upon Du (¶ 24–25). In contrast, Karlin describes Du's situation sympathetically: shopkeepers like Du seem unable even to accuse customers of shoplifting without fear of being assaulted.

Second, Karlin states that under the statute she is to consider "criminal sophistication" in deciding the propriety of probation. Although the consideration is meant to apply to the criminal sophistication of the *defendant*, Karlin ultimately balances Harlins's criminality against Du's criminal sophistication against the victim's alleged criminality (¶ 27). Karlin describes Du as lacking "any degree of criminal sophistication in her offense," as a woman "who would not be here today" but for "unusual circumstances" (¶ 28–29). Judge Karlin believes that Harlins, on the other hand, would have had charges filed against her had she "not been shot" and had the "incident which preceded the shooting been reported" (¶ 26).

Karlin further reinforces her social hierarchy through the use of gendered images of Du and Harlins. Du is portrayed as a good wife—loyally working in the family store. She is even more dramatically portrayed as a good mother—volunteering to work in the store to protect her son. Karlin also focuses attention on Du Soon Ja's status as spouse and wife by never directly mentioning Du's husband. There are references to Du's family and her son, but her husband is omitted. The context for these images is the traditional stereotype of the family as a strength of Asian cultures.

By contrast, any of the available positive gendered images of Harlins as dutiful daughter, church member, and student are ignored and she is portrayed as a criminal. This contrast between Du and Harlins reinforces the social hierarchy through the greater social distance from Judge Karlin—a female lawgiver.

The Model Minority

In this section, I argue that Karlin's racial characterizations of Du and Harlins are more than a by-product of Judge Karlin's personal sympathy or antipathy toward the two individuals. Karlin's racial stereotypes involve a racial map that includes more than just Du and Harlins as representative of Asian American and African American. By differentially distancing herself from Du and Harlins, she is producing a three-tier racial hierarchy that reinforces an existing set of stereotyped images.

The change from older stereotypes to the "model minority" can be seen by describing some of the older images that evolved in the early twentieth century and that have been only partly superseded today. At least one author has speculated on the connection between Edward Said's development of the complex construction of Oriental "otherness" to Europe and the West.[11] John Kuo Wei Tchen argues that British authors Sax Rohmer, creator of Fu Manchu in 1911, and Thomas Burke, author of "Limehouse Nights," set in the opium dens and shabby corners of London's small Chinese quarter, were themselves Orientalists, engaged in constructing racialized images of Chinese that would define American and British identity.[12]

As examples of demeaning stereotypes, Tchen points to Rohmer's Fu Manchu as embodying "evil incarnate," to caricatures of Chinese laundrymen who appeared as comic relief in early films, and to Sessue Hayakawa as an enslaving Japanese antique dealer in Cecil B. DeMille's 1915 film *The Cheat*. The images are not, however, uniform in their attitudes. Tchen examines D. W. Griffith's 1919 film *Broken Blossoms* and finds that Griffith "eschews the standard stereotype of the 'heathen Chinee' already well established in the previous century, and adapts the alternative image of the hardworking, good-for-the-West 'John Chinaman.'"[13]

A much more unrelentingly harsh set of images is seen in John Dower's examination of the mutually hostile propaganda campaigns of Japan and the United States throughout World War II, *War without Mercy*. During the war, "yellow hordes" of Japanese were portrayed as apes, monkeys, and insects.

These images constituted the collective set of stereotypes and constructed identities of Asian Americans, accumulated over a century of U.S. Asian immigration. The transformation of the Asian American from the "heathen Chinee" and the "yellow horde" into a "model minority" has been dramatic and rapid.

The sharp change began in the mid-1960s with the appearance of several articles in major national news media commenting favorably on the success of the Asian Americans, at that time mostly second- and third-generation Japanese and Chinese Americans.[14] Especially noteworthy was a 1966 *New York Times Magazine* article entitled "Success Story: Japanese American Style."[15] Those early articles, however, emphasized overcoming adversity, rather than focusing on their economic success.

In the past decade the stereotype has shifted to emphasize economic success based on an extremely aggressive work ethic and strong family cohesion. Lisa Lowe has described the model-minority myth as including the image of Asians as "aggressively driven overachievers" who "assimilate well."[16] This version of the "model minority" places Asian Americans in a reasonably well-to-do class position vis-à-vis other minorities, especially African Americans.

In the modern context, the image of the Korean grocery-store owner has become the dominant media image of an Asian American.[17] Sales transactions between Korean grocers and African-American patrons are now exemplary of all social interaction between Asians and African Americans, and the actions of Korean grocers are exemplary of all Asian-American cultures.

The racial stratification provided by the "model minority" thus provides Judge Karlin with an ideological framework both to distance herself from Latasha Harlins individually and to absolve non-Blacks generally, especially those in the highest tier of the three-tiered system of the "model minority," of any social responsibility for the effects of racial subordination on African Americans.

Conclusion

In conclusion, I offer some questions and suggestions for further exploration. One group of questions concerns the use of cultural forms to create
ideological constructions like the "model minority." Another surrounds the
difficulty of a racial analysis of Asian Americans and the troubling implications for political coalition.

Karlin's colloquy both reflects the myth of the "model minority" and
advances it by providing greater specificity. Karlin ascribes to a Korean grocer a certain class privilege (shopkeeper status), higher social status (strong
family), and high moral worth (law-abiding). These are balanced against
the demonized Latasha Harlins, who lacks them. The result is that Korean
Americans—and, by implication, Asian Americans—are defined by this
short list and the resulting narrow stereotype. Omitted is any sense of personal or social history, community or real family life, religion or spirituality,
all of which would be part of any historically textured description of Asian
Americans.

This entire effort took place in the midst of a now familiar media circus,
with full broadcast and print-media coverage. Karlin's efforts were therefore
not limited to the courtroom or even to traditional legal texts, but became
part of our everyday popular cultural discourse.

Work on the slippery terrain of popular culture and mass media is always
difficult. Hampering efforts have been the near-total absence of academic
and popular studies of the representation of Asian Americans.[18] Presenting
the varied and broad range of experiences encompassed by persons of Asian
ancestry in America while combating both model-minority and yellow-peril
stereotyping will require a depth of understanding and analysis that is only
now emerging.

Perhaps even more difficult is the question of the depth of reality behind
the "model minority." If one accepts that there really is a privileging of Asian
Americans and that the "model minority" is not simply a fabricated illusion,
then an examination of the racial status of Asian Americans in a multiracial
model becomes intensely complex.

If one takes the position that "Asians have problems, just like African
Americans," then one is implicitly using an analytical framework that says
the racial status of Asian Americans is identical to that of African Americans—both are subordinated by Whites. This two-category (White/non-
White) framework suggests that the only "real" differences between Asian

Americans and African Americans are minor variations in culture and economic achievement.

If, however, Asian Americans are coming to occupy a class position between Whites and African Americans, then a different analysis is needed. A further exploration of Asian-American as an intermediate racial category would examine whether or not social and economic privileges attach to those persons classified as Asian-American. For example, in economic relations, research could determine whether real property values declined when an Asian American integrated a formerly all-White neighborhood. One could compare whether the decline in values, and any associated racial "tipping," was more severe for African Americans than Asian Americans. An analysis of social attitudes might also reveal a differential between African Americans and Asian Americans around such issues as crime and morality. Similar studies could be carried out in other areas such as income, job discrimination, and portrayals in popular culture.

Recognizing that there is some truth in the "myth of the model minority" seems to me a better starting point for examining whether there is an emerging Asian-American racial category. The difficulty comes in attempting to situate this racial category without succumbing to the "model minority" stereotype. On the one hand, if a real class privilege is emerging for Asian Americans, then long term political coalitions cannot turn on simple calls for recognizing a common history of racial oppression by a White majority. Instead, one must explore more carefully the deeply intertwined issues of class and group privilege to explore where one can find both short- and long-term common interests.

What should not be forgotten amidst these complexities, however, is that interracial and interethnic conflict cannot be divorced from the broader American historical context of racial subordination. One of the historical axes of social subordination in America has been White privileging over African Americans. Even as the possibilities of racial stratification and the embedded ideological constructions of Orientalism are examined, awareness of the continuation of that basic axis of power and privilege must continue.

Sentencing Colloquy

Los Angeles Daily Journal, 22 November 1991: 7: a transcript of remarks by Los Angeles Superior Court Judge Joyce A. Karlin in the sentencing of Soon Ja Du.

[¶ 1] One thing I think both sides will agree on is that nothing I can do, nothing the judicial system can do, nothing will lessen the loss suffered by Latasha Harlins' family and friends. But the parties involved in this case and anyone truly interested in what caused this case can make sure that something positive comes out of this tragedy by having Latasha Harlins' death mark a beginning rather than an end—a beginning of a greater understanding and acceptance between two groups, some of whose members have until now demonstrated intolerance and bigotry toward one another.

[¶ 2] Latasha's death should be a catalyst to force members of the African American and Korean communities to confront an intolerable situation by creating constructive solutions. Through that process, a greater understanding and acceptance will hopefully result so that similar tragedies will not be repeated.

[¶ 3] Statements by the district attorney, (which) suggest that imposing less than the maximum sentence will send a message that a black child's life is not worthy of protection, (are) dangerous rhetoric, which serves no purpose other than to pour gasoline on a fire.

[¶ 4] This is not a time for revenge, and my job is not to exact revenge for those who demand it.

[¶ 5] There are those in this community who have publicly demanded in the name of justice that the maximum sentence be imposed in this case.

[¶ 6] But it is my opinion that justice is never served when public opinion, prejudice, revenge or unwarranted sympathy are considered by a sentencing court in resolving a case.

[¶ 7] In imposing sentence I must first consider the objectives of sentencing a defendant:

1) To protect society.
2) To punish the defendant for committing a crime.
3) To encourage the defendant to lead a law-abiding life.
4) To deter others.
5) To isolate the defendant so she can't commit other crimes.
6) To secure restitution for the victim.
7) To seek uniformity in sentencing.

[¶ 8] The question becomes, are any of these sentencing objectives achieved by Mrs. Du being remanded to state prison?

[¶ 9] Let us start with the last objective first: uniformity in sentencing. According to statistics gathered for the Superior Courts of California, sentences imposed on defendants convicted of voluntary manslaughter last year ranged from probation with no jail time to incarceration in state prison for several years.

[¶ 10] Because of the unique nature of each crime of voluntary manslaughter, and by that I mean the uniquely different factual situations resulting in that crime, uniformity in sentencing is virtually impossible to achieve.

[¶ 11] Which, then, of the other sentencing objectives lead to the conclusion that state prison is warranted?

[¶ 12] Does society need Mrs. Du to be incarcerated in order to be protected? I think not.

[¶ 13] Is state prison needed in order to encourage the defendant to lead a law-abiding life or isolate her so she cannot commit other crimes? I think not.

[¶ 14] Is state prison needed to punish Mrs. Du? Perhaps.

[¶ 15] There is, in this case, a presumption against probation because a firearm was used.

[¶ 16] In order to overcome that presumption, the court must find this to be an unusual case, as that term is defined by law.

[¶ 17] There are three reasons that I find this is an unusual case:

[¶ 18] First, the basis for the presumption against probation is technically present. But it doesn't really apply. The statute is aimed at criminals who arm themselves when they go out and commit other crimes. It is not aimed at shopkeepers who lawfully possess firearms for their own protection.

[¶ 19] Second, the defendant has no recent record, in fact, no record at any time of committing similar crimes or crimes of violence.

[¶ 20] Third, the defendant participated in the crime under circumstances of great provocation, coercion and duress. Therefore, this is, in my opinion, an unusual case that overcomes the statutory presumption against probation.

[¶ 21] Should the defendant be placed on probation?

[¶ 22] One of the questions a sentencing court is required to ask in answering that question is "whether the crime was committed because of unusual circumstances, such as great provocation." I find that it was.

[¶ 23] I must also determine the vulnerability of the victim in deciding whether probation is appropriate. Although Latasha Harlins was not armed with a weapon at the time of her death, she had used her fists as weapons just seconds before she was shot.

[¶ 24] The district attorney argues that Latasha was justified in her assault on Mrs. Du. Our courts are filled with cases which suggest otherwise.

[¶ 25] Our courts are filled with defendants who are charged with assault resulting in great bodily injury as a result of attacks on shopkeepers, including shopkeepers who have accused them of shoplifting.

[¶ 26] Had Latasha Harlins not been shot and had the incident which preceded the shooting been reported, it is my opinion that the district attorney would have relied on the videotape and Mrs. Du's testimony to make a determination whether to file charges against Latasha.

[¶ 27] Other questions I am required to address in determining whether probation is appropriate are "whether the carrying out of the crime suggested criminal sophistication and whether the defendant will be a danger to others if she is not imprisoned."

[¶ 28] Having observed Mrs. Du on videotape at the time the crime was committed and having observed Mrs. Du during this trial, I cannot conclude that there was any degree of criminal sophistication in her offense. Nor can I conclude that she is a danger to others if she is not incarcerated.

[¶ 29] Mrs. Du is a (51)-year-old woman with no criminal history and no history of violence. But for the unusual circumstances in this case, including the Du family's history of being victimized and terrorized by gang members, Mrs. Du would not be here today. Nor do I believe Mrs. Du would be here today if the gun she grabbed for protection had not been altered. This was a gun that had been stolen from the Du family and returned to them shortly before the shooting.

[¶ 30] The court has been presented with no evidence, and I have no reason to believe that Mrs. Du knew that the gun had been altered in such a way as to—in effect—make it an automatic weapon with a hairpin trigger.

[¶ 31] Ordinarily a .38 revolver is one of the safest guns in the world. It cannot go off accidentally. And a woman Mrs. Du's size would have to decide consciously to pull the trigger and to exert considerable strength to do so.

[¶ 32] But that was not true of the gun used to shoot Latasha Harlins. I have serious questions in my mind whether this crime would have been committed at all but for a defective gun.

[¶ 33] The district attorney would have this court ignore the very real terror experienced by the Du family before the shooting, and the fear Mrs. Du experienced as she worked by herself the day of the shooting. But there are things I cannot ignore. And I cannot ignore the reason Mrs. Du was working at the store that day. She went to work that Saturday to save her son from having to work. Mrs. Du's son had begged his parents to close the store. He was afraid because he had been the victim of repeated robberies and terrorism in that same store.

[¶ 34] On the day of the shooting Mrs. Du volunteered to cover for her son to save him one day of fear.

[¶ 35] Did Mrs. Du react inappropriately to Latasha? Absolutely.

[¶ 36] Was Mrs. Du's over-reaction understandable? I think so.

[¶ 37] If probation is not appropriate, and state prison time is warranted, then a short prison term would be an injustice. If Mrs. Du should be sent to prison because she is a danger to others or is likely to re-offend, then I could not justify imposing a short prison term.

[¶ 38] But it is my opinion that Mrs. Du is not a danger to the community and it is my opinion that she will not re-offend. She led a crime free life until Latasha Harlins walked into her store and there is no reason to believe that this is the beginning of a life of crime for Mrs. Du. But if I am wrong, Mrs. Du will face severe consequences.

[¶ 39] For all of these reasons it is hereby adjudged that: on her conviction for voluntary manslaughter, Mrs. Du is sentenced to the midterm of 6 years in state prison. On the personal use of a firearm enhancement, the defendant is sentenced to the midterm of 4 years, to run consecutive to the 6 years for a total of 10 years. Execution of this sentence is suspended.

[¶ 40] Mrs. Du is placed on formal probation for five years on the following terms and conditions:

[¶ 41] Mrs. Du is to perform 400 hours of community service. I strongly recommend that for the maximum impact on Mrs. Du and for the community, this service should be in connection with efforts to various groups to unite the Korean and African American communities.

[¶ 42] Mrs. Du is to pay $500 to the restitution fine [sic] and pay full restitution to the victim's immediate family for all out of court expenses for Latasha Harlins' funeral and any medical expenses related to Latasha Harlins' death.

[¶ 43] Mrs. Du is to obey all laws and orders of the probation department and the court.

[¶ 44] If I am wrong about Mrs. Du and she re-offends, then she will go to state prison for 10 years.

Notes

1. Superior Court of Los Angeles County, no. BA037738; *People v. Superior Court (Du)* 5 Cal.App. 4th 822 (1992).

2. The titles of the superior court case and the reported opinion use "Soon Ja Du" and place Du's surname last. In referring to defendant Du in this article, I will follow standard Korean usage in my placement of the family surname.

3. Appeal, at p. 829.

4. See, for example, "Blacks Voice Outrage over Sentence in Girl's Death; Reaction: Some

Fear That Fragile Truce between Korean Merchants and African-Americans Could Be in Danger," *Los Angeles Times,* 17 November 1991: 1; "Blacks Seek to Channel Anger over Sentence," *Los Angeles Times,* 17 November 1991: 1.

5. Largely fueled by sentiment against her sentence in *People v. Soon Ja Du,* three challengers opposed Karlin in her confirmation election. A majority of voters, however, reelected her to a full judicial term. She is not currently assigned to try cases in the criminal division of the Los Angeles Superior Court.

6. References to the sentencing colloquy are by paragraph and are not footnoted.

7. See generally, my discussion in "A Critique of 'Our Constitution Is Colorblind,'" *Stanford Law Review* 44 (1991): 1.

8. Judge Karlin does not mention the choice by Du and her family to operate a store in a racially particularized neighborhood. The appeals court noted that the Du family sold one business and chose to purchase this business in a "bad neighborhood" (Appeal, at p. 828). Had Karlin recognized a "consenting shopkeeper" instead of an "innocent shopkeeper," Karlin could then have allowed an inference that Du understood some of the dangers of operating a small business in a poor neighborhood. Du's use of the revolver would take on a more calculated character. Instead of Du as the innocent victim of a "defective" revolver, her use of the revolver was part of the difficult and sometimes harsh environment in which the Du family had chosen to work. I am not suggesting that self-defense, including armed self-defense, is inappropriate. At issue here is Judge Karlin's understanding of the context for the use of firearms and how Karlin has characterized Du Soon Ja's use of the weapon as completely without fault.

9. Appeal, 829 n. 7.

10. This "measurement" of Du is an aspect of a judge's traditional sentencing function.

11. Edward W, Said, *Orientalism* (New York: Random House, 1978).

12. John Kuo Wei Tchen, "Modernizing White Patriarchy: Re-Viewing D. W. Griffith's *Broken Blossoms,*" in *Moving the Image: Independent Asian Pacific American Media Arts,* ed. Russell Leong (Los Angeles: UCLA Asian American Studies Center and Visual Communications, 1991), 133. See also John W. Dower, *War without Mercy: Race and Power in the Pacific War* (New York: Pantheon, 1986), 147–80; Dennis M. Ogawa, *From Japs to Japanese: An Evolution of Japanese-American Stereotypes* (Berkeley: McCutchan Publishing, 1971). More traditional treatments are found in Stuart Creighton Miller, *The Unwelcome Immigrant: The American Image of the Chinese, 1785–1882* (Berkeley: University of California Press, 1969), and Stuart Creighton Miller, *"Benevolent Assimilation": The American Conquest of the Philippines, 1899–1903* (New Haven: Yale University Press, 1982).

13. Tchen, "Modernizing White Patriarchy," 136–37.

14. Bob Suzuki, "Education and the Socialization of Asian Americans: A Revisionist Analysis of the 'Model Minority' Thesis," *Amerasia Journal* 23 (1977): 4.

15. William Petersen, "Success Story: Japanese American Style," *New York Times Magazine,* 9 January 1966: vi–20. Similar articles included Julian Makaroff, "America's Other Racial Minority: Japanese Americans," *Contemporary Review* 210 (1967): 310–14; Barbara Varon, "The Japanese Americans: Comparative Occupational Status, 1960 and 1950–," *Demography* 4 (1967): 809–19. A recent article that discussed the model minority is Don T. Nakanishi, "Surviving Democracy's 'Mistake': Japanese Americans and the Enduring Legacy of Executive Order 9066," *Amerasia Journal* 19 (1993): 7–35.

16. Lisa Lowe, "Heterogeneity, Hybridity, Multiplicity: Marking Asian American Differences," *Diaspora* 1:1 (spring 1991): 24–44.

17. More recently, the *Los Angeles Times* presented a photo essay with accompanying text about Korean grocers and African-American patrons: photographs by Chang W. Lee, article by John W. Lee, "Counter Culture: In Los Angeles, Korean-American Stores Are Sometimes the

Flash Point of Racial Animosity—But They Are Also the Proving Ground for Tolerance" (*Los Angeles Times Magazine*, 17 October 1993: 20–21).

18. I am aware of only two book-length treatments of Asians in popular culture: James S. Moy, *Marginal Sights: Staging the Chinese in America* (Iowa City: University of Iowa Press, 1993), and Darrell Y. Hamamoto, *Monitored Peril: Asian Americans and the Politics of TV Representation* (Minneapolis: University of Minnesota Press, 1994).

CHAPTER SIXTEEN

The Erotic Zone

Sexual Transgression on the U.S.-Mexican Border

RAMÓN GUTIÉRREZ

The images middle-class San Diegans have of Mexicans in general are often shaped by the immediate impressions and images they form of Tijuana. Like the Tijuanenses, who have deep kinship, social, and economic ties to San Diego and to southern California, San Diegans have deep-rooted and long-standing ties to Tijuana. Indeed, since the end of the nineteenth century, Tijuana's growth as a city, in large part, has depended more on prominent capitalists in San Diego than on those farther south in central Mexico. Tijuana's businesses were created with American technology to meet consumption demands located in San Diego and Los Angeles. The Santa Fe Railroad link, which by 1890 connected Los Angeles, San Diego, and Tijuana, is but one early example of this. The telephone wires and electric lines, which by 1914 tied Tijuana to an American economic infrastructure based in San Diego, is another.[1]

The line that marks the boundary between Mexico and the United States is a border that both binds and separates two spaces, two national territories that once were one, and two peoples of numerous classes and multiple ethnicities that are now quite impossible to pull apart. Thousands of Tijuanenses cross into the United States every day to work, to study, and to pass their leisure time shopping in fancy shops in La Jolla, strolling through Balboa Park, or stashing away their millions in San Diego's banks. Commerce and capital move ever more frenetically in the opposite direction as well. Billions of U.S. dollars flow into the *maquiladoras* just across the border. Millions of American tourists visit Tijuana yearly in search of inexpensive leather goods and black velvet paintings of Jesus Christ, Michael Jackson, and Che Guevara. Many San Diego boys count the days until they reach manhood with dreams of Tijuana's bestial sex acts, its drinking and debaucheries, which good Protestant mothers constantly caution their sons will only lead to hell, furry palms, and dissipation.

Educated middle-class San Diegans who understand the social and economic dynamics of the cultural space they inhabit, or whose daily lives are profoundly touched by Mexicans, know that Mexico's human geography is a complex and multifaceted universe never easy to describe in one breath or image. But for the majority of San Diegans, the less educated and more ignorant ones, Mexico and Mexicans are more a concept than a tangible reality. Caricatures, stereotypes, and images, born of ignorance, fed by fantasy, shaped and distorted by the media, and explained by folk aphorisms, are the currency of popular discourse. Whatever the genesis of these perceptions, distorted as they are, they shape the way middle-class Americans refract reflections of themselves onto the "illegal aliens," those nonhuman creatures from another world called Mexico, who constantly threaten to invade sovereign United States space and destroy the essence of American life.

My task here is to explore the way middle-class San Diegans express their fears, the way they construct "illegal aliens," imaginary Mexican enemies at their borders. Let me proceed with my most complex point regarding how Americans shape and organize their symbols of national identification, and conversely, how they shape national others, citizens of other nation-states.

David Schneider, the respected cultural anthropologist, in his book, *American Kinship*, argues that the symbol of "conjugal sexual intercourse" was the key symbol that shaped how middle-class white Americans understood kinship, or that complex set of human relationships that structures how individuals are related to each other:

> Sexual intercourse as an act of procreation creates the blood relationship of parent and child and makes genitor and genetrix out of husband and wife. But it is an act which is exclusive to and distinctive of the husband-wife relationship: sexual intercourse is legitimate and proper only between husband and wife and each has the exclusive right to the sexual activity of the other.... Sexual intercourse between persons who are not married is fornication and improper; between persons who are married but not to each other is adultery and wrong; between blood relatives is incest and prohibited; be-

tween persons of the same sex is homosexuality and wrong; with animals is sodomy and prohibited; with one's self is masturbation and wrong; and with parts of the body other than the genitalia themselves is wrong. All of these are defined as "unnatural sex acts" and are morally, and in some cases, legally, wrong in American culture.[2]

The products of sexual intercourse, children born of shared blood and substance, are related to their parents naturally, or by the natural order of things. Father, mother, brother, sister, uncle, aunt, grandfather, and grandmother are related by blood, through acts that originate in intercourse and by a process that is deemed to be natural. People are also related through marriage and marriage is an institution rooted in law and custom. A husband and wife are related and duty-bound to each other through human laws. They are husband and wife, and their parents are in-laws (father-in-law, sister-in-law, son-in-law, etc.).

Middle-class white Americans organize their kin relationships around two orders: the order of nature, which is human and biological, and the order of law, which is based on the rule of reason. These two basic elements—nature and law—on which American notions of relatedness rest, are the basic oppositions through which spatial, political, philosophical, and zoological categories are often constructed and understood. One only has to take for an example how the United States of America defines citizenship and nationality to see this point. Americans are either born into the nation (the order of nature) or they enter it through a legal process (the order of law) and become citizens through a process we call "naturalization." Three types of citizens are possible in the United States: (1) those who are born American but are naturalized citizens of another country, (2) those who are born elsewhere but "naturalized" as Americans (quite frequently by marrying an American citizen), and (3) those who are American by birth and law.[3] Nature and law thus create citizens.

The nature/law code that derives from the domain of kinship creates other basic dichotomies, which are anchored to the symbol of conjugal sexual intercourse and are used to differentiate us/them, insider/outsider, male/female, law-abiding/criminal, human/animal, clean/dirty.

To form a mental picture of how American middle-class stereotypes of Mexico and Mexicans are logically constructed, we can begin at the spatial level, examining how Tijuana first developed as an escape valve for the sexually repressed and regulated American Protestant social body of San Diego. In this case, the international boundary between Mexico and the United States has long been imagined as a border that separates a pure from an impure body, a virtuous body from a sinful one, a monogamous conjugal body regulated by the law of marriage from a criminal body given to fornication, adultery, prostitution, bestiality, and sodomy.

Indeed, Tijuana really came into its own as a city in the 1920s primarily as a haven for American illegal activities. When Prohibition, the outlawing of the production and consumption of alcoholic beverages, was instituted in the United States in 1920, San Diegans rushed across the border to Tijuana to construct their gin mills and their saloons. Soon there were brothels, gambling houses, and all those pleasures and pains prohibited in respectable California society. San Diego newspapers frequently lambasted these activities. "Tia Juana Is a Disgrace to Mexico, a Menace to America," the *Los Angeles Examiner* announced in its headline, continuing that "Tia Juana is a plague spot and ought to be eradicated."[4] Although cries of shock and revulsion similar to these filled the pages of local tabloids, historian Vincent Z. C. de Baca argues that until the early 1940s, much of Tijuana's vice activity was owned and operated by American citizens who lived in Los Angeles and San Diego.[5] Prohibition was eventually abolished in 1935, but by that date the caricature of Tijuana as a den of vice and decadence—as a place of unruly and transgressive bodies—had been firmly fixed in the American psyche.

Shaping the images Americans have of the "other," of the Mexican that inhabits the deepest recesses of fantasy, are a series of concrete events that constantly crystallize the fear that seems to characterize sociocultural relations between San Diegans and Tijuanenses. Whether it be in the 1920s, the 1950s, or the 1990s, the Mexican rapist figures prominently in those fears. One can begin as early as 1926, with the famous Peteet case, to see how the fear and fantasy of rape constantly repeat themselves. The events of this case started on Saturday, 31 January 1926, when Thomas and Carrie Peteet and their two daughters, Clyde and Audrey, checked into Tijuana's San Diego Hotel. The family had crossed into Mexico for five days of vacation. A little gambling and a little drinking was all they had in mind. And, according to local witnesses, they did plenty of that. On Wednesday evening, 3 February, Thomas Peteet and his daughters entered the Oakland Bar, and before long Peteet, apparently drugged, passed out. His daughters met a similar fate, and in that state were abducted and raped. Mr. Peteet came to later that night, discovered by his wife in the street outside the Oakland Bar. The ordeal the girls had suffered was known the next day. Deeply humiliated and shamed when they returned home, the family committed suicide together. The case became a cause célèbre in San Diego. What sorts of outrages were being perpetrated on Americans across the border? Civic, religious, and temperance groups demanded a closed border. "Remove the menace of Tijuana and keep San Diego County a clean, safe, law-abiding community," the San Diego Law Enforcement League constantly proclaimed.[6] Eventually the furor died down, but before it did, this celebrated rape case had created an image of Tijuana and the Mexicans living there as brutes governed by lust and given to crime.[7]

Since the famous Peteet case, the shape of reporting on Tijuana has not changed very much. What is noted in stories are the unregulated sexual activities of American youth. The crimes they commit in Tijuana are rarely noticed; what is done to them makes the evening news.[8] As a headline in a recent story in the Orange County Register noted: "Tijuana's wild nights of partying lure teens south, where beatings, robbery and death sometimes await."[9] The story chronicles how young American boys and girls escape the natural-law authority of parents over children with trips to Tijuana where minors are served alcohol, indulge their sexual desires and fantasies, and create a disorder that is never permitted at home. At home, they would be breaking the law. The law codes that order and regulate the body and kinship in American thought stem from the symbol of conjugal marital intercourse. In Tijuana, American boys and girls desecrate marriage by soliciting prostitutes or by becoming the victims of rape. In American middle-class minds, Tijuana is a marginal area that lies beyond the border of the American body politic governed by nature and law. Mexico is a place where vice thrives. There, gambling, liquor, drugs, prostitution, and unnatural sexual activities flourish. And these activities constantly threaten to spill across the border to corrupt the American body politic.

If we cross the border into San Diego County to explore how middle-class San Diegans speak about and imagine the Mexican workers who actually cross the border to cook their meals, to clean their streets, to nurse their babies and to build their homes, we find again a related set of stereotypes best understood by looking at the ways in which nature and law create the moral community of kinship.

The dominant rhetoric concerning Mexican workers in the San Diego area has been marked by two major depictions. First, Mexican workers are "illegal aliens" and thus a menace to public safety. They break the law. They engage in illegal acts, such as seeking work. In times of economic difficulty, they take away jobs that are meant for Americans, and thus are the reason for economic hardship. This argument is well known, and so are its fallacious assumptions, but it nonetheless gets reinformed continually because the Immigration and Naturalization Service, seeking illegals, frequently stages raids at factories and fields. The second depiction of Mexican workers is that they are physically dangerous because they are rapists, the source of drugs and diseases such as AIDS, and a menace to public health because they live in squalor and unsanitary conditions.

Regarding Mexican illegality, consider the 1989 survey sent to voters in San Diego by the American Immigration Control Foundation. The Foundation asked recipients of the survey for their opinions on "America's illegal alien crisis," informed them of what it considered the facts on "illegal aliens," and solicited their dollars. Full of xenophobic rhetoric, the leaflet posed a variety of questions. Question 3 asked: "Which of the problems associated with illegal aliens are the most personally disturbing to you?" The options, to name but the most inflammatory, were: "bilingual public education, bring in diseases like AIDS, loss of jobs for American citizens, drug trafficking and crime." The opening statement of the cover letter that accompanied the poll, stated:

> My forefathers and yours entered America legally. They understood through hard work, obeying the law and contributing to the nation's good, they would EARN the right of citizenship in this great land of opportunity. But what we're dealing with today is quite different. Statistics show our borders have become a floodgate for millions . . . who think little of breaking our laws and living off taxpayers like you and me.[10]

The "illegal alien" as a physically dangerous rapist is a stereotype that has a long history in U.S.-Mexican relations that goes back to the 1926 Peteet case. But more recently, paranoid fantasies about Mexican rapists have reemerged in American public discourse. In September 1986, hysteria over school-aged children who attended the Kelly School in Carlsbad, California, in the northern part of San Diego County, exploded as a result of two incidents. The first involved several migrant workers and a fifteen-year-old girl near the Kelly School. Apparently the girl was walking near the school when three Mexican migrants started to approach her from the front, and three more from behind. An acquaintance of the girl saw the men approaching her and immediately called out to the girl, thus avoiding a "bad situation." Community concern had already been fanned by a newspaper story in the 19 September 1986 issue of the *San Diego Union*. "Aliens Said Preying on School Kids," the headline read. The story quoted Border Patrol Assistant Chief Gene Smithburg reporting that "A new type of crime is being perpetrated by undocumented aliens, extorting lunch money from schoolchildren . . . it's really too bad that something like this happens. The kids are really intimidated." A public outcry was quickly heard and it led to a "roundup" conducted on horseback, helicopter, and all-terrain vehicles. Some three thousand "illegal aliens" were apprehended and returned to Mexico. The idea of adult single men, dark-skinned men, who congregated near innocent children, was more than parents could take. As one resident said, "We hit a nerve that runs through San Diego County."[11]

One sees another permutation of the fear of the Mexican rapist in the "Light Up the Border" campaign that was started in San Diego in 1989 by Muriel Watson, a middle-class white widow of a former U.S. border patrol agent. The main activity of "Light Up the Border" was to get citizens to drive in their cars to Dairy Mart Road, just off Highway 5, about one mile north of the Tijuana-San Diego border, and, at sunset, to turn on the headlights of their cars toward the border. The campaign was a huge success, counting over five hundred cars and some 2,500 participants. These individuals came to "Light Up the Border," says Watson, because "they just share my concern, they all had [newspaper] clippings: 'Oh, look at this, this 16-year-old girl was raped and her throat was slit and they rescued her just in time.' . . . So this was what motivated me . . . pure and simple."[12] Using body metaphors to describe her goals, Watson explained, "The light . . . was just meant to light up this area. . . . This is a main artery, this is a very tender spot."[13]

Many sensationalistic things have been written and reported about "Light Up the Border." This probably is due to the fact that the movement is composed of many desperate elements, among them neo-Nazis and skinheads who are motivated by racist and xenophobic ideas. But, in the mind of Muriel Watson, the movement's founder, her actions are born of a concern for the "aliens." She wants to protect the "aliens" from border rapists. Her intentions are totally altruistic. She and her followers, Watson says, are "good Americans" motivated only by the desire to uphold law and order. Certain physical things had to take place, and one of them was the message to the alien: "Look, you're crossing the border and it is against the law.[14] "Light Up the Border," says Watson, was started to create

> a certain modicum of control. It's just like your own yard in your own house. If you have a fence up, then you keep kids from running across your lawn. . . . If you see somebody coming on, you're more aware of it and you're able to better control the flow of whatever goes across your own property. . . . I still ask the question: 'Why are they coming the way they are?' and that has to be resolved. And there's no reason that between two reasonably civilized nations, that the border can't be respected.[15]

The idea that the nation's front yard is being littered with the refuse of rapists, robbers, and petty criminals has been expressed in much of the literature describing the tensions in the northern townships of San Diego County. Here, one of the constant complaints of Americans is that the "aliens" congregate at shopping centers and local business establishments, waiting for work. Gloria Carranza, Transient Issues Coordinator for the City of Encinitas, summed up this fear well:

> The businesses were complaining that the large number of migrants was actually a negative impact to them because they were walking through the establishments or "hanging out" in the morning, looking for employment. In the afternoon they were hanging out, they would be drinking . . . just the intimidation factor of large groups of Hispanic males was an intimidation . . . [it was] a public safety issue.[16]

The composition of the Mexican workforce in Encinitas was large, single, and male—men who did not duplicate the American ideal of compulsory heterosexuality. Nina LeShan, a social worker, described this population and the root of the problem well when she said: "Most of the time, men come up here, and without their family or without any women."[17]

The image of the disease-infested Mexican is often juxtaposed and incorporated in public-safety arguments. In San Diego County the stereotype of the disease-spreading Mexican has become particularly potent primarily because the large-scale development of middle- and upper-class housing has suddenly put the residents of these new tracts in face-to-face contact with the cardboard and plastic shantytowns Mexican workers have constructed as their own shelters. These workers' camps have long existed, but went unnoticed when the area was still predominately rural. There they lived in the most rudimentary and rustic of conditions, without toilets, without running water, without heat or electricity. Then housing starts began. And as the number of Mexican workers arriving to build these fancy houses increased, so too the friction, fueled by the belief that the area was being overrun and that the encampments were a health menace to Americans. The city of Encinitas took the most strident measures against these "illegals." Using force, it proceeded "to clean them [the camps] up," stationing guards to assure that such squatter communities did not develop again. It is significant that the city of Encinitas wanted "to clean up" the camps, for, as Nina LeShan, a social worker and midwife to the Mexican migrants in the area stated, the Mexican were seen "as filth."[18]

In the public and official discourse of the city of Encinitas and its residents, the distinction between "us" and "them," between Americans and Mexicans, between citizens and "aliens," between persons who obey the law and those who are criminals, has been cast as "cleanliness" versus "dirt," as a distinction between healthy bodies and those infested with disease. "Dirtiness" represents the physical threat to the ideal order, to the orderly functioning of society.

Mary Douglas, the cultural anthropologist, in her book *Purity and Danger*, writes that symbolic schemes preoccupied with disease, hygiene, and dirt are often implicit comments about the ideal order of society. Douglas notes:

> If we can abstract pathogenicity and hygiene from our notions of dirt, we are left with the old definition of dirt as matter out of place. . . . It implies two conditions: a set of ordered relations and a contravention of that order. Dirt, then, is never a unique, isolated event. Where there is dirt, there is a system. Dirt is the by-product of a systematic ordering and classification of matter, in so far as ordering involves rejecting inappropriate elements.[19]

What I have been arguing is that in the dominant Anglo-American middle-class culture of the United States, the symbol of marital sexual intercourse is the fundamental foundation on which the moral community rooted in nature and law rests. This is a moral community that grants citizenship principally to those persons who mirror its body order, and resists penetration and excludes those who do not—"illegal aliens," rapists, dirt, and so on. Cultural historian Sander Gilman has noted that coitus creates in all of us a sense of abandonment, an abandonment of the highly ordered and controlled world. Such moments represent the potential loss of control, not only of self, but of our private and public worlds. "Such disorder cannot be contained within the self. It must be expelled into the world. The projection of such disorder, a disorder exemplified by the sexual, . . . [often] take[s] the form of the thought-collective's fantasies about the Other, whether the 'sexual' or the 'racial' Other."[20]

In Mexico, the process of nation building began when single Spanish males raped Indian women. The result was cultural, social, and biological *mestizaje*, the heritage of race mixture that remains the dominant conquest legacy for Mexicans. In the United States, the nation was founded atop Puritan and Calvinist foundations, based on a strict morality and beliefs about what was natural and unnatural, who were and who were not kin by blood and marriage. That legacy of nature and law, which is at the very core of American middle-class kinship ideas, explains how Americans project their hysterias and anxieties and thereby symbolically construct Mexicans.

Notes

1. Vincent Z. C. de Baca, "Moral Renovation of the Californias: Tijuana's Political and Economic Role in American-Mexican Relations, 1920–1935" (Ph.D. diss., University of California, San Diego, 1991), 1–4.

2. David Schneider, *American Kinship: A Cultural Account* (Chicago: University of Chicago Press, 1980), 38.

3. David M. Schneider, "Kinship, Nationality, and Religion in American Culture: Toward a Definition of Kinship," in *Symbolic Anthropology: A Reader in the Study of Symbols and Meanings*, ed. Janet L. Dolgin, David S. Kemnitzer, and David Schneider (New York: Columbia University Press, 1977), 67–68.

4. "Tia Juana Is a Disgrace to Mexico, a Menace to America," *Los Angeles Examiner*, 11 February 1926; quoted in de Baca, "Moral Renovation of the Californias," 12–13.

5. De Baca, "Moral Renovation of the Californias," 10.

6. Quoted in ibid., 8.

7. Ibid., 13–16.

8. See, for example, "Mexican Accuses U.S. of Disinformation Campaign," *San Diego Union*, 21 November 1986; "Pressure, Payoffs Curb Mexican Press," *Los Angeles Times*, 4 March 1987; "Views Differ over Coverage by U.S. Press of Mexico," *San Diego Union*, 11 October 1986.

9. *Orange County Register*, 1 December 1991: K1.

10. Quoted in Isabelle Fauconnier, "Perceptions of and Reactions to Undocumented Workers in San Diego" (senior thesis, University of California, San Diego, 1991), 5.

11. Daniel Wolf, *Undocumented Aliens and Crime: The Case of San Diego* (La Jolla, Calif.: Center for U.S.-Mexican Studies, 1988), 21.

12. Muriel Watson interview, transcript in Fauconnier, "Perceptions," 92.

13. Ibid., 91.

14. Ibid., 42.

15. Ibid., 48, 88.

16. Gloria Carranza interview, transcript in ibid., 53–54.

17. Nina LeShan interview, transcript in ibid., 70.

18. Ibid., 74.

19. Mary Douglas, *Purity and Danger: An Analysis of the Conceptions of Pollution and Taboo* (London: Praeger, 1966), 35.

20. Sander L. Gilman, *Sexuality: An Illustrated History, Representing the Sexual in Medicine and Culture from the Middle Ages to the Age of AIDS* (New York: John Wiley and Sons, 1989), 3.

CHAPTER SEVENTEEN

Site-seeing through Asian America
On the Making of Fortune Cookies

RENEE TAJIMA

I should have seen it coming the day I picked up the *Wall Street Journal* and read that one of the leading Communist Party formations on the Asian-American left was planning a hostile takeover of Shearson Lehman-American Express.

As the 1980s rolled into the 1990s, the changes were already in motion. Chinatown storefronts were now Vietnamese, Burmese, Malay. College admission struggles were being waged around the overrepresentation of Asian Americans, rather than their underrepresentation, as when I was a college student during the 1970s. A new generation of youthful gangsters surfaced in places like New Orleans and Iowa City, while Japanese companies became major players in Hollywood. In Brooklyn, the Red Apple grocery boycott gave national visibility to a decade of escalating tension between Asian immigrants and African Americans. The established Asian-American left—dominated by Chinese and Japanese Americans who had come of age during the Third World mobilizations of another era—were caught off guard. And they would remain ambivalent about their role in succeeding crises of interethnic strife.

It was becoming impossible to get a handle on who the Asian American was, or who we were as a collective. Prior to the 1980s the Asian American was fairly simple to define. We were predominantly Chinese, Filipino, and Japanese; the majority of us were American-born and English-speaking. We shared a common history of labor immigration and racial discrimination, and this history was the crux of our political identity—as Asian Americans and as an aggrieved racial minority. At a time when the struggle for equality was focused on legal protections, the construction of this common identity was the political currency upon which gains in equality were achieved. But demographics ultimately catapulted Asian Americans into the post-civil rights era. The Asian-American population quadrupled during the 1970s and 1980s, and the growth was characterized by a diversity in nationality, language, religion, culture, and class, the likes of which we had never seen before. As we entered the 1990s, the rules of the game had changed irrevocably.

At about this time, I found myself in Los Angeles at a state-of-Asian-America conference sponsored by the Asia Society. The fact of the tony Asia Society's involvement was bewildering enough. Then there were the scores of veteran activists wandering about the Biltmore Hotel like rebels with a caseload, not a cause. Former Marxist-Leninists had become city commissioners, corporate responsibility flaks, public television producers, and party officials. Democratic Party officials. We were The Suits now—still dominating the conference sessions with rhetoric from the 1970s, while new immigrants who represented the voice of the second millennium waited on the sidelines. A *Los Angeles Times* reporter asked me to define the common denominator linking all these disparate Asian nationalities. All I could think of is we all eat rice.

I decided to make a film about this new Asian America, and it turned out to be a road documentary called *Fortune Cookies: In Search of Asian America* (working title).

My life on the road began more than thirty years ago in a fire-engine-red Ford Fairlane in which I could stand to my fullest height and spy on America, traveling by like one long, manic theme park on wheels. The World's Fair. The Weeki Wachi mermaid show at Bucaneer Bay. Abe Lincoln's cabin. Tony the Tiger cereal samples, free for the asking at the Kellogg's factory in Battle Creek. The Four Corners. Devil's Peak at dusk.

The fact that the car was this bright, blazing color was an event in itself, because in all other matters, bland was our family motto. Our first real home was a ranch-style split-level on a tract of identical beige split-levels. We shopped the Sears catalog. We were Presbyterians, for god's sake, and I knew from the moment I could comprehend such things as fate and destiny that mine was sealed. I would be an average Jane floating along with the tide. Put it this way: no one has ever been moved to daredevil feats, to wail the blues, or to plumb the soul in psychoanalysis because they need to come to grips with growing up *Presbyterian.*

We were dull by design. My mother Marie had grown up on Los Angeles's Skid Row and spent her teenage years in the Heart Mountain, Wyoming, Relocation Center. Heart Mountain, the camp that ruptured the dignity of my mother and my uncles. And that my grandfather—who worked sixteen hours a day as a custodian at Bullocks and as a houseboy for rich people— regarded as a blessed event. An extended, all-expense paid vacation. Grandpa, who was mightily disappointed when Japan lost the war, and who later developed an intense fascination for women's professional Roller Derby competition. Grandpa had a dark side.

My father, named for Calvin Coolidge, was a high-school linebacker who once played in the state finals at the Coliseum, and the son of a preacher. A Presbyterian preacher, naturally, who counseled the Japanese community to go quietly to the camps. My father went into the Army. As fate would have it, his entire unit was felled by chicken pox and spent the remainder of the war quarantined at Fort Meade. Two months after V-day, my father finally made it to Germany, where he got to meet Ingrid Bergman. He has pictures.

Like most Nisei, once my parents returned to civilian life after the war, they weren't about to do anything to draw attention to themselves. And so the split-level and split identities. We became a family of Oriental Blandings, American Japanese.

Sacramento

The first thing I do before setting off to shoot *Fortune Cookies* is go to meet the actor Victor Wong. I plan to shoot a documentary film about Asian-American identity that is narrated by a fictionalized central character. I need a lead. I loved Victor in *Chan Is Missing*, so I go off to Sacramento to see him. I discover life is stranger than fiction.

Victor is the son of the late Sir King Wong, San Francisco's "Mayor of Chinatown," a prominent businessman, and the veritable crown prince of the prewar MSG business. Photo credit: Quynh Thai

Victor was a rebel. As a teenager he was born again and preached fire and brimstone on Grant Avenue, much to the chagrin of his strict Confucianist father. Worse yet, he went to art school. That was followed by four marriages, to one black woman and three white women. Not one of them a Chinese. He was every Chinese parent's nightmare.

"You put yourself into limbo because you reject one whole thing, which is the Chinese tradition. You have nothing to replace it with. It puts you into a terrible vacuum."
Photo credit: Renee Tajima

Victor is the same age as my own father, but they couldn't have lived more different lives. My father dared to buy a red sedan in a rare moment of devil-may-care, but he was a cautious driver all the way. Victor ran with Jack Kerouac and the Beats, lived dangerously, and once trekked all the way across country just to try out the chilis of various states. He knew he was breaking his father's heart, but Victor couldn't help himself. Although he savored tradition, he found it toxic in large doses. And besides, Victor was born in the same year Babe Ruth hit his sixtieth home run. He married Olive Thurman, the daughter of a famed black theologian, in the year of *Brown v. Topeka Board of Education*. He was a denizen of North Beach, a Chinese Beat, an American in Chinatown. Victor Wong was already having an Asian-American identity crisis in the days when the rest of us were still calling ourselves Orientals.

New York

My casting trip to Sacramento turns into a pilgrimage, with Victor Wong a road guru urging me on my search for Asian America. I do away with any notion of a fictionalized character. No amount of make-believe would match Victor's real-life story anyway. Inspired by Victor, I decide instead, right then and there, that I will drive the same highways I traveled as a child to see for myself how much we've changed. I begin my journey in New York City.

From all outward appearances, Chang Y. Choi is just another small-time businessman who makes fortune cookies in New York's Chinatown. Look beneath the surface, and his Chrystie Street factory is a web of complex economic relationships and social histories that signifies what Asian America has become.

Choi's Golden Star factory manufactures fortune cookies, a confection originated in America but generally served as an after-dinner treat at Chinese restaurants. Photo credit: Quynh Thai

Mr. Choi says he wants to retire by the time he's forty. "I want to make money five year and retire. OK? I young I can have energy now, I can work, okay? I don't want a ... Like a forty, fifty, or too old I can't do anything, right? So, I want a keep up about five year, that's it." It could be said that Choi is driven by a Confucian work ethic—and that is the key to success for Asian immigrants like him. But retire by forty? That doesn't come from Confucius. What is it, in the tangled cultural lineage of Choi's many lives from Vietnam to Hong Kong to New York that is the source of his ambition? The Calvinist work ethic imported via Christian missionaries? An innate entrepreneurialism inherent to Chinese diaspora survival? Greed?

And what is the source of my own addiction to Publisher's Clearinghouse and *Reader's Digest* sweepstakes contests? I've even taken to ordering the subscriptions offered, to save me the humiliation of returning my entry under cover of the wretched "No" sticker pasted on the front of the return envelope. My reply is "Yes." Yes, I will take one year of *People* at the low introductory rate of $9.97 in just four easy payments. Yes, I want a shot at millions, at the chance of greeting Ed McMahon and the Prize Patrol at my door, bearing a ticket to independent wealth.

I agonized for years while living in New York because I knew in my heart that they probably toss out all of the Manhattan entries anyway. Winners usually live in places like Indiana, in a single-family residence with a name like Miller festooned on a mailbox hand-painted with roosters and vines, the ample Mrs. Miller shrieking with surprise, wiping away tears of delight on her apron. I couldn't picture the Prize Patrol caravan double-parked on 38th Street to see me, as I peered through a crack in the door behind three dead bolts. "Who's there, *Ed McMahon*? Right. Slip your I.D. under the door."

There are certain prizes in American life that will always be off-limits. Asians need not enter. Nevertheless, something leads me to the mailbox each year, armed with my entry and hopes. Is it the stubborn persistence of the American Dream, ingrained in the immigrant psyche? An Oriental penchant for gambling? Greed? And why, after such industry and hard work, did our Mr. Choi choose to take the ultimate risk? One year after filming in Chinatown, I was to discover that the life of this model immigrant had taken a sordid turn—one that I never would have imagined. But that's for the movie.

It was Wood Moy, not Victor Wong, by the way, who actually played the lead in *Chan Is Missing.* He just looks like Victor, so I must have gotten them confused. Somewhere along the road I realize my error. But nothing is as you remember it anyway, and part of the glory of a road trip is allowing the accidents of fate to propel you along.

New Orleans

Our family travels when I was a child rarely took us south. It was too confusing. Which toilets do we use, the ones for "Whites" or for the "Coloreds"? My
mother always told us to use the cleaner one, but that solution never satisfied. Even in childhood I realized there was no place for us in the larger
drama of American life. The South only magnified our irrelevance.

I drive to New Orleans in hopes of meeting Harry Lee, the "Chinese
Cajun Sheriff" of Jefferson Parish. Sheriff Lee is the highest-ranking Asian-
American law-enforcement officer in the nation. He is also the brother of
China Lee, the first ever Asian-American *Playboy* centerfold, circa 1964. At
over three hundred pounds, Lee is the quintessential good ol' boy and a force
in local politics. No one calls Harry Lee irrelevant. He virtually declared war
on the *Times-Picayune* when they reported, one Christmas season, that Lee
had ordered his deputies to arrest any blacks they spotted driving through
the parish at night. Harry certainly knew which side of the latrine to stake
his interests on.

I do get to meet the ubiquitous sheriff, however briefly, and he loads me
up with Harry Lee souvenir drinking cups and Harry Lee Mardi Gras coins.
Unfortunately, he is out on a quail-hunting trip by the time I'm ready to film
and I'm left with these long unanswered questions. How have Asians accom-
modated themselves to the racial climate of the region? What shape does
Asian-American identity take far from the diaspora centers on the East and
West coasts?

My luck turns when I run across a local scholar named Marina Espina,
who has unearthed the history of the first Asian immigrants to America. I'm
taken aback when she tells me they were actually Filipinos who settled in
Louisiana as early as 1756. They were sailors who had been indentured by the
Spaniards and forced to work the galleon trade from Manila to Acapulco.
Weary of the brutal conditions on board, they jumped ship in the Louisiana
bayou and formed a colony, named Manila Village, on Barataria Bay. *The
young generation, they all know. They grew up knowin' they part Filipino. Well
because, we heard it. We heard it so they can hear it. When they're grandparents
they can tell it to their children. And we have it all written down. All kinds of
stories. . . . Well, if we don't know where we come from how do we know where
we going?*

The Burtanog sisters are from the oldest Filipino family around New Orleans. They go back
eight generations and know just about everyone and everything around here.
Photo credit: Quynh Thai

In the popular imagination, a gathering of Asian-American women typically surrounds a pot of tea or a mah-jongg game. The worlds of literature
and cinema prefer Asian-American stories when they are, in reality, stories
of Asia, and the tellers only once-removed by migration or birth. It is as if
the hugeness of the Asian drama alone can make our lives here in America
matter. War, exotica, the sweep of history, the tremors of grand conflicts as
cultures are renegotiated. But what of the rest of us, who claim four, five,
even eight generations in America, as the Burtanogs do? There are no mah-
jongg games and trans-Pacific memories here in the Burtanog household.
The defining cultural equation is Five-card Stud and a six-pack of Bud
(Lite). The talk is ex-husbands, voodoo curses, and the complicated racial
design of New Orleans society.

Sister Mae was the queen
of the Caballeros de
Dimas-Alang Mardi Gras
carnival ball in 1946, the
last year that a Filipino
float would win the
coveted Grand Prize
from the Elks Krewe of
Orleanians.
Photo credit:
Quynh Thai

In the Jim Crow South, Filipinos were considered white by dint of their
Spanish ancestry. They could intermarry, attend school with, and get buried
next to, below, or on top of the more conventionally white citizenry. Audrey
says her brother Walter use to play with another boy on the block named
Willy. But as soon as Walter turned eighteen, Willy, being black, had to start
calling his friend Mr. Walter. Of course the South is no more a nucleus of
racial enmity than the North. Benita Burtanog points out that her Filipino
cousins in California could not marry Caucasians because of antimiscegenation laws that classified Filipinos as Mongolians. It is a testament to
America's perpetual ambivalence toward Asian Americans that miscegenation laws, and attitudes, differ so wildly region by region and state by state.

Of course, nothing is more labyrinthine than Asian Americans' own rules and rankings for proper marriages. Ask a random sampling of Asian parents for their own mating formulas and you will hear any combination of the following: Parent A: "It's OK to marry Japanese or Filipino, but no Korean. Then comes white, then Vietnamese, then Puerto Rican. No black." Parent B: "Korean, Chinese, Indian for my son. Don't care about my daughter as long as he's not white." Parent C: "Chinese OK, then white, then Korean. No Japanese, no Mexican, no black." Parent D: "White or Oriental, I don't care which. Hispanic and Indian people maybe. No black." Parent E: "Must be northern Chinese. Period."

The common denominator is often: African Americans need not apply. When Victor Wong married his first wife, Olive, in 1954, the triumph of *Brown v. Topeka* had no discernible impact on his father, Sir King. Wong Sr. called Olive to an interview, and warned her that the Chinese do not intermarry, that the children would be funny looking. There is a painful irony to Asian bigotry, as we owe so much to the black movement. Antimiscegenation laws that persecuted Asians were struck down when a black woman and her white husband, aptly named the Lovings, went all the way to the Supreme Court to validate their marriage. A whole slew of legal guarantees for Asian Americans were born out of African-American struggles for equality. Voting rights, fair housing, desegregation of schools, affirmative action set-asides, civil rights protections. Even the right to be here.

A legal scholar named John Hayakawa Torok sends me a file of citations on the 1965 immigration reform act. Congress struck down race-based quotas in the so-called Asia-Pacific Triangle, and the Asian-American population multiplied sevenfold within the span of a single generation.

The Immigration and Nationality (McCarran-Walter) Act of 1952, as Amended to 1965

By MARION T. BENNETT

—for compassionate reasons. For other thousands of aliens here illegally, be adjusted their status to that of lawful immigrants. Other thousands were permitted to come in "under parole." Further, the 1952 Act contained a basic inconsistency in that it had such huge loopholes for nonquota immigrants that for the next thirteen years two out of every three immigrants would be classed as nonquota and entered without numerical restriction. This immediately threw the national-origins plan out of balance. It permitted the creation of such large voting blocs from other than the favored area of northern and western Europe that they soon politically controlled major urban centers in the United States, a good many electoral votes, and Congressional districts. By 1965 the political atmosphere would change completely, and in an era of expanding civil rights for minorities, our pluralistic and egalitarian-bent society would reject, through Congress by public law, the concept that white, Anglo-Saxon, western European culture need remain the cornerstone of a truly viable democratic society or was worthy of preservation though none denied it the nation's debt and honor.[9]

LEGISLATION, 1953–1964

The successful legislative strategy of antirestrictionists in the years 1953–1964, inclusive, is reflected in the fact that in this short period Congress enacted thirty-two public laws, the overall effect of which was to widen the loopholes in the national-origins system to such an extent that it was effectively nullified, although not repealed until 1965. Almost half a million immigrants were permitted to come in as special exceptions to the national-origins formula in these years. They were admitted largely as nonquota immigrants from outside the areas of northern and western Europe, which were given approximately 80 per cent of the quotas under the 1952 Act. The total of exceptions was substantially augmented by administrative waivers of exclusion, adjustment of status, and suspension of deportation. The refugee-parole provisions of the McCarran-Walter Act were also used extensively. Congress, in addition, enacted 4,273 private bills on behalf of individual immigrants, per-

Marion T. Bennett, A.B., LL.B., Washington, D.C., is Chief Commissioner of the United States Court of Claims; a former Member of Congress from Missouri (1943–1949); a Colonel in the Air Force Ready Reserve; author of American Immigration Policies: A History (1963) and of articles on legal subjects in various journals; and consultant to authors of the Immigration and Nationality Act of 1952 and the Judiciary Committees of Congress.

VOLUME 367   SEPTEMBER 1966

THE ANNALS

of The American Academy of Political and Social Science

THORSTEN SELLIN, *Editor*
RICHARD D. LAMBERT, *Associate Editor*

THE NEW IMMIGRATION

Special Editor of this Volume
EDWARD P. HUTCHINSON

Professor of Sociology
University of Pennsylvania

© 1966, by
THE AMERICAN ACADEMY OF POLITICAL AND SOCIAL SCIENCE
All rights reserved

PHILADELPHIA
1966

Arkansas and Mississippi

Hattiesburg, Mississippi, is a direct shot up Interstate 59 from New Orleans. I go there to meet Bill and Yuri "Mary" Kochiyama, the legendary Japanese-American activists from New York City. The trip is a second honeymoon for the Kochiyamas. They first met here some fifty years ago, when Bill was in basic training with the 442d battalion at Camp Shelby. Yuri at the time was interned at the Jerome, Arkansas, relocation camp just across the Mississippi River. Theirs was the kind of love affair memorialized in music of the era: "I'll be seeing you in all the old familiar places that this heart of mine embraces, all day through . . ." Bill, a young soldier fighting against fascism in Europe, and Yuri a USO volunteer anxious for his safe return. Unlike other wartime couples though, the bride waited behind barbed wire.

The conventional wisdom is that the Nisei never spoke of the internment camps. Not so the Kochiyamas, or my own family. When I was a child, the camps were a constant source of family stories, even vehicles for value lessons of the "when-I-was-young-we-had-to-live-in-barracks" variety. In one of our more rambunctious years as children, my parents tried to prove their point by driving us to the site of the Heart Mountain Relocation Center—a desperately barren place, even in summer. The camp experience has always been ingrained in our family lexicon. To this day, whenever I meet another Japanese American, I ask by way of introduction, "What camp was your family in?" It is a way of breaking the ice and establishing connections. In my lifetime, I have rarely met another Japanese American with whom I did not have some link, via the camps, family, friends of friends, or our family homestead in Japan.

I first met Yuri Kochiyama when I was a student at Harvard-Radcliffe and she was a featured speaker during our annual Malcolm X Weekend. In those days, Asian-American, Latino, and African-American student organizations regularly collaborated on progressive activities. As a veteran of antiracist and human rights struggles and a contemporary of Malcolm X, Yuri was an obvious choice to deliver the keynote. I had produced a three-screen slide show commemorating Third World solidarity for the event, and Yuri, as is her custom, invited me, a complete stranger, to visit her home the next time I was in New York. A few months later, I was on her doorstep—one of thousands of students she and Bill have fed, housed, matched up with prospective romances, and inspired.

Naturally, one of Yuri's first questions was, "Where were your parents in camp?" When I told her my mother Marie (née Ujiiye) was first detained at

Santa Anita Park, the racetrack-turned-detention center in Arcadia, California, a light went on in Yuri's mind and she withdrew to her ubiquitous backroom to fetch a file. Now Yuri is a figure bigger than life because of her great conviction and the boundless energy with which she has battled for equality during four plus decades. But what makes her memorable is her warmth and numerous eccentricities. My sister remembers joining her to watch a National Geographic special on the ant world. When the red ants started subjugating the white ants, Yuri was beside herself with indignation. Then there is the extensive teddy bear collection to which she is intensely devoted—much of which was given to her by luminaries in the arts, letters, and the left.

Yuri remembers virtually everything, and records the rest. She prodigiously notes every name, address, and memorable quality of the legions of people she meets, then takes a snapshot. During the war, she hand-wrote the lyrics to all her favorite romantic ballads—"Stardust," "Mood Indigo," "Rhapsody in Blue." So when I mentioned my mother's name, Marie Ujiiye detainee at Santa Anita Park, Yuri was able to find her listed in a battered diary from 1942. As it turns out, Yuri was my mother's Sunday School teacher and leader of the Crusaders, a group of teenage girls who wrote letters to the Japanese-American GIs stationed overseas.

When Bill was stationed overseas, Yuri wrote him three letters a day.
Photo credit: Quynh Thai

It's not an easy time for Bill and Yuri. They have just lost their daughter Aichi, who was hit by a taxi in midtown Manhattan. They have already buried one child, their eldest son, Billy. I drive the Kochiyamas west across the state to Rosedale, a small town on the Mississippi Delta where Billy lived during the Freedom Summer of 1965. It is fitting that Billy came back here to do civil rights work. Mississippi, during the Jim Crow years of World War II, was a large influence on his parents' passion for equality.

We take a tour through the old training grounds at Camp Shelby with Herb Sasaki, a 442d battalion veteran and retired officer here. "I've told Yuri many times, I wonder why I survived because I was just a plain rifleman, infantry. And all my buddies were wounded or killed and I was one of the very few remaining ones." Bill recalls the shock of racism for Nisei soldiers when they arrived as fresh recruits. African-American GIs, even in full uniform, couldn't get a ride on the Hattiesburg city bus. One day, a group of 100th battalion boys from Hawaii got fed up with the practice. They literally picked the driver up off his seat and threw him off the bus, invited all the black GIs on board, and took over the wheel themselves. The Hawaii Nisei were known for such antics—they hadn't come to Hattiesburg weighted down with the same baggage of racial intimidation as the mainland "Katonks." Herb doesn't remember the antics as fondly as Bill: "Well, we had to stay on the white side. You had to make up your mind. The reason why they had the problems during the war years is because the Hawaiians wouldn't comply with that. They said 'Nobody is going to tell us who we can associate with,' so they did as they pleased."

It turns out the Davises, the family Billy stayed with in Rosedale, still live across the street from city hall. We knock on their door and crowd inside the tiny, veneer-paneled living room, where as many as twenty young activists lived during that Freedom Summer. The Davises all remember Billy, and show us the big Barco-lounger that was his favorite chair. They had no idea he had died.

Bill swaps old war stories with a new generation of soldiers at Camp Shelby.
Photo credit: Quynh Thai

James Ernest Ellington's
family owns the land
where the War Relocation
Authority built the
Jerome internment camp.
He always thought the
camps were an injustice,
and so he makes it a
point to greet all the
Nisei who pass through
for one last look at the
site.
Photo credit:
Quynh Thai

When we travel as children, everything is new. I remember the American landscape as being full of places I never knew before, and places I might conquer someday in my future. But older travelers, like the Kochiyamas, or Victor and the Burtanog sisters, are drawn to the venues of their past, inhabited by the ghosts of people long dead. As a filmmaker, I regularly ask people to reveal their deepest pain, the tragedy of their lives. But in Rosedale, I can't bring myself to ask Bill and Yuri to talk about Billy. On our drive back to Hattiesburg, I remember the day my parents came to New York and invited the Kochiyamas out for a reunion dinner. We ran into another old friend from the camp days, the minister of our family's church and his wife. Each couple had endured the war together. But it strikes me that the strongest bond between them was that each had buried a son. Our minister's son, and Billy, to suicide. My brother Bobby at the wrong end of a drugged-out hit-and-run driver. With all the people I meet during my travels, there is a constant interplay of the particulars of race and history and the universality of death, love, family, dreams that determines the shape of their lives. As if, in striving to assert our singular identity, what we want people to know is that we grieve too.

Before we leave the site of the relocation camp at Jerome. Mr. Ellington has one last story to tell of the incarcerated Japanese. "Lookee here," he says, "when the War Department come and bringing those messages here about the dead, they cry just like the white people. They lost many a son, and a husband."

Chicago

I was a Cubs fan long before I ever considered myself Asian-American.

I was born before the immigration reforms of 1965, a time when Cubbies undoubtedly did outnumber Asian Americans. Our first home in Chicago was a second floor apartment on Roscoe Street in the northside, a fly ball's distance away from Wrigley Field. Those were the glory days of Ernie Banks, voted Most Valuable Player even when his team was in last place. We children were all die-hard loyalists in the footsteps of my father, a man who has waited patiently over a span of forty-five summers for the Cubs to take a pennant. There is something poignant about being a Cubs fan, which prepared me well for being Asian-American. Always waiting, hopelessly, for your ship to come in.

About the time we were moving to our new split-level in the suburbs, Victor Wong was heading for Chicago to perform with the improvisation troupe, Second City Theater. Second City is famous for its comedic alumni like Joan Rivers and *Saturday Night Live* regular John Belushi and company. Victor came on board in 1961, its early days, and he has been one of the only Asian-American members since then. If there is a group that has never been ready, or rather acceptable, in prime time, I suppose we Asian Americans are it. Victor's memories of Second City are not happy ones. "They didn't know what to do with a Chinese character," he says. I'm told by a cast member from those days that when a skit was doing poorly with the audience, the other actors use to hang Victor upside down by his ankles. Not a proud moment for a man whose acting debut was in a Lyon Phelps play directed by his first wife, and who named his son after Anton Chekov.

My first stop in Chicago is the northside—old haunts of Wrigley Field, our old apartment, and finally, Second City. I find Victor's name on the wall of fame in the theater, lonely among all the others both famous and obscure. Then I bring the crew to Roscoe Street to film a shot of my first home. It is far different from what I remember. The red brick facade and concrete steps of our old home movies seem to have been altered unrecognizably by time, reminding me that you can never go home again. As I meditate about the day later in my motel room, my mother calls me to tell me that she's given me the wrong address on Roscoe Street. They say you can't go home again, but if you want to try, make sure you get the right address.

On my way north from Chicago, I stop in the town of Barrington to pay a visit to my Uncle Bill and Aunt Barbara, who have two of everything. Two power mowers, two turkeys on Thanksgiving Day, two VCRs and two TVs stacked one on top of the other in the family room, two sons, two daughters, two freezers, and so on. Some years back my Aunt Barbara converted to Mormonism and it's no wonder. Mormons customarily keep a one-year supply of basic essentials in preparation for Armaggedon, and it was an easy adjustment for my Barbara to upgrade to keeping two dozen of everything.

Barrington is a sheltered, affluent Chicago suburb—the type in which John Hughes typically sets his comedies. As we drive into my aunt and uncle's property, I can see a Christmas tree sparkling through the front window and my aunt peeking through the door. It reminds me of the time twenty-some years ago when my four cousins gathered behind that same window in fright as two slovenly, bushy-haired strangers pounded on the front door. Memories of Charles Manson and the Tate-La Bianca murders were still fresh, and owners of sprawling, self-contained homes in places like Barrington were thinking twice about security in isolation. With this in mind, my cousins were about to call the police when they realized the stranger was actually my brother Mark and his friend Dave. Mark and Dave were on their way from college in Northfield, Minnesota, to an antiwar rally in Chicago and stopped by for a home-cooked meal.

What a difference a
war makes.

I don't know why we took such divergent turns from our Chicago cousins. It is typical of Asians of my generation for some to have rebelled, and others to have blended in. My cousins went on to become, respectively, a dentist, a CPA, a registered nurse, and a salesman of scientific measuring instruments. Our own record of adult pursuits includes my sister Marsha, who spent twelve years in college analyzing miniature Indian mogul paintings, and my brother Bobby, who once ran off to a Moonie camp but was kicked out because the Moonies thought he was nuts.

It could have been our move to California in 1966 that set us off on a different course. We left behind a homogenized Mount Prospect, once home to one of the Grand Dragons of the Ku Klux Klan, for Altadena, an integrated southern California community and home at one time or another to, among others, Sirhan Sirhan, David Lee Roth, and Rodney King. Mark and Marsha went off to college in time for the Summer of Love, and there was no turning back for any of us to our Mount Prospect days, or ways. The social revolution wasn't easy on my parents, and especially my father, a lifelong Republican. From 1968 to 1973 or so, roughly the period between Martin Luther

King's assassination and the Paris Peace Talks, my parents stopped taking pictures of us, with the exception of a single snapshot every Christmas. I don't know if it was the hair, the beards, or the general aura of disdain we wore on our faces.

About the only time I was nearly slapped by an aunt was during these years. By the age of fourteen, I had read *The Wretched of the Earth* and *The Autobiography of Malcolm X*, and formed an unbendable ideology of class and race oppression, which gave me no compunction at smirking at my elders' chosen lifestyles, what I perceived as their misguided patriotism, their failure to engage in armed struggle against the internment camps, and other such perceived crimes. Now, my mother and most of my aunts had done domestic work as young women. Those lucky enough to get jobs with wealthy families learned how to entertain and decorate their own homes from the ladies they worked for. They were proud of the lives they had made for themselves, especially this one particular aunt. What set her off might have been a snide remark about the bourgeois aspirations of the Nisei, second-generation Japanese Americans, or some tirade on the general malaise of capitalism. But my aunt could no longer stomach my attack on the lives the Nisei generation had so painfully reconstructed after the Depression and after the camps.

As I write this today, now the same age as my aunt was then, I am, of course, repentant. After all, my sweepstakes and lottery endeavors signify nothing less than my own dreams of a nice home, money for car payments, good colleges for the kids. In those days I use to flinch at that adage, "You'll get more conservative as you get older." I am now forced to admit there is truth in it. But I have also witnessed the political evolution of the Nisei, including my parents and aunts and uncles, in their own right. The redress and reparations movement of the 1980s was a milestone. All of my Nisei relations participated in some way, with a defiance I had never seen before. Through the testimony delivered to the Commission on Wartime Relocation and Internment Camps, we Sansei came to appreciate the context of the times, and the depth of the personal nightmare our parents faced. And during the mobilization for redress and reparations, I believe the Nisei came to rely on the activism and organizing skills their children had developed in the antiwar movement and campus struggles.

Victor Wong has told me in his interview that he never felt he could be a Chinese American, a part of America, until the civil rights movement. The political mobilizations for racial equality and construction of Asian-American identity during the 1960s and 1970s were a turning point for our participation in the public life of the nation. When Alexis de Tocqueville traveled nineteenth-century America, he observed the citizenry's penchant for forming like-minded associations—the organizing units for enacting democracy. He could have added any number of Asian-American mass organizations, labor groups, cultural clubs, and the like, to his list of teetotalers and yeoman's guilds. I don't think there is an Asian American who lived during that period of change who has not been touched by the stunning advances in education, housing, jobs, creative expression, and all sectors of public life.

But there has always been a strain of elitism in the movement, which was encapsulated in my aunt's exasperation with her highfalutin nieces and nephews. Still today, when we, as largely college-educated artists, activists, and scholars, gather to articulate hopes and aspirations of Asian Americans, it is often in a language most Asian Americans would not understand. Nor should they bother to. And there is the estrangement from new immigrants. Just as Asian-American activists were starting to solidify our own ideologies during the 1980s, we were confronted with the arrival of new immigrants and refugees. Among them were virulent anticommunists who associated Marxism and Mao with the Khmer Rouge and the Cultural Revolution. There were refugees who took no particular stock in the notion of Third World solidarity, and were just as likely to regard their black and brown neighbors as antagonists, not brothers and sisters in struggle. There were immigrants who clung tenaciously to the myth of the American Dream—one that we had already rejected in theory, if not entirely in practice. More annoying yet, some went on to achieve that dream, building successful businesses, sending their children to prestigious schools, and supplying real-life material for Model Minority stories in the mainstream press. These new Asian Americans did not fit our vision of an enlightened constituency. Perhaps that is why we found ourselves perplexed by the turn of events of the 1990s.

The Heartland

I can never figure out how Asian immigrants end up in the places where they end up. I recently met two Sikh brothers—at a Passover, naturally—whose parents first settled in a small town in Oklahoma, then relocated to my husband's hometown in the Rio Grande valley of Texas. I've had friends from glamorous cities like Tokyo and Hong Kong who traveled thousands of miles to attend a junior college somewhere in Iowa. How did they even find out about these schools?

On the road in Wisconsin.
Photo credit: Quynh Thai

Volunteers at the Sheboygan Historical Society.
Photo credit: Quynh Thai

In Sheboygan, Wisconsin, on the shores of Lake Michigan, I meet Charlie Ma, a local restaurateur who came here from Hong Kong as a young man to do just that, study, then work at the local technical college. When he arrived in 1970, he was about the only Chinese in town, but quickly endeared himself by joining the Lion's Club, ringing bells for the Salvation Army during Christmastime, and teaching Chinese cooking classes. "Ma" in Chinese means "horse," so his English name actually translates to Charlie Horse. Mr. Ma's place serves northern Chinese fare cooked by Hmong workers, a decent selection of Rhinelander wines, and offers karaoke singing on a stage next to the main dining room. I don't know if you ever traveled through Wisconsin twenty-five or thirty years ago, as I did when I was a child. But I can tell you, the mere idea of finding Sheboyganites in the home of the Jaycees Bratwurst Days, partaking of such entertainment as karaoke over a bowl of Mabo Tofu, is enough to double my eyelids on a cold day. Of course, during the 1960s, there were only about six thousand plus Asians living in the entire state. Today, the population is sizable enough that some Wisconsin towns have an Asian gang problem. Here in Sheboygan, I find the moniker "Asian Diciples" (sic) scrawled along the main street underpass.

Most of the Hmong refugees were brought to Wisconsin towns like Eau Claire and Wausau by church sponsors. They were welcomed in small numbers, but as children were born and relatives arrived, some of the locals began to have second thoughts. I wonder what the reaction has been in Sheboygan. Mr. Ma is an irrepressible town booster—a Chinese-American Babbit for the nineties—and he puts a positive spin on race relations here. The town already has a long immigrant history, Germans, Slovenians, and Greeks among them, and also European Jews. The comic Jackie Mason is a native, and his father was a rabbi. But as I leave town I pass the Hebrew cemetery, which is now gated and locked. Vandals have taken to desecrating the graves.

I continue my trip north through Minnesota, bypassing Minneapolis to get to Duluth in time for St. Patrick's Day. Duluth, by the way, is where Geno Paulucci launched his Chung King food empire. In a converted factory building owned by Mr. Paulucci, I meet a Hmong woman named Pang-ku Yang. She sews high-school varsity jackets and athletic wear in a small garment shop, along with a half dozen other Laotian women. I wonder if they understand the significance of the varsity versus junior varsity letters, or the rituals behind the cheerleading skirts and the numbered jerseys they stitch together.

At home in the Harbor View housing project on the northside of town,

Pang-ku shows me a suitcase full of clothes that constitute the entirety of her possessions from home. Only the festival headdress, which she made herself, still fits. Pang-ku also brings out a pile of quilts hand sewn by herself and her sister. There are small pieces embroidered with idyllic scenes of farm animals and country life. The biggest one is epic in size and in the tale it tells. The entire history of the family's journey from the hills of Laos to Minnesota is woven into yards of cotton. The story begins in November of 1978, on the night of their baby daughter's funeral. As relatives gathered for the burial, a cousin showed up to warn Pang-ku's husband that North Vietnamese soldiers were on their way to the village to kill him. He had been a soldier for eleven years, since the age of fifteen, fighting the CIA's secret war in Laos. Mr. Yang fled to Thailand, and after a month, returned to help Pang-ku and the three remaining children escape.

Pang-ku had never seen snow before arriving in Minnesota,
but her granddaughter, Maya, has known it all her life.
Photo credit: Quynh Thai

For a time, Mr. Yang had
a part-time job at the
Mama Sera spaghetti
sauce factory.
Photo credit:
Quynh Thai

When we escape, the
older, they know, because
we teach them. That if
you yell or you cry even
out loud, then everybody
must be, got killed. And
they, they afraid to and
they quiet. But, they
small, they don't know
and they crying.
Photo credit:
Quynh Thai

Quilts like Pang-ku's are now a popular item at crafts fairs wherever there are Laotian refugee communities. They generally depict happy scenes of the life the Hmong left behind, rather than the ravages of war. For those who know, the dissonance between their distant past, before the war, and their lives since then can be read between the lines of thread. But most buyers and collectors probably do not comprehend the symbolism or meaning woven into the quilts.

In the Thailand refugee camps, even the men learned to sew the quilts. It was the only work available, and it ameliorated the boredom. The Yang family has been in the United States since 1980, and has spent most of their years here on welfare. Mr. Yang is trained only as a soldier and subsistence farmer, and so has little in the way of transferable skills for the American workplace. But Pang-ku can sew, and her piecework earnings go a long way toward supporting the couple and the four sons and granddaughter who still live at home.

Pang-ku has been married before, to another man who was a Hmong soldier and who was killed during the war. She has lost four children in all, and many more family members. Three of her living sons were born in Laos and a Thailand refugee camp, and are named Ping, Chu, and Ong. The two born here in the United States are named Tom and Jerry. Tom, who wears a safety pin on his shoe for style, reads me a story he wrote for school called "Magic Tree." "In a clearing in a forest you find a magic tree. To have cash, you have to say please. Then the cash comes out like a machine. It never gets run over because it's a magic tree. Its leaves are always green. The first kid was John. He wished he could have money. He had a penny. These kids came out and said, 'Can I have your penny?' And they took it and ran away. John said, 'They could have said please.' And cash came out from the tree."

The Yangs first lived in Minneapolis, in a housing project on the poor side of town. On the night George Bush was elected president, in November 1988, three men broke into their apartment, threatening the family and yelling what Pang-ku could only make out to be "Where's Cholo? Where's Cholo?" Mr. Yang managed to shoot one of the robbers in the leg, which earned the Yangs a feature story on the evening news the next day. Ten years to the month after Mr. Yang was forced to leave his village in Laos, the family decided to pick up and move to the safer environs of Duluth.

The West

When my family moved to California in 1966, we ended up in a town that had a large Japanese-American community and more cousins alone than the entire nonwhite population of Mount Prospect. Since then, I have always associated the West Coast as something of an Asian-American homeland, where familiar food and relations are plentiful. As I drive through the West, I remember that white supremacists have a similar idea. The states of Idaho, Montana, Wyoming, Oregon, and Washington are considered the "white homeland" of the Aryan Congress.

I drive through the Mount Hood area of Oregon, the home of the Yasui family. Min Yasui was the crusading Japanese-American lawyer and plaintiff in the infamous Corum Nobus case. Although I have never been here before, it is a place I remember well from the documentary *Family Gathering*, made by his filmmaker niece, Lise Yasui. Spectacular country that can become as ugly and bigoted a place as one would find anywhere on the map. On the edge of the Mount Hood Wilderness Area, near the towns of Orient and Boring, I pass through Sandy, Oregon. At one time, it was the home of Patrick Purdy, a drifter and mass murderer. One day in January 1985, Purdy dressed in camouflage gear and, during recess, shot up an elementary school in Stockton, California. Five Cambodian and Vietnamese children were killed, and many more were injured. Afterward, local law enforcement denied the shooting was a hate crime, but Asian Americans all over the country assumed it was one of the more tragic examples of escalating anti-Asian violence. Had he gone to trial, the question of a racial motive would have certainly been the focus of the proceedings. But Purdy killed himself outside a classroom after he finished spraying the playground.

Victor Wong describes the Asian as being "the face of the enemy" in the popular American imagination. It is as if Bataan, Kaesong, and Da Nang are etched across our faces. This fact was never more clear to Asian Americans of my generation than during the Vietnam War. Like many others, I was weaned and raised on a steady diet of television. But the Vietnam War provided the first sustained, public picture of Asians that I had ever experienced in my lifetime. The first time something close to my own image had ever reflected back at me. The war came to symbolize the penultimate in anti-Asian racism. Agitation against the war, or any form of U.S. military action in the Third World for that matter, was central to the principles of our political identity.

And so I am intrigued when I arrive in Seattle and meet Michael Park, a progressive twenty-one-year-old militant activist, rap singer, cultural nationalist, and Marine recruit. Michael, aka Psycho Mike M.C., performs rap with his brother Rafael, a junior Tae Kwon Do champion who himself is also known as the Golden M.C. Their stage name is, aptly, the Seoul Brothers.

Yo, here's a taste of something delicious / And by the way it's also nutritious / Not made for the ears of a child / But for the ladies to go buck wild / You see, the rhyme is like Kentucky Fried Chicken / So get with me, huh, I'm finger-licking . . . (from "Taste of Honey," by Rafael Park, aka the Golden M.C.).

I first learned about the Park brothers in a local Asian-American newspaper, the *International Examiner,* and was attracted to their story because they are rappers. The Seoul Brothers name didn't hurt either. But it was their multiple identities that intrigued me the most: college students, singers, activists, one an up-and-coming martial artist and future lawyer, the other an aspiring journalist and Marine reservist. Both defiant youths and good Korean sons at the same time. They have promised their mother that they will marry Korean women.

Contrary to conventional wisdom, Michael and Rafael are rebellious because of their upbringing, not in spite of it. The two brothers were born in South Korea, but were raised in an integrated neighborhood on the north-

SITE-SEEING THROUGH ASIAN AMERICA   291

side of Seattle. Their mother, a deeply religious woman, was a nurse in Korea. Their father is trained as a political scientist, but has devoted most of his twenty years in America to helping out other Korean immigrants, often for little or no pay. The boys recall the years of living in a tiny apartment, which had modest furnishings but seven telephones. Mr. Park wanted to make sure people could always get through to him if they needed him.

Mr. and Mrs. Park were not happy that Michael had joined the Marine reserves, and they had quite a scare when the Persian Gulf War broke out in 1991. In fact, the couple left Korea because of compulsory military service. Mrs. Park remembers, "When I was a child in the fourth grade, the Korean War started. That's why I understand how tragic a war can be. At that time my third brother died. He was in his second year of college when he died. The People's Army took him away and that's why I don't like soldiers. I hate war." Mr. Park himself had been stationed in the demilitarized zone as a student conscript. As a youth, he was a staunch backer of the war who felt the South Korean dictatorship was necessary for stability in the region. Today, Mr. Park, like his wife, is a pacifist and firm believer in democratic freedoms. While I was there, he sat down with his sons to watch a videotaped speech of the Nation of Islam leader, Louis Farrakhan, and then engaged them in a friendly debate over his ideology.

Mr. Park reminded me of my own father. He was a Goldwater man in 1964, and was a hawk for most of the Vietnam War. Today he spends his retirement time volunteering for progressive organizations, and recently traveled to Sacramento with my mother to march in solidarity with the United Farm Workers. I am not sure when or how my father began to change. There were fiery debates over the Vietnam War, but they were debates nonetheless. I remember when a Japanese exchange student witnessed one such skirmish. In a traditional Asian household, the youngest daughter would certainly have no place challenging the patriarch over any issue. But my parents, like the Parks, and like Victor, sought dual ground in the best of both cultures.

With my parents, still on the road.

When I was young, I always looked at my life as being too marginal even to discuss. Like Mike and Rafael, I landed in a racially integrated neighborhood and became a child of multiple worlds—Asian, black, white, brown—not simply the dual cultures we conventionally ascribe to the Asian-American experience. But that experience always seemed too singular, too weird to be an American story—too singular to be worthy of any telling beyond private memories. The Park brothers are supremely at home with the mixed bag of cultural influences that shape them. They are not distinguished by their level of assimilation, in the way we used to look at Americanization—conforming to a homogeneous norm. America seems to have caught up with the experience of young people like the Parks. In the making of *Fortune Cookies,* I set out to find who the Asian American is. Looking back at the Burtanog sisters of New Orleans, the Kochiyamas, Pang-ku, the Parks, even Mr. Choi, I realize the cumulation of stories speaks loudly of America itself. The question is no longer, "How do people become Americans?" but rather, "How has America become its people?"

List of Completed Works by Renee Tajima

Fortune Cookies: In Search of Asian America (working title). Producer/director/writer. Projected completion, 1995, feature-length color film, sound. Cross-country road trip in a rollicking search for the Asian-American identity. Commissioned by the Corporation for Public Broadcasting and coproduced by Quynh Thai.

Declarations: All Men Are Created Equal? Senior producer. 1993, 1-hour color video, sound. Public affairs special featuring television essays on equality by legal activist and author Derrick Bell, writer Beverly Donofrio, conservative free enterprise activist Robert Woodson, and education activist Demetrio Rodriguez. Directed segment "The Ballad of Demetrio Rodriguez" about his twenty-five-year struggle for public school equality in Texas. Produced for PBS.

Jennifer's in Jail. Director/writer. 1992, 1-hour color video, sound. Documentary about teenage girls in trouble with the law, focusing on Asian girl gangs, homeless, street kids in Hollywood, and incarcerated teenagers. Produced for Lifetime Television.

Special Olympics International. Director/writer. 1991, 10 minutes, color film, sound. Chronicle of rock musician Bob Seger's visit to Kathmandu for the Nepal National Games of the Special Olympics, the sporting event for athletes with mental retardation. Produced for ABC.

The Best Hotel on Skid Row. Producer/director/writer. 1990, 47 minutes, color film, sound. Documentary narrated by writer Charles Bukowski, profiles the denizens of a Skid Row singles hotel in downtown Los Angeles. Produced for Home Box Office, and premiered at the Cannes Film Festival.

What the Americans Really Think of the Japanese (*Americajin no Tainichikanjo no Tatamae to Honne*). Producer/director/writer. 1990, 90 minutes, color video, sound. (Japanese with no subtitles.) Documentary special on American attitudes toward Japan during the height of trade tensions between the two countries. Produced for Fujisankei.

Yellow Tale Blues. Executive producer/director. 1990, 30 minutes, color film, sound. Documentary explores the conflict between media myth and the reality of Asians in America. Features profiles of the families of filmmakers Renee Tajima and Christine Choy.

Monkey King Looks West. Producer/writer. 1989, 42 minutes, color film, sound. Documentary about the tales behind and within the Chinese Opera in America, focuses on three classically trained, immigrant opera performers who work day jobs as a butcher, an Atlantic City tour guide, and a Chinatown arts administrator.

Who Killed Vincent Chin? Producer/director. 1988, 82 minutes, color film, sound. Academy Award-nominated film in the Best Feature Documentary category, and winner of the Peabody Award and Dupont-Columbia Award. Documents the controversy over the beating death of a Chinese American in Detroit, Vincent Chin, by a Chrysler autoworker and the subsequent civil rights prosecution. Produced for PBS.

Haitian Corner. Producer. 1987, 75 minutes, color film, sound. Dramatic feature film, directed by Raoul Peck. Story of a Haitian poet living in self-exile in Brooklyn, New York. Winner of the Grand Prize at Festival du Cinéma "Images Caribes," and premiered at the Berlin International Film Festival. Produced for ZDF-Germany.

Permanent Wave. Producer. 1986, 20 minutes, color film, sound. Dramatic short film directed by Christine Choy as a part of the American Film Institute Women Directors Workshop, about a day in the life of a beauty shop. Stars Anna Marie Horsford and Lauren Tom.

Grenada. Producer/director. 1979, 14 minutes, color video, sound. Chronicle of the first anniversary of the New Jewel Movement in the Caribbean nation of Grenada, features interviews with former Prime Minister Maurice Bishop. Produced for the Harvard Forum.

PART IV

Multi-Capitalism

CHAPTER EIGHTEEN

Multiculturalism and Flexibility

Some New Directions in Global Capitalism

RICHARD P. APPELBAUM

Marx is dead, buried, all but forgotten. The headlong global rush to embrace capitalism, with (as Marx might have said) all its warts and pimples, has left only Cuba and North Korea as the standard-bearers of state-sponsored versions of socialism. Perhaps, if we stretch the definition of socialism a bit, we might include Myanmar. Vietnam? No way. With the Clinton administration ready to finally inter the last traces of MIA remains, Vietnam is poised to become a vast factory of low-wage, highly-skilled labor for American firms. China has already moved well down the capitalist road, and its southern Guangdong province is the fastest-growing economic region in the world—perhaps in world history. In China, in fact, both local and foreign capitalists have the best (or worst) of both worlds: the heavily subsidized and virtually captive workforce characteristic of what used to be called socialism, combined with a cowboy capitalist labor regime based on piecework, zero job security, and prohibitions against antimanagement organization.

But wait! Is Marx really to be relegated to the scrap heap of modernist history, displaced by a decentered postmodern global economy in which the seductions of capitalism and the global assembly line have rendered class struggle all but moot? Have science, technology, and information replaced labor-intensive factory production as the basis of global wealth? Are we truly entering a postindustrial world in which the labor theory of value has been

RICHARD P. APPELBAUM

298

superseded, with ordinary workers increasingly replaced by what U.S. labor secretary Robert Reich calls "symbolic analysts," people who work with their heads rather than their hands?

I think the news of Marx's death is premature. I say this not only as a realist who suspects that the Russian people may be having second thoughts about the virtues of unbridled capitalism, but also as a scholar who remains convinced that Marxist theory continues to have relevance for understanding the nature and limits of global capitalism. Moreover, these observations have implications for the future of multiculturalism; for as capitalism reasserts itself on a global scale, race, ethnicity, and gender are occupying a central role in the restructuring of capitalist relations.

The following theoretical observations grow out of a long-term study of changes in global capitalism. Alongside the explosion of low-wage factory jobs in what were once peripheral countries has come the reperipheralization of the core—the coming home of sweatshops to take advantage of the home market and cheap immigrant labor. Consider the fact that the only manufacturing industry in the United States that experienced a growth in employment in 1991 was the apparel industry, one that depends increasingly on a subminimum wage workforce from Mexico, Central America, and Southeast Asia. What does it mean that Los Angeles alone employs some 120,000 workers in five thousand sweatshops that are for the most part owned by ethnic minorities?[1]

Global capitalism has meant the feminization of labor worldwide, and the ethnicizing of labor on the home front. Class differences are overlaid with differences based on race and ethnicity in a highly volatile multiculturalism predicated on exploitation rather than mutual understanding. This essay is an attempt to reinsert a bit of forgotten Marxist materialism into the discourse of multiculturalism. It is organized into three theoretical moments, divided by two historical interludes, and followed by some reflections on capitalism and multiculturalism in both Los Angeles and the world capitalist economy. It is accompanied by a brief visual travelogue (see chapter 20) that will take us to apparel factories in Los Angeles, Hong Kong, China, Macau, and Vietnam.

Theory 1: Marx's Theory of Industrial Capitalism

In volume 1 of *Capital* Marx elaborates on his theory of capitalist production.[2] Drawing on the labor theory of value, Marx distinguishes between constant capital, variable capital, and surplus value as constitutive of the value of individual commodities as well as commodities in the aggregate (the wealth of nations). To briefly summarize his distinction, constant capital represents sunk investment in machinery and equipment, a fruit of past or congealed labor that comprises the principal means of producing wealth in capitalist society. Marx terms this form of capital "constant" because its value is given once in use; it can create no additional value on its own. Constant capital represents a fixed cost that must be paid off whether or not it is actually productively employed. To introduce a distinction that will become of central importance in the ensuing discussion, capital costs are essentially inflexible; once machines are bought they must be paid for whether they are running twenty-four hours a day or idled by labor strife or a sluggish economy.

Variable capital represents the cost of living labor, as indicated by the wage bill. In Marx's view, this is a form of "capital" because, under the capitalist mode of production, workers are equivalent to machines, objects to be used up in production in the most efficient ways possible. By this Marx means that workers are treated as appendages to the machines they operate, their labor power to be scientifically reorganized and managed until all conscious and self-controlling aspects have been rationalized away. Marx regards this quasi-human form of capital as "variable" because unlike constant capital, its value can vary according to the degree of exploitation: variable capital is capable of creating new value, in the form of variable amounts of surplus value, which are then appropriated by the capitalist. Furthermore, it is useful to see variable capital as varying in yet another way, which Marx elaborates in his analysis of the dynamics of capitalist production: workers, unlike machines, can be hired and fired to suit the momentary needs of production. Living labor can be broken down into nearly infinitesimal increments, enhancing the capitalist's flexibility in responding to changing market conditions. Workers can be hired or fired; they can be paid by the piece or the hour, according to the needs of the moment.

Surplus value is, of course, the difference between the value produced and the value of the capital (both constant and variable) required to produce it. Drawing on the labor theory of value, Marx argues that since only productive labor can make machinery, provide the raw materials required to quench its hunger, and then set it in motion to produce commodities, surplus value represents the unpaid labor extracted by the capitalist. Surplus value results from inequitable social relationships, which permit one class of people to exploit the labor of another. Among other things, it is the source of the capitalist's profit, which is what keeps the capitalist in business. When surplus value is threatened, by pressures from either rising capital costs or declining sales, the capitalist goes out of business. The story of the development of capitalism is the story of the struggle between labor and capital over the allocation of these costs of production.

Labor, then, provides capitalists with infinite flexibility, although of course labor's part in class struggle is to seek to reduce that flexibility by speaking with one voice, thereby taking on the "lumpy" character of constant capital. If all workers are treated as one, they are then equivalent to a single machine, a constant cost that must be incurred regardless of the needs of the capitalist. Marx predicts that capitalists will resist these efforts on the part of variable capital to simulate the power of constant capital through technological innovations that render such simulations moot: replacing them with actual machines. In Marx's terms, over time constant capital replaces variable capital, leading to a long-term rise in the ratio between the two (what Marx termed capital's "organic composition"). Marx recognized that built-in structural pressures for automation would result from both price competition between capitalists, which dictates a strategy of reducing unit costs through raising productivity, and class struggle, which dictates a parallel need to control living labor by substituting more tractable machinery.

Although Marx couldn't fully anticipate the end point of this process, it is clear that he foresaw the possibility of the fully robotic factory with continuously running machinery operated by a relative handful of highly trained engineers and technicians. The mixed consequences of this long-term tendency toward automation were also anticipated by Marx. On the one hand, automation would reduce costs and increase the amount of surplus that could be extracted from a diminishing workforce, while disciplining the remaining workers by threatening to render them superfluous. On the other hand, automation would lead to an increasing concentration of capital as enterprises became ever larger, fewer, and more capital-intensive. While this concentration would increase the power of gigantic monopolies, it would also increase their vulnerability, since vast amounts of capital would be tied up in machinery that must be kept running constantly in order to turn a profit. Labor actions could prove increasingly strategic in this regard, since a well-placed strike could send shock waves through the entire economy. Furthermore, the growing army of workers displaced by machines are a poor market for the goods those machines were churning out, leading to chronic and growing problems of overproduction and underconsumption. Devastating labor stoppages and economic stagnation were two of the prices capital would eventually pay for automation.

Interlude 1: The Transition to Postindustrial Capitalism

In the past twenty years, since Intel's 1971 invention of the microchip, capitalism has gone truly global. Communication and information technology has made it possible to coordinate most activities with a virtual disregard for time and space. The global assembly line has emerged, on which no country can leave its exclusive stamp. From cars to clothing to electronics, the hands that produce our goods and services reveal the exploitative side of multiculturalism: they are hands of color, of women, of impoverished Third World peoples driven by hardship and hunger to labor in the global factory.

The theories of the transition to a postindustrial world order have recognized the emerging global nature of capitalism. These theories, which have emerged in response to the rapidly shifting conditions of global production, have successively emphasized dependency,[3] the possibility of dependent development,[4] the new international division of labor,[5] and the world capitalist system.[6] Common to all of these theories is the recognition that capital is increasingly footloose on a global scale—that in their search for profits, transnational businesses have emerged that have a truly global reach.

Yet in different ways all of these theories share a number of assumptions that reflect the paradigm of industrial society out of which they grow, rather than a new framework based on a postindustrial world order. First, in varying degrees they all assume that the nation-state remains sovereign. One consequence of this assumption, for example, is an analysis of the class system reproduced at the global level, resulting in a world system of upper- (core), lower- (peripheral), and middle-class (semiperipheral) nations, with surplus flowing up and exploitation flowing down. Second, they all assume that physical labor remains the principal source of the wealth of nations. What drives the global economy, in the view of most of these theorists, is the search for cheap labor to run the global assembly line.

Theory 2: The Theory of Postindustrial Capitalism: Karl Marx Meets Robert Reich

In the *Grundrisse*, his 1857-58 notebooks that were to become the foundation of volume 1 of *Capital*, Marx advanced the notion that in the final stages of capitalism, science and knowledge would replace labor as the source of value in production:

> The tendency of capital is thus to give a scientific character to production, reducing direct labor to a simple element in this process. . . . The production

302 RICHARD P. APPELBAUM

process has ceased to be a labor process in the sense that labor is no longer the unity dominating and transcending it.

Direct labor and its quantity cease to be the determining element in production and thus in the creation of use value. It is reduced quantitatively to a smaller proportion, just as qualitatively it is reduced to an indispensable but subordinate role as compared with scientific labor in general. . . .

Labor does not seem anymore to be an essential part of the process of production. The human factor is reduced to watching and supervising the production process.

Invention then becomes a branch of business.[7]

Thus, in what must rate as one of the most prescient passages on the future of industrial society written at the time of its birth, Marx anticipates the postindustrial theorists. From Secretary of Labor Robert Reich to Harvard business economist Michael Porter,[8] from the post-Fordist Marxist geographers to Daniel Bell,[9] all seem agreed: we are entering a period in which information itself, rather than the physical production of goods, holds the key to wealth.

Using the terminology if not the assumptions of the original labor theory of value, economists, sociologists, and social geographers from left to right agree that "value-added" results increasingly from the application of knowledge, and not from the hands that make the goods. Reich, for example, in his postmodern rereading of Adam Smith, argues that the wealth of the twenty-first-century nation will be found in the work of its citizens, with work redefined in purely symbolic terms. This is the labor theory of value turned on its head: intellectual rather than physical labor holds the key to success in the global economy. Invention, design, marketing, retailing, networking, and other forms of "symbolic analysis" are the true source of value in the postindustrial world.

Needless to say, Marx and Reich drew opposite conclusions from these anticipated futures. In Marx's view in the *Grundrisse*, to the extent that the logic of capitalist development rendered labor superfluous, capitalism's ideological nature would be revealed for all to see: why should workers continue to slave away at meaningless, poorly paid, and increasingly unnecessary jobs, enriching a small group of capitalists and their professional-managerial entourage?[10] If machines could do the work, so be it; all that remained was to shatter the system of oppressive social relations that kept one class perpetually in thrall to another.

Reich, on the other hand, envisions a postindustrial utopia populated entirely by capitalists and members of the professional-managerial class, symbolic analysts all. In Reich's "can-do" world of people who use their minds to make things happen, there are no workers to be found—at least not in those nations that invest sufficiently in their most valuable resource, their people. Woe be unto the nation that fails to so invest, however, since that nation's semiskilled and unskilled workers are competing with an infinitely substitutable global workforce, one that will drag its wages down to a global level. Reich never makes entirely clear whether or not he believes that the United States, to take one national example, could in fact develop a workforce of one hundred million or so symbolic analysts who would be effectively insulated from the potential loss of their jobs through global competition. But it does seem clear that he is not overly concerned about the hands that will eventually wind up doing the detail labor, particularly if they are found half a world away.

Let us take one set of such hands—an actual case study of a woman who labors in one of Nike's six Korean-run Indonesian shoe factories. Sadisah (the pseudonym provided by *Harper's Magazine*, which first told the tale) earns about fourteen cents an hour, raking in just under forty dollars each month by laboring sixty-plus-hour workweeks manufacturing athletic shoes.[11] The shoes she makes sell for about eighty dollars a pair, of which her value-added contribution is a full eleven cents. There are various types of arithmetic that can be performed on these data. For example, it is easy to compute that it would take Sadisah two months to earn enough money to buy back the shoes she makes, although it is unclear where she would find the time for cross-training at the local athletic club. An even more interesting calculation is that Sadisah would only have to work an estimated 44,492 years to earn the $20 million multiyear endorsement fee Michael Jordan commanded before his short-lived retirement from professional basketball. It should be pointed out in this regard that Nike's 1991 profits reached $287 million on $3 billion in sales, a figure that is of course calculated after Michael Jordan and all of Nike's designers, advertising agencies, marketing services, managers, and owners have taken their cut.

This is a handsome rate of return, and reveals the "rational kernel" underlying Reich's reasoning: Michael Jordon's value-added alone is estimated at 10 percent of Nike's sales, roughly equivalent to the company's total annual profit. From a strictly capitalist viewpoint, his $20 million fee was a bargain, perhaps even more so than Sadisah's eleven cents. After all, there is only one Michael Jordan, and there are probably a billion or so Sadisahs around the globe, all hungry and available for work. Although it is unclear whether or not Michael Jordan truly qualifies as a symbolic analyst, there can be no question that he is a potent symbol to millions of consumers.

Nike's highly paid in-house ad agency, which constructed one of the most effective ad campaigns in history around this particular symbol, performs the very sort of symbolic analysis that Reich believes will fuel the global economy of the future.

Interlude 2: Globalizing and Localizing Forces in Global Capitalism

As capitalism embarks on its information-driven postindustrial phase, its contours are shaped by forces that simultaneously result in the spatial disaggregation of production on a global scale as well as the localization of production in tightly integrated economic regions. The former, centrifugal forces are driven by the search for cheap and controllable labor and are abetted by modern information technology. Bar scanners, electronic mail, telephones, fax machines—all permit a global coordination of just-in-time production and delivery systems.

The latter, centripetal forces are driven by the advantages that continue to accrue to spatial concentration of production in dense metropolitan industrial districts. Even in this high-technology age of information, there is no substitute for a hands-on approach to integrated design, marketing, retailing, buying, financing, and even production. It is hard to put several heads together to come up with a new design or advertising campaign or marketing plan if the heads are spread out around the globe. At the manufacturing level, the printed circuit must be inspected to determine if it meets company standards; the fabric must be felt to know if the garment will hang properly. Other things being equal, it is still better to have the company headquarters, research and development teams, factories, and principal customers close to one another. Labor costs are only one consideration among many in the changing geography of global capitalism.

Perhaps virtual reality simulations will eventually do away with time and space altogether, finally enabling quality-control officers or designers or company presidents to beam themselves aboard wherever they think they are really needed. But for the present time, face-to-face relations still confer quick turnaround and flexibility. When the presence of low-cost Third World labor is found in core country metropolitan areas, capital finds the best of both worlds: it needn't go too far from home to find cheap labor. Such "global cities" as Los Angeles, New York, London, and Tokyo combine core and periphery in a single centrally located region, constituting a form of black hole that swallows up the otherwise globalizing networks of postindustrial capitalism.[12]

Theory 3: Flexibility, Subcontracting, and Contradictions

Let us try to bring some of these ideas together by drawing on several theoretical frameworks that seem to be grappling with a common set of issues.

First, an increasingly globalized economic dispersion has occurred through the creation of global commodity chains, "network[s] of labor and production processes whose end result is a finished commodity."[13] These commodity chains consist of such pivotal points in the production process as raw materials extraction and processing, production and manufacturing, export, retailing, financing, marketing, and design—the entire spectrum of activities required to make a commodity.[14] While commodity chains are conceptualized as being dispersed over time and space, they must eventually "touch down" at different times and in different places, with different impacts on different locales. Commodity chain analysis shifts the framework for analyzing production; manufacturing is conceptualized as a dynamic process among interconnected firms, rather than as a static property of nations or nation-based corporations.

Commodity chains are particularly likely to be highly dispersed in such labor-intensive, cost-sensitive, retailer-driven production as apparel, athletic shoes, electronic assembly, toys, dolls, and so forth.[15] The companies that fabricate such commodities are truly manufacturers without factories, who source production through globally distributed subcontracting arrangements. Production is typically done in low-wage areas, from Indonesia to Los Angeles. In commodity chain analysis, core, periphery, and surplus value extraction are not conceptualized as attributes of nations, but as aspects of the commodity chain itself. There are core and peripheral activities; where each touches down, it will leave its stamp on the economic region. In the Reichian world of the information-based economy, core activities are those that require symbolic analysis, while peripheral activities are those that require physical labor. Often, contrary to Reich's utopian vision, they occur side by side in the same industrial district. Factory production may have been key to surplus value extraction and hence capitalist development during the phase of industrial capitalism, but in the postindustrial world this is no longer necessarily the case. Sadisah's factory may never induct her into the aristocracy of labor, nor will Indonesia's export processing zones necessarily ever elevate that country into core or even semiperipheral global status.

Second, it is clear that economic concentration in industrial districts continues to benefit capitalist production, as has been recognized since Al-

fred Marshall.[16] Industrial districts consist of dense concentrations of economic actors, who rely on one another to get the job done. They consist of
elaborate subcontracting arrangements, often based on a handshake, and
are characterized by speed, trust, and quick lines of communication. "Networks of trust" are typically mediated by intense familistic and ethnic ties; as
one of the leading figures in the Los Angeles apparel industry explains it,
"We're an information business."[17] Such "transaction-intensive networks"
confer the flexibility required for efficiency and competitive advantage in a
global economy.

It will be useful at this point to distinguish two meanings of "flexibility."
The first meaning takes us back to our original discussion of Marx: flexibility entails the creation of truly variable capital through global subcontracting.[18] Labor can be taken on and cast off according to the momentary requirements of the marketplace. Surplus can be realized in one place, such as
a Los Angeles design studio or marketing firm, while labor exploitation can
occur in another—in the factory down the street or across the Pacific Ocean.

Since manufacturers subcontract labor rather than own their own factories, they are no longer legally responsible for wages, factory conditions, or
the exploitation of labor; as the production manager for a major U.S. apparel manufacturer put it, "I'm not the sheriff."[19] Thus, costs and risks can be
externalized: there is no danger of strikes closing down one's factory or
idling one's machines, since one can always switch to more hospitable contractors elsewhere. Manufacturers no longer need worry about local or national health, safety, or labor regulations; they can always find a new subcon-
tractor in a different state or a different country. Worries about health
insurance, lawsuits, workers' compensation, and the other evils of class
struggle can similarly be externalized. There is not even any serious danger
of rising wages: somewhere in the world there is a factory where the price is
right. Flexibility thus defines a contemporary moment in the class struggle,
a means acquired by capitalists to once again render labor a truly variable
form of capital just as it seemed to be gaining some measure of constancy.

This first, organizational form of flexibility is made possible by a second,
more technological form: flexibility as the ability to respond instantly to
changes in market conditions. During the industrial phase of capitalism,
businesses relied on vertical integration to achieve quick response. Organi-
zationally, it typically made sense for large firms to own or otherwise directly control as many forward and backward linkages as possible, from raw
materials extraction to final sales. Because communications technology was
rudimentary, only such internalized control and coordination seemed to

afford the possibility of avoiding bottlenecks as well as intermediate layers of surplus value extraction.

In the postindustrial phase, however, a high degree of coordination can be achieved through advanced information technology without the need for vertical ownership or management. One American clothing giant, the Gap, can deploy more than five hundred factories around the globe, none of which it owns. When a shopper buys a Gap shirt at the local mall outlet, information about the purchase is scanned into a computer at the point of sale, where it joins a stream of thousands of other sales in a centralized computer in Hong Kong. There, the Gap's overseas buying office analyzes the pattern of sales, placing its orders with factories from Egypt to Hong Kong, from the Philippines to Mauritius. In the words of James Cunningham, the Gap Far East's Vice President for Offshore Sourcing, "the best retailers will be the ones who respond the quickest, the best . . . the time between cash register and factory shipment is shorter."[20] The Gap is an example of a buyer-centered commodity chain, a firm that is organized around retailing and sales rather than internalized sources of supply.[21] It is typical of many labor-intensive industries, from clothing to electronic assembly. I believe it is the organizational form of the future, one that will increasingly come to characterize all forms of production.

The growth of subcontracting is abetted by the recent acceleration of information technology, which has made possible just-in-time delivery, long-distance coordination and control, and a radical disaggregation of the commodity chain. The firm of the future will avoid investing in large amounts of constant capital and the workers to set it in motion. In the postindustrial world, "lean and mean" are the watchwords.[22] In the words of management guru Tom Peters associate Jim Kouzes, "contract out everything but your soul—what you do better than everybody else."[23] For many businesses it is better to have a small in-house design office, advertising agency, and perhaps retail outlet, and subcontract for everything else.

If modern information technology provides the means, subcontracting provides the organizational vehicle for a truly postmodern form of lean, mean capitalism in which only the profit centers remain in-house. Depending on the size of the firm, its organizational resources, and the nature of its business, subcontracting networks can extend down the street, throughout the metropolitan area, or around the world. An estimated thirty million Americans today work at subcontracted jobs, including temporary workers, part-timers, independent subcontractors, and other forms of contingent workers. One out of five nonmilitary workers put in fewer than thirty-five hours a week. It is estimated that as many as a third of U.S. workers fall into this category today, a number that may reach half by the end of the century, approaching the percentage in Japan.[24] Manpower, Inc., the world's largest temporary employment agency, handles more workers each day than General Motors or IBM. Manpower and similar agencies now handle 1.5 million workers, three times as many as a decade ago.[25]

Thus, thanks to modern technology, capitalism has the best of both worlds—it can globalize and/or localize to maximize its flexibility in both senses of the word. It can obtain organizational flexibility from subcontracting, reducing labor to truly variable capital, maximizing surplus extraction while minimizing costs and risks. And it can attain the technological flexibility needed to respond quickly to market changes, while retaining complete control over the labor process.

As with all structural contradictions of capitalism, this postindustrial resolution of the problems of labor's growing power during the industrial phase carries with it its own complications. I will mention two in passing, before turning in greater detail to a third that bears directly on the question of multiculturalism.

First, while subcontracting solves capital's growing problem of internalized labor costs, it also multiplies layers of profit centers. Every layer of subcontracting must have its cut in order to stay in business. During global expansionary times this may not pose a problem for capital, but during global recessionary times such as the present there is a severe profit squeeze. Kouzes's "soul of the business" may find itself acting in a very unsoulful manner, mercilessly cutting the prices it pays to its vendors, who in turn do the same to their own subcontractors, and so on down the line. Smaller subcontractors may be severely hurt, and workers will ultimately bear the brunt of the cost cutting. With each layer marching to the orders of the layer above it, and each layer taking its own cut, there is less and less left over for the people whose labor ultimately makes the goods. The only difference between exploitation in the industrial and postindustrial age is that during the latter, the soulful managers at the head of the line are spared the sight of the workers, who are now somebody else's problem.

Second, it should be obvious that the purpose of subcontracting (like all capitalist relations) is to cut costs to the capitalist. As I have indicated, subcontracting is specifically intended to chasten labor, destroying the once-proud "aristocracy of labor" in core countries by rendering it competitive with a low-paid global workforce. To the extent that this strategy is successful, Marx's problem of underconsumption once again rears its head, although now on a global scale. The so-called global economic recession, which currently plagues Japan and Germany as well as the United States, is in fact largely the result of this organizational restructuring of capitalism. The long boom in the global economy of the 1960s through the mid-1980s, during which time the four Asian dragons and other newly industrializing countries came of age, actually marked the undermining of the very global economic order that had made such "economic miracles" possible.[26] The Pacific shift was based in large part on the growing buying power of European and American workers, which it eventually undermined. Indonesian women workers, earning thirty-five dollars a month from Nike, are hardly a viable market for Air Jordans—nor are garment workers in Los Angeles, whose subminimum wages are in part repatriated to their families in Mexico or El Salvador or Guatemala.

The New Multiculture of Capitalism: The Case of Los Angeles

The third contradiction of postindustrial capitalism, which I will illustrate with the example of the Los Angeles apparel industry, is that it has promoted the ethnicization of capitalism on a global scale. As capitalism becomes a multitiered machine of many subcontracting arrangements, the faces and hands at the different levels differ in color from one another.

Beginning a generation ago, high and rising costs in the unionized apparel industry of the northeastern United States began to drive factories out of the region, first to the south, then to Mexico and the Caribbean, to Asia, to the world—and today back home to Los Angeles, where an abundance of impoverished immigrants from Mexico and Central America render long-distance subcontracting in search of cheap labor less necessary. This is not the place to explain the reasons for this reperipheralization of the core, which has to do with the failed economies in Mexico and Central America, as well as civil warfare and repressive governments in Guatemala and El Salvador. (Our own involvement in these causes is less well understood, particularly our support—through international lending organizations—of austerity programs that have driven wages down and contributed to the enormous cross-border wage disparities.)[27]

In Los Angeles county there are an estimated 125,000 garment workers laboring in some five thousand factories.[28] As many as a quarter of the workers are undocumented immigrants, and an unknown (but probably larger) percentage of the factories are unlicensed. Los Angeles today accounts for nearly a tenth of total U.S. employment in apparel.[29] The city's spatially concentrated downtown garment district—as well as numerous other similar concentrations spread throughout Los Angeles, Orange, and San Bernardino counties—confers multiple synergies for garment manufacturing.

Downtown Los Angeles provides a combination of working conditions associated with peripheral country status and postindustrial core country opulence, one that affords a disturbing vision of the emerging "global city" of the twenty-first century. On one side of the downtown divide—flanked by man-made barriers (the Harbor and Hollywood Freeways) that reinforce the existing hilly topography—lies the business, financial, governmental, and cultural heart of Los Angeles. Here one finds the city's centers of culture— the Music Center, the Dorothy Chandler Pavilion, the Mark Taper Forum. Just south of the Hollywood Freeway lie the principal federal, state, and local government agencies, including city hall, the central police station, and the courthouse. The corporate headquarters of the *Los Angeles Times* are found here, as are the towering spires of the major banks and financial institutions of the Pacific Rim economy: First Interstate World, ARCO Plaza (now Bank of America), Union Bank Square, Wells-Fargo, Home Savings, Citicorp, the World Trade Center, and the Pacific Stock Exchange. For the small part of the Pacific Rim economy that constitutes the garment industry, many of these institutions help provide capital, accounting, and other financial services. Nearby are the hotels, malls, and plazas of the Bunker Hill redevelopment project, "one of the largest postwar urban designs in North America."[30] "Little Tokyo" is found on the eastern fringe of this upscale portion of downtown; Chinatown is just across the Hollywood Freeway. All in all, one can locate some two dozen government buildings, an even greater number of banks, cultural institutions, and trade centers of various sorts, and nearly as many first-class hotels catering to the business traveler. The visual image is one of towering steel and glass, gerbil-like pedestrian walkways set several floors above street level, and integrated parking plazas that remove any need for ground-level pedestrian traffic. This antipedestrian downtown design was far from accidental, but rather was intentionally constructed so as to prevent any danger of human spillover from the surrounding impoverished slums and factory districts into the citadels of global capitalism.

As one moves south and east of Bunker Hill, this small area of capital and the symbolic analysts who serve it quickly gives way to the teem and dirt of the garment district, where one finds the hands that make the goods. The modern California Apparel Mart, at the corner of Los Angeles and 9th Streets, symbolizes the transition. In a neighborhood filled with factories, discount clothing stores, and the enormous open-air "knock off" apparel bazaar at Santee Alley, this thirteen-story structure, which claims its own zipcode, houses the showrooms of some fifteen hundred manufacturers, including some of the most celebrated labels in the fashion business. A few blocks east of the California Mart lies the Fashion Institute of Design and Merchandising, training the future designers and marketers of the "California look," while providing interns for the local apparel manufacturers.

The garment district for the most part is characterized by low, eight- to twelve-story buildings, mainly constructed during the 1930s, and many in need of repair. These buildings house the small factories (average size: sixteen workers) that produce the "California look."[31] A contractor may occupy an entire floor, or share the floor with others; a building may house as many as a dozen or more different sewing factories, all using the same bathroom. Not far from the sewing factories are a handful of buying offices that shop wholesale for the country's principal retailers. Here also are found yarn factories, fabric providers, and related fabric services; the flower, produce, and jewelry marts; sewing schools; immigration services, lawyers, and others serving or living off of the largely immigrant workforce.

The apparel industry in Los Angeles is spatially concentrated and ethnically stratified in a way that reveals the push-pull forces at work in the global economy. The industry has grown in Los Angeles because the concentration of industry-related professional, managerial, financial, and technical services, design and manufacturing capability, and a low-wage immigrant workforce—in the heart of the world's largest apparel market—has for many manufacturers overcome the attractiveness of yet-cheaper labor at a greater distance. Local production also enables manufacturers to avoid quotas and tariffs, which add especially to production costs outside the Mexico-Central America-Caribbean Basin region. (This region benefits from special programs designed to pay duties only on the value added in production, which, because of the low labor costs, is typically minimal.) Finally, local production enjoys the flexibility that results from subcontracting, in a system of labor control that divides the industry along ethnic lines.

The principal profits in the industry are realized by those who design the clothing, the firms that provide necessary financial and legal services, and those engaged in its sales. These include the manufacturers (more correctly designers, since they seldom engage in actual manufacturing of final products); bankers and accountants who specialize in apparel-related financing; the factors who buy up the retail accounts receivable from the manufacturers, freeing up money for fabric purchases; and retailers and retail buying offices. This upper stratum of the industry is almost entirely white, largely but not exclusively male, and disproportionately Jewish. It goes back to the turn of the century, when shepherding and apparel manufacturing began in Los Angeles. Union Bank, which continues to finance apparel manufacturers, was founded at that time as a repository for funds generated by the fledgling industry. Wealth generated in large part by the industry's founders gave rise to two of Los Angeles's principal hospitals, City of Hope and Cedars-Sinai. Family, friendship, and religious community ties that originated at that time continue into the present.

But the original founders of the industry have been largely supplanted by immigrants, first from New York City, then from the Middle East, and most recently from Asia. The apparel manufacturing community still remains relatively small and largely known to one another. Its core members—those longtime Angelinos, as well as East Coast transplants from one or two generations ago—honor one another at charitable fund-raisers, sit on the same boards, and belong to the same civic organizations and commissions. The interlopers—Middle Eastern Jews and Koreans—are less well integrated into the community. Such dense networks contribute to a Marshallian industrial district where apparel is "in the air." Here a deal is easily made over lunch at the outside patio of the California Mart, a design is readily imitated from among the thousands of wholesale lines on display within a few city blocks. Competition and personal rivalries complement a strongly shared culture, fostering an unending spin-off of fashion ideas and marketing strategies.

The other half of the local industry is concerned with the fabrication of clothing. The thousands of small factories are run mainly by small immigrant entrepreneurs, many of whom are barely a rung on the ladder above the workers they exploit. Turnover is estimated at 50 percent or more a year, as immigrants from Mexico, Guatemala, El Salvador, Korea, Taiwan, Hong Kong, and South Korea scramble for a toehold in the apparel economy. The factory owners constitute a layer between manufacturer and worker, often a layer of yellow skin between white and brown. The workers are almost entirely immigrants, predominantly female (although increasingly male), and, to an unknown extent, undocumented. Because manufacturers subcontract to factory owners they have until recently been treated as legally exempt from factory violations, so long as they employ licensed contractors; because contractors are small, economically unstable, and can easily procure fictitious licenses, they are virtually impossible to hold accountable.

The result is an industry where no one is likely to be held responsible for labor abuses—where there are no sheriffs. It is an industry ready-made for exploitation along lines of race and ethnicity, in which a white manufacturer might place an order to a struggling Korean contractor, who employs a Latino workforce that can neither understand his language nor fathom his culture. Such a situation is ripe for racial and ethnic resentment, an explosive situation in an already explosive city.

Conclusion: Race, Ethnicity, and Gender in Global Capitalism

Capitalism has always reinforced class divisions with divisions based on race, ethnicity, gender, and other forms of ascription. In any system based to a large degree on the exploitation of one group of people by another, such distinctions provide a useful basis for justifying inequality. Not only does this foster a "divide-and-conquer" ideology among those who otherwise might find common cause, but it also helps to foster a standard of exploitation based on what is accorded the least common denominator—whichever group finds itself at the bottom of the economic heap.

Since modern industrial capitalism originated in northern Europe, its racialization until recently has tended to divide along white and nonwhite lines. Today, with Japan a global capitalist player and the emerging Asian dragons (including China) in hot pursuit, we can expect this historically fundamental racialization to be overlaid by new and innovative forms. The Japanese are well known for their racial attitudes and corresponding practices toward Japanese-born Koreans, for example, while Koreans have themselves acquired a well-deserved reputation for their own brand of racialized economic exploitation in Central America and Los Angeles.[32] No racial or ethnic group is exempt from the possibility of developing its own brand of racism as a rationalization for its class practices. Racism preceded capitalism, and will likely survive it. But capitalism benefits from racism, and so gives it a particular focus and direction depending on the circumstances.

Capitalism may often appear to be color-blind. If African-American superstar athletes can sell athletic shoes, they will be elevated into the upper tier of the class structure by shoe companies. If Latinos constitute a growing market for goods, then goods will be produced and sold for Latinos. Yet capitalism continues to reinforce racial and ethnic divisions, albeit in different ways and on a global scale. What has occurred is a scrambling of the racial topography. The black-white made-in-America model of racialization is supplanted by a rainbow constellation of exploitative race relations, reinforcing class divisions with often virulent differences across racial and ethnic lines.

In the United States, where several decades of legislation and judicial decisions have outlawed most forms of overt discrimination, only those truly at the margins remain completely unprotected: newly arrived (and undocumented) immigrants, and inner-city African-American males. The former provide the local battalions of the reserve army of the global proletariat, while the latter are simply sacrificed, the frontline casualties of global economic restructuring joined with a national policy of economic triage. In both cases, racism and sexism play key justificatory roles; but the causes are at root economic. Within the American production system, race, ethnicity, and gender continue to serve class divisions. As I have sought to show in the example of the Los Angeles garment industry, one encounters a rainbow coalition of conflicting interests: Asians against Latinos, whites against people of color, documented against undocumented workers.

Globally, the lowest stratum of the class structure is comprised disproportionately of women, rural immigrants to urban areas and export processing zones, and racial and ethnic minorities as defined in a particular country. Although exploitation of these groups undoubtedly preceded their incorporation into the global economy, it has now taken on new forms, designed to keep their wage demands low and their interests divided. It is perhaps a telling irony that while the most egregious types of exploitation are formally illegal in the United States, American businesses continue to profit from such exploitation elsewhere in the world, where even the effort to struggle against exploitation is often ruthlessly suppressed.

Flexibilization and subcontracting facilitate these global patterns of exploitation, since not even paternalistic loyalties or corporatist leanings are permitted to detract from the hard-nosed pursuit of profit in the fast-moving information age. If businesses today are counseled to retain only their soul, will that soul include people whose color or gender differs from that of the few remaining soulful managers? It seems that as capitalism moves into its information-driven stage, it will find new and creative ways to reproduce its old racial, ethnic, and gender differences on a global scale.

Notes

1. Richard P. Appelbaum and Edna Bonacich, *A Tale of Two Cities: The Garment Industry in Los Angeles* (Los Angeles: Report to the Haynes Foundation, 1993).

2. Karl Marx, *Capital*, vol. 1: *A Critique of Political Economy* (New York: International Publishers, 1967 [1867]).

3. Samir Amin, *Accumulation on a World Scale* (New York: Monthly Review Press, 1974); A. Emmanuel, *Unequal Exchange: A Study of the Imperialism of Trade* (New York: Monthly Review Press, 1972); and Andre Gunder Frank, *Latin America: Underdevelopment or Revolution?* (New York: Monthly Review Press, 1969), *World Accumulation: 1492–1789* (New York: Monthly

Review Press, 1978), and *Dependent Accumulation and Underdevelopment* (London: Macmillan, 1979).

4. Fernando H. Cardoso and Enzo Faletto, *Dependency and Development in Latin America* (Berkeley: University of California Press, 1979); Peter Evans, *Dependent Development* (Princeton, N.J.: Princeton University Press, 1979); Tom Gold, "Dependent Development in Taiwan" (Ph.D. diss., Harvard University, 1981); Hyun-Chin Lim, *Dependent Development in Korea, 1963–1979* (Seoul, South Korea: Seoul National University Press, 1985).

5. Folker Frobel, Jurgen Heinrichs, and O. Krege, *The New International Division of Labor: Structural Unemployment in Industrialized Countries and Industrialization in Developing Countries* (Cambridge: Cambridge University Press, 1980), and "The Current Development of the World Economy: Reproduction of Labour and Accumulation of Capital on a World Scale," *Review* 5:4 (1982): 507–55; Dieter Ernst, *Innovation, Industrial Structure and Global Competition: The Changing Economics of Internationalization* (New York: Campus Verlag, 1987), and *The New International Division of Labour, Technology and Underdevelopment: Consequences for the Third World* (New York: Campus Verlag, 1980); and A. Lipietz, "New Tendencies in the International Division of Labor: Regimes of Capital Accumulation and Modes of Regulation," in *International Capitalism and Industrial Restructuring*, ed. R. Peet (Boston: Allen and Unwin, 1986).

6. Immanuel Wallerstein, *The Modern World-System* (New York: Academic Press, 1974), *The Capitalist World Economy* (Cambridge: Cambridge University Press, 1979), and *The Modern World-System II* (New York: Academic Press, 1980); and Terence K. Hopkins and Immanuel Wallerstein, "Commodity Chains in the World Economy Prior to 1800," *Review* 10:1 (1986): 157–70.

7. Karl Marx, *Grundrisse*, trans. Martin Nicolaus (New York: Vintage Books, 1978 [1857–58]), 375–80.

8. Robert Reich, *The Work of Nations* (New York: Alfred A. Knopf, 1991); Michael E. Porter, "The Competitive Advantage of Nations," *Harvard Business Review* (March–April 1990): 73–93, and *The Competitive Advantage of Nations* (New York: Free Press, 1990).

9. Allen J. Scott, "Flexible Production Systems and Regional Development," *International Journal of Urban and Regional Research* 12 (1988): 171–86; Allen J. Scott and Michael Storper, eds., *Production, Work, and Territory: The Geographical Anatomy of Industrial Capitalism* (Boston: Allen and Unwin, 1986); Michael Storper and Richard Walker, *The Capitalist Imperative: Territory, Technology, and Industrial Growth* (New York: Basil Blackwell, 1989); Michael Storper and S. Christopherson, "Flexible Specialization and Regional Industrial Agglomeration: The Case of the U.S. Motion Picture Industry," *Annals of the Association of American Geographers* 77 (1987): 104–17; Daniel Bell, *The Coming Crisis of Post-Industrial Society: A Venture in Social Forecasting* (New York: Basic Books, 1973), and "The Third Technological Revolution and its Possible Socioeconomic Consequences," *Dissent* (spring 1989): 164–76.

10. Barbara Ehrenreich and John Ehrenreich, "The Professional Managerial Class," in *Between Labor and Capital*, ed. Pat Walker (Boston: South End Press, 1979).

11. Jeffrey Ballinger, "The New Free Trade Hell: Nike's Profits Jump on the Back of Asian Workers," *Harper's* (August 1992): 46–47.

12. Saskia Sassen, *The Global City: New York, London, Tokyo* (Princeton, N.J.: Princeton University Press, 1991).

13. Hopkins and Wallerstein, "Commodity Chains in the World Economy Prior to 1800," 159.

14. See the essays in Gary Gereffi and Miguel Korzeniewicz, *Commodity Chains and Global Capitalism* (Westport, Conn.: Greenwood Press, 1994).

15. Gary Gereffi, "The Organization of Buyer-Driven Global Commodity Chains: How U.S. Retailers Shape Overseas Production Networks," in ibid., 95–122.

16. Scott, "Flexible Production Systems and Regional Development"; Scott and Storper, *Production, Work, and Territory*; Storper and Walker, *The Capitalist Imperative*; Storper and

Christopherson, "Flexible Specialization and Regional Industrial Agglomeration"; Porter, "The Competitive Advantage of Nations"; Michael J. Piore and Charles Sabel, *The Second Industrial Divide: Possibilities for Prosperity* (New York: Basic Books, 1984).

17. Sidney Morse, personal interview, 28 October 1992. Morse was the largest owner and director (in 1992) of the California Mart. (Two years later the mart was foreclosed and is currently under new ownership.)

18. Jeffrey Pfeffer and James M. Baron, "Taking the Workers Back Out: Recent Trends in the Structuring of Employment," *Research in Organizational Behavior* 10 (1988): 257–303.

19. Mitch Glass, personal interview, 14 August 1991. Glass was the vice president of production, Cherokee Corporation.

20. James Cunningham, personal interview, 28 November 1991. Cunningham was the Vice President for Offshore Sourcing, the Gap Far East, Hong Kong.

21. Gereffi, "The Organization of Buyer-Driven Global Commodity Chains."

22. Tom Peters, *Liberation Management: Necessary Disorganization for the Nanosecond Nineties* (New York: Alfred A. Knopf, 1992).

23. James M. Kouzes, *The Challenge of Leadership: How to Get Extraordinary Things Done in Organizations* (San Francisco: Jossey-Bass Publishers, 1987).

24. Robert Rosenblatt, "Benefits Studied for Part-Time Workers," *Los Angeles Times*, 16 June 1993: D14; Lance Morrow, "The Temping of America," *Time*, 29 March 1993: 40–41; Marco Orru, Gary G. Hamilton, and Mariko Suzuki, "Patterns of Inter-Firm Control in Japanese Business," *Organization Studies* 10 (1989): 549–74; and Michael Gerlach, *Alliance Capitalism: The Strategic Organization of Japanese Business* (Berkeley: University of California Press, 1992).

25. Janice Castro, "Disposable Workers," *Time*, 29 March 1993: 43–47.

26. Jeffrey Henderson and Richard Appelbaum, "Situating the State in the Asian Development Process," in *States and Development in the Asian Pacific Rim*, ed. Richard Appelbaum and Jeffrey Henderson (Newbury Park, Calif.: Sage Publications, 1992).

27. See Richard Rothstein, "Continental Drift: NAFTA and Its Aftershocks," *American Prospect* 12 (winter 1993): 68–84.

28. For a more detailed elaboration of these points, see Appelbaum and Bonacich, *A Tale of Two Cities*, and Bonacich in this volume.

29. Edna Bonacich and Patricia Hanneman, "A Statistical Portrait of the Los Angeles Garment Industry," unpublished manuscript (1991).

30. Mike Davis, *City of Quartz: Excavating the Future of Los Angeles* (London and New York: Verso, 1990), 229.

31. See Bonacich and Hanneman, "A Statistical Portrait of the Los Angeles Garment Industry."

32. Kurt Peterson, *The Maquiladora Revolution in Guatemala* (New Haven: Yale Law School, Orville H. Schell Jr. Center for International Human Rights, Occasional Paper Series 2, 1992; Appelbaum and Bonacich, *A Tale of Two Cities*; Gregg Scott, "Achieving Dignity and Embracing Hope: Daily Battles for Justice in the Los Angeles Garment Industry" (Santa Barbara, Calif.: UCSB Department of Sociology, Report to the Haynes Foundation, 1993).

CHAPTER NINETEEN

The Class Question in Global Capitalism

The Case of the Los Angeles Garment Industry[1]

EDNA BONACICH

The proponents of multiculturalism claim to address the issues of race, class, and gender, but in practice class often falls out of the picture. Multiculturalism's critique is aimed not only at "mainstream" academic discourse, but also at Marxism, which is seen as a Eurocentric, male-dominated approach to society. Marxism is accused of ignoring the peculiar experiences of women and people of color (including women of color in both categories), who have often been cut out of the "proletariat." By placing the proletariat at the center of its analysis of class struggle, Marxism tends to ignore the important struggles for social change engaged in by women and people of color.

Although bringing in the experiences and struggles of women and people of color as a central focus of attention is obviously a very important corrective to a narrowly conceived Marxism, I am concerned that sometimes too much of what Marxism has to offer gets thrown out. For instance, in shifting away from an emphasis on "shop-floor struggles," sometimes the importance of those struggles gets completely disregarded.

More important, the attack on Marxism is often framed as an attack on "structuralism," that is, a structural analysis of society that ignores the cultural component of experiences and struggles. A useful corrective has been introduced here, but again, I fear that some authors take it to extremes, disregarding social structure entirely in their shift toward emphasizing issues of culture, identity, and difference. (I acknowledge that there are some authors who study working women and people of color, including their shop-floor struggles, but their emphasis tends to be on "giving voice" to the workers rather than on analyzing the larger systems of oppression in which they find themselves.)

What happens too often, in my observation, is that "class" gets treated as a kind of cultural identity. A person is "working-class" because she came from a working-class background and is familiar with a working-class life-style. This enables university women to consider themselves to be working-class, even though they earn professional salaries and enjoy the advantages of being middle-class. The idea of class as a system of exploitation that is life-threatening to working people has fallen by the wayside. Instead, it has become another component of cultural identity, along with race and gender.

This transformation of class enables proponents of multiculturalism to feel comfortable about carrying on their debates within the confines of the university, since they can claim that race, class, and gender differences are all represented there. It is true that race and gender differences are present on university campuses, providing a rich milieu for challenging the university's Eurocentric and male-centered traditions. But the working-class is absent among the academic debaters (though not from the university as an institution in its employment of secretaries, janitors, food-service workers, etc.).

My hope in this short paper is to reintroduce the importance not only of class and class struggle, but of a Marxist structural analysis of the system. I do this by examining the garment industry in Los Angeles. Here we see the exploitative character of capitalism, and how it is being transformed and increased by globalization. Issues of race and gender are, of course, important for workers in this industry, but not so much as loci of identity and culture as ways in which their exploitation as workers is organized. In other words, race and gender are used by the capitalist class for the more effective exploitation of labor.

As I see it, racism grew out of the imperialist expansion of Europe. It was the ideology that accompanied Europe's colonial domination of the rest of the world. Imperialism and colonialism created a racially divided working class in which the colonized were relegated to various forms of coerced labor or were kept dependent on linked, noncapitalist economies. These relations were replicated in the United States when peoples of color were either conquered in the Americas or brought, under various degrees of coercion, into the country as workers. Although state-sanctioned racism has ended, racism continues to be replicated and is still of considerable use to the capitalist class in maintaining an especially disadvantaged sector of the working class. Thus, I am not saying that class is more important than race (or gender), but rather, that we must recognize the ways in which gender and race are intensely important elements of the system of class exploitation. In shunting aside the class dimension of race and gender, students of multiculturalism blind themselves to one of the most important engines of race and gender oppression.

The globalization of capitalism is making class relations more difficult to disentangle, a factor that may play a part in disregarding them. The lines of exploitation have become complex and obscure, not only at a global level, but even at a local level. For the remainder of this paper I examine class relations in the Los Angeles garment industry. I consider the question of fighting back: what is being done and what can be done to counter the power of capital? I end by considering what this says about the limitations of multiculturalism.

Class Relations in the Los Angeles Garment Industry

The Los Angeles garment industry is hierarchically organized. Workers are typically employed in small contracting shops, and the contractors appear to be their main exploiters. In reality, contractors work for manufacturers, who design and engineer clothing production, who purchase the textiles, and who wholesale the finished goods. Manufacturers merely contract out part of the labor, namely, the sewing and sometimes the cutting. In a sense, contractors serve as "labor contractors."

Garment manufacturers can contract out the sewing and cutting both locally and abroad. They are encouraged by certain U.S. government policies to contract in Mexico, Central America, and the Caribbean. Still, thousands of contracting shops exist in the United States, employing immigrant workers primarily from Asia and Latin America. The workers are mainly women, though a significant proportion is men. In Los Angeles the workers are frequently undocumented.

Contractors are also typically immigrants, with the majority from Asia. They are immigrant entrepreneurs, in fierce competition with each other. Manufacturers take advantage of the competition and are able to drive prices down to the bare minimum. The contracting system enables manufacturers to squeeze contractors and then claim they have no responsibility for conditions in the contracting shops because the contractors are "independent" businesses.

Despite their power in relation to contractors, manufacturers are generally powerless in relation to retailers, who in turn exercise control over them and take advantage of the competition among them. Clothing is typically not produced unless a retailer has placed an order. Manufacturers show their samples to retailers' representatives who choose whether or not to order them, at which point the clothing is put into production.

Retailing in the United States has undergone major restructuring in recent years, as stores have consolidated into giant chains, and huge discounters (like Wal-Mart) and specialty stores (like the Gap and the Limited) have emerged to challenge the traditional department stores. Not only do retailers have tremendous economic clout in relation to manufacturers, but they also have gone into garment manufacturing themselves. They produce clothing under their own "private labels" both locally and overseas, putting increasing pressure on manufacturers, whose market is shrinking.

The effect of this hierarchy, combined with international competition (which is partially generated by segments of U.S. capital that are producing clothing abroad), is to place extreme pressure on the workers. Los Angeles garment workers typically labor under onerous conditions. They often are paid less than minimum wage, are not paid overtime, and suffer from severe job insecurity as their employers go in and out of business. Child labor is sometimes found, and illegal homework is rampant.

Garment workers in Los Angeles are clearly "exploited," but by whom? Class relations are obscured by the hierarchy of contractors, manufacturers, and retailers, and are even more obscured by the many adjunct actors who participate in the industry. The industry resembles the food chain, with bigger fish eating fish that are a little smaller than them, and on down the line. How can class struggle be conducted under these circumstances, and against whom?

Another way to phrase the question is to consider where the surplus goes, because the definitive character of "exploitation" is the appropriation of the surplus generated by the labor of other people. In the Los Angeles garment industry surplus is extracted in two basic ways: by the classic system of returns to the ownership of private property in the form of profit, rent, and interest; and by the high salaries garnered by professionals and managers.

To give a couple of examples: among retailers, in 1991 the Gap, an apparel specialty store chain, made profits of $258.4 million, and its chief executive officer, Donald Fisher, received a salary of $2.48 million. Among the top sixty-three publicly held apparel retail chains, the average company earnings in 1993 were $92.35 million, and the average salary of their CEOs was $904,900.[2] Real-estate owners include, among others, the owners of the buildings where the contracting shops are located. Among them is Jack Needleman, owner of the Anjac buildings in the Los Angeles garment district, who is said to be worth at least $250 million.

High salaries go not only to direct employees of the industry, but also to adjunct professionals such as accountants, lawyers, and advertisers. For example, we visited two apparel CPAS, one of whom has an office in Santa Monica's Water Garden, which has a man-made lake and multiple fountains, and the other in a downtown office building with an indoor waterfall. These buildings are like temples to capital. We did not ask them how much they make, but it is clear that they are doing very well. The owners of the buildings they are in also collect rent, which ultimately comes from the industry.

We have been discovering that there is a power elite in the Los Angeles apparel industry—that is, the higher echelons tend to know each other and mix together. Their primary form of mixing seems to be through charitable organizations. They support such charities as Cedars-Sinai Hospital, the City of Hope, the United Jewish Fund, and Israel Bonds. They hold fund-raising dinners, where they get together and honor one of their members. People who sit on the boards of these organizations, and who attend their functions, include both owners of capital (e.g., the California Mart owners, big manufacturers, real-estate owners) and managers and professionals (e.g., bankers, accountants, buying officials, lawyers, retail managers, and top managers in large manufacturing firms). The distinction between capitalist and professional/manager seems unimportant at the social level.

The extraction of surplus is supported by ideology and the state. Ideological support is necessary because the tremendous differences in life circumstances between themselves and the workers must give the wealthy pause. How can they justify their tremendous privilege? They hold various beliefs to support themselves: This is an industry where anyone can rise. It is entrepreneurial. The workers, too, will be able to avail themselves of the opportunities the industry offers. Some claim that they themselves worked their way up from the bottom. They see garment work as an entry-level job. Workers will not have to stay there.

Part of their ideology is tinged with racism. Workers are seen as "primitive" people who do not even know how to use a toilet. Employers claim they are teaching the workers basic skills for living in a "civilized" society.

They believe strongly in the fact that there is a "free market," and that everyone is doing what they choose to be doing. The workers would not be doing these jobs if they did not want them. As one powerful manufacturer said: "No one is putting a gun to their heads." In other words, the employers accept inequality as a product of free choice and fail to acknowledge that there is any power or coercion exercised in the system. And they believe that inequality will "work itself out" through upward mobility.

Finally, their charitable activities help them to assuage their guilt. They see themselves as "giving something back" because they were among the lucky ones who made it in the system. They fail to recognize that their good fortune is predicated on the impoverishment of others.

The role of the state is complex. On the one hand, numerous protections for workers are built into the law, including the payment of minimum wage and overtime, the banning of child labor and homework, health and safety regulations, protections for the right to organize independent unions, anti-discrimination laws, and unemployment insurance. These kinds of laws are in the interests not only of workers, but of capitalists who want to prevent undercutting by other capitalists. In the apparel industry it is not untypical for a contractor to approach a manufacturer and offer to sew the goods for 10 percent less than what the manufacturer is paying, no matter what the price. The setting of minimal standards aims at preventing such deals.

In practice, however, these provisions are not enforced. The inspection agencies are woefully underfunded and understaffed and barely make a dent in preventing wholesale violations of the law. When the union has pushed for joint liability legislation to hold manufacturers responsible for conditions in their contracting shops, Republican governors have vetoed the bills. The National Labor Relations Act, protecting the right to form unions, is completely ineffective in this industry, as employers openly fire workers who show any desire to unionize. By the time a case works its way through the cumbersome bureaucracy, the shop will have closed, moved, changed its name, or taken other evasive action.

Apart from weak enforcement of protective laws, the state supports surplus extraction in three other major ways. It does so through immigration law, which creates an especially rightless group of workers who are subject to intimidation. It does so through the encouragement of capital flight to countries where labor standards are lower and where unions are suppressed, thereby increasing the profits of U.S. businesses. Most important, it does so by supporting the rights of private property, that is, the rights of owners of capital to garnish the socially generated surplus simply because of their ownership.

Fighting Back[3]

It is my impression, based on doing volunteer work with the International Ladies Garment Workers Union (ILG) in Los Angeles, that workers in this industry generally feel exploited. No doubt some feel grateful to be working at all, and to have a toehold in the United States. Others may also feel terrified of engaging in any struggle against their employers for fear of losing their jobs or, worse, being deported. Nevertheless, the potential for militancy on the part of immigrant garment workers is high, in my opinion.

Not only have garment workers participated in militant strikes, but immigrant workers in similar low-wage industries in Los Angeles have also shown their militancy. Sometimes they have won important victories, as in the Justice for Janitors campaign in Century City, which was able to overcome the contracting out of janitorial services by forcing the building owners to get their contractors to accept the union. Another extraordinary struggle was waged by drywallers, who were able, despite the fact that the workers were widely dispersed over several counties and hundreds of miles, to gain a union contract in an industry that had drastically reduced their wages and benefits. The Hotel Employees and Restaurant Employees (HERE) has shown its ability to make important gains against a set of union-busting hotel owners. They are currently (mid-1994) engaged in a campaign to organize several major downtown hotels at the same time, along with a parallel campaign to organize the hotels along Century Boulevard that serve the airport (LAX).

These movements show that Los Angeles's immigrant workers are ready to struggle for justice and respect. I do not want to minimize the effort that is required in organizing these workers; their commitment to unionization is not automatic. But the potential is certainly there. Consciousness is not the major stumbling block. Workers do not buy the dominant ideology that they are not oppressed. They feel their oppression intensely and have no illusions about it.

If the problem of fighting back does not lie in the workers themselves, where does it lie? It lies primarily in the problem of finding a winning strategy. The problem is that capital has developed new tools with which to crush labor. What was assumed to be an accommodation between capital and labor during the period when Keynesianism reigned has broken down. Now employers who used to accept unions as an inevitable, and even useful, part of the industrial landscape, have joined in a declaration of war to destroy the unions in this country (and everywhere else).

The processes we have been describing, including globalization and con-tracting out, are part of the effort to destroy worker self-organization and empowerment. Add to them the gutting of the National Labor Relations Board (NLRB) as a small corrective in the imbalance of power and the in-ability of Congress to pass a law prohibiting striker replacement. The class struggle is not dead; rather, the capitalist class is waging it with intensified fury.

Thus, the problem becomes, how does one develop a successful strategy in the face of this onslaught? Workers can be very militant, but their move-ments can be crushed, sometimes brutally. The dilemma is to find a way to fight and *win*. Fighting back occurs all the time, of course, both in everyday actions on the shop floor and in more visible mobilizations, such as marches and strikes. But these actions can often end in defeat and demoralization. Militancy can turn into resignation and despair unless a winning strategy can be developed.

As I have suggested, some unions working with immigrant workers in Los Angeles are beginning to put together campaigns that are showing signs of success. The strategic elements of these struggles include the following features:

First, the unions recognize that organizing solely at the contracting level will not work. Even if one succeeds in organizing such a shop, it will quickly go out of business because manufacturers will cease to send work to such a shop. It is thus necessary to organize larger groups of shops at the same time—for example, all the contractors of a single manufacturer, all the man-ufacturer-contractor complexes in a particular sector of the industry, or all the manufacturer-contractor complexes in a particular geographic location. Another approach involves including the retailer in the campaign, either as a direct producer of private label goods or as the recipient of sweatshop pro-duction. The inclusion of retailers enables the coupling of worker action with consumer boycott.

A second element in the new strategic thinking is the need to develop strong community support for one's campaigns. This includes two types of "community." First, the workers need the strong support of their own com-munities, including, importantly, their ethnic communities. Thus the move-ment for worker empowerment must join with other community-based movements, including movements for better housing, health care, environ-mental safety, and so forth. High on the list for Los Angeles workers is the movement for immigrant rights. The unions need to link with these other movements, as well as to demonstrate the importance of decent wages and working conditions to the general well-being of the ethnic communities that make up Los Angeles.

The second "community" whose support the workers need includes all those forces that are sympathetic to immigrant workers' struggles and can be mobilized on their behalf. These include political, religious, academic, consumer, and other groups that recognize the exploitation that is occurring and will lend their considerable social power in support of these struggles. For example, these forces can express their outrage against police efforts to crush strikes and demonstrations, and ensure that egregious antiworker tactics cannot be deployed by the capitalist class. They can exert pressure on political as well as economic actors by participating in demonstrations, by voting, by boycotting, by writing letters and articles for the press, and by making it clear to the hierarchy of employers that they are being watched. The "community," in this sense, can be an important moral force for checking the class struggle being waged by employers.

The moral case of garment workers (and of other workers in similarly exploitative industries) is certainly compelling. Their case is similar to that of the civil rights movement. A horrible injustice is being committed, but those who hold the reins of power, who live in considerable affluence, and who also control all the mass media of communication have no intention of allowing the system they have created to be challenged. A major battle must be waged to get the public to see the injustice and the necessity for supporting workers' movements. It is only when such a climate of public opinion has been created that a brutal crushing can be staved off.

A third strategic consideration concerns the unions themselves. There is a need for considerable internal reform on the part of unions. The demography of the workforce has changed dramatically, and the leadership of some unions has been very slow to reflect these changes. Some unions also became complacent during the postwar years, focusing on retaining the membership they had, and not bothering with organizing the unorganized. Unions need to change their orientation; some of them are.

For example, HERE Local 11 has a Latina president, Maria Elena Durazo, who brings to the union leadership not only a different demographic configuration, but also strategic development. Local 11 has broken down the distinction between representing existing members and organizing new members. All organizers represent, and all representatives organize. Existing members are active in recruiting new members and helping in the organizing struggle. By helping fellow workers put pressure on employers, the workers who have yet to win a contract are made individually less vulnerable. Meanwhile, workers who already have a contract know that their own contract will only improve if they can bring more of their industry under the union's control.

Another change that some unions are making is to give up on the NLRB as a defender of workers' rights to organize. Not only was the NLRB packed with pro-employer forces under the Reagan and Bush administrations, but it is also especially ineffective as a tool for organizing the kinds of industries that employ immigrant workers in Los Angeles today. The tremendous instability of employment connected with the contracting system makes drawn-out elections almost useless, let alone the fact that employers are able to avoid signing a contract even when an election has been won by a union. Even the filing of charges against employers for blatantly illegal practices is time-consuming, costly, and rarely assured of victory.

Consequently, unions are turning toward more direct action against employers, attempting to get them to come to the bargaining table without having to suffer through an extended legal procedure. This tactic is associated with greater militancy on the part of workers, as they take to the streets and make it impossible for employers to conduct business as usual.

The ILG has been pursuing some of this new strategic thinking by opening Garment Workers' Justice Centers. These centers enable workers to become associate members of the union and participate in the building of a mass workers' movement that will be able to put broad pressure on the industry as a whole. Meanwhile, Justice Center members engage in political demonstrations and help put pressure on one another's shops to deal with important grievances.

It is noteworthy that most of the recent union successes in Los Angeles have been in industries that are less likely to suffer the extreme mobility of the garment industry: janitorial services, hotels, construction. The garment industry, and manufacturing in general, faces the added threat that firms will leave if they are faced with the prospect of unionizing.

This challenge has limits, however. No doubt some of the apparel industry that has not already left will leave in response to NAFTA, and worse, should the latest GATT agreement be signed into law. However, certainly part of the industry will not leave, whatever threats it makes. The need for a quick turn, especially in the fashion sector of the industry, makes overseas production inefficient. Some of the industry is likely to remain regardless. More important, the threat of leaving creates local political contradictions that cannot be ignored. City, state, and federal governments cannot simply let all U.S. industry move abroad. They have to deal with the contradiction this implies for the well-being of society. Although crushing the local labor movement is one of their options, it is not one that is compatible with the democratic traditions of our country, and raises an important moral backlash that will have to be dealt with.

Ultimately, the U.S. labor movement will have to link forces with workers overseas. Tentative steps are being taken in this direction, especially with Mexican workers. The ILG is starting to treat the production systems of manufacturers, which they liken to an octopus, as simply having longer tentacles that stretch across borders. The principles involved in organizing such a structure do not change dramatically just because of its transnational nature. Of course there are special problems connected to the social and political situations in different countries. Still, the potential for cross-border actions is going to rise.

Another approach to organizing in the manufacturing industries of Los Angeles is a new project named LAMAP, the Los Angeles Manufacturing Action Project. Conceived by Peter Olney, who has worked for the ILG, the Furniture Workers, and Justice for Janitors, this project plans to develop a broad movement of immigrant workers who live and work in the multiple manufacturing shops that stretch south from downtown Los Angeles to the harbor along the Alameda Corridor. These industries have all suffered "restructuring" akin to that in the garment industry, including increased contracting out, the destruction of unions, and declining wages and working conditions. All rely heavily on immigrant workers. The goal of LAMAP is to create a coalition of relevant unions that will work together, building a movement that crosses traditional industry lines and is rooted in the community from which all the industries draw.

I do not want to suggest that these struggles are easy to wage. The power of capital is formidable. Employers are able to hire high-priced union-busting lawyers. They are often able to get the state to do their bidding. On the other hand, many immigrant workers are disenfranchised because they are undocumented and disqualified from voting, because they have not yet been able to gain citizenship, or because, even if they are citizens, they face institutional racism in the whole electoral system. Now these workers face a concerted campaign against them in a rising hysteria about immigration. They are being blamed for multiple social ills that they surely do not have the power to create; unfortunately, too many in the U.S. public are prepared to point blame downward as opposed to upward, where the real power lies.

Nevertheless, as I have tried to show, there are signs of movement. New ideas are bursting out all over, and some of them are being put into action.

Keep your eyes on Los Angeles: it may be the first place seriously to challenge the new hegemony that capital has achieved.

Conclusion

Let me relate this back to the issue of multiculturalism. Clearly class struggle is not dead. Even if the workers were completely passive, the capitalist class would be waging the class struggle fiercely. It is determined to cut the cost of labor, which it treats as merely a "cost of production," and not as living human beings.

Gender and race/ethnicity play important roles in the way the class struggle is being waged by capital. Employers do not shy away from using the historical oppression of women and oppressed racial/ethnic groups to their profitable advantage. They structure the workforce to take maximum advantage of divisions, legal disabilities, and any other edges they can gain. They seek out the point of least resistance anywhere it can be found in the world.

Workers must organize themselves and their communities around issues of race and gender oppression, as well as around strictly work-related issues. The best of the unions recognize this clearly and are moving ahead on a broad agenda that could be described as "multicultural." I remain disturbed, however, by some of the tendencies within the multicultural movement to disregard the importance of union struggles, and instead to focus exclusively on identity-based movements and identity politics. Feminism and nationalism, while important components of any working-class movement, sometimes seem to ignore or dismiss the importance of developing strong workers' movements and fighting against capitalism. The "enemy" gets defined as all men or all whites, while the class differentiation among gender and racial/ethnic groups is downplayed. Moreover, the class character of the advocates of this kind of multiculturalism is not critically examined.

I think it is important to acknowledge our own role in the system of oppression. We in the university are, of course, part of the professional-managerial stratum, taking out part of the social surplus through our relatively high salaries. Even when we try to align ourselves with the oppressed, we are still part of a system of exploitation and among the beneficiaries of it. If we are serious about abolishing the oppression of people like the garment workers, we need to consider our class's relationship to that oppression. Not only do we need to fight against the abuses of capital, but also to reclaim for the working class the expertise and control exercised by the professional-managerial stratum. We should be the servants of the working class, not its masters.

In sum, the goal (as I see it) is not to assert the equal importance of one's culture and gender within the nation's (and world's) capitalist institutions, but to overthrow capitalist rule, though surely with complete sensitivity to the special oppression and needs of women and people of color (including, of course, women of color). Too often, the advocates of multiculturalism lose sight of this goal. For this reason, multiculturalism can be co-opted by capitalist institutions, who see it as a nonthreatening movement. On the other hand, when we pursue class struggle, and fight for the end of the (white) capitalist system of expropriation of the social surplus based on ownership of private property, you can be sure that the opposition by the ruling class will be relentless and without accommodation.

The Marxist issues are as alive as they ever were in the experiences of garment workers in Los Angeles today. Perhaps we lose sight of them in the university because they are so difficult to deal with. It is easier to escape into issues of culture and identity and forget about the seemingly intractable problems of intense social, economic, and political inequality. Whether we look at it or not, the class question of global capitalism is utterly central to the lives of millions of people. We must be prepared to fight.

Notes

1. The research on which this paper is based is being developed by Richard Appelbaum and myself as a book manuscript that focuses on the apparel industry in Los Angeles. For my previous work on the apparel industry, see Edna Bonacich, Lucie Cheng, Norma Chinchilla, Nora Hamilton, and Paul Ong, eds., *Global Production: The Apparel Industry in the Pacific Rim* (Philadelphia: Temple University Press, 1994).

2. *Women's Wear Daily*, 7 July 1994: 5.

3. Many of the ideas presented in this section come from lengthy discussions with David Young of the International Ladies Garment Workers Union. I am also learning a great deal from serving on the community core group of Hotel Employees and Restaurant Employees Local 11, and on the core group of the Los Angeles Manufacturing Action Project.

CHAPTER TWENTY

Travelogue

The Garment Industry in Los Angeles and East Asia

RICHARD P. APPELBAUM AND GREGG SCOTT

Every story is a traveling story.
Michel de Certeau, *The Practice of Everyday Life*

What follows is a traveling story about the garment industry in the Pacific Rim, based on conversations and interviews with workers, managers, owners, and corporate executives. Our story begins in Los Angeles, where the explosion of apparel production signals the rebirth of old-time industrial manufacturing at a new time of postindustrial decline (see chapter 18). Our travels will take us to Hong Kong, South China, Macau, and Vietnam, and combine recollections from two visits.[1] Along the way we will encounter young women workers, low wages and long workweeks, and well-known American labels. We will find modern, open factories in Vietnam, and dingy, cramped workshops in Los Angeles. We shall see the industry that served as industrialization's original midwife performing much the same role in Asia two and a half centuries later.

Los Angeles

Louis Lujan's factory, just west of downtown Los Angeles. At the time of our July 1991 interview, Louis's hundred sewing machines were largely idle; his

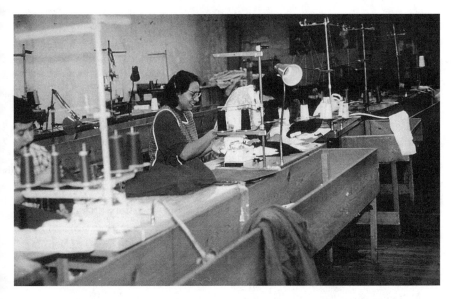

declining business supported fewer than fifty workers, mainly women from El Salvador and Mexico. Crammed into twelve thousand square feet of floor space (which cost him four thousand dollars a month), Louis was plagued by falling prices, growing competition from Asia and Mexico, workers' compensation claims, and two equipment thefts in a single year. Louis's thirty-seven years in the business had left him discouraged and disillusioned.

Louis's west downtown factory had been making clothing for more than a decade. Because of the intensity of competition among Los Angeles contractors, Louis told us he would "do anything" when it came to small-volume garment production, regardless of the nature of the task. His production output ranged from women's skirts to men's "jam" shorts, the latter a popular item among devotees of the widely exported Southern California beachwear look. Louis was also attempting to branch out into nonapparel manufacturing—for example, he had recently designed a combination seat cushion and beverage carrying case dubbed "cush 'n pak," which he hoped would appeal to sports fans and college students. He wondered aloud if our university store might be interested in placing an order.

Although Louis once priced his services on the basis of actual production costs, today he must take whatever the manufacturer offers. According to Louis, the commodity chain has a simple structure: the retailer sets the price for the manufacturer-designer, who in turn sets the price for the contractor, who must make the garment for whatever is offered. For example, Louis shows us a garment that retails for $32–$34. The retailer pays the manufacturer $15.75; the manufacturer pays Louis $3.50. Louis has only one place left to squeeze: the workers who produced the garment. The five who shared in its labor also share the $1.25 that remains after Louis takes his cut, which must cover all of his expenses as well as profits.

As far as Louis knows, despite their harsh conditions, not one of his workers has ever been involved with the union; in his candid opinion, "the union has no balls left." Louis himself may be running on borrowed time, unless "cush 'n pak" somehow manages to catch the public imagination. We have not yet seen it in any university store.

ABC Fashions, South Central Los Angeles. In this tiny shop, fifteen workers make garments ranging from women's skirts to children's beachwear. The physical working conditions are squalid; poor lighting, inadequate ventilation, unsanitary rest rooms, and a scarcity of "free space" for eating and resting are characteristics shared with many of the estimated five thousand factories in Los Angeles County.

Yet six of the workers we spoke with said that the physical environment only minimally affected their feelings about working at ABC. Rodolfo, the owner, migrated from El Salvador to Los Angeles in the early 1970s. He is reportedly generous, responsive, and sympathetic to the challenges facing Latino immigrant workers. Unlike many other contractors, Rodolfo claims to never pay less than the minimum wage; productive workers can earn much more. A few employees informed us that Rodolfo also offers interest-free loans to workers who are trying to assist family members in their migration to the United States. Because the owner's pleasant demeanor and overall "goodness" outweigh the unpleasant conditions that characterize the work setting, the workers in this factory said they feel a great deal of personal loyalty.

ABC Fashions carries three primary contracts, each of which was initiated informally with no more than a handshake binding the two parties. The sportswear made in Rodolfo's factory will retail in major discount department stores (like J. C. Penney and Mervyn's) for between $15 and $40 per item. Yet Rodolfo shares little of this return, and the price he pays for his economic marginality is an inability to compete for more lucrative contracts that require the special machinery (for example, sewing machines for denim) that he cannot afford. Rodolfo reports that contracts are harder and harder to come by, since his decision to pay minimum wage was rapidly pricing him out of the market. At the time of this writing (October 1994),

Rodolfo was trying to sell the factory to his wife's nephew. He hopes to stay on as production manager, a position that will afford him many of the same benefits he now enjoys, but without the associated anxieties of ownership.

Hong Kong

A nine-hour flight takes us to Hong Kong, a soon-to-be-former British colony and booming city-state on the southern tip of China. Asian-manufactured clothing making the return trip will require a bit longer, about two weeks in the truck-size "containers" that stack the decks of the enormous container ships that serve as the arteries of the world economy today. The transpacific flow has made Hong Kong the world's largest port, followed by Singapore; the combined ports of Los Angeles and Long Beach rank third. U.S.-Asian trade reached $361 billion by 1993; $144 billion in cargo passed through Los Angeles alone.

Hong Kong will become part of China in 1997, an inevitability whose economic significance is largely downplayed by local businesspeople. (The potential loss of political freedoms has been of somewhat greater concern, particularly since China crushed the Tiananmen uprising in 1989.) Hong Kong is an entrepreneur's paradise—a bastion of capitalist free enterprise whose towering high-rise apartments and offices are home to some of the world's most prosperous and powerful families. It is also a city of numerous low-wage workers, their ranks swollen by immigrants from nearby China. Yet despite its evident inequalities, Hong Kong unquestionably boasts a rising economic tide that carries most ships, not only the yachts of the business elites but the junks of many working people as well. It is for this reason that the garment industry is sunsetting in Hong Kong, even as it is sunrising to the east in Los Angeles.

Although the Hong Kong garment industry employs an estimated two hundred thousand people in nine thousand establishments, rising wages and land costs are driving labor-intensive industries north to China. Hong Kong is converting from a factory-based workhouse to a service economy of brokers and buyers, multinational corporate and financial headquarters, producer services and entrepreneurs. The enormous wage differentials between Hong Kong and China (garment workers earn $600–$800 a month in Hong Kong, $30–$50 a month just one hundred miles to the north) have had much the same effect as those between the U.S. and Mexico. Cross-border subcontracting in apparel is reinforced by the Out-Processing Arrangement, which permits Hong Kong firms to sew part of a garment in China, so long as the final sewing is done in Hong Kong factories (and therefore exported under Hong Kong quota).

Unlike the United States, Hong Kong has no mandated minimum wage, no employment security, no pensions, and no unemployment compensation. Furthermore, there is no legal right to collective bargaining; even in a fully unionized factory, the employer is under no obligation to comply with the union's demands, a situation that has recently led to wildcat strikes. Finally, there is no equal opportunity law here, so women cannot challenge their situation on the basis of sex discrimination.

Like Los Angeles, Hong Kong lacks a strong labor movement. Most unions in Hong Kong are nonoppositional; only the federation of Independent Trade Unions—and its affiliate, the Clothing Industry Workers General Union—can truly claim autonomy from governmental influence. But oppositional unions lack appeal to young, hip workers. According to labor activist and scholar Trini Leung, unions just cannot seem to shake their old-fashioned "frumpy" image: "We need a postmodern unionism to combat postmodern capitalism," she half-seriously jokes. In Leung's view, women should comprise the core of such a union. Given women's prevalence in the low-wage workforce, it is hard to contest her reasoning.

Unimix Industrial Centre, Hong Kong. A short ride on the Star Ferry brings us from Hong Kong island's sparkling waterfront office high-rises and seemingly endless shopping emporiums to their exact counterparts on the city's

mainland in Kowloon. Another fifteen minutes in an air-conditioned taxi brings us to the San Po Kong industrial district, its run-down buildings teeming with factories and tiny workers' apartments. The Unimix Industrial Centre is largely owned by Wing Tai, a Cheng family multinational corporation with a billion dollars of commercial, manufacturing, and real-estate interests throughout East Asia. (PCH, an Orange County-based, all-American active sportswear company originally known for its surf look, is one Wing Tai spinoff.)

Unimix's giant factory, the largest under a single roof in Hong Kong, makes both woven and knit apparel. In 1991, when the accompanying photograph was taken, its products bore some of the best-known European and North American labels, including Calvin Klein, the Chelsey Group, Horne Brothers (UK), the Burton Group, Structure, British Home Stores, Marks and Spencer, Yves St. Laurent, Perry Ellis, Nino Cerrutti, the Gap—a moderately pricey clientele that could still afford Hong Kong's rising labor costs. Yet although the Unimix factory once boasted three thousand workers, by 1991 the number had declined to two thousand, and currently stands at around fifteen hundred. As Paul Tsang, Unimix's general manager, explained it, with wages running at roughly US$3 per hour and rents at US$1.10 a square foot, floor space was more profitably used for offices than sewing machines. Workers could always be picked up in China.

The Unimix factory is clean, well lit, and modern, although its vast expanses of sewing machines—all operating at full throttle—contribute to a nerve-racking din whose only barrier appears to be the ubiquitous portable radio with headphones. We see machines that display the fabrics for visual inspection, as well as computerized CAD-CAM machines creating the patterns for cutting. Paul's running narrative could easily be a page taken from Frederick Winslow Taylor: "This is where the brains are. We de-skill— we separate the planning from the actual execution, saving us money." Harry Braverman could not have put it more accurately.[2]

We are told that men do the standing work, women the sitting work. We see mostly the latter. The workers are mainly young women, many Chinese immigrants, most lacking the skills, education, and class background to get jobs as multilingual secretaries in multinational offices.

China

From the crowded terminal adjacent to the Prince Hotel in Kowloon we catch a modern, air-conditioned bus that fights the heavy traffic in Hong Kong's New Territories, China's New Economic Zone, and eventually China.

We are joined by Victor Leung, an assistant production manager for Wing Tai Garment International, whose job it is to oversee production at Wing Tai's FuWah factory in Dongguan, China. We are joined by a busload of businessmen, all of whom seem to own cellular telephones that ring constantly and operate seamlessly on both sides of the border.

The three-plus-hour trip takes us through a landscape that is hard to fathom and harder still to describe. The terrain—less than two decades ago dominated by rice paddies and sleepy agricultural towns—is now wall-to-wall high-rise: factories, dormitories, apartments, offices. Cities of a million people seemingly sprout up overnight, connected by a growing and already overtaxed system of superhighways. We are traversing southern Guangdong Province between Hong Kong and Guangzhou, the fastest-growing economic region in the world today, perhaps ever. We are truly on the capitalist road, one never subjected to an environmental impact statement.

We stop for lunch after arriving in the Dongguan Hillside Hotel, which features a miniature artificial waterfall cascading down an exterior landscaped wall. We eat in the non-Chinese restaurant upstairs, rather than the Chinese one downstairs, a preference of our host. Among other things, Victor discusses the virtues of fast-food restaurants, now a popular feature of efficiency-minded Hong Kong. Victor argues that McDonald's offerings are healthier than Chinese food, a somewhat surreal assertion that seems to fit nicely with our Chinese travel thus far.

FuWah Garment Factory, Dongguan, People's Republic of China. FuWah's principal client is a highly critical Japanese manufacturer, who is concerned with what he perceives as the factory's low-quality work. Victor, as Wing Tai's overseer for the factory, has the unhappy task of mediating between the workers, his production staff, and the eight Japanese quality control inspectors. More specifically, his job is to get the factory itself to adopt the "Japanese method" of quality control, which involves a time-consuming, detailed, systematic inspection of every garment that is produced.

FuWah employs nearly two hundred sewing-machine operators and an equal number of workers who do trimming, cutting, bagging, shipping, and other activities. Most of the workers are young and female. The machinery used here is less automated than what we saw at Unimix, and therefore more labor-intensive. But then, the Japanese client requires hand-stitched waistbands on its jeans, and labor is cheap.

The young female workforce generally comes from outlying regions of China. The women—girls, really—labor from 8:00 A.M. to 8:00 P.M., with an

hour off for lunch and another hour for dinner; this goes down as eight hours on their time cards. They work seven days a week, and after work they sleep in company dormitories behind the factory, which we are not permitted to visit. They eat company food, for which they contribute a nominal amount. They are paid by the piece, with rates reportedly adjusted downward if pushed upward by rising productivity. Pay ranges from US$26 to $52 a month. They get a month off to go home during Chinese New Year, and a sizable bonus (US$13) if they return. Among other things, they are producing jeans that bear the suggestive label "Gapstar," whose exterior leather patch announces "authentic denim, European reference, built with the spirit of America."

Not so long ago, labor was protected in communist China: workers were permanently attached to a work unit, which provided them with a job, health care, a place to live, and script to buy food. But now there is a mixed system. A "free" labor market has been introduced, and the girls work by "choice," which gives them a much higher degree of independence than ever before. But they can also be fired, in which case they find themselves without any of the old protections.

Working conditions in the FuWah factory seem harsh to us. Only recently, for example, were workers permitted to have a cup of water or tea at their work station, provided that they did not soil the garments they were sewing. It is extremely hot in south China, and this would hardly seem to be a luxury. Unlike workers in other factories we have visited, the girls here do not smile at us as we pass through the factory.

Macau

Macau, a Portuguese colony, is a city-state like Hong Kong. It lies fifty miles distant, across the wide expanse of water where the Pearl River reaches the South China Sea. The journey is accomplished in less than an hour by hovercraft, a jet-powered ferry boat that skirts commuters between the two colonies. As we approach Macau, we are struck by its similarity to Hong Kong; albeit scaled down. In both places the skylines are dominated by high-rise offices and apartments; in both places, the Bank of China is the predominant feature. Macau itself sounds like a vast construction site, as it builds and rebuilds itself.

We were encouraged to visit Macau by U.S. Customs special agent Thomas Gray, whose territory includes Hong Kong and Taiwan as well. Macau, he pointed out, imports a large number of workers from China under a special work permit program. The program was originally intended to stem the illegal production of Macau garments in China, by bringing the Chinese workers to Macau instead. These workers—again, mainly young women from the rural hinterlands—earn far less than the native workers with whom they labor, and they get no benefits. They are recruited by contracting agents, to whom they pay 10 percent of their wages for housing. They agree to work for a specified period of time, usually two years, a term of indenture that is virtually assured by the fact that they surrender their passports to the agent when they arrive in Macau. As he packed his bags for a return trip to the United States, special agent Gray characterized these immigrant workers as "two-year subcontracted slaves."

Wintex Garment Factory, Macau. Located on the ninth floor of the Fok Tai Industrial Building on Macau's Estrada Marginal, Wintex is in a bustling industrial district where brand-new high-rise workers' apartments are replacing shanties and slums. Wintex is owned and run by Eulalia Cheong and her husband, K. L. Mok. She used to run a small import-export business; he was an architect. Their combined skills are evident in the open, airy design of the factory: immaculate rooms with colorful red ceiling fans, white and black wire bins at each work station to keep materials off the floor, strong neon lighting. Most of the clothing sells in the European Community, although some American labels are found here as well. Their sweaters wholesale for

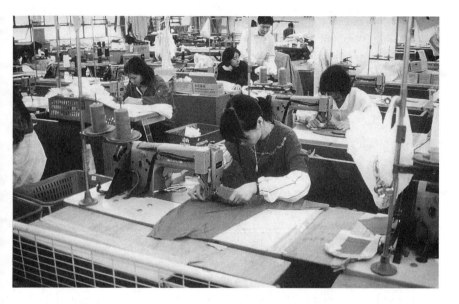

twenty dollars, and retail for at least twice that amount in U.S. department stores. We pass a bench where Esprit logos are being silk-screened onto T-shirts.

According to Mr. Mok, there is a labor shortage in Macau's apparel industry, which has led him to import Chinese workers under the above-mentioned contracting agreements. He tells us, however, that his Chinese workers make the same as the locals, about US$500–$600 monthly, except during a brief initial probationary period during which they earn half that amount. Contrary to what are apparently prevailing stereotypes in Macau, he reports that his immigrant workers are neither dumb, lazy, nor unmotivated. They certainly seem to us to be working very hard. Almost all the very young women we encounter working at sewing machines are from China (those at knitting machines tend to be from Macau). Workers live in the nearby high-rise flats, and frequently go home for their ninety-minute lunch break. Sewers are paid by the piece, and are allowed occasional breaks, such as fifteen minutes for tea or coffee in the afternoon, taken at a tea table. Ms. Cheong explains that they "set down the rules from day one with the workers, so they wouldn't establish bad habits," and that "this made for harmony and understanding later on."

Mr. Mok reports little labor turnover, and the factory is running at full capacity. As we pass a small Buddhist shrine constructed for his workers, he tells us they are like a closely knit family, that he pays them 10 to 15 percent more than the prevailing rate, and that he throws twice-yearly banquets for everyone. We come across a woman working on an overlock sewing machine; her productivity is such that she reportedly earns as much as US$800 per month. Wintex's decor would seem to resemble a trendy office more than a factory. The noise level is low, and workers focus on their machines but do not seem cut off from one another—perhaps because, since the portable radios with headphones appear to be absent, they are able to engage in conversation. The mood seems friendly, and we walk through to smiles.

Vietnam

We return to Hong Kong, and are soon aboard a Cathay Pacific 747 bound for Vietnam. The plane is filled not only with businessmen, but with a number of Vietnamese who are visiting their homeland for the first time after years of exile in Europe or North America. We speak with one man who is anxiously awaiting a reunion with parents he hasn't seen since he fled Vietnam in 1975. At that time he had only the army uniform on his back and a small bag containing a few possessions. Although he spoke no English, like hundreds of thousands of his compatriots he wound up in southern California. Today he is a successful Silicon Valley engineer.

The drama of flying to Ho Chi Minh City (still Saigon to its residents) is heightened by the presence of a large screen in the front of the passenger cabin, on which an emormous image of Indochina is being projected. In a style reminiscent of the original Indiana Jones movie, our route somehow traces its way forward on the map, snaking southward and then westward, rapidly closing in on Ho Chi Minh City. Our excitement mounts as lush jungle gives way to rice paddies and then the city itself, symbol of so much that decentered the United States a quarter century ago.

Hiep, a Vietnamese-born American from Orange County, meets us at the airport with his Vietnamese cousin Bao. Incongruously, Hiep speaks English with a flawless Baltimore accent. Today he is passing as a local, however, having returned to the country in hopes of making his fortune in the import-export business now that the United States plans to lift its long-standing trade embargo. Bao, who speaks almost no English, is an accomplished pianist specializing in European classical music. He lives marginally, barely making a living doing odd jobs and giving piano lessons.

Soon after checking into the Korean-owned Festival Hotel a couple of miles from the city center, we find ourselves on the back of Hiep's and Bao's motor scooters headed downtown. Although it is a sultry evening, the broad, French-designed boulevards are alive with countless living and moving parts. Thousands of bicycles, motor scooters, and occasional trucks converge at intersections long bereft of traffic signals or any other form of traffic control. Like a living organism, surging lanes of traffic somehow merge, cross one another, continue onward. The energy is palpable: a city of young people on the move, anxious to make a buck, hopeful that their former ally will once again establish full economic relations and provide markets for their factories and products.

Vietnam's apparel industry has a long history, although in the recent past state-owned factories produced millions of virtually identical garments for soldiers and workers in the former Soviet bloc, a manufacturer's dream where styles never changed and markets were perfectly predictable. Today, in its quest to become globally competitive, the industry is rapidly privatizing in order to better court foreign capital and clients.

Legamex State Factory, Ho Chi Minh City, Vietnam. One such rapidly privatizing factory is Legamex, a state-owned complex of six factories whose modern sewing equipment includes six computerized embroidery machines. At the time of our 1993 visit, Legamex was raising capital to privatize from a variety of sources, including Habitex of Belgium (its main apparel customer), the German DEG Bank, and the Hong Kong-based Chiap Hua Com-

342   RICHARD P. APPELBAUM AND GREGG SCOTT

pany. For Legamex, privatization means diversification as well—not only into other products and markets, but also into commercial real-estate investment, piggybacking on partner Chiap Hua's current ventures. They already hold a share in the "Villa Project," a planned urban development in which they hold a 30 percent stake; a shopping center is also being considered.

Legamex accounted for a tenth of Vietnam's clothing exports in 1990, thanks to the labor of six to eight thousand people working two shifts in the company's eight adjoining factories. Its annual sales were about $25 million—a modest figure by American standards, perhaps, but a small fortune in a country where the average annual income is less than US$500.

Ms. Nguyen Thi Son, Legamex director, reports that her family had been in the textile-apparel business for generations before her original factories came under state control. After a stint as vice-director of the State Trading Company, she took over Legamex when it was founded in 1987. Her twenty-three-year-old daughter, Nguyen Du Hong Van, heads the production planning department, where productivity graphs and time-motion charts adorn the walls. Although the rest of management is largely male, more than three-quarters of the workers are young Vietnamese women. Director Son was quoted in the September–October 1992 issue of *Vietnam Today* as attributing the dearth of women in top management positions to the fact that women must do all the housework even when employed outside the home, a fact that limits their professional mobility.

Legamex's main product consists of expensive Patagonia-style jackets, which sell in the European Community for US$250–$300. Workers average forty-eight hours during a six-day week, although Sunday overtime work (reportedly compensated) is not unusual. They are provided with one meal a day, mainly to keep them from leaving for their nearby flats. Within the factory is a worker canteen, educational facilities for the employees' children, and training programs for workers who wish to advance their knowledge and position within the company.

The average pay for workers is US$35–$40 monthly, and we are told that skilled workers can make as much as US$70. Managers, according to Ly Chanh Dao, the regional director of the Import and Export Department, do not make much more, although that will change with privatization.

Even before the United States formally lifted the trade embargo against Vietnam, well-known American manufacturers had been visiting the Legamex factory, eager to court business in a country where high-quality work can be had for a low price. Nor is this entirely a one-way street: director Son had already planned a trip to New York City to study the American market. As we conclude our interview, Mr. Dao inquires how he might come to the United States to study management—and asks me to send him some "critical path software for time motion study" (IBM compatible). If nearly two decades of communism have made an impact in what was once called South Vietnam, it is not evident in the Legamex factory complex.

Daewoo's Vietnam factories, Ho Chi Minh City, Vietnam. Daewoo is one of Korea's *chaebols*, the large conglomerates that dominate the Korean economy. Shinsung Tongsang Company Ltd., one of Daewoo's many holdings, recently decided to test the waters of Vietnamese apparel manufacturing, and dispatched Mr. Dong-Hyun Park to see if local factories could be brought up to Korean quality and productivity standards.

Mr. Park and his driver pick us up at the Festival Hotel shortly after noon, and devote the remainder of the day to braving the kinds of traffic jams that can only occur when nothing whatsoever interferes with the free flow of humans, vehicular traffic, and animals. As Mr. Park drives us to Daewoo's three factories on the outskirts of Ho Chi Minh City, he candidly admits that he is not entirely happy about this assignment. Vietnam is truly a hardship post by his standards, and even the country club atmosphere of Ah Phu Village—an expatriate residential enclave with tennis courts and other amenities—cannot shield him from the hot, tropical weather and harsh conditions of life. Mr. Park's attitude might be colored by the impending

birth of his first child, for which his wife planned to relocate home to Korea for at least six months.

Daewoo has been in Ho Chi Minh City for the past year and a half, attracted by the low cost and relatively high quality of labor. Yet productivity is low—perhaps half of Korean standards—so it is a mixed blessing. Moreover, given the extremely low salaries of government officials, bribery is regarded as a routine cost of doing business, adding (for example) US$100 to the cost of every twenty-foot container that leaves the country.

Two of Daewoo's factories work under subcontract; the third is a joint venture with the Vietnamese government. Daewoo's factories primarily manufacture highly standardized polo shirts for the Japanese and European markets. All of the fabric is imported, largely from Daewoo's Korean textile mills. When we ask Mr. Park if Korea plans to open textile plants in Vietnam, he pauses thoughtfully, laughs, and then says "no comment."

Two of Daewoo's factories are newly constructed, their remote suburban location reflecting the much lower land costs. Their location, however, requires a long daily commute for Mr. Park, compounded by the fact that he must frequently return home during the day to place his telephone calls and faxes. (Long-awaited phone lines have not yet been installed.) The Vietnamese government provides the building and facilities; Daewoo the sewing machines, which revert to Vietnam in four years. The first factory we visit is a large, clean, open cinder-block and corrugated steel structure, with bright fluorescent lights hanging low over each work station. We remove our shoes and don slippers as we enter.

Mr. Park tells us that workers are paid "Korean-style"—by the month, not the piece; wages are pegged to a target level of output, based on a forty-eight-hour workweek. Almost all the sewers are young women. If workers exceed their quota, they get a bonus; if not, they work overtime. Monthly pay begins at US$20, but once workers get up to speed—say, in six months—they may earn US$35–$40. Although productivity is only 30 percent of target in this factory, the two full-time Korean technicians on the premises are there to assure that it triples within half a year.

Some three hundred to four hundred people labor in a single open room, using the characteristic Korean assembly-line process rather than the more common bundle method (in which each worker receives a bundle of cut fabric, performs the same operation on each piece, reties the bundle, and passes it to the next worker). Each worker completes a detailed operation, such as a pocket attachment, and passes the changed garment ahead for the next enhancement. The four production lines run the length of the factory, each spitting out 550 pieces each day. There are productivity norm signs along each line, to encourage workers to meet their long-term goal of fifteen hundred pieces. The noise is loud and the heat oppressive as the women labor under the watchful eyes of ten quality-control inspectors.

Conclusion

The apparel industry is rapidly globalizing. In the early 1960s, global apparel exports barely totaled $2 billion; today they have surpassed the $100 billion mark. Five Asian countries—China, Hong Kong, South Korea, Japan, and Taiwan—account for more than a third of the world's apparel exports; Hong Kong alone accounts for an eighth. The United States, in parallel fashion, has become the world's leading apparel importer; in most categories, from a quarter to a half of all the clothing we wear is made outside of the country.

During the coming decade, Hong Kong and Japan will diminish in importance as apparel exporters, relative to such low-wage giants as China, Vietnam, and the many other nations around the world where poverty and hardship drive young women from the countryside to cities in search of work. Their labor, arguably, will help their nations to industrialize—just as it did in Hong Kong, South Korea, Taiwan, and Singapore a generation ago. At the same time, their working conditions will be harsh, their wages low, and their rights nonexistent. They will be competing with their American immigrant counterparts on the global labor market, a fact that will push apparel wages downward in the United States, contribute to sweatshop working conditions, and make it difficult for unions to organize workers.

It is more than ironic that postindustrial society has brought in its wake a reindustrialization on a global scale. Today's globe-trotters often marvel at the similarities they encounter in once "exotic" places: from Hyatts to hamburgers, the world of the traveler looks increasingly the same no matter where one is. This similarity also holds true of the workplace, where First and Third World appear to be merging—at least for those whose physical labor produces the goods we consume.

Notes

1. The trips were made by Richard Appelbaum in November–December 1991 and April-May 1993. Unless anonymity was specifically requested by the interviewees, we have used their personal and business names.

2. Taylor was the father of "scientific management" at the turn of the century; his approach—calling for workers' de-skilling and separation from any vestige of control over the labor process—is critically analyzed in Harry Braverman's classic work, *Labor and Monopoly Capital: The Deregulation of Work in the Twentieth Century* (New York: Monthly Review Press, 1976).

CHAPTER TWENTY-ONE

Unified Capital and the Subject of Value

PAUL SMITH

The Frankfurt School—notably Horkheimer, it could be said—used to insist that fascism was a form of state capitalism and that the racism and anti-Semitism that marked the years of National Socialism could be understood only by way of that fact; that is, racism as such should not be treated as essential, but as a specifiable set of social relations under capitalism. Expressing a different but related view, Malcolm X once remarked, "You can't have capitalism without racism."[1]

In Britain in the 1980s the Thatcher government, in its attempts to construct the proper "English" subject to be the agent of its born-again laissez-faire capitalism, continually came a cropper on the question of race—particularly with its infamous definition of all nonwhites as "black." And the last few years in newly unified Germany have seen the emergence of various virulent strands of racism and xenophobia accompany the extension of the free-market system to the former German Democratic Republic (GDR).

The temptation for many right now—especially since the collapse of "actually existing socialism" and in the laboratory of the New World Order—is to attempt to combat racism in and of itself, as if it could be properly viewed, analyzed, and understood apart from its overdetermined relations to many other elements in the social. For instance, the tendency in Germany, in the wake of the unification of East and West, has been to think of the current anti-Semitism, xenophobia, and racism of a generalized stripe as some-thing essential to German national culture; that is, the recent and ongoing social struggles around race, nationality, and ethnicity there are often ex-plained as some kind of "return of the repressed" in Germany's collective unconscious, some kind of historical struggle over the soul of the nation and its fate or destiny. The links between the present moment and the 1930s are posited by way of an almost mystical conception of the German psyche, rather than by any reference to the history of the changes in capitalist for-mations that call up and deploy the forces of racism and so on.

It seems to me that, if we are to look on multiculturalism as a force or as an ideology that can seriously combat racism (or indeed, any of the other ways of construing otherness within the capitalist cultures of the North), then it will be necessary to think of it very much in terms of its specific his-torical and ideological relation to capitalism's condition at any given junc-ture and in any given culture or set of cultures. This is not to suggest that racism does not exist outside the parameters of capitalism, but rather to at-tempt to talk of racism as one available component (even a necessary and necessarily available component) of capitalist structure. The case of Ger-many is especially interesting in the present discussions of multiculturalism because of the way in which a certain (and perhaps rather unexpected) op-portunity for economic unification under capitalism has been accompanied by the increased need for what we might call a "uniculturalism" in the newly unified nation. In the German context, that is, I think we can see rather clearly how the effort of capitalism to unify itself (an effort, I would argue, that is being played out across the whole of the North in the early 1990s) en-tails the construction of particular kinds of subjects and ideologies to serve its ends; the process—or the history—of such constructions seems to me important for any multiculturalist project to take note of.

One might look, then, with some profit at some of the events and cultural phenomena that follow upon the collapse of the Berlin Wall and the subse-quent unification of Germany—a process that led to a number of crucial political-economic effects. My starting point, however, is not quite those events themselves, but rather some particular representations of them. I begin with two in particular, both texts that in their own way were best-sellers in Germany immediately after unification: one from the left, Elmar Altvater's *Future of the Market;* and one from the mainstream of economic commen-tary, Gerlinde Sinn and Hans-Werner Sinn's *Jumpstart: The Economic Unifi-cation of Germany.*[2]

It is remarkable that both from the left (Altvater) and from the middle

right (Sinn and Sinn) the diagnosis of the collapse of actually existing socialism in the Eastern bloc, and particularly in the former GDR, rests on a
common claim: namely, that in the communist bloc some kind of debilitat-
ing relationship had been established between, on the one hand, economic
structuration and, on the other, the processes of civic life. For Altvater the
problem is that civic and political culture had not been allowed to develop in
such a way as to allow subjects to participate in decision-making processes;
in other words, while certain levels of equality and of participation had been
the norm (had even been required) in the GDR's economic life, the GDR itself
was profoundly undemocratic. Altvater's assumption is that the GDR effectively mishandled the question of people's political desire by keeping it dis-
junct from issues of their economic survival and well-being. The political
and the economic, in other words, were disjunctive.

For Sinn and Sinn the problem with actually existing socialism had been
precisely the absolute collusion between the suppression of people's political
desire and the eradication of what they understand as their fundamental
economic nature. That nature apparently consists in what they call economic motivation and the desire to "do better" in materialistic terms. Actually existing socialism had established a civic and political system that was
exactly designed to suppress the fundamental nature of the subject—its
"natural" economic desire—by refusing to provide "incentives" for the subject's motivations. Such a close alliance of the political and the economic
was predestined to fail, they claim: "Communist ideology, unlike that of
Christianity, assumes that people are fundamentally good; but unfortunately they are not—they are fundamentally selfish. An economic system
based on wishful thinking rather than on a realistic view of human nature
cannot hope to succeed" (Sinn and Sinn, *Jumpstart*, 3). Thus Sinn and Sinn
trot out the most hackneyed and untheorized notions of the subject as
(paradoxical) accompaniment to their insistence on the "iron laws of economics." Altvater's diagnosis, predicated less on the appetite of the subject
and more on its needs, is thereby perhaps more pertinent than the "human
nature" discourse of Sinn and Sinn. But even there it is remarkable that the
subject remains almost entirely *presumed*. In their divergence these two approaches share a lack of theorization of the subject even as they both register
a problem with the relationship established in actually existing socialism between the political subject and the economic subject.

One difference between them, however, is that while Sinn and Sinn quite
wrongly regard actually existing socialism as "Marxism in action," Altvater
more realistically thinks of it as the Frankfurt School did—that is, as a par-

ticular form of state capitalism. For him, therefore, its development depended on (but also finally collapsed because of) a factitious separation of
the political and economic realms. Indeed, like the Frankfurt School's descriptions of that older form of state capitalism, National Socialism, Altvater's version suggests that the totalitarianism of actually existing socialism
is best seen as an extension of the logic of capitalism itself as it tries to keep
the political and the economic apart—in other words, that there is a direct
correlation between the intensity of the attempt to keep the political and the
economic separate and the need for repressive state control.

These two texts, in their similarity and difference, then, provide two fundamental problematics. First, there is the issue of the relation between the
political and the economic, where the supposed logic of the market dictates
the necessity of a disjuncture between the two. And second, there is the issue
of the nature of the subject. As regards the latter issue, it should be pointed
out that the assumptions about—or the presumptions of—the subject that
are to be found in Sinn and Sinn are more or less standard and normative
within the field of economics; that is, more elaborate or theorized descriptions of the subject are scarce in the works of economists who by and large
depend on this presumptive, "commonsense" version of a subject defined almost exclusively as a function of some kind of original appetitive desire.
Mainstream economists almost never bother to go beyond this notion of the
subject, although, on the left, some economists have recently begun to think
of the constitution of subjectivity as germane to their understanding of economic processes. For instance, Jack Amariglio and Antonio Callari have proposed that capitalism works for the preparation of an "individual" who
might be (1) endowed with an ultimately self-interested rationality, (2) convinced of the principle of equality, and (3) dedicated to the concept of private property.[3]

Obviously a lot more needs to be said about this "subject of capitalism,"
especially since Amariglio and Callari necessarily confine their remarks to
delineating its epiphenomenal characteristics without addressing the complex (and largely cultural) processes of subject construction that might enable such characteristics to appear and to function as normative (to seem,
that is, somehow "natural"). But Amariglio and Callari do help us grasp the
importance of thinking about the factitious nature of the subject that is assumed and presumed in economic theory. One suggestive elaboration of
their work would be to begin to define their "subject of capitalism" and its
characteristics more specifically and historically in terms of capitalism's various processes of extracting surplus value. Indeed, one might be tempted to

think of this subject as the "subject of value"—the requisite subject, that is, for specifiable regimes and modes of value production.

It is of course over and against such a "subject of value"—or in dialectical arrangement with it—that capitalism also construes various orders of otherness. The present essay is drawn from a larger project, called "Bearing North," in which I attempt to show how capitalism's current effort to unify itself in the North has entailed—and continues to provoke—a culturally gradated structure of otherness; that is, for the unification of capitalism to occur, there must exist not simply an equal and opposite kind of other for the subject of value, but a series of others. For instance, the national, racial, or ethnic composition of otherness is a variable; and at the same time the subject of value is implicitly masculine, so it has always a gender dimension. However, it is a characteristic of the supposedly universal logic of market capitalism that it can produce only a partial or imperfect socialization of its preferred subjects. Thus, even as a unifying capitalism profers and presumes both its subject of value and a deployed structure of otherness, actual agents knowingly and unknowingly resist those proferrings and presumptions. The current mode of capitalist unification in the North can be generalized as one where it has become increasingly necessary to *legislate* the "subject of value" (as in, for instance, the British government's attempts to criminalize propertyless subjects) and thus consolidate such a subject as a norm.[4]

With those thoughts or those themes in mind, let me return to the political and economic effects of German unification. These feature for the GDR what even mainstream economists have understood as "one of the worst and sharpest depressions in European history. . . . It continues unabated."[5] And for the new Germany what begins is the latest phase in what is often taken to be a chronic struggle over the stakes and forms of an authentic German culture, and along with this a whole series of disturbances and often violent rearrangements in the civic life of the newly unified nation. The cultural context would tend to demonstrate that the issue of race that has so spectacularly reemerged from and for German history is directly a function or symptom of a massive shift in the organization of the means of production (the economic unification of the two states). In that light I would suggest that the logic of unification or integration needs to be understood as an overdetermined construction of economic, civic, and ideological, as well as cultural, elements.

Something of a methodological watchword here can be suggested by recalling Adorno's admonitions to Benjamin during their exchange over the latter's work on Baudelaire: Adorno accuses Benjamin of explaining cultural forms merely by positivistic reference to "adjacent" social events and processes; and Adorno suggests that "materialist determination of cultural traits is only possible if it is mediated through the total social process."[6] No one would suggest—except perhaps Adorno himself—that the preferred schema of materialist determination would be an easy task to construe. But it can be said that the necessarily overdetermined condition of the "total social process" simply does not lend itself to the predominantly positivistic frames and paradigms of the methodologies of the current social sciences. Thus I begin by narrativizing some part of the particular crisis in capitalism and its cultures that is attendant upon the economic unification of the two Germanys. I want to take a first cue from Marx, who (in the course of a discussion admittedly somewhat oblique to my own) considers the role of overproduction in the emergence of capitalist crisis; he posits a definition of crisis that I think is generally applicable: "Crisis is nothing but the forcible assertion of the unity of phases of production which have become independent from each other."[7]

Now, in the United States and Europe economists have regularly suggested that both the economic promise and the political problems of German unification reside in the joining of West German capital with East German labor: "Capital is scarce in East Germany, but skilled labour (and labour that can quickly become skilled) is abundant," say Sinn and Sinn (*Jumpstart*, 43). Another commentator suggests that "Economic integration can be interpreted as the addition of qualified labour . . . and an obsolete capital stock to the West German economy."[8] And in the same vein (but with more sanctimony and with at least a hint of an old-fashioned colonialist voice) Birgit Breuel, head of the Treuhand (about which I'll speak in a moment) enumerates the virtues of this new labor force to which West German capital will be added: "They work hard and loyally . . . they have high intelligence and are well-trained, but they are not at all used to modern machinery."[9]

Capital and labor, then, are taken in my account as the two "phases" of the production process that had been kept apart and I suggest that their recent integration in the unification process is in fact the *origin of an imposed crisis*—the forcible assertion of the unity of separate phases of production. The crisis of unification will thus offer lessons about the cultural and civic mediation of capital's fundamental needs and the practices it designs to meet those needs. As the North struggles to unify itself, German unification can suggest some of the formations and consequences of capital's deep and complex imperatives; among these will be the necessary re-formations of social relations in terms of gender and race, not to mention class, in a situation where crisis at the economic level entails a reshaping of what I've called the structure of otherness. The particular reshapings can be understood as both the consequence of and the necessary condition of a major and enforced shift in the economic system. It might also be worth bearing in mind here one of Altvater's asides, to the effect that indeed "crisis symptoms in the capitalist West have been pushed into the background by the dissolution of the actually existing socialist societies" (*The Future of the Market,* 18); that is, and as always, the symptoms of capitalist crisis are played out at levels other than the economic, and to ideological effect.

My work has been using as point of entry into all this another event, in March 1990, before unification proper: the founding of an institution called the Treuhandanstalt. The Treuhand was established by the Federal Republic with the connivance of the transitional GDR Modrow government and immediately became the biggest holding company in the world (with an impeccable sense of taste, it was housed in the former Luftwaffe building in Berlin). Nominally, the Treuhand was a joint stock association given control of the privatization of the old GDR industrial Kombinate—220 of them broken up into about 8,000 smaller concerns, some of which have since themselves been broken down into hundreds of small enterprises and either privatized by Treuhand or put out of business altogether. By August 1992 Treuhand had sold off about 6,000 companies, and had over 2,000 remaining under its care. About a year later, and because of its habit of breaking up companies into smaller units, Treuhand still had about 2,000 companies, but had privatized a total of 8,422, and liquidated a further 2,578. By the time it closed its doors at the end of 1994, it had disposed of all but about a hundred concerns.[10]

The founding of the company occurred even before monetary unification in July 1990, but it got into full operation in August 1990 when Detlev Rohwedder, former head of Hoesch steel, took over as head. Part of his task was to turn around the company's reputation of being an uncontrolled operation beset by various scandals of influence peddling and favoritism. But Rohwedder did not last long as head of the Treuhand, and thereby hangs one strand of my tale of German unification. Rohwedder was assassinated in April 1991 by the Red Army Faction. The Red Army Faction is known in CIA documents as "the fourth generation of the Bader-Meinhof gang" and had been relatively active in 1991 (including its firebombing of a Treuhand office just before Rohwedder's killing). The activity of the Red Army Faction is one part of the narrative that I can't elaborate here. Suffice it to say that the terrorist murder of Rohwedder can be understood as one particular registration or symptom of civic and cultural reaction to the economic effort of integration. Both before and immediately after unification, the RAF was active in opposition to what it called "reactionary Great Germany and Western European plans to suppress and exploit people here and in the third world," and it justified Rohwedder's murder as ridding the world of another "imperialist beast."[11] The Red Army Faction has woven its activities into the civic and cultural consciousness of the new Germany and has in a sense provoked new terrorist activities (such as those of the recent organization of leftist radical groups in Autonomen, but also of various right-wing groups).

Rohwedder's position at Treuhand was taken over by Birgit Breuel, who remained its head for the life of the Treuhand; its role in effecting the crisis of unification was conducted mostly under the leadership of Breuel. She is —not surprisingly—a confirmed believer in the free market and has described herself as a committed Friedmanite. In 1991, attendant upon the opening of a Treuhand office in New York, Breuel submitted to numerous interviews and laid out for the U.S. business community some of the problems associated with the Treuhand's task of privatization and with unification in general. Interpreting Breuel's statements on that occasion, it would seem that the problems of the Treuhand in the processes of unification boiled down to three in particular.

First, there was a problem with persuading Ossis of the proper principles of private property. For instance, Breuel complained about the simple-mindedness of those East Germans who assumed that property nationalized by the GDR could be simply returned to them; a further difficulty arose when the Treuhand offered mere pecuniary compensation for such property claims.

Second, the Treuhand became willy-nilly an active agency in the carrying out of labor policy. Directed by the political concerns of the government, the Treuhand was compelled to impose various conditions and restrictions on potential investors and buyers so as to ensure continued employment in the old GDR businesses.

Third, a whole series of practical and philosophical difficulties arose simply because of the imposition of a system of value production on a people that had historically not shared or been part of that system. The forced assertion of the unity of West German capital and East German labor entails literally the devaluation of the former GDR economy. In other words, as the Treuhand swept away the value system of a defeated economy, it often proposed the notion that the East German economy was essentially *without value*. The assumption here—an assumption shared by many other economists, whether consciously or not—suggests that only capitalism can produce value. The notion is clearly an absurdity: any economic system, however vilified it might be, or however undesirable it actually is, produces value, defined through the particular form of its expropriation of labor.

At any rate, each of these problems or sets of problems meant that the Treuhand was forced to play a double role in the unification process. Contradicting the Treuhand's own official view of the efficacy of the automatic economic mechanisms of the free-market system (the regime of what Sinn and Sinn call the "iron laws of economics"), the Treuhand *also* became a political and ideological apparatus; that is, the familiar free-market theory, with its doctrinaire opposition between market and planned economies, subverted itself in the practice of the Treuhand. One way in which this contradiction was played out is in the question—much debated by economists, the Treuhand, and the government—as to whether there should be investment and restructuring of GDR industries before their sale. The restructuring option—a de facto planning and thus a subversion of undisturbed market forces—was, for example, the tactic favored by the Thatcher government when it undertook privatization of nationalized industries in Britain in the 1980s. And this is effectively the option the Treuhand was forced to adopt by a government concerned with the political and civic consequences of wholesale privatization. As Breuel ruefully admits, "The social aspect enters into every decision we make."[12]

My point here is that the Treuhand was fully a political entity even while it offered itself as a benign conduit for the easy operation of the economic principles of the free-market system. Indeed, the Treuhand was designed to usher in a properly unpoliticized or depoliticized vision of the market. In that sense it was a contradictory and even embarrassing phenomenon—the embarrassment appears when Breuel says that "we want to make ourselves superfluous as soon as possible."[13] Indeed, one way of focusing on this double role of the Treuhand is to contrast it to another such trust company, the National Trust in Britain, which buys and owns (in order to preserve) private land for the nation. Patrick Wright has said of the National Trust that it "has provided the state with a way out of the conflict between public interest and private property. The two are now negotiated but at a displaced level: as a registered company, the Trust holds property privately, and yet it does so in what it also works to establish as the national and public interest."[14] The Treuhand negotiated the same contradictory role and with the same ideological concern for some putative "public interest." Its goal, however—distinct from the conservation function of the National Trust—was precisely to disappear, to finally have the public and national interest both expressed and realized in the fait accompli of total privatization. Breuel again: "We will cushion East German workers, but eventually the logic of the free market must change their very existences."[15] Clearly, as Breuel's remark promises, the much-vaunted rationality of the free market reaches its goal of magical and objective self-regulation through the interpellation of subjects fit for or apt for a set of economic forces that themselves must be manipulated. The denial of the linkage between the political and the economic is played out across the bodies of subjects that must be pulled into the right place.

The selling off of the assets of the GDR, in what Treuhand itself described as "the sale of the century," is an event of huge significance at the political-economic level, even if only because it is the most extensive privatization program ever conducted (exceeding by far the post-Allende privatization in Chile, and on a different scale and of a different nature than anything in the new republics of the former Soviet Union). But, notably, it is not simply an attempt to convert a planned economy to a market one; it is rather a process whereby a planned economy is colonized and integrated into a market one. As such, the unification of the two Germanys might be (and has been) seen as the very Aufhebung of the historical dialectic of socialism and capitalism! More modestly and realistically, the unification is undoubtedly of interest as the locus for the application of a principle that abounds in political and economic thinking in the North: the principle that the market system is inherently different from and, obviously, superior to planned economies.

The confidence of this principle can be seen quite clearly in the discourses that have surrounded the economic unification in the United States and in Europe. To take stock of some of this, I've been looking at three different registers of economic discourse: business and trade journals, academic economics, and the documents of policy groups and think tanks such as the Brookings Institute or institutions like the World Bank or the International Monetary Fund. I won't be discussing here the trade and business journals—journals such as *Mergers and Acquisitions, Journal of Business Strategy,* or *International Management,* which throughout 1991 were stuffed with articles with titles like "A Buyer's Guide to East Germany's Company Bazaar." Nor will I discuss one of the most influential—if controversial— policy discussions carried out in the United States at the Brookings Institute by the Berkeley economists Akerlof, Rose, Yellen, and Hessenius; or the way the Brookings Institute functions thereby as a component of American involvement in the attempt to unify the capitalist North.[16]

As far as the academic economic discourse is concerned, one of the most remarkable contributions I found is by Horst Siebert in the *European Economic Review*. It is one of the few that overtly attack what it calls the "political economy of integration" for its being a compromised confusion of a market economy and a planned economy. Looking ahead to the prospects for successful integration, Siebert stresses the necessity of depoliticizing the market and delineates the proper nature of the "subject of value": "Moving from a centrally planned economy with government ownership of the means of production to a market economy will increase economic efficiency. This is because the motivation of people will change. . . . Economic decisions will be delegated to the market and will thus be depoliticized" (Siebert, "The Integration of Germany," 598–99).

Siebert thus exhibits the same kind of faith in people's motivation—the whole capitalist notion of incentive—as quoted earlier from Sinn and Sinn, and, like Breuel, he insists on the necessary divorce of politics and the market. His position is repeated in a different way by Lawrence Brainerd, a consultant for the IMF, who claims that success in unification depends on the conversion of East Germans to the necessity of putting themselves at risk. This, it appears to him, is the essential difference between market economy and planned economy: in the latter subjects are not agents; capitalism, by contrast, works through the construction of subjects who come to see themselves as "responsible"—and responsible because they "naturally" protect their own stake in private property.[17]

Siebert, for his part, elaborates on the necessary depoliticization of the market that will restructure and reorganize the GDR economy into something more efficient. This is to be done by "eliminating the production of intermediate inputs that can be provided more cheaply by markets, by discarding repair departments and by giving up social services like Kindergarten." Siebert's fear, throughout his whole analysis, is that "there is a definite risk that the political process will dominate the privatization." Already, he suggests, the process of currency unification in the two Germanys "had not relied on market forces" and thence had led to a weakening of the prospects for increased ex-GDR efficiency (Siebert, "The Integration of Germany," 600–601).

The combination of this view of the subject of value and a fear of the politicization of market forces can be taken as an indication not only of the immense but fundamental ideological task that market capitalism sets itself to undertake, but also of the contradictions embedded within that system. Despite the compromises, the fears, and the contradictions, none of these economic discourses will ultimately demur from Birgit Breuel's final words on the subject of economic integration: "Privatization is the best restructuring."[18] Indeed, like the nineteenth-century economists whom Marx derides in *Capital*, it is the habit of contemporary bourgeois economists to denounce "every conscious attempt to control and regulate the process of production socially as an inroad upon such sacred things as the rights of property, freedom, and the self-determining genius of the individual capitalist," while at the same time undertaking exactly the social control and regulation of the economic process.[19] The obfuscatory claims about the "naturalness" of a capitalist notion of value and about the "nature" of the subject are taken as givens (here, perhaps, as the right of the victor) and emerge, as I say, in the form of an incredible insistence on the part of economists that the GDR economy was essentially valueless and that it did not serve the interests and needs of a normative human subject, the subject of value.

In the former GDR, women were prime beneficiaries of a whole array of state provisions and civic privileges of the sort that still cannot be guaranteed to women in most democracies in the North. These seem to have been intended to persuade women to reconcile their active role in the GDR economy with their presumed role in reproduction and the family. But restructuring has massively displaced women from the workforce, and consequently has allowed the removal of the rights and benefits they received under the communist system. This is not to suggest that the condition of women in the GDR was altogether satisfactory; certainly they were encouraged as workers and had legal equality in civic society, but at the same time their additional role as mothers was not only installed into legal and constitutional discourse but was also culturally mythologized—and this despite the fact that, as Barbara Einhorn has shown, no conception of the private sphere was encouraged for women in the GDR.[20] But perhaps it can be suggested that women have now reverted to an even less satisfactory role in the new unified economy; there they are returned from the civic to the private while traditional ideas of motherhood and femininity are reinstalled as the "family values" of the private sphere that has become theirs to safeguard and nurture. Thus, in the economic conditions of the new, and in the ideological climate, there has been a diminution of women's citizenship and their economic status. But, as Einhorn has also remarked, many women right now are embracing their new condition "as welcome respite from the rigours of the double or triple burden to which they were subjected by state socialism" (ibid., 7). To put this another way, the new economy, bringing with it the capitalist definition of the subject of value, sees East German women as precisely *not* that subject. If one definition of the subject of value is that it be endowed with an ultimately self-interested rationality, women are now returned to the traditional nonself-interested roles of reproduction, child rearing, and homemaking. If another definition is that the subject of value be convinced of the principle of equality, women have had to explicitly abandon the equalities bestowed by the GDR state constitution. If a third is that the subject be dedicated to the concept and system of private property, women have little or no role to play in that system. In the same way as capitalist unification declares the GDR economy "valueless," GDR women cannot be constituted as the proper subject of value.

In the transition toward a unified Germany, perhaps the most remarkable symptoms of capitalism's provision of the subject of value arise around issues of race. Before unification, West Germany's economic system had been highly reliant upon low-paid foreign "guest workers," economic and political refugees from many parts of the world. The opening up to West German capital of a new, cheap labor force in the shape of the Ossis immediately meant (to put the matter crudely) that the existing cheap labor became economically superfluous. More important, perhaps, it facilitated the revival of the slogan "Germany for the Germans"; now that the Ossis could be seen as a properly German source of labor, the economically unified new nation might be able to unify its culture too. Thus, one of the immediate consequences of unification was the debacle in 1991 and 1992 surrounding guest workers and asylum seekers.

The issue first arose in earnest, one might say, in the spring of 1991 when thousands of Poles arrived in eastern Germany, an event that provoked so-called neo-Nazi forces into the open to protest and presaged a "long hot summer ahead."[21] The influx of foreign workers and asylum seekers (from countries such as Romania, Armenia, Turkey, Vietnam, Yugoslavia, Bulgaria) resulted in about a quarter of a million requests for asylum during the first part of 1992. The ensuing debates led not only to the Kohl government's extreme tightening of Germany's asylum provisions (with the connivance of the Social Democratic Party, it should be said), but also to the reporting of over two and a half thousand incidents of racist and xenophobic violence in 1992. Those reported incidents are generally believed to be only the tip of the iceberg, and in any case were serious enough that they included seventeen homicides.

In that context, it's hardly a surprise that, as an Infas Research Institute survey showed in September 1992, 51 percent of Germans believed that the slogan "Germany for the Germans" was "largely justified."[22] Of course, the particular political-economic nature of racism and xenophobia is likely to be differently constructed in the two different halves of the country: it might be surmised, at least, that Ossi racism is in part a resistance to the effects of unification, whereas in the West it is by and large a way of embracing unification. In both sides of the country, however, the problem of racism and xenophobia has continued right up to the moment of writing in 1995. The state's attempts to deal with such an alarming situation have only tended to sustain the proposition that racism and xenophobia, seen as entirely political and not as economic issues, are symptoms of the effort to construe the proper subject of value. The tightening of asylum rules, for instance, was clearly legislation intended to stabilize the population as a population of white Germans and provided, furthermore, the opportunity to demonize nonwhites, blaming the victim. Helmut Kohl's concession at the time to the effect that he could understand popular concern over a massive influx of asylum seekers sets the same tone, refusing to acknowledge that such "popular concern" was a symptom rather than a cause of his government's policies.[23] The unwillingness of the government even to name the problem as a problem of racism reached its acme in one sense when a 1993 report ascribed the social violence experienced simply to the temporary difficulties of people in both halves of the country (especially young people) in coming to terms with new situations. The report carefully skirts most of the salient economic circumstances of the new racism, preferring to see the issue either as political or as part of Germany's "bad conscience" about its past. At the same time, the implication is that the improper subjects who perpetrate violence should not be tolerated (not "cushioned," perhaps, to adopt Breuel's language quoted earlier in relation to Ossi workers) for long in the drive toward a common cultural identity in the two Germanys.[24]

With these briefly elaborated examples (which should be understood only as parts of a draft of a longer and less gestural essay) I am simply suggesting that the forcible assertion of the unity of Germany provokes crisis, or takes the deliberate risk of civic and cultural disturbance, in the interests of the directives of capitalism itself. The alarming symptoms in civic and cultural life are not only varied and overdetermined in and of themselves, but are also inextricably part of the economic crisis. The cultural and civic formations of what we might call a desired *uniculturalism* are intimately tied to the nature of this capitalist crisis. And since, as Marx insists, crisis is a moment at which the contradictions of what he calls "the bourgeois economy" of capitalism are paramount, any struggle against "uniculturalism" is bound to uncover at some point and at some level exactly those contradictions. What we can perhaps see in the German context is a playing out of some of the fundamental contradictions of capitalism and a display of the logics of late twentieth-century capital. Even though the collapse of actually existing socialism in other places has led to a set of quite different scenarios (most of which tend toward the chaotic rather than the unified, as in the former Yugoslavia), the German situation can be taken as a pure instance or a model by dint of the fact that there is indeed this forcible assertion of unity—this forcible assertion that is quite specifically controlled and managed by actually existing capitalism. Now, in that process we can glimpse the way in which the economic realm is articulated with the civic and the cultural; equally we can see the forging of a double-headed effort first to produce the appropriate subject of value, and second to deny or simply elide the connectedness of the political and economic realms. From such propositions it would not be hard to conclude that any effective political, civic, or cultural strategy produced by multiculturalism will be struggling not just against a reluctance of white culture to "integrate" racially or ethnically "diverse" cultures, but equally—perhaps more thoroughly—against a set of formations and ideologies that are crucial to capitalism's development and its current effort to unify itself in the North.

Notes

Some citations have been taken from electronic versions of newspaper and magazine reports, and in those cases I do not cite page numbers.

1. Quoted in Manning Marable, Race Reform and Rebellion: The Second Reconstruction in Black America, 1945–1990, 2d ed. (Jackson: University Press of Mississippi, 1991), 90.

2. Elmar Altvater, The Future of the Market (London: Verso, 1994); Gerlinde Sinn and Hans-Werner Sinn, Jumpstart: The Economic Unification of Germany (Cambridge: MIT Press, 1994).

3. Jack Amariglio and Antonio Callari, "Marxian Value Theory and the Problem of the Subject," Rethinking Marxism 2:3 (fall 1989): 1–30.

4. For the notion of the presumption of the subject, see my Discerning the Subject (Minneapolis: University of Minnesota Press, 1988). The use of the term "to profer" is explained in my Clint Eastwood: A Cultural Production (Minneapolis: University of Minnesota Press, 1993), xvi.

5. George A. Akerlof, Andrew K. Rose, Janet L. Yellen, and Helga Hessenius, "East Germany in from the Cold: The Economic Aftermath of Currency Union," Brookings Papers on Economic Activity 1 (1991): 1.

6. Fredric Jameson, ed., Aesthetics and Politics (London: New Left Books, 1977), 129.

7. Karl Marx, "Crisis Theory," in The Marx/Engels Reader, ed. Robert Tucker (New York: W. W. Norton, 1978), 448.

8. Horst Siebert, "The Integration of Germany: Real Economic Adjustment," European Economic Review 35 (1991): 592.

9. Washington Post, 1 August 1991.

10. Figures for 1992 and 1993 quoted from United Press International, 25 September 1992

and 23 May 1993, respectively. The following passage (from the *Economist*, 24 December 1994), reporting on the closure of Treuhand in 1994, is interesting for the way that it replicates the assumption that the GDR economy was valueless at the moment of unification, but also because it succinctly relays some of the contradictions of the Treuhand's project: "In 1990 the Treuhand was the world's biggest holding company, with 12,370 businesses from coal pits to a down-at-heel Berlin horse track. Since then, all but 100 or so have been sold or liquidated. A gaggle of smaller agencies remains, mainly to enforce contracts, manage the few companies left and dispose of the Treuhand's property portfolio. The big companies went mainly to western German or other European investors which were in the same industry; many smaller ones were bought by their managers. The Treuhand leaves behind a flourishing economy (eastern Germany grew by around 9% in 1994) and thousands of firms with at least a chance of surviving in the world market.

"Yet the cost was high. More than six out of ten of the 4m people Treuhand firms once employed have been sacked. What is left of East German industry is dominated by western owners. In its early days the Treuhand thought it would raise DM6000 billion ($370 billion) from privatisation; instead, it will raise about a tenth of that amount and hand the state a debt of DM270 billion. After a string of scandals, the federal auditor has assailed the Treuhand for exercising lax controls. According to a poll published recently in *Süddeutsche Zeitung*, a Munich-based newspaper, 91% of eastern Germans have a low opinion of it."

11. *Newsweek*, 15 April 1991; *Independent*, 3 April 1991.

12. *Christian Science Monitor*, 12 November 1991.

13. Ibid.

14. Patrick Wright, *On Living in an Old Country* (London: Verso, 1985), 52.

15. Breuel, quoted by InterPress Service, 24 February 1992.

16. See Akerlof et al., "East Germany in from the Cold," 1–105. Yellen's recent elevation to the Federal Reserve Board by the Clinton administration gives an idea of the influence of this group of economists.

17. Lawrence Brainerd, quoted in *IMF Survey*, 7 January 1991: 11–12.

18. Quoted in *International Herald Tribune*, 2 April 1994.

19. Karl Marx, *Capital*, vol 1: *A Critique of Political Economy* (New York: Vintage Books, 1977), 477.

20. Barbara Einhorn, *Cinderella Goes to Market* (London: Verso, 1994), 23.

21. *Daily Telegraph*, 13 April 1991.

22. Infas Survey Report, quoted by United Press International, 11 September 1992.

23. Quoted by United Press International, 9 September 1992.

24. See *Dossier on Xenophobia in Germany*, Germany Foreign Press Office, January 1993. Angelina Peralva, in her contribution to the book *Racisme et xénophobie en Europe* (Paris: La Découverte, 1994) has a more optimistic reading of this report (159–212). It does appear that the Kohl government has been more willing in 1994 and 1995 to crack down on right-wing groups.

CHAPTER TWENTY-TWO

Living on the Edge

Everyday Lives of Poor Chicano/Mexicano Families

PATRICIA ZAVELLA

The growth of multiculturalism in the U.S. academy has been fueled, in part, by the development of respective fields of study on those originally ex-cluded from the canon—people of color, women, and gays and lesbians. Afro-American Studies, Asian-American Studies, Chicano Studies, Femi-nist Studies, Queer Studies, Puerto Rican Studies, and their respective vari-ant titles (as well as departments and research institutes on white ethnics) were initiated within the context of the social movements of the late sixties and early seventies. Led by so-called radicals, there was debate over the inat-tention to social problems—poverty, racism, the Vietnam War, sexism, ho-mophobia—by the social sciences and how academic work seemed out of touch with the profound contradictions existing in society. The impetus for change had come from the Great Society legislation, the civil rights move-ments—especially in providing access to educational institutions—and the nationalist, counterculture, feminist, and gay movements. Often led by stu-dents, faculty, and staff who engaged in strikes, fasts, and demonstrations demanding new programs, we in Ethnic Studies embarked on a concerted effort to make intellectual work "relevant," to analyze the pressing problems in our communities. The generation of knowledge itself—the construction of paradigms, the very research questions asked, and by whom—were all seen as reflections of power and privilege.[1]

Once established as academic programs or departments, the initial work of scholars working within Ethnic Studies often was to critique the then dominant theories, which, as was fashionable at the time, looked for internal cultural explanations of the social problems experienced by Chicanos.[2] Highly influenced by Marxism, early critics made challenges to structural functionalism and its variant, cultural determinism, with their ahistorical disregard for the structural bases of the oppression of people of color.[3] Within Chicano Studies, many of us saw our work as asserting the importance of race in theorizing about the Chicano experience—which meant framing and contextualizing the structural basis of racial inequality. With this project at hand, a generation of scholars began looking at history to understand how contemporary patterns of institutional racism and sexism were set in motion in historically specific ways.[4]

Now, in the early nineties, as the numbers of homeless and people experiencing poverty increase in the wake of the Reagan-Bush economic policies, the field of poverty studies has burgeoned once again. As during previous times when cultural analyses held sway, there are theoretical approaches to studying poverty that hold up the importance of internal cultural features of the poor. In studies that have been largely outside of Ethnic Studies discourse and placed within mainstream academic venues, the culture of the poor—particularly their values and behaviors—is being emphasized over structure and power. I will argue that such an approach limits our understanding of those currently living in poverty, particularly women and immigrants from Latin America.

Poverty Studies in the Nineties

Do "strong family values" determine how Mexicans adapt to living in poverty? Some researchers argue that in contrast to poor Blacks, Mexicans are more "stable" because poor Mexicans are more likely to live in nuclear families; because teenage pregnancy is a source of opprobrium, so if girls get pregnant, young men are pressured to marry and form nuclear households; and because extended family ties are important and, for cultural reasons, the main source of support for poor people.

Richard Taub argues that poor Mexicans in Chicago have very strong values about work, which include appreciating those who have two jobs, having women do industrial homework to increase their income or make crafts or garments at home to sell for extra income, and realizing that for women, hard work includes being responsible for housework after a day on the job.

Moreover, Mexicans (presumably immigrants, although he does not specify) expect men to be breadwinners, but also realize that men will be tired
and often drink after work, and may engage in extramarital affairs.[5] The
African Americans that he interviewed, on the other hand, specify that they
resent being asked to perform work when it's not part of their job description, are critical of exploitative working conditions, and angry about the lack
of promotions. Clearly, Taub is comparing two populations in different structural positions (immigrants and a subordinated racial group) and arguing
that they have different cultural values. They may indeed have divergent
value systems, but that can only be ascertained if they are asked the same
questions, which does not seem to have been done. Part of Taub's evidence is
that within a four-block area within a Mexican barrio in Chicago where he
did ethnographic research, there were fifteen bridal shops, bakeries, caterers,
and florists who specialized in weddings, but there is no such proliferation
in Black neighborhoods. When he interviewed people, they agreed that a
couple *should* get married when the woman gets pregnant.[6] With this data,
Taub concludes that Mexican Americans have an intense commitment to
the marital bond and to work, whereas Blacks do not, presumably because of
cultural differences between the two populations. The implicit conclusion is
that if Blacks just had different attitudes, they would have better lives.

Taub's and others' work falls within the dominant theoretical approach
about the "urban underclass" that has become prominent in the social sciences. The term itself was coined by journalists and there is debate about
who constitutes the underclass.[7] Probably the most influential formulation
is that of William J. Wilson, a self-avowed liberal who aims to counteract
conservative formulations that emphasize individual attributes within a culture of poverty.[8] Wilson focuses on the poor located in urban ghettos, who,
because of severe racial segregation, are predominantly Black. He argues
that because of restructuring in the economy with plant closures and deindustrialization in rust belt cities, Black men in the inner cities face chronic
joblessness. With the departure of industry from major cities and the rise of
the service sector, the remaining jobs provide low pay and few possibilities
for promotion. Without the ability to support their families, fewer couples
get married when women become pregnant. Accompanying the movement
of capital out of the inner city came the flight of the Black middle class to the
suburbs, followed by the exodus of stable working-class Blacks. Closely associated with the remaining socially isolated, impoverished neighborhoods
are "concentration effects," where the sense of community is replaced by social disorganization. Those who remain in the inner city form an urban "un-

derclass," made up of mainly poor single mothers—particularly teenage mothers—who rear children isolated from mainstream norms and behavior, and unemployed men.

Although Wilson claims he "draw[s] attention to the structural cleavage separating ghetto residents from other members of society and to the severe constraints and limited opportunities that shape their daily lives,"[9] he and other underclass theorists focus on the behavior and deduced values of the poor.[10] Thus, to understand high Black male unemployment, researchers do not interview employers about their perceptions of Black men, but unemployed men themselves, who then get cast as young men not developing a strong "work ethic" and losing their sense of masculine "honor"—valor, respect, appearance, and independence—which is rooted in Southern aristocratic tradition.[11] Rather than interrogating a firm's relocation policies about uprooting work sites or suburban tax benefits for relocating factories out of rust belt cities into the sun belt (or abroad), the inner cities are portrayed as bleak social spaces, where men "hang out" on the streets, engage in drug use to numb their feelings of powerlessness, and resort to crime to provide some income. Without discussion of the cutbacks in funding for agencies providing birth control and the controversy over parental consent for abortions for teenagers, adolescent females are presented as objectified and as being duped into sex with young men and then ending up on welfare.[12] Instead of documenting those programs that aim to involve ghetto parents in schools or offer innovative curricula, children are seen as having few "positive role models" with the departure of bourgeois Blacks. The influence of grassroots or community-based organizations—which address issues ranging from stopping gang violence to providing education regarding sexually transmitted diseases—is left unrecognized, without analysis of these groups' abilities to affect local policies or provide resources for the poor. Members of the urban underclass are portrayed as having lost all human agency or ability to contest the problematic features of poor neighborhoods, and similar dysfunctional attributes of wealthy or middle-class neighborhoods (such as drug use or the rise of white teenage pregnancies) are ignored, implying that social problems are exclusive to ghettos.

Embedded in the underclass approach are moral judgments about women's sexuality and men's work ethics. "Shiftless" men and "welfare queens," the putative models of individuals who are out of control, underlie much of the discussion of "family values" in relation to poverty. This view sees socialization, particularly the inculcation of the work ethic and of values about controlling one's sexuality, as taking place within families (or occasionally churches), where women and men are taught "proper" behavior and encouraged to marry.[13] The assumption is that if women would just control their sexuality, they would not be in the predicament of having illegitimate children and being pushed into dependency on the state. Moreover, this view assumes that if men would only hustle for stable jobs and form conventional households of nuclear families, they would not fall into poverty.

The ideological nature of this argument can be seen in the conservative media harangues that use underclass imagery to denounce the poor. In almost the same breath, media pundits bemoan the culture of poverty among welfare recipients and worry whether the "brown hordes" of Mexican and Central American immigrants, with their high fertility rates, will soon deplete American jobs and social services.[14] Recurrent pummeling of the immigrant poor also comes from state officials. California governor Pete Wilson's attacks on immigrants and welfare cheats, and the 1994 California initiative that would "Save Our State" from immigrant inundation, are part of a long history of blaming immigrants for the structural dislocations that plague this country. The cultural trope "Just say no" has taken on a political meaning far beyond Nancy Reagan's original slogan against drug use, as Blacks and Latinos are advised to change their behavior.[15] The influence of the media on people's behavior can be seen in the debate between Vice President Dan Quayle and the fictional television character Murphy Brown. The U.S. Census Bureau reports that about three hundred thousand births were unreported, apparently the result of parents lying to surveyors and either not admitting they had a child or claiming they were married when they were not. It took months before the Census Bureau was able to verify this underreporting through other sources, and the bureau attributes this "glitch" to the Quayle-Brown debate.[16]

The focus on value orientations and the behavior of the poor is problematic in several respects. The most obvious is that for these underclass theorists, poverty gets collapsed into family structure. They ignore the high number of families that include at least one employed adult, the so-called working poor. In 1991, 28 percent of Latino families, 22 percent of white families, and 12 percent of Black families below the poverty level had at least one adult who worked full-time during the whole year.[17] Clearly, finding the right mate will not preclude being poor. Focusing on family values ignores the fact that not all poor people engage in dysfunctional behavior or have weak family values.[18]

Moreover, socialization about marriage and sex also takes place in peer groups, in schools, and, especially for youths living in poverty, "on the streets,"[19] and lack of access to family planning may have more impact regarding bearing children out of wedlock than do women's desires. The assumption that pregnant teenagers would be better off within the bounds of marriage is belied by the high divorce and separation rates of young couples and by domestic violence rates that increase when men feel pressured through job loss or the increase of responsibilities beyond their means to meet them. This view also ignores the relationships that poor unwed fathers do have with their children, including the labor and other resources provided by his kin,[20] and it ignores the women who, despite strong family values, are abandoned by men who migrate in search of work.

The portrayal of inner city men is problematic, ignoring the intense activities for "getting paid," which range from finding legitimate employment to eventually moving into real jobs after brief experiences with street crime in neighborhoods where opportunities are few.[21]

This perspective on families of the poor also assumes that single women with children are heterosexual and would want to marry men, when some single mothers prefer to have sexual relationships and rear children with other women. It is difficult to estimate the number of women who are in these circumstances. A significant number of lesbians are experiencing their own "baby boom" and should be considered in the discussion of single parents. It is now clear that lesbian mothers often experience poverty, and must construct their own support systems and communities,[22] and some autobiographical writings illustrate the social isolation of lesbians from their extended families.[23] Like their heterosexual counterparts, lesbian single parents will suffer from "welfare reform" that is based on assumptions that the real problem is women's lack of conformity with "family values" and then pushes them off social programs and into the nexus of support networks.

With its jump cut to values and behaviors of the poor, the underclass perspective replicates the flawed "culture of poverty" argument of previous eras.[24] Yet the underclass framework has set the terms of debate in studies on Chicanos and Latinos living in poverty. Wilson himself suggested that "Hispanics" would show a steady increase in joblessness, crime, teenage pregnancies, female-headed families, and welfare dependency that characterize the underclass, while his followers simply lump Blacks and "Hispanics" together.[25] They ignore the scholars who show that the demographic profile of poor Chicanos is varied and does not match that of the "underclass," even those who live in the most poverty-stricken neighborhoods.[26] More important, an underclass perspective ignores the regional political-economic conditions that produce poverty. Wilson apparently has disavowed the term "underclass," yet his conservative followers use the politically charged image of welfare cheats to argue for policies that would push women into the labor force or training programs with limited child care to support their children before they are left without social benefits, and denigrates those who resist this path. Thus it becomes critical for us to provide alternatives to the "poverty of discourse about poverty."[27]

Latinos in Poverty

Indeed, Latinos have high and growing poverty rates. In California, approximately 22 percent of Latino families lived in poverty in 1992, compared to 22 percent of Blacks, 18 percent of Asians, and 7 percent of Anglo families.[28] Like their counterparts in different racial categories, households of Latina single mothers and their children are more likely to be poor.[29] Pérez and Martínez state that "the relationship between gender and poverty is critical to the discussion of Latino poverty, because almost one-half of all Hispanic poor families (45.7%) are maintained by a woman."[30] It behooves us to pay attention to the dynamics—economic, political, or cultural—that push increasing numbers of Latinas into single parenthood and that make supporting their children very difficult.

Female-headed households are a critical component of Latino poverty, but they are only one part of the story. When Latino men and women are included in the same national sample, we find consistent differences, with women generally having higher incidences of poverty, lower incomes, lower-paying jobs, higher unemployment rates, and higher incidences of domestic violence, all of which push them into dire living conditions.[31] In their random survey of Latinos in California, Hayes-Bautista and his colleagues found that the poverty rates among a sample of predominantly immigrants remained significant even by those of the third generation born in the United States, and that women consistently had higher poverty rates than men within each generation.[32] Clearly, large numbers of Latinos do not escape the bottom of the social structure and find the American dream by moving out of poverty.

Table 1. Latino poverty rates by generation and gender

	First generation		Second generation		Third generation	
	Male	Female	Male	Female	Male	Female
Poverty rate	34%	43%	27%	36%	20%	35%

Perhaps because of assumptions that Mexicans are culturally distinct, re-searchers, in their rush to focus on family values, often ignore the structural changes that Wilson points out. Some researchers of the Chicano/Latino population have used the logic of the underclass model to argue its in-verse—that poor Latinos have "good" values and behavior. Their evidence for this conclusion is often inferences made from people's statements on surveys. For example, Testa and Krogh found that Mexicans had strong cul-tural norms against premarital sexual relations and that they initiated sex later than Blacks; therefore Mexicans' "higher levels of conventional mar-riage compared to blacks would appear to be related to slightly longer delays in the initiation of sexual activity."[33] But, of course, having sex and getting married are entirely different things.

Others find sociodemographic patterns and ask questions about family values, then leap to the conclusion that values determine behavior. Hayes-Bautista and his colleagues conducted a large random survey of Latinos in California. They found that Latino males have high labor force participation rates, and, despite consistently high unemployment rates, do not leave the labor force as "discouraged workers." Compared to Blacks and whites, Lati-nos receive the lowest amount of cash derived from income-transfer pro-grams such as Social Security, welfare, and unemployment and other social programs.[34] Latinos in their sample are more likely to form nuclear house-holds than Anglos, Blacks, or Asians.[35] Hayes-Bautista and his colleagues conclude that since Latinos have large families, they are "quite committed to fulfilling their parental roles and assuming familial obligations," and when Latinos agreed that extended kin are important, they were seen as "imbued with rich family values."[36]

These findings are very useful, but their interpretations are ahistorical and provide no context for making sense of their data.[37] They ignore the fact that undocumented immigrants are not eligible for welfare (Aid to Families with Dependent Children), food stamps, Social Security, unemployment compensation, or supplemental security income, despite their paying state and federal income taxes and state sales taxes.[38] Many immigrants avoid so-cial services because they can jeopardize their amnesty status; they fear that applying for benefits will lead to deportation.[39] Moreover, Latinos have had a disproportionately higher increase in the percentage of families headed by women during the 1980s.[40] Hayes-Bautista and his colleagues also ignore the forces that created a decline of nuclear families in all groups over the past decades (e.g., Asians had immigration restrictions on women, so nuclear households have been impossible for some). They also do not take into consideration the structural changes occurring in California, including the flight of manufacturing in historically Black neighborhoods, or employers' discrimination against Blacks and Asians, which may have more to do with higher Latino employment than their own values.[41] In their zeal to refute the underclass model for Latinos, these researchers imply that Blacks or other groups do not have strong family values or a work ethic, and, ironically, they ultimately reinforce the model itself.

It is important to note that the high official rate of intact nuclear families among Mexicans masks the fluidity of family life and can be misleading. Indeed, recent ethnographic research shows that the "intact" nuclear family among Mexican immigrants can range from fictitious common-law marriages where "husbands" are in name only and women are very independent, often providing the sole economic support for the household, to cases where the women occasionally reside in Mexico, or where they cannot leave abusive marriages.[42] Other "intact" Mexican families include farmworker women who, because of employment discrimination in the United States and indigenous cultural norms rooted in Mexico, only migrate with male sponsorship and thus are pressured into remaining with their spouses.[43]

Nuclear families also include undocumented immigrant women and female "conditional residents"—those allowed to remain in the United States provided they stay wedded to their citizen or legal permanent resident spouses—who are at particular risk for spousal abuse once they settle in the United States.[44] These women sometimes find themselves married to men who use the threat of deportation as a weapon in the abuse of their wives. These men experience the conditions that often push men to abuse—high unemployment, layoffs, or low income, exacerbated by alcohol or drug use—and stresses associated with migration itself, such as anxiety about family members left at home, thefts from "old-timers" in new locales, or crowded living conditions.[45] The number of immigrant women coerced into remaining with abusive spouses is difficult to estimate, but various reports suggest that the population of abused immigrant women is disproportionately large. Data from a random sample survey of undocumented Latinas in the Washington, D.C., metropolitan area indicates that 60 percent report that they are battered by their spouses; agencies that provide resources to victims of domestic violence report that extremely high percentages of their clients are conditional residents.[46] The women forming this "hidden population," as it is being labeled, are often economically, linguistically, and psychologically dependent on their spouses. Like their fellow battered women who are citizens, women conditional residents are likely to experience a severe decline in resources if they leave their batterer spouses.[47] Furthermore, immigrant women migrate from Latin American countries not only to flee economic misery and political repression, but to *escape* domestic violence, sexual assault, or incest, often at the hands of their own partners or relatives.[48] Unfortunately, "strong family values" are often missing from Latino families as well.

The idea that Latinos have "good, stable nuclear families" says more about the discourse about poverty than about the conditions in the United States and Latin America under which migrants live. Moreover, it is not simply the type of data that is crucial. Some critics suggest that the shortcomings of underclass theory stem in part from the "difficulties inherent in using census data to measure a complex social reality."[49] As we have seen, underclass theory can be supported with ethnographic, census, or survey data. We could dismiss this as being faulty research, but there is an underlying ideological message: Mexicans are becoming the new "model minority," and our "good values" are being pitted against Blacks and others in poverty.[50] This kind of thinking is insidious and must be challenged.

We must be careful not to cast our analyses as value judgments (in this case positive ones), for this puts us in an analytic black hole: Mexicans' or Latinos' "rich" values are derived from their culture—and we are back full circle to cultural determinism. This perspective begs the question: if Latinos have such upstanding values and "stable" families, why are they disproportionately poor even by the third generation? Moreover, the policy implications of this thinking are benign neglect—just leave them alone because they're good citizens, or keep those policies that support positive values. What about those poor Latinos and Latinas who do use welfare and other social services? Do we condemn them as having dysfunctional values and unstable families? What about those who need social services but avoid applying because of language barriers or their fear of being deported?

Clearly we need an alternative perspective, one that analyzes the history of placement of groups in the local political economy, that provides some context for understanding differences between immigrants and U.S.-born Latinos, Asians, and Blacks who generally are concentrated in low-wage jobs, have few benefits or opportunities for occupational mobility, and in some cases are being displaced by technology or runaway shops. We need comparative historical analyses of the processes that concentrate certain populations in or push them out of particular sectors of the economy.

Regional Analyses

The current economic situation is one of structural change, in which fragmentation of the labor process, global integration of production sites and
markets, and permanent layoffs of white- and blue-collar workers in the
United States are part of the strategies for firms to remain competitive. The
effects of these changes in late-capitalist enterprises, however, have been different for particular racial populations or regions. Mercer L. Sullivan states,
"Despite the fact that economic restructuring has occurred nationally, its effects have not been uniform. Both African Americans and Latino Americans
have suffered disproportionately from economic restructuring, but there are
significant differences among minority communities in how they have been
affected and how they have responded."[51]

To understand these processes, we must move to perspectives that capture the heterogeneity of Latinos, while noting common structural experiences. Each Latino group has its own history in different regions of the
country, where particular structural processes—conquest and subordination, waves of migration and settlement, the specific nature of industrialization and urbanization, and discrimination toward racialized others—have
produced particular configurations of segregation and economic vulnerability as lived experience. This segregation can be seen in Latino participation in regional labor markets, in settlement and housing patterns, in migrant streams as people move in search of work and community, and in
particular groups' participation in regional or local politics. The case studies
in Moore and Pinderhughes, Morales and Bonilla, and others demonstrate
that the causes of Latino marginality in one sector of the economy may not
be replicated in other regions.[52]

Once we focus on regions, I believe that we need to socially locate people,
that is, examine groups' social makeup, including their entrance into the
United States. Obviously, Cubans who were welcomed as political refugees
into an ethnic enclave with established small-business owners had a different experience than undocumented Mexican migrant laborers in the same
region.[53] For each region we need to understand whether there are significant numbers of citizens versus undocumented immigrants, note the gender
composition and labor market opportunities of migrants and settlers, and
pay attention to salient features of race relations, including discrimination
against those with distinct racial features, and how their meaning changes
over time. We should take note of other bases of internal differentiation, including generation, age, language use, or sexual orientation.[54] Juan Vicente

Palerm argues, for example, that immigrant farmworkers in California are increasingly diverse, and over the decade of the 1980s through the early 1990s, at least five types developed: "old, middle, new, recent," and a collection of specialized workers who follow specific crops (e.g., *los lechugueros*), who are regular sojourners from Mexico.[55] Examining the experiences of subcategories of Latinos should illuminate how some people are restricted to marginal sectors of the economy while others can experience some mobility in the labor market.

Moreover, looking at fine-scaled internal differences leads to more nuanced understandings of how Latinos' experiences reshape structural processes. For example, even among the most economically vulnerable immigrants there are differences based on time of migration. Immigrants who arrived a decade ago find different labor market opportunities than do more recent immigrants.[56] Mexican immigrants often establish "niches" within particular industries or occupations (say, citrus picking or as busboys) that contrast with American-born Mexican Americans, and may preclude the entrance of succeeding cohorts of Mexican immigrants.[57] Leslie Salzinger shows how Central American women immigrants, through the formation of work cooperatives that help "professionalize" domestic work, influence the creation of an upper tier of the housekeepers' labor market with better pay and working conditions.[58] Thus it is important to examine in detail how immigrants, U.S.-born Chicanos, and other Latinos are integrated into a regional economy, and the implications for their being forced into poverty. Paying attention to the bases of the heterogeneity of Latinos, while grounding this in structural changes, will provide a historicized analysis.

Besides regional analyses with attention to gender differences, households should be an important unit of analysis for understanding Latinos living in poverty. Even though Latinos have varied placement in labor markets, racial differences, different migration histories, and so on, they have similar patterns of using extended kin as sources of social support—for finding resources such as jobs, housing, training, or day care and for getting emotional support. Thus it is important to understand how Latino households are structured, how household structure changes in concert with different economic circumstances, whether households function in a similar manner in all Latino groups, and whether particular types of households are more vulnerable to being poor. Rather than posing a polarized analysis showing that Blacks are different from Latinos, I suggest that we examine particular regions to understand whether and how Latinos and Blacks have had different experiences of segregation (in housing and in the labor market), discrimination, and poverty. Then we can move on to an examination of how these structural forces are experienced in daily life and how the participants perceive their circumstances and manage the daily travail of being poor.

Poor Chicano and Mexicano Households

Carlos G. Vélez-Ibañez and James B. Greenberg's work on "binational" Mexican families provides a good point of departure for understanding intrafamilial dynamics within poverty-stricken Chicano populations and how these families adapt to poverty.[59] They find that Mexicans living in conditions of poverty form "household clusters," networks of households that revolve around a nuclear family of grandparents or another key relative, with other kin and their households forming "peripheral" households. These household clusters contain "funds of knowledge," ranging from skills related to car repair to how to heal illnesses without resorting to doctors to information about dealing with social services. These funds of knowledge, transmitted through "thick" social relations with kin, enable Mexicans to share the burden and cope with poverty. Key features of household clusters include the exchange of goods and services, and ritual celebrations, where knowledge is shared. Vélez-Ibañez and Greenberg argue that the economic and political context of the border facilitates the establishment of these households, and in the case of Tucson, Mexican households span the U.S.-Mexico border. Their work confirms others' findings that Chicanos are "familistic," that is, that they place a high value on living close to relatives (more so than Anglos), that kin are an important source of resources and social exchange, that Chicanos often migrate with the help of kin, and that they believe extended family members are the best source of emotional support.[60]

Palerm also argues that a significant portion (13 percent) of his sample of Mexican farmworker families constitutes "binational" families—those who maintain occupied homes on both sides of the U.S.-Mexico border:

> Families settled on the U.S. side of the border continue to provide a bridgehead for both new immigrants and seasonal migrants from Mexico. In fact, a large proportion of the seasonal migrants . . . were temporarily contained within the household structure of U.S.-settled families. Settled family members, moreover, continue to return to their home communities in Mexico, not only to visit kin and friends, but also to oversee farms and businesses owned there. Wage remittances to Mexico continue to characterize the behavior of the California-based farm workers; they not only assist and support family members living in Mexico, but also pay for home and farm improvements and invest in local businesses.[61]

These families often find that their kin networks in Mexico can provide greater emotional and material support than those in the United States, especially for women.[62]

How do Mexican immigrant or binational households differ from those that include U.S.-born Mexican Americans? Hurtado and her colleagues found that there are important differences between first-generation immigrants (born in Mexico) and second-generation (born in the United States but parents born in Mexico) and third-generation (born in the United States and parents born in the United States) Chicanos.[63] Those from the first generation are more likely to value living close to relatives than those of the second or third generation. Keefe and Padilla, on the other hand, find that in the Santa Barbara region this familistic behavior *increases* by the third generation because Chicanos have more relatives living in the area than Mexicans of the first generation.[64] Clearly, the role of extended kin in providing support to low-income Chicanos and Mexicanos is important, but needs further analysis.

Poverty in Albuquerque

Phillip B. Gonzáles argues that the historical causes of poverty in Albuquerque stem from the incorporation of rural Hispano villages, whose inhabitants were made vulnerable to labor market restructuring in a peripheral economy. Albuquerque went through four major restructuring phases beginning in the late nineteenth century: the city shifted from an obscure frontier outpost to the state's commercial center with the construction of the railroad; World War II fueled the development of regional air bases and weapons development and atomic research facilities, which became major employers; the Cold War saw the expansion of military-related manufacturing; and, beginning in the late sixties, there was an expansion of manufacturing primarily based on electronics and garment industries. During each of these phases, the Mexican-American population experienced neighborhood poverty in different ways. In the first phase, rural villages with their traditional cooperative labor practices were incorporated into the city of Albuquerque. Between 1941 and 1960, Mexican Americans from other southwestern states and from Mexico settled in the village areas. Beginning in the 1960s, the Mexican-American population continued to disperse throughout the city, even into neighborhoods long reserved for whites. Albuquerque was never a large settlement area for Mexican immigrants, primarily because of the lack of major industry. Only during the late 1980s did a significant number of Mexican immigrants begin to settle in Chicano barrios. Gonzáles argues that during each historical period, in different neighborhoods of the city, restructuring meant different experiences of poverty for Mexican Americans.[65]

In researching Albuquerque's electronics and apparel industrialization, my colleagues and I found that the location of production facilities within a primarily service economy and the recession of the early 1980s set up contradictory forces.[66] Relying on a gender division of labor already in place throughout the wage and skill hierarchy of the electronics and apparel industries worldwide, managers hired women to fill the large number of assembly jobs that were created as part of each new plant's production process. Mainly because managers of Albuquerque's electronics and apparel factories employed women who had high-school education or even some vocational training from the local community college, immigrant women did not form a large part of the labor force. Mexican-American women made up a greater proportion of the high-school-educated labor force in Albuquerque, and were recruited to these jobs in higher numbers than Anglo, Black, or Indian women. In a deliberately antiunion strategy, managers of these factories paid higher than minimum wages—our informants averaged between five and six dollars an hour—and provided good benefits that included medical insurance, maternity leaves, paid holidays, and, in some cases, profit sharing. We found that women's work in these factories brought important changes in family life as women became coproviders, mainstay providers, or, in the case of single parents, sole economic providers for their families.[67]

At the same time that women were recruited to electronics and apparel jobs in Albuquerque, jobs in mining, the oil industry, construction, and transportation were declining or subject to seasonal layoff. Thus men were increasingly economically vulnerable as unemployment rose during 1982 and 1983, and Hispanic men had higher unemployment rates than white men. Thus Hispana women had moved a step up within the working class, while sometimes their own spouses had skidded down. Those families fortunate enough to have women working in electronics or apparel industries, then, were low-income, since they relied on women's wages for family support. Yet these families were above the poverty level, and, with the women's excellent job benefits (particularly medical insurance), experienced some economic stability.

There are indications that the phenomenon of increased male dislocation in the economy may now be more widespread than in the 1982–83 recession when we did our research. In one recent survey of national unemployment rates, Latino males had higher rates than females.[68] Unfortunately, the restructuring of the economy often means that industries expand in one area of the globe only to contract in another. These gendered dynamics, where women are able to secure stable industrial jobs (albeit low-paying) while men are subject to high unemployment, are found along both sides of the U.S.-Mexico border.[69]

I will discuss the experiences of one woman from our Albuquerque study who was the exception to the rule, in the sense that she was the only female Mexican immigrant we interviewed. Upon migrating to Albuquerque, Marta Astorga was able to secure a job in an apparel factory. Her experiences illustrate the links between poverty and political economy, the importance of kin as support networks, the perceived differences between Mexican immigrants and Chicanos, and the dangers of jumping to conclusions about cultural values.

The Case Study

A mestiza born in Durango, Mexico, forty-one-year-old Marta Astorga was a single head of family with three children, ages ten, eight, and six. Like so many other unskilled men in Albuquerque's economy, her husband could not find steady employment until he moved to another city. Marta was a sewing operator at a large nonunion factory in Albuquerque that was highly segregated by race/ethnicity and gender. She estimated that 97 percent of her coworkers were women, and the majority were Chicanas. Because of Reagan's recession, Marta had been working short weeks, sometimes able to get only twelve hours of work a week to support her family. Moreover, she claimed that there was discrimination, so that operators who were the "favorites" of the supervisor—that is, Mexican-American women—would get the better jobs.

Five months before our interview, Marta was forced out of the labor force because of her many problems at work: her machine kept breaking, causing her to lose wages and slow up the production line for others; her eyes became inflamed from the dust and chemicals, which further slowed her pace; and her supervisor was not supportive. After several written warnings, Marta was pressured to quit. She believed that if she had spoken English well, she might have been able to keep her job. Hesitantly, she observed: "Lots of times they don't give the heavier work to the Chicanas because they know that the Chicanas will cry and they don't want to do the heavier work.

And the Mexicans that don't understand much, so as not to argue and lose time, do not protest against it as much." She did not state the obvious—that immigrants would be more vulnerable in a depressed labor market, so they did not contest the discrimination. Marta had not adjusted to her new unemployed status and called herself "a housewife, I think." She seemed somewhat disconcerted when describing her circumstances, almost as if she couldn't believe how things had become so bad.

Marta's family is the product of the economic restructuring and demographic changes of the 1980s. She and eventually many of her extended kin migrated to Albuquerque from Juárez, Mexico, in search of work, to "better" themselves. Initially Marta claimed she had immigrated with a visa and that she felt free to occasionally visit her mother, four siblings, and their families on the other side of the border. Yet when I tried to ask about the circumstances of her immigration, she became tense and did not want to discuss it in detail, implying that she might have come "without papers" or that her visa had lapsed. She believed that her factory job was good because it had provided health benefits and, when working full-time, enough wages to support her children and to bring out a sister, who then provided day care while Marta worked.

After losing her factory job, Marta's search for another job was unsuccessful in Albuquerque's depressed labor market. To support her three children, she was working one or two days a week cleaning house for a wealthy Anglo family, earning wages of $30–$60. Her ex-spouse sent money about four times a year, with each payment averaging about $150. Marta survived by budgeting her income scrupulously, making clothes for her children and some for herself. And, she observed, "We eat lots of beans." She was behind on her rent, had no insurance of any kind, and was struggling to pay off her medical and dental bills. She rented a tiny house on the edge of town from her employers, who did not press her for the back rent.

Marta's ex-spouse would return for occasional visits of a few days or a few months. Marta knew that he was living with another woman in a nearby state and had "several families," but did not know his address or how many children he had. She was very angry with him but made it a point to say she was not separated or divorced. Marta spoke wistfully of the early days of their marriage, when she had been happy, and would not represent herself as a single woman.

Marta epitomized traditional family values: she believed that men should support the family, that men should earn more than women, that women should stay home with the children when they are little, and that she missed some of the best experiences of her children's early development because she was away from them while working. She had contested this traditional configuration somewhat. When she was married, Marta performed a double day—doing housework and child care after her long day of wage work—and she believed that this was an "injustice." Her contestation, however, had remained repressed. Unlike other single parents in our study who had children to support, Marta, without a steady job, was not ready to denounce her children's father.

Marta did not receive welfare or even food stamps, nor, because she had "quit," any unemployment benefits. Besides her meager wages from domestic work, Marta relied on seven siblings living in Albuquerque who provided occasional gifts of food or clothing for the children. Her kin, especially her sisters and sisters-in-law, also provided emotional support and were the source of weekend socializing and entertainment, as well as frequent phone calls.

Despite her bleak situation, Marta was no demoralized victim. She hoped to return to the regular labor market for the higher wages and medical benefits it offered and realized that working boosted her self-esteem: "Since I started working, that's when I found out that I can be useful and that I can fend for my own self. That I shouldn't let myself be mistreated by other persons, that I should feel worthwhile for my own self. I feel more confident, and I have learned so much. It was so hard, but I learned." She found the hardest part of her life "being alone," raising her children and trying to make ends meet without a spouse. Ever practical, Marta looked blank when I asked what the government could do to help families like hers. She apparently did not see government aid as an option for her because of her legal status. Her former company, however, was another story: "They [the managers] could switch all the people who have been working there for too many years to jobs that are not as hard, especially for older people. They aren't useless. It's simply that they've been on the job for too long. But they're tired now. It's impossible to keep on going so much, especially in a place like that. It's very hard." Nevertheless, Marta hoped to leave the informal sector and was looking for another factory job because of the higher pay: "I have to keep looking for work."

Marta Astorga indeed lived on the edge and struggled to make ends meet with very few resources. The culture of her daily life was one of isolation and fear of freely seeking institutional support because of language barriers and her unclear legal status. Although she did not live in a binational household herself, she was integrated into a household cluster and maintained close contact with kin in Mexico who apparently did. Marta was managing with the help of emotional support from and material exchange with her kin, who spanned both sides of the border. Despite her strong family values, she was unable to find a good job that would bring her household out of poverty.

Conclusion

Marta Astorga's life is similar to the lives of thousands of women on both sides of the U.S.-Mexico border who struggle to support their children with very few labor market options. These women endure the transcultural process of men leaving and establishing new households when they cannot find work; they must create nurturing social relations for themselves and their children. In many ways, Marta's life is the product of economic restructuring and demographic changes that Wilson deems as important. Like thousands of other immigrant women, she had migrated north in search of work, then experienced economic dislocation when her spouse could not find a job in the secondary labor market and she lost her own job in recessionary conditions. The informal economy, with its extremely low pay and lack of benefits, except for those provided through the paternalism of her employers, was her only recourse. Marta is also like the respondents in Hayes-Bautista's survey—someone who has "strong family values," avoids social services, and makes sure that her children are educated. Yet she is neither welfare queen nor model minority. Marta's "traditional values" include deference to her wealthy Anglo benefactors, repression of her anger toward her ex-spouse, and reliance on self and kin rather than on institutional support, such as job-training opportunities, or even food stamps. With these kinds of material changes, Marta could have supported her children and perhaps even eventually fulfilled her desire for a nuclear family by reuniting with her spouse on the basis of her steady employment.

In the current debate over the causes of poverty and the "underclass," there is no public policy advocate for Marta Astorga and other immigrant families in similar circumstances.[70] Moreover, in their rush to denigrate the values and behaviors of female single parents, underclass theorists have not fully contextualized the experiences of all types of poor people or considered why some women end up in single-parent households despite strongly supporting family values.

Clearly, poor Mexicans like Marta Astorga present a challenge to academics who now realize that our multicultural society includes many different types of families, households, cultures, and experiences. As we attempt to understand the "new immigrants" and their relations with already settled populations of varied cultural expressions, it is critical that we not fall into the American bog of family ideology, based on myths of the homogeneous nuclear family as the norm. Poor people have always lived flexible lives, migrating in search of work, living with extended kin, taking in boarders, doubling up with friends when they become homeless or need temporary help. The nuclear family of breadwinner pop and cookie-baking mom does not even typify white middle-class families. In refuting the underclass model, we must present careful analyses of local political economies, of how some groups have found labor market niches and others have been marginalized. In short, institutional discrimination and exclusion based on race, ethnicity, class, and gender—not family values—explain the persistence of poverty and create the context for how Mexicans adapt to being poor. Just as the underclass model has been problematic for understanding Blacks in poverty, we rush to cultural models about Latinos in poverty at our peril. Structural and cultural analyses of international *and* local levels will be necessary to understand Mexicans who are poor.

Notes

Thanks to Gloria Cuadraz, Micaela di Leonardo, Avery Gordon, Ramón Gutiérrez, Aída Hurtado, Josie Méndez Negrete, Christopher Newfield, Melvin Oliver, Adolph Reed Jr., Denise Segura, and Lynet Uttal for their helpful critical comments on different versions of this paper. Conversations with Felipe Gonzáles also helped in formulating this analysis.

1. See Raymond V. Padilla, "Chicano Studies at the University of California, Berkeley: En Busca del Campus y la Comunidad" (Ph.D. diss., University of California, Berkeley, 1975); Carlos Munoz, "The Quest for Paradigm: The Development of Chicano Studies and Intellectuals," in *History, Culture and Society: Chicano Studies in the 1980s*, ed. Mario T. García et al. (Ypsilanti, Mich.: Bilingual Press, 1983).

2. For an overview of how these political contestations affected theories pertaining to race, see Michael Omi and Howard Winant, *Racial Formation in the United States: From the 1960s to the 1980s* (New York and London: Routledge, 1986).

3. Estevan T. Flores, "The Mexican-Origin People in the United States and Marxist Thought in Chicano Studies," in *The Left Academy: Marxist Scholarship on American Campuses*, vol. 3, ed. Bertell Ollman and Edward Vernoff (New York: McGraw-Hill, 1986), 103–38.

4. For a full discussion of the paradigm shift in the social sciences within Chicano Studies, see Tomas Almaguer, "Ideological Distortions in Recent Chicano Historiography: The Internal Colonial Model and Chicano Historical Interpretation," *Aztlán* 18: 1 (1989): 7–28. See also Patricia Zavella, *Women's Work and Chicano Families: Cannery Workers of the Santa Clara Valley* (Ithaca, N.Y.: Cornell University Press, 1987), 6–11.

5. Taub fails to describe any background information about his informants, to indicate when he is referring to Mexican immigrants or informants born in the United States, or to specify how many individuals he has interviewed. He does indicate that he is unsure how representative his sample is for Mexicans in Chicago. See Richard Taub, "Differing Conceptions of Honor and Orientations toward Work and Marriage among Low-Income African-Americans

and Mexican-Americans" (paper presented at the Chicago Urban Poverty and Family Life Conference, University of Chicago, 23 August 1991).

6. See also Mark Testa and Marilyn Krogh, "Nonmarital Parenthood, Male Joblessness and AFDC Participation in Inner-City Chicago" (final report prepared for the Assistant Secretary for Planning and Evaluation, November 1990).

7. For an excellent genealogy of the term and how it has become popularized, see Adolph Reed Jr., "The Underclass as Myth and Symbol: The Poverty of Discourse about Poverty," *Radical America* 24 (January 1992): 21–40.

8. William Julius Wilson, *The Truly Disadvantaged: The Inner City, the Underclass, and Public Policy* (Chicago: University of Chicago Press, 1987). A MacArthur prize fellow, Wilson heads the Center for the Study of Urban Inequality at the University of Chicago.

9. William Julius Wilson, "The Underclass: Issues, Perspectives, and Public Policy," in *The Ghetto Underclass: Social Science Perspectives*, ed. William Julius Wilson (Newbury Park, Calif.: Sage Publications, 1993), 1–24, 2.

10. Some of the debate over the underclass can be found in Michael B. Katz, ed., *The "Underclass" Debate: Views from History* (Princeton, N.J.: Princeton University Press, 1993), and Bill E. Lawson, ed., *The Underclass Question* (Philadelphia: Temple University Press, 1992).

11. Testa and Krogh, "Nonmarital Parenthood"; Taub, "Differing Conceptions of Honor."

12. With the authority provided by using the ethnographic present and ignoring variability, Elijah Anderson validates the political rallying cry for "personal responsibility" by presenting young men's quest for "getting over" and the logic of young women's "irresponsibility" as consuming mothers. See Elijah Anderson, *Street Wise: Race, Class and Change in an Urban Community* (Chicago: University of Chicago Press, 1990), 112–37.

13. L. B. Schorr, *Within Our Reach: Breaking the Cycle of Disadvantage* (New York: Anchor Press, 1988); Wilson, *The Truly Disadvantaged*.

14. For one example of this hysteria, see Michael Meyer, "Los Angeles 2010: A Latino Subcontinent," *Newsweek*, 9 November 1992: 32–33.

15. The "True Love Waits" campaign launched in 1993 by the Southern Baptist Convention sex-education program hoped that up to five hundred thousand teenagers would sign covenants vowing to remain chaste until marriage. See David Briggs, "No Sex Till Marriage, Teens Vow: Campaign Hopes to Sign up 500,000," *San Jose Mercury News*, 24 September 1993.

16. See "Family Values Skewed Census Data: Political Debate Left 300,000 Births Unreported, Government Survey Says," *San Jose Mercury News*, 3 January 1994.

17. Sonia M. Pérez and Deirdre Martínez, *State of Hispanic America 1993: Toward a Latino Anti-Poverty Agenda* (Washington, D.C.: National Council of La Raza Report, 1993), iii (figures rounded).

18. Rina Benmayor, Rosa M. Torruelas, and Ana L. Juarbe present a wonderful ethnographic study about Puerto Rican women welfare recipients who enroll in a literacy program and then, through writing about family life, experience gratifying changes in how they perceive themselves and their neighborhoods. See "Responses to Poverty among Puerto Rican Women: Identity, Community and Cultural Citizenship" (Report to the Joint Committee for Public Policy Research on Contemporary Hispanic Issues of the Inter-University Program for Latino Research and the Social Science Research Council, 1992).

19. Diego Vigil, *Barrio Gangs: Street Life and Identity in Southern California* (Austin: University of Texas Press, 1988); Joan W. Moore, *Going Down to the Barrio: Homeboys and Homegirls in Change* (Philadelphia: Temple University Press, 1991).

20. Carol Stack, *All Our Kin: Strategies for Survival in a Black Community* (New York: Harper Colophon Books, 1974).

21. Mercer L. Sullivan, *"Getting Paid": Youth Crime and Work in the Inner City* (Ithaca, N.Y.: Cornell University Press, 1989).

22. Ellen Lewin, *Lesbian Mothers: Accounts of Gender in American Culture* (Ithaca, N.Y.: Cornell University Press, 1993).

23. Gloria Anzaldúa, *Borderlands/La Frontera: The New Mestiza* (San Francisco: Spinsters/Aunt Lute, 1987); Cherríe Moraga, *Loving in the War Years, lo que nunca pasó por sus labios* (Boston: South End Press, 1983).

24. For very early formulations, see Daniel Patrick Moynihan, *The Negro Family: The Case for National Action* (Washington, D.C.: U.S. Department of Labor, 1965); Oscar Lewis, *La Vida: A Puerto Rican Family in the Culture of Poverty—San Juan and New York* (New York: Vintage Books, 1965); and William Madsen, *Mexican Americans of South Texas* (New York: Holt, Rinehart, and Winston, 1964). For critiques, see Adolph Reed Jr., "Equality: Why We Can't Wait," *Nation*, 9 December 1991: 733–37; Adolph Reed Jr., "The Underclass as Myth and Symbol"; Douglas S. Massey, "Latinos, Poverty, and the Underclass: A New Agenda for Research" (Social Science Research Council-commissioned paper, 1992); Stack, *All Our Kin;* Charles A. Valentine, *Culture and Poverty: Critique and Counter-Proposals* (Chicago: University of Chicago Press, 1968).

25. Wilson, *The Truly Disadvantaged*, 35; Schorr, *Within Our Reach*, 17.

26. David E. Hayes-Bautista et al., *No Longer a Minority: Latinos and Social Policy in California* (UCLA: Chicano Studies Research Center, 1992); Joan Moore, "An Assessment of Hispanic Poverty: Is There a Hispanic Underclass?" (Working Paper, Tomás Rivera Center, 1988); Refugio I. Rochin and Adela de la Torre, "Economic Deprivation of Hispanics" (Working Paper, Tomás Rivera Center, 1989); Fernando M. Treviño et al., "The Feminization of Poverty among Hispanic Households" (Working Paper, Tomás Rivera Center, 1988).

27. Reed, "The Underclass as Myth and Symbol," 21.

28. Hayes-Bautista et al., *No Longer a Minority*, 13.

29. Diana Pearce, "Women, Work, and Welfare: The Feminization of Poverty," in *Working Women and Families*, ed. Karen Wolk Feinstein (Beverly Hills, Calif.: Sage Publications, 1979), 103–24; Treviño et al., "The Feminization of Poverty among Hispanic Households."

30. Pérez and Martínez, *State of Hispanic America 1993*, 12.

31. Ibid., 12–15.

32. Hayes-Bautista et al., *No Longer a Minority*. These researchers surveyed 1,086 Latinos, of whom 84 percent were of Mexican origin and 15 percent from other Latin American countries. They use "Latino" to refer to the entire sample. See also Aída Hurtado et al., *Redefining California: Latino Social Engagement in a Multicultural Society* (UCLA: Chicano Studies Research Center, 1992), 7 and 53.

33. Testa and Krogh, "Nonmarital Parenthood," 99.

34. Hayes-Bautista et al., *No Longer a Minority*, 166; also see Testa and Krogh, "Nonmarital Parenthood," 83.

35. By 1980, 47 percent of Latinos formed nuclear households, compared to 38 percent for Asians, 25 percent for Anglos, and 22 percent for Blacks. See Hayes-Bautista et al., *No Longer a Minority*, 19.

36. Ibid., 17. I am not contesting the finding that Latinos are more likely than whites or Blacks to reside in intact nuclear families or less likely to use social services. Rather, I am questioning the interpretation of those findings. Hayes-Bautista writes: "In spite of such *socially responsible* behavior in both the public and private spheres, Latinos are the most likely of any group to live in poverty" (ibid., xi; emphasis mine). This implies that groups other than Latinos living in poverty do not have socially responsible behavior, and it implies that the behavior of the poor themselves, rather than the behavior of and decisions by employers, teachers, or government officials, leads to poverty. For a review of the literature on Latino families, see Aída Hurtado, "Variations, Combinations, and Evolutions: Latino Families in the United States," in *Latino Families: Developing a Paradigm for Research, Practice, and Policy*, ed. R. E. Zambrana and M. Baca Zinn (Thousand Oaks, Calif.: Sage Publications, in press).

37. In another project, Franklin J. James compared seven census tracts in Denver with poverty rates exceeding 40 percent to understand "the possible roles of concentration effects, job market conditions and other factors in producing poverty and deprivation among neighborhood residents" ("Persistent Urban Poverty and the Underclass: A Perspective Based on the Hispanic Experience" [paper prepared for a conference on persistent poverty convened at Trinity University, San Antonio, by the Tomás Rivera Center, 8 April 1988], 18).

38. The only public services that undocumented immigrants can receive are emergency medical care, prenatal care, and K–12 education. See Estevan T. Flores, "Research on Undocumented Immigrants and Public Policy: A Study of the Texas School Case," *International Migration Review* 18:3 (1984): 505–23.

39. Immigrants whose status was legalized under the 1986 amnesty program are disqualified from Aid to Families with Dependent Children or Medi-Cal for five years after obtaining legal, permanent residency.

40. The overall percentage of families headed by females was highest for Blacks, at 47.7 percent, followed by 29.3 percent for Hispanics and 17. 4 percent for whites. However, between 1980 and 1985, the *increase* in female-headed families was 50.7 percent for Hispanics, followed by 22.6 percent for whites and 14.2 percent for Blacks. It appears that Latinos and whites are catching up to the high rates of Black single parents, regardless of their values. See U.S. Bureau of the Census, *Current Population Report*, Series P–60, cited in James, "Persistent Urban Poverty and the Underclass," table 12.

41. Melvin L. Oliver, James H. Johnson Jr., and Walter C. Farrell Jr., "Anatomy of a Rebellion: A Political-Economic Analysis," in *Reading Rodney King, Reading Urban Uprising*, ed. Robert Gooding-Williams (New York: Routledge, 1993), 117–41.

42. Julie Goodson-Lawes, "Changes in Feminine Authority and Control with Migration: The Case of One Family from Mexico," *Urban Anthropology*, Special Issue on Latino Ethnography 22: 3–4 (1993): 277–89; Adelaida Del Castillo, "Negotiating the Structure and Cultural Meaning of Sex/Gender Systems: Mexico City's Women-Centered Domestic Groups," *Urban Anthropology*, Special Issue on Latino Ethnography 22:3–4 (1993): 237–58. For descriptions of domestic violence in a migrant Mexican-American family, see Fran Leeper Bus, ed., *Forged under the Sun/Forjada bajo el sol: The Life of María Elena Lucas* (Ann Arbor: University of Michigan Press, 1993).

43. Alicia Chavira-Prado did research on Tarascan Indian migrants from Mexico who engaged in chain migration between Cherán, in the state of Michoacán in Mexico, and Cobden, in southern Illinois. See Alicia Chavira-Prado, "Work, Health, and the Family: Gender Structure and Women's Status in a Mexican Undocumented Migrant Population," *Human Organization* (spring 1992): 53–64; Alicia Chavira-Prado, "The Female Undocumented Experience" (paper presented at the Association of Latina and Latino Anthropologists-sponsored session, "*Rompiendo Barreras de Género*: Social Constructions of Gender in U.S. Latino Communities," American Anthropological Association Annual Meetings, San Francisco, November 1992).

44. Michelle J. Anderson, "A License to Abuse: The Impact of Conditional Status on Female Immigrants," *Yale Law Journal* 102:6 (1993): 1401–30.

45. For a discussion of these problems, see Ramón "Tianguis" Pérez and Dick J. Reavis, trans., *Diary of an Undocumented Immigrant* (Houston: Arte Público Press, 1991).

46. Anderson, "A License to Abuse," 1403.

47. Legislation has been proposed that would allow female conditional residents to file their own applications for status as permanent residents. As of September 1994, such legislation has not passed. See Carolyn Jung, "Enduring Abuse to Get Legal Residency: Immigrant Women Hostages to Husbands," *San Jose Mercury News*, 3 January 1994: 1.

48. Lourdes Arguelles and Anne Rivero, "Violence, Migration, and Compassionate Practice: Conversations with Some Women We Think We Know," *Urban Anthropology*, Special Issue on

Latino Ethnography 22:3–4 (1993): 259–76; Rosalía Solórzano-Torres, "Female Mexican Immigrants in San Diego County," in *Women on the U.S.-Mexico Border: Responses to Change*, ed. Vicki L. Ruiz and Susan Tiano (Boston: Allen and Unwin, 1987), 41–60.

49. Joan Moore and Raquel Pinderhughes, eds., *In the Barrios: Latinos and the Underclass Debate* (New York: Russell Sage Foundation, 1993), xv.

50. In an otherwise careful critique of underclass theory, Moore and Pinderhughes observe: "By contrast with [William Julius] Wilson's portrayal of the decay of the black family and other institutions, Latino institutions were generally viable" (ibid., xvi).

51. Mercer L. Sullivan, "Puerto Ricans in Sunset Park, Brooklyn: Poverty amidst Ethnic and Economic Diversity," in *In the Barrios*, 1–26, 3.

52. Moore and Pinderhughes, *In the Barrios;* Rebecca Morales and Frank Bonilla, eds., *Latinos in a Changing U.S. Economy: Comparative Perspectives on Growing Inequality* (Newbury Park, Calif.: Sage Publications, 1993). See also Louise Lamphere, ed., *Structuring Diversity: Ethnographic Perspectives on the New Immigration* (Chicago: University of Chicago Press, 1992); Louise Lamphere, Patricia Zavella, Felipe Gonzáles, and Peter B. Evans, *Sunbelt Working Mothers: Reconciling Family and Factory* (Ithaca, N.Y.: Cornell University Press, 1993); and Robert Lee Maril, *Poorest of Americans: The Mexican-Americans of the Lower Rio Grande Valley of Texas* (Notre Dame: University of Notre Dame Press, 1989). For two excellent case studies of racial differences in Los Angeles and the multiracial rebellion following the acquittal of Rodney King's assailants, see Melvin L. Oliver, James H. Johnson Jr., and Walter C. Farrell Jr., "Anatomy of a Rebellion," and Manuel Pastor Jr., *Latinos and the Los Angeles Uprising: The Economic Context* (Claremont, Calif.: Tomás Rivera Center, 1993).

53. Alejandro Portes and Robert L. Bach, *Latin Journey: Cuban and Mexican Immigrants in the United States* (Berkeley: University of California Press, 1985).

54. Patricia Zavella, "Reflections on Diversity among Chicanas," *Frontiers, a Journal of Women's Studies* 13:2 (1991): 73–85.

55. Juan Vicente Palerm, "Farm Labor Needs and Farm Workers in California, 1970–1989" (Report for the State Employment Development Department, U.S. Department of Labor, 1991), 5.

56. Leo R. Chávez, *Shadowed Lives: Undocumented Immigrants in American Society* (New York: Harcourt Brace Jovanovich, 1991).

57. Wayne Cornelius, "Mexican Immigrants in the San Francisco Bay Area: A Summary of Current Knowledge" (Research Report Series 40, San Diego: University of California, Center for U.S.-Mexican Studies, 1982).

58. Leslie Salzinger, "A Maid by Any Other Name: The Transformation of 'Dirty Work' by Central American Immigrants," in *Ethnography Unbound: Power and Resistance in the Modern Metropolis*, ed. Michael Burawoy et al. (Berkeley: University of California Press, 1991), 139–60.

59. Carlos G. Vélez-Ibañez and James B. Greenberg, "Formation and Transformation of Funds of Knowledge among U.S.-Mexican Households," *Anthropology and Education Quarterly* 23:4 (1992): 313–34. See also Carlos G. Vélez-Ibañez, "Ritual Cycles of Exchange: The Process of Cultural Creation and Management in the U.S. Borderlands," in *Celebrations of Identity: Multiple Voices in American Ritual Performance*, ed. Pamela R. Frese (Westport, Conn.: Bergin and Garvey, 1993), 119–43.

60. M. Jean Gilbert, "Extended Family Integration among Second-Generation Mexican-Americans," in *Family and Mental Health in the Mexican American Community*, ed. J. Manuel Carlos and Susan E. Keefe, monograph no. 7 (Los Angeles: Spanish-Speaking Mental Health Research Center, 1978), 25–48; Hurtado et al., *Redefining California;* Susan Emley Keefe, "Urbanization, Acculturation, and Extended Family Ties: Mexican Americans in Cities," *American Ethnologist* (spring 1979): 349–65; Susan Emley Keefe, "Real and Ideal Extended Familism among Mexican Americans and Anglo Americans: On the Meaning of 'Close' Family Ties," *Human Or-*

ganization 43:1 (1984): 65–70; Susan E. Keefe, Amado M. Padilla, and Manuel L. Carlos, "The Mexican American Extended Family as an Emotional Support System," in *Family and Mental Health in the Mexican-American Community,* 49–68; Susan E. Keefe and Amado M. Padilla, *Chicano Ethnicity* (Albuquerque: University of New Mexico Press, 1987); Joan Moore, "Mexican Americans and Cities: A Study in Migration and the Use of Formal Resources," *International Migration Review* 5:3 (1971): 292–308.

61. Palerm, "Farm Labor Needs and Farm Workers in California," 89.

62. Goodson-Lawes, "Changes in Feminine Authority and Control with Migration."

63. Hurtado et al., *Redefining California,* 20.

64. Keefe and Padilla, *Chicano Ethnicity.*

65. Phillip B. Gonzáles, "Historical Poverty, Restructuring Effects, and Integrative Ties: Mexican American Neighborhoods in a Peripheral Sunbelt Economy," in *In the Barrios,* 149–72.

66. Lamphere, Zavella, Gonzáles, and Evans, *Sunbelt Working Mothers.*

67. Coproviders earned wages nearly equal to those of their spouses, while mainstay providers were the primary breadwinners in their families. We also have a category of secondary providers, which includes wives who earn less than their spouses.

68. Pérez and Martínez, *State of Hispanic America 1993.*

69. María Patricia Fernández-Kelly, *For We Are Sold, I and My People: Women and Industry in Mexico's Frontier* (Albany: State University of New York Press, 1983); Vicki L. Ruiz and Susan Tiano, eds., *Women on the U.S.-Mexico Border: Responses to Change* (Boston: Allen and Unwin, 1987).

70. The National Council of La Raza suggests policy interventions such as equalizing educational outcomes for Latinos, ending housing and labor market discrimination against Latinos, making work "more rewarding" through increased minimum wage levels or better benefits, or increasing entitlement programs. See Pérez and Martínez, *State of Hispanic America 1993.*

PART V

Multiculturalism and the Production of Culture

CHAPTER TWENTY-THREE

Machine Talk

STEVE FAGIN

As with many of the presenters at the conference, I have the problem of condensing a much longer piece—in my case, a two-hour video, *The Machine That Killed Bad People*. The tape endures this fate in its own unique style, which, as is the California manner, I will "share" with you.

First of all, people get the wrong impression when seeing a segment of the tape. They presume "Oh yes, I've seen a bit. I'm sure if I saw the whole piece all of this mishmash would be a seamless coherence." No such luck. The piece works in a fragmentary style, trying to emulate the way television constructs meaning through fragmentation. The viewer is held together, or in the language of theory "is constructed," in the manner in which the caramel holds the chocolate and peanuts together in a Snickers bar, only then to bind the same elements to your teeth. Second, the order of the fragments works as a complex chain of commands. One opens the mind like one cracks a safe: three to the right, two to the left, five backward, spin the dial, and "Open Sesame!"—the mind is open to suggestion. TV functions this way, opening up the phatic, dysfunctional channels of our minds.

It is this need for ordering that insists that the piece be two hours long. Most independent videos range from 3 to 11 minutes long, in order to deal with the normal exhibition context of the art gallery or museum. I truly see the piece as being as short as I could make it. I often boast that it's like Roger

Bannister when he just broke the four-minute mile saying 3 minutes, 59.4 seconds: my tape is not 2 hours, it's 1 hour, 59 minutes, 42 seconds.

I should also point out that the piece is experimental, and by this I mean it's working on a question, exploring options. I see this as the responsibility of the independent arts. I must confess that this type of work is best when it comes out of a character affliction, not an ambition. One should never start off trying to be experimental; it ends up being kitsch like Dalí. One should be like Raymond Roussel, an artist I've done a piece on, trying only to make "the most popular piece in the world," or be like Victor Hugo, or, in my case, Steven Spielberg, ending up shocked at people's incredulity.

A lot has happened since the piece's inception with the overthrow of the Marcos dictatorship in February 1986. As it was happening, I thought, "What an extraordinary event I am watching!" The exclamation heralds the crossing of a great historical divide: the transition from Chicago 1968 and the truly narcissistic baby boomer motto "The whole world is watching." I remember "watching" in Istanbul (pass the opium, please!) with about as much social engagement as I could muster, seeing friends of mine being beaten. The space traversed from Chicago to Manila lurches from empathy to interactivity. As my piece was being completed in 1989, the 1986 overthrow of the Marcoses (what's called the Edsa Revolution in the Philippines, the first revolution to be named after a traffic jam) was beginning to be perceived as the prototypical TV revolution on an international scale. The event was being reconstructed as the pilot episode for the second-most popular show of that season, *From China to Ceausescu*, with Ted Koppel as the series host. Only the Simpsons were more popular.

As a prelude to showing my piece, and to bring you back to those thrilling days of yesteryear, I will give you a series of suggestions on how one might have watched some of the telehistorical events that have occurred between now, November 1992, and the completion of the piece in December 1989, challenging the baby boomer conceit that all events should be watched as if we were still in 1968 (even though I must concede my own nostalgia for opium in Istanbul).

I should make it very clear that I think the only history worth watching occurs on cable television, with Ted Turner emerging as a twenty-first-century Herodotus. I hold this to be immutable. I'll start with the most recent event, the presidential election, surfing stations. C-Span was definitely the station of choice, with Ross Perot dancing like Henry Fonda in *My Darling Clementine* into a visual sunset. Patsy Cline's song "Crazy" plays the whole time as people come in and out of frame, such a romantic gesture—

but the gesture goes on and on, durational TV turning the charming into a repetition compulsion. I start off humming along to Patsy Cline's "Crazy" and end up trapped in a labyrinthine chase film. Patsy Cline has been transformed into Joseph Lewis, no longer "crazy about you" but just plain "gun crazy." I begin to wish C-Span would have commercials. I need to go to the restroom.

The campaign itself, having taken so long (sort of like an academic job interview), had to be watched on different stations at different times of day. In the morning, with coffee, the networks, but as an amendment to my prohibition against anything but cable news I say, like Lot leaving Sodom, "Listen, but don't turn to watch." The insipid patter of *Good Morning America* gives a bottom beat worthy of the brilliant Cuban bassist Cachao. In the afternoon one had to be mobile, catching the syndicated shows: *Oprah, Donahue, Geraldo.* At night, the Arkansas Ornette Coleman Bill Clinton knew that it was either Arsenio on Fox or Rome itself, CNN. Even Bush figured this out, appearing on *Larry King Live* the Friday prior to the election.

Our next step backward comes to rest on Hurricane Andrew. Of course one would have watched the Weather Channel, but against the grain of its intention, without channel surfing. The Weather Channel, which I believe to be the most-watched cable station, is viewed on the average for thirty seconds per hit. The network's pacing assumes this and so they want people to switch the station. I must admit I watch this station only seasonally, in the winter, when living in California encourages my sadistic side to enjoy the Michelin snow reports from the East.

It is from the Weather Channel that I draw my model of history—much different from the Marxist dialectic (easterly winds) being assumed by many of the presenters in this conference. In my model of history, one is dominated by a bunch of gadgets, predictions that try to predict through means more folkloric than scientific. Once the storm is sighted and named, the process becomes a bit more ritualistic. If people have ever been involved in a hurricane, the response of people is quite the opposite of what I would have assumed. No one panics. Instead, people's lives become meticulous. Maps, tracking devices, shortwave radios, inch by inch, step by step, but then the hurricane hits and all becomes unpredictable. It stops, starts, jumps, and one just rides it out. I do think history works like this. We can know something is going to break, all the circumstances are right, but we cannot assume effects, only opportunities. Systems will hover off the coast, the Holy Roman Empire can last on the verge of collapse for five hundred years, gradually losing its holiness, its Romanness, its empireness, until all at once, it collapses into chaos, a black hole.

Likewise, dictatorships like Ceausescu's or Marcos's can hold on to power in their last stages for such a long period of time that it becomes a managerial style in itself. Capricious and erratic, but with the logic of the last-stages-style of management. When things crack, like a hurricane hitting land, everything becomes unpredictable. Where is the power going to turn next? It is this moment in history, the contact with land, that I am interested in engaging. Looking for a northwest passage but feeling like I'm going over Niagara Falls in a barrel.

Next event, the Rodney King uprising. This was best watched on local cable. Again, since I'm in southern California, I was able to watch the local Los Angeles stations. Now, this event was a beautiful study of dissonance being recuperated. During this type of brought-to-you-live event, one becomes painfully aware of the training of the local newscasters. All they know how to narrate is a five-alarm fire. Regardless of the origin and direction of the event, it eventually seeps to this level. At first, everything is a bit off: the wrong person is being interviewed, dark figures are running in and out of the frame, passers-by are contradicting the on-the-spot reporter. It is very interesting to observe how, over time, they turn it into one of the few stories they have been trained to tell, and when the eleven o'clock news comes on, it's all so comfy. Another fire story. Logo, then traffic copter view of "raging flames," cut to center frame, well-lit summary of damage to retailers, and finally talk to an eyewitness for fifteen seconds, the camera cutting before they even make eye contact with the camera. The coverage from eight to eleven, however—what a difference! Random camera movements, people competing to tell different types of stories, and the newscaster groping for a lead. It's truly extraordinary to watch it tilt and turn, a couch-potato game of pinball unraveling before your sour cream cherry-flavored bag of chips.

The Persian Gulf War. As stupid as it might sound, the only place on my eighty-three-channel TV set I could find people of color being slaughtered for no apparent reason was on ESPN. The Buffalo Bills were killing "the grey and black." The Raiders were being slaughtered. The Bills were using their "hurry-up" offense, the score was around 60 to 3 after a quarter, and I switched back to CNN to the TV moment of the war that first Saturday, before live coverage was thereafter quarantined. An oral virus was sweeping the airwaves, much more lethal than anything the Iraqis would ever release. It was during the coverage of a Scud attack, the camera frantically scanning the sky in a manner much more disorienting than anything from Michael Snow's experimental film *La*

Région Centrale. The newscaster, trying to talk through a gas mask, is looking like a character from a Soviet constructivist play, with costumes by Rodchenko. Bobbi Battista, hysterically shrieking into her knocked-askew-by-the-gas mask earplug that they had overheard from Dan Rather's assistant that there was a gas attack. This roller-coaster ride of rumor and disinformation is circulating like an oral tear-gas attack, the best experimental theater I've seen in years. It was like a new installment of a Wooster Theater Group performance. This was the last day this type of coverage appeared on the network. There were no more live Scud broadcasts after that.

The last events leading back to my tape are the TV revolutions of 1989: Berlin, Prague, Budapest, modeled after the Edsa Revolution in the Philippines. I must concede this was the last great moment of the major networks, watching before bed, horizontally, between one's toes. I'm sure that there has been some type of study that has shown that Ted Koppel's hair really looks sexy when seen between one's toes. The thing I most remember about this coverage was the radical time difference among the performers. It was always daytime for the people on screen during *Nightline*, or they were about to have breakfast, being awakened in the middle of the night. Truly, these events took place in a hybrid time more like a dream than waking life.

To the piece itself, *The Machine That Killed Bad People.* The piece grew out of an epiphany, which, like all wisdoms of that genre, is now on the verge of becoming a cliché. While watching the overthrow of the Marcoses it became apparent that there was no longer a conceptual separation among event, televising, and watching; the spatial separation had been imploded and now constituted a single complex multispatial/multitemporal event. During the Gulf War, many "well-meaning" people voiced their horror over the observation of this style of event: earth-shattering spectacle, televised, controlled by rumor and the intimacy of the frame. Television had revealed its disposition: a wanton creature not good for modern dance or *Masterpiece Theatre*, good only for assassinations, touchdowns, revolutions, and earthquakes. These are hypertraumas and dramas of the present tense.

Unlike these well-meaning people, I was not appalled by this observation. It seemed a squandered sentiment, as useful as being appalled by a thunderstorm. Instead of critiquing this mode of television, I wanted to study its scale and force and see if I could learn to ride, then change, its course. I saw the format as powerful and I wanted to figure out how to use it and alter the effect, keep the intensity but change the meaning. Too many papers in this conference have talked of resistance to spectacle, putting the cross in front of the vampire, or simply watching from the outside and saying "I told you so" over and over again, a rosary-stroking gesture that is often called critique. So I jumped in and tried to create a network of my own, trying to cross Bertolt Brecht with Ted Turner; I couldn't do any more harm than efforts to convert spring wheat into winter wheat: no one was going to starve to death because of my less than noble experiment. I wanted to tangle with this postmodern octopus, the CNN-ification of the planet.

Before showing some of the tape I would like to talk a bit about the different responses I've had to the piece among the Filipino communities. I've had basically two diametrically opposed responses. When I've shown it to intellectuals who were raised in the Philippines, the response has been intensely supportive. There is an appreciation of the piece's effort to acknowledge a complex Filipino identity, where there is no essential Filipino waiting to be released from imprisonment in First World pop culture. The brilliance of Filipino intellectuals is their ability to perform their identity not by some form of raw expressivity, but through subtle toning: irony, self-deprecation, and black humor allow them to resolve the seeming paradox of both embracing and liberating themselves from U.S. popular culture. Are Filipinos neocolonialized? "Yes, then no" or "No, then yes," depending on the individual. So these sophisticates have been a source of great support for my piece. On the other hand, when the piece has been viewed by young Filipino-

American college students, they have been disappointed or even angered. Why all the emphasis on Filipino involvement with U.S. culture? Where are the pure Filipino values they wish to embrace? I try to indicate to them that the piece is about the extraordinary twists and turns of this involvement, what's called the special relation that is the Filipino-U.S. liaison.

With regard to the formal strategies of the piece, the inspiration lies in work done in the 1930s. If one figure were to be singled out it would be the Portuguese-American novelist John Dos Passos, and his magnum opus *U.S.A.* In Dos Passos, the newspaper was seen as the complex site of how people construct their narrative relation to events through a patchwork quilt of visually simultaneous, self-canceling stories. Just look at the formal richness of a newspaper page: pictures, large and small typeface, stories all over the place, obituaries juxtaposed with statistics about the comparative literacy in developing nations. What an experimental form in terms of its grammar, though the semantics are reductive and most often conservative. The form encourages the opening up of the imagination and then its contraction. This is the issue that interested me. I wanted to transform this type of experimentation done in the thirties to the narrative image-site of the present: cable television. I worked off of cable television formatting, trying to take advantage of its grammatical resourcefulness, the way things are told and how they're juxtaposed, and redress the semantic redundancy and conservativeness. If an image-grammarian were to study my piece in the twenty-third century, it would be perceived as typical.

I'm going to show parts from all four sections of the piece and then take questions. I'll take the questions à la Donahue, and have someone go around the audience with a mike. It's that time of late afternoon when our appetite for truth has shifted: we no longer crave soap opera but the syndicated talk show. Our midday meal is dominated by melodrama, high tea by confession.

The following is excerpted from the script of *The Machine That Killed Bad People*:

Manila, December 7, 1972
Thousands watched on live television as she was carried off, her beige terno soaked in blood. Dr. Robert Chase, a hand expert from Stanford University flown in to consult, said he believed the First Lady survived due to her expertise at ping-pong. "She threw her arm up and danced back when he came forward, and that was part of her ping-pong capability."

It was in Leyte that she, Imelda Romualdez Marcos, had first heard of

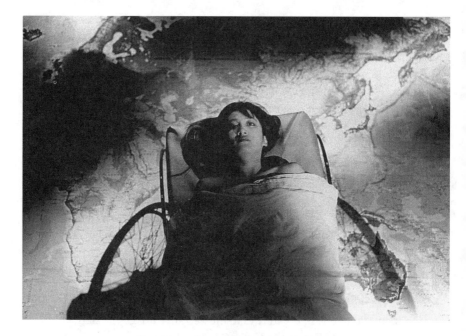

Europe. Brought by her widowed father to live in the family home, already nearly falling down. Her nun half sister told her the story of the opera singer Maria Malibran. As a little girl, her father, a famous tenor, had forced Maria to sing in the role of Desdemona in Rossini's *Othello*. This would be her debut. Her father told her that if she didn't sing perfectly he would strangle her to death. The critical scene of the opera occurred, his hand on Maria's throat. She couldn't tell if it was Desdemona being strangled to death by her jealous husband, or her own father trying to kill her. She sang perfectly.

Ten years later, Maria, now the most famous soprano in Europe, learns that she has but a few months left to live. She has only one request. Before she dies she wishes to play the lead in *Othello*.

Imelda arose, the morning after the assassination attempt, in the manner of the hysteric who, after a hectic day of being beaten, tortured, and defeated by her symptoms, awakes refreshed.

She had dreamed of mermaids, but this image was replaced by a more troubled one. Huge stones took shape before her, carved with strange etchings. It was a temple and a tomb, a royal tomb. A white vapor rose up from one of the pillars. It took the shape of a queen, a miracle of beauty. The woman smiled at Imelda and took her hand. Her hand slipped from the beautiful vision's grasp. Imelda tried to shout; she heard loud voices calling to her. At this moment she rejoined the living.

Later in the day, still watching the events broadcast in an endless loop on the television, she remained puzzled. Why had Ver's security, standing by, not rushed to her rescue? Ver politely explained that his men had wished to remain out of camera range, to give her center stage.

It was the custom in the Romualdez household to gather in the sala after supper for an evening of music. Don Vicente played the piano, one daughter played violin, and Imelda sang. After the Americans had retaken Leyte, several would gather to hear this pure voice soar over the accompaniment of the piano and violin. Eventually this was brought to the attention of Irving Berlin, touring the liberated South.

Although her range of songs was more distinguished, from the Abelardo Kundimans to selections from *The Desert Song*, Imelda sang to Berlin "You Are My Sunshine." She had been told this was the anthem of the American liberation. Despite Berlin's praises, Imelda decided not to pursue a singing career.

The tragedy of the twenty-first of August.

Marcos's trusted watchdog, General Fabian Ver, still lying on his back, his aides thinking him sound asleep, listened to their squelched laughter as they still told that joke. "No, you have it the wrong way 'round. Galman first committed suicide, then murdered Aquino."

They laughed.

All that remained on the tarmac to mark the bodies were thinly drawn chalk outlines, Ninoy's partially obscured by a muddied footprint. The body of Galman had been hastily removed, his blood both still wet and dried.

Eighteen bullets had pierced the body, entering both front to back and back to front. The Aquino corpse had but one bullet hole through the back of the neck. He had worn the same body armor as the American president.

General Ver turned onto his belly. He had dreamed of a battle, lasting not even a minute. Suspended in midair, their knives flashing. The slash in midair made thrice the damage as the one on the ground. He thought, "In the air they are angels, on the ground, merely fowl."

He returned.

The saving grace of the assassination was that it had been so perfectly bungled. He imagined the American ambassador saying, "Surely the work of amateurs." He would nod and mumble not even a word, but the letters N.P.A.

Cockfights.

The half-sleep reminded Ver of blue grass.

Kentucky.

Trained in torture, by experts, he bristled at their taunts. "Nothing but barbarism," they would say. He would smirk and remind them that "the cock had lost to the eagle by one vote when THEIR republic had selected its national symbol."

As he lay there, eyes fixed on the ceiling, he lost control. The Romans had derisively called cockfighting the Greek diversion.

The laughter had subsided.

His aides, fallen silent, turned toward him to listen, and he overheard his own voice saying into thin air, "Cocks are birds, it is us that have brought them down to earth."

This letter, dated December 17, 1951, was recently discovered quite by accident in an attic in Detroit, Michigan. At this time it would be best to withhold the author's name. We can, however, tell you a bit about him. He was Oliver North's hero and after his tour of duty in the Philippines he went on to Vietnam and finally Central America.

It has been said about him—no, about a character in a novel based on him—that he was determined to do good. Not to any individual, but to a country, a continent, a world.

Well, here's the letter.

Dear Dad,

Thanks so much for your letter dated October 13. Sorry to be so slow to respond but things take so long here, and I was off in the jungles of Luzon. But even there I heard that the Yankees had won the World Series; most everyone here, even the Flips, root for the Yanks. It didn't surprise me that the Yanks had won—what else is new?—but I was shocked to find out they had beaten the Giants. What the heck happened to the Dodgers? Well, your letter really filled me in on that. I must confess I took a certain unsavory pleasure in the way you described the excruciating details. I, like you, wondered why Dresson had put Branca in, after the Giants had murdered him all year and Thomson himself had hit a homer off him in game one. My favorite part of your letter, even more than the overpunctuated rendition of Russ Hodges saying over and over again, "The Giants win the pennant, the Giants win the pennant, the Giants win the pennant." Did it really need four exclamation points each time? Was the postgame interview with Dresson, him saying, without any punctuation in his voice, "I called the bull pen and they said Erskine just bounced a curve, Roc ain't ready, and Branca's throwing hard." He would have been better off consulting a numerologist. How can you put someone in, with the pennant on the line, who's wearing a big fat thirteen all over their back? Well, at least that turncoat Durocher lost the series.

As to some of your questions, yes, I'm still playing the harmonica and no, I don't like the Europeans any better; they seem so tired and cynical. They don't seem to see the importance of all this: oppression, communism, atheism . . . To them it seems like a mah-jongg game. I think they just come over to our officers' club because they think it's safe from the hand grenades. They are so easily amused, eating fried chicken and taking drugs. It's really true, the fate of the world is in our hands and we just have to round the Filipinos into shape. My advertising experience comes in handy and this seems to be the terrain that we can turn this thing around on. Magsaysay is a bit stupid, but at least he listened and does what we tell him. And the song I wrote, "Mambo, Mambo Magsaysay," is all the rage.

Sometimes this war makes me feel like a kid again back in Detroit. Often it's games and pranks that work. I concocted this eye of God scheme, borrowing it from the Egyptians—a little ancient history never hurt. We would, in the middle of the night, paint these evil eyes on the houses of suspected Huks. It would really scare the Huk out of them. Also, we have thought of a rather clever use of aircraft. We broadcast from the other side of the clouds, over loudspeakers, telling the natives not to feed the Huks. This voice of God seems to work better than the Voice of America.

Well, I guess by the time you receive this letter it will be a white Christmas. Here in the jungle, it's just green and more green. But at least it's a Christian country. They really carry on about Christmas. It seems to start up a week after the Fourth of July, reach full throttle Labor Day, and a crescendo level from Thanksgiving to Christmas Eve. It sure is festive, a bit too festive, almost pagan. Now I understand what McKinley meant when he said we had to Christianize them.

Wait till next year.

Your loving son

P.S.: Tell Mom to send some of her cookies; the desserts here are just too sweet. Also, around here you can't find any serious reading—only novels, plays, and poetry—so send me something, anything. I trust you.

Question and Answer

sf: I'll leave out the spectacular climax for another time, because time is up. That's the trouble with dealing with a two-hour piece in this context, so if we could have the lights, I'll try to expand or relate to something by taking questions. There's a mike that's supposed to come around.

r: I'd first like to introduce myself. I'm Rachel and I left the Philippines in 1984, right after Aquino left, uh, was assassinated. Again, the diaspora of Filipinos coming to the United States at that time trying to escape the economy, whatever we were afraid of, but the feeling that I got from this is, sort of, in between outrage. I'm angered because there is no narration.

sf: In fact, there's nothing but narration. The whole piece is governed by a series of stories. There's simply not a box narration. I mean, the most hideous narration in the world is actually NPR, and when I was talking about TV, the one thing I neglected to say is that the one channel I never look to for knowledge is PBS. On National Public Radio they say, "This person is going to say this," and then they say it. Instead, there's basically this cluster of different stories told over images, some of which I pull in one way, some of which overlap in other ways. Others contain others which resist. There's nothing but versions of narration. There's simply not a metanarration. The piece is an effort to take a cluster of discourses in narrations on many different levels and see if they could be juggled for politics. I suggest that politics should not be a universal, metadiscursive clarity but rather a constructed, rough-edged relation to differences.

v: I have to question who you're targeting as an audience because I don't know much about the Philippines, except for what I've read in the newspaper and then some stuff in journal magazines. If you're trying to target a general audience, which I assume that everyone is in here, I don't think that the message that you're trying to convey is coherently put together. It's very mumbo-jumbled and, frankly, I feel like it's very disorganized and I'm disappointed. I didn't get a lot out of it. Can you sort of explain this on a more general level and not use, like, artistic or whatever training that is behind the video? Because I don't understand.

sf: I think the point of this type of piece is really to say that to assume that there's a passive audience that you're supposed to target like some position on the dartboard is a mistake. I think the effort of experimental work is to try to construct a type of experimental text that raises types of questions in ways that enable people to open up to be able to organize information in different ways and, as I said before, the effort of the piece is to deal with the complexity without reducing it and still produce direction. The point with this type of work is to move away from some universal notion of video as a medium addressing an already existing monolithic audience. It's a question of expertise, I think, and not elitism, education and not arrogance, and a logic on another level as opposed to mumbo-jumbo.

List of Completed Works by Steve Fagin

Virtual Play: The Double Direct Monkey Wrench in Black's Machinery (1984)
An 80-minute video on Lou Andreas-Salomé.

The Amazing Voyage of Gustave Flaubert and Raymond Roussel (1986)
A 75-minute video on Flaubert and Roussel.

The Machine That Killed Bad People (1990)
A 120-minute video on the overthrow of the Marcos dictatorship in the Philippines.

Zero Degrees Latitude (1993)
A 60-minute video concerning the impact of North American evangelism in Ecuador.

All works available through Drift Distribution in New York and Video Data Bank in Chicago.

CHAPTER TWENTY-FOUR

"It's All Wrong, but It's All Right"

Creative Misunderstandings in Intercultural Communication

GEORGE LIPSITZ

Popular culture provides opportunities for escaping the parochialisms and prejudices of our personal worlds, for expanding our experience and understanding by seeing the world through the eyes of others. But popular culture can also trap us in its own mystifications and misrepresentations, building our investment and engagement in fictions that hide the conditions of their own production—the contexts of power, hate, hurt, and fear that give rise to seemingly neutral cultural texts. Gender, ethnicity, and race often serve as devices for building dramatic tension or supplying texture and meaning to cultural texts, but these representations can serve both progressive and reactionary purposes.

In its most utopian moments, popular culture offers a promise of reconciliation to groups divided by differences in power, opportunity, and experience. Commercial culture puts people from diverse backgrounds in contact with one another, creating contrasts that can call attention to existing social divisions as well as to the potential for eventual unity and community. But intercultural communication in popular culture can also create new sources of misunderstanding, misreading, and misappropriation that exacerbate rather than remedy social divisions.

Intercultural communication, like all communication, involves some measure of miscommunication. We can never really know how the world looks or sounds through the eyes and ears of others; we use metaphors to convey our experiences because of the impossibility of communicating our experiences to someone else directly. As scholars from many disciplines have argued in recent years, the inevitability of representation always involves the need for metaphors that make direct, unmediated, and perfect communication impossible. But although we can never know the exact dimensions, resonances, or consequences of any act of communication, we nonetheless have to make choices about cultural messages by analyzing their impact on our understanding of the world and our ability to act in it.

Critics of commercial culture often condemn the properties of mass media that encourage consumers to expropriate cultural creations for inappropriate purposes. Long ago, Walter Benjamin noted how the mechanisms of mass production ripped cultural practices from the sites and circumstances that gave them meaning, marketing them as mere novelties for uncomprehending consumers. Certainly these propensities account for the seamy history of exploitation and appropriation of folk cultures around the world by the culture industry, for the ways in which forms of expression connected to concrete social issues in particular places have circulated around the globe stripped of their local meanings.

On the other hand, many of these commodities have drawn the investment and engagement of consumers because their moral and political messages have gained even more power when applied to a new situation. Certainly the role of reggae music from Jamaica in articulating the aspirations of the African diaspora and the appeal of "magic realist" literature by Central American writers for European and American postmodern readers stem in part from the moral and political power of Caribbean and Central American strategies of signification and grammars of opposition to explain new realities for audiences encountering an increasingly cosmopolitan world. Even when listeners and readers have been ignorant of the exact original and local meanings of reggae or magic realism, they have often displayed advanced understanding about how they could use resonances of an "unfamiliar" culture to "defamiliarize" their own culture and then "refamiliarize" themselves and others with it on the basis of the new knowledge and critical perspectives made possible by cultural contrast.

The complexities of intercultural communication in popular culture compel us to look carefully at what might at first appear to be misunderstandings and mistakes. People who appear to be "mistaken" about another culture sometimes really know things that cannot be represented easily because their knowledge is illegitimate by existing standards and paradigms.

Especially on issues of identity involving nation, race, gender, sexuality, and class, "mistaken" ideas often contain important insights. Without minimizing the very real dangers of cross-cultural appropriations and misunderstandings, we must nonetheless be open to the kinds of knowing hidden within some "incorrect" perceptions.

Intercultural communication has been a foundational reality for North Americans for four hundred years. European exploration and settlement entailed the conquest, enslavement, and genocide of peoples of color, and vicious racial stereotypes in popular culture about Indians, Mexicans, Asians, and Blacks have functioned to obscure historical crimes and turn guilt and repression into entertainment and ideological domination. On the other hand, grassroots panethnic alliances have often given rise to popular culture products that present a utopian picture of potential interracial and interethnic cooperation. Culture in the United States has always been intercultural, and we can learn a great deal about both the promise and the peril of cross-cultural dialogue by exploring the cultural questions that have confronted specific cultural consumers and producers in our history.

Consider, for example, the case of eight-year-old Veronica Bennett (later Ronnie Spector of the vocal group the Ronettes) singing for her family in a flat in Spanish Harlem on a Sunday afternoon in 1951. One of her uncles put an electrician's light in a Maxwell House coffee can to make a "spotlight," and her father moved the coffee table to the middle of the room to make a "stage." Bennett recalls:

> That light seemed to focus all the warmth in the room on me as I belted out Hank Williams's "Jambalaya" in my eight-year-old voice. "Jambaylie, cold fish pie, diddly gumbo," I sang, with no idea what the words meant or if I even had them right. But when I looked around the room and saw all my aunts and uncles smiling and tapping their feet to keep time, I knew I must have been doing something right. In the middle of the song I stopped singing and improvised a little yodel. I was trying to imitate what all the cowboy singers used to do. And that was the beginning of the "whoa-oh-oh-oh-oh-ohs" that would become my trademark as a singer.[1]

Bennett mangled Hank Williams's lyrics in her rendition, changing "crawfish pie" into "cold fish pie" and substituting "diddly gumbo" for "filé gumbo." Her admission that she didn't know and didn't care what the words meant seems to provide strong support for critics concerned about the distracted and incomplete reception of intercultural messages in popular culture. Certainly, few people would imagine the maximally competent audience for Hank Williams's country-and-western song to be Ronnie Bennett's interracial family in Spanish Harlem. But further investigation reveals some interesting dimensions to Bennett's choices in singing this song.

Ronnie Bennett grew up as the daughter of an African-American/Native American mother and a Euro-American father. Her mother's sister Susu married a Puerto Rican, making Ronnie's cousin Nedra a mixture of African American, Native-American, and Puerto Rican ancestry. This extended family lived in a neighborhood that "had Chinese laundries, Spanish restaurants, and black grocery stores." At school, Black children teased Veronica about her light skin, calling her "skinny yellow horse" and yelling "Hey, half-breed, get your ass back to the reservation."[2] She later recalled:

> The blacks never really accepted me as one of them. The white kids knew I wasn't white. And the Spanish kids didn't talk to me because I didn't speak Spanish. I had a little identity crisis when I hit puberty. I remember I used to sit in front of the mirror, trying to decide just what I was. Let's see now, I'd think. I've got white eyes, but these are black lips. My ears—are they white ears or black ears?[3]

Bennett appropriated "Jambalaya" from Hank Williams, who was no stranger to the kinds of cultural questions that confronted Veronica Bennett. Williams grew up in a white working-class family, but received his first vocal training and guitar lessons from black street singers Big Day (Connie McKee) and Tee Tot (Rufus Payne). Williams habitually described himself as "part Indian," and his band, the Drifting Cowboys, included a Native American and a Mexican American. He wrote "Jambalaya" by taking the melody from the Cajun song "Grand Texas" and adding to it English lyrics that he thought sounded Cajun.[4]

So when the African-American, Native American, and Euro-American Ronnie Bennett sang "Jambalaya" for her Puerto Rican, African-American, Native American, and Euro-American family, she was imitating a version of a Cajun song written and recorded by an Anglo-American singer who thought of himself as a Native American trained by African Americans, and who played in a band with a Mexican American and a Native American. The "whoa-oh-oh-oh-oh-ohs" that Bennett took from "cowboy singers" and that became her trademark vocal signature as the lead singer of the Ronettes, came from Euro-American efforts to imitate the African-American musical sensibility expressed through changes in pitch and use of "impure" tones. [5]

Ronnie Spector may not have known the correct words to "Jambalaya," but her attraction to it reflected more than a simple misunderstanding. It functioned efficiently to evoke the kind of mixed subject position in music that Bennett had experienced her whole life. From one perspective, her rendition of the song might seem ignorant or incompetent, but from another it can be interpreted as an uninterrogated and perhaps unexpected form of intelligence and competence in finding a song that turned cultural contradictions into a creative expression of cultural hybridity.

Similarly creative "misunderstandings" about popular culture pervade an important scene in Cheech Marin's film *Born in East L.A.* An Immigration and Naturalization Service officer questions Marin's character, Rudy, to see if he is a U.S. citizen or an undocumented alien. Rudy protests that he was "born in East L.A.," so the officer tests his familiarity with U.S. culture, asking him the name of the president of the United States. Flustered by the question, Rudy replies, "That's easy, that dude that used to be on *Death Valley Days*—John Wayne." Rudy's failure to identify Ronald Reagan marks him as "incompetent" in his civic knowledge. But, of course, his conflation of Ronald Reagan with John Wayne reveals a larger truth: that Reagan's masculinist and paternalist politics and image "played" John Wayne for the American public.

In another scene in *Born in East L.A.*, Rudy attempts to teach some Mexican conjunto musicians "the most famous rock-and-roll song ever." He starts to play "Twist and Shout," but the other musicians hear the chord progressions and start singing "La Bamba." Rudy gets exasperated by their "incorrect" response, but the similarity between the two songs teaches the audience (if not the characters in the film) that Chicano identity is already sedimented within what might seem like a uniformly Anglo U.S. popular culture. In a film devoted to exploring the heterogeneous and composite nature of Chicano identity, it is appropriate that Rudy identifies "Twist and Shout," a song written for a Black singing group by Jewish songwriters who admired and attempted to copy Puerto Rican dance music, as his own, while missing its similarity to Mexican music. After the band shares "Twist and Shout" and "La Bamba," Rudy introduces them to other music that reveals the composite and dialogic nature of Chicano culture—a version of Jimi Hendrix's "Purple Haze," where they bill themselves, in an interlingual pun, as "Rudy and His New Huevos Rancheros," and "Roll Out the Barrel," a Czech song that Rudy sings in German (which he learned in the military) but whose polka form brings to the surface the similarities (and interactions) between German/Czech and Mexicano music in the United States.[6]

Wayne Wang employs similar strategies of creative misunderstanding in his film *Chan Is Missing*. While searching for Chan, cabdriver Joe tries to draw on his cultural roots by "thinking Chinese," while Joe's nephew and partner Steve is more "American" in his approach. But neither approach succeeds in understanding Chan, who is not only Chinese, but also likes to dance to mariachi music at the Manila Town Senior Center. Chan is Chinese, Chinese-American, and intercultural; no one narrative, however perfectly understood, can contain or explain him.

Japanese-American poet Lawson Fusao Inada presents another creative misunderstanding in his prose poem "Fresno," where he reflects upon the Asian-American, Armenian-American, and Mexican-American neighborhood in which he was raised. Inada talks about African-American music as the glue that held together these diverse groups. He remembers that for young people in Fresno Black music was the "lingua franca" that "enfranchised" and "conferred citizenship" on those who proved knowledgeable about it.[7]

On the surface, Inada's identification seems disastrously incorrect; how could identification with America's most disenfranchised group confer cultural citizenship on immigrants and their children? But taken less literally, his poem illumines a greater truth, what Albert Murray calls the "inescapably mulatto" nature of American culture. The Black music that Inada and his classmates regarded as quintessentially "American" was and continues to be one of the nation's great achievements, even if the credentialing institutions of society fail to recognize it as such.

Another kind of music offers an important insight in Oscar Zeta Acosta's *Autobiography of a Brown Buffalo.* The author wonders why the song "A Whiter Shade of Pale" holds such portent for him as he becomes more deeply involved in Chicano activism during the late 1960s. He hears it again and again on the radio, and it seems to speak directly to him. "The song moves me deeply. It reminds me of Luther's 'A Mighty Fortress Is Our God,'" he writes.[8]

Acosta never explains the importance of "A Whiter Shade of Pale," but in his confusion he leaves some clues. Of course, one possible connection comes from the song's psychedelic imagery and the massive quantities of hallucinogenic drugs that Acosta's book suggests he was taking. But "A Whiter Shade of Pale" also combines European forms—the melody is from Johann Sebastian Bach's "Air" from his Orchestral Suite No. 3 in D Major—with African-American styles (the soul ballad tradition exemplified in the singing of Sam Cooke) in a way that resonates with Acosta's presentation of Chicano identity as a mysterious and always surprising entity forged from dialogue between Euro-American, Afro-American, Spanish, Indian, and Chicano sensibilities. Acosta's references to "A Mighty Fortress Is Our God" also contain musical accuracy since many of the devices employed to build a sense of majesty in "A Whiter Shade of Pale" appear frequently in Lutheran hymns. Acosta is not simply "confused" or "incompetent" about "A Whiter Shade of Pale," but rather his confusion brings to the surface things that he knows but cannot articulate except through his identification with the song.

Ethiopian-American film scholar Teshome Gabriel offers an example of yet another kind of creative misunderstanding in a story about an African friend of his who grew up believing that Pete Seeger was Black. Gabriel's friend knew that the folksinger participated in the civil rights movement, that he sang freedom songs, and that he included Paul Robeson among his personal friends. When the African's view of Seeger's ethnicity got him involved in an argument after he came to the United States, his adversary showed him a picture of Seeger that clearly showed him to be white. But the African remained adamant. "I know that Pete Seeger is Black," he replied. "Why should I change my mind just because I see his face?" In this instance, blackness becomes a political position, something determined more by culture than by color. Although the African is factually wrong about the meaning of Seeger's identity within the context of U.S. culture, his "misunderstanding" also contains at least a strategic grain of truth.[9]

One can well understand how these kinds of "misunderstandings" allow people of color to see "families of resemblance" that reframe their separate experiences as similar, although not identical. But what about the danger of misunderstandings incorporated into Euro-American appropriation of the cultures of aggrieved populations? For example, Jefferson Starship's Marty Balin told an interviewer in 1983 that "I grew up with the beat era; when I was twelve years old, I'd go down to the clubs and watch John Coltrane and Miles Davis. I didn't know what I was doing, but I could feel something happening."[10]

Balin's recognition that he didn't know what he was doing seems to confirm the views of critics who stress the limits of reception and the barriers to intercultural communication. Part of what Balin didn't know at the age of twelve was the way that his experiences as a listener had been influenced by the history of Euro-American appropriation, colonization, orientalism, and primitivism. But, given the segregated nature of U.S. society, the censoring apparatuses of the culture industry and the state, and the systematic miseducation carried on by institutions of instruction, something else had to be happening in Balin's response to jazz at the same time. His sense that "something was happening" may also have been a recognition of the inadequacy of his existing language to know exactly how and why Coltrane and Davis affected him, how their music broke through the walls erected to keep them unknown to him, and how subversive their thinking might be to the culture in which he was raised. At the very least, it provided him with the inspiration to do more looking and listening, to see music as a potential site for the kinds of exciting and profound changes in human relations that Balin helped along in his capacity as a member of one of the leading bands of the 1960s counterculture.

Just as artists and audiences have been influenced positively by "creative mistakes," so too have artistic products themselves been enhanced by imperfect cultural exchanges. Artists from aggrieved communities have often profited from less than perfect knowledge about the exclusionary rules devised from within other cultures. Their "ignorance" of the intentions of others to exclude them has often served as an impetus to creativity; not knowing they were supposed to fail enabled them to succeed. Los Angeles Chicano artist Harry Gamboa Jr. remembers learning about art museums only after he had been painting for years. His inspirations and models came mainly from comic books, neighborhood graffiti, advertising, and prints used on calendars. When he discovered that museums exhibited "art," he took his drawings to the curator of the most prestigious local museum. They were rejected on the spot. Later, Gamboa went through more conventional channels, but got the same result. "We tried to get our work inside the museum, just like all the other Chicano artists in town," he recalls in reference to the origins of the guerrilla art group "Los Four." Gamboa and his friends found the art museum uninterested in their work, "so one night, we went over there and spray painted our names on the outside of the building. We felt that if we couldn't get inside, we would just sign the museum, and it would be our piece."[11]

Gamboa and Los Four titled their tagging of the museum "Pie in De-Face," and their action generated enthusiastic support among community artists and audiences because it articulated accumulated resentments about exclusion from the establishment definition of "culture." This action succeeded, at least in part, because from the start Gamboa "failed" to learn the lesson his society was trying to teach him—that "art" didn't include him. By remaining "ignorant," he positioned himself perfectly to challenge rather than accept that judgment.

Technical "misunderstandings" can also often be productive for artists. In the 1920s, Bix Beiderbecke could make changes on the trumpet and cornet that no one else could master because he taught himself the instruments and learned all the "wrong" fingerings. The way he fingered the instrument would have been a detriment to skillful playing for most music written within the Western symphonic tradition, but within jazz it enabled Beiderbecke to perform maneuvers that came easily to him but that seemed highly skilled to most other artists and to audiences. Similarly, Black jazz musicians in turn-of-the-century New Orleans often confounded classically trained musicians who tried to play with them because they played in so many "hard keys." They had no self-conscious intention of playing "difficult" music, but, like Beiderbecke, they were self-taught, and the black keys on the piano felt easier to play because they were physically farther apart on the keyboard. Consequently, they developed a style of playing in keys like F sharp, making extensive use of what other musicians had been taught to ignore or to treat as forbiddingly difficult. But these keys were only "hard" to those whose training started them in the key of C and others more commonly employed in the Western classical tradition.[12]

Charlie Parker's "mistakes" proved equally instructive. When he entered his first "cutting contest" (a bandstand battle where musicians tried to outplay each other), Parker didn't know about playing in key and was laughed off the stage. He took his saxophone with him to the Lake of the Ozarks, where he spent an entire summer teaching himself to play in every key—an education that better-schooled musicians might see as wasteful for someone in a dance band, where three or four keys were usually all that was required. But the ability Parker developed gave him exceptional resources as a musician, which he explored more fully in his years as a leader in bebop composing and playing. In a similar fashion, Roeland Roy Byrd, known professionally as Professor Longhair, used to confound nightclub owners by insisting on an upright piano rather than a grand piano. Most musicians considered the grand to be the superior instrument, but Longhair liked to kick the baseboard of the piano to help create the polyrhythms that made his playing so exceptional. His choice of instruments certainly added to the delight of his audiences, if not to that of club owners and their insurance companies when they discovered the damage that his kicks did to these instruments.

By calling attention to these creative mistakes, I am not dismissing the serious consequences of cultural appropriation and exploitation. Neither am I claiming that all or any people have perfect competence in decoding the materials they encounter through popular culture. I am not saying that it is better not to know than to know. We still need cultural studies scholarship that is grounded in history, that is ideologically attuned to understanding the limits of any one artist's or audience's subjectivity. But I do want to argue that people may know a lot even if they don't know the history of the literature they like or the names of the notes they play and hear, and that their imperfections as consumers of intercultural communication do not necessarily render them oblivious to effects of power or to the resonances of hate, hurt, and fear in the cultural creations they enjoy. People are more curious, more ingenious, and more intersubjective than their roles as consumers and citizens acknowledge or allow. Consequently, they often fashion fused subjectivities that incorporate diverse messages about who they are. Often, they make mistakes and they distort what they see and hear. Sometimes they do violence to others by stealing stories and appropriating ideas. But they also display a remarkable ability to find or invent the cultural symbols that they need.

It is important to document the harm done by uncomprehending appropriations of cultural creations, to face squarely the consequences of mistakes in the reception, representation, and reproduction of cultural images, sounds, and ideas. But the biggest mistake of all would be to underestimate how creatively people struggle, how hard they work, and how much they find out about things that people in power never intended for them to know.

Notes

I would like to thank Susan McClary, Rob Walser, Michael Omi, Janet Walker, Avery F. Gordon, and Christopher Newfield for their comments and criticisms of earlier drafts of this essay.

1. Ronnie Spector (with Vince Waldron), *Be My Baby: How I Survived Mascara, Miniskirts, and Madness or My Life as a Fabulous Ronette* (New York: Harper Perennial, 1990), 5.

2. Ibid., 1–2.

3. Ibid., 10.

4. Richard Leppert and George Lipsitz, "Everybody's Lonesome for Somebody: Age, Gender, and the Body in the Music of Hank Williams," *Popular Music* 9:3 (October 1990).

5. Spector describes her vocal maneuver as a "yodel," but while it gestures toward the yodeling tradition, it doesn't involve the full form as expressed in the music of yodelers like Elton Britt or Eddie Arnold. Instead, it involves the changes in pitch, impure tones, and instrumentalized-sounding vocals that cowboy singers appropriated from African-American music.

6. See Rosa Linda Fregoso, "Born in East L.A.," *Cultural Studies* 4:3 (October 1990).

7. Lawson Fusao Inada, "Fresno," American Studies Association meetings, Costa Mesa, California, 8 November 1992. Author's notes.

8. Oscar Zeta Acosta, *The Autobiography of a Brown Buffalo* (New York: Vintage Books, 1989), 35.

9. Teshome Gabriel, "Every Individual Is a Crowd," presentation at the University of California, San Diego, 12 April 1991.

10. Marty Balin, "Starship Interview," *Trouser Press* (March 1983).

11. "Interview with Harry Gamboa, Jr.," in *Murals: Sparc's Southern California Chicano Mural Documentation Project* (Santa Barbara: University of California, Santa Barbara Library, Special Collections, n.d.), 1.

12. Burton Peretti, *The Creation of Jazz* (Urbana: University of Illinois Press, 1992), 102, 104. Irving Berlin also never learned to read music and preferred to use these hard keys while composing at the piano.

CHAPTER TWENTY-FIVE

Imagining Los Angeles in the Production of Multiculturalism

LISA LOWE

Ridley Scott's science-fiction thriller film *Blade Runner* (1982) portrays Los Angeles in the year 2019 as a ruined, deteriorating city in postindustrial decay, a grand slum plagued by decaying garbage, dirt, ethnic ghettos, and radioactive rain. In composing this dystopic setting, the film represents L.A. as a pastiche of Third World, and particularly Asiatic, settlements: the storefronts are marked by neon Chinese ideograms, the streets filled with Chinese, Latino, Egyptian, and Cambodian faces. Everyone is talking "cityspeak," which the blade runner Deckard's voice-over narration describes as "a mishmash of Japanese, Spanish, German, French, what-have-you . . . I knew the lingo." Overlooking the city is a "Japanese simulacrum," a huge advertisement that alternates the image of a seductive Japanese woman's face and a Coca-Cola sign, a portentous emblem of future Japanese economic hegemony in the "city of angels."[1] The portrait of L.A. as a metropolis congested with poor Asian, Latino, African, and Arab immigrants projects the future of the First World *as* the Third World. In *Blade Runner*'s version of the twenty-first century, it is no longer necessary to travel out to see "the world"; "the world" has come, and now inhabits, indeed possesses, Los Angeles. At the same time, the film's predominant intrigue—a narrative in which the blade runner Deckard serves the law by hunting down replicants, but ultimately, in fleeing with his replicant lover Rachel, subverts the law that would

413

maintain the dominance of humans over androids—thematizes and critically opposes the very erasure of differences (the indistinguishability of machines and human beings, of species, race, and economic status) performed by the film's collapse of racial and economic difference in the representation of L.A. as ethnic ghetto. In other words, *Blade Runner*'s representation of a Third World invasion of L.A. does not perform a univocal homogenizing of difference, conflict, and otherness, but rather this representation is somewhat contested; the construction of Los Angeles as multicultural dystopia is put into question by the narrative in which Deckard comes to identify with the plight of the subordinated replicants, no longer seeking to kill them, but rather wishing to provide for their escape.

Against *Blade Runner*'s gloomy threat of multiculturalism, I wish to pose a more celebratory, but no less problematic, vision of Los Angeles as multicultural metropolis: the city represented in the September 1990 Los Angeles Festival of the Arts. For sixteen days, the festival represented the city as benevolent host to 550 performance events by artists and performers from twenty-one countries of Asia, the Pacific, and Latin America; as with *Blade Runner*, it may not be possible to constitute the festival as a univocal object. Part of the multiplicity of the festival-object is due to the sheer plenitude of performances, the uniqueness of the geography, the impossibility of having been at all sites, in all neighborhoods, at all times. My comments about the festival are directed more at a multiplicity produced by the variety of competing narratives that structured the presentation of events; among the different narratives vying for authority in the festival, I briefly address four, which I term, for convenience, the narratives of authenticity, genealogy, heterogeneity, and opposition. These narratives overlap and conflict, and I propose that it may not serve our inquiry to attempt to reconcile the narratives, or to determine one as dominant; rather, it seems that it is at the sites of conflict and antagonism between these different narratives that we find the most interesting, and most suggestive, moments in the production of multiculturalism.

I will be arguing that although film and festival representations register the increase of immigrant, racial, and ethnic populations in Los Angeles, both images of multiculturalism are problematic; neither topos reckons with the material differentiations of heterogeneous and unequal racial, ethnic, and immigrant communities in Los Angeles (or to extend our scope, in the state of California, where demographers declare that we are nearing a time in which more than 50 percent of the population will be Asian, Latino, African-American, and other "minority" populations). To the degree that multiculturalism claims to register the increasing diversity of populations, it precisely obscures the ways in which that aesthetic representation is not an analogue for the material positions, means, or resources of those populations; this is not so much a question of posing the figural against the literal, or the metaphorical against an essentialized notion of the "real," as it is a revelation of an undialectical confusion of historically differentiated spheres.[2] Although the concept of multiculturalism registers the pressures that demographic increases of immigrant, racial, and ethnic populations bring to all spheres, these pressures are registered only partially and inadequately in aesthetic representations; the production of multiculturalism instead diffuses the demands of material differentiation through the homogenization, aestheticization, and incorporation of signifiers of ethnic differences. Multiculturalism levels the important differences and contradictions within and among racial and ethnic minority groups according to the discourse of pluralism that asserts that American culture is a democratic terrain to which every variety of constituency has equal access and in which all are represented, while simultaneously masking the existence of exclusions by recuperating dissent, conflict, and otherness through the promise of inclusion.[3] Multiculturalism is central to the maintenance of a consensus that permits the present hegemony, a hegemony that relies on a premature reconciliation of contradiction and on persistent distractions away from the incommensurability of different spheres.[4] In this sense, the production of multiculturalism at once "forgets"—and in this forgetting, exacerbates—a contradiction between the concentration of capital within a dominant class group and the unattended conditions of a working class increasingly comprised of heterogeneous immigrant, racial, and ethnic groups.[5]

Both *Blade Runner*'s and the L.A. Festival's images of multiculturalism are, in a sense, driven by the increased presence of Third World people in Los Angeles; yet where *Blade Runner* produces a dystopic image of a decaying city engulfed, taken over by, Asians, Africans, and Latinos, the L.A. Festival presented the city as an aestheticized utopia of Third World artists. Multiculturalism in the L.A. Festival is represented as a polyvocal symphony of cultures; it is as if the festival's importing of selected "world" artists serves to "innoculate" L.A. against unmanaged "alien" invasions of the sort imagined by Scott's *Blade Runner*. A narrative of authenticity stressed the role of the city as a "curator" whose task was the salvaging and protection of pure cultural objects threatened with extinction in their native lands; this narrative identified originary places and moments of authentic culture (such as the Mayan, Chinese, or Aboriginal), located outside of the city, both temporally

and geographically "other" to the contemporary "fallen" milieu of Los Angeles. This narrative of authenticity surrounded, for example, the presentation
of the Kun Opera, exiled from communist China and protected by the city;
or the Court Performers from the Yogyakarta Palace of Java, whose performance was described as "the first time a Javanese court ensemble . . . and this
range of repertoire, has been seen outside Indonesia"; or the Balinese game-
lan players, Maori haka war dancers, and Ecuadoran folk musicians, which
the festival described as "resisting the disintegration of their culture in the
face of rapidly accelerating westernization of their Pacific homelands." In
this sense, "Los Angeles" was constituted as the Western curator/ethnogra-
pher who no longer needed to venture out to meet the exotic tribes, because
these cultures could now all be brought to Los Angeles.

At the same time that these authentic cultures were constituted as distant
and beyond the local sites of Los Angeles, a concomitant genealogical narrative tied L.A. to the ancient Chinese, Mayans, and Aborigines. The program
stated, for example: "Seen side by side, a new reality comes clear—that many
of the ideas, traditions, and practices of our colleagues are shared by the
artists living and working in Los Angeles today . . . the Festival celebrates
humanity and the cycles of life: the remembrance of *our* ancestors, *our*
hopes for the future." Yet, in conflating Third World artists and the general
population of the city, the precise relationship between Okinawan dance
and Black gospel music, for example, was "fudged," glossed over. The festival's staging of theater, dance, and music performances from Thailand,
China, Japan, Australia, the Philippines, Indonesia, Mexico, Central America, Chile, Panama—adjacent to work by artists from within the city of Los
Angeles itself—also enunciated to some extent this genealogical narrative
pronouncing the identity and continuity of "global" and "local" cultures.
The festival program read:

> 1990. We've arrived at the last decade of our century and it's a new world out
> there. With 85 languages spoken in the L.A. school system, it turns out that
> most of that new world is alive and living right here in this city. . . . We are
> living on the verge of the "Pacific Century." . . .
>
> This is a festival of new stories for a new America existing in a new
> world. . . . It's a delightful opportunity for Los Angelenos to travel to places
> where they don't usually go, to feel the presence of the multiple cultures that
> co-exist in our sprawling city. . . . After all, who owns culture?

Built upon the notion of connecting traditional non-Western cultural performance with the contemporary residents of Los Angeles, the city became a
living museum; the Chicano/Latino, Chinese, Japanese, African-American,

Thai, and Korean neighborhoods were opened up as locations for the performances by artists from Mexico, China, Japan, Africa, Thailand, and
Korea. These connections foregrounded new contrasts, invented new hierarchies, suggested new cultural mixtures and constellations. And as the final
question "After all, who owns culture?" implies, the juxtapositions were
aimed at thematizing the shift in hegemonic rule of Western art and culture
toward a newly invented syncretism of "Pacific culture." However, the production of multiculturalism as a *representation* of a changing cultural hegemony must be distinguished from shifts in the existing hegemony itself; the
synthetic production of multiculturalism unravels, and may be best contested, at the moments when the contradiction between the representational
economy of ethnic signifiers on the one hand, and the material economy of
resources and means on the other, becomes unavoidably clear. That is, what
the claim to "new stories for a new America" made dangerously invisible is
that to most African Americans, Asians, or Latinos living and working in Los
Angeles today, on the other 349 days of the year it may be very clear indeed
who "owns" culture: it is pronounced in the official language all must learn
to speak; it is declared if you can't afford to buy the garments that you are
employed to sew; it is evident if your call to 911 fails to bring emergency
assistance to your neighborhood.

   Antagonistic to the narratives of authenticity and genealogy—both of
which we might say are developmental narratives that depend on notions of
continuity, progression, and conversion—was a concurrent narrative of heterogeneity, whose formal characteristic was juxtaposition, pronounced in
apparently random contrasts between the ancient and the postmodern, the
arts of the street and the arts of the theater, "high" and "low," the Latin and
the Asian, the developing worlds and the overdeveloped worlds. A collection
of events at Griffith Park one weekend, for example, featured twenty different acts on five simultaneous stage locations in the park: Cambodian singers,
Flamenco dancers, Japanese puppet theater, mariachi bands, a Balinese children's choir—all performed at once. In relying on the structure of heterogeneous juxtaposition, this narrative tended to erase the history of each performance, by leveling the nonequivalent statuses of each particular form, genre,
and cultural location. Afro-Brazilian dancers, zydeco bands, performances of
Aborginal myths and legends, and Hawaiian hula were all accorded the same
relative importance. "Los Angeles" was represented as a postmodern multicultural cornucopia, an international patchwork quilt; while the means of
representation were the very uneven, unassimilable differences among these
diverse acts, the important signified was a notion of Los Angeles as multi-

cultural spectacle. In the process, each performance tradition was equated with every other, and its meaning leveled and generalized to a common denominator whose significance was the exotic, colorful advertisement of Los Angeles. Despite tensions between the narratives of authenticity, genealogy, and heterogeneity, all of these narratives may risk, in different ways, erasing and occluding the "material" geographies of L.A.; neither topos reckons with the practical relationships between heterogeneous and economically unequal racial, ethnic, and immigrant communities in Los Angeles, a city that is already the home to more people of Mexican descent than any other city outside Mexico, more Koreans than any other city outside Asia, and more Filipinos than any city outside the Philippines. There is a tendency, to varying degrees, to level the important distinctions and contradictions within and among racial and ethnic minority groups according to a pluralism that effectively continues to privilege the centrality of dominant culture. As Hal Foster argues, pluralism promotes a form of tolerance that leaves the status quo unthreatened; the margins are absorbed into the center, the heterogeneous is domesticated into the homogeneous.[6] It is pluralism's leveling of the material, and not simply aesthetic unevennesses of racial, ethnic, and immigrant cultures, as well as its erasure of exclusions, that I believe risks the depoliticization of multiculturalism. In this sense, it is the productive conflict and irresolution between pluralist and antipluralist narratives that mark, in my view, the most interesting moments of the festival.

Thus, while the aestheticizing and pluralizing tendencies of these narratives are problematic, it also seems clear that none of these narratives monolithically "colonizes" the radically nonequivalent populations and locales each seeks to include and represent; in this sense, the leveling of Asians, Latinos, and African Americans (each itself a contradictory grouping, crossed by differences of language, generation, class, national origin, gender, religion) is also at certain moments challenged by important pressures from resisting, or oppositional, narratives. The oppositional narrative made some use of the juxtapositions from the narrative of heterogeneity, but in the oppositional narrative, the contrasts were inflected differently; attention was drawn to the inequalities between cultural objects by attaching, when possible, the object to some cultural context of production and reception, thereby making the history of the object explicit. For example, narratives of resistance were made possible in the staging of the Thai Likay performers at the Wat Thai Temple in North Hollywood, or in the placement of the African Marketplace near West Central L.A.; that is, these stagings generated interesting connections between cultural performance and local communities and geography. In this way, a Black American community was attached to African cultural forms in a relationship that was not based on identity, but that was not entirely discontinuous either. In addition, disparate communities were introduced to one another—for example, relationships were articulated between the Thai and gay communities in North Hollywood. Where the narrative of heterogeneity could have juxtaposed and equalized the Korean shaman with mariachi bands, an oppositional narrative worked to attach the Korean shaman to the Korean-American community by staging his arrival in a Korean-American strip mall, suggesting a degree of dialectical relationship between object and community. Yet, ironically, while shamanism has an important history in Korea, many Korean Americans in Los Angeles are Christian, a disjunction occluded by the narrative of heterogeneity.

The eruption of riots in Los Angeles in 1992 following the verdict that freed four white policemen accused of beating a Black man, Rodney King, is a most vivid example of the contradiction between multiculturalism as the representation of the liberal state and the material poverty and disenfranchisement that are the conditions of those represented. Although the U.S. media consistently attempted to construct the riots as a racial conflict between Blacks and Koreans, the looters enraged by the King verdict were not only Blacks, but also Chicanos, Latinos, and working-class whites; all violently objected to the denial of brutally racialized economic stratification. I wish to locate a radical critique of multiculturalism in the 1993 documentary film *Sa-I-Gu* by Christine Choy, Elaine Kim, and Dai Sil Kim-Gibson, which deals with those events.[7] The film powerfully disrupts a developmental, genealogical narrative that assimilates an ethnic immigrant into the capitalist economy. The very different articulations of the Korean immigrant and Korean-American speakers contradict a notion of the homogeneous authenticity of immigrant groups. Thus, the film radically challenges the liberal myth of pluralist inclusion, both on the level of the speakers' testimonies and in terms of the interrupted, particularist form of the film itself.

Sa-I-Gu collects together heterogeneous interviews with Korean immigrant and Korean-American women speaking about the Los Angeles crisis in the aftermath of the King verdict.[8] The film is not a narrative, but a series of clips of Korean immigrant workers, shopkeepers, owners of grocery stores, liquor and convenience stores, laundries—women who speak about their losses and their disillusionment. Their testimonies are contradictory, unsynthetic, unhomogeneous. They speak about the lack of support from the Los Angeles Police Department and the National Guard during the uprisings. They speak about the shock of working long hours in order to eke out a living. They speak about losing sons, husbands, livelihoods, and opportunities. The film opens with an interview with the mother of Edward Jae Song Lee; Lee was shot and died during the crisis when he was mistaken by a store owner for a looter. Her testimony focuses on mourning the loss of her son, as well as her disillusionment with the promises of capitalism, inclusion, and protection by police or government. She says: "At the time, I thought it was one man who shot my son. But if I think broadly, it is not just an individual matter. Something is drastically wrong." Another woman interviewed states: "I would like to express my feeling about this after the riot. Right now I'm angry at everybody. Or on contrary, I'm angry at myself. Because I don't know to whom to where I should be angry at them. I am totally confused, totally confused." The statements of both of these women articulate the desire to grasp an explanation of the convergence of racism and capitalism, as much as their "confusion" attests to the unavailability of this convergence. Indeed, the Los Angeles crisis, in which Korean Americans became the recipients of violent anger that might well have been "better" directed at white capital in other parts of the intensely spatially segregated city, illustrates precisely how a society can mask the interlocking dominations of racism, patriarchy, and capitalism, not only by ideologically constructing multicultural inclusion, but by separating and dividing its objects—as Black youth, as Korean shopkeeper, as Chicana single mother. It is this isolation of objects that contributes to the fragmentation of social life in the advanced capitalist USA, and this isolation likewise contributes to the fragmentation of political organization against the interlocking dominations. The statement of "confusion" at not knowing where to focus blame implies a desire for an explanation for the convergences of dominations; at the same time, it articulates the difficulty of apprehending or seizing more than a fragment of that convergence. If structured domination and oppositional responses to it remain unavailable to groups and individuals, then domination functions and persists precisely through the unavailability of this structure. Multiculturalism is one ideological representation of the liberal imperialist state that enacts that unavailability. In the film *Sa-I-Gu* a powerful particularism—particular griefs, losses, and anger—demystifies multiculturalist inclusion and moves us toward an interrogation of the convergence of dominations of which multiculturalism is the ideological expression and resolution. *Sa-I-Gu* is a radical objection to multiculturalism and a forceful testimony about the conjunction of capitalism with racism and patriarchy in Los Angeles.

Let me conclude by stressing the importance of oppositional narratives

and practices, and by foregrounding their conflicts with the narratives of authenticity, genealogy, and heterogeneity, conflicts that build pressure against
the pluralist tendencies of a produced multiculturalism. If we do not stress
these oppositions, the geographies and histories of immigrant settlement in
Los Angeles are dangerously obscured, segregation of neighborhoods is
masked as spatial contiguity, and racial and class violence between groups is
aestheticized in a multicultural juxtaposition of ethnic images. Without
these tensions, multiculturalism fails to come to grips with the material
inequalities and strata of a city like Los Angeles: the separations, unevennesses of opportunity due to different groups' histories of labor, racism, and
poverty.[9] The narratives of multiculturalism that do not make these connections, or that do not make space for oppositional critiques, risk denuding
racial and ethnic groups of their specificity. Subject to the leveling operations of both postmodern pastiche and pluralism, African, Asian, and Latino
cultures become all equally other, are metaphorized as all equally different,
all whole without contradiction. These narratives, which suppress tension
and opposition, suggest that we have already achieved multiculturalism, that
we know what it is, that it is defined simply by the coexistence and juxtaposition of greater numbers of diverse groups; these narratives allow us to
ignore the profound and urgent gaps, the inequalities and conflicts, among
racial, ethnic, and immigrant groups; they let us off the hook. The suggestion that multicultural discourses might ultimately emphasize, rather than
domesticate, the productive irresolution, opposition, and conflict of these
various narratives is neither a call for chaos nor a return to traditional Western notions of art and high culture. It is rather an assertion that it may be
through contradiction that we begin to address the systemic inequalities
built into cultural institutions, economies, and geographies, and through
conflict that we call attention to the process through which these inequalities are obscured by pluralist multiculturalism.

Notes

1. See Giuliana Bruno, "Ramble City: Postmodernism and *Blade Runner*," *October* 42 (summer 1987): 61–74.

2. On the relationship between aesthetic culture and material economy, see David Lloyd,
"Analogies of the Aesthetic: The Politics of Culture and the Limits of Materialist Aesthetics,"
New Formations (spring 1990): 109–26.

3. On the logic of pluralism in critical discourse, see Ellen Rooney, *Seductive Reasoning: Pluralism as the Problematic of Contemporary Literary Theory* (Ithaca, N.Y.: Cornell University
Press, 1989).

4. Gramsci distinguishes hegemony from the violent imposition of rule and elaborates it as
the process through which a particular group gains consent to determine the political, cultural,
and ideological character of a state; pluralism elicits the consent of racial and ethnic groups

through the promise of equal participation and equal citizenship. See Antonio Gramsci, *Selections from the Prison Notebooks*, ed. and trans. Quintin Hoare and Geoffrey Nowell Smith (New York: International Publishers, 1971). However, Gramsci defines hegemony as always existing within the context of pressures from subaltern groups, pressures that can be articulated into counterhegemonic formations. For further discussion of how Gramsci's concept of hegemony also includes within it the possible challenges by emergent groups, see Stuart Hall, "Gramsci's Relevance for the Study of Race and Ethnicity," *Journal of Communication Inquiry* 10 (summer 1986); Radha Radhakrishnan's discussion of the Rainbow Coalition in "Towards an Effective Intellectual: Foucault or Gramsci?" in *Intellectuals*, ed. Bruce Robbins (Minneapolis: University of Minnesota Press, 1990); and Chantal Mouffe, "Hegemony and New Political Subjects: Toward a New Concept of Democracy," in *Marxism and the Interpretation of Culture*, ed. Cary Nelson and Lawrence Grossberg (Urbana and Chicago: University of Illinois Press, 1988).

5. The description of the "forgetting" of differentiated spheres recalls Horkheimer and Adorno's analysis of the "culture industry": "the idea of 'fully exploiting' available technical resources and the facilities for aesthetic mass consumption is part of the economic system which refuses to exploit resources to abolish hunger" (Max Horkheimer and Theodor Adorno, *The Dialectic of Enlightenment*, trans. John Cumming [New York: Seabury Press, 1972], 139). Benjamin comments also on the production of aesthetic culture as distraction: "Distraction as provided by art presents a covert control of the extent to which new tasks have become soluble by apperception. Since, moreover, individuals are tempted to avoid such tasks, art will tackle the most difficult and most important ones where it is able to mobilize the masses. . . . The public is an examiner, but an absent-minded one" (Walter Benjamin, "The Work of Art in the Age of Mechanical Reproduction," in *Illuminations*, trans. Harry Zohn [New York: Schocken, 1969], 240–41). However, for Horkheimer and Adorno, the analysis of the "forgetting" of historical differentiation is part of a critique of mass culture as deception and its undermining of society's emancipatory potential, whereas for Benjamin, technology and mass culture do not in themselves lead to deception or appropriation, but can also be means, as with Brecht, of initiating political action (in this, it might be said that Benjamin portends postmodernism's "antiaesthetic" celebration of mass culture, technology, and the crisis of representation, as means of calling attention to the end of the autonomous aesthetic object, a critique of official representations and narratives, and the possibility of destructuring the order of representation; see Hal Foster on a "postmodernism of resistance" in the introduction to *The Anti-Aesthetic: Essays on Postmodern Culture* [Port Townsend, Wash.: Bay Press, 1983]). For a very persuasive discussion of the ideological and utopian functions of mass culture, see Fredric Jameson, "Reification and Utopia in Mass Culture," *Social Text* 1:1 (1979): 130–48.

6. Hal Foster, "The Problem of Pluralism," *Art in America* (January 1982): 9–15.

7. *Sa-I-Gu*, produced by Christine Choy, Elaine Kim, and Dai Sil Kim-Gibson, Cross Current Media (1993); distributed by National Asian American Telecommunications Association, 346 Ninth Street, 2d floor, San Francisco, CA 94103.

8. *Sa-I-Gu*, meaning "4.29" or April 29 (the date of the Rodney King verdicts), alludes to the history of Korean nationalism, by putting the 1992 attack on Korean Americans in the context of other Korean nationalist struggles. Elaine Kim writes in "Home Is Where the Han Is," in *Reading Rodney King, Reading Urban Uprisings*, ed. Robert Gooding-Williams (New York: Routledge, 1993): "Situated as we are on the border between those who have and those who have not, between predominantly Anglo and mostly African American and Latino communities, from our current interstitial position in the American discourse of race, many Korean Americans have trouble calling what happened in Los Angeles an 'uprising.' At the same time, we cannot quite say it was a 'riot.' So some of us have taken to calling it *sa-i-ku*, April 29, after the manner of naming other events in Korean history—3.1 (*sam-il*) for March 1, 1919, when massive protests against Japanese colonial rule began in Korea; 6.25 (*yook-i-o*), or June 25, 1950, when the

Korean War began; and 4.19 (*sa-il-ku*), or April 19, 1960, when the first student movement in the world to overthrow a government began in South Korea. The ironic similarity between 4.19 and 4.29 does not escape most Korean Americans" (216). I wish to stress that Korean-American nationalism in the aftermath of the L.A. crisis is not a direct transference of Korean nationalism but a discontinuous rearticulation of it that includes the crucial consideration of the racialization of Korean immigrants in the United States as workers of color. For a powerful discussion situating the racialization of racial, ethnic, and immigrant groups in the United States in the negotiation between dominant institutional constructions of race and the political struggles of social movements, see Michael Omi and Howard Winant, *Racial Formation in the United States: From the 1960s to the 1980s* (New York and London: Routledge, 1986).

9. See Mike Davis, *City of Quartz: Excavating the Future in Los Angeles* (London and New York: Verso, 1990); George Lipsitz, *Time Passages: Collective Memory and American Popular Culture* (Minneapolis: University of Minnesota Press, 1990). Davis's and Lipsitz's works attach the different histories of racial and ethnic communities to neighborhoods, urban history, labor movements, and community practices, and to popular cultural forms such as rap, rock and roll, low-riding, or graffiti.

CHAPTER TWENTY-SIX

A Style Nobody Can Deal With

Politics, Style, and the Postindustrial City in Hip Hop

TRICIA ROSE

Multiculturalism—no doubt a complex and contested term—often refers to a process of incorporation of marginal groups' contributions into a mainstream or dominant culture. In this context, multiculturalism is pressed into service to highlight and legitimize the contributions of "others" to invisible yet omnipresent cultures of whiteness. Hence, multiculturalist efforts include revisions to the overwhelmingly white male author-based literary canon to include writers and oral masters of color and women, and rewritings of Christopher Columbus that transform him into an agent of imperialism rather than a heroic discoverer. In other words, the "multi" in "multicultural" frequently refers to multiple "others" knocking on a central gate of power.

Although these efforts have been important in challenging cultural and intellectual hierarchies, there are other modes of cultural dialogue that are not as easily seen from this vantage point. In the cases of contemporary popular culture and the diverse communities of young people who create, consume, and propel it, multicultural exchanges develop in several ways, most notably via day-to-day cross-cultural contacts, identification with mass-mediated images, similar cultural traditions, and shared lived experiences of oppression. In this sort of multiculturalism, a variety of groups are engaged in feisty and congenial dialogues that focus not only on resisting and/or critiquing dominant institutions, but also on developing forms that grow out of intercultural exchanges.

Hip hop continues to be a rich space for the development and exploration of these interactions. Most heavily (but not exclusively) shaped by multiple sources of Afro-diasporic cultural influences and the postindustrial urban New York terrain, hip hop emerges in the mid-to-late 1970s as a form of cultural affirmation and resistance. Puerto Rican, Dominican, and Cuban immigrants—whose musical and cultural traditions have strong ties to the Afro-diaspora—along with other Carribean Afro-diasporic cultures, such as Jamaicans and Haitians, were especially important actors in the multicultural development of hip hop. No doubt these "multiple others" are knocking at a central gate, but they are also hard at work in communication with each other, building cultural bridges and new identities that affirm and transform cultural traditions in new environments not only for purposes of staking societal claims, but also for pleasure and regeneration.

Life on the margins of postindustrial urban America is inscribed in hip hop style, sound, lyrics, and thematics.[1] Emerging from the intersection of lack and desire in the postindustrial city, hip hop manages the painful contradictions of social alienation and prophetic imagination. Hip hop is an Afro-diasporic cultural form that attempts to negotiate the experiences of marginalization, brutally truncated opportunity, and oppression within the cultural imperatives of African-American and Caribbean history, identity, and community. It is the tension between the cultural fractures produced by postindustrial oppression and the binding ties of black cultural expressivity that sets the critical frame for the development of hip hop.[2]

Worked out on the rusting urban core as a playground, hip hop transforms stray technological parts intended for cultural and industrial trash heaps into sources of pleasure and power. These transformations have become a basis for digital imagination all over the world. Its earliest practitioners came of age at the tail end of the Great Society, in the twilight of America's short-lived federal commitment to black civil rights and during the predawn of the Reagan-Bush era.[3] In hip hop, these abandoned parts, people, and social institutions were welded and then spliced together, not only as sources of survival but as sources of pleasure.

Hip hop replicates and reimagines the experiences of urban life and symbolically appropriates urban space through sampling, attitude, dance, style, and sound effects. Talk of subways, crews and posses, urban noise, economic stagnation, static, and crossed signals leap out of hip hop lyrics, sounds and themes. Graffiti artists spray-painted murals and (name)"tags" on trains, trucks, and playgrounds, claiming territories and inscribing their otherwise contained identities on public property.[4] Early breakdancers' elaborate technologically inspired street-corner dances involving head spins on concrete sidewalks made the streets theater-friendly and served as makeshift youth centers. The dancers' electric robotic mimicry and identity-transforming characterizations foreshadowed the fluid and shocking effect of morphing, a visual effect made famous in *Terminator 2*. DJs who initiated spontaneous street parties by attaching customized, makeshift turntables and speakers to streetlight electrical sources revised the use of central thoroughfares, made "open-air" community centers in neighborhoods where there were none. Rappers seized and used microphones as if amplification was a life-giving source. Hip hop gives voice to the tensions and contradictions in the public urban landscape during a period of substantial transformation in New York and attempts to seize the shifting urban terrain, to make it work on behalf of the dispossessed.

Hip hop's attempts to negotiate new economic and technological conditions as well as new patterns of race, class, and gender oppression in urban America by appropriating subway facades, public streets, language, style, and sampling technology are only part of the story. Hip hop music and culture also rely on a variety of Afro-Caribbean and Afro-American musical, oral, visual, and dance forms and practices in the face of a larger society that rarely recognizes the Afro-diasporic significance of such practices. It is, in fact, the dynamic and often contentious relationship between the two—larger social and political forces and black cultural priorities—that centrally shapes and defines hip hop.

The tensions and contradictions shaping hip hop culture can confound efforts at interpretation by even the most skilled critics and observers. Some analysts see hip hop as a quintessentially postmodern practice, while others view it as a present-day successor to premodern oral traditions. Some celebrate its critique of consumer capitalism, while others condemn it for its complicity with commercialism. To one enthusiastic group of critics, hip hop combines elements of speech and song, of dance and display, to call into being through performance new identities and subject positions. Yet to another equally vociferous group, hip hop merely displays in phantasmagorical form the cultural logic of late capitalism. I intend to demonstrate the importance of locating hip hop culture within the context of deindustrialization and to show how hip hop's primary properties of flow, layering, and rupture simultaneously reflect and contest the social roles open to urban inner-city youth at the end of the twentieth century.

In an attempt to rescue rap from its identity as postindustrial commercial product and situate it in the history of respected black cultural practices, many historical accounts of rap consider it a direct extension of African-American oral, poetic, and protest traditions, to which it is clearly and substantially indebted. This accounting, which builds important bridges between rap's use of boasting, signifying, preaching, and earlier related black oral traditions, produces multiple problematic effects. First, it reconstructs rap music as a singular oral poetic form that appears to have developed autonomously (e.g., outside hip hop culture) in the 1970s. Quite to the contrary, rap is one cultural element within the larger social movement of hip hop. Second, it substantially marginalizes the significance of rap as *music*. Rap's musical elements and its use of music technology are a crucial aspect of the use and development of the form and are absolutely critical to the evolution of hip hop generally. Finally, and most directly important for this discussion, it renders invisible the crucial role of the postindustrial city on the shape and direction of rap and hip hop and makes it difficult to trace the way hip hop revises and extends Afro-diasporic practices using postindustrial urban materials. Hip hop's styles and themes share striking similarities with many past and contiguous Afro-diasporic musical and cultural expressions; these themes and styles, for the most part, are revised and reinterpreted using contemporary cultural and technological elements. Hip hop's central forms—graffiti, breakdancing, and rap music—developed, in relation to one another, within Afro-diasporic cultural priorities, and in relation to larger postindustrial social forces and institutions.

What are some of the defining aesthetic and stylistic characteristics of hip hop? What is it about the postindustrial city generally and the social and political terrain in the 1970s in New York City specifically that contributes to the emergence and early reception of hip hop? Even as today's rappers revise and redirect rap music, most understand themselves as working out of a tradition of style, attitude, and form that has critical and primary roots in New York City in the 1970s. Substantial postindustrial shifts in economic conditions, access to housing, demographics, and communication networks were crucial to the formation of the conditions that nurtured the cultural hybrids and sociopolitical tenor of hip hop's lyrics and music.

The Urban Context

Postindustrial conditions in urban centers across America reflect a complex set of global forces that continue to shape the contemporary urban metropolis. The growth of multinational telecommunications networks, global economic competition, a major technological revolution, the formation of new international divisions of labor, the increasing power of finance relative to production, and new migration patterns from Third World industrializing nations have all contributed to the economic and social restructuring of urban America. These global forces have had direct and sustained impact on urban job opportunity structures, have exacerbated long-standing racial and gender-based forms of discrimination, and have contributed to increasing multinational corporate control of market conditions and national economic health.[5] Large-scale restructuring of the workplace and job market had its effects upon most facets of everyday life. It has placed additional pressures on local community-based networks of communication and whittled down already limited prospects for social mobility.

In the 1970s, cities across the country were gradually losing federal funding for social services, information service corporations were beginning to replace industrial factories, and corporate developers were buying up real estate to be converted into luxury housing, leaving working-class residents with limited affordable housing, a shrinking job market, and diminishing social services. The poorest neighborhoods and the least powerful groups were the least protected and had the smallest safety nets. By the 1980s, the privileged elites displayed unabashed greed as their strategies to reclaim and rebuild downtown business and tourist zones with municipal and federal subsidies exacerbated the already widening gap between classes and races.

Given New York's status as hub city for international capital and information services, it is not surprising that these larger structural changes and their effects were quickly and intensely felt in New York.[6] As John Mollenkopf notes, "during the 1970s, the U.S. system of cities crossed a watershed. New York led other old, industrial metropolitan areas into population and employment decline."[7] The federal funds that might have offset this process had been diminishing throughout the 1970s. In 1975, President Ford's unequivocal veto to requests for a federal bailout to prevent New York from filing for bankruptcy made New York a national symbol for the fate of older cities under his administration. The New York *Daily News*'s legendary headline "Ford to New York: Drop Dead" captured the substance and temperament of Ford's veto and sent a sharp message to cities around the country.[8]

Virtually bankrupt and in a critical state of disrepair, New York City and State administrators finally negotiated a federal loan, albeit one that accompanied an elaborate package of service cuts and carried harsh repayment terms. These dramatic social-service cuts were felt most severely in New York's poorest areas and were part of a larger trend in unequal wealth distribution and were accompanied by a housing crisis that continued well into the 1980s. Between 1978 and 1986, the people in the bottom 20 percent of the income scale experienced an absolute decline in income while the top 20 percent experienced most of the economic growth. Blacks and Hispanics disproportionately occupied this bottom fifth. During this same period, 30 percent of New York's Hispanic households (for Puerto Ricans it is 40 percent) and 25 percent of black households lived at or below the poverty line. Since this period, low-income housing has continued to disappear and blacks and Hispanics are still much more likely to live in overcrowded, dilapidated, and seriously undermaintained spaces.[9] It is not surprising that these serious trends have contributed to New York's large and chronically homeless population.

In addition to housing problems, New York and many large urban centers faced other major economic and demographic forces that have sustained and exacerbated significant structural inequalities. Although urban America has always been socially and economically divided, these divisions have taken on a new dimension. At the same time that racial succession and immigration patterns were reshaping the city's population and labor force, shifts in the occupational structure away from a high-wage, high-employment economy grounded in manufacturing, trucking, warehousing, and wholesale trade and toward a low-wage, low-employment economy geared toward producer services generated new forms of inequality. Earlier divisions in the city were predominantly ethnic and economic. "New York," Mollenkopf concludes, "has been transformed from a relatively well-off white blue-collar city into a more economically divided, multi-racial white-collar city." This "disorganized periphery" of civil service and manufacturing workers contributes to the consolidation of power among white-collar professional corporate managers, creating the massive inequalities in New York.[10]

The commercial imperatives of corporate America have also undermined the process of transmitting and sharing local knowledge in the urban metropolis. Ben Bagdigian's study *The Media Monopoly* reveals that monopolistic tendencies in commercial enterprises seriously constrain access to a diverse flow of information. For example, urban renewal relocation efforts

not only dispersed central-city populations to the suburbs, they also replaced the commerce of the street with the needs of the metropolitan market. Advertisers geared newspaper articles and television broadcasts toward
the purchasing power of suburban buyers, creating a dual "crisis of representation" in terms of whose lives and images were represented physically in
the paper and whose interests got represented in the corridors of power.[11]
These media outlet and advertising shifts have been accompanied by a massive telecommunications revolution in the information processing industry.
Once the domain of the government, information processing and communication technology now lie at the heart of corporate America. As a result of
government deregulation in communications via the breakup of AT&T in
1982, communications industries have consolidated and internationalized.
Today, telecommunications industries are global data transmittal corporations with significant control over radio, television, cable, telephone, computer, and other electronic transmittal systems. Telecommunication expansion coupled with corporate consolidation has dismantled local community
networks and has irrevocably changed the means and character of communication.[12] Since the mid-1980s, these expansions and consolidations have
been accompanied by a tidal wave of widely available communications products, which have revolutionized business and personal communications.
Facsimile machines, satellite-networked beepers, cordless phones, electronic
mail networks, cable television expansions, VCRs, compact discs, video cameras and games, and personal computers have dramatically transformed the
speed and character of speech and written and visual communication.

Postindustrial conditions had a profound effect on black and Hispanic
communities. Shrinking federal funds and affordable housing, shifts in the
occupational structure away from blue-collar manufacturing and toward
corporate and information services, along with frayed local communication
patterns, meant that new immigrant populations and the city's poorest residents paid the highest price for deindustrialization and economic restructuring. These communities are more susceptible to slumlords, redevelopers,
toxic waste dumps, drug rehabilitation centers, violent criminals, redlining,
and inadequate city services and transportation. This also meant that the
city's ethnic- and working-class-based forms of community aid and support
were growing increasingly less effective against these new conditions.

In the case of the South Bronx, which has been frequently dubbed the
"home of hip-hop culture," these larger postindustrial conditions were exacerbated by disruptions considered to be an "unexpected side effect" of a
larger, politically motivated "urban renewal" project. In the early 1970s, this

renewal (*sic*) project involved massive relocations of economically fragile people of color from different areas in New York City into parts of the South Bronx. Subsequent ethnic and racial transition in the South Bronx was not a gradual process that might have allowed already taxed social and cultural institutions to respond self-protectively; instead it was a brutal process of community destruction and relocation executed by municipal officials and under the direction of legendary city planner Robert Moses.

Between the late 1930s and the late 1960s Moses executed a number of public-works projects, highways, parks, and housing projects that significantly reshaped the profile of New York City. In 1959, city, state, and federal authorities began the implementation of his planned Cross-Bronx Expressway, which would cut directly through the center of the most heavily populated working-class areas in the Bronx. Although he could have modified his route slightly to bypass densely populated working-class ethnic residential communities, he elected a path that required the demolition of hundreds of residential and commercial buildings. In addition, throughout the 1960s and early 1970s, some sixty thousand Bronx homes were razed. Designating these old blue-collar housing units as "slums," Moses's Title I Slum Clearance program forced the relocation of 170,000 people.[13] These "slums" were in fact densely populated stable neighborhoods, comprised mostly of working- and lower-middle-class Jews, but they also contained solid Italian, German, Irish, and black neighborhoods. Although the neighborhoods under attack had a substantial Jewish population, black and Puerto Rican residents were disproportionately affected. Thirty-seven percent of the relocated residents were nonwhite. This, coupled with the subsequent "white flight," devastated kin networks and neighborhood services. Between the late 1960s and mid-1970s, the vacancy rates in the southern section of the Bronx skyrocketed. Some nervous landlords sold their property as quickly as possible, often to professional slumlords; others torched their buildings to collect insurance payments. Both strategies accelerated the flight of white tenants into northern sections of the Bronx and into Westchester. Equally anxious shopkeepers sold their shops and established businesses elsewhere. The city administration, touting Moses's expressway as a sign of progress and modernization, was unwilling to admit the devastation that had occurred. Like many of his public-works projects, Moses's Cross-Bronx Expressway supported the interests of the upper classes against the interests of the poor and intensified the development of the vast economic and social inequalities that characterize contemporary New York. The newly "relocated" black and Hispanic residents in the South Bronx were left with few city resources, fragmented leadership, and limited political power.

The disastrous effects of these city policies went relatively unnoticed in the media until 1977, when two critical events fixed New York and the South Bronx as national symbols of ruin and isolation. During the summer of 1977 an extensive power outage "blacked out" New York and hundreds of stores were looted and vandalized. The poorest neighborhoods (the South Bronx, Bedford-Stuyvesant, Brownsville, and Crown Heights areas in Brooklyn, the Jamaica area in Queens, and Harlem), where most of the looting took place, were depicted by the city's media organs as lawless zones where crime is sanctioned and chaos bubbles just below the surface. The 1965 blackout, according to the New York Times, was "peaceful by contrast," suggesting that the blackout that took place during America's most racially tumultuous decade was no match for the despair and frustration articulated in the blackout of the summer of 1977.[14] The 1977 blackout and the looting that accompanied it seemed to raise the federal stakes in maintaining urban social order. Three months later, President Carter made his "sobering" historic motorcade visit through the South Bronx to "survey the devastation of the last five years," and announced an unspecified "commitment to cities." (Not to their inhabitants?) In the national imagination, the South Bronx became the primary "symbol of America's woes."[15]

Following this lead, images of abandoned buildings in the South Bronx became central popular cultural icons. Negative local color in popular film exploited the devastation facing the residents of the South Bronx and used their communities as a backdrop for social ruin and barbarism. As Michael Ventura astutely notes, these popular depictions (and, I would add, the news coverage as well) rendered silent the people who struggled with and maintained life under difficult conditions: "In roughly six hours of footage—Fort Apache, Wolfen and Koyaanisqatsi—we haven't been introduced to one soul who actually lives in the South Bronx. We haven't heard one voice speaking its own language. We've merely watched a symbol of ruin: the South Bronx [as] last act before the end of the world."[16] Depictions of black and Hispanic neighborhoods were drained of life, energy, and vitality. The message was loud and clear: to be stuck here was to be lost. And yet, while these visions of loss and futility became defining characteristics, the youngest generation of South Bronx exiles was building creative and aggressive outlets for expression and identification. The new ethnic groups who made the South Bronx their home in the 1970s began building their own cultural networks, ones that would prove to be resilient and responsive in the age of high technology.

North American blacks, Jamaicans, Puerto Ricans, and other Caribbean people with roots in other postcolonial contexts reshaped their cultural identities and expressions in a hostile, technologically sophisticated, multi-ethnic, urban terrain. While city leaders and the popular press had literally and figuratively condemned the South Bronx neighborhoods and their inhabitants, its youngest black and Hispanic residents answered back.

Hip Hop

Hip hop culture emerged as a source of alternative identity formation and social status for youth in a community whose older local support institutions had been all but demolished along with large sectors of its built environment. Alternative local identities were forged in fashions, language, street names, and most importantly, in the establishment of neighborhood crews or posses. Many hip hop fans, artists, musicians, and dancers continue to belong to an elaborate system of crews or posses. The crew, a local source of identity, group affiliation, and support, appears in virtually all rap lyrics and cassette dedications, music video performances, and media interviews with artists. Identity in hip hop is deeply rooted in the specific, the local experience, and in one's attachment to and status in a local group or alternative family. These crews are new kinds of families forged with intercultural bonds, which, like the social formation of gangs, provide insulation and support in a complex and unyielding environment and may, in fact, contribute to the community-building networks that serve as the basis for new social movements.

The postindustrial city, which provided the context for creative development among hip hop's earliest innovators, shaped their cultural terrain, access to space, materials, and education. Although graffiti artists' work was significantly aided by advances in spray-paint technology, they used the urban transit system as their canvas. Rappers and DJs disseminated their work by copying it on tape-dubbing equipment and playing it on powerful, portable "ghetto blasters." At a time when budget cuts in school music programs drastically reduced access to traditional forms of instrumentation and composition, inner-city youth increasingly relied on recorded sound. Breakdancers used their bodies to mimic "transformers" and other futuristic robots in symbolic street battles. Early Puerto Rican, Afro-Caribbean, and black American hip hop artists transformed obsolete vocational skills from marginal occupations into the raw materials for creativity and resistance. Many of them were "trained" for jobs in fields that were shrinking or that no

longer existed. Graffiti writer Futura graduated from a trade school specializing in the printing industry. But, since most of the jobs for which he was
being trained had already been computerized, he found himself working at
McDonald's after graduation. Similarly, African-American DJ Red Alert
(who also has family from the Caribbean) reviewed blueprints for a drafting
company until computer automation rendered that job obsolete. Jamaican
DJ Kool Herc attended Alfred E. Smith auto mechanic trade school, while
African-American Grand Master Flash learned how to repair electronic
equipment at Samuel Gompers vocational high school. (One could say Flash
"fixed them alright.") Salt N Pepa (both with family roots in the West Indies)
worked as phone telemarketing representatives at Sears while considering
nursing school. Puerto Rican breakdancer Crazy Legs began breakdancing
largely because his single mother couldn't afford Little League baseball fees.[17]
All of these artists found themselves positioned with few resources in marginal economic circumstances, but each of them found ways to become
famous as entertainers by appropriating the most advanced technologies
and emerging cultural forms. Hip hop artists used the tools of obsolete industrial technology to traverse contemporary crossroads of lack and desire
in urban Afro-diasporic communities.

Stylistic continuities were sustained by internal cross-fertilization between rapping, breakdancing, and graffiti writing. Some writers, such as
black American Phase 2, Haitian Jean-Michel Basquiat, Futura, and black
American Fab Five Freddy, produced rap records. Other writers drew murals
that celebrated favorite rap songs (e.g., Futura's mural *The Breaks* was a
whole car mural that paid homage to Kurtis Blow's rap of the same name).
Breakdancers, DJs, and rappers wore graffiti-painted jackets and T-shirts.
DJ Kool Herc was a graffiti writer and dancer before he began playing
records. Hip hop events featured breakdancers, rappers, and DJs as triple-
bill entertainment. Graffiti writers drew murals for DJs' stage platforms and
designed posters and flyers to advertise hip hop events. Breakdancer Crazy
Legs, founding member of the Rock Steady Crew, describes the communal
atmosphere between writers, rappers, and breakers in the formative years
of hip hop: "Summing it up, basically going to a jam back then was [about]
watching people drink, [break]dance, compare graffiti art in their black
books. These jams were thrown by the [hip hop] DJ. . . . it was about piecing
while a jam was going on."[18] Of course, sharing ideas and styles is not always
a peaceful process. Hip hop is very competitive and confrontational; it
fosters both resistance to and preparation for a hostile world that denies
and denigrates young people of color. Breakdancers often fought other

breakdance crews out of jealousy, writers sometimes destroyed murals, and rapper and DJ battles could break out in fights. Hip hop remains a never-ending battle for status, prestige, and group adoration that is always in formation, always contested, and never fully achieved. Competitions among and cross-fertilization between breaking, graffiti writing, and rap music were fueled by shared local experiences and social position and similarities in approaches to sound, motion, communication, and style among hip hop's Afro-diasporic communities.

As in many African and Afro-diasporic cultural forms, hip hop's prolific self-naming is a form of reinvention and self-definition.[19] Rappers, DJs, graffiti artists, and breakdancers all take on hip hop names and identities that speak to their roles, personal characteristics, expertise, or "claim to fame." DJ names often fuse technology with mastery and style: DJ Cut Creator, Jazzy Jeff, Spindarella, Terminator X Assault Technician, Wiz, and Grand Master Flash. Many rappers have nicknames that suggest street smarts, coolness, power, and supremacy: L. L. Cool J (Ladies Love Cool James), Kool Moe Dee, Queen Latifah, Dougie Fresh (and the Get Fresh Crew), D-Nice, Hurricane Gloria, Guru, MC Lyte, EPMD (Erick and Parrish Making Dollars), Ice-T, Ice Cube, Kid-N-Play, Boss, Eazy-E, King Sun, and Sir Mix-A Lot. Other names serve as self-mocking tags or critique society, such as Too Short, The Fat Boys, S1Ws (Security of the First World), The Lench Mob, NWA (Niggas With Attitude), and Special Ed. The hip hop identities for breakdancers like Crazy Legs, Wiggles, Frosty Freeze, Boogaloo Shrimp, and Headspin highlight their status as experts known for special moves. Taking on new names and identities offered "prestige from below" in the face of limited legitimate access to forms of status attainment.

In addition to the centrality of alternative naming, identity, and group affiliation, rappers, DJs, graffiti writers and breakdancers claim turf and gain local status by developing new styles. As Dick Hebdige's study on punk illustrates, style can be used as a gesture of refusal, or as a form of oblique challenge to structures of domination.[20] Hip hop artists use style as a form of identity formation that plays on class distinctions and hierarchies by using commodities to claim the cultural terrain. Clothing and consumption rituals testify to the power of consumption as a means of cultural expression. Hip hop fashion is an especially rich example of this sort of appropriation/critique via style. Exceptionally large "chunk" gold and diamond jewelry (usually "fake") mocks yet affirms the gold fetish in Western trade; "fake" Gucci and other designer emblems, which are cut up and patch-stitched to jackets, pants, hats, wallets, and sneakers in custom shops, work as a form of sartorial warfare (especially when "fake" Gucci-covered b-boys and b-girls brush past Fifth Avenue ladies adorned by the "real thing"). Hip hop's late 1980s fashion rage—the large plastic (alarm?) clock worn around the neck over leisure/sweat suits—suggested a number of contradictory tensions between work, time, and leisure. Early 1990s trends—oversized pants and urban warrior outer apparel, as in "hoodies," "snooties," "tims," and "triple fat" goose-down coats—make clear the severity of the urban storms to be weathered and the saturation of disposable goods in the crafting of cultural expressions.[21] As an alternative means of status formation, hip hop style forges local identities for teenagers who understand their limited access to traditional avenues of social status. Fab Five Freddy, an early rapper and graffiti writer, explains the link between style and identity in hip hop and its significance for gaining local status:

> You make a new style. That's what life on the street is all about. What's at stake is honor and position on the street. That's what makes it so important, that's what makes it feel so good—that pressure on you to be the best. Or to try to be the best. To develop a new style nobody can deal with. [22]

Styles "nobody can deal with" in graffiti, breaking, and rap music not only boost status and elevate black and Hispanic youth identities, they also articulate several shared approaches to sound and motion that are found in the Afro-diaspora. As black filmmaker and cultural critic Arthur Jafa has pointed out, stylistic continuities between breaking, graffiti style, rapping, and musical construction seem to center around three concepts: *flow, layering,* and *ruptures in line.*[23] In hip hop, visual, physical, musical, and lyrical lines are set in motion, broken abruptly with sharp, angular breaks, and yet sustain motion and energy through fluidity and flow. In graffiti, long winding, sweeping, and curving letters are broken and camouflaged by sudden breaks in line. Sharp, angular, broken letters are written in extreme italics, suggesting forward or backward motion. Letters are double and triple shadowed in such a way as to illustrate energy forces radiating from the center— suggesting circular motion—and yet the scripted words move horizontally.

Breakdancing moves highlight flow, layering, and ruptures in line. Popping and locking are moves in which the joints are snapped abruptly into angular positions. And, yet, these snapping movements take place in one joint after the preceding one—creating a semiliquid effect that moves the energy toward the fingertip or toe. In fact, two dancers may pass the popping energy force back and forth between each other via finger-to-finger contact, setting off a new wave. In this pattern, the line is a series of angular breaks and yet sustains energy and motion through flow. Breakers double each other's moves (like line shadowing or layering in graffiti), intertwine their bodies into elaborate shapes, transforming the body into a new entity (like camouflage in graffiti's wild style), and then, one body part at a time, revert to a relaxed state. Abrupt, fractured, yet graceful footwork leaves the eye one step behind the motion, creating a time-lapse effect that not only mimics graffiti's use of line shadowing, but also creates spatial links between the moves that give the foot series flow and fluidity.[24]

The music and vocal rapping in rap music also privileges flow, layering, and ruptures in line. Rappers speak of flow explicitly in lyrics, referring to an ability to move easily and powerfully through complex lyrics, as well as of the flow in the music.[25] The flow and motion of the initial bass or drum line in rap music is abruptly ruptured by scratching (a process that highlights as it breaks the flow of the base rhythm) or the rhythmic flow is interrupted by other musical passages. Rappers alternately stutter and race through passages, always moving within the beat or in response to it, often using the music as a partner in rhyme. These verbal moves highlight lyrical flow and points of rupture. Rappers layer meaning by using the same word to signify a variety of actions and objects; they call out to the DJ to "lay down a beat," which it is expected will be interrupted, ruptured. DJs layer sounds literally one on top of the other, creating a dialogue between sampled sounds and words.

What is the significance of flow, layering, and rupture as demonstrated on the body and in hip hop's lyrical, musical, and visual works? Interpreting these concepts theoretically, it can be argued that they create and sustain rhythmic motion, continuity, and circularity via flow; accumulate, reinforce, and embellish this continuity through layering; and manage threats to these narratives by building in ruptures that highlight the continuity as they momentarily challenge it. These effects at the level of style and aesthetics suggest affirmative ways in which profound social dislocation and rupture can be managed and perhaps contested in the cultural arena. Let us imagine these hip hop principles as a blueprint for social resistance and affirmation: create sustaining narratives, accumulate them, layer, embellish, and transform them. But also be prepared for rupture, find pleasure in it, in fact, *plan on* social rupture. When these ruptures occur, use them in creative ways that will prepare you for a future in which survival will demand a sudden shift in ground tactics.

While accumulation, flow, circularity, and planned ruptures exist across a wide range of Afro-diasporic cultural forms, they do not take place outside of capitalist commercial constraints. Hip hop's explicit focus on consumption has frequently been mischaracterized as a movement *into* the commodity market (e.g., hip hop is no longer "authentically" black if it is for sale). Instead, hip hop's moment(s) of "incorporation" are a shift in the already existing relationship hip hop has always had to the commodity system. For example, the hip hop DJ frequently produces, amplifies, and revises already recorded sounds; rappers prefer high-end microphones; and both invest serious dollars for the speakers that can produce the "phattest" beats. Graffiti murals, breakdancing moves, and rap lyrics often appropriate and sometimes critique verbal and visual elements and physical movements from popular commercial culture, especially television, comic books, and karate movies. If anything, black style through hip hop has contributed to the continued blackening of mainstream popular culture. The contexts for creation in hip hop are never fully outside or in opposition to commodities; they involve struggles over public space and access to commodified materials, equipment, and products. It is a common misperception among hip hop artists and cultural critics that during the early days, hip hop was motivated by pleasure rather than profit, as if the two were incompatible. Yet, it would be naive to think that breakdancers, rappers, DJs, and writers were never interested in monetary compensation for their work. The problem was not that they were uniformly uninterested in profit; rather, many of the earliest practitioners were unaware that they could profit from their pleasure. Once this link was made, hip hop artists began marketing themselves wholeheartedly. Just as graffiti writers hitched rides on the subways and used its power to distribute their tags, rappers "hijacked" the market for their own purposes, riding the currents that were already out there, not just for wealth but for empowerment. During the late 1970s and early 1980s, the market for hip hop was still based inside New York's black and Hispanic communities. So, although there is an element of truth to this common perception, what is more important about the shift in hip hop's orientation is not its movement from precommodity to commodity but the shift in control over the scope and direction of the profit-making process, out of the hands of local black and Hispanic entrepreneurs and into the hands of larger white-owned, multinational businesses. And, most important, although black cultural imperatives are obviously deeply affected by commodification, these imperatives are not in direct opposition to the market, nor are they "irrelevant" to the shape of market-produced goods and practices.

Hebdige's work on the British punk movement identifies this shift as the moment of incorporation or recuperation by dominant culture and perceives it to be a critical element in the dynamics of the struggle over the meaning(s) of popular expression. "The process of recuperation," Hebdige argues, "takes two characteristic forms . . . one of conversion of subcultural signs (dress, music, etc.) into mass-produced objects and the 'labelling' and redefinition of deviant behavior by dominant groups—the police, media and judiciary." Hebdige astutely points out, however, that communication in a subordinate cultural form, even prior to the point of recuperation, usually takes place via commodities, "even if the meanings attached to those commodities are purposefully distorted or overthrown." And so, he concludes, "it is very difficult to sustain any absolute distinction between commercial exploitation on the one hand and creativity/originality on the other."[26]

Hebdige's observations regarding the process of incorporation and the tension between commercial exploitation and creativity as articulated in British punk is quite relevant to hip hop. Hip hop has always been articulated via commodities and engaged in the revision of meanings attached to them. Conversely, hip hop signs and meanings are converted and behaviors relabeled by dominant institutions. Graffiti, rap, and breakdancing are fundamentally transformed as they move into new relations with dominant cultural institutions.[27] In 1996, rap music is one of the most heavily traded popular commodities in the market, and yet it still defies total corporate control over the music, its local use, and its incorporation at the level of stable or exposed meanings.

These transformations and hybrids reflect the initial spirit of rap and hip hop as an experimental and collective space where contemporary issues and ancestral forces are worked through simultaneously. Hybrids in rap's subject matter, not unlike its use of musical collage, and the influx of new, regional, and ethnic styles have not yet displaced the three points of stylistic continuity to which I referred earlier; approaches to flow, ruptures in line, and layering can still be found in the vast majority of rap's lyrical and musical construction. The same is true of the critiques of the postindustrial urban American context and the cultural and social conditions it has produced. Today, the South Bronx and South Central are poorer and more economically marginalized than they were ten years ago.

Hip hop emerges from complex cultural exchanges and larger social and political conditions of disillusionment and alienation. Graffiti and rap were especially aggressive public displays of counterpresence and voice. Each asserted the right to write[28]—to inscribe one's identity on an environment that seemed Teflon-resistant to its young people of color, an environment that made legitimate avenues for material and social participation inaccessible. In this context, hip hop produced a number of double effects. First, themes in rap and graffiti articulated free play and unchecked public displays, and yet the settings for these expressions always suggested existing confinement.[29] Second, like the consciousness-raising sessions in the early stages of the women's movement and the black power movement of the 1960s and 1970s, hip hop produced internal and external dialogues that affirmed the experiences and identities of the participants and at the same time offered critiques of larger society that were directed to both the hip hop community and society in general.

Out of a broader discursive climate in which the perspectives and experiences of younger Hispanics, Afro-Caribbeans, and African Americans had been provided little social space, hip hop developed as part of a cross-cultural communication network. Trains carried graffiti tags through the five boroughs; flyers posted in black and Hispanic neighborhoods brought teenagers from all over New York to parks and clubs in the Bronx, and eventually to events throughout the metropolitan area; and, characteristic of communication in the age of high-tech telecommunications, stories with cultural and narrative resonance continued to spread at a rapid pace. It was not long before similarly marginalized black and Hispanic communities in other cities picked up on the tenor and energy in New York hip hop. Boom boxes in Roxbury and Compton blasted copies of hip hop mix tapes made on high-speed portable dubbing equipment by cousins from Flatbush Avenue in Brooklyn. The explosion of local and national cable programming of music videos spread hip hop dance steps, clothing, and slang across the country faster than brush fire. Within a decade, Los Angeles County (especially Compton), Oakland, Detroit, Chicago, Houston, Atlanta, Miami, Newark and Trenton, Roxbury, and Philadelphia had developed local hip hop scenes that linked (among other things) various regional postindustrial urban experiences of alienation, unemployment, police harassment, and social and economic isolation to their local and specific experience via hip hop's language, style, and attitude.[30] Regional, and increasingly national, differences and syndications in hip hop have been solidifying and will continue to do so. In some cases these differences are established by references to local streets and events, neighborhoods and leisure activities, preferences for dance steps, clothing, musical samples, and vocal accents. At the same time, cross-regional syndicates of rappers, writers, and dancers fortify hip hop's communal vocabulary. In every region, hip hop articulates a sense of entitlement and takes pleasure in aggressive insubordination. Like Chicago and Mississippi blues, these emerging regional hip hop identities affirm the specificity and local character of cultural forms as well as the larger stylistic forces that define hip hop and Afro-diasporic cultures. Developing a style nobody can deal with—a style that cannot be easily understood or erased, a style that has the reflexivity to create counter-dominant narratives against a mobile and shifting enemy—may be one of the most effective ways to fortify communities of resistance and simultane-ously reserve the right to communal pleasure. With few economic assets and abundant cultural and aesthetic resources, Afro-diasporic youth have designated the street as the arena for competition and style as the prestige-awarding event. In the postindustrial urban context of dwindling low-in-come housing, a trickle of meaningless jobs for young people, mounting police brutality, and increasingly draconian depictions of young inner-city residents, hip hop style *is* black urban renewal.

Notes

This essay is adapted from Tricia Rose, *Black Noise: Rap Music and Black Culture in Contemporary America* (Middletown, Conn.: Wesleyan University Press, 1994).

1. I have adopted Mollenkopf and Castells's use of the term "postindustrial" as a means of characterizing the economic restructuring that has taken place in urban America over the past twenty-five years. By defining the contemporary period in urban economies as postindustrial, Mollenkopf and Castells are not suggesting that manufacturing output has disappeared, nor are they adopting Daniel Bell's formulation that "knowledge has somehow replaced capital as the organizing principle of the economy." Rather, Mollenkopf and Castells claim that their use of postindustrial "captures a crucial aspect of how large cities are being transformed: employ-ment has shifted massively away from manufacturing toward corporate, public and nonprofit services; occupations have similarly shifted from manual workers to managers, professionals, secretaries and service workers" (John Mollenkopf and Manuel Castells, eds., *Dual City: Re-structuring New York* [New York: Russel Sage Foundation, 1991], 6). Similarly, these new post-industrial realities entailing the rapid movement of capital, images, and populations across the globe have also been referred to as "post-Fordism " and "flexible accumulation." See David Harvey, *Social Justice and the City* (Oxford: Basil Blackwell, 1988). For an elaboration of Bell's initial use of the term, see Daniel Bell, *The Coming of Post-Industrial Society* (New York: Basic Books, 1973).

2. My arguments regarding Afro-diasporic cultural formations in hip hop are relevant to African-American culture as well as Afro-diasporic cultures in the English- and Spanish-speak-ing Caribbean, each of which has prominent and significant African-derived cultural elements. While rap music, particularly early rap, is dominated by English-speaking blacks, graffiti and breakdancing were heavily shaped and practiced by Puerto Rican, Dominican, and other Spanish-speaking Caribbean communities that have substantial Afro-diasporic elements. (The emergence of Chicano rappers takes place in the late 1980s in Los Angeles.) Consequently, my references to Spanish-speaking Caribbean communities should in no way be considered incon-sistent with my larger Afro-diasporic claims. Substantial work has illuminated the continued significance of African cultural elements to cultural production in both Spanish- and English-speaking nations in the Caribbean. For examples, see Herbert S. Klein, *African Slavery in Latin America and the Caribbean* (New York: Oxford University Press, 1986); Ivan G. Van Sertima,

They Came before Columbus (New York: Random House, 1976); and Robert Farris Thompson, *Flash of the Spirit* (New York: Random House, 1983).

3. See Allen J. Matusow, *The Unraveling of America: A History of Liberalism in the 1960s* (New York: Harper and Row, 1984).

4. In hip hop, the train serves both as means of interneighborhood communication and as a source of creative inspiration. Big Daddy Kane says that he writes his best lyrics on the subway or train on the way to producer Marly Marl's house. See Barry Michael Cooper, "Raw Like Sushi," *Spin* (March 1988): 28. Similarly, Chuck D claims that he loves to drive, that he would have been a driver if his rapping career hadn't worked out. See Robert Christgau and Greg Tate, "Chuck D All over the Map," *Village Voice*, Rock 'n' Roll Quarterly 4:3 (fall 1991).

5. See John H. Mollenkopf, *The Contested City* (Princeton, N.J.: Princeton University Press, 1983), especially pp. 12–46, for a discussion of larger twentieth-century transformations in U.S. cities throughout the 1970s and into the early 1980s. See also Mollenkopf and Castells, *Dual City*; Michael Peter Smith and Joe R. Feagin, eds., *The Capitalist City: Global Restructuring and Community Politics* (London: Basil Blackwell, 1987); Michael Peter Smith, ed., *Cities in Transformation: Class, Capital and the State* (Beverly Hills, Calif.: Sage Publications, 1984); and Saskia Sassen, *The Mobility of Labor and Capital: A Study in International Investment and Labor Flow* (Cambridge: Cambridge University Press, 1988).

6. I am not suggesting that New York is typical of all urban areas, nor that regional differences are insignificant. However, the broad transformations under discussion here have been felt in all major U.S. cities, particularly New York and Los Angeles—hip hop's second major hub city—and critically frame the transitions that, in part, contributed to hip hop's emergence. In the mid-1980s, very similar postindustrial changes in job opportunities and social services in the Watts and Compton areas of Los Angeles became the impetus for Los Angeles's gangsta rappers. As Robin Kelley notes: "The generation who came of age in the 1980s was the product of devastating structural changes in the urban economy that date back at least to the late 1960s. While the city as a whole experienced unprecedented growth, the communities of Watts and Compton faced increased economic displacement, factory closures, and an unprecedented deepening of poverty. . . . Developers and city and county government helped the suburbanization process along by cutting back expenditures for parks, recreation, and affordable housing in inner city communities" (Robin D. G. Kelley, "Kickin' Reality, Kickin' Ballistics," in *Race Rebels: Politics and the Black Working Class* [New York: Free Press, 1994], 192). See also Mike Davis, *City of Quartz: Excavating the Future of Los Angeles* (London and New York: Verso, 1990).

7. Mollenkopf, *The Contested City*, 213.

8. Frank Van Riper, "Ford to New York: Drop Dead," *Daily News*, 30 October 1975: 1.

9. Philip Weitzman, "'Worlds Apart': Housing, Race/Ethnicity and Income in New York City," Community Service Society of New York (css) (1989). See also Terry J. Rosenberg, "Poverty in New York City: 1980–1985," css (1987); Robert Neuwirth, "Housing after Koch," *Village Voice*, 7 November 1989: 22–24.

10. Mollenkopf and Castells, *Dual City*, 9. See also Parts II and III of the collection, which deal specifically and in greater detail with the forces of transformation, gender, and the new occupational strata.

11. Ben Bagdigian, *The Media Monopoly* (Boston: Beacon Press, 1987). Despite trends toward the centralization of news and media sources and the fact that larger corporate media outfits have proven unable to serve diverse ethnic and racial groups, a recent study on New York's media structure in the 1980s suggests that a wide range of alternative media sources serve New York's ethnic communities. However, the study also shows that black New Yorkers have been less successful in sustaining alternative media channels. See Mitchell Moss and Sarah Ludwig, "The Structure of the Media," in Mollenkopf and Castells, *Dual City*, 245–65.

12. See Tom Forester, *High-Tech Society* (Cambridge: MIT Press, 1988), and Herbert

Schiller, *Culture, Inc.: The Corporate Takeover of Public Expression* (New York: Oxford University Press, 1989).

13. Similar strategies for urban renewal via "slum clearance" demolition took place in a number of major metropolises in the late 1960s and 1970s. See Mollenkopf, *The Contested City*, especially chapter 4, which describes similar processes in Boston and San Francisco.

14. Robert D. McFadden, "Power Failure Blacks Out New York; Thousands Trapped in Subways; Looters and Vandals Hit Some Areas," *New York Times*, 14 July 1977: A1; Lawrence Van Gelder, "State Troopers Sent into City as Crime Rises," *New York Times*, 14 July 1977: A1; Charlayne Hunter-Gault, "When Poverty Is Part of Life, Looting Is Not Condemned," *New York Times*, 15 July 1977: A4; Selwyn Raab, "Ravage Continues Far into Day; Gunfire and Bottles Beset Police," *New York Times*, 15 July 1977: A1; "Social Overload," *New York Times*, editorial, 22 July 1977: A22.

15. Lee Dembart, "Carter Takes 'Sobering' Trip to South Bronx," *New York Times*, 6 October 1977: A1; Richard Severo, "Bronx a Symbol of America's Woes" *New York Times*, 6 October 1977: B18; Joseph P. Fried, "The South Bronx USA: What Carter Saw In New York City Is a Symbol of Complex Social Forces on a Nationwide Scale," *New York Times*, 7 October 1977: A22.

16. Michael Ventura, *Shadow Dancing in the USA* (Los Angeles: J. P. Tarcher Press, 1986), 186. Other popular films from the late 1970s and early 1980s that followed suit included *1990: The Bronx Warriors* and *Escape from New York*. This construction of the dangerous ghetto is central to Tom Wolfe's 1989 best-seller and the subsequent film *Bonfire of the Vanities*. In it, the South Bronx is constructed as an abandoned, lawless territory from the perspective of substantially more privileged white outsiders.

17. Interviews by the author with all artists named except Futura, whose printing trade school experience was cited in Steve Hager, *Hip Hop: The Illustrated History of Breakdancing, Rap Music, and Graffiti* (New York: St. Martin's Press, 1984), 24. These artist interviews were conducted for my book on rap music entitled *Black Noise*.

18. Interview by the author with Crazy Legs, November 1991. "Piecing" means drawing a mural or masterpiece.

19. See Henry Louis Gates Jr., *The Signifying Monkey: A Theory of African-American Literary Criticism* (New York and Oxford: Oxford University Press, 1988). Gates's suggestion that naming be "drawn upon as a metaphor for black intertextuality" is especially useful in hip hop where naming and intertextuality are critical strategies for creative production (see pp. 55, 87).

20. Dick Hebdige, *Subculture: The Meaning of Style* (London: Methuen, 1979). See especially pp. 17–19, 84–89.

21. "Hoodies" are hooded jackets or shirts, "snooties" are skullcaps, and "tims" are Timberland brand boots.

22. Nelson George et al., eds., *Fresh: Hip Hop Don't Stop* (New York: Random House, 1985), 111.

23. Although I had isolated some general points of aesthetic continuity between hip hop's forms, I did not identify these three crucial organizing terms. I am grateful to Arthur Jafa, who shared and discussed the logic of these defining characteristics with me in conversation. He is not, of course, responsible for any inadequacies in my use of them here.

24. For a brilliant example of these moves among recent hip-hop dances, see *Reckin' Shop in Brooklyn*, directed by Diane Martel (Epoch Films, 1992).

25. Some examples of explicit attention to flow are exhibited in Queen Latifah's "Ladies First": "Some think that we can't flow, stereotypes they got to go"; Big Daddy Kane's "Raw": "Intro I start to go, my rhymes will flow so"; and Digital Underground's "Sons of the P": "Release your mind and let your instincts flow, release your mind and let the funk flow" (later, they refer to themselves as the "sons of the flow").

26. Hebdige, *Subculture*, 94–95.

27. Published in 1979, Hebdige's *Subculture* concludes at the point of dominant British culture's initial attempts at incorporating punk. My project examines the points of incorporation and responses that come after the initial moment of incorporation to which Hebdige's study is devoted.

28. See Duncan Smith, "The Truth of Graffiti," *Art & Text* 17: 84–90.

29. For example, Kurtis Blow's "The Breaks" (1980) was both about the seeming inevitability and hardships of unemployment and mounting financial debt and the sheer pleasure of "breaking it up and down," of dancing and breaking free of social and psychological constrictions. Regardless of subject matter, elaborate graffiti tags on train facades always suggest that the power and presence of the image is possible only if the writer has escaped capture.

30. See Bob Mack, "Hip-Hop Map of America," *Spin*, June 1990.

Annotated Bibliography

DARRYL B. DICKSON-CARR

As the myriad essays in this volume have demonstrated, the concept we know as "multiculturalism" has many different interpretations and manifestations. Its place in the evolution of global economics and politics is widely debated; as a result, information about how and where we may find examples of multiculturalism is relatively easy to find. On the other hand, discussions of the *origins* of multiculturalism are much less common. Where such discussions are found, scholars of race and ethnicity are locked in debate over where and when multiculturalism first found a foothold in sociopolitical consciousness. I refer the reader to the Introduction to this volume for one history of the concept.

This bibliography does not attempt to cover the entire history of the term multiculturalism or its antecedents and variants. That effort would require a bibliography easily several times the size of this one, and could only serve to overwhelm the reader with confusing choices. Rather, this bibliography surveys a selection of the more prescient and salient documents that explore the basic (and occasionally far more complicated) terms of the debate on multiculturalism and its social purposes. The categories that divide the bibliography are designed to touch upon those areas in American culture where different understandings of multiculturalism have been contested and (to one degree or another) implemented. Furthermore, the texts listed offer a sampling of some of the most common places where different brands of multiculturalism (ranging from corporate "diversity management" training to educational guidelines) are currently found and have been found over the last twenty-five years.

What becomes readily apparent as one surveys the resources listed here is that most discussants of multiculturalism or racial and ethnic matters are making serious attempts to achieve a semblance of social justice, whether that justice be achieved in the political, social, or economic arenas, or at least to make living and working communities appear more egalitarian. In the vast majority of these cases, the authors of a given book or article view *education* as the key to sociopolitical equity for a given racial or ethnic group. This education may take the form of education in the public school system, a university education, or a (re)orientation with the needs of racial/ethnic employees and business partners in the workplace.

Since education is the basic key to multiculturalism's success or failure in the public domain, it might be expected that the most abundant category for materials on multiculturalism is "Multiculturalism in Primary and Secondary Education." This is the area where ideas and discussions of multiculturalisms caused the least anguish and produced the most extensive work. Many of these works are direct or distant descendants of the integration-oriented civil rights era, during which, at least initially, the most pressing issue for politicians and educators was intelligent enforcement of school desegregation. As the civil rights movement became more complicated, however, educators began to perceive that inequities in schools and educational quality were the result not only of segregation but also of prejudices that teachers and administrators may have held against students of color and of the absence of a school system where people of color could have control of their own schools. The latter turned out to be a more radical notion of restructuring the school system, but the former has been served very well by the articles listed here, in which authors frequently demonstrate the many ways that educators have been biased against their constituencies and suggest methods for overcoming or correcting those biases.

As physical desegregation became a slightly more tangible reality in American schools, educators (particularly educators of color) began to reassess the means of making children from disenfranchised racial groups as well as their white counterparts feel more comfortable with one another and with their peers' histories, since the lessons in children's formative years regarding racial, ethnic, and other social matters are probably the most thoroughly entrenched. The period extending from the early 1970s through the mid-1980s saw a wealth of books and articles on multicultural education that attempted to encourage the changes in education already noted; in recent years (when the debate on multiculturalism has escalated) this wealth has become a veritable flurry. The reader, however, should be aware that most of the work on multicultural education seeks the common end of providing an education sensitive to the cultural situation of children of color. More often than not, differences occur in the strategy for attaining an egalitarian educational system rather than in the general goal itself. This does not mean, though, that it is not necessary to read a variety of texts to understand what needs to be set in motion for multiculturalism to succeed; not all of the strategies mentioned earlier are equally applicable to all parts of the populace, and most could use the supplementary views of alternative texts. In fact, the wisest reading strategy would be to pick texts from different periods (for example, one from the early 1970s, one from later in the decade, one from the early 1980s, and so on), inasmuch as it is helpful to review approaches that may have been discarded in favor of less controversial ideas.

Of further note should be the fact that even multicultural education at the public school level has come under fire in recent years, though not nearly to the degree that its cousin at the college level has. The idea of revising the manner in which colleges teach and hire (and, by extension, *who* they teach and hire and *what* they teach, as well as *how* they teach it) is one of never-ending debate, but the racial portion of this debate began to simmer in the late 1960s (especially at such campuses as Berkeley, the University of California, Santa Barbara, and Howard), when students and professors (many of color) registered some of the first demands for Black Studies and Chicano/Latino Studies departments and courses. Such demands had enormous implications, since the country's universities are generally considered training grounds and test labs for ideas that could affect the rest of the nation. Appropriately, then, the category of "Multiculturalism in Higher Education" signals a tenuous link between the topics of primary education and the others, inasmuch as it covers teaching methods, policy, educational opportunities, and hiring at the university level. A few of the authors that have worked on multiculturalism in primary schools have contributed to discussions of university policy and pedagogy (most notably Donna M. Gollnick). But by and large, the scholars writing about these areas tend not to exchange ideas. Perhaps one reason for this separation of resources is that the most sincere and widespread concern for making American institutions reflect the composition and needs of all levels of the nation's population has reached the university primarily within the last decade. In that time, educators have made penetrating observations and studies of the university environment and its potential for enacting multicultural policies. Central to the incorporation of multiculturalism into university policies and practices is the issue of affirmative action in all its permutations. Although most of the texts under the higher education rubric touch upon this issue along the way, it is one that needs further exploration, since affirmative action is perhaps the most divisive (and therefore the most crucial) component in the multiculturalism debate occurring within academia's halls.

In fact, multiculturalism-oriented policies in American universities have provided more grist for the antimulticulturalism mill than they have at any other societal level. It should come as no surprise, then, that most of the entries under "The Multiculturalism Debates" focus on the university. These articles or essays represent the more staunchly rhetorical, and (in some cases) even demagogic, voices concerned with American racial matters, especially those that emerged within the last decade in the forefront of the debates. We have culled most of these articles and books from the more "mainstream" portion of the mass media, such as newsmagazines or the more popular academic journals. Within these publications, the multiculturalism debate has engendered the most widespread attention (or notoriety), to say nothing of generating considerable heat. A substantial number of these polemics, however, are in want of serious historical scholarship, whether they be for or against multiculturalism. A curious facet of the debate waged in the popular press is an unsettling tendency for antimulticultural critics to lump multiculturalism in the same camp with Afrocentrism or other ethnocentric theories, even if those theories have demonstrated a marked aversion to being truly multicultural (that is, to looking at history from multiracial points of view). Not unlike the resistance to the physical integration of African Americans into the mainstream university environment, the antimulticulturalism approach in the polemics marks a stubborn and often poorly thought-out resistance to, even a backlash against, the integration of ideas fostered by African Americans. This trend is especially problematic insofar as the American public is led to believe that the work of Afrocentrists, whether right or wrong, is synonymous with multiculturalism, and this frequently leads to a rejection of multiculturalism at all levels of society, including primary and secondary education. These articles and their authors will probably continue to produce the most controversial statements and wield the greatest influence on public opinion as scholars continue to debate multiculturalism.

A less discussed, though no less essential, area of the multiculturalism phenomenon is "Multiculturalism in the Corporate World." One of the central demands of virtually all social protest movements, such as those that preceded and emerged from the activism of the 1960s, has been for jobs, or equal access to jobs, for oppressed groups. As the social, racial, and class dynamics of both the United States and the world in the 1960s transformed into those of the 1970s and 1980s, private corporations began to adjust their business policies to accommodate some of the demands and needs of a racially shifting labor pool, one that began to include significantly more African, Asian, and Latino Americans. Given the reluctance of the American workforce to include these groups in everyday operations, corporations were forced, whether by the government or from within, to make greater efforts to cope with a slightly more diverse workforce. These coping mechanisms, however, were and are not necessarily intended to be more inclusive corporate policies; rather, many of them are intended to defuse conflicts within the workforce, to enforce an artificial peace. Additionally, "diversity management" texts generally do not provide much more than cursory histories of corporate multiculturalism. Rather, they tend to act as instructional "textbooks" for implementing specific management methods. And pursuant to those goals, numerous authors (many of whom are full-time consultants) have produced volumes that explain these methods in incredible detail for managers of all levels in order to make their intra- and interbusiness relations run more smoothly through cultural awareness. Notable authors in this vein include Farid Elashmawi, Pierre Casse, and Muriel James. Of further note should be the recent publication dates of these authors' works. "Diversity management" is a relatively young development under the multiculturalism rubric, one that has yet to be extensively interrogated and explored.

On the other hand, the topic of "Multiculturalism in the Humanities," not unlike "The Multiculturalism Debates," has been extensively mined by academics. Given the fact that the focus of pro- and antimulticulturalism discourse has been on considerations of canonicity in literature, curriculum, and program structures in the university and of the infusion of divergent politics into everyday life on the American campus, it makes sense that those academic disciplines most apt to call for and extend these discourses should produce numerous texts on multiculturalism. Most of the works placed under this category fill considerable numbers of pages discussing, undermining, and revising the notion of multiculturalism or complicated issues of race tangential to the current debate. Very few, however, engage the logistical issues of *pedagogy* with the kind of rigor that Betty E. M. Ch'maj's

Multicultural America does. The predominant trend, instead, is to review the past and current policies and politics of integrating different definitions and practices of multiculturalism into the classroom. Henry Louis Gates Jr.'s collection of essays reviewing the controversy over canonicity offers a fair summary of the pedagogical issues on the American campus, while Reginald Martin's interview of author and scholar Ishmael Reed provides an insight into a definition of multiculturalism in the early 1980s. Additionally, the entire January–February 1992 issue of *Change* magazine includes some of the most insightful and practical histories and applications of multicultural pedagogy produced since the controversy around the term arose. Many scholars in this category have formulated their perspectives from different kinds of race theory, which, instead of discussing what multiculturalism might mean or how it might be practiced in general, revolve around *specific* racial and/or ethnic groups and question the very idea of "race" and its history as a social and political concept. Unfortunately, many serious race theorists (and the articles we have culled from them) are ensconced in ethnic or racial studies departments (and journals or presses), such as Black/African-American Studies, Asian-American Studies, or Chicano/Latino Studies programs and departments, which may prevent their work from receiving its due notice from the rest of the scholarly community. Additionally, many of these volumes have been produced within the last few years. This phenomenon is partially attributable to the fact that scholars of race and ethnicity have only recently begun to discuss the relation of racial histories to the concept of multiculturalism.

"Multiculturalism in Society and Public Policy," while a relatively short list, is as important as the education-oriented areas. Here, the majority of texts center on how federal, state, and local agencies and institutions might be able to address the problems that are endemic to particular racial or ethnic groups in the United States. Legislative bodies, welfare systems, the legal profession, and other forms of public social organization find themselves increasingly burdened with demands to accommodate the needs of different social or racial groups that cannot be covered through "blanket" measures. The reaction to this demand takes the form of increased study of the economic and political conditions that lead to certain groups' difficulties with navigating bureaucratic institutions. Such texts as Clausen and Bermingham's *Pluralism, Racism, and Public Policy* or Michael Omi and Howard Winant's *Racial Formation in the United States* help to delimit some of the general issues facing public policymakers. The remainder of the texts in this area, however, tackle more specific institutions and problems, the selection of which shall be left to the reader.

As the reader begins to pick and choose among these numerous rubrics, s/he will notice that the tone of the arguments, as well as the intentions of the proponents and opponents of multiculturalism, shift considerably between areas. For example, the sorts of issues at stake in implementing multiculturalism at the university level tend to be much more complex, or at least more acrimonious, than those at the primary educational level. This is not to say that one is somehow less important than the other by virtue of being less fraught. But whereas the primary and secondary levels are often concerned with pedagogical methods that accommodate a diverse general populace, the college and university levels are often concerned with diminishing resources, whether financial, cultural, ideological, or otherwise, for which a few impassioned groups must continually struggle. One of the principal concerns of corporate multiculturalism, on the other hand, is maintaining control of a potentially and practically volatile workforce.

So when, therefore, we encounter the term multiculturalism at any point in general public discourse or within these texts, we must force ourselves to consider the social realm in which the term appears. To transfer the same sorts of sociopolitical considerations from one area where they have full validity to another could prove to be disastrous and confusing. Although it is simultaneously true that some common ground exists between the various areas, such as the calls for education or affirmative action mentioned earlier, the relationships between each become more complicated beyond these few common points. Only by undertaking thorough and particularistic inquiries into the many uses of the concept and practice of multiculturalism could we discern to what degree it not only is working but *could* work with our support.

I. The Multiculturalism Debates

Adams, Willi Paul. "U.S. Fears of Multiculturalism are Unfounded." *Public Affairs Report* 32:2 (1991).

"An American Culture." *National Review* 43 (1991): 18.

Asante, Molefi Kete. *The Afrocentric Idea*. Philadelphia: Temple University Press, 1987.

———. *Afrocentricity: The Theory of Social Change*. Buffalo, N.Y.: Amulefi, 1980.

———. "Multiculturalism: An Exchange." *American Scholar* 60 (spring 1991): 267–72.

Auster, Lawrence. "The Forbidden Topic." *National Review* 44 (1992): 42–44. This article draws links between multiculturalism and immigration.

Brustein, Robert. "The Use and Abuse of Multiculturalism." *New Republic* 205 (1991): 31–34.

Contention: Debates in Society, Culture and Science 1:3 (1992).

Decter, Midge. "E Pluribus Nihil: Multiculturalism and Black Children." *Commentary* 92 (1991): 25–29.

Draper, Roger. "P.C. Pipe Dreams." *New Leader* 75 (1992): 16–17.
D'Souza, Dinesh. "Multiculturalism 101: Great Books of the Non-Western World." *Policy Review* 56 (1991): 22–30.
Erickson, Peter. "What Multiculturalism Means." *Transition: An International Review* 55 (1991): 105–14.
Fraser, Laura. "The Tyranny of the Media Correct." *San Francisco Bay Guardian* (17 April 1991).
Gates, Henry Louis, Jr. *Loose Canons: Notes on the Culture Wars.* New York: Oxford University Press, 1992.
Hacker, Andrew. "Multiculturalism and Its Discontents." *Black Scholar* 24:1 (1994): 16–17.
———. *Two Nations: Black, White, Separate, Hostile, Unequal.* New York: Scribner's, 1992.
Hughes, Robert. "The Fraying of America." *Time* 139:3 (February 1992): 44–49.
Jay, Gregory. "Liberalism and Multiculturalism." *Democratic Culture* 2:1 (1993): 10.
Jones, Malcolm. "It's a Not So Small World." *Newsweek* 118:9 (September 1991): 64–65.
Leo, John. "The Words of the Culture War." *U.S. News & World Report* 111 (28 October 1991): 31.
Marable, Manning. *Black America: Multicultural Democracy in the Age of Clarence Thomas, David Duke and the L.A. Uprisings.* Westfield, N.J.: Open Media, 1992.
Maudlin, Michael G. "Now That's Multicultural!" *Christianity Today* 36 (13 January 1992): 15.
Nelson, Cary. "Canon Fodder: An Evening with William Bennett, Lynne Cheney, and Dinesh D'Souza." *Works and Days: Essays in the Socio-Historical Dimensions of Literature and the Arts* 9:2 (1991): 39–54.
Plagens, Peter. "Multiculturalism or Bust, Gang." *Newsweek* 116 (24 September 1990): 68–69.
Ravitch, Diane. "Multiculturalism." *American Scholar* 59 (summer 1990): 337–54.
———. "Multiculturalism: An Exchange." *American Scholar* 60 (spring 1991): 267–76.
———. "Multiculturalism or Cultural Separatism: The Choice Is Ours." *New Perspectives Quarterly* 8 (fall 1991): 79.
Royal, Robert. *1492 and All That: Political Manipulations of History.* Washington, D.C.: Ethics and Public Policy Center, 1992.
Schlesinger, Arthur M., Jr. *The Disuniting of America.* The Larger Agenda Series. Knoxville, Tenn.: Whittle Direct Books, 1991.
———. "Multiculturalism or Cultural Separatism: The Choice Is Ours." *New Perspectives Quarterly* 8 (fall 1991): 79.
Siegel, Frederick F. "The Cult of Multiculturalism." *New Republic* 204 (18 February 1991): 34ff.
Stimpson, Catharine R. "Multiculturalism: A Big Word at the Presses." *New York Times Book Review* 96 (22 September 1991): 1ff.
Terkel, Studs. *Race: How Blacks and Whites Think and Feel about the American Obsession.* New York: Anchor Press, 1992.
Trachtenberg, Stephen. "Multiculturalism Can Be Taught Only by Multicultural People." *Phi Delta Kappan* 71 (April 1990): 610–11.
Walljasper, Jay. "Multiculturalism and Me." *Utne Reader* (November–December 1991): 154–55.
Willie, Charles Vert. "Multiculturalism Bashing: A Review of Magazine Coverage." *Change* 24 (January–February 1992): 70–73. The entire issue of *Change* (a magazine for educators) from which this article emerges is an excellent source for discussions of multiculturalism in education. It covers many of the primary points of the debates for any educator who is attempting to get a grasp of the current (that is, as of early 1992) political and logistical facets at all educational levels. This is *not*, however, an entirely pro-multiculturalism issue. Willie's article, unfortunately, does not live up to the title, if one is expecting a review of *all* recent magazine coverage. Instead, this article summarizes other articles that appeared in the *New Republic*'s 18 February 1991 special issue on multiculturalism. Willie picks out a

few of the more problematic antimulticulturalism articles and discusses their considerable leaps of logic and lack of proof. Interestingly, Willie is pretty polemical himself, especially at the end of the article, when he makes a very rough transition from his discussion of multiculturalism to political correctness.

II. Multiculturalism in Operation

A. In the Arts and Museums

Adams, Robert McCormick. "The Central Challenge for Museums Today May Be to Find Ways to Address the Increasing Diversity of Our Society." *Smithsonian* 23 (April 1992): 13–14.

Bamberger, Joan. "Reclaiming Traditions: A Symposium on Craft Revivals Points to the Multiculturalism of Today." *American Craft* 51 (August–September 1991): 74–77.

Cembalest, Robin. "Goodbye, Columbus?" *Art News* 90 (October 1991): 104–9.

Chong, Ping. "Notes for 'Mumbling and Digressions: Some Thoughts on Being an Artist, Being an American, Being a Witness. . . .'" *MELUS* 16:3 (1989): 62–67.

Ciani, Kyle Emily. "The Machado Quilt: A Study in Multi-Cultural Folk Art." *Uncoverings: Research Papers of the American Quilt Study Group* 12 (1991): 190–207.

Clinton, Michelle T., Sesshu Foster, and Naomi Quinonez, eds. *Invocation L.A.: Urban Multicultural Poetry.* Albuquerque, N.M.: West End Press, 1989.

Foster, Sesshu. "Fresh Harvest: New Multicultural Poetry by and about Workers." *Northwest Review* 28:2 (1990): 146–54.

Galinsky, Karl. *Classical and Modern Interactions: Postmodern Architecture, Multiculturalism, Decline, and Other Issues.* Austin: University of Texas Press, 1992.

Gibbins, John Joseph. "The American Theatre's Attempts to Achieve Multiculturalism on Stage through Non-Traditional Casting." Ph.D. diss., Northwestern University, 1992.

Glidden, Robert. "Finding the Balance." *Design for Arts in Education* 91 (May–June 1990): 2–13.

King, Edith W. "Using Museums for More Effective Teaching of Ethnic Relations." *Teaching Sociology* 20:2 (1992): 114–20.

La Duke, Betty. *Women Artists: Multi-Cultural Visions.* Trenton, N.J.: Red Sea Press, 1992.

Lippard, Lucy R. *Mixed Blessings: New Art in a Multicultural America.* New York: Pantheon Books, 1990.

Mason, Rachel. *Art Education and Multiculturalism.* London and New York: Croom Helm, 1988.

Multicultural Focus: An Exhibition of Photography for the Los Angeles Bicentennial: Municipal Art Gallery, Barnsdall Park, January 27–February 22, 1981. Santa Monica, Calif.: The Center, 1981.

Rodriguez, Fred. "Cultural Pluralism and the Arts: Designing Multicultural Materials for Music Educators." *Design for Arts in Education* 86 (March–April 1985): 38–42.

Rodriguez, Luis J. "Living on the Hyphen: Multicultural Diversity in the Arts." *Mid-American Review* 12:1 (1991): 3–7.

Sacramento Metropolitan Arts Commission. *New and Emerging Organizations Pilot Program: Phase I, Technical Assistance to Multi-Cultural Groups, 1987.* Sacramento, Calif.: Sacramento Metropolitan Arts Commission, 1987.

Schuman, Jo Miles. *Art from Many Hands: Multicultural Art Projects for Home and School.* Englewood Cliffs, N.J.: Prentice Hall, 1981.

B. In Primary and Secondary Education

Adler, Sol. *Multicultural Communication Skills in the Classroom.* Boston: Allyn and Bacon, 1993.

Alderson, Brian. "Lone Voices in the Crowd: The Limits of Multiculturalism." In *Cross-Culturalism in Children's Literature: Selected Papers from the Children's Literature Association, Carle-*

ton University, Ottawa, Canada, ed. Susan R. Gannon and Ruth Anne Thompson. New York: Pace University Press, 1988. 5–10.

American Association of Colleges for Teacher Education, Commission on Multicultural Education. *Directory of Multicultural Education Programs in Teacher Education Institutions in the United States, 1978.* Washington, D.C.: Accreditation Standards for Multicultural Teacher Education Project, AACTE, 1978.

The American Tapestry: Educating a Nation: A Guide to Infusing Multiculturalism into American Education. Alexandria, Va.: National Association of State Boards of Education, 1991.

Arora, R. K., and C. G. Duncan. *Multicultural Education: Towards Good Practice.* London and Boston: Routledge and Kegan Paul, 1986.

Au, Kathryn Hu-Pei. *Literacy Instruction in Multicultural Settings.* Fort Worth, Tex.: Harcourt Brace Jovanovich, 1993.

Bagley, Christopher. "Cultural Diversity, Migration, and Cognitive Styles: A Study of British, Japanese, Jamaican, and Indian Children." In Verma and Bagley, 217–46.

Baker, Gwendolyn C. *Planning and Organizing for Multicultural Instruction.* Reading, Mass.: Addison-Wesley, 1983.

Banfield, Beryle. *Black Focus on Multicultural Education: How to Develop an Anti-Racist, Anti-Sexist Curriculum.* New York: E. W. Blyden Press, 1979.

Banks, James A., and Cherry A. McGee Banks, eds. *Multicultural Education: Issues and Perspectives.* 2d ed. Boston: Allyn and Bacon, 1993.

Banks, James A., and James Lynch, eds. *Multicultural Education in Western Societies.* New York: Praeger, 1986.

Baptiste, H. Prentice, Jr. *Multicultural Education: A Synopsis.* 2d ed. Washington, D.C.: University Press of America, 1979.

Baptiste, H. Prentice, Jr., and Mira Lanier Baptiste, eds. *Developing the Multicultural Process in Classroom Instruction: Competencies for Teachers.* Washington, D.C.: University Press of America, 1979.

Bennett, Christine I. *Comprehensive Multicultural Education: Theory and Practice.* Boston: Allyn and Bacon, 1986.

Bodnar, John E., Vandra Masemann, and Ray C. Rist. *Multicultural Education: Perspectives for the 1980s.* Buffalo, N.Y.: Department of Social Foundations and Comparative Education Center, Faculty of Educational Studies, State University of New York at Buffalo, 1981.

Boyer, James. *Multicultural Education: From Product to Process.* New York: ERIC Clearinghouse on Urban Education, Institute for Urban and Minority Education, Teachers College, Columbia University, 1983.

Broadbent, John. *Assessment in a Multicultural Society: Community Languages at 16+: A Discussion Document.* York, England: Longman for Schools Council, 1983.

Brown, Daphne M. *Mother Tongue to English: The Young Child in the Multicultural School.* Cambridge, England, and New York: Cambridge University Press, 1979.

Bull, Barry L., Royal T. Fruehling, and Virgie Chattergy. *The Ethics of Multicultural and Bilingual Education.* New York: Teachers College Press, 1992.

California Association of School Librarians, Human Relations Committee. *Words Like Freedom: A Multi-Cultural Bibliography.* Burlingame: California Association of School Librarians, 1975.

California State Department of Education, Bureau of Intergroup Relations. *Guide for Multicultural Education: Content and Context.* Sacramento: California State Department of Education, 1977.

California State Department of Education, Office of Intergroup Relations. *Planning for Multicultural Education as a Part of School Improvement.* Sacramento: California State Department of Education, 1979.

Caliguri, Joseph P., Jack P. Krueger, and Young Pai. *An Annotated Bibliographical Guide to the Literature on Bilingualism and Multicultural Education.* Kansas City: School of Education, University of Missouri, 1980.

Cardenas, Jose Angel. *Multicultural Education: An Annotated Bibliography.* San Antonio, Tex.: Intercultural Development Research Association, 1976.

Chace, William M. "The Real Challenge of Multiculturalism." *Education Digest* 56 (May 1991): 34–36.

Chambers, Joanna Fountain. *Hey, Miss! You Got a Book for Me? A Model Multicultural Resource Collection Annotated Bibliography.* 2d ed., rev. and expanded. Austin, Tex.: Austin Bilingual Language Editions, 1981.

Cohen, David, and Monroe D. Cohen, eds. *Louis Armstrong Middle School (East Elmhurst, N.Y.) Resources for Valuing Diversity: The Louis Armstrong Middle School (I.S. 227Q) Multicultural Collection.* East Elmhurst, N.Y.: Louis Armstrong Middle School, 1990.

Colangelo, Nicholas, Dick Dustin, and Cecelia H. Foxley. *The Human Relations Experience: Exercises in Multicultural, Nonsexist Education.* Monterey, Calif.: Brooks/Cole Publishing Company, 1982.

———, eds. *Multicultural Nonsexist Education: A Human Relations Approach.* 2d ed. Dubuque, Iowa: Kendall/Hunt Publishing Company, 1985.

Cross, Dolores E., Gwendolyn C. Baker, and Lindley J. Stiles, eds. *Teaching in a Multicultural Society: Perspectives and Professional Strategies.* New York: Free Press, 1977. This anthology is divided into three parts, all devoted to arguing for multicultural education, but each with a different emphasis. The first contains essays that provide histories of and arguments for cultural diversity in general, and is eventually linked to the need for multicultural education, the focus of the second section. The third section outlines strategies for implementing the proposals of the second section. Three essays are particularly intriguing and informative: Meyer Weinberg's "A Historical Framework for Multicultural Education," James Deslonde's "You Know the Rules! Myths about Desegregation," and Asa Hilliard's "Intellectual Strengths of Minority Children," all of which argue for changes in teacher attitudes as precursors for improved education.

Current, Richard N. "The 'New Ethnicity' and American History: Wisconsin as a Test Case." *History Teacher* 15:1 (1981): 43–50.

Diaz, Carlos, ed. *Multicultural Education for the 21st Century.* Washington, D.C.: NEA Professional Library, National Education Association, 1992.

Diversity in Teacher Education: New Expectations. San Francisco: Jossey-Bass Publishers, 1992.

Everstz, Linda Cathryn. "Textbooks in a Multicultural Society: A Look at the 1990 Social Studies Textbook Adoption in the State of California." Ph.D. diss., University of California, 1992.

Ferguson, Henry. *Manual for Multicultural and Ethnic Studies: A Survival Manual for the Innovative Leader.* Thompson, Conn.: InterCultural Press, 1977.

———. *Manual for Multicultural Education.* 2d ed. Thompson, Conn.: InterCultural Press, 1987.

"Focus: Multiculturalism in Education." *Education Digest* 57 (December 1991): 3–16.

Forbes, Jack D. *The Education of the Culturally Different: A Multi-Cultural Approach.* Berkeley: Far Laboratory for Educational Research and Development, 1968.

Fradd, Sandra H. *Foundations of Multicultural Education.* Gainesville: Department of Special Education, University of Florida; Washington, D.C.: U.S. Department of Education, Office of Educational Research and Improvement, Educational Resources Information Center, 1990.

Gibson, Margaret Alison. "Approaches to Multicultural Education in the United States: Some Concepts and Assumptions." *Anthropology and Education Quarterly* 15:1 (1984): 94–120.

Gold, Milton J., Carl A. Grant, and Harry N. Rivlin, eds. *In Praise of Diversity: A Resource Book for Multicultural Education.* Washington, D.C.: Teacher Corps, 1977.

Gollnick, Donna M. *Profile of the Multicultural/Bilingual Education Activities of Professional and Related Education Organizations.* Washington, D.C.: American Association of Colleges for Teacher Education, 1978.

Gollnick, Donna M., and Philip C. Chinn. *Multicultural Education in a Pluralistic Society.* 3d ed. Columbus, Ohio: Merrill Publishing Company, 1990.

———, eds. *Multiculturalism in Contemporary Education. Viewpoints in Teaching and Learning* 56:1. Bloomington: School of Education, Indiana University, 1980.

Gomez, Gloria. *An Introductory Guide to Bilingual-Bicultural/Multicultural Education: Beyond Tacos, Eggrolls and Grits.* Dubuque, Iowa: Kendall/Hunt Publishing Company, 1982.

Grant, Carl A., ed. *Multicultural Education: Commitments, Issues, and Applications.* Prepared by the Association for Supervision and Curriculum Development, Multicultural Education Commission. Washington, D.C.: Association for Supervision and Curriculum Development, 1977. This volume is one of several that emerged just as the popular understandings of both cultural pluralism and multiculturalism were changing in the 1970s. As a manifesto calling for necessary changes in the educational system, it rejects the notion that multicultural education should reify a "dominant school culture." Rather, Grant sees an awareness of cultural pluralism's benefits as the direct antecedent to implementing a truly multicultural educational system. Most of the short essays included in the volume follow this basic philosophy, and tend to be written by scholars of color exploring such issues as funding, racial justice, stereotypes, and sexism in education.

———. *Sifting and Winnowing: An Exploration of the Relationship between Multi-Cultural Education and* CBTE [Competency-Based Teacher Education]. Madison: Teacher Corps Associates, University of Wisconsin, 1975.

Grant, Carl A., and Christine E. Sleeter. *Turning on Learning: Five Approaches for Multicultural Teaching Plans for Race, Class, Gender, and Disability.* Columbus, Ohio: Merrill Publishing Company, 1989.

Grant, Gloria, ed. *In Praise of Diversity: Multicultural Classroom Applications.* Omaha: Teacher Corps, Center for Urban Education, University of Nebraska, 1977.

Hallman, Clemens L. *Implications of Psychological Research for Assessment and Instruction of the Culturally Different: Bilingual Multicultural Education Training Project for School Psychologists and Guidance Counselors.* Gainesville: University of Florida Press, 1983.

Hallman, Clemens L., Antonette Capaz, and David Capaz. *Value Orientations of Vietnamese Culture: Bilingual Multicultural Education Training Project for School Psychologists and Guidance Counselors.* Gainesville: University of Florida Press, 1983.

Heid, Camilla A., ed. *Multicultural Education: Knowledge and Perceptions.* Bloomington: Indiana University, Center for Urban and Multicultural Education; Washington, D.C.: U.S. Department of Education, Office of Educational Research and Improvement, Educational Resources Information Center, 1988.

Hernandez, Hilda. *Multicultural Education: A Teacher's Guide to Content and Process.* Columbus, Ohio: Merrill Publishing Company, 1989.

Hill, Patrick J. "Multi-Culturalism: The Crucial Philosophical and Organizational Issues." *Change* 23:4 (1991): 38–47.

Hymowitz, Kay S. "Self-Esteem and Multiculturalism in the Public Schools." *Dissent* 39:1 (1992): 23–29.

Johnson, Lauri, and Sally Smith. *Dealing with Diversity through Multicultural Fiction: Library-Classroom Partnerships.* Chicago: American Library Association, 1993.

Kalantzis, Mary, and Bill Cope. "Pluralism and Equitability: Multicultural Curriculum Strategies for Schools." *Curriculum and Teaching* 4:1 (1989): 3–20.

Kendall, Frances E. *Diversity in the Classroom: A Multicultural Approach to the Education of Young Children.* New York: Teachers College Press, 1983.

Kohl, Herbert. "The Politically Correct Bypass Multiculturalism and the Public Schools." *Social Policy* 22:1 (1991): 33–40.

Kruse, Ginny Moore, and Kathleen T. Horning, with Merri V. Lindgren. *Multicultural Literature for Children and Young Adults: A Selected Listing of Books, 1980-1990, by and about People of Color.* 3d ed. Madison: Wisconsin Department of Public Instruction, 1991.

Kwak, Kyunghwa. "Second Language Learning in a Multicultural Society: A Comparison between the Learning of a Dominant Language and a Heritage Language." Ph.D. diss., Queens University, 1992.

Lambert, Wallace E., and Donald M. Taylor. "Assimilation versus Multiculturalism: The Views of Urban Americans." *Sociological Forum* 3:1 (1988): 72–88.

Lawless, Ken. *Harvesting the Harvesters. Book 10: Cooling Down the Melting Pot: Bilingualism and Multiculturalism.* Potsdam, N.Y.: MENTOR, Potsdam College, 1986.

Levine, Arthur, and Jeannette Cureton. "The Quiet Revolution: Eleven Facts about Multiculturalism and the Curriculum." *Change* 23:4 (1991): 24–29. This easily accessible article lays out the basic issues at stake in the multiculturalism debates. It offers an excellent starting point for those interested in discovering how multiculturalism is impacting or will impact education at all levels of the educational system.

Levy, Berlowitz Ruth. "Interpreting in Multicultural Settings." In *Interpreting—Yesterday, Today and Tomorrow,* ed. David Bowen and Margareta Bowen. Binghamton: State University of New York Press, 1990. 117–21.

Linskie, Rosella, and Howard Rosenberg. *A Handbook for Multicultural Studies in Elementary Schools.* San Francisco: R & E Research Associates, 1978. This book is an elementary teacher's guide for devising exercises that will incorporate the experiences and knowledge of ethnic/racial students into everyday classroom life. It includes illustrations, examples, and detailed, clear instructions.

Lipsky, William E., ed. *Planning for Multicultural Education: A Workshop Report.* Los Angeles: Curriculum Inquiry Center, University of California, 1977.

Love, Roni Lerner. "Motivating Teachers: An Individualized Approach to Implementing a Multicultural Curriculum." Ph.D. diss., University of California, Irvine, 1977.

Lynch, James. *Education for Citizenship in a Multicultural Society.* London and New York: Cassell, 1992.

———. *The Multicultural Curriculum.* London: Batsford Academic and Educational, 1983.

———. *Multicultural Education in a Global Society.* London: Falmer Press, 1989.

———. *Multicultural Education: Principles and Practice.* London and Boston: Routledge and Kegan Paul, 1986.

MacGregor, Molly Murphy. *National Women's History Week: A Multi-Cultural Infusion Model.* Santa Rosa, Calif.: National Women's History Week Project, 1985.

Male, George A., et al. "Policy Issues in the Education of Minorities: A Worldwide View." *Education and Urban Society* 18:4 (1986): 395–499. This special issue of *Education and Urban Society* is a collection of essays on the education of minorities in different countries around the world. There are no articles that deal exclusively with the United States, but the separate articles on Canada, the United Kingdom, and Australia are extremely useful for comparative purposes.

Manna, Anthony L., and Carolyn S. Brodie, eds. *Many Faces, Many Voices: Multicultural Literary Experiences for Youth: The Virginia Hamilton Conference.* Fort Atkinson, Wis.: Highsmith Press, 1992.

McCarthy, Cameron. "Multicultural Approaches to Racial Inequality in the United States." *Curriculum and Teaching* 5:1–2 (1990): 25–35.

————. "Multicultural Education, Minority Identities, Textbooks, and the Challenge of Curriculum Reform." *Journal of Education* 172:2 (1990): 118–29.

McCarthy, Cameron, and Warren Crichlow. *Race, Identity, and Representation in Education.* New York: Routledge, 1993.

McDiarmid, G. Williamson. *What to Do about Difference? A Study of Multicultural Education for Teacher Trainees in the Los Angeles Unified School District.* East Lansing, Mich.: National Center for Research on Teacher Education; Washington, D.C.: U.S. Department of Education, Office of Educational Research and Improvement, Educational Resources Information Center, 1990.

McKenna, Francis R. "The Myth of Multiculturalism and the Reality of the American Indian in Contemporary America." *Journal of American Indian Education* 21:1 (1981): 1–9.

Michigan Department of Education. *Position Statement on Multicultural Education.* Lansing: Michigan Department of Education, 1979.

Milton Van Brunt, Vida L., ed. *Black Students in a Multicultural Setting: Implications for Teacher Effectiveness.* Madison: Teacher Corps Associates, University of Wisconsin-Madison, 1979.

Modgil, Sohan, et al., eds. *Multicultural Education: The Interminable Debate.* London and Philadelphia: Falmer Press, 1986.

Montero, Martha, ed. *Bilingual Education Teacher Handbook: Language Issues in Multicultural Settings.* Cambridge, Mass.: Evaluation, Dissemination and Assessment Center for Bilingual Education, 1982.

————. *Bilingual Education Teacher Handbook: Strategies for the Design of Multicultural Curriculum.* Cambridge, Mass.: National Assessment and Dissemination Center, 1979.

Multicultural Education Center, College of Education, University of Arizona. *The Cultural Literacy Laboratory: A New Dimension in Multicultural Teacher Education.* Tucson: University of Arizona Press, 1973.

Multicultural Education: The Interdisciplinary Approach: A Summary of Conference Proceedings, April 1–3, 1976, San Diego, April 29–May 1, 1976, Oakland. Sacramento: California State Department of Education, 1977.

Multicultural Education Resource Guide: African Americans, Asian Americans, Hispanic Americans, and Native Americans. Lansing: Michigan State Board of Education, 1990.

Multicultural Teacher Education. Washington, D.C.: Commission on Multicultural Education, American Association of Colleges for Teacher Education, 1980.

National Study of School Evaluation, Multicultural/Multiracial Project. *Evaluation Guidelines for Multicultural/Multiracial Education, Designed Primarily for Secondary Schools.* Arlington, Va.: National Study of School Evaluation, 1973.

Nichols, Margaret S. *Multicultural Educational Materials in the Areas of Black, Mexican-American, American Indian, and Oriental Cultures: Supplement, November 1970, to Bibliography of a Demonstration Collection Assembled by Margaret S. Nichols for All Ages and Reading Abilities.* Stanford, Calif.: Multicultural Collection, Stanford University, 1970.

————. *Multicultural Materials: A Selective Bibliography of Adult Materials concerning Human Relations and the History, Culture, and Current Social Issues of Black, Chicano, Asian American, and Native American Peoples.* Rev. expanded ed. Stanford, Calif.: Multicultural Resources, 1974.

————. *Preliminary Edition Bibliography of Multicultural Materials for Educators: A Selective Listing of Materials concerning the History, Culture, and Current Problems of Racial and Ethnic Minorities in California.* Sacramento: California State Department of Education, 1973.

Nichols, Margaret S., and Margaret N. O'Neill. *Multicultural Bibliography for Preschool through Second Grade: In the Areas of Black, Spanish-Speaking, Asian American, and Native American Cultures.* Stanford, Calif.: Multicultural Resources, 1972.

Nieto, Sonia. *Affirming Diversity: The Sociopolitical Context of Multicultural Education.* New York and London: Longman, 1992. Nieto provides a compelling argument for implementing multicultural education at the primary and secondary school levels. Part of her argument rests on case studies of individual students that demonstrate the importance of well-informed and well-trained *teachers* in making multicultural education work. Nieto also includes a superb bibliography on multicultural education.

Pasternak, Michael G. *Helping Kids Learn Multi-Cultural Concepts: A Handbook of Strategies.* Champaign, Ill.: Research Press, 1979.

Pedersen, Paul. *A Handbook for Developing Multicultural Awareness.* Alexandria, Va.: American Association for Counseling and Development, 1988.

Perry, Theresa, and James W. Fraser, eds. *Freedom's Plow: Teaching in the Multicultural Classroom.* New York: Routledge, 1993.

Peters, Abe, ed. *Building the Bridges: Report of the National Conference on Multicultural Education, November 11–14, 1981, Winnipeg, Manitoba.* Regina, Sask.: L. A. Weigl Educational Associates, 1982.

Pizzillo, Joseph J., Jr. *Intercultural Studies: Schooling in Diversity.* Dubuque, Iowa: Kendall/Hunt Publishing Company, 1983.

Pusch, Margaret D., ed. *Multicultural Education: A Cross-Cultural Training Approach.* La Grange Park, Ill.: Intercultural Network, 1979.

Ramsey, Patricia G. *Teaching and Learning in a Diverse World: Multicultural Education for Young Children.* New York: Teachers College, Columbia University, 1987.

Ramsey, Patricia G., Edwina Battle Vold, and Leslie R. Williams. *Multicultural Education: A Source Book.* New York and London: Garland Publishing, 1989.

Redburn, Dennis B., and Charles Payne, eds. *Multicultural Education Clinic Papers: Proceedings of the Association of Teacher Educators Spring Clinic, 1975.* ATE National Multicultural Education Clinic, Ball State University, 1975. Muncie, Ind.: Ball State University, 1976.

Reyhner, Jon, ed. *Teaching the Indian Child: A Bilingual/Multicultural Approach.* 2d ed. Billings: Eastern Montana College, 1988.

Richardson, Richard C., and Louis W. Bender. *Fostering Minority Access and Achievement in Higher Education: The Role of Urban Community Colleges and Universities.* San Francisco: Jossey-Bass Publishers, 1987.

Rizvi, Fazal. *Ethnicity, Class and Multicultural Education.* Victoria, B.C.: Deakin University, 1986.

Rodriguez, Fred. *Education in a Multicultural Society.* Washington, D.C.: University Press of America, 1983. Rodriguez's text compares the different models upon which socialization between different racial and ethnic groups has been based. Its primary project is to map out ways to get American children (and by extension, American adults) to *value* cultural pluralism, not simply tolerate it. This book is especially significant inasmuch as it provides relatively clear, concise definitions of *what* "multicultural education" is (and is not) before it launches into its history of interethnic/racial relations.

———. *Mainstreaming a Multicultural Concept into Teacher Education: Guidelines for Teacher Trainers.* Saratoga, Calif.: R&E Publishers, 1983.

Simonson, Rick, and Scott Walker, eds. *Multi-Cultural Literacy.* Saint Paul, Minn.: Graywolf Press, 1988.

Sims, William E., and Bernice Bass de Martinez, eds. *Perspectives in Multicultural Education.* Washington, D.C.: University Press of America, 1981.

Sleeter, Christine E. *Empowerment through Multicultural Education.* Albany: State University of New York Press, 1991.

———. *Keepers of the American Dream: A Study of Staff Development and Multicultural Education.* London and Washington, D.C.: Falmer Press, 1992.

Sleeter, Christine E., and Carl A. Grant. *Making Choices for Multicultural Education: Five Approaches to Race, Class, and Gender.* Columbus, Ohio: Merrill Publishing Company, 1988.

Smoler, Fredric Paul. "What Should We Teach Our Children about American History?" *American Heritage* 43 (February–March 1992): 7, 45–52.

Trueba, Henry T., and Carol Barnett-Mizrahi. *Bilingual Multicultural Education.* Rowley, Mass.: Newbury House Publishers, 1979.

———. *Bilingual Multicultural Education and the Professional: From Theory to Practice.* Rowley, Mass.: Newbury House Publishers, 1979.

Verma, Gajendra K., "Multiculturalism and Education: Prelude to Practice." In Verma and Bagley, 57–77.

Verma, Gajendra K., and Christopher Bagley, eds. *Race Relations and Cultural Differences: Educational and Interpersonal Perspectives.* New York: St. Martin's Press, 1984.

Vold, Edwina Battle, ed. *Multicultural Education in Early Childhood Classrooms.* Washington, D.C.: NEA Professional Library, 1992.

Williams, Byron, et al. *Manual for Evaluating Content of Classroom Instructional Materials for Bilingual-Multicultural Education.* San Diego: Institute for Cultural Pluralism, School of Education, San Diego State University, 1977.

Wurzel, Jaime S., ed. *Toward Multiculturalism: A Reader in Multicultural Education.* Yarmouth, Maine: Intercultural Press, 1988.

C. In Higher Education

Auletta, Gale S., and Terry Jones, eds. "The Inclusive University: Multicultural Perspectives in Higher Education." *American Behavioral Scientist* 34 (1990).

Berman, Paul, ed. *Debating P.C.: The Controversy over Political Correctness on College Campuses.* New York: Laurel, 1992.

"A *Black Scholar* Special: Student Strikes: 1968–69." *Black Scholar* 1:3–4 (1970): 65–75.

Bunzel, John H. *Race Relations on Campus: Stanford Students Speak.* Stanford, Calif.: The Portable Stanford, 1992.

Butler, Johnnella, and Betty Schmitz. "Ethnic Studies, Women's Studies, and Multiculturalism." *Change* 24:3 (1991): 36–41.

Cahn, Steven M., ed. *Affirmative Action and the University: A Philosophical Inquiry.* Philadelphia: Temple University Press, 1993. This edition of scholarly papers on affirmative action does an excellent job of demarcating the most important philosophical issues surrounding university hiring and manages to cover many of the same issues pertinent to the multiculturalism debates.

Cotera, Martha, comp.; Nella Cunningham, ed. *Multicultural Women's Sourcebook: Materials Guide for Use in Women's Studies and Bilingual/Multicultural Programs.* Austin, Tex.: Women's Educational Equity Act Program, U.S. Department of Education, 1982.

"Cracking the Cultural Consensus." *Society* 29 (November–December 1991): 5–44.

Davis, Lenwood G. *A Bibliographical Guide to Black Studies Programs in the United States: An Annotated Bibliography.* Westport, Conn.: Greenwood Press, 1985.

Duster, Troy. "They're Taking Over!" *Mother Jones* 16 (September–October 1991): 30–33.

Erickson, Peter. "Rather Than Reject a Common Culture, Multiculturalism Advocates a More Complicated Route by Which to Achieve It." *Chronicle of Higher Education* 37:41 (1991): B1–B3.

Gollnick, Donna M., Frank H. Klassen, and Joost Yff. *Multicultural Education and Ethnic Studies in the United States: An Analysis and Annotated Bibliography of Selected ERIC Documents.* Washington, D.C.: American Association of Colleges for Teacher Education, 1976.

Harris, Robert L. *Three Essays: Black Studies in the United States.* New York: Ford Foundation, 1990.

Hassenger, Robert. "True Multiculturalism." *Commonweal* 119 (10 April 1992): 10–11.

Hawkins, John N. *Asian American Studies and Asian Studies: Interrelationships.* Los Angeles: Asian Pacific American Research Seminars, Asian American Studies Center, UCLA, 1980.

Hwang, David Henry. "Evolving a Multicultural Tradition." *MELUS* 16:3 (1989): 16–19.

Kelley, Don Philip. "Course of Study Outline in Multi-Cultural Studies." Ph.D diss., University of California, Irvine, 1976.

Kolenda, Konstatin. "E Pluribus Unum." *Humanist* 51 (September–October 1991): 40ff.

Loo, Chalsa M., and Garry Rolison. "Alienation of Ethnic Minority Students at a Predominantly White University." *Journal of Higher Education* 57:1 (1986): 58–77.

Nakanishi, Don T. *Asian American Studies and the Changing University.* Berkeley: National Association for Asian and Pacific American Education, 1980.

Nordquist, Joan, ed. *The Multicultural Education Debate in the University: A Bibliography: A Bibliographic Series.* Santa Cruz, Calif.: Reference and Research Services, 1992.

Olivas, Michael A. "Financial Aid Packaging Policies: Access and Ideology." *Journal of Higher Education* 56:4 (1985): 462–75.

Reflections on Political Correctness: A Collection of Student Papers on Multiculturalism, Speech Codes and "The Canon." Santa Cruz: University of California, Santa Cruz, 1992.

Richardson, Richard C., Jr., and Elizabeth Fisk Skinner. *Achieving Quality and Diversity: Universities in a Multicultural Society.* New York: American Council on Education: Macmillan; Toronto: Collier Macmillan Canada; New York: Maxwell Macmillan International, 1991.

Robbins, Bruce. "Othering the Academy: Professionalism and Multiculturalism." *Social Research* 58:2 (1991): 355–72.

Schoem, David, et al. *Multicultural Teaching in the University.* New York: Praeger, 1993. This anthology is perhaps the most cogent offering that attempts to do what the many early texts on multiculturalism in primary education have already accomplished: address the disparate areas in the contemporary American university where different forms of multiculturalism are needed, and *create strategies* for implementing them, as both policies and pedagogies. Of particular interest is David Schoem's essay on training teaching assistants to understand multiculturalism, as well as the definition of multiculturalism used here, which is not restricted to ethnicity and race; it also includes sexuality, which is a relatively new and welcome addition to the dialogue on making the university multicultural.

Smith, M. G. "Ethnicity and Ethnic Groups in America: The View from Harvard." *Ethnic and Racial Studies* 5:1 (1982): 1–22.

Stanford University Committee on Minority Issues. *Building a Multiracial, Multicultural University Community: Final Report of the University Committee on Minority Issues.* Stanford, Calif.: Stanford University, 1989.

Thomas, Gail E. *Black Students in Higher Education: Conditions and Experiences in the 1970s.* Contributions to the Study of Education, no. 1. Westport, Conn.: Greenwood Press, 1981. Thomas's book is intended both to review the history of the increased access for Black students in higher education and to assess the experiences, programs, and problems that either contributed to, continued, or eroded the barriers to college in the 1970s. This volume is similar to the revised California Master Plan for education, insofar as it determines which methods of qualifying, admitting, and retaining Black students are destined for success or failure. A wide range of educational scholars contributed to this volume, including Charles V. Willie and Ada M. Fisher.

UCLA Chicano Studies Center. *Chicano Studies Center, Growth and Development, 1969 to 1975: A Summary Statement.* Los Angeles: The Center, 1975.

Washburn, David E. *Ethnic Studies: Bilingual/Bicultural Education and Multicultural Teacher Education in the United States: A Directory of Higher Education Programs and Personnel.* Miami: Inquiry International, 1979.

What It Is: Multicultural Dorm Yearbook, 1975–1976, Merrill College, University of California. Santa Cruz, Calif.: n.p., 1976.

Williams, Patricia J. "Blockbusting the Canon." *Ms.* 2:22 (September–October 1991): 59–63.

Yarbrough, Larry. "Three Questions for the Multiculturalism Debate." *Change* 24:3 (1991): 64–69.

D. In the Corporate World

Alster, Judith, Theresa Brothers, and Holly Gallo, eds. *In Diversity Is Strength: Capitalizing on the New Work Force.* New York: Conference Board, 1992.

Betances, Samuel. "Diversity: Multiculturalism in Education and Business." *Vocational Educational Journal* 66:8 (1991): 22–23.

Casse, Pierre. *Training for the Multicultural Manager: A Practical and Cross-Cultural Approach to the Management of People.* Photographs by M. L. Bussaty. Washington, D.C.: Society for Intercultural Education, Training, and Research, 1982.

Coleman, Troy. "Managing Diversity at Work: The New American Dilemma." *Public Management* 72:9 (1990): 2–4.

Copeland, Lennie. "Learning to Manage a Multicultural Workforce." *Western City* 65 (1989).

Crabtree, Kristen M., and Ann Morrison. *A Practical Guide to Diversity Literature.* La Jolla, Calif.: Center for Creative Leadership, 1992.

Cross, Elsie. "Issues of Diversity." In *Sunrise Seminars,* vol. 2, ed. D. Vails-Weber and J. Potts. National Training Laboratories Institute for Behavioral Sciences, 1991.

"Cultural Diversity." *Working Woman* 16 (January 1991): 45ff.

Elashmawi, Farid, and Philip R. Harris. *Multicultural Management: New Skills for Global Success.* Houston: Gulf Publications, 1993.

Fine, Marlene Gail. "Cultural Diversity in the Workplace." *Public Personnel Management* 19:3 (1990): 305–19.

Friesen, John W. *When Cultures Clash: Case Studies in Multiculturalism.* Calgary, Alta.: Detselig Enterprises, 1985.

Gamst, Frederick. "Industrial Ethnological Perspectives on the Development and Characteristics of the Study of Organizational Cultures." *Studies in Third World Societies* 42 (1990).

Henderson, George. *Cultural Diversity in the Workplace: Issues and Strategies.* Westport, Conn.: Quorum Books, 1994.

Jackson, Susan E., et al., eds. *Diversity in the Workplace: Human Resources Initiatives.* Professional Practice Series. New York: Guilford Press, 1992.

James, Muriel. *The Better Boss in Multicultural Organizations: Guide to Success Using Transactional Analysis.* Walnut Creek, Calif.: Marshall Publishing, 1991.

Jamieson, David. *Managing Workforce 2000: Gaining the Diversity Advantage.* San Francisco: Jossey-Bass Publishers, 1991.

Johnson, William B., and Arnold H. Packer. *Workforce 2000: Work and Workers for the 21st Century.* Indianapolis: Hudson Institute, 1987.

Kauffman, L. A. "The Diversity Game." *Village Voice* (31 August 1993): 29–33.

Kessler, Lorence L. *Managing Diversity in an Equal Opportunity Workplace: A Primer for Today's Manager.* Washington, D.C.: National Foundation for the Study of Employment Policy, 1990.

Kliment, Stephen A. "Managing Diversity." *Architectural Record* 179 (February 1991): 11.

Leo, John. "The 'Us' versus 'Them' Industry." *U.S. News & World Report* 111 (16 December 1991): 42.

Mabry, Marcus. "Past Tokenism." *Newsweek* 115 (14 May 1990): 37ff.

———. "Pin a Label on a Manager—and Watch What Happens." *Newsweek* 115 (14 May 1990): 43.

March, Robert M. *Working for a Japanese Company: Managing Relationships in a Multicultural Organization.* Tokyo and New York: Kodansha International, 1992.

Nelton, Sharon. "A Tougher Challenge for Family Firms." *Nation's Business* 79 (June 1991): 65.

Reich, Robert. *The Work of Nations.* New York: Vintage Books, 1992.

Samuelson, Robert. "The Multicultural Corporation." *Washington Post* 112 (23 August 1989): A27.

Sowell, Thomas. "Cultural Diversity: A World View." *American Enterprise* 2:3 (1991): 44–55.

———. *Race and Economics.* New York: David McKay, 1975.

Strategic Plan for Human Resources Management. Washington, D.C.: U.S. Department of the Interior, ca. 1991.

Thiederman, Sondra B. *Bridging Cultural Barriers for Corporate Success: How to Manage the Multicultural Work Force.* Lexington, Mass.: Lexington Books, 1991.

———. *Profiting in America's Multicultural Marketplace: How to Do Business across Cultural Lines.* New York: Lexington Books; Toronto: Maxwell Macmillan Canada; New York: Maxwell Macmillan International, 1991.

Thomas, R. Roosevelt, Jr. *Beyond Race and Gender: Unleashing the Power of Your Total Work Force by Managing Diversity.* New York: American Management Association, 1991.

———. "From Affirmative Action to Affirming Diversity." *Harvard Business Review* (March–April 1990): 107–17.

Walton, Sally J. *Cultural Diversity in the Workplace.* Business Skills Express Series. Burr Ridge, Ill.: Irwin Professional Publications/Mirror Press, 1994.

White, J. P. "Diversity's Champion." *Los Angeles Times Magazine* 111 (9 August 1992): 14ff.

E. In the Humanities

Anderson, James M. "The Development and Conceptualization of Ethnic Studies in Michigan." *Ethnic Forum* 1:2 (1981): 23–28.

Barnes, A. E. "Blaspheming like Brute Beasts: Multiculturalism from an Historical Perspective." *Contention: Debates in Society, Culture and Science* 1:3 (1992): 37–58. Barnes argues that multiculturalism as we know it today, contrary to the views of Diane Ravitch and John Searle, was the initial condition of the "West" and became recessive only when northern Europe asserted its own cultural superiority to other regions on the basis of race. Cultural unity was historically an effect of a Northern supremacist project. Minority scholars, he concludes, should avoid the "romanticism" that infects these European nationalist projects.

Bernal, Martin. *Black Athena: The Afroasiatic Roots of Western Civilization.* New Brunswick, N.J.: Rutgers University Press, 1987. Bernal's most famous work, like Henry Louis Gates's below, is not a guidebook to multiculturalism itself, but it is perhaps the most widely discussed example of the sort of scholarly revisionism that has fueled antimulticulturalist critics (albeit some of the best scholarship), inasmuch as Bernal calls rather passively accepted accounts of ancient history into serious question with elaborately detailed research.

Braided Lives: An Anthology of Multicultural American Writing. St. Paul, Minn.: Minnesota Humanities Commission: Minnesota Council of Teachers of English, 1991.

Buenker, John D., and Lorman A. Ratner, eds. *Multiculturalism in the United States: A Comparative Guide to Acculturation and Ethnicity.* Westport, Conn.: Greenwood Press, 1992. Buenker and Ratner have collected essays discussing the histories of and processes through which American ethnic/racial groups have (or haven't) become assimilated into the American mainstream. Strangely enough, the editors omit several important racial/ethnic groups (which the editors admit is problematic). All of the essays, however, are written by scholars from the groups in question. The collection's purpose is to map out those cultural spaces that are particular groups' exclusive property and, conversely, where those same groups have acquiesced to the mainstream's demand that they sacrifice their ethnicity.

Burke, Ronald K., ed. *American Public Discourse: A Multicultural Perspective.* Lanham, Md.: University Press of America, 1992.

Cadzow, John. "The Growth of Ethnic Studies: The Kent State University Experience." *Ethnic Forum* 1:1 (1980): 25–27.

Carby, Hazel V. *Multicultural Fictions.* Birmingham: Centre for Contemporary Cultural Studies, University of Birmingham, 1979.

Chicago Cultural Studies Group. "Critical Multiculturalism." *Critical Inquiry* 18:3 (1992): 530–55.

Ch'maj, Betty E. M., ed. *Multicultural America: A Resource Book for Teachers of Humanities and American Studies: Syllabi, Essays, Projects, Bibliography.* Lanham, Md.: University Press of America, 1993.

Daniels, Lee A. "Diversity, Correctness, and Campus Life: A Closer Look." *Change* 23:5 (1991): 16–20.

Dasenbrock, Reed Way. "Intelligibility and Meaningfulness in Multicultural Literature in English." *PMLA* 102:1 (1987): 10–19.

Dennis, John. *O, Promised Land: A Multi-Cultural Reader.* Rowley, Mass.: Newbury House, 1982.

Dent, Gina, ed. *Black Popular Culture.* Seattle: Bay Press, 1992. Some articles compare and contrast Black popular culture with multiculturalism.

Devy, Ganesh N. "The Multicultural Context of Indian Literature in English." In *Creativity in the New Literatures in English: Cross/Cultures*, ed. Geoffrey V. Davis and Jelinek H. Maes. Amsterdam: Rodopi, 1990. 345–53.

DuBois, Ellen Carol, and Vicki L. Ruiz, eds. *Unequal Sisters: A Multicultural Reader in U.S. Women's History.* New York: Routledge, 1990.

Durham, Carolyn A. *The Contexture of Feminism: Marie Cardinal and Multicultural Literacy.* Urbana: University of Illinois Press, 1992.

Gates, Henry Louis, Jr. *Loose Canons: Notes on the Culture Wars.* Oxford: Oxford University Press, 1992.

———. *The Signifying Monkey: A Theory of African-American Literary Criticism.* New York and Oxford: Oxford University Press, 1988. Although Gates's magnum opus of African-American literary theory does not necessarily deal with multiculturalism per se, it operates under a related premise: we must reckon the history of a people through the internal logic of their culture in order to understand their achievements. This book has been elevated in the public mind as a symbol of what multiculturalism is doing or should do.

Geyer, Michael. "Multiculturalism and the Politics of General Education." *Critical Inquiry* 19: (1993): 499–533.

Glazer, Nathan. "In Defense of Multiculturalism." *New Republic* 205 (2 September 1991): 18ff.

Gunew, Sneja. "Postmodern Tensions: Reading for (Multi)Cultural Difference." *Meanjin* 49:1 (1990): 21–33.

Hull, Gloria T., Patricia Bell Scott, and Barbara Smith, eds. *All the Women Are White, All the Blacks Are Men, but Some of Us Are Brave: Black Women's Studies.* Old Westbury, N.Y.: Feminist Press, 1982.

Hunter, James Davison. *Culture Wars: The Struggle to Define America.* New York: Basic Books, 1991.

Kafka, Phillipa. "A Multicultural Introduction to Literature." In *Practicing Theory in Introductory College Literature Courses*, ed. David B. Downing. Urbana, Ill.: National Council of Teachers of English, 1991. 179–86.

———. "Another Round of Canon Fire: Feminist and Multi-Ethnic Theory in the American Literature Survey." *MELUS* 16:2 (1989): 31–49.

Lippert, Paul. "The Semantics of Multiculturalism." *ETC.: A Review of General Semantics* 48 (1991–92): 363–74.

Martin, Reginald. "An Interview with Ishmael Reed." *Review of Contemporary Fiction* 4:2 (1984): 176–87.
Miller, Wayne Charles. "Toward a New Literary History of the United States." *MELUS* 11:1 (1984): 5–25.
Moraga, Cherríe, and Gloria Anzaldúa, eds. *This Bridge Called My Back: Writings by Radical Women of Color.* Watertown, Mass.: Persephone Press, 1981.
Morton, Carlos. "Celebrating 500 Years of Mestizaje." *MELUS* 16:3 (1989): 20–22.
Nandan, Satendra, ed. ACLALS *Triennial Conference (5th: 1981: University of the South Pacific) Language and Literature in Multicultural Contexts.* Suva, Fiji: University of the South Pacific; Mysore, India: Association for Commonwealth Language and Literature Studies, 1983.
Pap, Michael. "NESA and the Status of Ethnic Studies in America." *Ethnic Forum* 1:1 (1980): 25–27.
Payne, James Robert. *Multicultural Autobiography: American Lives.* Knoxville: University of Tennessee Press, 1992.
Redding, Jay Saunders. "The Negro in American History: As Scholar, as Subject." In *The Past before Us: Contemporary Historical Writing in the United States,* ed. Michael Kammen. Ithaca, N.Y.: Cornell University Press, 1980. 292–307.
Rico, Barbara Roche, and Sandra Mano. *American Mosaic: Multicultural Readings in Context.* Boston: Houghton Mifflin, 1991.
Rose, Marilyn Gaddis. "The Multinational Curriculum: (Why We Need One and) What to Translate for It." In *New Literary Continents: Selected Papers of the Fifth* NDEA *Seminar on Foreign Area Studies Sponsored by the School of International Affairs, Columbia University, and Council on National Literatures,* ed. Anne Paolucci. Whitestone, N.Y.: Griffon House, 1984. 49–55.
San Juan, E., Jr. "Multiculturalism vs. Hegemony: Ethnic Studies, Asian Americans, and U.S. Racial Politics." *Massachusetts Review: A Quarterly of Literature, the Arts and Public Affairs* 32:3 (1991): 467–78.
Schmidt, Peter. "Introduction to Williams' 'Letter to an Australian Editor' (1946): Williams' Manifesto for Multiculturalism." *William Carlos Williams Review* 17:2 (1991): 4–12.
Sowell, Thomas. "A World View of Cultural Diversity." *Society* 29 (November–December 1991): 37–44.
———. "What 'Cultural Diversity' Means." *Wilson Quarterly* 16 (spring 1992): 16.
Taylor, Charles. *Multiculturalism and "The Politics of Recognition": An Essay.* Princeton, N.J.: Princeton University Press, 1992.
———, ed. *Guide to Multicultural Resources.* Madison, Wis.: Praxis Publications, 1989.
West, Cornel. *Beyond Eurocentrism and Multiculturalism.* Monroe, Maine: Common Courage Press, 1993.
Wolf, Bryan. "Firing the Canon: Introduction." *American Literary History* 3:4 (1991): 707–52.
Yarmolinsky, Adam. "Loose Canons: Multiculturalism and Humanities." *Change* 24:3 (1991): 6–9.

F. In Society and Public Policy

Abilock, Debbie. *A Database of Resources for Developing Multicultural Library Collections. HyperCard Conversion by Ray Olszewski.* California Bay Area Independent School Libraries, 1992.
Aguero, Kathleen, ed. *Daily Fare: Essays from the Multicultural Experience.* Athens: University of Georgia Press, 1993.
Allan, Lyle. "A Selective Annotated Bibliography of Multiculturalism." *Social Alternatives* 3:3 (1983): 65–72. This bibliography concerns itself primarily with definitions and policies and

practices of multiculturalism in Australia, with a few resources from New Zealand and Canada. Only the last section of the bibliography is devoted to overseas materials, including the United States. All of these resources, however, including the comparative insight that studies of multiculturalism in Canada and New Zealand contain, may prove useful in studies of multiculturalism as a global concept.

Appleton, Nicholas. *Multiculturalism and the Courts.* Bilingual Education Paper Series vol. 2, no. 4. Los Angeles: National Dissemination and Assessment Center, 1978.

Auster, Lawrence. *The Path to National Suicide: An Essay on Immigration and Multiculturalism.* Monterey, Va.: American Immigration Control Foundation, 1990.

Barkan, Elliott R. "Haven, Heaven, and Hell: America and Its Ethnic Minorities, 1945–1980." *Journal of American Ethnic History* 2:2 (1983): 83–92.

Bibliography on Multicultural Drug Abuse Prevention Issues. Rockville, Md.: U.S. Department of Health and Human Services, Public Health Service, Alcohol, Drug Abuse, and Mental Health Administration; National Institute on Drug Abuse, Division of Prevention and Treatment Development, Prevention Branch, 1981.

Bozeman, Adda Bruemmer. *The Future of Law in a Multicultural World.* Princeton, N.J.: Princeton University Press, 1971.

Braham, Peter, Ali Rattansi, and Richard Skellington, eds. *Racism and Antiracism: Inequalities, Opportunities and Policies.* London: Sage Publications, 1992.

Brooks, Roy L. *Rethinking the American Race Problem.* Berkeley and Los Angeles: University of California Press, 1990.

California Department of Mental Health, Citizens Advisory Council. *Multi-Cultural Issues in Mental Health Services: Strategies Towards Equity: Report.* Sacramento: State of California, Health and Welfare Agency, Department of Mental Health, Citizens Advisory Council, 1979.

California Ethnic Services Task Force. *Multicultural/Multilingual Resources: A Vendor Directory.* Inglewood, Calif.: California Ethnic Services Task Force, 1979.

California Legislature Joint Committee for Review of the Master Plan for Higher Education. *California Faces . . . California's Future: Education for Citizenship in a Multicultural Democracy.* M. Brian Murphy et al., consultants. Sacramento: California Legislature, 1988. This report is arguably the most thorough attempt to enact a policy of multicultural education in the United States, insofar as it actually includes wording for possible legislative bills (some of which have been proposed and passed). But its most intriguing features are a detailed and devastating analysis of California's economy, the status of the state's higher educational system, and current race relations (as of 1989), and a forceful, compelling argument that multiculturalism in education is both inevitable and desperately needed. It also fascinatingly documents what multiculturalism meant immediately before it became a highly controversial term.

Center for Policy Development. *Adrift in a Sea of Change: California's Public Libraries Struggle to Meet the Information Needs of Multicultural Communities.* Sacramento: Distributed by California State Library Foundation, 1990.

Clausen, Edwin G., and Jack Bermingham, eds. *Pluralism, Racism, and Public Policy: The Search for Equality.* Boston: G. K. Hall and Company, 1981. Clausen and Bermingham provide an overview of pluralism, circa 1980. The book is divided into three sections: the first reviews forms of inequality in America and how these forms have affected the United States' relations with other nations; the second offers suggestions for promoting pluralism in the schools; the third is devoted to sharp criticisms of pluralism and other purportedly antiracist agendas (especially those promoted by mainstream American liberalism). Some prominent authors in the volume are Douglas W. Lee, Maulana Ron Karenga, and Sucheng Chan.

Cohen, Neil A., ed. *Child Welfare: A Multicultural Focus.* Boston: Allyn and Bacon, 1992.
Community Education and Multiculturalism: Immigrant/Refugee Needs and Cultural Awareness. Washington, D.C.: U.S. Conference of Mayors, 1982.
Cox, David R. *Welfare Practice in a Multicultural Society.* Englewood Cliffs, N.J.: Prentice Hall, 1989.
Dana, Richard Henry. *Multicultural Assessment Perspectives for Professional Psychology.* Boston: Allyn and Bacon, 1993.
Dillard, John M. *Multicultural Counseling: Toward Ethnic and Cultural Relevance in Human Encounters.* Chicago: Nelson-Hall, 1983.
Eggington, Everett. "Ethnic Identification and Perception of Racial Harmony." *Urban Review* 12:3 (1980): 149–61.
Espiritu, Yen Le. *Asian American Panethnicity: Bridging Institutions and Identities.* Philadelphia: Temple University Press, 1992.
Feuer, Lewis Samuel. "From Pluralism to Multiculturalism." *Society* 29 (November–December 1991): 19–22.
Fishman, Joshua A. "Toward Multilingualism as an International Desideratum in Government." *Annual Review of Applied Linguistics* 6 (1985): 2–9.
Frideres, James S. *Multiculturalism and Intergroup Relations.* Contributions in Sociology no. 75. New York: Greenwood Press, 1989.
Furness, Anne-Marie. "Development of Local Services and Community Action on Behalf of Multiculturalism." *Social Work Papers* 17 (1983): 15–25.
Glazer, Nathan, and Daniel Moynihan, eds. *Ethnicity: Theory and Experience.* Cambridge: Harvard University Press, 1975.
Gollnich, Donna M., assistant project director, Frank H. Klassen, project director. *State Legislation, Provisions and Practices Related to Multicultural Education.* Washington, D.C.: Accreditation Standards for Multicultural Teacher Education Project, American Association of Colleges for Teacher Education, 1978.
Gordon, Milton M., ed. *America as a Multicultural Society. Annals of the American Academy of Political and Social Science* 454. Philadelphia: American Academy of Political and Social Science, 1981.
———. *Assimilation in American Life: The Role of Race, Religion, and National Origins.* New York: Oxford University Press, 1964.
Haddock, Mable, and Chiquita Mullins Lee. "Whose Multiculturalism? PBS, the Public, and Privilege." *Afterimage* 21:1 (1993): 17–20.
Horowitz, Tamara. "The Positive Legacy of Positivism." *Critical Quarterly* 33:1 (1991): 88–92.
Hurtado, Aída, et al. *Redefining California: Latino Social Engagement in a Multicultural Society.* Los Angeles: Chicano Studies Research Center, University of California, Los Angeles, 1992.
Jackson, Bailey W., and Evangelina Holvino. *Multicultural Organization Development.* Ann Arbor: University of Michigan Press, 1988.
Katz, Judith H. *Facing the Challenge of Diversity and Multiculturalism.* PCMA working paper, no. 13. Ann Arbor: Center for Research on Social Organization, University of Michigan, 1988.
Kukathas, Chandran. "Are There Any Cultural Rights?" *Political Theory* 20:1 (1992): 105–39.
Lambert, Wallace E. *Coping with Cultural and Racial Diversity in Urban America.* New York: Praeger, 1990.
Lenz, Gynter. *Crisis of Modernity: Recent Critical Theories of Culture and Society in the United States and West Germany.* Boulder, Colo.: Westview Press, 1986.
Lerda, Valeria Gennaro. *From "Melting Pot" to Multiculturalism: The Evolution of Ethnic Relations in the United States and Canada.* Biblioteca di cultura (Bulzoni Editore) 418. Rome: Bulzoni Editore, 1990.

Locke, Don C. *Increasing Multicultural Understanding: A Comprehensive Model.* Multicultural Aspects of Counseling Series. Newbury Park, Calif.: Sage Publications, 1992. Locke's book is aimed primarily at counselors and educators. It summarizes the common cultural experiences of most of the major American ethnic and/or racial groups in order for these professionals to respond sensitively to the concerns of their patients and students. Locke manages to carefully cover a smart array of groups and their historical experiences and concerns. Additionally, he wisely and continuously places caveats in his text to remind the reader that his models of understanding are not meant to cover all individuals in each group.

Lovrich, Nicholas P., Jr. "Continuity and Change in American Ethnic Politics." *Social Science Journal* 18:1 (1981): 107–13.

Magnarella, Paul J. "Justice in a Culturally Pluralistic Society: The Cultural Defense on Trial." *Journal of Ethnic Studies* 19:3 (1990): 65–84.

Messolonghites, Louisa. *Multicultural Perspectives on Drug Abuse and Its Prevention: A Resource Book.* Rockville, Md.: U.S. Department of Health, Education, and Welfare, Public Health Service, Alcohol, Drug Abuse, and Mental Health Administration, National Institute on Drug Abuse, Division of Research Development, Prevention Branch, 1979.

Mississippi Governor's Multi-Cultural Advisory Council. *Report of the Governor's Multi-Cultural Advisory Council.* Jackson: Mississippi Governor's Multi-Cultural Advisory Council, 1979.

Morgan, Gordon D. *America without Ethnicity.* Port Washington, N.Y.: Kennikat Press, 1981.

Multicultural Education and the American Indian. Los Angeles: American Indian Studies Center, University of California, 1979.

Norgren, Jill. *American Cultural Pluralism and Law.* New York: Praeger, 1988.

Peterson, William, Michael Novak, and Philip Gleason. *Concepts of Ethnicity.* Cambridge: Belknamp Press of Harvard University Press, 1982.

Pisano, Jane Gallagher. "After the Riots: Multiculturalism in Los Angeles." *National Civic Review* 81:3 (summer–fall 1992).

Smedley, Audrey. *Race in North America: Origin and Evolution of a Worldview.* Boulder, Colo.: Westview Press, 1993.

Smith, David E., et al., eds. *A Multicultural View of Drug Abuse: Proceedings of the National Drug Abuse Conference, 1977.* Cambridge: Schenkman Publishing Company, 1978.

Smolicz, J. J. "Cultural Alternatives in Plural Societies: Separatism or Multiculturalism?" *Journal of Intercultural Studies* 4:3 (1983): 47–68.

Takaki, Ronald. *A Different Mirror: A History of Multicultural America.* Boston: Little, Brown, 1993.

Toure, Kwame (formerly Stokely Carmichael), and Charles V. Hamilton. *Black Power: The Politics of Liberation in America.* New York: Random House, 1967. This book's reissue includes afterwords by Hamilton and Toure that describe Black Power as a "reformism" that failed. Some lessons for current-day multiculturalism may lie herein.

Trager, Oliver. *America's Minorities and the Multicultural Debate.* New York: Facts on File, 1992.

Triandis, Harry C. "The Future of Pluralism." *Journal of Social Issues* 32:4 (1976): 179–208.

Trueba, Henry T. *Healing Multicultural America: Mexican Immigrants Rise to Power in Rural California.* Washington, D.C.: Falmer Press, 1993.

Tumin, Melvin M., and Walter Plotch, eds. *Pluralism in a Democratic Society.* Praeger Special Studies in U.S. Economic, Social, and Political Issues. New York: Praeger, 1977. Intended to aid in curriculum reform in American schools, *Pluralism* is a volume for the "history teacher who wishes to introduce ethnic studies into the classroom" so that s/he may "deal with each ethnic group in the United States without twisting history totally out of context" (from the Foreword). The editors have divided the book into three sections: (1) "A Search for Definition" (cultural pluralism and the social scene); (2) "Psychological Background" (how acceptance or rejection of cultural pluralism is acculturated in the United States); (3) "Curriculum Development" (implications of cultural pluralism for curriculum reform). Most of the articles have extensive charts, tables, and graphs to help support their claims.

Wiebe, Robert H. *The Segmented Society: An Introduction to the Meaning of America*. New York: Oxford University Press, 1975. This book is a brief (200 pp.) history of the influx and subsequent mixing (or lack thereof) of the different ethnic and racial groups in the United States. As such, it "identifies three distinctive social systems" (one lasting until 1790, one from 1830 to 1890, and one from 1920 to 1975) that established policies circumscribing American ethnic and racial groups. Wiebe outlines the subtle differences between various types of race-centered socialization and traces their link to what we now call multiculturalisms.

~

Contributors

Norma Alarcón is associate professor of Chicano studies and ethnic studies at the University of California, Berkeley. She is the editor and publisher of Third Woman Press, and has published numerous essays and articles on Chicano literature and Chicana feminism. A leading feminist theorist, Alarcón has written a book on the Mexican feminist novelist and poet Rosario Castellanos, and has translated into Spanish the classic book, *This Bridge Called My Back*.

Richard P. Appelbaum is professor of sociology and director of the Center for Global Studies at the University of California, Santa Barbara. He is the author of *Karl Marx*, numerous articles and books on housing and urban policy, and the editor, with Jeffrey Henderson, of *States and Development in the Pacific Rim*. He is currently conducting research on global contracting in the garment industry, looking at the changing geography of capitalist production and its impact on labor.

Edna Bonacich is professor of sociology and ethnic studies at the University of California, Riverside. She is the author of *The Economic Basis of Ethnic Solidarity: Small Business in the Japanese Community* (with John Modell) and *Immigrant Entrepreneurs: Koreans in Los Angeles, 1965-1982* (with Ivan Light), and the coeditor of *Labor Immigration under Capitalism: Asian Workers in the U.S. before World War II* (with Lucie Cheng), *Global Production:*

The Apparel Industry in the Pacific Rim (with Lucie Cheng, Norma Chinchilla, Nora Hamilton, and Paul Org), and *The New Asian Immigration in Los Angeles and Global Restructuring* (with Paul Org and Lucie Cheng).

Wendy Brown is professor of women's studies and legal studies at the University of California, Santa Cruz. She is the author of *Manhood and Politics: A Feminist Reading in Political Theory* and *States of Injury: Essays on Power and Freedom in Late Modernity*.

Antonia I. Castañeda is assistant professor of history at the University of Texas at Austin. Her research focuses on mestizas in colonial California, on women of color in the nineteenth-century Spanish/Mexican/U.S. borderlands, on Chicana/o history, and on Chicana feminisms. In addition to her book-length manuscript entitled *Indias, Españolas, Mestizas, Mulatas, Coyotas, Lobas, y Chinas in Colonial California: The Gendered, Racial and Sexual Politics of Colonialism*, her current projects include an annotated bilingual edition, with a critical introduction, of nineteenth-century California narratives and a social history of Tejana farmworkers in Washington State.

Angie Chabram-Dernersesian is associate professor of Chicana/o literature at the University of California, Davis, where she teaches Chicana/o studies. She has authored articles in the areas of Chicana/o studies, criticism, and ethnography and is coeditor, with Rosa Linda Fregoso, of a special volume of *Cultural Studies* on Chicana/o cultural representation, which includes her essay "Chicana/o Studies as Oppositional Ethnography."

Jon Cruz is assistant professor of sociology at the University of California, Santa Barbara. He has written on historical aspects of African-American music, Filipino Americans, and conservative populism. He is completing a book on elite appropriations of black music in the nineteenth century and is coeditor of *Viewing, Reading, Listening: Audiences and Cultural Reception.*

Angela Y. Davis is professor of History of Consciousness at the University of California, Santa Cruz, where she was recently appointed Presidential Chair in African American and Feminist Studies. Her articles and essays have appeared in numerous journals and anthologies, both scholarly and popular. She is an internationally recognized writer, scholar, lecturer, and activist and the author of several books, including *Angela Davis: An Autobiography; Women, Race and Class;* and a forthcoming volume on black women's music and social consciousness. She currently is conducting research on incarcerated women, racism in the U.S. criminal justice system, and alternatives to jails and prisons.

Darryl B. Dickson-Carr is assistant professor of English at Florida State University. His dissertation, "Black Satire: The Revision of an Art Form in

Twentieth-Century America," studies the history of satire by African-American authors.

Steve Fagin has produced four video epics and has contributed photo-text pieces to such publications as *Social Text, Documents,* and *Breakthroughs.* His work has been extensively theorized in *Artforum, Camera Obscura,* and *October* as well as in several critical books. In 1994 a major retrospective of his work was held at the Museum of Modern Art in New York. A book on his work is forthcoming. He teaches at the University of California, San Diego.

Rosa Linda Fregoso is the author of *The Bronze Screen: Chicana and Chicano Film Culture* (University of Minnesota Press) and coeditor with Norma Iglesias of *Mirades de Mujeres* (forthcoming). Fregoso has published on film, cultural studies, and feminism in numerous anthologies and journals, including *Cultural Studies, Theory and Society, Cineaste,* and *Journal of Communication.* She is an associate professor of women's studies at the University of California, Davis.

Avery F. Gordon is assistant professor of sociology at the University of California, Santa Barbara. She is the coeditor of *Body Politics* (with Michael Ryan) and the author of *Ghostly Matters* (forthcoming from the University of Minnesota Press) and several articles on knowledge, gender, and race.

Neil Gotanda has written and lectured extensively on issues of race and legal ideology. His current work uses legal materials to explore questions of racial ideology, immigration, and Asian Pacific Americans. Educated at Stanford, Berkeley, and Harvard, he is professor of constitutional law at Western State University College of Law in Fullerton, California, and resides in West Los Angeles.

Ramón Gutiérrez is professor of history and chair of the Department of Ethnic Studies at the University of California, San Diego. Recipient of the prestigious MacArthur Foundation award, Gutiérrez is the author of *When Jesus Came, the Corn Mothers Went Away: Marriage, Sexuality, and Power in New Mexico, 1500-1846,* as well as numerous articles on Chicano history.

Cynthia Hamilton is the director of African and African-American studies at the University of Rhode Island. She has been an active participant in community affairs and a contributor to many journals and newsletters, and has produced news and commentary programs for public radio on the topics of civil liberties, culture, and politics.

M. Annette Jaimes Guerrero was a visiting professor in American Indian studies at Arizona State University in 1994–95. During the summer of 1995 she was a field researcher in a Native Researchers Cancer Control Training

Program at the University of New Mexico Health Sciences Center with the University of Arizona. In fall 1995 she joins the faculty of the San Francisco State University Women's Studies program.

George Lipsitz is professor of ethnic studies at the University of California, San Diego. A pioneer in the field of cultural studies, Lipsitz is the author of *Dangerous Crossroads*; *A Rainbow at Midnight*; *Time Passages: Collective Memory and American Popular Culture*; *Sidewalks of St. Louis*; *A Life in the Struggle: Ivory Perry and the Culture of Opposition*; and *Class and Culture in Cold War America*.

Lisa Lowe teaches comparative literature at the University of California, San Diego. She is the author of *Critical Terrains: French and British Orientalisms* (1991) and a book on Asian-American cultural production (forthcoming).

Wahneema Lubiano teaches in the Department of English and the Program in African-American Studies at Princeton University. She is the author of numerous articles on African-American women writers and on African-American popular culture and theory, including "Black Ladies, Welfare Queens, and State Minstrels: Ideological War by Narrative Means" in *Race-ing Justice, En-Gendering Power: The Anita Hill-Clarence Thomas Controversy and the Construction of Reality*, edited by Toni Morrison.

Christopher Newfield is associate professor of English at the University of California, Santa Barbara. He is the author of *The Emerson Effect: Individualism and Submission in America* and of articles on nineteenth-century American culture and contemporary society and culture. He has edited *After Political Correctness: The Humanities and Society in the 1990s* with Ron Strickland.

Michael Omi is currently associate professor of ethnic studies and chair of the Asian American Studies Program at the University of California, Berkeley. He writes about racial theory and politics, and is the coauthor, with Howard Winant, of *Racial Formation in the United States: From the 1960s to the 1990s*.

Lourdes Portillo is a filmmaker living in the Bay Area. Her most recent film is *The Devil Never Sleeps*. Her other films include *Las Madres: The Mothers of the Plaza de Mayo* and *La Ofrenda: The Day of the Dead*.

Cedric J. Robinson is chair of the Department of Black Studies and professor of political science at the University of California, Santa Barbara. Robinson is the author of *Terms of Order*, the pathbreaking *Black Marxism: The Making of the Black Radical Tradition*, and numerous articles on U.S., African, and Caribbean political thought, Western social theory, film, and the press. His most recent work is *The Anthropology of Marxism*. He is also an editor of the journal *Race and Class*, and the producer of *Third World News Review*, a local television program.

Tricia Rose is assistant professor of Africana studies and history at New York University. She is the author of *Black Noise: Rap Music and Black Culture in Contemporary America* and coeditor, with Andrew Ross, of *Microphone Fiends: Youth Music and Youth Culture*.

Gregg Scott is a Ph.D. candidate in the Department of Sociology at the University of California, Santa Barbara. He is currently doing fieldwork in Los Angeles for his dissertation, which is entitled "Globalization, Multiculturalism, and the Fashioning of Resistance: A Historical-Sociological Ethnography of Class Struggle in the Los Angeles Apparel Industry."

Paul Smith is professor of English at George Mason University. He is the editor, with Alice Jardine, of *Men in Feminism*, and, with Lisa Frank, of *Madonnarama*. He is the author of *Pound Revised, Discerning the Subject* (University of Minnesota Press) and most recently *Clint Eastwood: A Cultural Production* (University of Minnesota Press). His next book, *Bearing North: Essays in Cultural Studies*, is forthcoming, as is an edited collection of essays, *Boys: Culture and Masculinity*. He recently published a collection of translations from Jean Louis Schefer, *The Enigmatic Body*.

Renee Tajima is an Academy Award-nominated filmmaker who lives in Los Angeles and New York City. She is the director of the powerful documentary *Who Killed Vincent Chin?*; *The Best Hotel on Skid Row*; and *Jennifer's in Jail*. She is a commentator for National Public Radio's *Crossroads* series and has been a film critic for the *Village Voice*, associate editor of the *Independent Film & Video Monthly*, and editor of *Bridge: Asian American Perspectives*. Her most recent film-in-progress, to be broadcast on PBS, is entitled *Fortune Cookies: In Search of Asian America* (working title) and explores the search for Asian America.

Patricia Zavella is professor of community studies at the University of California, Santa Cruz. She is the author of *Women's Work and Chicano Families: Cannery Workers of the Santa Clara Valley* and *Sunbelt Working Mothers: Reconciling Family and Factory*, coauthored with Louise Lamphere, Felipe Gonzáles, and Peter B. Evans. She is currently researching poverty in Santa Clara County, comparing how Mexican immigrants, Chicanos, and whites adapt to the local labor market, and how economics and cultural notions about gender and sexuality affect the formation of poor households.

Index

COMPILED BY MARTIN L. WHITE

74; as monitored minority, 240–41;
Newton, 99; and New York's decline,
429, 431; as an outlaw group, 73;
poverty rate in California, 368; rap
music, 427; resistance to ideas fostered
by, 448; slavery, 26, 41, 71, 117; state
practices regarding, 26; stereotypes in
popular culture, 405; treatment while
serving in World War II, 277; trial of
Du Soon Ja, 238–52; two Americas for,
94–95; as an underclass, 364–68; values
about work, 364; working poor, 366.
See also civil rights movement
Afro-Caribbeans, 425, 426, 440
Afrocentrism, 90, 91, 93, 111n.40, 448
Alarcón, Norma, 210
Albuquerque, 375–80
Altvater, Elmar, 347–49, 352
Amariglio, Jack, 349
American Creed, 7–8
American Indian Movement (AIM), 54
American Indians: African Americans and,
71; Bering Strait theory, 62n.8; boarding school system, 52–53, 209; Bureau
of Indian Affairs, 51, 54–55, 62n.14;
certification of identity, 54–55, 62n.13;
children as translators for, 209; Civilization Fund, 52; colonization and Indian education, 50–54; and Columbus
Quincentenary, 222–23; Cornplanter,
50–51; decolonization to precede multiculturalism for, 49–50; distortions and
bias in scholarship on, 53–54; ethnic
cleansing of, 26; as an ethnic minority,
56; genocide of, 209; Indigenism,
50, 60–61; intellectualism of, 57–58; as
major American racial grouping, 1;
Malintzín, 209, 210; pending enrollments, 55; politicized reemergence of,
27; politics of Indian identity, 54–56; in
Portillo's *Mirrors of the Heart*, 193–95;
public school education mandated for,
54; as a race, 53, 62n.8; stereotypes in
popular culture, 405; treaties understood as bilateral by, 51
American Indian Studies, 49–63; multiculturalism and Indigenism in, 56–61
Americanization, 84, 168–69
Anglo-Saxon stock, 84–85
antidiscriminatory law, 168

antiessentialism, 20, 104–5, 113n.75, 134
antimiscegenation laws, 27, 272, 273
antiracism, 3–4, 8
Anzaldúa, Gloria, 130–31, 132, 135, 137, 138
apparel industry (garment industry): in
Albuquerque, 376; in China, 335–38,
345; commodity chain in, 305, 331–32;
globalization of, 345; in Hong Kong,
333–35, 345; in Macau, 338–40; mobility of, 326; retailing, 320; subminimum
wage workforce in, 298; in Vietnam,
340–45. *See also* Los Angeles garment
industry
Arendt, Hannah, 127–30, 137
Argentina, 191–93
Arkansas, 275–79
Asian Americans, 263–94; and African Americans, 47, 244, 263, 273; anti-Asian violence, 289; Asian Indians, 27, 181; associations of, 283; attempted exclusion
of, 27; civil rights movement's effect
on, 282; elitism among activists, 283;
Filipino Americans, 27, 180, 270–73,
394–95; in the Heartland, 283–88; immigration restrictions on women, 369;
as intermediate racial category, 246;
Laotian (Hmong) refugees, 285–88; as
major American racial grouping, 1;
marriage rules, 273; as model minority,
243–44, 245–46, 283; new immigrants,
283; in New Orleans, 270–73; Orientalism, 243, 246; overrepresentation in
higher education, 263; politicized
reemergence of, 27; poverty rate in
California, 368; racialization of, 180;
stereotypes in popular culture, 243–44,
405; two Americas for, 94–95; Vietnam
War and, 289; women in the popular
imagination, 271. *See also* Chinese
Americans; Japanese Americans; Korean
Americans
Asian Indians, 27, 181
assimilation: American culture of, 173;
Americanization, 84, 168–69; as antipluralist, 81; assimilationism distinguished from, 80; people of color not
improving their lives through, 108; of
white ethnics, 109n.15; whites opposing assimilation of people of color, 95
assimilationism, 80–83; American melting

culture: American culture of assimilation, 173; biculturality, 95; centrifugal capitalism and centripetal culture, 28–30; children as translators of, 201–14; classless culture, 172–74; commercial, 403, 404; commodification of, 167; cultural autonomy, 4–5; cultural fragments as new sites of concreteness, 25; cultural interaction, 90, 92–93; cultural nationalism, 99–101; cultural parity, 86, 88, 90, 92–93; cultural particularism, 46; cultural politics of difference, 138–46; cultural racism, 84–85, 88–89, 169; culture industry, 422n.5; economic globalism versus the cultural state, 26–28, 37; intercultural communication, 403–12; multiculturalism and the production of, 387–444; multiculturalism's cultural turn, 78–79; mistakes in understanding other peoples', 403–12; as not politically neutral, 47; and politics in multiculturalism, 6–7, 9; popular, 403–12, 424; as psychosocial currencies, 32; state influence on, 71–72; in the workplace, 168–72. See also common culture; core culture; cultural diversity; cultural pluralism
culture industry, 422n.5
culture of poverty, 73, 79, 364, 366, 367
Cureton, Ette, 87
"Curriculum of Inclusion, A" (New York State), 87

Dachau, 116–17
Daewoo's Vietnam factories, 343–45
Davis, Ray, 114n.80
deindustrialization, 28, 426–27
del Castillo, Adelaida, 210
Deloria, Vine, Jr., 51, 60
democracy: in American Creed, 7–8; appropriation of, 70–71. See also liberal democracy
democratic pluralism, 96
deregulation: economic, 28; social, 28–30
Derrida, Jacques, 128, 129, 133–34
Después del Terremoto (Portillo), 187, 189–91, 197
différance, 128, 129, 134, 137
differential consciousness, 136–37, 187
differential racism, 33

disappeared, the, 191–93
disciplinary power, 154, 155–56, 158
diversity management: in corporate multiculturalism, 41; multiculturalism as, 5–6; seen as response to excessive local control, 9; by the state, 31; texts on, 449
Dominicans, 425, 441n.2
drug economy, 72–73
drywallers' strike, 323
D'Souza, Dinesh, 116, 119, 120, 121
Du Bois, W. E. B., 109n.5
Duke, David, 184
Duluth, Minn., 285–88
Durazo, Maria Elena, 325
Duschene, Marlys, 57
Du Soon Ja, 238–52
Duster, Troy, 83

East Germany. See German Democratic Republic
economic deregulation, 28
economic globalization: American cities affected by, 428; in apparel industry, 345; cheap labor driving, 301; class relations made more difficult to disentangle, 319; the class question in global capitalism, 298, 317–29; differential effects of, 372; GATT and NAFTA, 326; globalizing and localizing forces in, 304; global multinational corporatism, 38n.11; multiculturalism in context of, 19; new directions in global capitalism, 297–316; race, ethnicity, and gender in global capitalism, 313–14; and the state, 26–28, 37, 301; stripping away liberal democracy's vision of society, 36–37; in telecommunications industry, 430
economic recession, global, 309
educational system: balkanization in, 179; colonization and Indian education, 50–54; after desegregation, 446–47; multiculturalism in, 42, 76, 94–98, 446–47; public school education mandated for American Indians, 54; toleration, pluralism, and diversity encouraged in, 32. See also academy, the
egalitarianism: building from multiculturalism toward, 37; in liberal democratic ideology, 32–33; and liberty in liberal-

ism, 157; in multiculturalism, 36. *See also* equality
elections, race card in, 184
Ellington, James Ernest, 278, 279
Encinitas, Calif., 260
English language, 184
Enlightenment, the, 20, 128
equality: in American Creed, 7–8; assimilationism militating against demands for, 81; cultural parity, 86, 88, 90, 92–93; cultural pluralism and political parity, 105–7; equity as a primary principle of multiculturalism, 108; and freedom in liberalism, 157; as identity for Kallen, 84; inequality, 24, 79, 322. *See also* egalitarianism
Espiritu, Yen, 180
essentialism: antiessentialism, 20, 104–5, 113n.75, 134; in Enlightenment rationalism, 20; essentializing on basis of race and female body, 131; in nationalisms, 104; ontologization of difference and, 133; and politics, 36; Portillo as an essentialist, 193; poststructuralist avoidance of, 22; in resistant texts of minoritized populations, 134
ethnicity: and class struggle, 328; dominant society's redefinition of, 8; ethnic coalitions, 5–6, 9, 405; ethnic cultures in the workplace, 169–72; ethnicizing of labor, 298, 309; ethnic pluralism, 109n.15; function of in America, 173–74, 175; in global capitalism, 298, 313–14; New York media resources for ethnic communities, 442n.11; occupational identity replaced by, 176; panethnicity, 103, 180–81, 183; and race, 174; revival of, 175–76; social-science views about, 173; Steinberg's iron law of, 92; used as cover for economic dominance, 168; white ethnics compared to people of color, 95
Ethnic Studies, 58, 59, 230, 362, 363
European Americans (whites): Anglo-Saxon stock, 84–85; anomie among, 173; antiessentialist understandings of white-majority institutions, 105; assimilation of people of color opposed by, 95; assimilation of white ethnics, 109n.15; cohesion in other groups

feared by, 175; crisis of white identity, 181–83; as defining model minorities, 240; as designers of the academic curriculum, 57; female-headed families among, 384n.40; flight from South Bronx, 431; German Americans, 169–70, 431; Greek Americans, 170; Hungarian Americans, 170; Irish Americans, 171, 431; Italian Americans, 170, 171, 431; in Los Angeles riots, 419; as major American racial grouping, 1; minority critique of nationalism rejected by, 99; neutral institutions as pro-white, 81, 89; Newton on, 99; as panethnic group, 183; Polish Americans, 169–70; poverty rate in California, 368; racialization of, 181–83; "white" as term of self-identity, 179; white bias in medical school admission, 113n.77; white ethnics compared with people of color, 95; whiteness as cultural, 79; working poor, 366. *See also* Western culture
existentialism, 128

Fagin, Steve: completed works of, 402; *The Machine That Killed Bad People*, 389–402
family: Asian marriage rules, 273; family values, 363, 365–66, 369, 381; female-headed, 369, 384n.40; household clusters, 374; nuclear, 370, 381, 383n.36
Fanon, Frantz, 121, 132–33, 169
farmworkers: diversity among, 373; Tejana, 205–7, 210–11
feminism: and class struggle, 328; essentialism in, 104; feminists of color, 103; film criticism of, 187; Habermas and, 145; ontologization of difference and, 133; socialist, 103; universalized concept of woman in, 129; U.S. Third World feminism, 135–36, 187
fetishization, 22, 23
Filipino Americans, 27, 180, 270–73, 394–95
flexibility, 31, 306–7
Ford, Henry, 168
Fortune Cookies: In Search of Asian America (Tajima), 263–94
Frankfurt School, 346, 348–49
Fraser, James W., 6

race: American Indians as a, 53, 62n.8; American society's refusal to confront, 174; and the American state, 26–28; as any group generally believed to be a race, 65; antiessentialist race consciousness, 104–5; Asian Americans as intermediate category, 246; binary constructions of, 47–48, 245–46; as both real and changeable, 104; capitalist use of, 318; class and, 43, 44, 65, 173, 319; and class struggle, 328; as complex of meanings constantly being transformed, 65; contemporary race relations as consequence of increasing anomie, 172–73; as cover for economic dominance, 168; cultural markers as substitute for, 240; discredited as biological term, 43; dominant society's redefinition of, 8; essentializing on basis of, 131; and ethnicity, 174; expanding significance in American life, 183; five major racial groupings, 1; as fundamental principle of identity and action, 179; gender and, 43, 133; and German unification, 358; in global capitalism, 298, 313–14; liberalism consenting to prevailing racial common sense, 108; in Marxism, 24; multiculturalism and racial stratification, 238–52; new racial subjects, 180–81; the race card in elections, 184; raced identities as most associated with multiculturalism, 35–36; race progressives, 81–82; racial backlash, 172, 175, 181–82, 184, 448; racial composition of America as changing, 181; reification of, 19–39; rethinking race politics, 40–48; Washington's "new race," 88. See also color blindness; racialization; racism
race progressives, 81–82
racialization, 179–80; in capitalism, 313–14; civil rights movement altering state strategies of, 27; historic consolidation of "black" and "white," 179; of politics, 183–85; in post-civil rights era, 178–86; white indifference to racialized dimension of institutional neutrality, 89; of whites, 181–83
racism: as abolished in United States, 15n.1; American society's refusal to confront,

174; antiracism, 3–4, 8; attempting to overcome without altering power structures, 43; and capitalism, 313, 319, 346, 347, 420; charges of, 44; cultural, 84–85, 88–89, 169; culturalism shifting attention from, 79; differential racism, 33; dual function in America, 173; in garment industry elite, 321; in Germany, 347, 358–59; growing out of imperialist expansion of Europe, 318; multiculturalism as oblivious to, 3–4; multiculturalism eliciting neoracist reaction, 139; scientific, 53; strategies to make marginalized cultures visible reproducing ideologies of, 40
Ramírez, Manuel, 96
rape, 258, 261
rap music, 427, 434, 437, 439–40, 441n.2
Ravitch, Diane, 6, 46, 91, 93, 119
reason, 20, 128
recession, global, 309
Red Apple grocery boycott, 263
Red Army Faction, 352–53
reggae music, 404
Reich, Robert, 38n.11, 298, 302–4, 305
Reiff, David, 115n.86
reification, 22, 24, 26, 31
ressentiment, 157–64
retailing, 320
revenge, 162, 163
Rodriguez, Richard, 208
Rohwedder, Detlev, 352–53
Roman, Leslie G., 106
Roosevelt, Theodore, 52
Rosedale, Miss., 277

Sa-I-Gu (Choy, Kim, and Kim-Gibson), 419–20
Sánchez-Albornoz, Nicolás, 225, 231, 235n.24, 236n.41
San Diego, 253–62
Sandinistas, 189, 191
Sandoval, Chela, 129, 135–37, 138
Sartre, Jean-Paul, 128, 132–33
"Save Our State" initiative (California), 366
Schiebinger, Londa, 118
Schlesinger, Arthur, Jr., 84, 88, 90, 93, 94, 109n.5, 140
scientific racism, 53
Scott, Ridley, 413